PHILOLOGICAL AND HISTORICAL COMMENTARY
ON AMMIANUS MARCELLINUS XXV

PHILOLOGICAL AND HISTORICAL COMMENTARY ON AMMIANUS MARCELLINUS XXV

BY

J. DEN BOEFT
J.W. DRIJVERS
D. DEN HENGST
H.C. TEITLER

BRILL
LEIDEN · BOSTON
2005

This book is printed on acid-free paper.

Library of Congress Cataloging-in-Publication Data

A C.I.P. record for this book is available from the Library of Congress.

ISBN   90 04 14214 2

© Copyright 2005 by Koninklijke Brill NV, Leiden, The Netherlands
Koninklijke Brill NV incorporates the imprints Brill Academic Publishers,
Martinus Nijhoff Publishers and VSP.

All rights reserved. No part of this publication may be reproduced, translated, stored in
a retrieval system, or transmitted in any form or by any means, electronic,
mechanical, photocopying, recording or otherwise, without prior written
permission from the publisher.

Authorization to photocopy items for internal or personal
use is granted by Brill provided that
the appropriate fees are paid directly to The Copyright
Clearance Center, 222 Rosewood Drive, Suite 910
Danvers MA 01923, USA.
Fees are subject to change.

PRINTED IN THE NETHERLANDS

CONTENTS

Preface	VII
Introduction	IX
A note on chronology	XV
Legenda	XXIII
Map	XXVI
Commentary on Chapter 1	1
Commentary on Chapter 2	39
Commentary on Chapter 3	57
Commentary on Chapter 4	111
Commentary on Chapter 5	169
Commentary on Chapter 6	197
Commentary on Chapter 7	219
Commentary on Chapter 8	251
Commentary on Chapter 9	279
Commentary on Chapter 10	307
Bibliography	345
Indices	369

PREFACE

Book 25 of the *Res Gestae* is the last of the books in which Julian plays a leading part. The commentary on this book is our sixth contribution to the series which was initiated by P. de Jonge. As in book 24, the precise chronology of the events and the numerous geographical details posed many problems. Owing to a lack of clear evidence, in a number of cases only tentative solutions were feasible.

We owe thanks to friends and colleagues for their helpful advice and to Ines van de Wetering, who corrected our English. The Fondation Hardt at Vandoeuvres (CH) again offered its hospitality for some periods of undisturbed study. Dr Vera Enke of the Berlin-Brandenburgische Akademie der Wissenschaften kindly gave us the opportunity to study the archives of the 'Arbeitsgruppe für spätrömische Philologie und Geschichte', led by Dr W. Seyfarth (1906–1985), the editor of the Teubner edition of the *Res Gestae*. This material made us aware of the difficulties he had to cope with in his scholarly work and also provided us with some welcome suggestions for our own task. Thanks are due to the Netherlands Organization for Scientific Research (NWO), which subsidized the correction of the English manuscript.

The cooperation with the publishing house Koninklijke Brill N.V. was efficient.

J. den Boeft
J.W. Drijvers
D. den Hengst
H.C. Teitler

INTRODUCTION

Book 25 of the *Res Gestae* is the last part of the trilogy on the Persian expedition. Book 23 describes the events in the first three months of 363, during which the final preparations were made at Antioch and the army marched to Cercusium on the Euphrates, where it invaded Persian territory. The march to Ctesiphon and the beginning of the northbound katabasis, a period of two and a half months, are dealt with in book 24. Remarkably, book 25 covers a larger space and more time than the two preceeding books put together: it takes the reader from a place about 35 kilometers north of Ctesiphon to Dadastana on the border between Galatia and Bithynia, a distance of more than 1700 kilometers. In time, it runs from June 17, 363 to February 17, 364, a full eight months.

Such bare calendrical and geographical details are, however, misleading: in fact, the first half of book 25 is devoted to a period of ten days, from June 17 to June 26, and its final pages, marked off as chapter 10, deal with around four months. Simple observations of this kind illustrate the huge difference between a purely chronological survey and historiography. A historian is rightly expected to pay careful attention to a correct chronology, but within this framework he selects the events to which he ascribes a particular importance, distinguishing them from any facts which he regards as less interesting or even not worth mentioning. Ammianus expresses this in these words: *carptim, ut quaeque memoria digna sunt, explicabo* (28.1.2) and, more precisely, *sufficiet enim veritate nullo velata mendacio ipsas rerum digerere summitates* (31.5.10). No reader will deny the historian the right or, indeed, the duty to proceed selectively (*carptim*) and to restrict himself to the truly crucial events (*ipsas rerum summitates*). Generally speaking, there is no reason for repeated complaints about Ammianus' strategy, although at times more precise and detailed information would have been desirable. Nevertheless, the historian's selection of material is as much determined by his interpretation of the past as is his presentation of the evidence in a well-composed account. These aspects of the historiographic art were hardly problematized by Ammianus, but they are today the object of critical scrutiny in philosophical analyses of historiography in general. Inevitably, the *Res Gestae* has also become the object of such critical examinations, and many scholars have tried to pinpoint the author's political principles and, more specifically, his biased views and prejudices, and some have even called his basic trustworthiness into question. In recent books and articles the second half of book 25, which describes the short reign of Jovian, is regularly exploited as evidence to demonstrate how Ammianus manipulated the facts.

The first pages of the book describe the continuation of the army's katabasis in a northern direction, which the author never openly calls a retreat. The Romans are continually harassed by the Persians, but they finally defeat their enemies in a pitched battle, during which Roman stamina gloriously overcomes Persian fragility. However, this success does not in any way alter another problem, viz. the acute shortage of food, which severely worries the emperor Julian. Suddenly two earlier threads, one in each of the books 23 and 24, come together: book 23 is characterized by a series of warning omina, neglected by Julian; in book 24 omina are absent, with one exception; instead we find a number of reckless acts committed by Julian, in which he exposes himself to mortal danger. In chapter 2 of book 25 Julian is first confronted with a nightly appearance of the Genius publicus, who had also appeared to him in Paris during the night before he was proclaimed Augustus. This time, however, the Spirit of the Commonwealth leaves his tent in a somber mood, with the horn of plenty veiled. Somewhat later Julian sees a shooting star. The divinatory experts, whom he consults, conclude that all further action ought to be postponed, but they fail to persuade Julian and therefore the next morning the army continues its march. When it is heavily attacked at various points, Julian involves himself personally in the necessary defensive actions, *sine respectu periculi sui* and forgetting to don a proper armour. Ammianus refrains from terms such as *temeritas*, but the reader cannot help fearing the outcome of this bravery. These fears come true: suddenly the emperor is severely wounded by a spear and he has to be brought back to his tent. This setback ignites in his soldiers a spirited determination and they gain the upper hand. Ammianus hails their success in panegyric phraseology, but has to admit that there were some costly losses on the Roman side.

In the meantime Julian has realized that his life is at its end. The author honours the man, whom, for all his shortcomings, he regarded as an outstanding ruler and general, in the best way he could think of, viz. by putting an impressive farewell address in his mouth. For the composition of this speech Ammianus draws on various literary traditions; the result is an admirable piece of writing, which honours the reputation of the only indisputable hero

INTRODUCTION   XI

of the *Res Gestae* and will move even those who are less convinced of
Julian's qualities and achievements. It is the highlight of a deathbed
scene for which the death of Socrates, as it is described on the final
pages of Plato's *Phaedo*, is the example. The necrology, which follows
in chapter 4, is somewhat disappointing, especially its first part,
where Julian's virtues are treated according to the rules of epideictic
oratory. The author's talents were, above all, suited to lively narrative,
gripping descriptions and appropriate speeches, but less adapted
to the rigid structure of a schematic survey. In the second part,
when describing Julian's weaknesses and the controversial Persian
expedition, the author performs much better. The necrology is
the definite closure of the entire history of Julian as Caesar and
Augustus. His career had begun in Milan on November 6, 355, when
Constantius II officially announced that he had appointed Julian as
his Caesar with specific tasks in Gaul, a scene described in chapter 8 of
book 15. Critical modern readers will probably acknowledge Julian's
successes in Gaul, but may doubt, whether he really could have
defeated Constantius, had it come to civil war, and will most certainly
blame him for the failure of the Persian expedition. This judgment,
should it be made, would fundamentally differ from Ammianus'
assessment. There is not a doubt in his mind that Julian's decision
to attack the arch-enemy was correct. Only his untimely death gave
the Lady Fortuna the opportunity to play one of her tricks and to
saddle the Roman empire with a successor who lacked the experience
indispensable for an emperor, with ghastly consequences.

The second half of the book begins on the day after Julian's
death. When the leading officers deliberate whom to appoint as
successor, they are unable to reach a conclusion. Their momentary
indecision is used by a group of supporters of Jovian, a thirty-one year
old officer of the protectores, to cause a disturbance, which results in
his surprise election as emperor. Ammianus gives a lively description
of these events, which has come in for much scepticism and criticism
in recent scholarly literature. In fact, as the commentary will show,
the only flaw in Ammianus' account is the absence of any information
concerning the identity of the troublemakers and the precise course
of events at the vital moment. From the outset, however, he is firm
in his judgment that Jovian was the wrong choice. It is imperative to
be quite precise regarding the reason for this judgment. Ammianus
did not regard Jovian as an utter nonentity, but as a man who simply
lacked the experience to fulfil his tasks properly. Consequently, he
was overpowered by fear of possible usurpers, Procopius in particular,
and this fear caused him to head immediately for Constantinople and

to send reliable envoys ahead in order to strengthen his position. This haste in its turn had fatal consequences: it deprived Jovian of the patience and perseverance needed to lead the army back to Roman territory amidst the dangers of Persian attacks and the shortage of supplies. This lack of mental strength manifested itself in an exasperating manner, when king Sapor, impressed by the spirit with which the Romans were coping with their manifold problems, unexpectedly sent envoys to negotiate peace. Instead of making full use of this opportunity in a dignified Roman style, Jovian reached an overhasty agreement with the king, which guaranteed the safety of the Roman army, but was dearly paid for by the loss of large sections of Roman territory around the upper course of the Tigris, among them even the historical stronghold Nisibis. This town had often played a decisive role in the conflicts with Persia. Ammianus is deeply scandalized by this surrender, which in his eyes was at odds with the entire history of the Roman empire. Fortune's whims proved expensive indeed. Modern scholars will be less sure and may be inclined to ask, whether Jovian was really in a position to fight it out to the end with any prospect of success. Ammianus shows his strong feelings when he describes the pathetic scenes of the inhabitants of Nisibis, who implore Jovian to call off the surrender and then leave their beloved town in great distress; in this description he alludes to some verses in book 2 of the *Aeneid*. Contemporary readers will not have failed to see the parallel with the plight of Troy. The historian's fierce indignation at the loss of Nisibis may also have been provoked by his personal memories. The first time he introduces himself as being part of the action in the *Res Gestae* is 14.9.1, where he states that in 354 he was serving in Nisibis under Ursicinus, whose task it was to guard the town. The loss of Nisibis, and of the other towns and regions involved, is the vantage point, from which he assessed Jovian's capacities and conduct.

From this moment haste becomes the prime characteristic of Ammianus' narrative. Jovian and his army are continually on the move. Modern readers are helped by scholarly reconstructions of the long journey, specifically contrived with the help of evidence available in the *Codex Theodosianus*; these reconstructions make it clear that although the new emperor did indeed resolutely travel westward, he moved at a far slower pace than is suggested by Ammianus. In fact, Jovian stayed for shorter or longer periods in several towns in order to attend to various governmental and ecclesiastical matters. This is in contrast to the speed of Ammianus' narrative, which finally culminates in the observation that all along it had been fate which

INTRODUCTION   XIII

drove him on towards his untimely end at Dadastana, where he was
suddenly found dead. The author assumes that his death was caused
by excessive gluttony, a huge difference with the noble end of Julian.
The brief necrology, which follows, is by no means hostile and even
hints at potential qualities. It also mentions for the very first time
that Jovian was a convinced Christian. This deserves to be noticed,
since some scholars have argued that, in his treatment of Jovian's
short reign, Ammianus is guilty of considerable anti-Christian bias.
If this were the case, it needs to be explained why he does not allude
to the emperor's religious faith anywhere except in the necrology.

As was stated above, book 25 is the third part of the Persian
trilogy, but this is not its only function. It also rounds off the
Julianic period of the *Res Gestae* in a grand manner, by paying
tribute to the emperor's greatness in four ways: first, his actual
courageous leadership, which showed that he still was *animosus contra
labores maximos* (16.12.28), then, the farewell speech, followed by the
necrology, and finally, in the second half of the book, the implicit
contrast with Jovian, who failed in one of his essential tasks: the
defence of the integrity of the Roman empire. In this respect book
25 can in itself be interpreted as a diptych, portraying the different
ways in which the highest office in the Roman world was performed.
Despite some weaknesses Julian was a true and experienced leader
of men, but Jovian lacked experience and was, above all, driven by
fear. They ended their lives correspondingly: Julian gloriously and
serenely, amidst his entire staff, Jovian alone, a disgraceful victim of
his own gluttony.

A NOTE ON CHRONOLOGY

Julian set off on the journey home on June 16, 363 (*sextum decimum kalendas Iulias*, 24.8.5). This is the only precise date in Book 24. The next we find in 25.5.1, viz. June 27 (*quintum kalendas Iulias*), the day which saw Jovian's accession, after Julian had been mortally wounded the day before. There is one more passage in Book 25 which furnishes a precise chronological datum: in 25.6.9 Ammianus tells us that the Romans reached a city called Dura (on the far side of the Tigris) on the first day of July (*cumque hinc kalendis Iuliis...civitatem nomine Duram adventaremus*). Taking these data as a starting point, with the help of Zosimus' account and some other sources, and taking into account expressions in Ammianus like *paulo postea, per biduum, eodem die* etcetera, an attempt to reconstruct the chronological order of events can be made. It should be stressed, however, that many dates in this reconstruction are no more than reasonable guesses. Brok 258–9 and Dodgeon-Lieu, 1991, 236–7 also give a chronological overview of the events described in Book 25.

The decision to start the katabasis must have been taken in the *stativa castra* mentioned in 24.7.7 (q.v.), possibly to be identified with Noorda. When the soldiers had broken camp on June 16 (24.8.5), they were soon startled by what seemed to be smoke, or a great whirling cloud of dust. Subsequently the march was interrupted and a camp was pitched near a stream (24.8.7), possibly the Douros (Diyala). Here the night was spent (*hanc quidem noctem...exegimus*, 25.1.1). Early the next morning (*ubi...primum dies inclaruit*, 25.1.1), i.e. on 17 June, it became clear that the Persians were near at hand. Some skirmishes followed (25.1.2–3), whereupon the Romans, via Barsaphthae (Zos. 3.27.1), reached Hucumbra/Symbra (*qua ex regione profecti ad Hucumbra nomine villam pervenimus*, 25.1.4; Zos. 3.27.2 προϊὼν δὲ εἰς κώμην ἐλήλυθε Σύμβραν). In this place they stayed two days, i.e. 18 and 19 June (*ubi per biduum...recreati discessimus*, ibid.). On the following day (*Postridie*, 25.1.5), i.e. June 20, the Persians suddenly attacked the rear, but a disaster was averted. On the same day (*eodem die*, 25.1.7) the *Tertiacorum equestris numerus* and some tribunes of other units, accused of cowardice, were punished. Probably still on 20 June they advanced some 13 km (*Progressi itaque septuaginta stadia*, 25.1.10) and reached Accete (Zos. 3.28.1), where, presumably, they spent the night. The following day, i.e. June

XVI   A NOTE ON CHRONOLOGY

21, they left Accete and marched towards Maranga/Maronsa, where (on June, 22) at daybreak the Persians, under the command of Merena and others, appeared (*hoc etiam loco relicto cum ad tractum Maranga appellatum omnis venisset exercitus, prope lucis confinia immensa Persarum apparuit multitudo cum Merena* etc., 25.1.11; Περαιτέρω δὲ προελθόντες εἰς Μάρωνσα παρεγένοντο κώμην, Zos. 3.28.2). The fight, which subsequently broke out, only ended after the soldiers had been wearied by the fiery course of the sun (*miles solis cursu flammeo diu lassatus...in tentoria repetit*, 25.1.18).

After this, three days were devoted to a truce (*Post quae triduo indutiis destinato*, 25.2.1), i.e. June 23, 24 and 25, during which period the Roman army probably advanced at a slow pace until it reached Toumarra by the evening of 25 June (Zos. 3.28.3 Παραδραμόντες δὲ κώμας τινὰς εἰς Τούμμαραν ἦλθον). During the night Julian thought he saw the Genius publicus (*obscuro noctis...vidit...speciem...Genii publici*, 25.2.3) and, some time later but still in the same night (*adulta iam...nocte*, 25.2.4), a blazing light like a falling star. From what follows it appears that Julian saw all this in the last night of the truce: he sent for Etruscan soothsayers before first light (*ante lucis primitias*, 25.2.7), who begged him to postpone his departure for some hours; nevertheless he broke camp in the morning (*exorto iam die promota sunt castra*, 25.2.8), i.e. in the morning of the day which would be Julian's last, 26 June 363. On that day the Romans marched from Toumarra northwards, at first secretly accompanied by the Persians (*Hinc nos egressos Persae...occulte comitabantur*, 25.3.1), later suddenly attacked from behind (*invasa subito terga pone versus arma cogentium principi indicatur*, 25.3.2) – according to Zos. 3.28.4 the Persian assault commenced at the end of the morning (Τῇ δὲ μετὰ ταῦτα ἡμέρᾳ περὶ πλήθουσαν ἀγορὰν οἱ Πέρσαι συνταχθέντες εἰς πλῆθος τοῖς οὐραγοῖς τοῦ Ῥωμαίων στρατεύματος ἀδοκήτοις ἐπέπεσον). In the ensuing battle Julian was mortally wounded (25.3.6–7) near a place which Ammianus calls Phrygia (*Phrygiam appellari locum, ubi ceciderat, comperit*, 25.3.9), to be found in the neighbourhood of modern Samarra. Brought to his tent the emperor expired in the dread hour of midnight (*medio noctis horrore, vita facilius est absolutus*, 25.3.23; περὶ τὴν ἕκτην καὶ εἰκάδα τοῦ Ἰουνίου μηνός...τὸν βίον κατέλυσεν, Socr. *HE* 3.21.18).

Early the following day, which was 27 June 363, consultations began about choosing a new emperor (*principio lucis secutae, quae erat quintum kalendas Iulias...collecti duces exercitus...super creando principe consultabant*, 25.5.1). Soon, presumably on the same day, these resulted in the election of Jovian (*Inter has exiguas ad tantam rem*

A NOTE ON CHRONOLOGY   XVII

moras...Iovianus eligitur imperator, 25.5.4; Malalas *Chron.* 13.333 αὐτὸν ἀνηγόρευσαν βασιλέα τῇ κζ τοῦ δαισίου τοῦ καὶ ἰουνίου μηνός, Socr. *HE* 3.22.1 τῇ ἑξῆς ἡμέρᾳ ἀναδεικνύουσι βασιλέα Ἰοβιανόν). Meanwhile the army prepared to set out (*et confestim indumentis circumdatus principalibus subitoque productus e tabernaculo per agmina iam discurrebat proficisci parantia*, 25.5.5). Immediately after the withdrawal was resumed, i.e. on 28 June, the Persians attacked again (*proinde egredi iam coeptantes adoriuntur nos...Persae*, 25.6.2) and killed some Romans, who were buried as well as circumstances allowed. Towards nightfall, while the troops were heading for a fortress called Sumere, Zosimus' Σοῦμα (3.30.2), modern Samarra, they found the body of the magister officiorum Anatolius, killed in the same battle which proved fatal to Julian (*prope confinia noctis, cum ad castellum Sumere nomine citis passibus tenderemus, iacens Anatolii corpus est agnitum*, 25.6.4). The next day (*Secuto deinde die*, 25.6.5), i.e. June 29, they camped in a valley, while in the following night, i.e. of 30 June, a place called Charcha was taken, presumably modern Karkh Fairuz or Karkh Samarra, some 11 km north of Samarra (*Egressi exinde proxima nocte Charcham occupavimus locum*, 25.6.8). From there they reached the still unidentified city of Dura on the Tigris, some 6 km from Charcha. This happened on the first of July (*cumque hinc kalendis Iuliis stadiis triginta confectis civitatem nomine Duram adventaremus*, 25.6.9).

In the region around Dura the Romans were constantly harassed by the enemy and prevented from moving on, which meant a delay of four days, i.e. 2–5 July (*in hoc loco Persarum obstinatione tritum est quadriduum*, 25.6.11; cf. Zos. 3.30.4 ἡμέρας δὲ τέσσαρας προελθόντες). In their despair, and thinking that Roman territory was not far away, the soldiers demanded to be allowed to cross the Tigris. Although Jovian tried to restrain them by pointing out that the river was in flood because the Dog Star had already risen (*tumentemque iam canis exortu sideris amnem ostendens*, 25.6.12), he finally consented that some Gauls and Germans should swim across, when the quiet of the night, i.e. of 5 July, made it possible to do this without being seen (*cum latendi copiam nocturna quies daret*, 25.6.14). This crossing was successful, but the rest of the army, eager to follow, was persuaded to wait till pioneers could construct bridges (25.6.15). However, since the force of the stream prevented these bridges from being made, the Romans spent two days, i.e. 6–7 July, of being miserable and hungry (*acto miserabiliter biduo furebat inedia*, 25.7.4). Then, while the Romans were still in the neighbourhood of Dura, Sapor, rather unexpectedly, sent envoys to negotiate peace, which took another four miserable days, i.e. 8–11 July (*dies quattuor sunt evoluti inedia cruciabiles et omni supplicio tristiores,*

XVIII
A NOTE ON CHRONOLOGY

25.7.7). After the peace was concluded (*pax specie humanitatis indulta*, 25.8.1), Jovian and his army finally crossed the Tigris (*tandemque universi praeter mersos ad ulteriores venimus margines*, 25.8.3). Taking into consideration that the preparations for the difficult crossing of the river (cf. 25.7.4), as well as the crossing itself took some time, one may conclude that the Romans had reached the right bank of the Tigris by 16 July.

The next place mentioned by Ammianus is Hatra, an old and, at the time, abandoned city, situated in the midst of a desert (*properantesque itineribus magnis prope Hatram venimus, vetus oppidum in media solitudine positum olimque desertum*, 25.8.5). On the way there the troops suffered from lack of food and water, since they had left the Tigris: *quoniam loca contigua flumini...vitabantur...potus inopia premebamur et cibi*, 25.7.14. The distance to Hatra from the spot where the army crossed the Tigris can be estimated at some 250 km. In view of the difficult circumstances we conjecture that the army wanted to speed up its march, but that at least a fortnight must have passed before the Romans reached the neighbourhood of Hatra, so that they may have arrived there about 30 July (cf. Elton, 1996, 245: 'A day's march obviously varied in length, but seems to have averaged 20 km'). Near Hatra they found out that worse was to come, for they had to march for seventy miles (*ad usque lapidem septuagensimum*, 25.8.6) across an almost completely dry and barren plain. Having taken some time to prepare themselves for this march (*vasa, quae portabantur, aquis impleta sunt dulcibus et mactatis camelis iumentisque aliis alimenta quaesita sunt*, 25.8.6), they left Hatra on, say, 3 August, and marched on for six days (3–8 August, presumably). Then, on 8 August, near the Persian fortress of Ur (probably to be identified with Zagura, close to the modern village of Ain Sinu), they met troops led by the dux Mesopotamiae Cassianus and the tribune Mauricius, who brought them food (*Et via sex dierum emensa...dux Mesopotamiae Cassianus et tribunus Mauricius pridem ob hoc missus ad Ur nomine Persicum venere castellum cibos ferentes*, 25.8.7). This food came from stores of the army corps which was under the command of Procopius and Sebastianus, who happened to be nearby (presumably in Nisibis) and came out to meet Jovian in Thilsaphata (*Profecti exinde Thilsaphata venimus, ubi Sebastianus atque Procopius...occurrerunt*, 25.8.16). Thilsaphata should probably be identified with Thebetha or Tebitha, known i.a. from the Peutinger Table (*Tab. Peut.* X 4), and, if so, lay at a distance of some 33 miles from Nisibis. It was outside Nisibis that Jovian put up a standing camp (*post quae itinere festinato Nisibi cupide visa extra urbem stativa castra posuit princeps*, 25.8.17). Since it would have taken some eight days to complete the total stretch of 106 miles from Ur (Zagura) to Nisibis, and the Romans probably stayed a few days in both Ur and Tilsaphata, it would seem that Jovian's army pitched its tents outside Nisibis by 19 August.

In the very night that he reached Nisibis Jovian saw to it that a possible rival was murdered, the notarius Iovianus (*ibi tunc vespera tenebrante raptus a cena Iovianus...ductusque ad devium locum et praeceps actus in puteum siccum obrutus est saxorum multitudine superiacta*, 25.8.18). On the following day, that is (if our calculations are correct) on August 20, the emperor permitted the Persian noble Bineses to make a start with the implementation of one of the terms of the peace treaty, and to plant the standard of his nation on the citadel of Nisibis as a sign that the inhabitants had to leave their native place (*Postridie Bineses...principe permittente Romano civitatem ingressus gentis suae signum ab arce extulit summa migrationem e patria civibus nuntians luctuosam*, 25.9.1; cf. 25.7.9–11 and, for *postridie*, τῇ ὑστεραίᾳ in Zos. 3.33.2). When the Nisibenes strongly protested against their fate, Jovian made the order to leave the city at once (*et vertere solum extemplo omnes praecepti*, 25.9.2) more specific: all had to depart within three days (*intra triduum omnes iussit excedere moenibus*, 25.9.4). Either this evacuation must have been executed very quickly or Jovian did not wait to see it carried out, if indeed, as Eunapius reports, the emperor stayed near Nisibis for only two days, i.e. 20–21 August (*fr.* 29.1 ἐλθὼν δὲ ἐς Νίσιβιν...δύο μόνον ἡμερῶν ἐνδιατρίψας αὐτῇ). But perhaps Eunapius should not be taken too literally. At any rate, after the inhabitants had gone and the city of Nisibis had been handed over to the Persians (*extractis civibus et urbe tradita*, 25.9.12), the tribune Constantius was sent to deliver the fortifications and regions which Rome had to cede to Persia according to the peace treaty (cf. 25.7.9), while Julian's relative Procopius was sent to Tarsus with Julian's mortal remains (25.9.12).

'After these arrangements had been made we came by hurried marches to Antioch' (*His hoc modo peractis discursisque itineribus Antiochiam venimus*), Ammianus writes in 25.10.1, not wasting a single word on the journey of some 450 km from Nisibis to Antioch. Zosimus is not very detailed either (Ἰοβιανοῦ δὲ σπουδῇ τὰς πόλεις διαδραμόντος, 3.34.3). Both authors emphasize Jovian's haste, but this is deceptive. On 27 September, that is more than a month since he left Nisibis, the emperor was still in Edessa (*Cod. Theod.* 7.4.9). The remaining distance to Antioch, some 250 km, must have been covered at a somewhat greater speed, for *Cod. Theod.* 10.19.2 was issued in the Syrian capital on October 22. Jovian's stay at Antioch

XX A NOTE ON CHRONOLOGY

was far from pleasant. On successive days a series of dreadful portents were seen (*per continuos dies...multa visebantur et dira*, 25.10.1), and he was ridiculed by the local populace (Eun. *fr.* 29). This may explain why the emperor wanted to depart soon (*Moratum paulisper Antiochiae principem curarumque ponderibus diversis afflictum exeundi mira cupiditas agitabat*, 25.10.4). He left Antioch in great haste (*nec iumento parcens nec militi...profectus*, 25.10.4), presumably at the beginning of November, for *Cod. Theod.* 11.20.1 places him at Mopsuestia on November 12; that Jovian left Antioch 'in the dead of winter' (*flagrante hieme die*, 25.10.4, q.v., χειμῶνος ὄντος, Eun. *fr.* 29.1, Joh. Ant. *fr.* 181), is an exaggeration.

Mopsuestia was at a distance of some 50 km from Tarsus, so that Jovian must have arrived there about 15 November (*Tarsum urbem Cilicum nobilem introiit*, 25.10.4; cf. Zon. 13.14.10). Still in a hurry (*exindeque egredi nimium properans*, 25.10.5), the emperor nevertheless properly furnished the tomb of his predecessor situated just outside the city on the road to the Cilician Gates (*exornari sepulchrum statuit Iuliani in pomerio situm itineris, quod ad Tauri montis angustias ducit*, 25.10.5, cf. 23.2.5 *in suburbano sepultum est* and 25.9.12–3). Jovian left Tarsus on, say, 17 November, and with forced marches reached Tyana (*Deinde Tarso profectus extentis itineribus venit oppidum Cappadociae Tyana*, 25.10.6), which is situated well over 100 km from Tarsus. To cover this distance would have taken some five days, so that Tyana may have been reached about November 22. The next halting place mentioned by Ammianus is Aspona, a small town in Galatia, modern Sarihüyük, 180 miles (i.e., as a rule, a sixteen days' march) away from Tyana (*Itin. Burdig.* 575.12–577.6; cf. *Itin. Anton. Aug.* 144.1–145.2, where a slightly shorter distance is given). In Aspona Jovian met a delegation of the Gallic army (*apud Aspona Galatiae municipium breve Gallicani militis visa principia...redire iubentur ad signa*, 25.10.10). If Jovian had left Tyana on, say, 24 November, and if the 180 miles from Tyana to Aspona were indeed covered in some sixteen days, the meeting at Aspona with the officers of the Gallic army took place about December 10.

Before the end of the year Jovian was in Ancyra. The distance between Aspona and Ancyra can be calculated as 96 km (*Itin. Burdig.* 575.5–12, cf. *Itin. Anton. Aug.* 143), which means a four or five days' march and a date in mid-December for the arrival in Ancyra. *Cod. Iust.* 1.40.5 was published at Ancyra on December 28. In Ancyra Jovian assumed the consulship on January 1, 364 (*cum introisset Ancyram imperator, paratis ad pompam pro tempore necessariis consulatum iniit*, 25.10.11, cf. Them. *Or.* 5). How long he stayed in the capital of

A NOTE ON CHRONOLOGY

Galatia is uncertain, but he probably prolonged his sojourn there until the beginning of February. He died at Dadastana on 17 February 364 (*cum enim venisset Dadastanam, qui locus Bithyniam distinguit et Galatas, exanimatus inventus est nocte,* 25.10.12; *Decessit...tertio decimo Kal. Mart.,* Eutr. 10.18.2; Socr. *HE* 3.26.5). Dadastana, on the border of Galatia and Bithynia, is 167.5 (*Itin. Burdig.* 574.5–575.4) or 187.5 (*Itin. Anton. Aug.* 142) km west of Ancyra, that is, on average, an eight or nine days' march.

The results of our reconstruction are shown below in a diagram, which suggests a high degree of accuracy, but appearances are deceptive. While some of these dates are reasonably certain, others are no more than educated guesses.

June 16, 363	Beginning of Julian's retreat (*sextum decimum kalendas Iulias,* 24.8.5)
June 17	Skirmishes with the Persians; march via Barsaphthae to Hucumbra
June 18–19	At Hucumbra
June 20	Persian attack on the rear; some tribunes punished; from Hucumbra to Accete
June 21	From Accete to Maranga
June 22	Battle of Maranga
June 23–25	Truce of three days; from Maranga to Toumarra
June 26	From Toumarra northwards; Julian is wounded near Phrygia and dies
June 27	Election of a new emperor: Jovian (*quintum kalendas Iulias,* 25.5.1)
June 28	Persian attacks near the fortress Sumere
June 29–30	From Sumere to Charcha
July 1	From Charcha to Dura on the Tigris (*kalendis Iuliis,* 25.6.9)
July 2–5	Delay caused by Persian harassments
July 5	Some Gauls and Germans swim across the Tigris at night
July 6–7	Another delay
July 8–11	Negotiations with the Persians, resulting in a peace treaty
July 12–16	Crossing of the Tigris
July 16–30	From the Tigris to Hatra
July 30-August 2	At Hatra
August 3–8	From Hatra to Ur
August 9–11	At Ur
August 12–19	From Ur via Tilsaphata to Nisibis

A NOTE ON CHRONOLOGY

August 20–21	Nisibis surrendered to the Persians
August 21-October	From Nisibis via Edessa to Antioch
Before September 27	Arrival in Edessa (*Cod. Theod.* 7.4.9)
Before October 22	Arrival in Antioch (*Cod. Theod.* 10.19.2)
Before November 12	Arrival in Mopsuestia (*Cod. Theod.* 11.20.1)
November 12–15	From Mopsuestia to Tarsus
November 15–16	At Tarsus
November 17–22	From Tarsus to Tyana
November 24-December 10	From Tyana to Aspona
Before December 28	Arrival in Ancyra (*Cod. Iust.* 1.40.5)
January 1, 364	Jovian assumes the consulship (*consulatum iniit*, 25.10.11, Them. *Or.* 5)
February	From Ancyra westwards
February 17	Jovian dies at Dadastana (*tertio decimo Kal. Mart.*, Eutr. 10.18.2, Socr. *HE* 3.26.5)

LEGENDA

1. The lemmata are taken from W. Seyfarth's Teubner-edition (Leipzig 1978), with one alteration: consonantial u is always printed as v (*venit* instead of *uenit*).

2. For references to Greek authors we follow the abbreviations and indications of books and chapters in H.G. Liddell and R. Scott, *A Greek-English Lexicon*. Passages in Latin authors are indicated according to the system of the *Oxford Latin Dictionary*. For later and Christian authors we follow the *Thesaurus Linguae Latinae*.

Some exceptions to these rules:

- In the case of Caesar, Sallust and Tacitus the division of the chapters into sections in the Teubner-editions has also been taken into account.
- Seneca's *Dialogi* are referred to with the title of the individual works.
- For the Panegyrici Latini Mynors' OCT-edition has been used.
- The *Epistulae* of Julian are quoted from Bidez' edition in the Budé-series.
- Eunapius' *History* is quoted from Blockley's edition (*The Fragmentary Classicising Historians of the Later Roman Empire*, vol. II, Liverpool 1983).

3. As to secondary literature the following rules are observed:

- References to the six volumes of De Jonge's commentaries and to our commentaries on Books 20, 21, 22, 23 and 24 are usually given with 'see (the note) ad...' or 'q.v.'.
- Books or articles are normally referred to with the name of the author(s), the year of publication and the page(s). The full titles can be found in the bibliography; e.g. Hagendahl, 1921, 64 refers to H. Hagendahl, *Studia Ammianea*, Uppsala 1921, page 64.
- Quotations from existing translations and secondary literature are given between double inverted commas ("..."). Our own explanations of words or phrases in Greek and Latin texts are given between single inverted commas ('...').
- Occasionally reference is made to commentaries on other authors, e.g. Austin's on Vergil and Koestermann's on Tacitus, or

XXIV   LEGENDA

to well-known editions like those in the Budé-series. As a rule
these works are omitted from the bibliography.
– Of the following books, which are referred to regularly, only the
name of the author and the page(s) are given:

Bitter   N. Bitter, *Kampfschilderungen bei Ammianus Mar-*
                    cellinus, Bonn 1976.
Blomgren   S. Blomgren, *De sermone Ammiani Marcellini quaes-*
                    tiones variae, Diss. Uppsala 1937.
Brok   M.F.A. Brok, *De Perzische expeditie van keizer Ju-*
                    lianus volgens Ammianus Marcellinus, Groningen
                    1959.
Ehrismann   H. Ehrismann, *De temporum et modorum usu Ammi-*
                    aneo, Diss. Strasbourg 1886.
Fesser   H. Fesser, *Sprachliche Beobachtungen zu Ammianus*
                    Marcellinus, Diss. Breslau 1932.
Fontaine   J. Fontaine, *Ammien Marcellin, Histoire, IV (Livres*
                    XXIII–XXIV), 2 vols., Paris 1977.
Harmon   A.M. Harmon, *The Clausula in Ammianus Mar-*
                    cellinus, New Haven 1910 (Transactions of the
                    Connecticut Academy of Arts and Sciences 16,
                    117–245).
Hassenstein   G. Hassenstein, *De syntaxi Ammiani Marcellini*,
                    Diss. Königsberg 1877.
Jones   A.H.M. Jones, *The Later Roman Empire 284–612. A*
                    Social Economic and Administrative Survey, Oxford
                    1964 (repr. 1986).
Kühner-Stegmann   R. Kühner and C. Stegmann, *Ausführliche Gram-*
                    matik der lateinischen Sprache, II Satzlehre, 2 vols.,
                    Hannover 1955[4], 1976[5].
Leumann   M. Leumann, *Lateinische Laut-und Formenlehre*,
                    Munich 1977.
Matthews   J.F. Matthews, *The Roman Empire of Ammianus*,
                    London 1989.
Paschoud   F. Paschoud, *Zosime, Histoire Nouvelle, II, 1 (Livre*
                    III), Paris 1979.
Sabbah   G. Sabbah, *La méthode d'Ammien Marcellin. Recher-*
                    ches sur la construction du discours historique dans les
                    Res Gestae, Paris 1978.
Seager   R. Seager, *Ammianus Marcellinus. Seven studies in*
                    his Language and Thought, Columbia 1986.

LEGENDA

Szantyr   J.B. Hofmann and A. Szantyr, *Lateinische Syntax und Stilistik*, Munich 1965 (repr. 1972).

Wagner-Erfurdt   J.A. Wagner, *Ammiani Marcellini quae supersunt*, cum notis integris Frid. Lindenbrogii, Henr. et Hadr. Valesiorum et Iac. Gronovii, quibus Thom. Reinesii quasdam et suas adiecit, editionem absolvit Car. Gottl. Aug. Erfurdt, 3 vols., Leipzig 1808 (repr. in 2 vols, Hildesheim 1975).

The following translations are often referred to with the name of the translator only:

Caltabiano   M. Caltabiano, *Ammiano Marcellino. Storie*, Milan 1998.

Hamilton   W. Hamilton and A. Wallace-Hadrill, *Ammianus Marcellinus: the Later Roman Empire (AD 354–378)*, Harmondsworth 1986.

Rolfe   J.C. Rolfe, *Ammianus Marcellinus*, with an English translation, 3 vols., London-Cambridge Mass. 1935–1939 (repr. 1971–1972).

Selem   A. Selem, *Le Storie di Ammiano Marcellino. Testo e Traduzione*, Turin 1965 (repr. 1973)

Seyfarth   W. Seyfarth, *Ammianus Marcellinus, Römische Geschichte. Lateinisch und Deutsch und mit einem Kommentar versehen*, II, Berlin 1983[5] and III, Berlin 1986[3].

Veh   O. Veh, *Ammianus Marcellinus. Das römische Weltreich vor dem Untergang*, übersetzt von Otto Veh, eingeleitet und erläutert von G. Wirth, Zurich-Munich 1974.

Viansino   G. Viansino, *Ammiano Marcellino. Storie*, 3 vols., Milan 2001–2002.

4. In cases where this is helpful for the reader or relevant for the interpretation the cursus is indicated as follows:

– *revocávit in státum*: cursus planus
– *sublátius éminens*: cursus tardus
– *fécit et vectigáles*: cursus velox

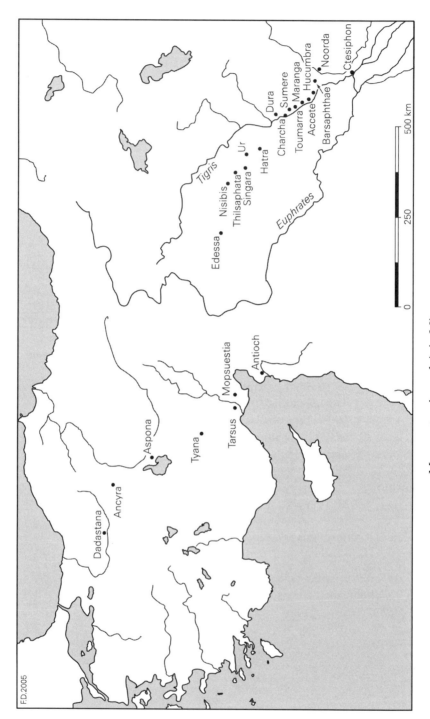

Mesopotamia and Asia Minor

CHAPTER 1

Introduction

The chapter begins in the darkness of a starless night, which causes tense uncertainty among the Roman soldiers. But as they march on in the next few days, they go from strength to strength, in spite of the difficulties they have to cope with: heat, continuous skirmishes with smaller or larger enemy units, cowardly behaviour of part of the cavalry, and finally a full-scale battle, in which Roman stamina gloriously overcomes Persian fragility. In the preamble of the rather brief description of this battle Ammianus takes the opportunity to expatiate once more on what had obviously struck him most in the Persians' armed forces: the ironclad warriors, the elephants and the archers.

Julian's presence is less pronounced than in book 24. Several details make clear that he is fully in control of the situation, but he stays away from the heat of the actions. Regarding topographical, chronological and other details, the chapter leaves much to be desired. Without Zosimus' parallel report it would be wellnigh impossible to reconstruct the particular stages of the katabasis referred to by the author.

Et hanc quidem noctem nullo siderum fulgore splendentem Amm. has a **1.1** prcdilcction for the sentence pattern in which *et hic* (or *ille*) *quidem* winds up an episode or a description, and a new development is introduced by *vero* (sometimes *sed* or *autem*). Some examples: *et hae quidem regiones...orientis vero limes* (14.8.4–5), *et haec quidem...Rex vero* (19.9.8–9), *et haec quidem Gallieni temporibus evenerunt. Iulianus vero* (23.5.3–4). The present case is remarkable in that it occurs right at the beginning of a book, but it can be explained by the author's wish to begin with the contrast between the anxiety during the dark night and the revived spirits at daybreak. It should also be noted that anaphoric *hic* is one of the first words in the majority of the books of the *Res Gestae*. It is only absent at the beginning of books 14, 15, 24, 28 and 29. In book 26 it appears in 1.3, directly after the author's new preface.

It was the night of June 16–17, 363. "Cette nuit du 15 au 16 juin 363" in Fontaine's n. 474 must be a slip. In 24.8.5 Amm. had given a date for the beginning of the katabasis: *sextum decimum kalendas*

Iulias, i.e. June 16. In the course of that day the march had been interrupted and a camp measured off (24.8.5–7). For Paschoud's proposal to identify this camp as Zosimus' Barsaphthae see below, ad § 3 *hinc recedentibus nobis*.

TLL VI 1.1515.25–50 lists a number of cases in which *fulgor* is specifically used of sun, moon or stars. As was noted ad 22.15.5, Amm. uses *sidus* for different celestial bodies, among them the moon. Presumably neither moon nor stars relieved the darkness of the night, as in 16.12.11 *nox senescente luna nullis sideribus adiuvanda*. The absence of any light in the nocturnal sky cannot be ascribed to the date: as has been explained in the note ad 24.5.8 *nox casu*, May 13 or 14, 363 witnessed full moon, so that in the night of June 16 new moon must be ruled out; in fact it was due on June 26 or 27. It may simply have been a clouded night, but the absence of any celestial glow could also have been caused by the huge cloud of dust described in 24.8.5–7.

ut solet in artis rebus et dubiis Cf. *ut solet in dubiis rebus* (15.5.31), *utque in rebus amat fieri dubiis* (16.12.40). See also Heubner ad Tac. *Hist.* 3.69.4 *artas res*: "vor Tac. anscheinend immer in der Form *rebus in artis*", i.a. Ov. *Pont.* 3.2.25, V.Fl. 5.324.

nec sedere quodam auso nec flectere in quietem lumina See for the late Latin use of *quidam* "in der Bedeutung von *quisquam*" Szantyr 197 and the note ad 24.4.22 *nec quodam*. The men remained standing all night, nobody dared to sit down, let alone lie down. The latter is substituted by a somewhat high-flown phrase. There seem to be no examples of *flectere* to denote the 'closing' of the eyes. Therefore, judging from such phrases as *quocumque oculos flexeris* (14.6.20), *nec dextra vultum nec laeva flectebat* (16.10.10), *flexis ad aedem ipsam luminibus* (22.11.7), here, too, one should assume a similar meaning: the soldiers did not dare to 'turn' their eyes away from the direction from which danger was expected, and to go to sleep (*in quietem*). Some other examples of people not turning their eyes away: Orpheus in Ov. *Met.* 10.52 *ne flectat retro sua lumina* (see Bömer ad loc.), and Tac. *Hist.* 2.70.4 *At non Vitellius flexit oculos nec tot milia insepultorum civium exhorruit.* See for *lumina*, 'eyes', the note ad 22.11.7. Brok 170 is right in drawing attention to *tutius quievimus* (24.8.7), which seems to contrast with the present text. However, in 24.8.7 the author expresses that in the given situation the men felt comparatively safe within their camp, whereas here their worries about the near future are expressed.

CHAPTER 1.1   3

ubi verum primum dies inclaruit I. e. the morning of June 17. The information in TLL VII 936.82 sqq. implies that this is the first time that the verb *inclarescere* is used "proprie" to describe the appearance of daylight. Obviously, the cloud of dust (cf. 24.8.5–7) had now disappeared.

radiantes loricae limbis circumdatae ferreis et corusci thoraces Amm.'s memories of military actions were filled with the glitter and shine of the armour worn by the various warriors; cf. the introductory note to 24.2.5 and phrases like *armorumque nitore conspicuus* (16.12.24), *radiantium armorum splendore perstricti* (18.8.4), *cum agmine catafractorum fulgentium* (20.7.2), *quem adesse coruscus nitor indicabat armorum* (24.7.8). According to Libanius *Or.* 18.264 the armour of the Persians glittered with gold (καὶ χρυσὸς πολὺς ἐν τοῖς ὅπλοις). This seems a bit exaggerated. Cf. Bliembach, 1976, 206: "Nur die Waffen des Königs und seiner Feldherrn werden vergoldet gewesen sein". But the glitter of the armour, whatever its cause, apparently had the expected effect intended by Vegetius: *plurimum...terroris hostibus armorum splendor importat* (*mil.* 2.14.8; cf. 31.10.9 *nitore fulgentes armorum imperatorii adventus iniecere barbaris metum*). Plutarch relates that the Parthians first covered their armour and then showed themselves in blazing helmets and *thoraces*: ἐξαίφνης τὰ προκαλύμματα τῶν ὅπλων καταβαλόντες ὤφθησαν αὐτοί...φλογοειδεῖς κράνεσι καὶ θώραξι (*Crass.* 24.1).

It is difficult to ascertain whether or not Amm. made a difference between *lorica* and *thorax* and, if he did, what precisely the difference was. Valesius suggested that the one was made of leather, the other of iron, referring to Plut. *Crass.* 25.7, but Plutarch there only speaks of *thoraces*, not of both *loricae* and *thoraces*: θώρακας ὠμοβύρσους καὶ σιδηροῦς. According to Wagner a *thorax* covered only the chest, a *lorica* also other parts of the body, but Heliodorus 9.15.1, speaking of *catafractarii*, says: οὐ τὰ στέρνα μόνον ἀλλὰ καὶ σῶμα τὸ ἄλλο ἅπαν τεθωράκισται (he then gives an extensive description of the way in which a *thorax* was made, 9.15.2–3). One could point to 16.10.8, where we find *loricae* used of infantrymen and *thoraces* of cavalry (*et incedebat hinc inde ordo geminus armatorum clipeatus atque cristatus corusco lumine radians nitidis loricis indutus sparsique catafracti equites, quos clibanarios dictitant, personati thoracum muniti tegminibus et limbis ferreis cincti*), but in 25.3.3 it is the mounted Julian who, when going into the battle which was to be his last, forgot to put on his *lorica*. Note further that according to Zos. 3.27.2 Julian on another occasion put on a *thorax*: ἐνδὺς τὸν θώρακα ὁ βασιλεύς.

4   COMMENTARY

In distinguishing the various types of *loricae* modern scholars coined the following names: *loricae hamatae* (consisting of ring mail), *loricae squamatae* (made up of small sections of metal sheet, less flexible than the *loricae hamatae*) and *loricae segmentatae* (made of strips of iron sheet articulated on leather straps). Although in the present text we are, of course, dealing with Persian troops, it is worth noting that the traditional view that Late Roman soldiers went into battle unprotected by body armour, in contrast to their colleagues during the Principate, is nowadays not held anymore. Cf. e.g. Grosse, 1927; Coulston, 1990; Bishop-Coulston, 1993, 59, 60, 85; Southern-Dixon, 1996, 96–9; Elton, 1996, 110–4; Stephenson, 1999, 32 ff. and the plates in Robinson, 1975. For Sasanian armour see Bivar, 1972 and Allan, 1987.

adesse regis copias indicabant Cf. Lib. *Or.* 18.264 τότε δὴ πρῶτον ὁρᾶται Περσικὴ παράταξις, πλῆθος οὐκ ἄτακτον. There had been much speculation among the Romans about the arrival of the Persian king with his troops. Cf. 24.5.7 *rex cum ambitiosis copiis passibus citis incedens propediem affore credebatur*, 24.7.7 *ut…viderentur advenisse iam regis auxilia* and 24.8.6 *nonnulli Persas nobis viantibus incubuisse firmabant.*

1.2   *hocque viso accensum* Cf. for *accendere* denoting the arousing of feelings *pugnantes accendens* (15.8.13), *Romanisque ad ducis vindictam accensis* (21.3.3).

dirimente fluvio brevi The *fluvius* here and the *rivus* of 24.8.7 are probably one and the same river, possibly the Douros (Diyala) mentioned by Zosimus in 3.26.4 (cf. Paschoud n. 75). So already Wagner: "Durus fortasse", but Brok 171 is sceptical. He thinks that one of the many irrigation canals in the region must be meant. Since other geographical details are lacking, it is hard to decide which of these suggestions is right. Anyway, in order to be able to take the royal road on the left bank of the Tigris leading north to Corduene (see the note ad 24.8.4), Julian's army must have crossed the Douros. If the *fluvius* of the present text and the *rivus* of 24.8.7 indeed denote the Douros, it follows that the Romans, after having crossed the stream, encamped not far from it. One might be inclined to render *brevis* with 'small' (see the note ad 23.6.16), but it may well mean 'shallow' (TLL II 2180.75 sqq.: "exiguae profunditatis"), as in Verg. *A.* 5.221 *brevibusque vadis* and Claud. 26 (*Bell. Get.*). 333 *primo fonte breves, alto mox gurgite regnant* (about the Danube and the Rhine). Mela 1.102

CHAPTER 1.2   5

uses it of the Black Sea. Cf. also the noun *brevia*, 'shallows', in 16.11.9 and 22.8.46 with the notes ad loc.

prohibuit imperator A notably brief and matter-of-fact phrase, which shows that Julian still had a keen eye for what was prudent and profitable in the situation.

et non procul a vallo ipso inter excursatores nostros et Persicos proelio acri conserto I.e. not far from the camp mentioned in 24.8.7 (*metatis…castris*). Cf. Zos. 3.26.5 Τῶν δὲ ἡγουμένων τοῦ στρατοῦ κατασκόπων εἰς χεῖρας ἐλθόντων μοίρᾳ τινὶ Περσικῇ. Pace Klotz, 1916, 497: "es wäre eine Verbindung durch *tamen* möglich, aber nicht das einfach anreihende *et*", there is no contradiction here. Julian forbade a large scale fight 'and' so hostilities remained limited to a struggle in which only the *excursatores* took part. See on these the note ad 24.1.2, the only other place in which the word occurs according to TLL V 2.1294.24–6.

Machameus cecidit, ductor unius agminis nostri The incident is referred to by Zosimus in the following way: Μακαμαῖός τις γυμνὸς ('not covered by armour') ὑπὸ προθυμίας ἐπιπεσὼν τέσσαρας μὲν ἀναιρεῖ, συστραφέντων δ' ἅμα πολλῶν ἐπ' αὐτὸν κατασφάττεται (3.26.5). Libanius *Or.* 18.264, cited ad §3, also mentions it, without giving the man's name. In *PLRE* I the *ductor unius agminis* is listed under the heading of Macameus. Note that the author of the lemma in the *PLRE* says that Macameus was fatally wounded "near Ctesiphon". This is not very precise, whether or not the *fluvius* of 25.1.2 is to be identified with the Douros.

    According to Malalas *Chron.* 13.329 Machamaeus, called Ἀκκαμέος in this excerpt of Magnus of Carrhae, and Maurus, for whom see the next note, had been left by Julian in charge of a garrison at Cercusium: καὶ ἐάσας καὶ ἐν τῷ Κιρκησίῳ κάστρῳ ὅσους εὗρεν ἐγκαθέτους ('whom he found stationed there') στρατιώτας ἑξακισχιλίους, προσθεὶς αὐτοῖς καὶ ἄλλους ὁπλίτας ἄνδρας τετρακισχιλίους μετὰ ἐξάρχων δύο Ἀκκαμέου καὶ Μαύρου (for Julian's stay in Cercusium in the beginning of April 363 see Amm. 23.5.1–5 with the notes; the passage of Malalas should have been mentioned there). It is not related how and when the two ἔξαρχοι had joined the main body of the army again.

    As to *ductor*, the noun in Amm. most often denotes an emperor, as e.g. in 23.5.24, 25.3.10, 31.5.17, or a high-ranking general (cf. e.g. 14.9.1, 28.6.26). In 23.6.2 the Parthian Arsaces is referred to

6 COMMENTARY

with *latronum...ductoris*. Sometimes it means 'guide', as for example in 17.10.2 and 24.7.3. In the present text and in 25.1.8 (q.v.) it would seem that it is equivalent to *tribunus*. So e.g. Ensslin, 1930, *PLRE* I, Macameus, although with a question mark, Brok 171 and Paschoud n. 76. For *agmen*, 'army unit', cf. 17.13.6 (q.v.) *in agmina plurima clam distributo exercitu*, 25.3.2 *laxis...agminibus*, 26.7.13 (ni) *agmina duo praeire iussisset, quibus nomina sunt Iovii atque Victores*.

In his note 76 Paschoud appears to be "irrésistiblement" reminded of the episode of Nisus and Euryalus, but there are no verbal parallels at all to the relevant passage *A.* 9.422–45, and, moreover, Maurus' shoulder wound was not fatal.

cui propugnaturus Maurus frater, dux postea Phoenices Cf. 27.6.9 *castris...propugnabit*, 31.10.12 *caritatibusque suis...propugnabant*. Cf. also Apul. *Met.* 9.37 *propugnare fratri*. Libanius *Or.* 18.264, although referring to the death of Machameus (see the preceding note), is silent about the heroic action taken by his brother Maurus (*PLRE* I, Maurus 1). Zosimus does mention Maurus (Μαῦρος δὲ ἀδελφὸς ὢν αὐτοῦ, 3.26.5), but omits to relate that he later became *dux Phoenices*, one of the seven zone commanders on the eastern frontier. When precisely Maurus held this position is not known. Perhaps he was the successor of the Alamannic king whom Amm. mentions in 21.3.5 (q.v.): *Vadomarius...postea quoque ducatum per Phoenicen regens*. In *PLRE* I the Maurus of the present text (Maurus 1) is distinguished (rightly, it would seem) from Maurus 2, the *draconarius* of the Petulantes who at the pronunciamiento of Paris in 360 took off his *torques* and put it on Julian's head (20.4.18) and who many years later, as a *comes*, managed the situation at the pass of Succi (31.10.21) badly. Woods, 1998, however, argues for the identification of these two Mauri.

cum germani trucidasset interfectorem, obvium quemque perterrens infirmatus et ipse umerum telo pallescentem morte propinqua Machameum extrahere pugna viribus valuit magnis Cf. Zos. 3.26.5 τὸ σῶμα ἰδὼν ἐν μέσοις κείμενον Πέρσαις, ἁρπάζει τε αὐτὸ καὶ τὸν πρῶτον παίσαντα κτείνει· καὶ οὐκ ἀπεῖπε βαλλόμενος, ἄχρις ὅτε τὸν ἀδελφὸν ἔμπνουν ἔτι τῷ Ῥωμαίων στρατῷ παρέδωκεν. The verb *interficere* does not primarily occur in contexts of battles and warfare, but it is sometimes used in such passages: *interfecto Punico praesidio* (Liv. 23.7.6), *plerique et vulnerati et interfecti sunt* (Liv. 35.29.3), so that the fact that Amm. uses it in this way is not surprising: *quos...nec interficere nec corripere...potuerunt* (18.2.13), *interfectis quibusdam viros cepere nonnullos* (24.5.9). As the list in TLL VII 2190.35–74 shows, the nomen agentis *interfector* hardly

CHAPTER 1.3   7

ever occurs in passages of warfare; Liv. 44.40.9 (not mentioned in the list) is a rare exception: *ad persequendos interfectores transgressi sunt.* Two of Amm.'s instances, the present text and 25.1.6, do belong to this category; in the third, 27.10.4, it means 'assassin'. Amm. probably saw no difference in usage between the verb and the noun.

Zosimus expresses *pallescentem morte propinqua* much more factually with ἔμπνουν ἔτι. This is the only example of *pallescere* in Amm. and according to TLL X 1.126.68–73, there are only two other cases in which the verb occurs in a context of death. However, the phrase is primarily, if not irresistibly, reminiscent of Verg. *A.* 4.644 *pallida morte futura* and 8.709 *pallentem morte futura.*

Et cum fatiscerent vix toleranda aestuum magnitudine crebrisque congressibus partes   The torrid heat of Mesopotamia in June, for which see Kaegi, 1991, 587–91, is mentioned more than once, cf. 24.8.3 *per eas terras vapore sideris calescentes* and 25.1.18 *miles solis cursu flammeo diu lassatus.* From TLL VI 353.35 sqq. it appears that *fatiscere* (or *fatisci*) in the sense "fatigari, deficere" occurs mainly in archaic and post-classical Latin; cf. e.g. Acc. *trag.* 330 *haut fatiscar quin,* Tac. *Ann.* 14.24.1 *per inopiam et labores fatiscebant,* Amm. 18.6.13 *equo iam fatiscente.* In Amm. the plural of *aestus* is used more often than the singular, even if Heraeus' emendation *intemperantia aestuum* (19.4.8) is not counted. The plural is interpreted as "poetic" by De Jonge ad 17.7.12 and 18.9.2, but the relevant lemmata in TLL and OLD show that the plural is by no means uncommon; some examples: *ferventissimis aestibus* (Plin. *Ep.* 8.1.1), *aestuum magnitudinem* (Ambr. *hex.* 4.5.23), *in aestibus...diei* (August. *C.D.* 21.5). In the present text one may regard it as expressing the hot hours of the day. See for *partes,* 'the two fighting parties', the note ad 19.2.14. Other examples are 20.11.24 *partesque discesserunt ad otium breve,* 21.12.5 *partes accensae in clades mutuas,* 24.4.15 *strepebant utrimque partes.* **1.3**

ad ultimum hostiles turmae gravi sunt repulsa discussae   Here *turmae* is used of enemy troops, as in 15.4.9, 18.9.3, 19.2.2, 26.8.5, 27.1.4, 29.1.3, 31.13.5. For *turmae* in the Roman army see the notes ad 23.3.4 and 24.3.1. Zosimus is silent about the outcome of the struggle, but according to Libanius the Persians fled immediately: πεσόντος δὲ ἡμετέρου τινὸς προμάχου (i.e. Machameus) καὶ συμπεσόντων ἁπάντων οὔθ' ἱππεὺς οὔθ' ὁπλίτης ἤνεγκε τὰς παρ' ἡμῶν ἀσπίδας, ἀλλ' εὐθὺς ἐγκλίναντες ἔφευγον (*Or.* 18.264).

The original meaning of *repulsa* is 'electoral defeat', as in 28.4.21 *ob repulsam praeturae.* In a metaphorical sense it can express "rebuff"

8 COMMENTARY

(OLD s.v. 2), e.g. in Ov. *Met.* 3.289 *nullam patiere repulsam.* Amm. 26.10.17 *marini fremitus velut gravati repulsam* (in the description of an earthquake) might also be an instance, but it is more likely that this metaphor is prompted by Amm.'s unexpected use of *repulsa* in a military sense: 'beating off an attack'. The other instance of this is 19.5.8 *gentes acri repulsa disiectae.* In his note ad loc. De Jonge refers to 24.4.7 *a cohortibus nostris repulsoriis*, where the adi. is a hapax.

hinc recedentibus nobis According to Zosimus, who, in the passages corresponding to chapters 1 and 2, gives more geographical details than Amm., the army reached a city called Barsaphthae, where it was discovered that the Persians had burnt all fodder for the horses: Ἐλθόντες δὲ εἰς πόλιν Βαρσαφθὰς τὸν χιλὸν εὗρον ὑπὸ τῶν βαρβάρων καταπρησθέντα (3.27.1).

In Zosimus' account the arrival at Barsaphthae took place after the fight in which the brothers Machameus and Maurus distinguished themselves by their courage. Paschoud in n. 76 (cf. n. 77 and 82) suggests that Zosimus mistakenly reversed the chronological order. In his view Barsaphthae was the name of the place where the Romans encamped in the night of June 16–17 (for the date see above, ad §1 *Et hanc quidem noctem*). Otherwise, according to the Swiss scholar, one has to admit that Barsaphthae was not a port of call for the Romans and this would be bizarre.

Paschoud's suggestion is not without problems. In the first place, if we were to follow him, we would have to assume that Julian encamped in or near a city, for Zosimus calls Barsaphthae a πόλις. However, in Amm.'s description of the place where the army camped in the night of June 16–17 there is no hint of a city: *in valle graminea prope rivum...metatis tutius quievimus castris* (24.8.7). More importantly, the Romans had measured off a camp in a grassy valley, while Zosimus says that the Persians near Barsaphthae had burnt all fodder. The identification of the *castra* of 24.8.7 as the πόλις Barsaphthae therefore does not seem very likely. What about the alternative? Is it really bizarre that Zosimus mentions Barsaphthae although the Romans did not actually stop at this city? We think not. It is perfectly understandable that precisely for the reason which Zosimus gives, viz. the burning of the fodder, Julian passed by the city and marched on till he found a place to stay in Hucumbra/Symbra, where there was plenty of food (25.1.4, Zos. 3.27.2–3).

The use of *recedere* for the victorious party is slightly surprising: it seems more appropriate for those who are defeated or thwarted, e.g.

CHAPTER 1.3   9

hostes a moenibus recessere (Liv. 6.28.4). Translators tend to smoothe over the difficulty, e.g. with "Daraufhin zogen wir von hier aus weiter" (Seyfarth).

longius Saraceni secuti sunt et nostrorum metu peditum repedare compulsi paulo postea innexi Persarum multitudini tutius irruebant Romana impedimenta rapturi Zosimus' version is rather close to that of Amm.: μοίρας δέ τινος Περσῶν ἅμα Σαρακηνοῖς ἐπιφανείσης, καὶ οὐδὲ ἄχρι θέας τὸν Ῥωμαϊκὸν στρατὸν ὑποστάσης ἀλλ᾽ αὐτόθεν ἀφανοῦς γενομένης, κατ᾽ ὀλίγους εἰς ταὐτὸ συνιόντες οἱ Πέρσαι συνειλεγμένοι τε εἰς πλῆθος ἤδη παρεῖχον ὑπόνοιαν ὡς ἐπελευσόμενοι τοῖς ὑποζυγίοις (3.27.1). It was noted ad 23.3.8 (q.v.) that Saracens fought in the Persian army as well as on the Roman side and that the Romans experienced a lot of difficulties as a result of their actions, cf. 25.6.8–10 and 25.8.1. For Saracens in general see the notes ad 22.15.2 *Scenitas* and 23.3.8 *Saracenorum*. Add to the literature cited there Gatier, 1999.

Without doubt in V's *longius sunt saraceni et* a part. perf. in the nom. pl. is missing. Seyfarth adheres to Clark's *secuti*, which is more attractive than Günther's tentative *insidiati* (1891, 69), in that it forms a better combination with *longius* ('at a considerable distance'). However, Heraeus' *visi* (before *longius*) is also worth considering, viz. as a case of haplography after *nobis*; moreover, this tallies with the participle ἐπιφανείσης in Zos. 3.27.1, quoted above. The nearness of *viso imperatore* argues against this solution.

See for *repedare* the note ad 24.4.30. Although the use of *innectere* is quite bold here, the emendation *innixi*, proposed by Günther, 1888, 42–3 is not felicitous. The verb *inniti* does not occur anywhere else in Amm., and the required meaning 'to rely on the protection provided by' would be at least equally bold. Moreover, *sibique vicissim innexi* (16.12.38) is akin to the present phrase. Although the dat. is usual as a complement with *innectere*, the abl. should not be ruled out, especially in the passive: the Saracens were completely enclosed within and by the Persian host: V's *multitudine* can be kept. Cf. for *irruere* about attacking an army train 24.1.2 *ne quis repentinus irrueret*. Strictly speaking, the addition of *Romana* is superfluous, but presumably the author wanted to prevent any misunderstanding. With *rapturi* he characterizes the Saracens: these men were no warriors, but brigands, only eager for booty; in 14.4.1 they are compared to birds of prey: *milvorum rapacium similes*; cf. also 24.2.4, where one of their leaders is contemptuously called a *latro*.

10 COMMENTARY

viso imperatore ad alas subsidiarias reverterunt Since the burning of
the ships (24.7.6) Julian's presence is far less conspicuous than
in the report of the march towards Ctesiphon (chapters 1–6 of
book 24). Here the deft touch of *viso imperatore* is remarkable.
Although it does not conflict with Zos. 3.27.2 Τότε δὴ πρῶτος ἐνδὺς
τὸν θώρακα ὁ βασιλεὺς παντὸς προέδραμε τοῦ στρατεύματος, οἱ Πέρσαι
δὲ οὐχ ὑπέμειναν, ἀλλ᾽ εἰς τοὺς αὐτοῖς ἐγνωσμένους ἀποδρᾶναι διέγνωσαν
τόπους, Amm.'s laconic phrase has a different flavour: the emperor's
mere presence does the trick.

As to *ala*, this is "another typically Roman word for a Persian
party of riders" (De Jonge ad 18.6.12, the only occurrence of *ala* in
Amm. apart from the present text.). This is Amm.'s only instance
of *subsidiarius*, which in classical Latin is a normal term to denote
forces which are 'kept in reserve', e.g. Caes. *Civ.* 1.83.2 *subsidiariae*
(cohortes), Liv. 37.42.1 *auxilia...subsidiaria*. In 14.6.17, 27.10.15,
29.5.47 and 31.7.12 Amm. has *subsidialis*.

1.4 *qua ex regione profecti ad Hucumbra nomine villam pervenimus* It would
seem that Hucumbra is Zosimus' Symbra. However, Zosimus' description of Symbra is rather puzzling. According to him it was situated
right in the middle between two cities, Nisbara and Nischanadalbe,
which were separated from each other by the Tigris but joined by
a bridge. To take this literally seems rather odd: "il faudrait placer
Symbra sur une île du Tigre" (Paschoud n. 78). Zosimus' text certainly is hard to understand: προιὼν δὲ εἰς κώμην ἐλήλυθε Σύμβραν, ἥτις
ἐν μέσῳ δυοῖν κεῖται πόλεων, αἷς ὀνόματα Νίσβαρα καὶ Νισχαναδάλβη.
Διαιρεῖ δὲ ταύτας ὁ Τίγρις, καὶ γέφυρα ἦν, ἣ τὰς ἐπιμιξίας τοῖς ἀμφοτέρων
οἰκήτορσιν ἐδίδου ῥᾳδίας καὶ συνεχεῖς (3.27.2–3). He must have been
confused by what he found in his source. However, there is no need
to assume with Dillemann, 1961, 145–6 that Zosimus invented the
existence of Nisbara and Nischanadalbe. We may conclude then that
Julian's army on its march north along the Tigris passed these twin
cities not far from Hucumbra/Symbra, but that their position with
regard to this place is unknown.

As to Hucumbra/Symbra, note that Zosimus speaks of a κώμη,
a village. In their various languages the translators agree about the
meaning of Amm.'s *villa* here: "estate" (Rolfe), "domain" (Hamilton), "Landgut" (Seyfarth), "tenuta" (Caltabiano), "domaine" (Fontaine). They all keep to the classical meaning, which is correct for
e.g. the occurrences in 14.9.8, 19.9.7, 30.10.4, but neither here nor
in 18.7.9 *cumque Bebasen villam venissent* can be regarded as satisfactory. It is better to heed Souter's opportune reference to August. *cat.*

CHAPTER 1.4

rud. 22.40, where this word is used to denote Bethlehem: *inter omnes Iudaeae civitates ita erat exigua ut hodieque villa appelletur.* So around 400 the term could denote a 'village' or 'rural settlement', a meaning which suits the present text.

The wording of both Zosimus and Amm. implies that Hucumbra/Symbra was rather small and therefore speaks against the identification of this κώμη or *villa* as the city of 'Ukbara, proposed by Streck, 1913, 2517 and accepted by e.g. Herzfeld, 1948, 64–5 and Fontaine n. 482 (but rejected by Paschoud n. 78). 'Ukbara, of which the ruins are still to be seen, is now on the west bank of the Tigris, but up to the 13th century, when the course of the river moved, it was situated on the east bank. The city lay some 50 km north of modern Bagdad (and perhaps 20 km north of Amm.'s Hucumbra). If we are to believe the *Chronicle of Se'ert*, pp. 220–1 Scher (quoted in a German translation by Winter-Dignas, 2001, 258–9), "Marw Habur (= Shapur), that is, 'Ukbara", was founded by Sapor I, but other Arabic sources, referred to in Oppenheimer, 1983, 453 n. 5, hold Sapor II responsible for its foundation. Julian's army did pass 'Ukbara a couple of days later.

ubi per biduum omnibus ad usum congruis et satietate quaesita frumenti ultra spem recreati discessimus The two days spent in Hucumbra were 18 and 19 June. Zosimus also points to the abundance of food found in Hucumbra/Symbra. He further relates that Persian units were put to flight by Roman foragers: ἔνθα (i.e. in Symbra) που λόχοι Περσῶν ἀναφανέντες ὑπὸ τῶν προνομευόντων κατασκόπων ἐτράπησαν· καὶ ἅμα τροφὴν ἄφθονον ὁ στρατὸς εὑρὼν ἐν ταύτῃ τῇ κώμῃ...τὸ περιττὸν ὅσον ἦν ἅπαν διέφθειρεν (3.27.3). For a similar two days' rest with plenty of provisions see 24.5.3 *exercitu omni per aquarum et pabuli opportuna biduo recreato.*

Petschenig, 1891, 353 argues against the conjecture *esum* in these terms: "Also ausser hinlänglichem Getreide noch alle mögliche Esswaren? Selbstverständlich ist mit V *usum* zu lesen". The conclusion is better than the argument. Amm. has no other examples of *esus* and, moreover, *usui congruus* occurs in 20.6.1 (q.v.), 23.2.5 and 30.3.3. See also the note on *congruus* ad 22.12.5. From the parallel in 23.6.65 *satietate frugum...exuberat* it appears that *satietas* means "abundance" (OLD s.v. 1) here; cf. also *alimentorumque in isdem satias condita* (18.2.4, q.v.). Cf. for *quaerere*, 'to obtain', 24.1.15 *quaesitis dextris propriis utebantur* (q.v.), 27.4.11 *sex provinciae sunt quaesitae.* The present phrase can be best explained as an abl. abs. consisting of two heads and one participle which is formally adapted to one of

12   COMMENTARY

them. Two other examples of this in Amm.: *opibus et necessitudine omni recuperata* (19.9.7), *pabulo absumpto et frugibus* (24.8.2).

quae tempus vehi permisit This is an intriguing phrase. It is not the capacity of the wagons and the beasts of burden which limits the amount of corn to be transported (cf. § 10 *ut quisque vehere potuit* and the introduction to chapter 2), but *tempus*. Does this imply that they were in a hurry? But the next day the army marched *sedatius* (§5). If *tempus* denotes the 'circumstances', almost the same question can be asked. Zos. 3.27.3 phrases the restriction in a different way: the army ὅσα πρὸς τὴν χρείαν ἧρκει λαβών, τὸ περιττὸν ὅσον ἦν ἅπαν διέφθειρεν. In this case another question arises: how much was sufficient to meet their needs? According to Josephus *BJ* 3.95 it was the norm to carry rations for three days, but Amm. 17.9.2 and HA *AS* 47.1 speak of supplies for seventeen days, while in *Cod. Theod.* 7.4.5, Amm. 17.8.2 and Lib. *Or.* 18.264 rations for twenty days are spoken of.

1.5 *Postridie* I.e. June 20.

exercitu sedatius procedente Amm. uses *sedatius* in quite different contexts in 17.3.4 (q.v.) and 22.12.3 (q.v.). Its occurrence here lends a touch of peaceful leisure to the march, which contrasts with the unexpected Persian attack.

extremos, qui eo die forte cogendorum agminum officia sustinebant, necopinantes Persae adorti As we may conclude from Amm.'s use of *forte*, the task of bringing up the rear rotated. If, as seems likely (cf. the note ad §6 *in hac*), Zonaras 13.13.12 refers to the present situation and if his information is correct, the rear was protected by troops from Gaul (τοὺς Γάλλους δ᾽ ὀπισθοφυλακοῦντας). See Veg. *mil.* 3.6.1 sqq. for the importance of protecting an army on the march against enemy attack.

Zosimus relates that the Persian attack took place between the cities of Danabe and Synce and that many Romans, but still more Persians lost their lives: Ἐπεὶ δὲ μεταξὺ Δανάβης πόλεως καὶ Σύγκης ἐγένοντο, τοῖς φύλαξι τῆς οὐραγίας τοῦ στρατοπέδου συμπεσόντες οἱ Πέρσαι πολλοὺς ἀπέκτειναν, πλείους δὲ ἀποβαλόντες ἐτράπησαν, καὶ ἄλλως ἐλαττωθέντες (3.27.4). Nothing is known about the location of Danabe and Synce, but there is no need to follow Dillemann, 1961, 146 and regard these cities as inventions of Zosimus. Eunapius *fr.* 27.8 is perhaps a parallel to the present text rather than to 25.1.12 sqq., about the battle at Maranga/Maronsa, or 25.3.4 about

CHAPTER 1.6   13

the opening attack in the battle in which Julian was killed: τότε δὲ ἴλη τῶν καταφράκτων ἱππέων ὑπὲρ τοὺς υ ʼ ('over four hundred strong') ἐς τοὺς ὀπισθοφύλακας κατερράγη. So Blockley, 1983, 134 n. 56.

The classical expression *cogere agmen*, 'to bring up the rear', also occurs in 24.1.2 and 24.1.13; *officium sustinere* is not a common combination: the phrase also occurs in Cic. *Fam.* 2.65 *Ego ni te videre scirem...quantum offici sustinerem*, HA *AS* 61.3 *qui scutarium officium sustinebat* and *Dig.* 49.1.21.2.

negotio levi As is noted ad 16.12.22 and 20.10.2, this expression only occurs in Amm.

ni proximus equitatus...reppulisset Kellerbauer, 1873, 131 regards *ocius* instead of V's *acutius* as "unzweifelhaft richtig". He may have overlooked the fact that *intellegere* can imply sensory perception (cf. TLL VII 2.2097.60 "mente et sensibus", e.g. Fest. p. 110M *quia non tam facile noctis horae quam diei possint intellegi*), so that *acutius* does not pose any problem whatsoever: cf. 21.16.19 *cernensque acutum* (q.v.), 22.15.20 *acutius cernens* (q.v.). Having spotted the danger, the cavalry, with among them, possibly, the cavalry troop called *Tertiaci* (see below, ad §7), which happened to be nearby spread through the broad valleys and neutralized the surprise attack. See for *patulus* in a geographical sense TLL X 1.796.3–36, and cf. *patulae valles* (15.10.5). In the note ad 20.6.5 *certaminum mole* the present text is quoted as an instance in which *moles* denotes "the weight of problems and dangers". See for *supervenire* indicating a surprise attack the note ad 19.6.7 *supervenire ipsi regiae...meditabantur*.

in hac cecidit pugna Adaces, nobilis satrapa, legatus quondam ad Con-   **1.6**
stantium principem missus ac benigne susceptus The same information about Adaces (*PLRE* I, Adaces) is given by Zosimus, who calls him Daces (presumably a case of haplography): ἀνῃρέθη γὰρ ἐν ταύτῃ τῇ μάχῃ σατράπης τις τῶν ἐπιφανῶν ὄνομα Δάκης, ὃς ἔτυχε πρότερον ἐπὶ πρεσβείαν πρὸς τὸν βασιλέα Κωνστάντιον ἀπεσταλμένος, εἰρήνης πέρι καὶ καταλύσεως τοῦ πολέμου διαλεξόμενος (3.27.4). For *satrapa* see the note ad 25.3.13 *quinquaginta*. It would seem that Zonaras 13.13.12 refers to the same occasion. After having stated that the enemy attacked the Romans, Zonaras relates that troops from Gaul, which protected the rear (cf. above, ad §5 *extremos*), drove the Persians back and killed many of them, not only common soldiers (οὐ τῶν τυχόντων μόνον), but also some nobles (ἀλλὰ καὶ τῶν παρ᾽ ἐκείνοις ἐπιφανῶν).

14   COMMENTARY

It is not clear to what embassy to Constantius Amm. alludes. Wagner points to that of 357/8, mentioned by Amm. in 17.5.2 (q.v.), but rightly remarks that Amm. there speaks not of Adaces, but of Narseus (*missoque cum muneribus Narseo quodam legato litteras ad Constantium dedit* sc. Sapor; cf. Petr. Patr. *fr.* 17 ὁ δὲ τῆς πρεσβείας ἡγεμὼν Ναρσῆς), whom we encounter again in 24.6.12 (*Pigrane et Surena et Narseo potissimis ducibus*) and who most probably is to be identified with Zosimus' Ἀνάρεος (3.25.5). Paschoud n. 79 glosses over this problem: "Je me demande s' il ne faut pas combiner tous ces textes et faire un seul personnage de Dacès-Adacès-Narseus-Narsès-Anaréos", but it is perhaps better to assume either that Narseus in 357/8 was not the only envoy or that Adaces was sent as an ambassador to Constantius on another occasion. We know that in 358 Constantius twice sent a delegation to Sapor, first Prosper, Spectatus and Eustathius (17.5.15 and 17.14.1), later Lucillianus and Procopius (17.14.3). There is no reason to doubt that Sapor, like Constantius, may have sent more than one embassy. See for Constantius' diplomatic contacts with Persia the note ad 21.6.7 *ad Transtigritanos reges*.

Sometimes Amm. reports explicitly that a person is well received, in accordance with the relevant conventions. Such a statement always has a specific significance. In 20.9.6 Constantius' envoy Leonas was *susceptus ut honoratus et prudens* by Julian, who in this way showed appropriate benevolence; in 20.11.1 *summaque liberalitate susceptum* shows how much value Constantius attached to the loyalty of the Armenian king. Other instances are 18.2.16, 18.6.21, 22.7.3, 22.9.13, 25.8.16, 29.5.16. In the present case the purpose of the phrase is unclear. Does Amm. intend to emphasize the contrast between dignified diplomacy, which came to nothing, and the cruel risks of the inevitable war?

cuius exuviis interfector Iuliano oblatis remuneratus est, ut decebat See for *exuviae* the note ad 24.4.4 *spoliatisque ambobus*. The verb *remunerare* (*remunerari* in classical Latin) occurs only here in Amm. The phrase *ut decebat* either means 'according to the rule which requires that such feats are rewarded' (cf. 18.2.16 *leniter susceptus est, ut decebat*) or 'with the level of honour which such a hero should receive' (cf. 15.8.16 *infra quam decebat*).

The anonymous *interfector* was either decorated (cf. the notes ad 24.4.24 and 24.6.15) or, more probably, rewarded in cash (cf. the notes ad 20.11.12 and 24.3.3). Cf. also 25.10.10 concerning officers from Gaul, who, after having received rewards, were told to

CHAPTER 1.7–9   15

return to their posts (*munerati redire iubentur ad signa*). The soldier who killed Adaces resembles Q. Occius, nicknamed Achilleus, who distinguished himself by his courage in Spain about 140 B.C. This Occius, after killing a Celtiberian, took his victim's armour and brought it triumphantly to the Roman camp: *Celtiberum...interemit detrectasque corpori eius exuvias ovans laetitia in castra retulit* (V. Max. 3.2.21).

In spite of the clarity of *eodem die* (§7) it is difficult to determine the precise place in the sequence of events of the episode described in §7–9. There is no parallel report in Zosimus. In Amm.'s account the infantry's irritation cannot have been caused merely by the events of §5–6, since the cavalry won the day and there is no mention of any large-scale fighting against the enemy's battle formation (§7 *adversas...acies*). Possibly the complaints were prompted by a general dissatisfaction with (part of) the cavalry's performance.   **1.7–9**

eodem die Tertiacorum equestris numerus a legionibus incusatus est Since   **1.7**
Amm. explicitly says that the accusation against the *Tertiaci* was uttered *eodem die* (i.e. still on June 20), it is likely that the complaint against the cavalrymen had to do with their behaviour earlier that day, i.e. during the attack of the Persians on the Roman rear mentioned in section 5. Probably the legions of the present text belonged to the troops *qui eo die forte cogendorum agminum officia sustinebant* (§5), while it had been the task of the *Tertiaci* to protect that rear. Another, less likely possibility would be that the cavalrymen, although belonging to the *equitatus noster* which caused the Persians to withdraw (ibid.), did not do their duty properly. Anyway, the *Tertiaci* apparently failed to provide the necessary support for their fellow soldiers, and even gradually disappeared from the battlefield (*paulatim dilapsi*). As becomes clear in §8–9, however, they were not the only soldiers who fell short of expectations.

The fact that a unit of *Tertiaci* is attested nowhere else while *Tertiani* are, viz. in the *Notitia Dignitatum*, has led to the suggestion that instead of *Tertiacorum* perhaps *Tertianorum* should be read. So e.g. Lindenbrog, Rolfe, and Fontaine n. 485 (cf. Zuckerman, 1998, 255: "in the military nomenclature of the *Notitia* the suffixes -*ianus* and -*iacus* are interchangeable"). In that case, it is argued, the *equestris numerus* (see for the term *numerus*, covering units of all kinds, the note ad 20.1.3) belonged to the *legio comitatensis tertia Italica*, which still existed at the time when the *Notitia Dignitatum* was compiled and whose soldiers are called *tertiani* in this document (cf. *Occ.* 5.88,

16 COMMENTARY

5.237 and 7.53). *Legiones comitatenses*, however, consisted mainly of infantrymen (cf. Nicasie, 1998, 53). It is more likely therefore that the *Tertiacorum equestris numerus* formed part of the cavalry proper, and that these cavalrymen, in view of the element '*tertius*' in their name (whether *Tertiaci* or *Tertiani*), are to be identified as *equites tertio Dalmatae* or *equites tertii stablesiani* or *equites tertii clibanarii Parthi* – note that "die lateinischen Autoren, wie etwa Ammianus Marcellinus und Claudianus, [sich] nur selten an die Fachsprache halten" (Hoffmann, I, 5).

The *equites tertio Dalmatae* and the *equites tertii stablesiani* are mentioned in the *Notitia Dignitatum* (*Or.* 7.27 and 7.30, respectively), the *equites tertii clibanarii Parthi* are not (unlike the *equites primi clibanarii Parthi*, the *equites secundi clibanarii Parthi* and the *equites quarti clibanarii Parthi*, cf. *Or.* 5.40, 6.40 and 7.32; see for *clibanarii* the notes ad 20.7.2 and 24.2.5). However, precisely the fact that the *tertii clibanarii Parthi* are missing in the *Notitia* is the reason why they, and not the *tertio Dalmatae* or the *tertii stablesiani*, are perhaps to be identified as the *Tertiaci* (so Hoffmann, I, 275–6). As Amm. tells us in § 8, Julian had the standards taken from the *Tertiaci* and their lances broken. He forced the cavalrymen themselves to march from now on among the baggage-train with the prisoners. In other words, he dissolved the unit, which therefore naturally does not occur in the *Notitia*, as was already pointed out by Mommsen, 1889, 268.

As to *legionibus*, in his narrative of Julian's Persian expedition Amm. mentions the following legions by name: *Lancearii* and *Mattiarii* (21.13.16), *Victores* (24.4.23, 25.6.3), *Zianni* (25.1.19), *Ioviani* and *Herculiani* (25.6.2) and *Iovii* (25.6.3). See the notes ad loc., the note ad 24.1.2 *excursatores* and in general Hoffmann I, 207, 307–8 and Tomlin, 2000.

cum ipsae…exercitus Perhaps *cum…irrumperent* should be regarded as an iterative clause: each time the infantry got engaged in heavy fighting with the enemy, the Tertiaci failed to provide the necessary support and even gradually disappeared from the battlefield. See for *alacritas* denoting 'fighting spirit' the notes ad 19.2.6 and 24.1.1.

1.8 *ad indignationem iustam imperator erectus* See the relevant note ad 24.3.3.

ademptis signis hastisque diffractis The text which Seyfarth prints, as do Clark and Fontaine, is that of Gelenius; instead of the first three words V has only *adeptisque*. This is the third time that Amm. speaks

CHAPTER 1.8

of the punishment of a military unit during the Persian campaign. The first time was in 24.3.2, q.v., the second in 24.5.10, q.v. (see for a curious story about Julian resorting to disciplinary measures when he was Caesar in Gaul Zos. 3.3.4–5, with Paschoud n. 10). Julian's action, i.e. the taking away of the standards, the breaking of the lances and the degradation of the cavalrymen (see below) probably added up to the disintegration of the *Tertiacorum equestris numerus* (cf. the relevant note above).

The technical meaning of a *signum* is to be distinguished from that of an *aquila*, a *vexillum* and a *draco* (cf. 15.5.16 *cultu purpureo a draconum et vexillorum insignibus...abstracto*, 20.5.1 *signis aquilisque circumdatus et vexillis* and the note ad 24.3.1 *unum rapuisse vexillum*). It is "aus einem Schaft gefertigt, der ursprünglich in einer offenen Hand aus Holz oder Bronze endete, später in einer einfachen Spitze. Darunter hielt eine Querstange zwei Gehänge oder...einen quadratischen Stoff, auf dem in Goldbuchstaben die Namen der Kaiser geschrieben oder Medaillons gestickt waren. Darunter waren unmittelbar am Schaft Phalerae mit dem Bildnis eines Kaisers oder einer Gottheit angebracht. Sodann folgte...ein Stoff, der den Namen der Kampfeinheit trug" (Seston, 1969, 693–4). But Amm. sometimes, as in the present text, seems to use the plural *signa* more loosely for all kinds of military banners and standards, including *vexilla* ('square pieces of cloth, hung from a crossbar carried on a pole') and *dracones* ('hollow, open-mouthed dragon's masks'). Cf. e.g. 15.8.4 (tribunal) *quod aquilae circumdederunt et signa* and 18.2.17 *Macrianus...inter aquilas admissus et signa*. See in general for standards and *insignia* Babuin, 2001.

To decorate a soldier by giving him a *hasta (pura)* was quite common (cf. Festus p. 101M *Romani fortes viros saepe hasta donarunt* and Maxfield, 1981, 84–6), but the breaking of lances as a form of punishment is not attested anywhere else. The closest parallel is provided by Festus' definition (p. 54M) of *censio* ('i.q. animadversio', TLL III 796.52) *hastaria: cum militi multae nomine ob delictum militare indicebatur, quod hastas daret*. As to the interpretation of this text, Müller's note ad loc. is to the point: "intelligitur e Pauli verbis, non admodum disertis, milites hoc iudicio hasta esse privatos, quod ea indigni censerentur". Mommsen's explanation on the other hand (1887³, II 396–7 n. 2, reading *quot* instead of *quod*) is quite absurd: "Sie wird darin bestanden haben, dass dem fehlbaren Soldaten aufgegeben wurde eine bestimmte Zahl von Lanzenschäften zu hauen und zuzurichten, und heisst darum 'Abschätzung', weil je nach dem Mass des Vergehens die Zahl der Schäfte abgestuft ward".

18   COMMENTARY

qui fugisse arguebantur The verb *arguere* should here be interpreted according to *Dig.* 50.16.197 (Ulpianus) *'indicasse' est detulisse: 'arguisse' accusare et convicisse.*

inter impedimenta et sarcinas et captivos agere iter disposuit The *Tertiaci* were positioned in the place allotted to those who fell short of military standards; cf. *Sarcinas vero et calones et apparitionem imbellem impedimentorumque genus omne* (24.1.4). The combination of *impedimenta* and *sarcinae* occurs also in 31.11.6 and 31.12.10. Cf. Liv. 25.13.12 *sarcinis omnibus impedimentisque Beneventi relictis.* See for literature on degradation of soldiers the note ad 24.5.10 *dignitatibus imminutis.* As to *captivos*, from 24.8.1 it appears that Persian captives were taken along, perhaps "um sie in einem Triumphzug vorzuführen" (Bliembach ad Lib. *Or.* 18.264). See further the note ad 24.1.9 *reliqui vero…transmissi sunt* (add to the literature cited there Kettenhofen, 1996 and Winter-Dignas, 2001, 257ff.).

See for *disponere*, 'to decide', the note ad 20.4.9. About V's *inposuit* Kellerbauer, 1873, 131 rightly notes: "Sinn und Sprachgebrauch erfordern *disposuit*".

ductore eorum, qui solus fortiter decertarat, aliae turmae apposito, cuius tribunus turpiter proelium deseruisse convincebatur The word *ductor* here appears to be the equivalent to *tribunus* (cf. the note ad 25.1.2 *Machameus*). It appears from the present text that not all members of the *Tertiacorum equestris numerus* had failed to do their duty. On the other hand, not only the *Tertiaci* were to blame. The *turma* mentioned here (see for this word the note ad 25.1.3) and the tribunes of §9 had committed a *flagitium simile.*

See for dat. fem. sing. *aliae* Neue-Wagener 2.535–6, where three instances in Gellius are mentioned (4.10.8, 9.4.8, 17.9.3) and Fest. p. 27M: *Aliae rei dixit Plautus pro eo, quod est ali rei*, evidently a reference to *Mil.* 802. Cf. for *apponere*, 'to appoint (as commander of)', 22.7.7 *rectores militibus diu exploratos apponens.*

1.9   *abiecti sunt autem sacramento etiam alii quattuor ob flagitium simile vexillationum tribuni* See on the soldiers' oath and their release from it, either as a demotion or honourably, the note ad 24.3.2. For 'releasing' Amm. also uses *exuere* (28.2.9), *removere* (15.7.7, in a metaphorical phrase) and *solvere* (16.7.1, 24.3.2, 28.6.25, 30.7.3). For *tribuni*, a general term for commanding military officers, see the notes ad 23.3.9 and 24.3.1. This is Amm.'s only instance of *vexillatio*, which according to Veg. *mil.* 2.1.2 is a synonym of *ala: quae*

CHAPTER 1.9

nunc vexillationes vocantur a velo, quia velis, hoc est flammulis ('small banners'), *utuntur.* In Amm., however, *ala* is only used of enemy troops (see above, ad 25.1.3 *verum viso imperatore*). For a Roman cavalry unit Amm. prefers *turma* or *numerus*, as e.g. in §3 and 7, respectively. See further Southern-Dixon, 1996, 30–1.

hoc enim correctionis moderamine leniori impendentium consideratione difficultatum contentus est imperator The reader perhaps expects capital punishment in the case of officers who have been found guilty of desertion. The emperor himself (see for *imperator* the note ad 21.4.4) once wrote in a letter to Oribasius (*Ep.* 14, 385 c) that soldiers, who deserted their post, should be put to death and denied burial, while earlier in the Persian campaign he actually had executed some men who had fled from the battlefield (24.3.2, q.v.). However, Julian did not put the officers of those soldiers to death. He only released them from their oath (*tribunos sacramento solvit ut desides et ignavos*, ibid.), as he did in the present case with respect to the four tribunes who had been guilty of cowardice (*abiecti sunt autem sacramento etiam alii quattuor...tribuni*). On another occasion too, Julian, although *ira gravi permotus* (cf. 24.5.6 *iratus et frendens* and 24.5.7 *concitus ira immani*) had refrained from punishing cowardly behaviour with the death penalty (24.5.10, q.v.).

Neither in 24.3.2 nor in 24.5.10 does Amm. make any comment on Julian's measures. Here, with *enim*, he at least introduces a point of view which might make the reader understand Julian's behaviour. Apart from *correctione titubantium benivola et sollerti* (19.11.3, q.v.), where according to TLL IV 1028.69sqq. *correctio* is a synonym of "restitutio", in the other cases in Amm. this term means 'rebuke': 22.10.3 (q.v.), 27.7.9 and the present text. It is a very mild term in view of the 'outrage' (*flagitium*) and it is made even milder by *moderamine leniori.* The noun has the same meaning as in 15.10.7, 22.16.22 and 30.9.5: 'moderation', 'restraint'; *leni* would have created a regular cursus, so that the choice of the comparative seems to be deliberate. Presumably, *correctionis* is a genitivus inversus and the entire phrase could therefore be rendered as 'a rather mild and moderate reproof', a procedure which was not inappropriate for an emperor to whom, as Seager 19 puts it, "leniency was a guiding principle" and who was even lenient towards those who were openly his enemies (25.4.9 *constat eum in apertos aliquos inimicos insidiatores suos ita consurrexisse mitissime, ut poenarum asperitatem genuina lenitudine castigaret*; cf. Brandt, 1999, 189–93). The reason of his leniency at this particular moment was Julian's 'taking account of the impending dif-

20 COMMENTARY

ficulties' (cf. 25.4.8 *pro rerum hominum distinctione*): it would be unwise
to provoke the soldiers' anger in view of the hardships to come, the
more so because their morale and physical condition had already
been flagging lately, owing to a growing lack of supplies (24.7.7, Zos.
3.27.1) and the deleterious effects of the climate (24.8.3; cf. Crump,
1975, 90). Whether Amm. fully agreed with Julian's measures is
another matter. As was noted ad 24.3.2, in a later book the author
defends the harsh punishment of a cohort by general Theodosius
with the words: *admonemus hanc cohortem et facto fuisse et exemplo adver-
sam* (29.5.23) – Theodosius had at first pretended to be content with
a somewhat mild punishment of deserters, degrading them to the
lowest class of service: *ut contentum se supplicio leniori monstraret, omnes
contrusit ad infimum militiae gradum* (29.5.20), but later turned some
soldiers of the *Constantiniani* over to their colleagues to be killed
in the old-fashioned way, had the hands of the officers of a *cohors
sagittariorum* cut off and the rest of this cohort slain.

The only other instance of an abl. of the comparative ending
on -*i* in Seyfarth's edition is *leniori* in 29.5.20, quoted above. In the
relevant section of Neue-Wagener, II 264–9, it appears that, although
there are more examples, even in classical Latin, it is a comparatively
rare phenomenon. See also Courtney ad Juv. 13.48 *minori*.

1.10 The facts, which are reported in this section, are difficult to understand, because Amm. fails to mention the circumstances which led
to the burning of grass and grain. The parallel section in Zosimus is
far clearer.

Progressi itaque septuaginta stadia I.e. they advanced some 13 km
(see for *stadia* the note ad 24.2.3). From Zosimus' words in 3.28.1
(Ἰδόντες δὲ αὐτούς οἱ πολέμιοι πλησιάζοντας Ἀκκήτῃ πόλει) it can be
deduced that the army then reached the city of Accete. Presumably,
this was still on June 20 (cf. Paschoud n. 80). Where precisely Accete
is to be sought, is not known, pace Mazzarino, who for that matter
himself admits that his identification of Accete as Akkad is somewhat
surprising ("la mia proposta, di identificare Akketes polis con Akkad
a oriente del Tigri, maraviglierà molti", 1962², 471). However, there
is at any rate no reason to follow Dillemann, 1961, 147 in assuming
that Zosimus invented the place.

attenuata rerum omnium copia herbis frumentisque crematis For *attenuare*
in similar phrases cf. *attenuatis omnium opibus* (19.11.3, q.v.) and the
note ad 21.12.17 *attenuatis...subsidiis*. The verb can also be used to

CHAPTER 1.11   21

describe the victims of dearth: 31.3.8 *populi pars maior...attenuata necessariorum penuria*, 31.13.7 *Romanos magis attenuatos inedia*, and it occurs in an entirely different context in 20.3.1 and 24.1.3. All kinds of supplies were 'exhausted', because grain and grass had been burnt. The results were soon noticeable, see 25.2.1 *inedia cruciabat iam non ferenda*, with the note. Zos. 3.28.1 explicitly mentions who were responsible for this: οἱ πολέμιοι...τοὺς ἐν τῇ γῇ καρποὺς ἐπυρπόλουν. Cf. Zos. 3.27.1, cited ad 25.1.3 *hinc recedentibus nobis*.

ex flammis ipsis raptas fruges et pabula, ut quisque vehere potuit, conservavit Cf. Zos. 3.28.1 οἷς ἐπιδραμόντες οἱ Ῥωμαῖοι τὸ πῦρ κατέσβεσαν καὶ τῶν καρπῶν τοῖς λειπομένοις ἐχρήσαντο. Amm. has expressed the nervous haste of the action by *ex flammis ipsis raptas*, whereas Zosimus restricts himself to the more factual ἐπιδραμόντες. The third person sing. *conservavit* is caused by *quisque*. Blomgren 49 notes that Amm. uses the 'normal' plural in some comparable cases: 27.8.5 *violabant*, 31.10.9 *iniecere*. However, in these instances the distance between the 'formulaic' *quisque...potuit* and the predicate of the main clause is much larger.

hoc etiam loco relicto Zosimus' Accete, no doubt (see above, ad § 10).   **1.11**

cum ad tractum Maranga appellatum omnis venisset exercitus On June 21, presumably. See for *tractus*, 'region', the note ad 16.3.1. Zosimus gives the place a slightly different name, calling it a 'village': εἰς Μάρωνσα παρεγένοντο κώμην (3.28.2). The exact site of Maranga/Maronsa is not known. According to Herzfeld, 1948, 65 the place is be identified with modern Tell-Hir, some 54 km from Samarra, but this identification is disputed. Cf. Brok 174, Pachoud n. 81 and the note on chronology.

prope lucis confinia immensa Persarum apparuit multitudo The similar phrase *prope lucis confinia* occurs in 19.6.11 and 27.2.8; cf. also Apul. *Met.* 2.17 and see Hagendahl, 1921, 102–3 for a full list of Amm.'s phrases denoting daybreak; cf. 25.6.4 *confinia noctis* with the note. Here the morning of June 22 must be meant. Both *immensus* and *multitudo* occur frequently in Amm., though seldom in combination. Here *immensa...multitudo* sets the tone for a description of a full-scale battle in § 12–18, which markedly differs from Zosimus' very brief report on scrimmages at the rear of the Roman column: ἢ (i.e. in Maranga/Maronsa) τοῖς τὴν οὐραγίαν τοῦ στρατοῦ φυλάττουσιν ἐπιθέμενοι Περσῶν λόχοι συνέπεσον (3.28.2). According to Libanius

22   COMMENTARY

(*Or.* 18.265) there were no pitched battles either after the one in which Machameus died, only ambuscades and attacks on the rear by small parties of horsemen.

cum Merena equestris magistro militiae filiisque regis duobus et optimatibus plurimis The presence of such highly placed persons adds to the importance of the attackers' force. They do not play any part in the subsequent description of the battle, but in the fierce battle described in ch. 3 fifty aristocrats and satraps fall and also Merena (25.3.13), whose title, *equestris magister militiae*, in 23.6.14 (q.v.) was given as *vitaxa*: *Sunt autem in omni Perside hae regiones maximae, quas vitaxae, id est magistri equitum, curant et reges et satrapae.* His name, related to Mithrana/Mithra/Mihran (cf. Justi, 1895, 214 and Gignoux, 1986, nr. 630), indicates that he probably belonged to the family of Mihran, one of the seven privileged families in Sasanian Iran whose family-tree went back to Arsacid times (*PLRE* I, Merena). As in the case of Surena or Surên (cf. the note ad 24.2.4), Merena seems to have been both a personal name and a title. Compare for this e.g. Procop. *Pers.* 2.30.7 Πέρσης δὲ ἀνήρ, Μιρράνης ὄνομα, ὅσπερ τοῦ ἐν Πέτρᾳ φυλακτηρίου ἦρχεν (cf. *PLRE* III B, Mirrhanes) with Procop. *Pers.* 1.13.16 Πέρσης ἀνήρ, μιρράνης μὲν τὸ ἀξίωμα (οὕτω γὰρ τὴν ἀρχὴν καλοῦσι Πέρσαι), Περόζης δὲ ὄνομα (cf. *PLRE* III B, Perozes).

The evidence concerning Sapor's sons is discussed in the note ad *regis filius* (24.4.31). See the notes ad 20.6.3 and 21.13.4 on *optimates* denoting the aristocracy of non-Roman peoples.

1.12–18   More than half of the following report on the second full-scale battle with a large Persian force – the first one was described in book 24, chapter 6 – consists in a detailed description of the enemy's lines (§ 12–15). The battle itself is described in general terms in § 17–18, after a succinct sketch of the Roman line-up in § 16. One cannot avoid the impression that the author eagerly seized the opportunity to expand once more on the three parts of the Persian armed forces which had impressed him most: the ironclad warriors, the skill of the archers and the frightening appearance and size of the elephants. In contrast, the brief description of the battle shows that the entire Persian line-up for all its impressive outward appearance simply lacked the necessary power to withstand genuine Roman stamina. As will be shown in the notes, part of the text consists of variations of phrases and expressions used in previous descriptions.

CHAPTER 1.12   23

erant autem omnes catervae ferratae See the notes ad 16.2.6 *caterva-* **1.12**
tim and 20.7.14 on Amm.'s use of *caterva* about non-Roman or
mercenary troops. Hor. *Carm.* 4.14.29–30 *ut barbarorum Claudius*
agmina/ ferrata vasto diruit impetu is the first example of *ferratus*
meaning "ferreis armis indutus" (TLL VI 572.72–82); more recent
examples are *ferrati...viri* (Claud. *carm. min.* 28.571) and *ferratasque*
acies (Prud. c*ath.* 5.48). Normally Amm. uses *ferratus* in descriptions
of arrows (16.12.46, 24.2.13), towers (19.5.1, 19.7.2, 19.7.5) and
bolts or doors (21.12.13, 30.5.17). Cf. also *ferreus equitatus* (19.1.2,
q.v.) and *ferrea...facie omni* (24.2.10, q.v.). For literature on *catafrac-*
tarii/clibanarii see the notes ad 20.7.2 *primo...impetu* and 24.2.5
visi tunc primitus. Cf. also 25.1.1 *radiantes loricae...et corusci thoraces*
with the note. According to Dillemann, 1961, 147 Eunapius *fr.*
27.8 corresponds to the present text, but see the note ad 25.1.5
extremos.

ita per singula membra densis lamminis tectae, ut iuncturae rigentes com-
pagibus artuum convenirent This is what fascinated the author most
of all: the suits of armour completely covered the men's bodies, fitting them to perfection, but without hampering the flexibility and
movement of the joints. Julian, in his description of Constantius'
mail-clad cavalry (*Or.* 1.37 c–d), compares the horsemen with statues, whose limbs were fitted with armour that followed closely the
outline of the human form (οἷς συνήρμοστο τὰ μέλη κατὰ μίμησιν τῆς
ἀνθρωπίνης φύσεως) and says that the covering of their hands was so
flexible that they were even able to bend their fingers (τῶν χειρῶν
τοῖς ὑφάσμασι τούτοις σκεπομένων ('covered') πρὸς τὸ καὶ καμπτομένοις
ἐπακολουθεῖν τοῖς δακτύλοις, ibid. 38 a). Amm.'s fascination with this
has inspired him to use his full stylistic resources for three different descriptions. The other two are 16.10.8 *quos* ('these warriors')
lamminarum circuli tenues apti corporis flexibus ambiebant per omnia mem-
bra diducti, ut, quocumque artus necessitas commovisset, vestitus congrueret
iunctura cohaerenter aptata, and 24.2.10 *ferrea nimirum facie omni, quia*
lamminae singulis membrorum liniamentis cohaerenter aptatae fido operi-
mento totam hominis speciem contegebant. Apart from these complete
pictures the same armour is more briefly sketched in 24.4.15 and
24.6.8; see the relevant notes ad loc. All five descriptions have the
term *lam(m)ina*, 'plate of metal', in common. As in 16.10.8, *iuncturae*
denotes the 'joinings' of the individual parts of the harness; although
they were hard and stiff (*rigentes* has a concessive connotation), they
were adjusted (*convenirent*) to the joints (*compagibus*) of the body's
limbs. The noun *compages* occurs quite often in Amm., but the plural

24 COMMENTARY

only in two other places: 17.7.14 (in a digression on earthquakes) and 17.13.28 (about the joints on a bridge); *artuum* could also be interpreted as a gen. identitatis.

humanorumque vultuum simulacra ita capitibus diligenter aptata This explicit attention to the wellnigh complete protective covering of the warriors' heads is functional, because at this point the author wants to emphasize the fact that their bodies have no unprotected spots whatsoever. As in the case of the rest of the body, the iron armour exactly fitted the head (see on the verb *aptare*, which occurs in most of the passages mentioned, the note ad 24.6.8), which gave the covering the 'likeness of a human face' (eyes, nose, mouth); cf. also the note ad 16.10.8 *personati*.

imbratteatis corporibus solidis TLL VII 1.425.68–71 mentions only Amm.'s three instances of *imbratteare*, 'to cover with sheets of metal': 14.6.8 on covering bronze images with gold, and 17.4.15 idem of a bronze globe; *brattea* denotes a sheet of metal, often, but not necessarily, of gold. Cf. for *solidus*, 'entire', 23.6.80 *particulatim vel solidas*, Verg. *A.* 6.253 *solida…viscera*, Ov. *Met.* 8.552 *trabes solidas*.

qua per cavernas minutas et orbibus oculorum affixas parcius visitur Cf. Lucr. 3.410 *luminis orbem*, Verg. *A.* 12.670 and Tac. *Hist.* 1.81.1 *oculorum orbes*. Sabbah 284–5 with n. 142, pointing to the close resemblance with Lib. *Or.* 59.69, argues that Libanius was perhaps Amm.'s model. In this passage he says that Constantius clad his cavalry in iron, but not totally: ὥστε τὸν μὲν ἐκ κεφαλῆς εἰς ἄκρους πόδας, τὸν δὲ ἐκ κορυφῆς εἰς ἄκρας ὁπλὰς κεκαλύφθαι τοῖς φυλακτηρίοις, ὀφθαλμοῖς δὲ μόνοις ἀνεῷχθαι χώραν εἰς ὄψιν τῶν πραττομένων καὶ ταῖς ἀναπνοαῖς τοῦ μὴ ἀποπνίγεσθαι, '(he wished) that his men should be covered and protected from top to toe and the horses from head to hoof, except for an opening at eye level, through which they could see what happened and, a precaution against suffocation, could take breath.' Cf. for the remark about the *catafractarius*' range of vision also Hld. 9.15.1 ἐκ κορυφῆς εἰς αὐχένα πάντα πλὴν τῶν ὀφθαλμῶν εἰς τὸ διοπτεύειν σκεπόμενος ('covered'). The phrase *parcius visitur* is slightly awkward, in that it suddenly switches the focus to the bearer of the armour: his range of vision is restricted.

per supremitates narium The word *supremitas* occurs only here and in an entirely different phrase in 31.13.17, where it means 'death'.

CHAPTER 1.13 25

At first the static character of the description continues (*stabat* **1.13**
immobilis), but then the scene develops into one of action (*tende-*
bant...evolabant).

quorum pars contis dimicatura stabat immobilis See for *contus* TLL IV
809.25–58: "hasta longissima, equitum potissimum et barbarorum".
With this meaning it also occurs in 25.3.4 and 31.7.6, and in a
number of passages in Veg. *mil.*, e.g. 3.24.7 about the cavalry: *contos*
et cassides frequenter tergere et curare. The word can also denote a long
pole used for other purposes: 18.5.6 (q.v.), Veg. *mil.* 2.25.6. It was the
catafractarius' weapon par excellence: μία γὰρ ἀλκὴ τῶν καταφράκτων
κοντός (Plut. *Luc.* 28.3), τὴν μὲν δεξιὰν κοντῷ μείζονι λόγχης ὁπλίζει
(Hld. 9.15.1, cf. 9.15.6, Tac. *Hist.* 1.79.3, Plut. *Crass.* 24.3, 25.7,
25.8, 25.12, 27.1, 27.2, D.C. 40.15.2, 40.22.2–3, 40.24.1). See Coulston, 1986, 65–6 for the question whether this lance was wielded
with one hand or with two. Note the future of *dimicatura*: they are
not in action yet. As to *stabat immobilis*, the *catafractarii/clibanarii* are
often compared to statues, cf. 16.10.8 *ut Praxitelis manu polita crederes*
simulacra, Claud. *in Ruf.* 2. 359–60 *credas simulacra moveri/ ferrea cog-*
natosque viros spirare metallo, Hld. 9.15.6 σιδηροῦς τις ἀνὴρ φαινόμενος
ἢ καὶ σφυρήλατος ('wrought with the hammer') ἀνδριὰς κινούμενος,
Jul. *Or.* 1.37 c–d καθάπερ ἀνδριάντας ἐπὶ τῶν ἵππων ὀχουμένους...τὸ
δὲ κράνος αὐτῷ προσώπῳ σιδηροῦν ἐπικείμενον ἀνδριάντος λαμπροῦ καὶ
στίλβοντος παρέχει τὴν ὄψιν, Jul. *Or.* 3.57 c ὥσπερ ἀνδριάντες ἐπὶ τῶν
ἵππων φερόμενοι. In Theophylactus Simocatta *Hist.* 3.14.5 we not
only find the comparison with statues, but also the Greek equivalent of Amm.'s *immobilis*: δίκην ('in the way of') ἀνδριάντων ἀκινήτως
ἐχόντων.

ut retinaculis aereis fixam existimares The word *retinaculum* occurs seven
times in Amm. In 14.6.5, 14.11.26, 28.1.15, 30.4.4 and 30.9.2 it is
used in a figurative way, to denote some form of restraint. In 29.6.18
it denotes the natural barriers of a river. As to its meaning in the
present text, Brok 175 interprets it as 'cord' or 'cable' and refers to
some passages in classical poetry in which the word is used about
the moorings of a ship, e.g. Verg. *A.* 4.580 *strictoque ferit retinacula*
ferro. Fontaine n. 495 suggests that the term evokes the race course,
e.g. when during the race the charioteer can no longer rein in his
team of horses: *et frustra retinacula tendens/ fertur equis auriga* (Verg.
G. 1.513–4). Neither solution is satisfactory. In view of the fact that
catafractarii/clibanarii are often compared to statues (cf. the previous
note) and that in Amm.'s three other instances of *aereus* (14.6.8,

26   COMMENTARY

17.4.15, 25.10.2) the adi. concerns works of art, one should rather think of statues, "held fast by clamps of bronze" (Rolfe). It would seem that in *Dig.* 33.7.12.23 such statues are mentioned. It is stated there that, if statues were *adfixae* (cf. *fixam* in the present text and *fixae* in 19.2.5 *acies immobiles stabant ut fixae nullo variato vestigio*), they did not belong to moveable property but formed part of the house: *sigilla et statuae adfixae instrumento domus non continentur, sed domus portio sunt.* Cf. Vitr. 10.2.13 *metuentes ne caderet ea statua et frangeretur, locaverunt ex eisdem lapidicinis basim excidendam.* In Cic. *Rep.* 6.8, quoted in Macr. *comm.* 1.4.2, it is not bronze, but lead with which the statues are fixed: *statuas plumbo inhaerentes.* Cf. LSJ s.v. μολυβδοχοέω 2: "c. acc. fix with molten lead, e.g. a statue on its pedestal", Ar. *Ec.* 1109–10 τὼ πόδε μολυβδοχοήσαντες κύκλῳ περὶ τὰ σφυρά, IG II².1670.5, II².1672.176, 7.3073.179, 7.4255.15, TAM 2.437. See also E. *Andr.* 266–7 καὶ γὰρ σ' ἔχοι / τηκτὸς μόλυβδος, ἐξαναστήσω σ' ἐγώ, "Y fusses-tu tout alentour soudée par du plomb fondu (sc. comme une statue fixée à son socle), je saurai t'en faire lever", tr. Méridier.

iuxtaque sagittarii, cuius artis fiducia ab incunabulis ipsis gens praevaluit maxima It is unclear what precisely is meant by *iuxta*: are they lined up 'beside' the men with the long pikes or only 'in their vicinity'? In 16.12.7 we also find mounted *sagittarii* mentioned in the same breath with *catafractarii* (*pedestres copiae…earumque lateri equestres iunctae sunt turmae, inter quas catafractarii erant et sagittarii, formidabile genus armorum*), but there they belong to the Roman forces. See for the trouble (Parthian) archers could cause a Roman army Plut. *Crass.* 24.3 sqq. The complicated structure of the relative clause is mirrored in the different translations. Although the content is not difficult to understand, grammatically speaking, *cuius artis* is a bold example of a reference to what is only implied in the antecedent (*sagittarii*), viz. 'archery'.

Within the structure of the clause *ab incunabulis ipsis* refers to the Persian people (*gens*). This is the view taken in TLL VII 1078.47 and in Seyfarth's rendering: "Auf deren Kunst verliess sich dieses Volk von seinem Ursprung"; cf. 14.6.4 about the Roman people: *ab incunabulis primis.* Yet, somehow one has the feeling that Amm. meant to say that the archers were trained in this particular skill 'from early childhood'; cf. Hdt. 1.136 on the education of Persian boys from the age of five: παιδεύουσι δὲ τοὺς παῖδας ἀπὸ πενταέτεος ἀρξάμενοι μέχρι εἰκοσαέτεος τρία μοῦνα, ἱππεύειν καὶ τοξεύειν καὶ ἀληθίζεσθαι. Hamilton's translation phrases this very clearly: "practised from the very cradle in a skill in which that people especially excells".

CHAPTER 1.13   27

As it stands, *maxima* could belong to either *gens* or to *fiducia*. Although the former might perhaps be compared with *cum plebe maxima* (25.3.13), such a solution seems out of place here. On the other hand, the remarkable hyperbaton with *fiducia* is also suspect. Presumably, such reflections prompted Petschenig, 1891, 353 to propose: "Lies *maxime*; *praevalere* bedeutet im Spätlatein nicht mehr als das einfache *valere*". He suggests the same correction for 26.9.3, where both Clark and Seyfarth follow suit. For the present text Seyfarth does not even mention the proposal in his app. crit. It must be said that there are good parallels in Amm. for the emendation *maxime* in 26.9.3, but its final position here would be unparalleled. Be this as it may, both Rolfe and Hamilton silently agree with *maxime* in view of their "especially". As to Petschenig's argument, it should be noted that *praevalere* does not often occur in late Latin. There are only two other instances in Amm.: 17.12.11 (q.v.) and 18.8.4. In both places the verb has its normal meaning 'to have the upper hand'.

tendebant divaricatis brachiis flexiles arcus, ut nervi mammas praestringerent dexteras, spicula sinistris manibus cohaererent See for the various bodily postures expressed by *divaricatus* the note ad 22.11.8 *divaricatis...pedibus*, and for *praestringere*, 'to touch lightly', the note ad *praestrinximus* (21.7.2). Discussing the functions of the parts of the body, Cicero says that men's *mammae* only exist *quasi ad quendam ornatum* (*Fin.* 3.18); cf. also *erat praecinctus supra mammas zonam auream* (Firm. Mat. *err.* 24.7, in a quotation of Apoc. 1.12–8). In a brief, but admirable note on the various techniques used by archers, Valesius i.a. quotes Hom. *Il.* 4.123 νευρὴν μὲν μαζῷ πέλασεν, τόξῳ δὲ σίδηρον.

As to *flexiles arcus*, Amm. in chapter 8 of book 22 refers six times to the Scythian or Parthian bow (§ 10, 13, 20, 37, 42 and 43, q.v.), which differed from that of other races (we may assume that the Sasanians used the same type of bow as the Parthians). Cf. the note ad 24.2.13 *quibus panda*. The Parthian opponents of Crassus made "vigorous and powerful shots from bows which were large and mighty and curved so as to discharge their missiles with great force" (εὐτόνους δὲ τὰς πληγὰς καὶ βιαίους διδόντες ἀπὸ τόξων κραταιῶν καὶ μεγάλων καὶ τῇ σκολιότητι τῆς καμπῆς ἠναγκασμένον τὸ βέλος ἀποστελλόντων, Plut. *Crass.* 24.5, tr. Perrin). *Spiculum* can be used as a pars pro toto: "sharply pointed weapon" (OLD s.v. 2), e.g. *pars spicula gestat/ bina manu* (Verg. *A.* 7.687–8), *creberrima spicula funditantes* (Amm. 24.4.16), but in Amm. it more often denotes the head of a spear or arrow, e.g. *inter spiculum et harundinem* (23.4.14). Note that the points of the arrows 'formed

28 COMMENTARY

an undivisible unity with' (*cohaererent*) the archers' hands: in this way Amm. expresses the skill of true professionals, who act in full harmony with their instrument. The expression also leads up to the next phrase which deals with their excellently trained fingers.

summaque peritia digitorum pulsibus argutum sonantes harundines evolabant Cf. *sagittarii...tela summa peritia dispergebant* (19.5.5, q.v.), *ut nervi digitorum acti pulsibus violentis harundines ferratas emitterent* (24.2.13, q.v.). The structure of the present phrase is far more complicated, mainly because of the absence of a part. perf. pass. like *actae* or *missae* (cf. Fontaine's "décochés sous l'impulsion de leurs doigts"). Nevertheless, it seems best to regard the ablativi *summa peritia* and *pulsibus* as denoting manner and cause respectively, unless *digitorum* is an extreme case of the gen. inversus: 'by the impulse of their extremely skillful fingers'. See Kühner-Stegmann 1.281 for the acc. neutr. of adjectives and pronouns with verba "des Tönens und Rufens" and cf. *catenisque sonantibus triste* (28.1.55).

1.14 *post hos elephantorum fulgentium formidandam speciem et truculentos hiatus vix mentes pavidae perferebant* Fear is the main theme in this section: *formidandam, pavidae, terrebantur*. Cf. Bitter 25 n. 71: "Den Einsatz der Elefanten schildert Ammian weniger aus taktischen Gründen, sondern vielmehr, um Stimmungen und Affekte zu erzeugen". Cf. App. *Pun.* 43 (about the battle of Zama): οἱ μὲν ἐλέφαντες κατῆρχον τῆς μάχης, ἐς τὸ φοβερώτατον ἐσκευασμένοι.

For *fulgentium* Meurig Davies, 1951 refers in the first place to *Elephantis...auro purpura argento et suo ebore fulgentibus* (Flor. 2.8.16). Cf. for *fulgere* in Amm. e.g. *fulgentem...augusto habitu* (20.4.22, q.v.) and *indumentis...lumine colorum fulgentibus vario* (23.6.84). She points further to some other passages where we read about the beautiful outfit of war elephants, J. *BJ* 1.42 ὁ ἀδελφὸς αὐτοῦ προϊδὼν τὸν ὑψηλότατον τῶν ἐλεφάντων πύργῳ τε μεγάλῳ καὶ περιχρύσοις προτειχίσμασι κεκοσμημένον, B. *Afr.* 72.4 *ornatusque ac loricatus...elephans*, B. *Afr.* 86.1 *elephantosque lxiiii ornatos armatosque cum turribus ornamentisque capit*, Hld. 9.18.8, Polyaen. 8.23.5 and Plin. *Nat.* 8.5.12. Cf. also *fulgentem...augusto habitu* (20.4.22, q.v.), *indumentis...lumine colorum fulgentibus vario* (23.6.84). See for *hiatus* denoting an animal's wide open jaws the list in TLL VI 3.2683.6–49 "de ore animantium". Amm.'s only other instance of this meaning is 16.10.7 about the dragon-like imperial standards: *hiatu vasto perflabiles*. Cf. also Claud. *carm. min.* 24.353 (in a section on elephants) *patulos exarmat hiatus*.

CHAPTER 1.15   29

ad quorum stridorem odoremque et insuetum aspectum magis equi terrebantur
This is obviously inspired by Liv. 30.18.7 *ad quorum stridorem odoremque
et adspectum territi equi.* See the detailed note ad 24.6.8 *elephanti* on
the various aspects of Amm.'s descriptions of the elephants' role on
the battlefield. Their frightening smell and sound also appear in
25.3.4 *faetorem elephantorumque stridorem impatienter tolerantibus nostris*
and 25.6.2 *ad quorum faetorem inaccessum terribilemque equis inter initia
turbatis et viris* (q.v.). For *insuetum* cf. Hld. 9.18.4 on horses who
panicked πρὸς τὸ ἄηθες τῆς τῶν ἐλεφάντων ὄψεως.

This section shows the other side of the picture. Elephants are an   **1.15**
asset, when they strike terror into the enemy's ranks, but they are
difficult to control and their deployment entails considerable risks.
Amm. illustrates this with two examples, one from the recent past,
the other from the war with Hannibal.

*quibus insidentes magistri manubriatos cultros dexteris manibus illigatos
gestabant* Cf. for *magister* with the meaning 'mahout' *regere magistri
non poterant* (19.7.7, q.v.) and see TLL VIII 84.69sqq. on the use of
the word "de doctore, domitore, rectore bestiarum". TLL VIII 337.28
–30 mentions only one other instance of *manubriatus* (i.q. *manubrio
ornatus*): Pallad. 1.42.2 *serrulas manubriatas*, 'small handsaws
equipped with a handle'. The sources differ as to the number of
persons riding on an elephant during a battle. Philostr. *VA* 2.12
mentions turrets large enough to carry ten or fifteen archers, while
Heliodorus 9.18.5 speaks of six men, two in front and an equal number on the left and the right side. According to Aelian, however, a
war elephant carried in its tower or on its bare back three armed
men, and a fourth who held "the goad with which he controls the
beast, as a helmsman or pilot of a vessel controls a ship with a rudder": τέταρτον δὲ τὸν τὴν ἅρπην ἔχοντα διὰ χειρῶν καὶ ἐκείνῃ τὸν θῆρα
ἰθύνοντα, ὡς οἴακι ναῦν κυβερνητικὸν ἄνδρα καὶ ἐπιστάτην τῆς νεώς (*NA*
13.9, tr. Scholfield; cf. Strabo 15.1.52, 709C ὁ δὲ τοῦ ἐλέφαντος ἡνίοχος
τέταρτος, τρεῖς δ' οἱ ἀπ' αὐτοῦ τοξεύοντες).

acceptae apud Nisibin memores cladis See for a succinct survey of Nisibis'
history from 165 A.D. the notes ad 14.9.1 *Nisibi* and 25.9.3 *Iovianum
inter*, and in general for this *orientis firmissimum claustrum* (25.8.14),
modern Nusaybin, Oppenheimer, 1983, 319–34 and Kessler, 2000.
The city had been unsuccessfully besieged three times by Sapor II
(Ruf. Fest. 27 *Ter...a Persis est obsessa Nisibis, sed maiore sui detrimento
dum obsidet hostis adfectus est*). The first time was in 337 (so e.g. Barnes,

30   COMMENTARY

1985, 133, Blockley, 1989, 470 n. 24 and Barnes, 1998, 136 n. 33) or
338 ("either that year or 337 is chronologically possible", Matthews
499 n. 15). See most recently Burgess, 1999, who opts for 337. The
second siege was in 346 (cf. e.g. Blockley, 1989, 475 with n. 59:
"The attempt of A. Olivetti…to redate this second siege to 348 is
unconvincing"), the third in 350. Relevant evidence can be found
in Dodgeon-Lieu, 1991, 164–70, 190–2 and 193–207 respectively
(see further Kawerau, 1985, 74 ff.). Brok 185, followed by Fontaine
n. 498, surmises that Amm. refers to the third siege, which is by far the
best documented (cf. Maróth, 1979 and Lightfoot, 1988). Dodgeon
and Lieu incorporate the present section among their texts about
the siege of 350. However, as will be pointed out in the note ad *ut
tunc acciderat*, only the available reports on the first siege contain a
detail about the elephants which comes close to Amm.'s allusion.

ferociens animal Amm. uses *ferocire* mostly about human beings; its
only other instance concerning animals is 17.12.2 (stallions); the
verb denotes following natural instincts in a violent way. Cf. Curt.
9.2.19 *Quod pertinet ad elephantos, praesens habemus exemplum: in suos
vehementius quam in nos incucurrerunt.*

ut tunc acciderat Theodoretus twice describes the course of the siege
of 338: *HE* 2.30 and *h.rel.* 1.11. When Nisibis was in dire straits,
bishop Jacob, ὁ θεσπέσιος ἄνθρωπος (*HE* 2.30.12; cf. for him Peeters,
1920 and Krüger, 1968), σκνιφῶν αὐτοῖς καὶ κωνώπων ἐπιπέμψαι νέφος
ἱκετεύσε τὸν θεόν (*h.rel.* 1.11). The 'cloud of insects and mosquitoes'
indeed arrived and caused havoc among the besiegers: they settled in
the trunks of the elephants and the ears and noses of the other animals, who could not bear this and then τοὺς ἐποχουμένους κατήνεγκαν,
καὶ τήν τε τάξιν συνέχεαν τό τε στρατόπεδον καταλιπόντες ἔφυγον κατὰ
κράτος (*HE* 2.30.14). Since Jacob died soon after the siege of 337/8,
this end of the actions only fits the first siege. The presence of flies
and mosquitoes could well have been caused by the swampy sur-
roundings. Lieu, 1986, 98 points to Herodian 3.9.5, where we are
told that in earlier days the citizens of nearby Hatra flung containers
of insects at the forces of Septimius Severus. See for insects as warfare
agents in the ancient Middle East Neufeld, 1980.

venam, quae caput a cervice disterminat, ictu maximo terebrabant 'The
blood-vessel which marks off the head from the neck' is a dubious
piece of anatomy. One can understand Gelenius' *vertebram*, which
would be the only instance in Amm., but this does not suit the

CHAPTER 1.16   31

curious verb *terebrare*, a hapax in Amm. It could be a surgical term. Orosius and Zonaras relate more or less the same story, but say that the elephants were wounded *inter aures* (Oros. *hist.* 4.18.12 *fabrili scalpro inter aures adacto necabantur*) or ὑπὸ τὸ οὖς (Zon. 9.9 οἱ ἐλέφαντες...σιδηρίῳ τινὶ ὑπὸ τὸ οὖς νυττόμενοι, 'stabbed', ἐκτιννύοντο).

exploratum est enim aliquando ab Hasdrubale Hannibalis fratre ita citius vitam huiusmodi adimi beluarum This clearly refers to Liv. 27.49.1–2 (in the report on the battle at the Metaurus in 207 B.C.); this passage needs to be quoted in full here: *Elephanti plures ab ipsis rectoribus quam ab hoste interfecti. Fabrile scalprum cum malleo habebant; id, ubi saevire beluae ac ruere in suos coeperant, magister inter aures positum ipsa in compagine qua iungitur capiti cervix quanto maximo poterat ictu adigebat. Ea celerrima via mortis in tantae molis belua inventa erat ubi regendi spem vi vicissent, primusque id Hasdrubal instituerat, dux cum saepe alias memorabilis tum illa praecipue pugna.* Cf. Oros. *hist.* 4.18.12 *Id genus occidendae cum opus esset beluae idem dux Hasdrubal primus invenerat* and Zon. 9.9 παρήγγειλεν ὁ Ἀσδρούβας τοῖς ἐπ' αὐτῶν καθημένοις τοὺς τιτρωσκομένους τῶν θηρίων παραυτίκα σφάζειν. Hasdrubal is mentioned by Amm., apart from the present text, in 15.10.11; for Hannibal see the note ad 22.9.3. For Hannibal's elephants see now Edwards, 2001.

In a few other cases too Amm. uses *huiusmodi* as a synonym of anaphoric *is* or *hic*: 18.1.3 *in huiusmodi controversiis*, 'in the quarrels just mentioned', 18.7.5, *huiusmodi bestiis*, 'the beasts which are the subject of this section (viz. lions)'.

quibus non sine magno terrore perspectis Amm. does not conceal the fact   **1.16**
that the elephants did inspire fear on the Roman side, because he wants to contrast this with the cool confidence of the emperor, who concentrates on an efficient positioning of his men.

stipatus armatarum cohortium globis cum primatibus fidentissimus imperator Cf. for the stereotyped picture of the general amidst his forces *saeptusque tutius armatarum cohortium globis* (20.5.1, q.v.), *multitudine stipatus armorum* (21.13.6, q.v.). Note also the caricature *stipatusque mulierculis* (22.14.3). See for *primates*, 'highest ranking officers', the note ad 24.7.1. There is no reason to assume that *fidentissimus* denotes hybris. Julian relied on his men and his own military insight and the outcome of the battle proved him right.

ut flagitabat maior vis et atrocior Some translators interpret this phrase as expressing the "desperate nature of the situation" (Hamilton),

32   COMMENTARY

but it is difficult to understand how *vis* can have such a meaning. It seems far more natural to assume that *vis* here means "a large body or number…, often implying potential violence" (OLD s.v. 8a). The absence of a genitive *hostium* is slightly surprising, but after all the enemy's forces have been extensively described in the previous sections. Moreover, the present clause explains why Julian chose a 'round' line-up for his forces, "um besser gegen Flankenangriffe der starken feindlichen Reiterei geschützt zu sein" (Kromayer-Veith, 1928, 597, on the present section). There is nothing wrong with Caltabiano's "come esigeva la forza maggiore e più temibile degli avversari". See for *flagitare* with the relevant situation as subject the note ad 20.10.1.

lunari acie sinuatisque lateribus occursuros hosti manipulos instruebat From TLL VII 2.1838.47–62 it can be inferred that this is the only instance of *lunaris* in a military sense; cf., however, Fron. *Str.* 2.3.4 *lunata acie.* It seems that a similar formation is meant with *in bicornem figuram acie divisa* (16.2.13), *infusis utrimque cornibus* (27.10.13) and *aciem rotundo habitu figuratam opponit* (29.5.41; but see for this last passage Kromayer-Veith, 1928, 597 and Fontaine n. 500). Cf. also Elton, 1996, 252 and Nicasie, 1998, 212, 214. See further Veg. *mil.* 3.19.3 on the danger of being surrounded: *unum remedium est, ut alam cornuque replices et rotundes.* The only other example of *sinuatus* in Amm. is 22.8.37 where it relates to the 'Scythian bow' (i.e. the Black Sea). See for his outdated use of *manipulus* and comparable terms the notes ad 21.13.9 and 24.6.8.

1.17 *nostrorum cuneos* See for *cuneus* the note ad 25.6.7.

illatis concitatius signis spiculorum impetum fregit The military phrase *signa inferre*, 'to advance', used by Amm. only here, occurs frequently in Caesar and Livy; cf., however, especially Fron. *Str.* 2.1.9 *Philippus ad Chaeroniam…languentibus iam Atheniensibus concitatius intulit signa et ipsos cecidit.* TLL IV 69.7–26 assumes two meanings for *concitate*: *celeriter* and *vehementer, acriter.* The present text is wrongly put in the second category; Julian wants to thwart the dangerous archers immediately by a swift manoeuvre the objective of which is *ne possint emittere* (24.2.5, q.v.), as Ventidius tried to do against the Parthians: *ita procursione subita adeo se admovit ut sagittas, quibus ex longinquo usus est, comminus adplicitus eluderet* (Fron. *Str.* 2.2.5). See further 24.6.11 with the note and Hdt. 6.112.

CHAPTER 1.18   33

datoque ad decernendum sollemniter signo See for *decernere* as a synonym
of *pugnare* the note ad 20.11.12 and for *sollemniter* as a synonym of
ex more the note ad 16.12.36 *Dato...sollemniter signo.*

denseti Romani pedites confertas hostium frontes nisu protruserunt acerrimo
This is the heart of Julian's strategy: he is relying on the sheer bodily
strength and weight of his infantrymen to push the enemy off the
battlefield. They lived up to his expectations. See for *denseti* the note
ad 22.6.2 and for *nisu acerrimo* comparable phrases like *virorum for-
tium acrior nisus* (20.11.19), *acri nisu* (29.6.11), *nisu valido* (14.2.6,
14.11.1, 15.10.4). Note that not skill or shrewd tactics, but pure physical effort (*nisus*) is used to 'push away' the enemy; see for *protrudere*
the note ad 19.6.9 *protrusi*, and cf. *umbo trudebat umbonem* (16.12.37),
pulvis...arma armis corporaque corporibus obtrudebat (16.12.43) and Bitter 146.

This section contains an impressionistic sketch of the battle proper   **1.18**
and its outcome, in a long and complicated sentence and a shorter
and straightforward one. In fact, only the first half of the first
sentence describes the fighting; the second part, consisting of more
than twenty words, has the status of an appendix, in which the
Persians' lack of perseverance in man-to-man fighting is explained.
The most remarkable aspect of the entire sentence is the fact that
the loud noise of the battlefield functions as the Agens of the actions.
The various sounds of trumpets and armour and the men's warcries
regularly occur in Amm.'s descriptions of battles (see Bitter 147–
8), but it is a daring stylistic move to make the noise into the
performer of the action, bolder than *pulvis* being the Agens in a
brief clause in 16.12.43, which was quoted at the end of the last note
on §17.

fervente certaminum mole The same phrase occurs in 20.6.5 (q.v.). Cf.
also *anceps pugna diutius fervens* (24.4.20), *fervente...proelio* (31.7.13)
and see the note ad 20.11.7 *ante fervorem certaminum.*

armorumque lugubre sibilantium fragor Cf. *iaculorum...stridentium crebritate* (16.12.43) and *stridentibus iaculis* (21.12.6). Other phrases in
Amm. about deathly sounds are *ferum ululantes et lugubre* (16.11.8),
horrendo fragore scutorum lugubre concrepantium (26.6.16), *lugubre cla-
mante praecone* (28.2.13), *ululantibus lugubre barbaris* (28.5.6), *subrau-
cum et lugubre strepens* (31.16.6). As was announced in the introduction to this section, *sonitus et...fragor* are the grammatical subject and

34   COMMENTARY

indeed the Agens of the predicate *contexit*: 'noise covered the fields with blood'. By this remarkable device, which resembles an extremely blown up genitivus inversus construction, the author wants to impress the overpowering horror of the ghastly noise on his reader, whose other senses are more implicitly aroused by the 'heat' of the battle, the smell of 'blood' and elephants, and the sight of fallen soldiers everywhere (*effusius*).

nihil perpetiens iam remissum Cf. *proeliorum ardor nihil perpeti poterat segne* (16.10.3; see the note ad loc. for parallels in Sallust and Tacitus). See for *remissus*, 'slack', 'without energy', also *cum enim remissius pugnaretur* (20.11.25), (civitas) *obsideri remissius coepta est* (21.12.15).

effusius cadentibus Persis Translators agree with Seyfarth's rendering of *effusius*: "in grösserer Anzahl". TLL V 2.227.54–5 lists the present text and 22.4.2 under the heading "i.q. copiose, large, effrenate", in section d ("varia"). However, it is more likely that *effusius* denotes wide space: Persians were falling everywhere on the battlefield; cf. *effuse disiecti sunt* (20.7.15; cf. 22.8.18). This indeed implies the greater number of the fallen, but *effusius* gives a more graphic representation of this aspect of the scene.

quibus saepe languidis in conflictu artius pes pede collatus graviter obsistebat Note the careful phrasing of this crucial part of the battle, which invites the reader to visualize the scene and to understand the sharp contrast between true Roman stamina and barbarian fragility. The Persians often lack the necessary staying power (*languidis*) in the direct clash (*conflictu*) with their opponents (cf. 23.6.80, 23.6.83, 24.8.1); *conflictus* is sometimes a mere synonym of *pugna* (see the note ad 19.5.2), but here it clearly denotes the physical collision between the warriors (cf. Cic. *Caec.* 43 *conflictu corporum*), when their feet are placed very closely (*artius*) against one another. See the note ad *dextrae dexteris* (16.12.37) for other examples in Amm. of polyptoton expressing reciprocity. The phrase *pedem conferre*, which apart from a number of instances in Livy is less frequently used than some scholars seem to assume, also occurs in 16.2.13 and 27.2.6. One would expect *cum pede*, as in Livy 28.2.6 *tum pes cum pede conlatus*, but Amm. has no use for the preposition here, since the terse juxtaposition *pes pede* has an iconic value. In fact, this juxtaposition has a long history, which begins with Enn. *Ann.* 584 Sk.: *premitur pede pes atque armis arma teruntur* (restored from *B. Hisp.* 31.7).

CHAPTER 1.18   35

See Skutsch's extensive and invaluable note for further instances, among which Verg. *A.* 10.361 *concurrunt: haeret pede pes densusque viro vir* (see Harrison ad loc., who refers condescendingly to Skutsch's "useful note"). The adverb *graviter* is preferred to words like *acriter, fortiter, strenue*, because it brings out the 'weight' of the strong Roman legs, which formed a physical barrier (*obsistebat*). It is as if Amm. is depicting a gigantic rugby maul.

pugnare fortiter eminus consuetis The entire 'Nachsatz', up to *deterrere*, serves as an explanation of *saepe languidis in conflictu*; cf. *eminusque terribiles* (23.6.80): the Persians were redoubtable adversaries only at a distance.

si inclinatas suorum copias senserint The first instance of *inclinare*, "to cause (troops) to waver in battle, drive back" (OLD s.v. 6a) is Enn. *scen.* 172 (= 333 Jocelyn) *nostram acrem aciem inclinatam*. Other examples are *Romana inclinatur acies* (Liv. 1.12.3), *inclinatam vidit Pompeianorum aciem* (Vell. 2.52.4), *acies inclinatae nostrorum* (Amm. 31.13.7).

cedendo in modum imbrium pone versus directis sagittis hostes a persequendi fiducia deterrere "After Carrhae the Parthians' ungentlemanlike tactics became a stock theme" (Nisbet and Hubbard ad Hor. *Carm.* 1.19.11). Cf. e.g. Verg. *G.* 3.31 *fidentemque fuga Parthum versisque sagittis*, Plut. *Crass.* 24.6 ὑπέφευγον γὰρ ἅμα βάλλοντες οἱ Πάρθοι, καὶ τοῦτο κράτιστα ποιοῦσι μετὰ Σκύθας and Lib. *Or.* 18.264 εὐθὺς ἐγκλίναντες ἔφευγον ἐν εὖ τοῦτο ἠσκηκότες τοῦ πολέμου τὸ μέρος. See for the abl. gerundii as the equivalent of the part. praes the note ad 20.4.22 *diu tacendo*. Enn. *Ann.* 266 Sk. *Hastati spargunt hastas. Fit ferreus imber* is the first Latin example of the metaphor 'shower of missiles'; see Skutsch's note ad loc. The last three words are quoted in Verg. *A.* 12.284. See further the short list in TLL VII 1.423.46–56 and cf. also the notes ad *saxorum manualium nimbis* (24.2.14) and *missilium nube* (24.5.6).

Fiducia with the gen. of the gerundi(v)um denotes confidence in the successful realization of the action concerned: *fiducia rei bene gerendae* (Caes. *civ.* 2.38.2), *fiducia caput gentis Artaxata adgrediendi* (Tac. *Ann.* 13.39.6), *fiducia nandi* (Amm. 14.2.10), *revertendi fiducia* (23.5.5), *pugnandi fiducia* (29.6.16). Before Amm. *pone versus*, 'backwards', only occurs twice in Cato (*orat.* fr. 15 and 16 Iordan = 36 and 37 Malcovati, in these cases as a preposition). Amm.'s other instance (25.3.2) is also adverbial. Cf. also *pone versum coactus* (Apul. *Met.* 9.2).

36 COMMENTARY

pulsis igitur pondere magnarum virium Parthis Cf. *armorum pondere pulsus loco Romanus* (16.12.48). However, in his note ad loc. De Jonge combats the common view that the enemy's weapons are meant: "dejected and worn out by his heavy armour" is his interpretation. Krylová, 2001 shows that Amm.'s use of *ergo* and *igitur* does not differ markedly from classical usage. The discourse function of *igitur* in classical Latin has been defined by Kroon, 1989, 236–8 as marking "important new steps...after the fulfilment in the preceding context of a necessary precondition for that step". This fits the present text: the soldiers repair to their tents to prepare themselves for further actions. This new phase was made possible by their defeat of the Persians, as reported in the preceding text. For Amm.'s use of *Parthi* instead of *Persae* see the note ad 23.3.2.

solis cursu flammeo diu lassatus See the note ad 20.6.3 *signo per flammeum erecto vexillum* for Amm.'s use of *flammeus*, which here expresses heat. About the verb *lassare* TLL VII 2.989.39 notes: "vox maxime poetica". All six occurrences in Amm. are forms of the part. perf., i.a. 17.2.3 *inedia et vigiliis et desperatione postrema lassati*, 28.1.17 *Carthaginiensibus victus inopia iam lassatis*. For the heat see 24.8.3 *per eas terras vapore sideris calescentes* and 25.1.3 *aestuum magnitudine*.

in tentoria repetit ad audenda deinceps maiora sublatus There is a small note on *tentoria* ad 24.3.9. Clark and Fontaine follow Valesius' *repedat*, in spite of Hagendahl, 1922, 83–4, who defends V's original *repetit* with some instances of (*re*)*petere in* in late Latin. However, in view of *tentoria repetit* (17.13.34), (ut) *tentoria repeterent* (19.5.8), *tentoria repetivit* (20.7.15), *repetitis post haec tentoriis* (24.3.9) and *repetunt tentoria* (31.7.15) the preposition in the present text is very suspect. On the basis of the correction *repetat* by V's second hand *repedat* seems an obvious emendation, but the very list of passages quoted above makes this less certain. A mistaken repetition of the preceding *in* is more likely. The soldiers' morale has now risen sky-high, they are ready for even greater exploits; some comparable phrases in Amm. denoting such a state of mind: 16.12.3 *ad maiora stimulati fiducia*, 27.5.3 *sublatus fiducia*, 27.8.9 *ad audenda maiora prospero successu elatus*, 31.7.7 *incentivum audendi maiora*, 31.10.5 *maioraque conceptantes*.

1.19 In this section Amm.'s report rejoins that of Zosimus (cf. the note ad § 11 *prope lucis confinia*). Note that Zosimus is totally silent about the successes which, according to Amm.'s § 12–18, took place near Maranga. He only reports an attack by the Persians on the Roman

CHAPTER 1.19   37

rear in which Vetranio among others died: ἀπώλεσαν ἄλλους τε στρατιώτας καὶ Βετρανίωνα τὸν ἡγεμονίαν ἔχοντα τοῦ λόχου...καὶ ἀνδρείως ἀγωνισάμενον (3.28.2). On the other hand, Zosimus in 3.28.2 gives some information which is not found in Amm., viz. the unexpected capture by the Persians of boats which were far behind the land forces: καὶ πλοῖα δὲ ἥλω κατόπιν πολὺ τοῦ στρατοπέδου τοῖς πολεμίοις περιπεσόντα (ibid.). Libanius *Or.* 18.263 also speaks of the loss of ships, but not in the manner of Zosimus' narrative (cf. Paschoud n. 81). That there still were some boats left can be deduced from 25.8.3 *brevibus lembis, quos post exustam classem docuimus remansisse* (cf. further the notes ad 24.7.4 *praeter minores duodecim*, 24.7.5 *duodecim tantummodo* and 25.2.1 *Post quae triduo indutiis destinato*).

Persarum maior, ut dictum est, apparuit strages This refers to *effusius cadentibus Persis* (§ 18).

eminuit tamen inter varios certaminum casus Vetranionis mors, viri pugnacis, qui legionem Ziannorum regebat Cf. the following parallels: 14.1.3 *eminuit autem inter humilia...Clematii cuiusdam Alexandrini nobilis mors repentina*, 19.11.16 *mors tamen eminuit inter alios Cellae Scutariorum tribuni*, 27.7.5 *Eminuit tamen per id tempus inter alias humilium neces mors Dioclis ex comite largitionum Illyrici*, 28.1.14 *praeter multa cruda et immitia...mors Marini causarum defensoris eminuit*, 31.13.18 *In hac multiplici virorum illustrium clade Traiani mors eminuit et Sebastiani*. Nobody seems to have picked up the hint in TLL V 2.492.5–6 and noticed that the kernel of the various sentences is derived from Luc. 7.599–600 *mors tamen eminuit clarorum in strage virorum/ pugnacis Domiti*. When the present text is compared with the five other passages quoted from Amm., the presence of *pugnacis* is striking. If the adverbial form *pugnaciter* (14.6.25) is included, this word occurs only seven times in Amm., so that one almost feels tempted to assume that the author had recently reread the relevant passage in Lucan. The phrase (*inter*) *varios certaminum casus* is repeated in 27.12.12; cf. also *proeliorumque varios casus* (15.9.1), *post bellorum assiduos casus* (18.5.7, q.v.), *multiplices casus* (23.5.20, 28.4.35, 29.2.21).

Vetranio (*PLRE* I, Vetranio 2) is only known from this text and Zos. 3.28.2, quoted above – the lacuna in Zosimus' text, indicated by Mendelsohn and adopted by Paschoud, must have contained the name of the Zianni. The legion which Vetranio commanded (as a *tribunus*, presumably) was, at the time when the *Notitia Dignitatum* was compiled, a *legio comitatensis* in Thrace (*Not. Dign. Or.* 8.17,

38 COMMENTARY

8.49). Its name points to a Caucasian people, which, according to Eustathius' note ad D.P. 766, was called Sanni or Tzanni (cf. Procop. *Pers.* 1.15.21 τὸ Τζανικὸν ἔθνος…Σάνοι ἐν τοῖς ἄνω χρόνοις καλούμενοι), but in former days Macrones (known from e.g. Hdt. 2.104, 3.94 and X. *An.* 4.8). Justinian claims to have brought them under Roman rule for the first time (*Nov.* 1 pr., *Nov.* 28 pr., cf. Procop. *Pers.* 1.15.25), but already in the fourth century they apparently furnished the Roman army with troops. Cf. Hoffmann, I 225 and 308.

CHAPTER 2

Introduction

After the battle of Maranga the Persians and the Romans decided to interrupt their military activities for a period of three days, a break both parties used to recover from the wounds they had inflicted upon each other. Although Ammianus uses the term *indutiae*, it is very much open to doubt whether the warring parties agreed on a formal truce. It is more likely that they just abstained from further attacks.

The scorched earth policy practiced by the Persians now takes its full and devastating effect. Julian tries to mitigate it by putting the food reserves, meant for the officers and his personal staff, at the disposal of the common soldiers. This self-effacing attitude of the emperor is given due praise and is explained as being the result of his general abstemiousness. In this way the author anticipates the elogium in Chapter Four, in which this aspect of Julian's character receives much attention.

In a typically smooth transition from general description to factual narration, Ammianus tells us in section three how Julian, during his nocturnal meditations, saw the Genius publicus depart from his tent. Just as the beginning of Julian's reign was marked in 20.5.10 by the apparition of the Genius asking to be admitted, now its end is announced by this sudden disappearance. Ammianus uses the same structural device in the introduction to the deaths of Constantius (21.14.2) and Valentinian (30.5.18), but it should be noted that only in Julian's case is the apparition called explicitly Genius publicus, c.q. – populi Romani. The identification of the personal Genius with the Genius of the Roman people is a signal honour attributed to Julian alone.

While the emperor, in the middle of the night, sacrifices to the gods to avert this omen, he sees a 'shooting star' or meteor furrowing the sky. Like comets, meteors often announce the death of rulers. What frightens Julian above all is that he sees this as a sign of the anger of Mars, whom he had treated so disrespectfully after the god had refused to send him good omens (24.6.16). The two signs, the disappearance of the Genius and the shooting star, leave no doubt that Julian's death is near. Before Ammianus reaches this climax in

40 COMMENTARY

his history, he offers the reader a short digression on the nature of the latter phenomenon, thereby emphasizing its importance as an omen.

The last two sections of this chapter show how conceited and obstinate Julian could be in his dealings with the *haruspices*, who warned him not to ignore such unmistakable signs. Even their plea for a delay of a few days was not honoured by the emperor. A catastrophe was now inevitable, and Julian had in no small measure personally contributed to his downfall.

2.1 *Post quae triduo indutiis destinato* After the battle of Maranga, which involved heavy fighting, as appears from the preceding chapter, the two armies observed a three days' truce. These days fell on 23, 24 and 25 June (see the note on chronology).

Zosimus does not mention any period of rest. According to him the Roman army advanced after the battle at Maranga and passed some villages until it reached Toummara (3.28.2–3). The suggestion of Dillemann, 1961, 145 that Zosimus' Σοῦμα (3.30.2), his Τούμμαρα (3.28.3) and Amm.'s Sumere (25.6.4) are one and the same city should be rejected, as Paschoud n. 82 has shown. Zosimus also mentions that the Romans regretted having burnt their ships since the pack animals were not capable of carrying the supplies – note that according to Amm. the Romans had not burnt all their ships (24.7.4 *praeter minores duodecim*, q.v.; cf. also the note ad 24.7.5 *duodecim*) and that in 3.28.2 Zosimus had said that some ships had been taken by the Persians and furthermore, that the Persians had stored the food in fortified places to which the Romans had no access. Moreover, Zosimus refers to a battle not mentioned by Amm., in the course of which the Romans killed many Persians.

As Paschoud n. 82 rightly observes, a formal truce between the Romans and the Persians at this stage is very difficult to imagine. One might add that for such an agreement Amm.'s usual phrase would have been *pactis indutiis*, as in 28.5.4 *pactis indutiis et datis ex condicione proposita* and 29.1.4 *pactis indutiis ex consensu*. Paschoud tries to reconcile Amm. and Zosimus by arguing that the three days' rest should be interpreted as an advance at a slow pace: "Pendant ces trois jours, les Romains avancent lentement vers le nord, couvrant une distance qui n'excède pas 40 km." According to him, the Roman army should have reached Toummara by the evening of 25 June.

For other instances of *indutiae* indicating a pause in the fighting and a cessation of hostilities, formally or silently agreed upon by both parties, see the notes ad 16.12.19, 17.3.1, 19.2.14, 19.6.13,

CHAPTER 2.1   41

20.7.5, 20.8.9 and 20.11.9. It can also indicate a more longstanding armistice; e.g. 27.9.7 *per indutias pacem sibi tribui poposcerunt*. For *destinare*, 'to destine', cf. 29.6.9 *cum...noctem proximam destinasset in fugam* and ps. Sol. 53.12 *noctis partem quieti destinant*.

dum suo quisque vulneri medetur vel proximi For a similar scene see 19.2.15 *medebatur ergo suis quisque vulneribus pro possibilitate vel curantium copia*. *Mederi* is also found in a metaphorical sense in Amm., e.g. 23.5.18 *ut medeamur praeteritis*. For *dum* with present indicative see the note ad 20.6.1.

commeatibus nos destitutos This applies of course to the Roman army in general, but especially to the common soldiers, since it appears from the end of this section that the tribunes and comites still have food which they are sharing with these ordinary soldiers.

inedia cruciabat iam non ferenda This is the result of the action of the Persians described in 25.1.10 *herbis frumentisque crematis*, repeated below with the words *frugibus exustis et pabulis*. The Persians had applied their scorched earth tactics as soon as the Romans started the return journey; see 24.7.7 *Quo cognito hostes, ut inedia nos cruciarent, herbas cum adultis segetibus incenderunt*. Occasionally the Romans were able to procure grain, as in Hucumbra (25.1.4, q.v.), but these supplies probably did not last long. Scarcity of food and the threat of starvation are recurrent themes in this book; see also 25.7.4, 8.1, 8.7 and 8.15. The Romans were in such dire straits that they eventually killed camels and other pack animals in order to stave off hunger (25.8.6). According to Greg. Naz. *Or.* 5.12 the army, blaming Julian for all its troubles, not only had a shortage of food but was in utter despair: ἡ τροφὴ δὲ οὐκ εὔπορος· ἐν ἀθυμίῃ δὲ ὁ στρατός, καὶ δι' ὀργῆς εἶχον τὸν βασιλέα.

Thdt. *HE* 3.25.3–4 likewise points to the soldiers' hunger and thirst caused by Julian's folly, as does John Chrysostom in *pan. Bab.* 2.122. The latter, moreover, says that the Romans were forced to eat their horses: ὥστε ἱππείων ἀπογεύσασθαι κρεῶν. Amm. also speaks of the eating of slaughtered horses, but only in 25.8.15, when Jovian had become emperor after the death of Julian.

The phrase *non ferendus* is used frequently by Cicero. Usually it refers to unacceptable behaviour, as in Cic. *Ver.* 4.45 *Superbum est enim iudices, et non ferendum*, but he also uses it of intolerable pain, as in Cic. *Tusc.* 5.32 *cum cruciaretur non ferendis doloribus*. There is no parallel for *iam non ferendus*, in which *iam* indicates that a new stage

42   COMMENTARY

in the development of the action has been reached, but cf. Cic. *Sest.* 2 *nihil minus est ferendum quam quod iam non per latrones suos...sed per vos nobis...periculum inferre conantur*, Quint. *Inst.* 8.6.40 *Cetera iam non significandi gratia, sed ad ornandam non augendam orationem adsumuntur.* Claud. *in Eutr.* 2. 487–8 is very similar: *nec iam revocabile damnum / eventu stolidi serum didicere magistro.*

tribunorum...et comitum For tribunes see the notes ad 22.11.2 and 23.3.9. For the title of *comes*, see the note ad 20.4.18 *postea comes* and in general for *comites* Scharf, 1994.

imae quoque militum plebi penitus indigenti The expression *ima plebs* is extremely rare. In Amm. the only parallel is 31.6.2 *imam plebem omnem...armavit.* Cf. Juv. 8.47–8 *tamen ima plebe Quiritem / facundum invenies.* For Amm.'s use of *plebs* to designate the common soldiers see the note ad 20.6.6. Thompson, 1947, 3 although not referring to this passage, detects "a note of contempt throughout Ammianus' history for the fortunes, habits, and speech of common soldiers".

2.2 *et imperator, cui non cuppediae ciborum...parabatur* Julian was in many respects a moderate man, and definitely with regard to food the emperor observed *temperantia*, as Amm. elaborately mentions in 25.4.4. Already in 16.5.1 the author had referred to the moderation of Julian, who behaved as if he was bound by the sumptuary laws of Lycurgus; cf. also 21.9.2 *nullius cibi indigens mundioris, sed paucis contentus et vilibus*, q.v. See Brandt, 1999, 37 and 397. *Cuppedia* in the singular is mentioned as one of the vices in Cic. *Tusc.* 4.26 *avaritia, ambitio, mulierositas, pervicacia, ligurritio, vinulentia, cuppedia et si qua similia.* The plural is used "de lautioribus cibis", TLL IV 1436.8. In all probability Amm. imitates Gel. 7.13.2 *coniectabamus ad cenulam non cuppedias ciborum, sed argutias quaestionum.* Amm. uses the word again in 26.7.1 *cuppediarum vilium mercatores* and 30.1.20 *cumque apponerentur exquisitae cuppediae.*

sub columellis tabernaculi párcius cenatúro There are no other instances of *columella* used of a tent, but the term is easily understood of poles supporting the canvas. The emperor takes his meal in the open, for all to see, which is a sign of his *civilitas. Parcius* is the reading of Gelenius, either found in the Hersfeldensis or conjectured by himself. The comparative produces a cursus velox, which makes this reading even more attractive. In 27.3.15 provincial bishops are characterized by their *tenuitas edendi potandique parcissime.* Cf. also 25.8.7 *cibos*

CHAPTER 2.2   43

ferentes ex his, quos relictus cum Procopio et Sebastiano exercitus parcius victitans conservarat.

pultis portio parabatur For the alliteration, a device which Amm. uses sparingly, see the notes ad 20.4.8 *procurare* and the introduction to 21.7.1. It is continued in the next section: *ad sollicitam suspensamque quietem paulisper protractus* and contributes to the panegyrical tone of sections 2–4, which prepare the reader for the death scene in the next chapter. This is the only time Amm. uses the word *puls*, a porridge made of meal, prepared with water and salt; Hug, 1959. It was the primitive food of the Romans before they became acquainted with bread; Var. *L.L.* 5.105 *De victu antiquissima puls*; Plin. *Nat.* 18.83 *pulte autem, non pane, vixisse longo tempore Romanos manifestum*. Poets like Juvenal (11.58; 14.171) and Martial (5.78.9, 13.8) refer to it as the most simple form of food in contrast to the delicacies of their day. It was also used in sacrifice; Plin. *Nat.*18.84 *et hodie sacra prisca atque natalium pulte fitilla* ('cake') *conficiuntur*. Cato, *R.R.* 85 gives a recipe for *puls Punica*. The *pultes Iulianae*, mentioned by Apicius (5.186), may have something to do with Julian, according to Staesche, 1998, 81: "Es ist höchst zweifelhaft, ob Julian das Gericht wirklich selbst kreierte. Wahrscheinlicher ist, dass es sich um ein 'normales' Rezept für einen recht unaufwendig zubereiteten Getreidebrei handelte, das der Kompilator mit dem Namen 'Julian' – dessen einfacher Geschmack bekannt war – überschrieb". The fact that Julian eats this simple food characterizes him as a Roman who adheres to the old Roman ways, and testifies to his self-restraint; cf. V. Max. 2.5.5 *erant adeo continentiae attenti ut frequentior apud eos pultis usus quam panis esset*. Furthermore, it emphasizes that Julian ate the same food as his soldiers; cf. 16.5.3 *munificis militis vili et fortuito cibo contentus*; 25.4.4 *per varios autem procinctus stans interdum more militiae cibum brevem vilemque sumere visebatur*. In this respect, too, Julian resembled Hadrian: HA *H* 10.2 *cibis etiam castrensibus in propatulo libenter utens, hoc est larido caseo et posca*.

The staple diet of soldiers consisted of baked bread combined with sour wine, as appears from one of Julian's letters to Libanius (*Ep.* 98, 402 b). *Cod. Theod.* 7.4.6 (= *Cod. Iust.* 12.37.1), dated to 17 May 360, tells us in more detail what the regular food was for soldiers on campaign: *Repetita consuetudo monstravit expeditionis tempore buccellatum ac panem, vinum quoque atque acetum, sed et laridum, carnem verbecinam etiam, milites nostros ita solere percipere: biduo buccellatum, tertio die panem; uno die vinum, alio die acetum; uno die laridum, biduo carnem verbecinam.* See in general for the military diet Davies, 1989.

44 COMMENTARY

munifici...gregario Cf. 16.5.3 *munificis militis.* In the military hierarchy these are the soldiers of the lowest rank; Veg. *mil.* 2.7.12 *Reliqui munifices appellantur, qui munera facere coguntur.* Amm. calls the common soldiers also *inferior miles* (20.5.8) or *gregarius miles* (14.6.10; 15.1.2). Kromayer-Veith, 1963, 589 suggest that the foreign soldiers in the army looked down their noses at the rustic national food of Roman soldiers.

quidquid ad ministeria postulabatur, per contubernia paupertina sui securus egessit The abstractum pro concreto for *ministri* is common, as the list in TLL VIII 1013.20–9 shows. Löfstedt, 1911, 112–3 gives many examples from Late Latin. The emperor's personal servants are designated as *ministeria vitae secretioris* (14.11.3, 18.4.4). As Fontaine n. 510 observes, the plural is best understood as referring to the various personal servants of the emperor rather than to the service of the emperor in general. In view of expressions like *res, tempus postulat* (TLL X 2.268.40–78), *postulabatur* here must mean 'was required.' The *contubernia paupertina* are the tents of the common soldiers. Cf. 14.6.25 *Ex turba vero imae sortis et paupertinae* and 23.6.61 about the Scyths *assueti victu vili et paupertino.* The phrase *sui securus,* for which see the note ad 21.9.8 *recreatus tandem,* sums up the emperor's self-effacing behaviour. At the same time it prepares the reader for the death scene. When Julian had been seriously wounded he wanted to return to the battlefield *ut reviso proelio suorum fiduciam repararet ac videretur sui securus alienae salutis sollicitudine vehementer astringi* (25.3.8).

2.3 *ad sollicitam suspensamque quietem paulisper protractus* The phrase *suspensa quies* is an oxymoron, probably modelled on Vergil: *A.* 4.379–80 *scilicet is superis labor est, ea cura quietos / sollicitat* and 11.253–4 *quae vos fortuna quietos / sollicitat?* The same applies to *suspensa,* in view of *A.* 4.9 *Anna soror, quae me suspensam insomnia terrent!* and Liv. 28.31.5 *dum quidnam de seditione statueretur scirent, suspensi quieverunt.* The two adjectives are combined in [Quint.] *Decl.* 10.17 *'Tuae tamen' inquit, 'hoc quieti praestiti, ne attonitis agitata terroribus sollicitas semper ageres suspensasque duceres noctes.'* *Protractus* suggests that Julian unwillingly gave in to sleep.

somno, ut solebat, depulso In 16.5.4 Amm. reports that Julian, in imitation of Alexander the Great, divided his nights into three parts: rest, state affairs and business relating to the Muses: *Hinc contingebat, ut noctes ad officia divideret tripertita, quietis et publicae rei et Musarum,*

CHAPTER 2.3   45

quod factitasse Alexandrum legimus Magnum. Cf. the references ad 25.4.6 *et si nocturna.*

quaedam sub pellibus scribens Cf. Jul. *Ep.* 28 and Lib. *Or.* 18.175.

ad aemulationem Caesaris Iulii Apart from this section Julius Caesar is mentioned four times by Amm.: 21.16.13, q.v. (see also Szidat's commentary ad loc.), 22.16.13, 28.4.18, 29.2.18. However, only in this section does Amm. present Caesar as a man whom Julian tried to emulate. Plin. *Nat.* 7.92 has the unbelievable report that Caesar used to read, write, dictate and listen simultaneously, and that he was able to dictate four, and sometimes seven, letters at once. Suet. *Jul.* 56.5 tells us that Caesar wrote his *de Analogia* while crossing the Alps, his *Anticatones* around the time of the battle of Munda, and a poem *Iter* during his journey from Rome to Spain. Plut. *Caes.* 17 relates that Caesar, while travelling, dictated to a slave at his side and that during his Gallic campaigns he dictated letters on horseback keeping two scribes busy at the same time.

cum...obscuro noctis altitudine sensus cuiusdam philosophi teneretur Again Vergil may have been in Amm.'s mind, e.g. *A.* 6.268 *ibant obscuri sola sub nocte per umbram* and *G.* 1.477–8 *simulacra modis pallentia miris / visa sub obscurum noctis. Altitudo* is brought under the heading of βαθύτης in TLL I 1769.43, which is wrong, since in the parallel description of the emperor's philosophical meditations during the night in 16.5.6 we read: *quasi pabula quaedam animo ad sublimiora scandenti conquirens per omnia philosophiae membra prudenter disputando currebat.* Cf. also Macr. *comm.* 2.17.16 *at cum de motu et immortalitate animae disputat...illic ad altitudinem philosophiae rationalis ascendit.*

Sensus is a gen. inversus. The use of *cuiusdam* does not necessarily mean that Amm. has a particular philosopher in mind, since he does not distinguish between *quidam, aliquis* and *quisquam.* See the note ad 25.1.1 *nec sedere.*

vidit squalidius, ut confessus est proximis Amm. has related elsewhere, practically in the same words, similar visions by Julian himself in the night before he was made an Augustus (in early February 360; cf. Szidat I 93): 20.5.10 *iunctioribus proximis rettulerat imperator per quietem aliquem visum, ut formari Genius publicus solet,* by Constantius on the eve of his death: 21.14.2 *confessus est iunctioribus proximis,*

46   COMMENTARY

quod tamquam desolatus secretum aliquid videre desierit, quod interdum affuisse sibi squalidius aestimabat, et putabatur Genius esse quidam tutelae salutis appositus, and finally by Valentinian: 30.5.18 *nocteque, quam lux ereptura eum vita secuta est, ut per quietem solet, videbat coniugem suam absentem sedere passis capillis amictu squalenti contectam; quam aestimari dabatur Fortunam eius esse cum taetro habitu iam discessuram.* On *squalere* and its derivatives see the note ad 21.14.2. For dreams announcing the death of Julian in pagan and Christian authors see Weber, 2000, 476–82. The number and diversity of these dream visions testify to the deep impression which the premature death of Julian has made on his admirers as well as on his opponents. With regard to the circumstances of the dream Weber correctly observes that this time Julian is wide awake when he sees the Genius. Fögen, 1997, 151–71 starts her highly illuminating study of Amm.'s views on divination and the attitude of the emperors towards those who practised it with a discussion of the dreams mentioned above. For the concept of the δαίμων / *genius* see the notes ad 20.5.10. Although the personal Genius of the emperor was identified with the Genius populi Romani, it is not accidental that only in Julian's case Amm. explicitly mentions the Genius publicus, c.q. – populi Romani. In describing the approaching deaths of Constantius and Valentinian, Amm. only mentions their personal Genius (*Genius...quidam tutelae salutis appositus* and *Fortunam eius* respectively). For the reference to (*iunctioribus*) *proximis* as Amm.'s source see the note ad 21.14.2.

speciem illam Genii publici, quam, cum ad Augustum surgeret culmen, conspexit in Galliis See the preceding note. Amm. has a variety of expressions for 'to be raised to the purple', e.g. 14.1.1 *ad principale culmen...provectus,* 15.5.16 *ad culmen imperiale surrexit* (cf. 21.16.11), 15.5.17 *ad Augustum culmen evectum* (cf. 20.8.21, 25.8.8) and 22.1.2 *qui eum ad culmen extulerat celsum.*

velata cum capite cornucopia To cover one's head was a sign of mourning. See Waltz, 1939 for many illustrations from Greek and Roman literature. By analogy, covering the *cornucopia* probably indicated an end to prosperity, as Brok 178 says. For representations of the Genius in the visual arts see the Supplement to *LIMC* (VIII 2), figs. 61 and 63 and the *Enciclopedia dell'arte antica,* vol. III fig. 1008 on p. 813.

per aulaea tristius discedentem By *aulaea* the tent is meant. TLL II 1460.45–56 quotes August. *quaest. hept.* 2.177.13 *eadem dicit aulea, quae tentoria.* In 14.9.3 *reginae exsertantis ora subinde per aulaeum* a

CHAPTER 2.4 47

curtain is meant behind which queen Constantia followed judicial interrogations. For this behaviour of the queen see now Wieber-Scariot, 1999, 115ff.

ad momentum For this rare phrase see the note ad 22.16.7. **2.4**

haesit stupore defixus Again borrowed from Vergil, *A.* 1.495 *dum stupet optutuque haeret defixus in uno* and 7.249–50 *talibus Ilionei dictis defixa Latinus / optutu tenet ora soloque immobilis haeret.* Weber, 2000, 42 n. 101 mentions reactions of this kind as standard elements in dreams like this.

ventura decretis caelestibus commendabat Cf. the melancholy words in the elogium 25.4.26 *si consiliis eius et factis illustribus decreta caelestia congruissent.* For a list of comparable expressions see Camus, 1967, 142–3 and cf. 21.1.8 *fixa fatali lege decreta* with the note. Fontaine n. 514 rightly considers *decreta caelestia* a "pompeuse périphrase pour désigner les *fata*". Amm., however, uses the phrase on purpose, since heaven promptly sends a warning in the form of a shooting star. The imperfect *commendabat* between the two forms in the perfect tense (*haesit, existimavit*) can be interpreted as describing the attitude (*omni...superior metu*) on the basis of which Julian acted as he did.

relictoque humi strato cubili For Julian's Spartan lifestyle see 16.5.5 *exsurgens non e plumis vel stragulis sericis ambiguo fulgore nitentibus, sed ex tapete et sisyra* ("a rough blanket and rug", Rolfe), *quam vulgaris simplicitas susurnam appellat* with De Jonge's note.

adulta iam excitus nocte For this and similar expressions see the note ad 20.1.3 *adulta hieme* and Heubner ad Tac. *Hist.* 3.23.3.

numinibus per sacra depulsoria supplicans The preposition phrase is unique. There is only one parallel for *depulsorius* in a literary text, viz. Plin. *Nat.* 28.11 *alia sunt verba impetritis, alia depulsoriis* (sc. precationibus). In inscriptions the adj. is found as an attribute of Jupiter and Mercurius (ἀλεξίκακοι), TLL V 1.619.56–8. Evidently, Julian tries to ward off the evil omen. For Amm.'s use of *numen* see the note ad 23.5.4 *nondum pace.*

flagrantissimam facem cadenti similem visam In V a noun, to go with *flagrantissimam*, is missing. Gelenius has *facem*, which he may have found in the Hersfeldensis, and which is, moreover, a usual term

48   COMMENTARY

for both a comet and a meteor ('shooting star'). Fontaine n. 515 thinks *flammam* an attractive alternative for *facem*. That, however, does not occur in the mss., so the note in his edition "flammam fortasse *reponendum*" is something of an overstatement. Cf. also Vell. 2.48.3 *Bello autem civili...non alius maiorem flagrantioremque quam C. Curio tribunus pl. subiecit facem* and Sen. *Her. O.* 1005 *quid me flagranti dira persequeris face?*

Taisne, 1992, 245–6 points out that Tacitus, one of Amm.'s role models, interpreted comets as unfavourable omens; e.g. *Ann.* 14.32.2. Apart from Amm., the *Epitome* is the only source in which a similar portent is mentioned on the eve of Julian's death: (ut) *ne noctu quidem visus ingens globus caelo labi ante diem belli cautum praestiterit* (43.8). The phrasing suggests a comet (*ingens globus*) rather than a meteor, but that is a minor detail. What is important is that this, admittedly topical, detail was part of the tradition surrounding Julian's death. Given the fact that it is unlikely that the *Epitome* used Amm. (see Schlumberger, 1974, 212–3), a common source for both accounts is a plausible hypothesis.

Amm. writes *cadenti similem* instead of simply *cadentem* to avoid being considered an ignoramus. For the same reason Ov. says in *Met.* 2.321–2 *ut interdum de caelo stella sereno, / etsi non cecidit, potuit cecidisse videri* and Sen. *Nat.* 2.55.3 *emicare ignes stellis transversis et cadentibus similes.* In the last resort this harks back to Arist. *Mete.* 342 a 10 ὥστε καὶ εἰς τὴν γῆν καὶ εἰς τὴν θάλατταν φαίνεσθαι πίπτοντα. See the note on *nec cadens umquam* in the next section.

aeris parte sulcata The metaphor of the furrow for the trail of a comet or a meteor is traditional. Cf. e.g. Verg. *A.* 2.697–8 *longo limite sulcus / dat lucem* and Luc. 5.562/3 *traxere cadentia sulcos / sidera.* Amm. has the phrase *sulcare latera* for 'to torture' in 26.10.5 *lateribus sulcatis acerrime* and 28.1.10. In 31.2.2 it refers to a custom of the Huns, who give their young boys the 'Mensur': *infantum ferro sulcantur altius genae, ut pilorum vigor tempestivus...hebetetur.*

horroreque perfusus est, ne ita aperte minax Martis apparuerit sidus The emperor was struck by fear 'that it was the star of Mars that had shown itself in this threatening way'; cf. the speech of Proculus in Liv. 1.16.6 *cum perfusus horrore venerabundus adstitissem* e.q.s. Amm. continues with a *ne*-clause, since *horrore perfusus est* is treated as a verb of fearing. The meaning must be that Julian contemplated the possibility that the meteor was a manifestation of the anger of the god Mars caused by his irreverent declaration in 24.6.16 *Iovemque*

CHAPTER 2.5   49

testatus est nulla Marti iam sacra facturum. It is, however, strange that
an educated person like Julian would have mistaken a shooting star
for the planet Mars. Gundel (1929, 2444) suggested that perhaps the
meteor, like the planet, had a reddish colour. It may also be relevant
that Mars was in opposition on 22 September of the year 363, which
means that the planet not just on that day, but also in the weeks
preceding it was exceptionally bright (for the astronomical data see
Goffin, 1976 and Drummen & Meeus, 2003, 106–7). It seems more
likely, however, that we are confronted here with a fabrication ex
post facto by the author.

   The next two sections contain a digression on shooting stars or
meteorites. It has the usual structure of the scientific digressions
in the *Res Gestae*, for which see Den Hengst, 1992, 41. First the
phenomenon is described (*flagrantissimam facem...visam*, §4); then
follows a doxography (*fit autem hic habitus modis compluribus, e quibus
sufficiet pauca monstrare*, §5); a concluding phrase is lacking this time.
The digression is balanced by an excursus on comets at the end
of book 25 (10.3). The two subjects are akin, both as astronomical
phenomena and in regard to their ominous character. At the outset
of his discussion on meteors, Seneca (*Nat.* 1.1.3) reminds his readers
that this phenomenon accompanied the deaths of Augustus, Seianus
and Germanicus.

Erat autem nitor igneus iste, quem diaissonta nos appellamus If, as seems   **2.5**
likely, *nitor igneus iste* is the antecedent of the relative clause, it seems
best to take it as a subject complement with the unexpressed subject
of *erat* ('this phenomenon'). In a flattering description of the young
Stilicho, Claudian speaks of the *nitor igneus* of his outer appearance
(*Cons. Stil.* 1.45). For the relative clause see Den Boeft, 1992, 12
about expressions like these, which "betray the value which the
author set on the Greek language", διαΐσσων being the standard term
for a meteor in Greek, comparable to *stella transcurrens, transvolans*
or *transiens* in Latin. When these meteors are in the sublunary region
they seem to fall down, which is expressed by verbs such as *cadere* and
(de)labi.

*corpora enim qui credit caelitus posse labi, profanus merito iudicatur et
demens* Strong language, which may well derive from Sen. *Nat.* 1.1.9
Illud enim stultissimum, existimare aut decidere stellas aut transilire. The
emphasis here is on *stellas*; the fiery objects we see in the sky should
not be called stars. For *caelitus labi* cf. 22.9.7 *figmento deae caelitus lapso,*

50 COMMENTARY

which ironically happens to refer to a meteorite. *Profanus* is a hapax in Amm. It refers to those who are uninitiated into the mysteries of science, as in Apul. *Soc.* 122 *profana philosophiae turba imperitorum.*

fit autem hic habitus modis compluribus, e quibus sufficiet pauca monstrare On *habitus* see De Jonge ad 17.13.9. He gives as its meaning here "appearance", which suits the context well. Amm. uses *habitus* also for the phases of the moon in 20.3.11 *quem habitum vocamus* ἀπόκρουσιν. Fontaine n. 517 aptly quotes Sen. *Nat.* 7.11.3 *inter spectantes de habitu illorum* (comets) *non convenit.* Both here and in 20.3.11 the choice of words leaves something to be desired, in that *habitus* designates a state, whereas both ἀπόκρουσις and *fit* imply a process. Amm., however, does not mean to say that meteors come into being in a variety of ways, but that there are different theories about their origin. It would have been clearer if Amm. had written something like: *huius habitus faces variis modis oriri existimantur.* For *monstrare* see Sabbah 388–90.

2.6 *scintillas quidam putant ab aetherio candentes vigore parumque porrectius tendere sufficientes exstingui* This is the first δόξα, which goes back to Anaxagoras, as Von Scala, 1898, 128 has shown. See Aetius 3.2.9 Ἀναξαγόρας τοὺς καλουμένους διάττοντας ἀπὸ τοῦ αἰθέρος σπινθήρων δίκην καταφέρεσθαι, διὸ καὶ παραυτίκα σβέννυσθαι ('Anaxagoras says that the so-called shooting stars fall down from the ether like sparks. For that reason they go out almost immediately'). As Gilbert, 1907, 688–9 explains, Anaxagoras was the first to surmise the true nature of meteorites, which according to him were made of the same material as the earth itself. The phrase *aetherius vigor* emphasizes the heavenly origin as well as the superior character of the fiery element. According to Claudianus (*in Eutr.* 2.490–500) Prometheus added aether to the clay from which he fashioned men (*multumque innexuit aethera limo* 493), whereas Epimetheus failed to do so, with the result that his creatures *pecudum ritu non inpendentia vitant / nec res ante vident* (499–500). Also according to Macrobius (*comm.* 1.21.35) men depend on that element: *nam quia terra aqua et aer infra lunam sunt, ex his solis corpus fieri non potuit quod idoneum esset ad vitam, sed opus fuit praesidio ignis aetherii, qui terrenis membris vitam et animam sustinendi commodaret vigorem, qui vitalem calorem et faceret et ferret. Sufficere* 'to have enough power to' is found for the first time in Vergil *A.* 5.21–2 *nec nos obniti contra nec tendere tantum / sufficimus,* which Amm. may have had in mind, cf. also Luc. 5.153–4 *nec vox antri complere capacis / sufficiens spatium.* On *porrectius* see the note ad 20.3.10.

CHAPTER 2.6   51

vel certe radiorum flammas iniectas nubibus densis acri scintillare contactu This is the δόξα of Metrodorus, according to Aetius 3.2.10: Μητρόδωρος τὴν εἰς τὰ νέφη τοῦ ἡλίου βίαιον ἔμπτωσιν πολλάκις σπινθηρίζειν. In Amm.'s version βίαιος ἔμπτωσις becomes *acer contactus*. In classical Latin *vel certe* is used to correct or mitigate a preceding statement which might be regarded as too bold, as in Cic. *de Orat.* 2.232 *quis enim haec non vel facile vel certe aliquo modo posset ediscere?* Amm. sometimes uses the expression in this way, e.g. 21.7.1 *finito propiore bello vel certe mollito* and 22.6.1 *ut levari debito possit, vel certe commodius per dilationem inferre.* In other places, however, Amm. uses *vel certe* to express the 'loaded alternative', a different explanation, which Amm. regards as the most likely one, as in this case and in 14.8.3 about Tarsus: *hanc condidisse Perseus memoratur...vel certe ex Aethiopia profectus Sandan quidam.* Cf. also the digression on the pest 19.4.5 *aliis placet auras, ut solent, aquasque vitiatas foetore cadaverum vel similibus salubritatis violare maximam partem vel certe aeris permutationem subitam aegritudines parere leviores* and 20.8.13 *Laetos quosdam, cis Rhenum editam barbarorum progeniem vel certe ex dediticiis, qui ad nostra desciscunt*, q.v. See also 25.10.3 *vel certe stellas.* See for this use of *vel certe* Löfstedt, 1936, 103 and TLL III 939.75. *Radiorum flammas* refers of course to the rays of the sun which are, so to speak, trapped in a thick cloud, from which they cannot escape. This theory also plays a part in the digression on the rainbow, which is formed *cum altius delatae nubi crassae radii solis infusi lucem iniecerint liquidam, quae non repperiens exitum in se conglobata nimio splendescit attritu* (20.11.29).

The comparison of meteors with sparks is also found in the short passage which Manilius devotes to the subject (1.847–51) *praecipites stellae passimque volare videntur, / cum vaga per liquidum scintillant lumina mundum / exsiliuntque procul volucris imitata sagittas / ardua cum gracili tenuatur semita filo.*

aut, cum lumen aliquod cohaeserit nubi This vague phrase is connected sloppily with the preceding AcI-clauses. It looks like a continuation of *fit autem hic habitus*, disregarding the intervening *putant.* As to its contents, it could be a paraphrase of the third δόξα presented by Aetius 3.2.11: Ξενοφάνης πάντα τὰ τοιαῦτα νεφῶν πεπυρωμένων συστήματα ἢ κινήματα ('Xenophanes held that all these phenomena were due to clouds set on fire and set in motion'). We can only guess what it was that lit up the clouds: the rays of the sun, fiery particles from the ether or the hot vapours rising from the earth (ἀναθυμάσεις), which in the opinion of Aristotle accounted not only for meteors and comets, but for thunder and lightning as well.

52   COMMENTARY

id enim in stellae speciem figuratum decurrit quidem, dum viribus ignium sustentatur It is not clear what *id* refers back to. If to *lumen*, the sentence continues the exposition of Xenophanes' theory. Since, however, *decurrit* applies to all meteors, regardless of the theories about their origin, it seems preferable to take *id* to mean 'this phenomenon'. Amm. is at times rather imprecise in the use of anaphoric pronouns; see the notes ad 23.4.2 *et hac* and 24.2.4 *hac quoque*. This would imply that Amm., after enumerating the δόξαι in his source, ends here with a summary of his own: a meteor looks like a star and it moves downward until it burns itself up completely. For *in stellae speciem figuratum* cf. 26.8.9 *quod machinae genus...ideo figuratur hac specie, ut* and Mart. Cap. 8.842 *Centaurique pars, quae in equi speciem figuratur.*

   The *dum*-clause recalls *ab aetherio candentes vigore* in the first δόξα, just as the following words *amplitudine spatiorum exinanitum* correspond to *parum porrectius tendere sufficientes*. This means that the trail of the meteor is visible as long as its fiery power remains intact. In Sen. *Nat.* 7, the opinion of Aristotle (and the Stoics) that meteors and comets are like fire in that they consume the surrounding aërial matter is expressed repeatedly: 7.8.1 *tam diu manet splendor ignis expressi quamdiu alimenta sufficiunt, quibus desinentibus et ipse subsidit*; 7.20.2 (lightning quickly disappears) *alii vero ignes diu manent nec ante discedunt quam consumptum est omne quo pascebantur alimentum*; 7.21.2 *Quare ergo non stat cometes sed procedit? dicam: ignium modo alimentum suum sequitur; quamvis enim illi ad superiora nisus sit, tamen deficiente materia retro iens ipse descendit.* It would have been clearer if Amm. had written *decurrit quidem, dum igneae vires* (of the meteor) *sustentantur* (sc. *alimento*).

in aerium solvitur corpus ad substantiam migrans, cuius attritu incaluit nimio The fiery substance of the meteor is finally swallowed by the surrounding *aer*, the frictional resistance of which had made it glow. *Corpus* here has the sense of 'element', for which see TLL IV 1024.11–62, where i.a. Ov. *F.* 1.105–6 is quoted: *aer et quae tria corpora restant, / ignis, aquae, tellus.* For *migrare ad* in the sense of 'to change into' cf. TLL VIII 938.4–19. The phrase *attritu nimio* is found also in 20.11.29 *in se conglobata nimio splendescit attritu.* In the note ad loc. it is stated that friction is the common element in the descriptions of the rainbow and the meteor. In the case of the former it causes the sun's rays to glow inside a cloud, in the latter it causes the transmutation of the fiery sparks into the element of *aer.*

CHAPTER 2.7   53

Amm.'s words here are strongly reminiscent of Ovid's description of Caesar's katasterismos at the end of the *Metamorphoses*, 15.845–9 (Venus) *Caesaris eripuit membris nec in aera solvi/ passa recentem animam caelestibus intulit astris, / dumque tulit, lumen capere atque ignescere sensit / emisitque sinu: luna volat altius illa / flammiferumque trahens spatioso limite crinem.* Less well known, but very similar is Stat. *Theb.* 5.284–6, where Dionysus disappears after giving advice to his son Thoas: *ita fatus in aera rursus / solvitur et nostrum, visus arcentibus umbris, / mitis iter longae claravit limite flammae.* If, as was suggested above ad §4 *horroreque perfusus est*, the digression on the meteor has been inserted here to throw into relief the death of Julian, which Amm. is about to narrate, it is quite understandable that associations like these have coloured his description of the phenomenon. One might go one step further and consider a connection between the element *aer*, into which the meteor disappears and the future abode of Julian. In *C.D.* 7.6 Augustine mentions *aer* as the region where, according to the *theologia naturalis*, the heroes dwell: *inter lunae vero gyrum et nimborum ac ventorum cacumina aerias esse animas, sed eas animo, non oculis videri et vocari heroas et lares et genios,* while in the opening phrase of Julian's elogium (25.4.1) he is called *vir profecto heroicis connumerandus ingeniis.* However, this is very speculative and, moreover, the comparison with Caesar's apotheosis in Ovid would imply that Julian was assigned a place after his death, which Venus thought unworthy of her offspring (*nec in aera solvi passa*). That would be a dubious honour.

Julian's attitude towards the *Etrusci haruspices* as described in sections   **2.7**
7 and 8 should be compared to the passage 23.5.8–14, where the warnings of these experts, based on the handbooks of their profession, were also totally disregarded by the emperor. In that episode Julian is said to have yielded to the philosophers in his retinue, who with a fatal combination of arrogance and ignorance managed to undermine the authority of the *haruspices.* In the account that follows here, the emperor acts completely on his own.

Confestim itaque ante lucis primitias Amm. reverts to the events reported before the digression. The fact that Julian did not wait till morning, but immediately called his *haruspices*, proves that he took the sign very seriously. This is the early morning of 26 June; see the note on chronology. On the variety of expressions used by Amm. for daybreak see Hagendahl, 1921, 100–1.

54   COMMENTARY

Etrusci haruspices   See for the Etruscan soothsayers Briquel, 1998 and Haack, 2002. They were part of Julian's retinue, cf. the notes ad 21.1.10, 23.1.7 (*horum periti*) and 23.5.10.

vitandum esse cautissime responderunt, ne   In 15.8.13 (the only parallel for *cautissime* in the *Res Gestae*) *pugnantes accendens praeeundo cautissime turbatosque subsidiis fulciens* the adverb refers to the behaviour of the commander. For that reason it is preferable to link it here also with *vitandum esse*, not with *responderunt*, as Fontaine does. For other instances of *ne*-clauses after *vitare* see OLD s.v. 4a.

Tarquitianis libris   These books were translated by M. Tarquitius Priscus from Etruscan into Latin at the end of the Republic; see the note ad 23.1.7, to which may be added Macrobius *Sat.* 3.7.2 *Est super hoc liber Tarquitii transcriptus ex Ostentario Tusco* ('translated from an Etruscan book on prodigies') and 3.20.3: *Tarquitius...Priscus in Ostentario arborario* ('a book on signs from trees') *sic ait.* The books by Tarquitius are perhaps the same as those by a certain Tages, mentioned by Amm. in 17.10.2 (with the extensive note by De Jonge) and 21.1.10 (q.v.; see also Szidat's commentary ad loc.).

in titulo   'Under the heading'. Cf. Gaius *Inst.* 4.46 *quae sub titulo 'de in ius vocando' propositae sunt.*

quod...non oportebit   For Amm.'s use of the future indicative instead of imperfect subjunctive see the note ad 20.8.10 *quod...libens.*

2.8   *quo etiam id inter alia multa spernente orabant haruspices*   Since there are no unambiguous instances of active *orare* with personal object, the abl. abs. preceding *orabant* is not surprising. Amm. reports time and again that Julian (to whom the relative refers) attached great importance to soothsaying and divination. He even seems to have been besotted by it. See the notes ad 21.1.6 *coniciens eum*, 21.2.4 *haruspicinae auguriisque*, 22.1.1 *Iulianus inter* and cf. also 22.1.2–3. Even on his deathbed Julian professed his belief in divination: *interiturum me ferro dudum didici fide fatidica praecinente* (25.3.19). Amm. compares Julian's propensity to divination with that of Hadrian; cf. 22.12.8, q.v, and 25.4.17 *praesagiorum sciscitationi nimiae* (or rather *nimium*) *deditus, ut aequiperare videretur in hac parte principem Hadrianum* (q.v.). Julian, however, regularly ignored bad omens like those which happened while he was in Antioch preparing the Persian campaign (23.1.5–7) or during the expedition (e.g. 23.2.6, 8; 23.5.6, 8–9,

CHAPTER 2.8   55

12–3). The emperor listened rather to the philosophers in his retinue than to the Etruscan haruspices; cf. e.g. 23.5.10–1 and 23.5.14 with the notes. In this case, we must assume that the emperor made his own decision. In any case, scorning the advice of the soothsayers had very serious consequences since Julian died on that same day, as is described in the next chapter.

imperatore omni vaticinandi scientia reluctante Heraeus conjectured *scientia* for V's *sententia*. Češka, 1983 tries to defend V's reading by adducing as a parallel Cic. *Leg.* 2.11 *in ipso nomine legis interpretando inesse vim et sententiam iusti et veri legendi.* According to him, the soothsayers resisted Julian 'with everything *vaticinatio* stood for'. Without the addition of *vis* this seems very forced. *Scientia* on the contrary is highly attractive, since it is used in a similar context by Seneca: *Nat.* 2.32.2 *Tuscos, quibus summa est fulgurum persequendorum scientia.* Cf. moreover 22.12.7 *scientiam vaticinandi professus.* The text of the Teubner edition would mean that Julian 'making use of all knowledge of divination' resisted the experts, in which case one would rather expect *sua* to be added, to contrast the emperor's expertise with that of the soothsayers. This is pointed out correctly by Selem, 1973, 401, who compares 23.5.11, where it is said of the self-willed and ignorant philosophers: *ut probabile argumentum ad fidem implendam scientiae suae, id praetendebant* e.q.s. Alternatively, and starting from V's reading *reluctantes*, one might read *imperatori* with Fontaine, in which case the meaning is that the soothsayers are disregarded, although they used all their knowledge to resist the emperor, which is linguistically impeccable. Still, after *quo id inter alia multa spernente*, which calls attention to the emperor's obstinacy, one would expect a comment on his stubborn resistance to his advisers rather than a remark about the soothsayers' determined opposition to the emperor. For these reasons Lindenbrog's *scientiae reluctante*, which requires only a minor change of V's *scientia reluctantes*, seems to be the best solution: the emperor resists all the expertise offered by his advisers.

CHAPTER 3

Introduction

In this chapter Ammianus describes the events of one of the most memorable days in the *Res Gestae*: June 26, 363.

While the Roman army continues its katabasis, the Persians move on through the hilly country on either side, continually looking for chances to lay ambushes. Therefore the Romans remain on the alert, but the conditions of the country make it difficult to march constantly in serried ranks, and at a certain point the Persians in quick succession attack first the rear, then the van and finally the centre of the Roman column. In contrast to his prudent conduct in the first phases of the katabasis, described in chapters 1 and 2, Julian this time involves himself personally in the actions, and this without donning a proper armour. It proves a fatal mistake, for he is severely wounded in the liver by a spear and has to be transported to his tent. Shocked by this disaster the Roman soldiers rouse themselves to a fanatical fighting spirit. They win the day, inflicting considerable losses on the enemy, but also suffering some themselves.

In the meantime both Julian and his staff have realized that the injury which he has sustained is lethal. He holds a valedictory speech, pointing out that the guiding principles of his life and career as Caesar and Augustus have kept his soul pure. Therefore, bidding farewell at a glorious moment is not a reason for tears, but for gratitude. After the speech Ammianus depicts Julian's final moments in terms which seem directly inspired by Plato's *Phaedo*. The description ends with some details about his origins, which form a smooth transition to the necrology in chapter 4.

In itself this brief survey of the bare facts in Ammianus' report reveals how momentous the events of the day were, but there is more to be said. The author has made a considerable effort to exploit his talent for conveying his personal experiences and impressions to the reader. Here his strategy is essentially based on a consistent focus on the protagonist, who, both in his perilous courage on the battlefield and in his laudable conduct when faced by the inevitability of death, continually figures at the heart of the proceedings. Until the very end the varied events and reactions are depicted around the centre of the stage which is sovereignly occupied by Julian. Even when he is

58 COMMENTARY

unable to partake in the battle described in § 10 sqq., it is the soldiers' anger at the fact that their commander has been wounded which stirs them to a fanatical fighting spirit and a subsequent victory.

Ammianus' approach results in a lack of precision regarding some of the details, especially where the fighting is concerned. In the present case this seems less inconvenient for the reader than on some other occasions. Moreover, it is a price worth paying. In a way the chapter can be compared with the impressionistic description of Julian's journey from Constantinople to Antioch in chapter 9 of book 22. That description consists of a number of scenes and short episodes which intend to show the emperor's particular qualities. Similarly, in the present chapter the various aspects of Julian's personality are shown in telling actions and words. From the scenes of his courage and his sense of responsibility for his men, in which respects he surpassed no lesser man than Epaminondas, the reader is led from his acceptance of fate's decision and the carefully worded declaration of the principles of his life to the lofty serenity of his final moments.

The structure of the chapter serves the historian's message: June 26, 363 was a terrible day, but also a day which for the last time brought out the practical, intellectual and spiritual resources of a truly admirable man. The end was bitter for all those who realized his greatness; for himself it came at the right time to lend the finishing touches to precisely this greatness. During his life he had preserved the purity of his soul, and the gods now granted him a departure from the world at the height of his glory. No doubt, the valedictory portrait which Ammianus has drawn bears testimony to his own positive judgment about the controversial emperor, but since his treatment of the evidence is basically sober, it is a relief between the extremes of eulogy and abuse indulged in by some of his contemporaries.

Some parts of this chapter require a rather extensive elucidation or, in the case of the Julian's farewell speech, a specific introduction. The reader will find these at the relevant places.

3.1 *Hinc nos egressos* In the note ad 25.2.1 it has been argued, with reference to Paschoud n. 82, that by the evening of 25 June the Roman army had reached Toummara. It is from this resting place that the army marched northwards on the morning of 26 June (see the note on chronology).

Persae, cum saepe afflicti peditum stabiles pugnas horrerent The Persian army indeed tried to avoid open infantry battle with the Romans.

CHAPTER 3.1   59

Its infantry, definitely the weakest contingent, was not a standing but a drafted army; it consisted of peasant soldiers; see 23.6.83 and the notes there. The Persians rather relied on their bowmen and cavalry, as well as on surprise attacks when the Roman army was on the march. See for *stabiles* the note ad 20.8.1 *statariae pugnae*. Amm.'s four other examples of *horrere* with direct object ('to tremble at') may show the depth of the Persians' fear: 14.2.19 (famine), 14.11.8 (the terrible Gallus), 22.8.14 (Phineus' fear of the Harpies), 29.1.13 (people awaiting trial).

structis insidiis occulte comitabantur Throughout Julian's campaign bushwacking the Romans, following them on their march as well as avoiding open battle, had been the strategy of the Persians; see 24.2.4, 24.3.1, 24.5.5, 24.7.7, 25.1.5. It was only when the Roman army retreated and was weakened by a shortage of supplies that the Persians dared to engage in more open battle with their cavalry, infantry, bowmen and elephants, as appears from e.g. 25.1.11 and 25.6.2 as well as from this section. The phrase *insidias struere*, which judging from TLL VII 1.1893.34–5 is not very common, occurs also in 17.1.6, 24.2.4 and 28.5.5. In the present text *structis insidiis* is best regarded as expressing repeated actions simultaneous with *comitabantur*; cf. Fontaine's "en nous tendant des ambuscades". Note that *occulte comitabantur* is a paradox. Normally the presence of those who are accompanying is clearly visible.

altrinsecus viantes catervas a celsis collibus explorando The fact that the Persians kept an eye on the marching Roman army from high hills, suggests that the Romans did not march close to the river Tigris, but marched a bit more inland, away from the river bank; Paschoud n. 83; cf. Greg. Naz. *Or.* 5.14, who reports that Julian lay wounded on the river bank; see the last part of the note ad *invasa subito* (§ 2). As is noted ad 20.7.11, in Amm. *altrinsecus* always means 'on both sides'. See for the late Latin verb *viare* the note ad 19.8.10.

miles ad usque perpetuum diem nec vallum erigeret nec sudibus se communiret From TLL X 1.1639.53–5 it appears that Amm. may have borrowed the phrase *usque perpetuum diem*, 'throughout the day', from Plaut. *Most.* 765. The clarity of Amm.'s report leaves something to be desired, since it appears from § 7 of this chapter that there was a military camp to which Julian was brought back when he was wounded in battle (*relatus in castra*). According to *epit.* 43.2 a camp was already being built from which Julian hastily set out to join

60   COMMENTARY

the fight: *Illic a transfuga quodam in insidias deductus, cum eum hinc inde Parthi urgerent, e castris iam positis, arrepto tantum clipeo, procurrit.* Possibly the camp was being built when the battle had already started and before Julian joined it. Veg. *mil.* 1.25.1 explains that under threat of an enemy attack the cavalry and half of the infantry are drawn up to repel the enemy, whereas the rest of the army builds the camp: *si hostis incumbat, tunc omnes equites et media pars peditum ad propulsandum impetum ordinantur in acie, reliqui post ipsos ductis fossis muniunt castra.* Vegetius also advises, in case the enemy threat is serious, to fortify the camp with a proper fosse and a wall of wooden stakes (1.24.2–4: *Sed ubi vis acrior imminet hostium, tunc legitima fossa ambitum convenit munire castrorum...supra quam sudes de lignis fortissimis, quas milites portare consueverunt, praefiguntur*).

3.2   *teguntur firmiter latera*   See 16.2.6 (*confertis lateribus*) and 16.12.37 (*muniret latera sua firmius pedes*) for protecting the flanks in situations of a serious enemy threat. Possibly the flanks were so well strenghtened in order to protect the baggage train; cf. Veg. *mil.* 3.6.14 *A lateribus quoque pari armatorum manu impedimenta claudenda sunt; nam insidiatores alii in alio loco impulsant, transversos frequenter incursant.* See for *firmiter* the note ad 17.2.1. The survey in TLL VI 819.75–84 shows that from early Latin onwards *firmiter* occurs more often than *firme.*

exercitus pro locorum situ quadratis quidem, sed laxis incedit agminibus Cf. *pro captu locorum* (25.6.5). For *quadratis* see the note ad 24.1.2. The nearby presence of the enemy in the surrounding hills (§1) was no doubt the reason why the Roman army marched in this formation. The word *laxis* does not mean 'elongated', as Brok 182 suggests – this would be hard to combine with the *agmen quadratum*–, but implies that the soldiers marched in "gelockerter Formation" (Seyfarth), or "en formations...peu serrées" (Fontaine), possibly due to the circumstances of the terrain.

invasa subito terga pone versus arma cogentium The pleonastic phrasing 'the backs (*terga*) of those who at the end (*pone versus*) were forming the rearguard (*arma cogentium*)' is, presumably, meant to emphasize the treacherous habits of the Persians, who made up for their lack of courage by cunning: *magis artifices quam fortes* (23.6.80). See for *pone versus* the note ad 25.1.18. According to Eun. *fr.* 27.8 a squadron of four hundred catafracts attacked the rear guard. Amm. only says that the attack happened suddenly but does not provide a time, as does Zos. 3.28.4, who mentions that the Persian assault, which

CHAPTER 3.2   61

he calls unexpected, commenced at the end of the morning: Τῇ δὲ
μετὰ ταῦτα ἡμέρᾳ περὶ πλήθουσαν ἀγορὰν οἱ Πέρσαι συνταχθέντες εἰς
πλῆθος τοῖς οὐραγοῖς τοῦ Ῥωμαίων στρατεύματος ἀδοκήτοις ἐπέπεσον.
According to Malalas *Chron.* 13.332 Julian was injured about the
second hour (περὶ ὥραν δευτέραν), which would imply that the battle
had started early in the day. In § 12 Amm. tells us that the darkness
of night ended the battle (*nox diremit certamina iam tenebrosa*); hence
the battle took the best part of the day. Lib. *Or.* 18.268 has a
completely different description of the events from that of Amm.
and Zosimus. He relates that the Persians had already decided to
plead for peace the following day and were even prepared to accept
a peace settlement on terms set by Julian. But then part of the Roman
column became detached from the main body and its situation
was worsened because of a sudden storm, which encouraged the
Persians to continue their unpremeditated attack; cf. Ruf. Fest. 28,
who mentions that Julian could not see his men anymore because of
a dust storm (*excito pulvere erepto suorum conspectu*). Libanius' version
is most unlikely considering the desperate situation the Roman army
was in as described by Ammianus and Zosimus; Malosse, 1998, 65
considers this as one of Libanius' "thèmes de son propos sur Julien":
Julian dies at the moment of triumph. Nor can Libanius be right
about the attack being not intended (see the note ad 25.3.4 below).
Ammianus does not give any indication here about the location of the
battle, but he says in 25.3.9 that the place where Julian was mortally
wounded was called Phrygia; see the note ad loc. Paschoud n. 83
suggests that the battle took place "à quelques kilomètres au sud
de Samarra"; he identifies the *castellum Sumere* mentioned by Amm.
in 25.6.4 (q.v.), and which was situated north of the battleground,
with Zosimus' Σοῦμα (3.30.2); the latter, in its turn, was identified by
Herzfeld, 1948, 66 with Samarra. According to Greg. Naz. *Or.* 5.14
Julian, when he lay wounded ἐπὶ τῇ ὄχθῃ τοῦ ποταμοῦ, remembered
that in the past many men of great renown had contrived to pass
away without being seen and subsequently were regarded as gods.
He therefore tried to throw himself into the river with the help of
a few faithful followers. His attempt was thwarted and the world was
spared the birth of a θεὸς νέος. The story breaks down because of the
simple fact that Amm., who was an eyewitness, reports that during
their march the Romans were surrounded by high hills.

inermi etiamtum It is difficult to decide what Amm. intends to express
by the addition of *etiamtum*. One can hardly assume that it is used
merely factually, as in 21.16.20 *Iovianus etiamtum protector domesticus.*

62   COMMENTARY

It either implies that Julian should already have donned his armour, or, as an excuse, that there had as yet been no compelling reason to do so. The latter solution does not tally well with *ad speculanda anteriora progresso*. According to Libanius (*Or.* 18.268) Julian was without armour because he was certain of his success: ἄοπλον, τῷ γάρ, οἶμαι, σφόδρα κρατεῖν οὐδὲ ἐφράξατο. Zonaras' account that Julian did not wear his armour because of its weight and the heat makes more sense: ἔτυχε δὲ διὰ βάρος καὶ τὴν ἐκ τοῦ ἡλίου φλόγωσιν (θέρους γὰρ ἦν ὥρα) τὸν θώρακα ἐκδυσάμενος (13.13.17). But Amm. may have the best explanation: shocked by the sudden danger and in a hurry, Julian forgot his armour and only grabbed a shield (25.3.3).

3.3 Suddenly we are back with the Julian of book 24, who more than once indulged in acts of rashness: *ut propius temeritatem multa crebro auderet* (24.6.4). The various phrases of the section all express that he acts emotionally rather than rationally.

loricae See the note ad 25.1.1.

scuto inter tumultum arrepto Cf. *epit.* 43.2: *arrepto tantum clipeo*.

properans ultimis ferre suppetias revocatur alio metu See for the archaic *ferre suppetias* the note ad 20.4.1. This must be a bold instance of the metonymical use of *metus* (TLL VIII 910.77 sqq.: "res timorem faciens"). Seyfarth renders "Schreckenbotschaft", Fontaine has "nouvelle alarmante".

antesignanos See the note ad 23.5.19 *imperator et antesignanus* on Julian's presence in the vanguard. Zos. 3.28.4 only mentions an attack on the rearguard of the Roman column and is silent about an assault on the vanguard.

3.4 *quae dum sine respectu periculi sui redintegrare festinat* There is no specific word to which *quae* refers; it probably denotes the parts of the army which were threatened by the enemy.
    The phrase *sine respectu periculi* occurs in an entirely different context in 21.12.20 and 22.9.8. In the note on the latter instance it is stated that by this and similar phrases considerable recklessness is denoted. From a strictly rational point of view this tallies with the present text: Julian ought to have taken care of himself. However, the addition of *sui* should not be overlooked. Amm. wants to show that in his last battle Julian first and foremost attended to the perilous

CHAPTER 3.4   63

situation of his men; cf. the phrase in §8 *ut...videretur sui securus alienae salutis sollicitudine vehementer astringi*. See also 16.12.29, where V's *cautior sui* is printed by Seyfarth, with De Jonge's approval (see his note ad loc.), but Clark and Galletier prefer *incautior sui*, a conjecture which Langen, 1867, 22 put forward, i.a. on the basis of the present text and the beginning of §6. This conjecture was defended by Cornelissen, 1886, 247: "Loci sententia flagitat nimirum 'incautior sui', cf. Stat. *Theb.* 6. 766 '*at ille nocendi prodigus incautusque sui ruit*'."

ex alia parte I.e. another part, not the rear guard which the Persians had attacked first (§2). Now they assaulted the marching army in the middle section from the left side, as appears from the following *centurias adoritur medias ac sinistro cornu inclinato acriter superfusus.* Cf. Zon. 13.13.15 who mentions, contrary to Amm., that the Romans kept their lines on the left flank but had to give way on the right flank: καὶ κατὰ μὲν τὸ εὐώνυμον κέρας ἐκράτουν Ῥωμαῖοι, κατὰ δέ γε τὸ δεξιὸν ἡλαττοῦντο. From the report of Amm. it may be surmised that the onslaught on the rear was only the beginning of a full-scale Persian attack by catafract troops, archers and elephants on the left flank and the front of the marching Roman army. The fact that the ensuing battle ended only when darkness fell, and that many Persian *optimates* and common soldiers fell (§13), corroborates the impression that the Roman-Persian confrontation was not a mere scrimmage. So this was not an unpremeditated attack, as Libanius (*Or.* 18.268) wants us to believe nor an attack only on the rear as Zos. 3.28.4 says, but a major battle; see Matthews 181. Eun. *fr.* 27.8 is perhaps a parallel to the present text, but see the note ad 25.1.5 *extremos.*

catafractorum Parthicus globus centurias adoritur medias For the *catafracti* see the notes ad 20.7.2 and 24.2.5. For *Parthicus* designating Persian/Sasanian see the note ad 23.3.2. For *globus* see the notes ad 16.12.49, 20.5.1 and 24.4.9. Pace Brok 182 and Fontaine n. 525 the word *centuria* is probably an archaism; see the note ad 21.13.9 and Nicasie, 1998, 52.

sinistro cornu inclinato acriter superfusus Cf. for *cornu* about an army on the march Tac. *Ann.* 13.40.2 *in cornibus pedes sagittarius et cetera manus equitum ibat.* See for *inclinato* the note ad 25.1.18 *si inclinatas.* One just wonders whether the present text is influenced by Luc. 7.365–6 *nonne superfusis collectum cornibus hostem/ in medium dabimus*, which, of course, is different in that *superfusis...cornibus* means 'pouring our

64 COMMENTARY

wings (over them)'. See for the literal sense of *superfundere* 17.1.10 *superfusae nives opplevere montes*, 22.15.7 *superfusis fluctibus*, and for a translated sense 30.7.9 *catervas superfusorum hostium*.

faetorem elephantorumque stridorem There is no need to change *faetorem elephantorumque stridorem*. See the relevant note ad 20.4.5 *vigore corporumque levitate*. For the use of elephants by the Sasanians in battle as well as the fear which their size, smell and trumpeting inspired in the Roman soldiers, see the notes ad 24.6.8, 25.1.14 and 15.

contis et multiplicatis missilibus decernebat For *contus* see the note ad 25.1.13. In addition to the cavalry and infantry, the Sasanian army had contingents of experienced (mounted) archers; see the note ad 25.1.13 *iuxtaque sagittarii*. Also Schippmann, 1990, 104–5; Wiesehöfer, 1994, 263–5. See for *decernere* as a synonym of *pugnare* the note ad 20.11.12.

3.5 *verum principe volitante inter prima discrimina proeliorum* Amm. uses *volitare* about military actions in two other instances: 16.12.15 (q.v.) and 30.4.8, where it is a metaphor. This could well be a Vergilianism: *et circumfuso volitabant milite Volsci* (*A.* 11.546), *ductores auro volitant ostroque superbi* (*A.* 12.126), *multa virum volitans dat fortia corpora leto* (*A.* 12.328). Cf. Zos. 3.28.4: τοῦ βασιλέως ᾗπερ εἰώθει περιόντος καὶ εἰς θάρσος τὰς τάξεις ἐγείροντος; 3.29.1: Ἐπεὶ δὲ εἰς χεῖρας ἅπαντες ἦλθον ἀλλήλοις ἐπιὼν τοὺς ταξιάρχους καὶ λοχαγούς, ἀναμεμιγμένος δὲ τῷ πλήθει, πλήττεται. *Epit.* 43.3 (*Cumque inconsulto ardore nititur ordines ad proelium componere*) and Ruf. Fest. 28 (*cum incautius per agmen erraret*) consider Julian's behaviour in battle irresponsible; Hier. *Chron.* a. 363 speaks of *inconsultius*. See also Zon. 13.13.14. Cf. 25.3.6 *cavendi immemor*. As is suggested in the note ad 23.6.22 *post discrimina varia proeliorum*, the present phrase could be regarded as a gen. inversus: 'during the first dangerous scrimmages'. Another explanation would be gen. part.: 'the first dangers of the fighting'.

exsiluit nostra succinctior armatura The verb *exsilire* denotes the sudden appearance of a person or a thing, which one had not expected: 16.12.49 *Exsiluit itaque subito ardens optimatium globus*, 21.9.6 *e navi exsiluit improvisus*, 23.6.24 *labes primordialis exsiluit*. Amm. uses the term *armatura* several times. In most instances it refers to infantry in the Roman army (14.11.3, 21.16.7, 24.6.9) or in the army of Rome's enemies (17.12.1 – Quadi and Sarmatae; 23.6.83 – Persae; 31.2.17 – Alani). It consisted of light-armed troops, as appears from

CHAPTER 3.6   65

14.6.17 *leves armaturas*. For *succinctior* Brok 183 refers to 20.11.20 *dimicare succinctius parans*, 'preparing to fight at short distance', and then argues that it does not mean 'light-armed'. This seems disputable in view of 30.1.11 *cum sagittariis mille succinctis et levibus*. In two cases Amm. possibly refers to *armaturae* as units of the *scholae palatinae*: in 15.5.33 he mentions Silvanus' desertion *cum armaturis* to Constantius, and in 27.2.6 he calls *Balchobaudes armaturarum tribunus*; see Barlow and Brennan, 2001, 247–9. Afric. *Cest.* 1.18 advises to employ light-armed forces against elephants; Nicasie, 1998, 212.

beluarum suffragines concidebat Veg. *mil.* 3.24.7–16 describes a variety of ways in which elephants can be resisted in battle, but not the hacking at their knee joints – most likely to cut their sinews so that they would collapse – as Amm. describes in this passage. Curt. 8.14.28 describes similar tactics against elephants – cutting off their feet – deployed by the soldiers of Alexander in his battle against the Indian king Porus: *Anceps ergo pugna nunc sequentium, nunc fugientium elephantos…donec securibus – id namque genus auxilii praeparatum erat – pedes amputare coeperunt.* In this context the word *suffrago* means knee joint, knee bend, see the notes ad 19.6.2 and 24.6.12 (*aciem*) *egit*. See for this apparently common military practice also 31.7.13: *et sequebantur equites hinc inde fugientium occipitia lacertis ingentibus praecidentes et terga itidemque altrinsecus pedites lapsorum timore impeditorum secando suffragines.*

Iulianus cavendi immemor In the vast majority of cases *immemor* **3.6** means 'forgetting (to do) something which one is expected not to forget'. This is true for the other four instances in Amm.: 15.4.12 *cavendi*, 22.7.3 *dicti*, 30.6.3 *beneficiorum*, 31.13.5 *salutis*. Criticism by the author is not necessarily implied. In the present text he may want to express that Julian was only concerned with the plight of others. See the note ad *sine respectu periculi sui* in § 4.

diffluxisse trepidos elatis vociferando manibus aperte demonstrans Cf. for *diffluxisse* 29.5.26 *foedo diffluxere terrore*, which shows that the verb denotes spreading out in disorderly flight. The raising (and waving?) of the hands is probably to be interpreted here as a gesture of success and of encouragement; 25.6.14 *efficacis audaciae signum elatis manibus contortisque sagulis ostendebant* (q.v.). In 18.6.13 Amm. himself made clear to his fellow Roman soldiers at the fortress Amudis that the enemy was near by extending his arm far forward and waving his

66   COMMENTARY

cloak: *porrecto extentius brachio et summitatibus sagi contortis elatius adesse hostes signo solito demonstrabam.*

irasque sequentium excitans audenter effunderet semet in pugnam See for the rousing of the soldiers' anger the note ad 24.2.5 *ira tamen acuente virtutem.* With *effunderet semet in pugnam* Amm. uses a very strong expression: see TLL V 2.226.29sqq. (*effundi* and *se effundere* as synonyms of *se dedere*) and OLD s.v. *effundo* (refl. or pass. "to break out into"). Some examples: Liv. 29.23.4 *Numidae effusi in venerem,* Tac. *Hist.* 2.80.2 *in adulationem effusos,* Tac. *Ann.* 14.13.2 *seque in omnes libidines effudit,* Amm. 14.11.2 and 30.8.3 *effusior ad nocendum.* Julian has completely lost control of himself.

candidati, quos disiecerat terror A group of forty men from the *scholae palatinae,* supervised by the *magister officiorum,* who served as the emperor's personal guard and did not leave his side in the field. They probably wore white uniforms, hence their name. Amm. is the first source to mention them in 15.5.16 (with the elaborate note by De Jonge); they are also mentioned in 31.13.14, 16. One should not confuse them with the *candidati duplares* and *candidati simplares* mentioned by Vegetius (*mil.* 2.7.11), who are lower ranking officers; Milner, 1996², 39, n. 6. It seems that a considerable number of the *candidati* were barbarians; 31.15.8; Hier. *Vit. Hil.* 22. See further Seeck, 1899; Jones 613.
   The relative clause *quos disiecerat terror* provides indispensable information: Julian had been left unguarded by the men whose specific task it was to protect him. Combined with his own rash behaviour, this simply invited a catastrophe. Apparently the *candidati* were to stick close together in their protection of the emperor. Lib. *Or.* 18.268 mentions that, when Julian rushed to repair the ranks, he had with him only one attendant as an escort (σὺν ἑνὶ θεράποντι).

ut fugientium molem tamquam ruinam male compositi culminis declinaret As Fontaine n. 528 plausibly suggests, these words recall the bad omen which had occurred earlier in the campaign: the collapse of a stack of chaff as a result of which fifty soldiers were killed (23.2.8 *mole maxima ruinarum,* q.v.).

incertum unde Very disappointingly, precisely at this crucial point V's text is deficient, in that it only has *incertum,* which by itself does not make any sense. Four solutions have been proposed: a) Wagner is absolutely sure about *incertum*: "e margine irrepsisse in contex-

CHAPTER 3.6   67

tum", b) Hermann, 1865, 25 sq. proposes *interdum* as a synonym of *interim*, referring to examples in Apuleius and Justinus. It is true that in later Latin *interdum* can have such a meaning (see the list in TLL VII 1.2181.76–2182.28); in Apuleius' *Metamorphoses* this is in fact usually the case (see Van der Paardt ad *Met.* 3.1), but of the thirty-odd cases in Amm. none has this meaning; even in 25.9.3, the only instance of the *Res Gestae* in the TLL list just mentioned, *interdum* means 'from time to time', c) Haupt's addition *unde*, accepted by Gardthausen and subsequent editors until Fontaine. The combination *incertum unde* also occurs in 16.8.3, where the text is not entirely certain, 19.8.10 and 24.2.4. The remarkable similarity with Zonaras 13.13.20 ἄδηλον δ᾽ εἶναι ὅθεν ἡ αὐτὸν πλήξασα αἰχμὴ κατ᾽ ἐκείνου ἐβέβλητο favours this solution; cf. also Malalas *Chron.* 13.332 ὁ βασιλεὺς Ἰουλιανὸς...ἐτρώθη ἀδήλως ('mysteriously' according to the translation of Jeffreys e.a.), d) Fontaine conjectures *incertam* to go with *ruinam*, defending this solution with a reference to Sen. *Nat.* 6.9.3 *fastigia deferuntur et incerta sunt*, which is not a parallel at all, unless one regards *incertam* as a remarkable case of enallage. For the *candidati*, who were warning Julian, the danger was entirely real and not 'uncertain'. It is an unconvincing solution of the problem, in contrast to the persuasive ones of Wagner and Haupt. One cannot help feeling that the predilection of editors and other scholars for the third solution is at least partly prompted by the attractive corollary of the author taking a clear stand in the battle of speculations about Julian's death: "most editors have supplied 'unde' after V's 'incertum'...thereby allowing to Ammianus explicit expression of the view that the origin of the fatal spear was unknown" (Matthews 507, n. 4). He thus provides the precise details about the wound with an almost medical diagnosis, but adds that nobody knows by whom it was inflicted. It must, however, be admitted that the text can easily do without *incertum* and, moreover, that in Wagner's solution *subita* gains in importance: it does not have to share the emphasis with *incertum* (*unde*). This aspect derives more weight from the fact that the entire sentence has a '*cum* inversum'-structure: *clamabant...et...haesit*. In such a structure the *cum* clause can include adjectives like *repens* and *subitus* (Kühner-Stegmann II 339) and quite often hypotactical *cum* is substituted by paratactical *et*; see the examples in Kühner-Stegmann II 167 and consult also Szantyr 481. Unfortunate though this may be, the final verdict can only be: *non liquet*. It is perhaps worthwhile to put forward one other suggestion: *in certamine*. The noun is quite frequent in Amm., and occurs most often in a military context. It is true that the plural prevails and that in the sin-

68   COMMENTARY

gular an accompanying adj. is usual, though not invariably so: e.g.
17.1.1 *ante certamen*. Livy has six cases of *in certamine*: 2.61.4, 6.37.7,
28.21.9, 29.34.7, 40.12.18, 40.32.3, and it suits the present text:
Julian threw himself into the fighting; his bodyguards were shouting
that he should avoid the mass of fleeing soldiers, when during the
battle he was suddenly hit.

The discussion as to where the weapon came from, and hence
who inflicted the mortal wound on Julian arose immediately after the
death of the emperor and has not stopped raising curiosity until this
day. The account given by Amm. about Julian's death is the fullest
there is. Matthews 182 notes that Amm. wrote from a "personal
acquaintance with the circumstances" and was well-informed "on
many of the more intimate details".

Gregory of Nazianzus, who wrote his two *Orationes contra Julianum*
not long after Julian's death, already summed up in his *Oratio* 5.13
four of the then apparently existing hypotheses: 1. the emperor was
killed by a lance thrown by a Persian; 2. he was killed by an enraged
Roman soldier who had overheard Julian saying that it was a pity
to have to lead all the soldiers back to Roman territory; 3. Julian
was killed by a barbarian buffoon who followed the army for the
entertainment of the soldiers. Baldwin, 1986 suggests that Gregory
may have wilfully misunderstood the Latin word *scurra* (military slang
for a guardsman of barbarian origin; see Amm. 29.4.4 and 30.1.20)
as 'buffoon'. This suggestion is accepted by Matthews 507 n. 3; 4.
the emperor was killed by a Saracen – Gregory does not inform us
on which side the Saracen fought. Gregory does not indicate which
of the four hypotheses he considered the most likely one. Also Zon.
13.13.20 reports that it was unclear who was responsible for throwing
the weapon that killed Julian: an enemy, someone from Julian's own
ranks, or a divine power. Other writers took more explicit stands and
several traditions concerning the killer of Julian can be distinguished.
According to Malalas *Chron.* 13.332 it was unclear (ἀδήλως) who had
mortally wounded the emperor. Like Amm., Zosimus is neutral about
who was responsible for the mortal wound: 3.29.1: πλήττεται ξίφει
παρ' αὐτὴν τῆς μάχης τὴν ἀκμήν. There is the tradition, represented
by Festus, the *Epitome* and Eutropius, a participant in Julian's Persian
expedition, that he was killed by an enemy. Ruf. Fest. 28: *cum
incautius per agmen erraret, excito pulvere erepto suorum conspectu ab obvio
hostium equite conto per ilia ictus inguinum tenus vulneratus est. Epit.* 43.3:
*Cumque inconsulto ardore nititur ordines ad proelium componere, ab uno
ex hostibus, et quidem fugiente, conto percutitur.* Eutr. 10.16.2 *remeansque
victor, dum se inconsultius proeliis inserit hostili manu interfectus est VI*

CHAPTER 3.6   69

Kal.Iul. imperii anno septimo aetatis altero et tricesimo, atque inter Divos relatus est. According to another tradition, which started to spread on the day after the emperor's death, Julian was killed by a Roman. The Persians heard about Julian's death from a deserter only the following day (25.5.8, q.v.), which is remarkable, and the rumour among them spread that he had been killed by one of his own people. In insulting language they accused the Romans of being traitors and murderers of an outstanding ruler: *verbis turpibus incessebant ut perfidos et lectissimi principis peremptores; audierant enim ipsi quoque referentibus transfugis rumore iactato incerto Iulianum telo cecidisse Romano* (25.6.6, q.v.). Libanius (*Or.* 18.274–5) also argues that the killer was a Roman since none of the enemy received any reward for killing Julian. Libanius implies that a Christian was responsible for Julian's death. The Christians had already for some time been conspiring against Julian since they considered him a threat and could not accept the fact that he had paid honours to the gods; moreover, they were wicked people according to Libanius; see Malosse, 1998, 67. Libanius has a completely different story in *Or.* 24.6. Here a Taiene, that is a Tayy Arab or in Amm.'s words a Saracen, inflicted the fatal blow acting on his leader's command. This action, Libanius continues, would secure for the chief of the Taienes a reward from those who were keen to have Julian killed. It is not clear who "those" are to whom Libanius refers: they could either be the Persians or the Christians within the Roman army. Both armies had contingents of Saracen mercenaries as part of their forces; see the note ad 23.3.8. Bowersock, 1978, 117 notes that Libanius' information is confirmed by Philost. *HE* 7.15, who even added that the Saracen was a member of auxiliary cavalry spearmen fighting on the Persian side; Bowersock therefore concludes that "Julian was most probably felled by a spear from the Persian army from a Saracen hand." Paschoud n. 84 and Hunt, 1998, 77 also consider this probable.

    Julian's death gave rise to an ideological debate between Christians and pagans, reflected in the sources, in which the former saw in Julian's death the hand of God; see Hahn, 1960 and the references in Teitler, 2000, 71, n. 3. According to Ephrem Syrus (*HcJul.* 3.13–4) it was a godsend when "the spear of justice passed through his belly" (trans. Lieu, 1989, 120). Sozomen (*HE* 6.2.1), picking up Libanius' suggestion, says that Julian was killed by a Christian as an act of divine vengeance and that it is not improbable that this Christian came from the Roman ranks. Socrates (*HE* 3.21.14), citing the *protector domesticus* Callistus, says that the wound of which Julian died was inflicted by a demon. Socrates thinks it more likely that Julian

70　　　　　　　　　　　　COMMENTARY

was killed by one of his own men rather than by a Persian. Meulder, 1991, 473 ff. strangely suggests that Amm. thought of Julian's death as caused by "une intervention personnelle" by Mars, and hence as an act of divine vengeance.

In spite of all the speculations as to who inflicted the mortal wound of which Julian died, and for which reasons, it is most likely that it was just bad luck that the emperor was hit in the turmoil of the battle and that no one knew who threw the fatal spear; no preconceived scheme by Christians or other opponents to kill Julian should be supposed.

A Sasanian rock relief in Taq-I Bustan possibly shows the defeated Julian. The prostrate figure on this relief is identified by Trümpelmann, 1975 as Julian; he is trampled upon by Sapor II and Ahura Mazda. The relief symbolizes of course Sapor's victory and Julian's failure. The fourth figure on the relief, the god Mithras – associated in Iranian tradition with treaties, oaths and boundaries – is, according to Azarpay, 1982, 186 "surely a reference to the territorial concessions made to Sapur by Julian's successor Jovian". See also Nicholson, 1983 and, for another attempt to identify Sapor's victory over Julian in a work of art, MacDonald, 1978–1979, about the Cunningham chalcedony in the British Museum.

equestris hasta About the weapon which wounded Julian the sources likewise differ. Greg. Naz. *Or.* 5.13 αὐτὸν κατηκοντίσθαι φασίν refers to a spear. According to Zos. 3.29.1 Julian was hurt by a ξίφος, a sword; cf. also Thdt. *HE* 3.25.7. John Lydus, *Mens.* 4.118 speaks of a ῥομφαία (a long, broad sword). The other sources speak of a long spear, javelin or lance: Ruf. Fest. 28 (*contus*), Lib. *Or.* 18.268 (δόρυ ἱππέως), Lib. *Or.* 17.23 (λόγχη), Socr. *HE* 3.21.12 (ἀκόντιον), Zon. 13.13.18 (δόρατι βάλλεται). The weapons mentioned by these latter sources are closer to Amm.'s *equestris hasta* than the weapons referred to by the former. Paschoud n. 84 thinks Zosimus may have confused a sword with a lance. However, as in the case of the question as to who inflicted the mortal wound on Julian, the sources do not allow for a final conclusion about the murder weapon: it could have been a sword, a spear, a lance or a javelin. It had been predicted that Julian would die by a weapon, if we are to believe the emperor's words as put into his mouth by Amm.: *interiturum me ferro dudum didici fide fatidica praecinente* (25.3.19).

cute brachii eius praestricta costis perfossis haesit in ima iecoris fibra Of the sources which refer to Julian's death, Amm. is the most detailed as

CHAPTER 3.7   71

to which limbs and internal organs of the emperor were damaged by the *equestris hasta*. Concerning the details of the wound it should be noted that this is the only time Amm. uses *cutis* in such a context, *costa* occurs once more, in 28.6.14, about a man falling in a well, and *fibra* (Greek λοβός, 'lobe') only here. One of the two other occurrences of *iecur* (14.11.24) is also in a medical context. The clarity of Amm.'s brief 'medical' description leaves nothing to be desired. This does not prove its correctness, but emphasizes the author's wish to let the bare facts speak their horrible message. See for Amm.'s interest in medical matters Salazar, 2000, 83 and 92–3. Libanius, *Or.* 18.268 mentions that the spear went through his arm into Julian's side: διὰ τοῦ βραχίονος δραμὸν εἰς τὴν πλευρὰν εἰσέδυ; Lib. *Or.* 24.6 Ἐδέξατο μὲν ὑπὸ τῇ πλευρᾷ τὴν πληγὴν Ἰουλιανός.

A somewhat different tradition makes its appearance in Ruf. Fest. 28 *per ilia ictus inguinum tenus*, Philost. *HE* 7.15 κατὰ τὸ περιτόναιον, 'in the peritoneum' (with the result that part of the excrements came out together with the blood caused by the wound: κόπρος τις ἐπηκολούθησε συνεπισπωμένη τῷ αἵματι), *Art. pass.* 69 βέλος ἐπ' αὐτὸν ὡς ἐπὶ σκοπὸν ἀφιὲν καὶ διὰ τῶν λαγόνων ('through his flanks') ὁρμῆσαν διαμπερὲς ἔτρωσεν αὐτὸν εἰς τὰ ὑποχόνδρια ('in the abdomen'), Lyd. *Mens.* 4.118 κατὰ τοῦ ἤτρου ('in the abdomen').

quam dum avellere dextra manu conatur, acuto utrimque ferro digitorum   **3.7**
nervos sensit excisos   TLL V 2.1243.77–8 interprets this instance of *excidere* as a synonym of *dissecare*. Amm. is the only source which has this information.

provolutus iumento   This is the only instance in Amm. of *provolvere*; *provolutus* is a strong term, which not merely indicates that he fell from his horse: he was 'thrown headlong'; cf. Tac. *Hist.* 1.41.2 *Galba proiectus e sella ac provolutus est.* Cf. for *iumentum*, 'mount', 16.12.35 *Chnodomarius iumento statim desiluit*, 24.2.8 *equites vero cum iumentis armati*, 29.5.15 *iumento desiluit*. Libanius *Or.* 18.269 (καὶ πεσὼν ἐπὶ γῆς ὁ γενναῖος) and 24.7 (ὁ δὲ εὐθὺς κατέπεσεν) has this same information but adds that Julian, while concealing his wound, remounted. He was, however, unable to hide his wound because of the bloodstains, but assured his soldiers that it was not fatal. Subsequently, he lost consciousness.

veloci concursu relatus in castra medicinae ministeriis fovebatur   Note the contrast between *veloci concursu* and *disiecerat* in §6. *Epit.* 43.4: *Relatusque in tabernaculum.* Lib. *Or.* 18.269 κομίζεται πρὸς τὴν σκηνὴν.

72   COMMENTARY

According to Zos. 3.29.1 Julian was carried to his tent on a shield: ἐπιτεθεὶς ἀσπίδι φοράδην ἐπὶ τὴν σκηνὴν ἄγεται. From Amm.'s words it may be surmised that somehow during the battle the Roman soldiers had been able to construct a camp; see the note ad 25.3.1. In its other three instances (16.8.2, 21.1.13, 22.16.18) *medicina* denotes the art of medicine in general. The present case can be regarded as abstractum pro concreto (see the note ad 25.2.2 *quidquid ad*): Julian was being treated by the services of medical experts, among whom no doubt Oribasius; cf. the note ad 25.3.15 *Quae dum.*

3.8 *magno spiritu contra exitium certans arma poscebat et equum, ut reviso proelio suorum fiduciam repararet* Without doubt *magno spiritu* expresses high praise; cf. 16.12.49 *proelium maiore spiritu repetivit* (Julian's soldiers at Strasbourg), 22.12.5 *maioris praeter ceteros spiritus* (Julian at Antioch), 24.1.1 *celso praeter alios spiritu* (Julian entering Assyria). The lethal wound could not quell the emperor's lofty spirit. Cf. *epit.* 43.4: *rursusque ad hortandos suos egressus.*

videretur This is one of the details which testify to the author's precision in his report on Julian's conduct in his last hours: he wanted his soldiers to 'see' him being 'bound' (*astringi*) by his care for their well-being. See for *sui securus* the note ad 25.3.4.

licet in negotio dispari Cf. 23.6.88 *licet dignitate dispari*, as should be printed there instead of *suppari*; see the note ad loc.

Epaminondas ille dux inclutus The way in which the Theban general Epaminondas died in the battle of Mantinea (362 B.C.) was considered exemplary. Like Julian, he was mortally wounded by a spear or lance, was carried to the camp, and after giving a speech (D.S. 15.87.6) eventually died. On his deathbed Epaminondas asked where his shield was – the fact that Julian had only carried a shield and not his full armour in his last battle may have been Amm.'s source of inspiration to relate the story about Epaminondas' shield. D.S. 15.87.5–6: Ἐπαμεινώνδας δ᾽ ἔτι ζῶν εἰς τὴν παρεμβολὴν ἀπηνέχθη, καὶ τῶν συγκληθέντων ἰατρῶν ἀποφηναμένων, ὅτι πάντως, ὅταν ἐκ τοῦ θώρακος ἐξαιρεθῇ τὸ δόρυ, συμβήσεται καὶ τὸν θάνατον ἐπακολουθῆσαι, εὐψυχότατα τὴν τοῦ βίου καταστροφὴν ἐποιήσατο. πρῶτον μὲν γὰρ τὸν ὑπασπιστὴν προσκαλεσάμενος ἐπηρώτησεν εἰ διασέσωκε τὴν ἀσπίδα; Iust. 6.8.11–2.

Amm. is fully justified in introducing Epaminondas as an example for a Roman readership. His death in the battle of Mantinea

CHAPTER 3.8   73

(362 B.C.) occurs already in Cicero: *Fam.* 5.12.5 *Quem enim nostrum ille moriens apud Mantineam Epaminondas non cum quadam miseratione delectat? qui tum denique sibi evelli iubet spiculum, posteaquam ei percontanti dictum est clipeum esse salvum; ut etiam in vulneris dolore aequo animo cum laude moreretur*; *Tusc.* 2.59, *Fin.* 2.97; the first and third references contain his preoccupation with his shield. It seems more likely, however, that Amm. himself was inspired by V. Max. 3.2 *ex.* 5, although this passage like *Fin.* 2.97, apart from the shield, mentions another question by Epaminondas: *Epaminondas...traiectus hasta, sanguine et spiritu deficiens recreare se conantes primum an clipeus suus salvus esset, deinde an penitus fusi hostes forent interrogavit.* Being reassured in both respects, he died in peace. Evidently, Amm. found it less appropriate to refer to this second question in the present context. This is precisely the dissimilarity of both men's situation. For if, as seems likely, the proviso *licet in negotio dispari* does not merely express that in making comparisons between historical events one should always proceed 'mutatis mutandis', the question arises which specific difference Amm. is hinting at. In all probability Julian's primary concern was the fact that his men were having a hard time and needed encouragement. Therefore, as a result of this difference Julian concentrated on his men's morale and well-being, whereas Epaminondas was anxious about his personal honour. Brok 186 surmises that Amm. did not know Nepos' biographical sketch of Epaminondas, since in that case he would have done better by referring to it: Nep. *Ep.* 9.3: *at Epaminondas, cum animadverteret mortiferum se vulnus accepisse simulque, si ferrum, quod ex hastili in corpore remanserat, extrahisset, animam statim emissurum, usque eo retinuit, quoad renuntiatum est vicisse Boeotios.* Amm., however, was better served by Epaminondas' preoccupation with his shield, in contrast to Julian's more lofty thoughts. The comparison with an admirable hero of the past is a subtle way of expressing Julian's superiority. His example could now replace the one set by the famous Theban leader. Note the difference between imperfect *amittebat* and perfect *formidavit*. When Epaminondas was dying without fearing death, he did express one specific anxiety.

    Near the end of his 'Funeral oration over Julian' Libanius also briefly introduces Epaminondas, in a prosopopoeia in which Julian addresses the mourners: ἔτι τοίνυν μηδὲ τὸ ἐν πολέμῳ καὶ διὰ σιδήρου δεινὸν ὑμῖν δοκείτω, οὕτως ἀπῆλθε Λεωνίδας, οὕτως Ἐπαμινώνδας (*Or.* 18.297).

scutum...clipei Although these were two different sorts of shield, Amm. does not seem to distinguish between the two types; see the

74   COMMENTARY

note ad 21.2.1 *quatiens scutum*. On the whole he uses – as Brok 186 already observed – *scutum* as the generic word for shield. However, for the sake of variation he also uses *clipeus*; 15.8.15 (*scutum, clipeus*); 16.12.54, 62 (*scutum*), 57 (*clipeus*); 24.2.12 (*scutum*), 5 and 14 (*clipeus*); 24.6.7 (*scutum*), 10 (*clipeus*); 29.5.38 (*scutum*). For crossing a river either a *scutum* (16.11.9) or a *clipeus* was used (16.12.57). In 16.12.22, 36 and 31.12.12 Amm. mentions that the cavalry uses a *scutum*; in 24.2.5 and 6.10 the infantry wears a *clipeus*. An infantry shield was different from that of a cavalryman as may be surmised from Amm.'s adding of *pedestre* to *scutum* in 20.4.17. A testudo was generally formed by *scuta*, but in 20.11.8 by *clipei*. Apart from *scutum* and *clipeus* Amm. also used the word *parma* for shield; 16.12.37, 29.5.39, 31.5.9.

cura…sollicita Heraeus' emendation is satisfactorily supported by Hagendahl, 1924, 164 n. 4 and 203. He i.a. refers to *sollicitior cura* in 22.4.5, where *sollicitior* is an obvious emendation, and 31.2.19.

vi vulneris interiit Note in *interiit* the accent required by the cursus velox.

3.9 *cum vires parum sufficerent voluntati* The most famous example of this contrast is *ut desint vires, tamen est laudanda voluntas* (Ov. *Pont.* 3.4.79). Some other examples are: *Non omnes ad bonum propositum easdem adferunt vires,…voluntas ipsa rectum petens laudanda est* (Sen. *Ben.* 5.2.2), *ut scias…nec voluntatem ei,…sed ingenium ac vires defuisse* (Tac. *Dial.* 21.2), *maiore scilicet voluntate quam facultate* (Apul. *Fl.* 20). It can also be the other way round: *plus facultatis habuit ad dicendum quam voluntatis* (Cic. *Brut.* 245).

sanguinisque profluvio In 23.1.5 Amm. had reported a macabre joke of the Antiochenes after the deaths of the *comes sacrarum largitionum* Felix and Julian's uncle Iulianus. The former died suddenly *profluvio sanguinis*. The entire sequence of events proved to be ominous, *ut docuit exitus*.

mansit immobilis It is not clear what Amm. wants to convey by this phrase. When used about a person the adi. can denote inability to move, as in Sen. *Contr.* 1.17.10 *ego in senectute immobilis*. This meaning suits the context: Julian's loss of physical strength and the haemorrhage made it impossible for him to perform the actions he intended. Amm., however, now adds another reason: the place where the battle

CHAPTER 3.9   75

was raging had been predicted to him as the place where he would die. He therefore gave up all hope to remain alive, and this adds another meaning to *mansit immobilis*. It now seems to denote mental strength, as in the case of the orator Eusebius, who under torture *fundato pectore mansit immobilis* (14.9.6), and to remind the reader of other situations in which Julian had shown his imperturbability: hearing the Alamans' arrogant demands, he laughed at them and *in eodem gradu constantiae stetit immobilis* (16.12.3); when he addressed his soldiers at the beginning of his campaign against Constantius, he reminded them how he had coped with the attacks on Gaul from the German side: *stando immobilis* (21.5.3); at Antioch his detractors, who wanted the Persian expedition to be called off, *frustra virum circumlatrabant immobilem* (22.12.4). See further Fontaine, 1982, 538–42.

ideo spe deinceps vivendi absumpta, quod percunctando Phrygiam appellari locum, ubi ceciderat, comperit. Hic enim obiturum se praescripta audierat sorte This does not mean that Julian was petrified by desperation. He reacted entirely rationally to the answer he received, when asking the name of the place. At first sight *deinceps vivendi* seems a curious phrase to express 'remaining alive', but the adverb can be used "implying continuance" (OLD s.v. 3) and, moreover, it emphasizes the precise moment at which Julian concluded that his life was destined to end there and then. With *percunctando* Amm. adds a telling detail: Julian did not hear the name by chance, he had asked a deliberate question, and on hearing the answer he calmly drew the inevitable conclusion and gave up his wish to return to the battlefield: *mansit immobilis*.

As Paschoud n. 83, following Herzfeld, 1948, 65–6, concluded there is no known place named Phrygia in the region, i.e. some kilometers south of Samarra; this, however, does not imply that such a place could not have existed ("rien n'empêche de croire qu'il y avait un site nommé Phrygia."). Ridley, 1973, 323 remarks that Phrygia "would seem the best evidence we have for the site of Julian's last battle, although the name may well be only an approximation of its native form". The traditions, many of them representations of dreams, about the location of Julian's death are unclear and far from unanimous. Zon. 13.13.29–30 is the only other source which mentions Phrygia; he reports that Julian, while in Antioch, was told by a blond young man, who had appeared to him, that he would die in Phrygia. Malalas *Chron.* 13.331 says that Julian and his army, after having been led astray by Persian deceivers, pitched camp on 25 June near the ancient ruins of Boubios (Babylon according to

76   COMMENTARY

Paschoud n. 83) and Asia; a day later Julian would meet his death there. This coincides with a strange story told by Eutychianus, and cited by Malalas *Chron.* 13.332, that Julian had a dream in Asia, not far from Ctesiphon, in which he died by a spear; when he woke up he was mortally wounded. According to *Chron. Pasch.* a. 363 Julian died at Rasia, Rassia or Radia, possibly a scribal error for Asia; see Herzfeld, 1948, 65–6. The information these sources provide us with does not make it possible to establish where exactly Julian died, as Paschoud n. 83 already noted. The only conclusion which the source material allows us to draw is that the site where Julian was killed was a day's march south of Sumere (25.6.4)/Σοῦμα (Zos. 3.30.2).

There is a resemblance between the predictions given to Julian and to Cambyses as described by Hdt. 3.64.3–5. Hdt. mentions that it had been predicted to Cambyses that he would die in Ecbatana. Cambyses had supposed that this would mean that he would pass away in Ecbatana in Media. However, when he had mortally wounded himself by accident and asked in which city he was, he was told that he was in Ecbatana, this being the Syrian Ecbatana. He then realized that the prediction had been fulfilled. Julian may have thought that the oracle given to him meant that he would meet his fate in Phrygia in Asia Minor, whereas he realized the true meaning of the prediction when told that he was in Phrygia in Persia.

Amm. has not mentioned this prediction before. However, with *enim* he appeals to the reader's empathy, expecting him to link the prediction with the situation. Moreover, and perhaps more importantly, *hic* clearly must be the first word, which rules out the use of *nam*. Cf. for *praescripta...sorte* 15.3.3 *praescriptum fatorum ordinem*, 23.5.5 *quod praescripsit fatalis ordo*, 25.10.12 *praescriptus vitae finiendae dies*, examples of the use of *praescribere* to denote "quae secundum fatum constituta sunt" (TLL X 2.825.56–66). *Sors* can mean a person's destiny, as in *fatali decesserat sorte* (17.11.5), *fatali sorte decessit* (27.5.10).

3.10 *reducto ad tentoria principe* This repeats *relato in castra* (§7) and the report now returns to the actions on the battlefield.

incredibile dictu est, quo quantoque ardore miles ad vindictam ira et dolore ferventior involabat Cf. *incredibile quo quantoque ardore* (16.5.6) and similar phrases in 14.4.4 and 31.10.18, all three in different contexts. See the notes ad 24.2.5 and 24.4.20 on the soldiers' anger as a praiseworthy source of inspiration. This instance of *involare* differs from the other four in Amm. In 16.12.36 (q.v.), 19.2.6, 21.4.8 (q.v.)

CHAPTER 3.10   77

and 24.2.5 it occurs with a direct object. Here it either forms a curious combination with *ad vindictam,* for which there are no parallels, or is used without any direct object or complement: 'they rushed to attack'. However, it seems more feasible to regard V's *hostes* as the direct object of *involabat* and to assume the loss of *hastis* or *hastas* as caused by haplography; syntactically, *ad vindictam* could be regarded as complement to *ferventior* after the example of 21.3.3 *Romanisque ad ducis vindictam accensis* and 28.3.6 *ad vindictam compertorum erectus.* It is, however, perhaps more convincing to interpret it as a satellite: 'in order to take revenge'. The only disadvantage of this solution is the absence of a regular cursus in *involabat hostes.*

Verg. *A.* 1.25 *causae irarum saevique dolores* is perhaps the most famous instance of the combination of *ira* and *dolor,* but it occurs often in various literary genres; some examples: *ira et dolore succenso militi* (Amm. 24.4.20, q.v.), *veterani ira et dolore incensi* (*B. Afr.* 25.6), *dolor iraque surgit* (V.Fl. 2.165), *exedere animum dolor iraque demens* (Stat. *Theb.* 2.319), *dolorem iramque Bedriacensis pugnae retinentes* (Tac. *Hist.* 2.86.1, see Heubner ad loc.).

hastis ad scuta concrepans The plausibility of Kiessling's conjecture *hastis* is not enhanced by his argument: "wie der acc. *hastas* grammatisch zu rechtfertigen sein soll sehe ich nicht ein; der sprachgebrauch verlangt den ablativ *hastis,* vgl. XIV 2, 17 *hastisque feriens scuta.* XV 8, 15 *cum hastis clipei feriuntur.* XX 5, 8 *hastis feriendo clipeos,* und auf dies führt auch das *hostes* der ms." (Kiessling, 1871, 493). Fontaine n. 534 adds *hastis illidendo scuta* (16.12.13), but in all these cases the verb in question is combined with a direct object. This is also the case in Petr. 59.3 *hastisque scuta concrepuit.* On the other hand, Kiessling could have adduced Liv. 28.29.10 *gladiis ad scuta concrepuit,* and this is perhaps decisive. For *concrepans,* mostly used to indicate the sound of wind instruments or of arms, see the notes ad 20.4.14 and 20.5.8. By clashing their spears against their shields the soldiers showed their eagerness for battle; 16.12.13 *ardoremque pugnandi hastis illidendo scuta monstrantes.* It was also meant to rouse hatred and resentment, and to show anger; 14.2.17 *hastisque feriens scuta, qui habitus iram pugnantium concitat et dolorem;* 15.8.15 *cum hastis clipei feriuntur, irae documentum est et doloris.* It appears from Amm. that, when the soldiers heard about Julian's fatal wound, they took up the fight even more furiously and energetically. This is in contrast to Libanius (*Or.* 18.270) who says that the soldiers began to wail, beat their breasts and shed tears when they heard that Julian was dying, and that in their sorrow they cast aside their weapons.

78   COMMENTARY

etiam mori, si tulisset fors, obstinatus Cf. *si copiam fors dedisset* (and
similar phrases) in 15.10.10, 16.9.3, 29.5.32, 30.5.2, 31.7.6, *si iuvisset
fors* (16.11.9, 16.12.45) and *si qua fors iuvisset* (19.3.1). The present
phrase is paralleled by *si fors ita tulisset* (27.10.10). The subjunctive
expresses that the quoted words were the soldiers' thoughts, if not
their actual words. As was stated in the note ad 20.4.8 *obstinatissime*,
the word *obstinatus* is by no means only used in a deprecatory sense.
Here it means "fest entschlossen" (Seyfarth) rather than "opiniâtres"
(Fontaine).

offundebatur oculis altitudo pulveris Kühner-Stegemann 1.334–6 lists
a number of verbs with two possible constructions, dat. and acc.
or acc. and abl.; *offundere* is mentioned in Anmerkung 13. Cf.
tenebrae stupentibus offunduntur oculis (Sen. *Contr.* 7.1.6) and *offunditur
densioribus tenebris caelum* (Amm. 20.3.5). Presumably, *altitudo pulveris*
is a bolder instance of the gen. inversus than *altitudo...fossarum*
(24.2.11, q.v.): 'a high-whirling cloud of dust'. It is not obvious
whether the clouds of dust were due to the fighting of the soldiers or
to a natural cause (sc. a dust storm), as mentioned by Lib. *Or.* 18.268
αἰγίδος δὲ ἐξαίφνης λαμπρᾶς κόνιν τε ἐπεγειρούσης καὶ νέφη συναγούσης.
Cf. also Ruf. Fest. 28 *excito pulvere*. See the note ad 24.6.10 for clouds
of dust as a recurrent theme in Amm.'s descriptions of battles. Veg.
mil. 3.14.1 advises that commanders, in drawing up the lines, should
be attentive to clouds of dust because they fill and close the eyes
(*pulvis...oculos implet et claudit*).

aestus calescens officeret alacritati membrorum The verb *calescere* also
occurs in 24.8.3 *terras vapore sideris calescentes*. About these two instances TLL III 150.12–4 wrongly notes: "utroque loco vis inco-
hativa deest", since in both cases the increasing heat is expressed.
Because *alacritas* is normally used to describe a mental state, the
combination with *membrorum* is somewhat surprising, but, as appears
from OLD s.v. *alacer*, already in classical Latin the adjective is used
to describe physical movement. See also the note on *alacri gradu*
(20.4.12). Ehrismann 45 notes the occurrence of *offundebatur* and
officeret in one clause as an example of inexplicable combinations of
modes.

velut exauctoratus amisso ductore This is evidently inspired by Liv.
25.20.4 *velut exauctoratus morte ducis*. In 24.3.2 *exauctorare*, 'to dismiss
from service', is used in its literal sense. Here the absence of their
general makes the soldiers feel as if they are no longer obliged to

CHAPTER 3.11   79

obey any command, and they rush blindly and uncontrollably into the battle. See for *ductore* the note ad 25.1.2.

sine parsimonia ruebat in ferrum See for *ruere in* the note ad 20.11.16 and cf. especially 14.2.15 *ruitura...in ferrum*. In 15.4.8, 17.10.6, 19.11.14 and 29.6.8 *sine* (*ulla*) *parsimonia* occurs in a context of indiscriminate slaughter. Probably Amm. wants to express that in their fury the soldiers spared neither their adversaries nor themselves (*in ferrum*).

animosius See the note ad 24.4.11, where it is stated that the adjective **3.11** means 'confident' or 'courageous'. The comparative may well have its full meaning: the Persians added a little extra; cf. Fontaine's "avec une ardeur accrue". Cf. *sagittarum undique volantium crebritate* (19.6.9, q.v.). Amm.'s surprising use of *rapere* with dat. is perhaps inspired by the normal complement of *eripere*; cf. *quam mihi febricula eripiet una* (24.3.7).

quos elephanti tardius praecedentes The structure of the entire period leaves something to be desired. Only at the end does the reader perceive that *quos* is the object of *praecedentes* and does not refer to *oppositis*, but to *Persae*. This insight makes Brok's suggestion that *praecedentes* is here the equivalent of *procedentes* impossible. Brok 187 suggested this because he found it hard to imagine that the elephants went before the bowmen, since the risk of getting struck by the arrows of their own *sagittarii* would have been immense. However, it could be that the arrows were shot in a curve over the elephants to the enemy ranks. For war elephants see the notes ad 24.6.8 and 25.1.14, 15. See Blomgren 142–6 for other passages in which the relative pronoun is placed at a considerable distance from the antecedent.

magnitudine corporum cristarumque horrore Cf. Liv. 37.40.4 about elephants: *Ingentes ipsi erant; addebant speciem frontalia et cristae.* In order to look more impressive and fearful the elephants were wearing plumes on their heads. As Brok notes, Daremberg-Saglio II 1, 1892, 540–1 n. 128 refers to this passage in comparison with the present one. Fig. 2626 provides a picture of coins with elephants wearing plumes; elephants were depicted regularly on coins; see Scullard, 1974, Pls. XIII–XVI and XXI–XIV. Fletcher, 1937, 396 does not explicitly refer to this evidence, but rightly makes use of it in defending V's *cristarum* against Heraeus' curious *crustarum*, which is supposed to tally with *rugosis...corporibus* (19.2.3) and to denote the elephants' rough hide.

80 COMMENTARY

3.12 *concursus itaque armatorum et cadentium gemitus, equorum flatus, tinnitus ferri procul audiebatur* Amm. neither describes nor summarizes the further course which the fighting took. He only registers some of the sounds which could be heard from a distance. Cf. *gemituque caesorum* (19.6.8), *morientium gemitus* (31.13.4); *equorum flatus* is a quotation from Verg. *A.* 11.911 *flatusque audivit equorum* (see the commentaries of Thomas and Mynors ad Verg. *G.* 3.111 *flatuque sequentum* for possible Greek models); in 24.4.22 *ferri tinnitus* is caused by the chisels of the sappers. TLL X 2.1559.28–67 provides a list of instances in which *procul* is combined with a term denoting sensory perception. As might be expected, Amm. has such a combination in a number of passages, but the present phrase *procul audiebatur* deserves close attention: the four preceding brief phrases do not denote anything seen, but the sounds of what was happening at a distance. This may well be a sign of the personal memory of the historian, who at the time did not take part in the fighting, but heard the various noises from afar, perhaps in the neighbourhood of the tent in which Julian lay.

quamdiu satietate vulnerum partibus fessis nox diremit certamina iam tenebrosa See for *satietas*, 'abundance' the note ad 25.1.4; here, however, the term clearly implies that they had now endured enough, as in *satias aerumnarum* (19.2.14, q.v.). Enn. *Ann.* 160 Sk. *bellum aequis manibus nox intempesta diremit* is the likely origin of a long series of phrases in which *dirimere* has *proelium, bellum* or *certamen* as direct object. Livy has many instances. See TLL V 1.1258.82–1259.12 and also Bitter 168 n. 533 and 534. Other passages in Amm. in which nightfall ended the fighting: *nox finem caedibus fecit* (19.2.14), *ut vero certaminibus finem vespera dedit incedens* (20.11.24), *noxque adventans ad quietem invitos retinebat* (31.7.8). The translators take *tenebrosa* with *nox*, which is quite possible, also in view of *tenebrosae noctis* (15.4.8). However, the remarkable hyperbaton and the presence of *iam* make one wonder whether the adi. does not belong to *certamina*: 'the hostilities upon which darkness was already coming down'. According to Zos. 3.29.2 the battle only ended when the Roman soldiers heard of their emperor's death. Amm.'s chronology of events is more plausible (Paschoud n. 85: "C'est évidemment Ammien qui a raison."): 1. the emperor is mortally wounded; 2. the battle continues and is won by the Roman army at the end of the day; 3. Julian dies.

3.13 *quinquaginta tum Persarum optimates et satrapae cum plebe maxima* Zos. 3.29.2 corresponds closely with Amm.: τῶν Ῥωμαίων ὁ στρατὸς ἐπὶ

CHAPTER 3.13   81

τοσοῦτον ἐκράτησεν ὥστε πεντήκοντα μὲν τῶν ἐν μεγίστῃ δυνάμει σατρά-
πας πεσεῖν, καὶ ἐπὶ τούτοις Περσῶν ἄπειρον πλῆθος. For the use of the
term *optimates* for non-Romans see the notes ad 20.6.3 and 21.13.4.
Satraps, governors of the territorial/provincial subdivisions of the
Persian empire, undoubtedly belonged to the Persian *optimates* as
did the *vitaxae* and *reges* mentioned in 23.6.14 (with the note). For
the administration of the Persian satrapies, see Christensen, 1944[2],
136–40.

Merena et Nohodare potissimis ducibus interfectis See for Merena the
note ad 25.1.11. Nohodares is also mentioned in 14.3.1, 18.6.16,
q.v., 8.3. Amm. considers Nohodares a proper name, whereas it is
a Persian title (*nakhvadhār*); see Christensen, 1944[2], 21 n. 3; *PLRE*
I, Nohodares. The phrase *potissimis ducibus*, 'most eminent leaders',
also occurs in 19.1.6 and 24.6.12. Cf. Symm. *Ep.* 2.18.2 *Eusebius,
medicorum potissimus.*

obstupescat magniloquentia vetustatis At various points in his report
on the Persian campaign Amm. airs a rivalry with the military feats
of the venerated Greek and Roman past. See 24.2.16–7, 24.4.5
and especially 24.6.14, where the exploits of ancient times are
challenged to a comparison with the great battle near Ctesiphon.
A similar phrase with a 'defiant' adhortatory subjunctive is used here
in *obstupescat magniloquentia vetustatis*. Although *magniloquentia* is not
necessarily a deprecatory term, its combination with *adulatorum* in
15.5.37 and 16.12.69 and the phrase *magniloquentia socordi coalitus*
(27.2.6) about an incompetent officer, make it probable that Amm.
uses it in this way here too: TLL VIII 114.41–50 rightly includes
Amm.'s four instances in the list of *magniloquentia* as a synonym of
iactatio or *ostentatio*.

    Brok aptly refers to Claud. *in Ruf.* 1.283–4 *taceat superata vetus-
tas,/ Herculeos conferre tuis iam desinat actus.* See for other parallels in Claudian Levy ad loc. and Heus ad Claud. *carm. min.* 30
(= *Laus Serenae*), 42. This type of formula is called "Überbietung"
by Curtius, 1978[9], 171, according to whom it was introduced into
Latin literature by Statius' frequent use of it. In a note ad Stat.
Silv. 2.2.60–2 Van Dam agrees with this. Another variant of the
formula is Claud. *Olyb.* 197–8 *talem nulla refert antiquis pagina lib-
ris/ nec Latiae cecinere tubae nec Graia vetustas;* see Taegert's note ad
loc. Not surprisingly, such "Überbietung" also occurs in panegyrical prose: *cedat his terris terra Cretensis parvi Iovis gloriata cunabulis
(Pan.* 2.4.5), *Eat nunc sui ostentatrix vetustas et illa innumeris litte-*

82 COMMENTARY

rarum vulgata monimentis iactet exempla (*Pan.* 2.17.1), *Cedat tibi non recentium saeculorum modo, sed totius memoriae vetustas* (*Pan.* 4.15.1), *tibi habe, vetustas, redemptas saepe centurias et gratiosas Quiritium classes* (Symm. *Or.* 1.9). It can be concluded that Amm. has borrowed a stylistic device from laudatory texts. Its introduction into his historiographic work is like the 'we-style' a token of his personal involvement.

From Valesius onwards commentators have noticed the great similarity of the rest of § 13 and § 14 with Solinus 1.102–7. However, Wagner's "fere totum exscripsit Ammianus" is somewhat exaggerated, if only because of the different number of battles fought by M. Claudius Marcellus. In the case of L. Sicinius (often Siccius; thus Münzer, 1923) Dentatus it is not impossible that *ornatum militarium multitudine coronarum* is derived from V. Max. 3.2.24, Plin. *Nat.* 7.101–2 or Gel. 2.11. In the cases of M. Sergius Silus and Catilina the direct dependence on Solinus is indeed undeniable.

Thus the source of the material and the general purpose of the passage are fairly clear, but it is far more difficult to establish what Amm. wants to express specifically. In contrast to the comparisons in book 24, in the present text the precise point(s) of comparison are not mentioned. Does he mean to say that the many battles fought by the three Roman heroes of the past are outweighed by the battle at Phrygia or rather by the series of battles fought during the campaign? And why is the notorious villain Catilina introduced? In order to make the reader realize that for all the glorious feats of its past, the Roman republic was finally confronted by the horrors of civil war? Is some parallel with contemporary history envisaged? There is no answer to such questions and the verdict can only be that this particular example of Amm.'s "Überbietung" leaves much to be desired.

proelia viginti Marcelli M. Claudius Marcellus, consul in 222 B.C. and one of Rome's leading generals in the Second Punic War; see Broughton, 1951, 222–3. Plin. *Nat.* 7.92 mentions thirty-nine battles, and so does Sol. 1.107.

Sicinium Dentatum L. Sicinius Dentatus, also called L. Siccius Dentatus, was *tribunus plebis* in 454 B.C.; Broughton, 1951, 43; 1986, 199. He was considered to be an exemplary soldier who according to V. Max. 3.2.24 fought in 120 battles, saved the lives of fourteen compatriots, received forty-five wounds in his chest (and none in

CHAPTER 3.13

his back), participated in nine triumphs and received many awards: *praeferebantur enim aureae coronae octo, civicae quattuordecim, murales tres, obsidionalis una, torques octoginta tres, armillae centum sexaginta, hastae octodecim, phalerae quinque et viginti, ornamenta etiam legioni, nedum militi satis multa.* Gel. 2.11 calls him the Roman Achilles. See further Liv. 3.43; Plin. *Nat.* 7.101; Dion. Hal. 10.37; Sol. 1.102. In 27.10.16 Amm. compares a *scutarius* by the name of Natuspardo with Sicinius and Sergius (see below): *Natuspardo...exsertus ita bellator, ut Sicinio veteri comparetur et Sergio.* For the use of exempla by Amm., see Blockley, 1975, ch. IX, Blockley, 1994 and Wittchow, 2000, 15–71 and 154–226.

Sergium M. Sergius Silus, greatgrandfather of Catilina. Plin. *Nat.* 7.104 describes his courageous deeds in the Second Punic War; however, his good name was somewhat diminished by his greatgrandson: *M. Sergio...nemo quemquam hominum iure praetulerit, licet pronepos Catilina gratiam nomini deroget*; also Sol. 1.105.

cuius posteritatis ultimus Catilina claras gloriarum adoreas sempiternis maculis obumbravit The use of the words *posteritas, adorea* and *obumbrare* clearly betrays its origin in Sol. 1.105 *nisi heres in posteritatis eius successione Catilina tantas adoreas odio damnati nominis obumbrasset.* Amm., however, has adapted the original sentence, with *sempiternis maculis* for *odio damnati nominis* as the most conspicuous substitution: not merely the bad reputation of the discredited name Sergius, but eternal stains darkened M. Sergius Silus' glory. See for *adorea* the relevant note ad 20.4.1; *gloriarum* can be regarded as a gen. identitatis. Cf. for *sempiternus* in a negative context 14.5.6 *facinus impium, quod Constanti tempus nota inusserat sempiterna*, for *maculis* 16.12.31 *elutis pristinis maculis* and for *obumbravit* 15.2.10 *iustitia concinnatis mendaciis obumbrata.*

In Late Antiquity Catilina remained *the* example of villainy; cf. Eutr. 6.15.1 *ingenii pravissimi*, HA *AC* 3.5 *nec defuerunt qui illum Catilinam vocarent, cum et ipse se ita gauderet apellari, addens futurum se Sergium si dialogistam occidisset, Antoninum hoc nomine significans*, August. *Conf.* 2.5.11 (in the well-known passage on the theft of pears): *vaecordi et nimis crudeli homine*, Prud. *c. Symm.* 1.529–30 *multos Catilinas/ ille domo pepulit*, Sidon. *epist.* 2.1.1 *Catilina saeculi nostri.* Perhaps the most remarkable example of this ongoing bad reputation is Sulpicius Severus' use of Sallust's portrait of Catilina as a model for his assessment of the notorious heretic Priscillian; see Fontaine, 1975.

84   COMMENTARY

3.14   The description of events in this section corresponds with that of
Zos. 3.29.2–4, although the latter has other details than Amm.,
among them that troops led by Hormisdas were attacked by a Persian
contingent, that the Romans were put to flight, and that sixty Roman
soldiers managed to capture a Persian fortress, to be identified with
Amm.'s Sumere (25.6.4) which they were able to hold for three days.
See Paschoud n. 86.

deformabat tamen tristitia laetiores eventus   The best parallel for this
instance of *deformare*, 'to spoil', is Liv. *per.* 18 *res…prospere gestas
deformaverunt naufragia classium.*

post discessum ducis   One might be tempted to interpret *discessum* as a
euphemism for 'death', as in Cic. *Div.* 1.47 *'O praeclarum discessum,'
inquit, 'e vita'*, but this would not tally at all with the author's
presentation of the sequence of events. In his report Julian died
after the end of the fighting. See for *dux* in a general, non-technical,
sense ('commander') the note ad 21.7.1.

cornu dextro   Cf. Zon. 13.13.15; see the note above ad 25.3.4 *ex alia
parte.* The left wing had to give way in the Persian attack, as Amm. had
reported in §4 of this chapter. The right wing put up more resistance
and was able to chase the Persians and to capture a fortress (25.6.4).
It is not immediately evident what Amm. means by *cornu.* As he had
reported in 25.3.2, the army was marching in an *agmen quadratum*
formation. The latter was built up of various units; see Nicasie, 1998,
199ff. In all probability *cornu dextro* refers to the units marching on
the right flank and *cornu sinistro* to those on the left flank, closest to
the Tigris.

Anatolio interfecto, qui tunc erat officiorum magister   See for Anatolius
the note ad 20.9.8 *libellis antea respondentem.* Zos. 3.29.2–3 adds that
Anatolius was killed after forces from a Persian fortress had attacked
Roman forces led by Hormisdas: λόχοι δέ τινες ἀπὸ φρουρίου Περσικοῦ
τοῖς ὑπὸ Ὁρμίσδην τεταγμέμοις ἐπιθέμενοι κατέστησαν εἰς χεῖρας. Μάχης
δὲ καρτερᾶς γενομένης ἔπεσεν Ἀνατόλιος ὁ τῶν περὶ τὴν αὐλὴν ἡγούμενος
τάξεων, ὃν καλοῦσι Ῥωμαῖοι μάγιστρον. Anatolius' body was found later
and buried hastily at the fortress Sumere; 25.6.4 *cum ad castellum
Sumere nomine citis passibus tenderemus, iacens Anatolii corpus est agnitum,
quod tumultuaria opera terrae mandatum est.* Zos. 3.30.4 ἐν τούτοις
εὑρόντες τὸ Ἀνατολίου σῶμα, ταφῆς ἠξίωσαν ἧς ὁ καιρὸς ἐδίδου. For
the function of *magister officiorum* see the note ad 20.2.2.

CHAPTER 3.14

Salutius praefectus actus in exitium praeceps et opera sui apparitoris ereptus
For Salutius see the notes ad 22.3.1 and 23.5.6. In this book we
meet him again in 25.3.21, 25.5.3 and 25.7.7; for his office see the
notes ad 21.6.5 *Anatolio* and 23.5.6 *quem praefectus*; cf. now also Migl,
1994; Moro, 1996; Gutsfeld, 1998. Zosimus 3.29.3 says that he fell
from his horse and that he, as Amm. also reports, was saved by an
adjutant (whose name is not known): Σαλούστιος ὁ τῆς αὐλῆς ὕπαρχος,
ἐκπεσὼν τοῦ ἵππου, μικροῦ κατεσφάγη τῶν πολεμίων ἐπικειμένων, εἰ μὴ
τῶν ὑπηρετῶν τις ἀποβὰς τοῦ ἵππου δέδωκεν αὐτῷ ῥαστώνην φυγῆς. See
for *actus in exitium praeceps* the note ad 22.11.7 and for *apparitor* the
note ad 23.5.6.

Phosporio amisso consiliario Phosphorius (*PLRE* I, Phosphorius 1) is
only known from this passage. The term *consiliarius* usually denotes
'a person who provides advice', but as a t.t. it can also mean 'a
member of the consistorium'; see the note ad 21.9.8. In the absence
of other information about Phosphorius it is impossible to establish
the specific meaning in the present context.

*et fugam…palatini quidam militesque per multa discrimina occupato castelli
vicini praesidio post diem denique tertium iungi exercitui potuerunt* Zosimus relates that because of the Persian attack the Romans were put
to flight, among them Salutius, together with two contingents of
Scutarii. According to Zos. 3.29.4, sixty Roman soldiers managed
to occupy the Persian fort, (apparently the φρουρίον Περσικόν of
which Zos. 3.29.2 speaks), for three days, after which they were
released by a considerable Roman army. Cf. 25.6.4 *hic et* [sc. Sumere]
*milites sexaginta cum palatinis recepimus, quos in munimentum † vaccatum
confugisse rettulimus.* Many apparently made it back to the Roman
camp; Salutius, at least, was present when Julian died (25.3.21).
V's impossible *et fugam quidam militesque* has given rise to various
conjectures. Because 25.6.4 *milites sexaginta cum palatinis* evidently
refers to the present passage, Mommsen has proposed to replace *et
fugam* by *palatini*. Petschenig, 1892, 681 says: "Es ist zu schreiben casu
evasit et pagani (fu = pa, m = ni) quidam militesque. Denn von den
Entkommenen heisst es später 6,4 hic (im Kastell Sumere) et milites
sexaginta cum palatinis (dies waren die Civilpersonen) recepimus".
This solution may be clever from a paleographical point of view,
but it would result in Amm.'s only instance of *paganus*. Češka, 1974,
95, apart from proposing a different punctuation *aderat, casu evasit*,
suggests *et fuga⟨ti palati⟩ni quidam*, which has persuaded Fontaine,
perhaps rightly.

86 COMMENTARY

Kellerbauer, 1871, 20–1 is quite sure that in 25.6.4 one should read *vacuum* and here *vacui*: "dass das betr. Blockhaus leer gewesen, bedarf wol kein Beweisführung". There is, however, in itself nothing wrong with *vicini*: cf. 14.11.15 *in vicinis oppidis*, but cf. the note ad 25.6.4 *hic et milites*. See for *iungi* the note ad 21.12.22 *bellicoso iungi rectori*.

3.15–20 Julian entered the stage of the *Res Gestae* in chapter 8 of book 15, when Constantius introduced the *elucentis industriae iuvenem* (15.8.8) to his troops. At that moment he was only a κωφὸν πρόσωπον, whispering to himself a verse from the *Iliad*. Although he will remain a point of reference and comparison in the rest of the *Res Gestae*, here his active role ends and the author honours him in the best way possible, by letting him take the floor for a valedictory speech. In this speech Julian expounds the fundamental principles which had guided him throughout his life and his reign as emperor. Of course, the speech has been composed by the author, and, by making a competent use of motifs from literary and philosophic traditions, Amm. goes out of his way to lend Julian's *ultima verba* an impressive and persuasive power. Specific details are not touched upon, the speech is entirely about truly basic guidelines. In this respect the passage differs markedly from the necrology in chapter 4, where for all the author's biased feelings towards his hero, a pragmatic appraisal of Julian's weak and strong points dictates the structure of the passage. In the present chapter the protagonist is given every opportunity to explain in person his main concerns.

Libanius is the first author to compare Julian's last hours with Socrates' final night in prison: ἐῴκει δὴ ἡ σκηνὴ μὲν τῷ δεξαμένῳ δεσμωτηρίῳ τὸν Σωκράτην, οἱ παρόντες δὲ τοῖς ἐκείνῳ παροῦσιν, ἡ πληγὴ δὲ τῷ φαρμάκῳ, τὰ ῥήματα δὲ τοῖς ῥήμασι, τῷ δὲ μὴ δακρῦσαι τὸν Σωκράτην μόνον τὸ μηδὲ τοῦτον, "the tent in which he was laid down was like the prison that had held Socrates, the company like the company there, his wound the poison, and his words those of Socrates. Socrates was the only one not to be in tears; so was he" (*Or.* 18.272, tr. Norman). Following in these steps, many scholars have assumed that the entire deathbed scene is derived from Plato's *Phaedo*, specifically the last part of this dialogue. See for the similarities between Plato and Amm. Scheda, 1966, 380–1, who lists the resemblances between Socrates' and Julian's last moments.

Blockley, 1975, 102 n. 158 thinks that "the scene could be authentic, since Julian...may well have tried to imitate Socrates." Considering his erudition and familiarity with philosophic ideas,

CHAPTER 3.15–20

Julian would have been able to hold the fine speech which Amm. gives to him; Matthews, 506–7: "Julian was well able to conceive such a scene." However, it is not very likely that his physical condition would have allowed him to do so. Geffcken, 1914, 168 has sincere doubts about the Socratic presentation of Julian's death: "Ich habe hier meine Zweifel gegen Ammian... Die antike Geschichtsschreibung lässt auch Andere so sokratisch sterben." The same opinion is expressed by Bowersock, 1978, 116: "Whether he made a wise, philosophic discourse to his friends from his death-bed, as Ammianus would have us believe, is open to doubt. The Socratic parallel is too obvious." "Ammianus' representation of Julian's last moments...is a highly artistic handling of the facts that had been passed down to him [Ammianus], and he evidently displays his familiarity with other authors who wrote on the deaths of famous men, Plato in the first place" (Teitler, 2000, 75). However, it is perfectly possible that Julian did converse with those standing around his deathbed and that philosophical ideas about death and dying and reflections on life were part of that conversation. Maybe Amm. included Julian's remarks in this speech which he composed, in order to portray the philosopher-king and to make up the balance of his life as well as of his political and military actions.

Other sources of inspiration for our author may have been the famous death scenes of Cato (e.g. Plut. *Cat. Min.* 69–70), and the last moments of Seneca and the Stoic Thrasea Paetus as described by Tac. *Ann.* 15.63–4 and 16.34–5. Taisne, 1992, 247–8 sees in Julian's last hours an evocation of Tacitus; he considers the deathbed scene in general to be a contamination of various stories given by Tacitus about Seneca, Thrasea and Otho *(Hist.* 2.46–9): "il est remarquable que la mort de Julien, à la fois prince et philosophe, représente en quelque sorte une *contaminatio* des différents récits de Tacite". On these last moments, and especially on the last words which famous figures from Antiquity are recorded to have spoken, consult Schmidt, 1914.

In some of the various views reported above there is a distinct tendency to overlook that the farewell speech as such does not contain anything particularly reminiscent of the *Phaedo*. In fact, the speech should above all be regarded as the climax in the series of speeches held by Julian in the *Res Gestae*: 16.12.9–12, 20.5.3–7, 21.13.10–5, 23.5.16–23, 24.3.4–7, a climax as well as a contrast: the earlier speeches focused on tasks immediately at hand, the present one reviews the constants in the whole of his career. As will become evident in the notes, Amm. employs topoi from various genres.

88   COMMENTARY

3.15 *Quae dum ita aguntur, Iulianus in tabernaculo iacens circumstantes allo-
cutus est demissos et tristes* See for the stereotyped temporal clause
the note on 21.3.1. The *circumstantes* must have been those who
were close to Julian. Among them were the philosophers Priscus and
Maximus (25.3.23), the prefect Salutius (25.3.21) and no doubt
Julian's doctor Oribasius (Philost. *HE* 7.15, Lyd. *Mens. 4.118*). If he
had not already been killed, Anatolius would have been there; see
25.3.21. See for *demissos et tristes* the note on 20.5.10 *ibo demissus*
and cf. Hagendahl, 1924, 176 for some similar cases of 'Synonymenhäufung'. Zosimus does not mention a deathbed speech; Ruf. Fest.
28 alludes to it without saying anything about its contents: *animam
multa suos adlocutus efflavit.* Agozzino, 1972, 130 refers to Tac. *Ann.*
2.71.1 about the dying Germanicus: *adsistentes amicos in hunc modum
adloquitur;* on p. 198 he brings out the sharp contrast between the
two speeches.

advenit, o socii, nunc abeundi tempus e vita The interjection *o* is very rare
in Amm.; its only other occurrences are 16.12.30 *o socii*, 22.5.5 and
29.2.18. It signals a heightening of the emotion, which is appropriate
at this crucial and sollemn moment. The phrase *abire e vita* also occurs
in 21.15.3 and 22.14.7; in 14.5.8, 14.11.27, 21.1.6 and 23.6.44 one
finds the more usual *excedere e vita*, and in 28.4.15 *discedere e vita*. Cf.
also Socrates' words in Pl. *Ap.* 42 a: ἀλλὰ γὰρ ἤδη ὥρα ἀπιέναι.

impendio tempestivum This is a powerful version of a topos in consolationes, viz. the opportunity of death; see Johann, 1968, 108–9.
However, Julian's development of the idea differs considerably from
the usual pattern, in which the protection against possible future
adversity is stressed. At the end of the speech it becomes fully clear
why Julian is so certain that his departure is timely. See for *impendio*
the note ad 20.7.1. The combination *impendio tempestivus* also occurs
in 19.8.6, 26.6.11, 27.2.3, 28.5.15. Here, however, in combination
with the 'figura etymologica' *tempus...tempestivum* it emphasizes the
paradox of a 'timely death'. See for this phrase Aus. *Ludus sapientium*
61 *sed καιρὸς iste tempestivum tempus est,* and 204.
    Julian himself in his *Hymn to Helios* had expressed the wish not
only for a virtuous life and for wisdom, but also for a gentle death
at a fitting hour; *Or.* 11, 158 b εὔχομαι...θεῖον νοῦν ἀπαλλαγήν τε τὴν
εἱμαρμένην ἐκ τοῦ βίου πραοτάτην ἐν καιρῷ τῷ προσήκοντι. In his *Hymn
to Cybele* he had prayed for a painless and glorious death; *Or.* 8, 180
c τὸ τοῦ βίου πέρας ἄλυπόν τε καὶ εὐδόκιμον. See also Jul. *Ep.* 201, 412
c, addressed to a certain Himerius on the occasion of the death of

CHAPTER 3.15   89

the latter's wife, where Julian refers to the topoi about death, i.e. that it happens to us all, and that we have to accept it and overcome our grief; it should be noted that the authenticity of this letter is not certain (Bidez, 1972³, 221). In his letter to the Alexandrians (*Ep.* 59, 443 b) where he refers to Constantius' death, he says that death is one's fate: ἐπεὶ δὲ ἐκείνῳ συνέβη θεῶν ἐθελόντων ἐνθένδε ἐκεῖσε πορευθῆναι τὴν εἱμαρμένην πορείαν.

The Christian sources show a Julian who did not accept his death, but an emperor who died full of anger because the Christians had got their way; Thdt. *HE* 3.25.7 Νενίκηκας Γαλιλαῖε; *Art. Pass.* 69 νενίκηκας, Χριστέ. χοράσθητι, Γαλιλαῖε; Zon. 13.13.21 κορέσθητι, Ναζωραῖε.

quam reposcenti naturae ut debitor bonae fidei redditurus exsulto Apart from Prop. 2.1.71 *quandocumque igitur vitam mea fata reposcent*, by far the clearest parallel is Sen. *Cons. Pol.* 11.3 *quisquis ad vitam editur, ad mortem destinatur. Gaudeamus eo quod dabitur, reddamusque id cum reposcemur.* Cf. also Cic. *Tusc.* 1.93 *Pellantur ergo istae ineptiae paene aniles, ante tempus mori miserum esse. Quod tandem tempus? Naturaene? At ea quidem dedit usuram vitae tamquam pecuniae nulla praestituta die.* Personified *natura* reminds one of the famous prosopopoeia in Lucr. 3.391 sqq., where her speech, of course, has an Epicurean flavour. See for *bona fides* in a context of obligations TLL VI 1.681.35–65. Inexplicably, Valesius refers to M. Ant. 3.5.2 οἷος ἂν εἴη τις περιμένων τὸ ἀνακλητικὸν ἐκ τοῦ βίου εὔλυτος, "as one who awaits the signal of recall from life in all readiness" (tr. Haines), and notes "eadem utitur metaphora qua Iulianus hoc loco." In fact, Julian's metaphor belongs to an entirely different sphere, viz. monetary or commercial transactions. Cf. Sen. *Cons. Marc.* 10.2 in a passage on man's possessions: *nos oportet in promptu habere quae in certum diem data sunt, et appellatos sine querella reddere: pessimi debitoris est creditori facere convicium.*

The verb *exsultare* is quite frequent in Amm. and not always used 'in bonam partem', as is shown by Seager 44–5, who also explicitly mentions some positive cases, among which the present text and e.g. 23.3.7 *exsultans pernoctavit et laetus* (q.v.).

ut quidam opinantur This parenthesis is puzzling. One can hardly assume that Julian means 'as some (of you?, of my enemies?) are supposing at this very moment'. It is better to interpret the words as shorthand for 'as some people are inclined to think, when a comparatively young person at the height of his career is suddenly confronted with death'. Or is the author making Julian react to

90 COMMENTARY

later stories about his feelings in the face of death? In any case, the attentive reader will have noticed the sharp contrast with Constantius: *deflebat exitium* (21.15.2).

philosophorum sententia generali perdoctus Julian owes his fundamental conviction to his thorough study (*perdoctus*) of those philosophers who share the principle of the soul's superiority over the body.

laetandum esse potiusquam dolendum Cf. *negotium laetitiae fuit potiusquam timori* (31.4.4). Julian's reasoning can be rephrased as follows: when (what is in) a better state is separated from (what is in) a worse state, there is reason for joy; the soul is a happier entity than the body; ergo, I have no reason to be dejected. The reason of the 'happiness' of Julian's soul will become fully clear in § 17. In *Or.* 7, 223 c (*To the Cynic Herakleios*) Julian remarks that death is not an evil: τίνα ἐθεράπευσας πενθοῦντα, τῷ λόγῳ διδάξας, ὅτι μὴ κακὸν ὁ θάνατος μήτε τῷ παθόντι μήτε τοῖς οἰκείοις αὐτοῦ; this remark is made in the context of a discussion about (the lack of) personal achievements of Herakleios.

illud quoque advertens, quod etiam dii caelestes quibusdam piissimis mortem tamquam summum praemium persolverunt Note that *illud quoque advertens* is a specifically religious addition to the preceding philosophical argument which is decisive in its own right. With *etiam* Amm. explicitly adds the practical decisions of the gods to the philosophers' reflections. This is quite similar to the pattern in (ps.?) Plutarch's *Consolatio ad Apollonium* 14. After a philosophical argument about the advantage of being liberated τῆς τοῦ σώματος ἀφροσύνης in ch. 13, the author continues with Λέγεται δὲ τούτοις μαρτυρεῖν καὶ τὸ θεῖον. Πολλοὺς γὰρ παρειλήφαμεν δι' εὐσέβειαν παρὰ θεῶν ταύτης τυχόντας τῆς δωρεᾶς (108 e). Then follow the traditional examples of Cleobis and Biton, and Trophonius and Agamedes; Cic. *Tusc.* 1.113–4 based resp. on Hdt. 1.31 and Pind. *frg.* 2.3. They died after honouring the gods. Cic. *Tusc.* 1.115–6 has more examples – derived from the *Consolatio* of Crantor (*c.* 335–275 B.C.) – of happy and noble deaths.

The 'heavenly gods' also occur in 19.10.3 and 21.14.5: in both cases in the words or reflections of others. Amm. himself prefers the singular; see Rike, 1987, 31–4. He makes Julian also use it in 21.5.3, but the plural of the present text is quite natural on the lips of a man who honoured so many gods and who in the prayer at the end of his treatise *Hymn to Cybele* i.a. asked her: δίδου πᾶσι μὲν ἀνθρώποις εὐδαιμονίαν, ἧς τὸ κεφάλαιον ἡ τῶν θεῶν γνῶσίς ἐστι (*Or.* 8.180 a).

CHAPTER 3.16 91

munus autem id mihi delatum optime scio, ne difficultatibus succumberem **3.16**
arduis Cf. for the structure of the sentence Tac. *Ann.* 3.65.1 *prae-*
cipuum munus annalium reor ne virtutes sileantur and also Cic. *Fin.* 4.38
hoc munus est ut efficiat ut etc. TLL II 2117.5–34 lists a number of cases
in which *bene* is used in combination with verbs of knowing (*nosse,*
intellegere, scire), and *ego me nunc volo ius pontificium optime scire* (Cato
fr. 197 Malcovati = Gel. 1.12.17) could be regarded as a clear example for *optime* as an adverb of degree. Such a sense suits the present
context too, but less so than in the case of Cato, where a thorough
knowledge of an extensive dossier is expressed. Add to this the fact
that in none of Amm.'s instances of *scire* any adverb of degree occurs.
Such reflections give rise to the question whether *optime* should not
be interpreted as an "Urteilsadverb" (Szantyr 827); cf. *bene dispereo*
(Plaut. *Stich.* 753), *male terrore veneratio adquiritur* (Plin. *Ep.* 8.24.6).
Here *optime scio* could express 'it fits in very well that I know'.

Amm.'s only other instance of *succumbere* is 15.8.2, where Constantius declares *succumbere tot necessitatibus tamque crebris unum se*, a
curious contrast with Julian's words here.

neve me proiciam umquam aut prosternam Hagendahl, 1924, 185 lists
the two verbs as a case of 'Synonymenhäufung'. See Szantyr 552 on
departures from the rules of the *consecutio temporum*. Perhaps here
Julian's past life is referred to with imp. s*uccumberem* and the present
situation with *proiciam* and *prosternam*.

expertus, quod dolores omnes ut insultant ignavis, ita persistentibus cedunt
In their translations Rolfe ("for experience teaches me") and Hamilton ("for I have learnt from experience") rightly make this the
explicit source of Julian's knowledge that it is his task never to give in
to problems from outside (*difficultatibus*); for experience has shown
him that emotional reactions (πάθη), e.g. distress (*dolores*), rejoice
in weaklings, but keep out of the way of those who stay the distance.
Cf. Cic. *Tusc.* 2.54 *ut onera contentis corporibus facilius feruntur, remissis*
opprimunt, simillime animus intentione sua depellit pressum omnem pon-
derum, remissione autem sic urgetur ut se nequeat extollere.

Whereas the preceding section concerned the way in which Julian **3.17**
coped with the arduous problems he was confronted with, here the
focus is on what he did on his own initiative.

recordatio stringit See for *stringere* the note ad 20.11.2. Agozzino ad
loc. aptly quotes Cic. *Sen.* 9 *conscientia bene actae vitae multorumque*

92   COMMENTARY

benefactorum recordatio iucundissima est (see also Powell's note ad loc.)
and the remarkable words which the Spartan Chilo, one of the seven
sages, *in vitae suae postremo* spoke *ad circumstantis amicos*: *'Dicta' inquit
'mea factaque in aetate longa pleraque omnia fuisse non paenitenda, fors
sit ut vos etiam sciatis. Ego quidem in hoc certe tempore non fallo me, nihil
esse quicquam commissum a me cuius memoria mihi aegritudini sit'* (Gel.
1.3.1–3); see also the much shorter version in D.L. 1.71: φασὶ δ᾽ αὐτόν
ποτε γηραιὸν ἤδη ὄντα εἰπεῖν ὡς οὐδὲν συνειδείη ἄνομον ἑαυτῷ ἐν τῷ βίῳ.

vel cum in umbram et angustias amendarer, vel post principatum susceptum
Julian obviously contrasts the nadir and the zenith of his life, and the
former in all probability refers to his years in Macellum, pace Brok
193, who thinks that this is an allusion to Julian's period as Caesar and
the difficulties he encountered in Gaul. Julian was exiled to Macellum
in Cappadocia by Constantius; Fontaine n. 548. The date of this exile
is debated; 342–8 is plausible (e.g. Hunt, 1998, 44; Bowersock, 1978,
25–7), but Fontaine, n. 548, following Bidez, 1930, 22 and 38–9,
has 341/342–7 and Browning, 1975, 42 has 344–50. However, the
precise text is a moot point. Seyfarth agrees with Clark, but Amm.
has no other instances of *in* + acc. with *amendare* and Fontaine n. 548
rightly points to 16.12.58 *in secretis…secessibus*, 26.10.16 *sub immensis
gurgitibus*, 27.10.15 *silvarum latebris*: in all these cases the abl. occurs
with the verb. His *in umbra et angustiis* is preferable. The second of
the nouns is due to Bentley; *angustiae* occurs often in Amm., and
at least once in the sense required here: 17.5.13 *contrusi in orientales
angustias*, "confined within the narrow limits of the East" (Hamilton).
Kiessling, 1871, 501, applauded by Michael, 1874, 17 thinks that
"vielmehr *in umbra et angulis* zu lesen ist mit beziehung auf Julians
zurückgezogenes studienleben: vgl. Cic. *de or.* I 13, 57 *de his rebus
in angulis otii consumendi causa disserant*, Seneca *Ep.* 95, 23 *liberalia
professi…desertis angulis praesident.*" Indeed, Leeman-Pinkster ad *de
Orat.* 1.57 point out that *in angulis* is a sort of topos, denoting the
four corners of a room or a lecture-hall. However, *angulus* occurs only
twice in Amm.: 27.4.8 and 30.4.14, and a reference to learned studies
seems less in place here. Fontaine's text is the best; in any case Amm.
refers to Julian's confinement in a place far removed from the action.

post principatum susceptum In Amm. the term *principatus* does not
have an ideological meaning but "s'applique à un pouvoir de fait";
Béranger, 1976, 53 and the note ad 20.4.8. *Principatus* in this passage
does not, therefore, solely denote Julian's reign as Augustus, but also
his period as Caesar.

CHAPTER 3.17   93

animum tamquam a cognatione caelitum defluentem immaculatum, ut existimo, conservavi V's text has an undeniable lacuna here: *conservavi* requires a direct object. In his 1636 edition Valesius inserted *quem* after *susceptum*. This implies that Julian's status as Caesar and emperor was derived from a kinship with the heavenly gods. Although he does not accept Valesius' textual correction, Fontaine n. 549 tries to make the idea plausible and regards the addition of *animum* by Madvig, 1884, 268 as "arbitraire". Instead he restricts himself to a more modest solution, viz. the insertion of "le petit mot *me*" after *immaculatum*. However, in the structure of the text a high-flown qualification of *principatum* is out of place. Moreover, Fontaine's interpretation is intricate and puzzling. He does not regard the text which he advocates as a more 'theological' variant of βασιλείαν ἐκ τοῦ οὐρανοῦ κατέπεμψεν εἰς τὴν γῆν ὁ θεός (Them. *Or.* 19.2, 228 a), but renders it thus: "en tant qu'il découlait de ma parenté avec les êtres célestes". Such an emphasis on his personal divine origins is definitely out of tune with the spirit of Julian's speech. Apart from this, the verb *defluere*, as will presently be shown, fits far better, where the human soul's kinship with the gods is concerned. This kinship is a decisive reason to keep it 'without blemishes' (*immaculatum*). TLL VII 1.437.14–6 notes that, apart from Luc. 2.736, Amm. 19.12.9, 21.14.5 and the present text are the only non-Christian instances of the adj. In 19.12.9 a former consul is punished with banishment, but *corpore immaculato*, "with a whole skin" (Rolfe); 21.14.5 is far more interesting: the genii who are linked with the human souls protect them *docentque maiora, si senserint puras et a colluvione peccandi immaculata corporis societate discretas*. See the note ad loc. This passage expresses a clear Platonic spirit, in that it is implied that the soul's association with the body is dangerous. Purity and purification of the soul by philosophic methods, and later by theurgy, are a hallmark of Neoplatonism; cf. Plot. *Enn.* 1.7.3 ὥσπερ τοῖς θεοῖς ἀγαθὸν μέν ἐστι, κακὸν δὲ οὐδέν, οὕτως οὐδὲ τῇ ψυχῇ τῇ σωζούσῃ τὸ καθαρὸν αὐτῆς, Jul. *Or.* 8.166 d (about Heracles' soul) ψυχῆς ἀχράντου καὶ καθαρᾶς, and Augustine's long discussion with Porphyry about the purification of the soul in *De civitate Dei* 10.23 sqq. The present text concentrates primarily on morally correct conduct, although Julian explicitly refers to the soul's origin as the reason for this: *tamquam* "expresses the feelings" of the speaker: see the note on 24.4.11 *tamquam superatura*. Cf. for the idea of heavenly kinship Plot. *Enn.* 6.4.14 Ἦ καὶ πρὸ τοῦ ταύτην τὴν γένεσιν γενέσθαι ἦμεν ἐκεῖ ἄνθρωποι ἄλλοι ὄντες καί τινες καὶ θεοί, ψυχαὶ καθαραί.

94 COMMENTARY

Cf. for *defluere* Sen. *Ep.* 120.14 *mens dei, ex quo pars et in hoc pectus mortale defluxit.* It is also a very apt verb to express 'emanation' in the Neoplatonic sense (e.g. Plot. *Enn.* 2.1.5 about the World-Soul: ἀπὸ δὲ τῆς οὐρανίας ἴνδαλμα αὐτῆς ἰὸν καὶ οἷον ἀπορρέον ἀπὸ τῶν ἄνω τὰ ἐπὶ γῆς ζῷα ποιεῖν). According to the *novi quidam viri*, "certain upstarts" (McCracken), opposed by Arnobius, *uno ex fonte omnium nostrum defluunt animae* (Arn. 2.15); Augustine, who was less dogmatic about this subject, refers to those *qui putant animas in corpora sponte defluere* (*Ep.* 143.10). Walter, 1913, 94 suggests *spiritum* instead of *animum*, but a reference to Tac. *Ann.* 16.34.1 is his only argument: there Thrasea Paetus is engaged in a discussion *de natura animae et dissociatione spiritus corporisque.* The suggestion is not implausible, but *animus* and *anima* seem to be more usual equivalents of ψυχή. It is difficult to define Amm.'s use of *anima* and the more frequent *animus.* The former can express '(breath of) life', as in 23.1.6 *animamque...efflavit*, 24.3.7 *contempturus animam* (q.v.), 31.3.3 *animam effudit*, but it is also used to indicate the immortal soul: *pronuntiarunt animas immortales* (15.9.8), *errantium...animarum* (19.12.14), *si senserint puras* (21.14.5, q.v.). In view of this it might be better to substitute Madvig's *animum* by *animam*, and consequently to read *immaculatam.*

ut existimo As in three other instances in Julian's speeches, 20.8.17 *ut aestimo* (q.v.), 21.5.6 *ut puto*, 23.5.19 *ut reor* (q.v.), the parenthesis mitigates a statement of some considerable pretension.

civilia moderatius regens et examinatis rationibus bella inferens repellens Amm. presents Julian as a good and moderate emperor who had virtues which a good monarch is expected to have, and which are described by Julian himself in his *Oratio* 3, 86b–92d ('The Heroic Deeds of the Emperor Constantius, or, On Kingship'); also Pl. *Plt.* 296e–297b; Arist. *EN* 1160 b; Cic. *Off.* 1.25, 85. Julian wanted to be regarded as a *civilis princeps*; 25.4.7 *civilitati admodum studens, tantum sibi arrogans, quantum a contemptu et insolentia distare existimabat*; see further Neri, 1984. The phrase *civilia regere* is also used in 21.16.3 and 26.8.12. In his speech to his soldiers in 21.5.2 sqq. Julian also states his moderation in domestic affairs: *domi moderatus visus sum et tranquillus* (21.5.5).

Julian is neither a hawk nor a dove. In military matters he acts in a calculated manner, carefully balancing the accounts. Translators fail to bring out the financial metaphor. See Seager 79 on Julian's military prudence. As might be expected, Blomgren 13–4 defends

CHAPTER 3.18   95

the asyndeton *inferens repellens*, using 30.9.4 *Ad inferenda propulsanda bella sollertissime cautus* as a convincing parallel. The explicit statement that wars were only started or averted after profound deliberations, may also be intended to answer those who had criticized Julian for having embarked on the Persian expedition.

tametsi prosperitas simul utilitasque consultorum non ubique concordent This is a contamination of *simul accidant* and *ubique concordent*. OLD s.v. *utilitas* 3 precisely expresses what Julian means: "the consideration of what is advantageous". Brok 193 interprets the present text as an excuse for the failure of the Persian expedition. However, in this general overview this campaign is not the only action envisaged. See Seager 79 for some other cases in which prudent plans "did not come out as intended".

quoniam coeptorum eventus superae sibi vindicant potestates This is the polytheistic version of "man proposes, God disposes". Cf. Sen. *Ep.* 14.16 *initia in potestate nostra sunt; de eventu fortuna iudicat*. TLL X 2 319.47 sqq. provides a list of cases in which *potestas*, often in the plur., denotes "dei, daemones, angeli". Verg. *A.* 10.18 *o hominum rerumque aeterna potestas* is the first example. Amm.'s other instance is 28.4.24 *superas potestates*; cf. also *substantiales potestates* (21.1.8, q.v.). See further the note ad 25.4.26 *triumphum exinde*. At no point in his speech does Julian refer explicitly to the Persian expedition. Nevertheless, the present general remark might imply the recognition that its failure was due to the higher powers. However, in books 23–25 Amm. time and again depicts Julian as ignoring the ominous signs which these powers had sent.

Discussing the present text, Roca Alamá, 1997, 246 interprets its contents as clearly belonging to the category of "verdades establecidas". The use of *quoniam* therefore tallies with classical usage in this case. See, however, the note ad 25.10.17 *et quia*.

iusti esse finem imperii oboedientium commodum et salutem Julian's basic **3.18** principle when exercising his imperial functions is here expressed in a phrase which is preceded by a long history. In Plato's *Republic* Socrates shows Thrasymachus that no ruler in his actions as a ruler τὸ αὑτῷ συμφέρον σκοπεῖ οὐδ' ἐπιτάττει, ἀλλὰ τὸ τῷ ἀρχομένῳ (*R.* 342 e); cf. further βασιλέως ἀγαθοῦ τοῦτο ἔργον ἐνόμιζε, τὸ τοὺς ἀρχομένους ὡς πλεῖστα ἀγαθὰ ποιεῖν (X. *Ag.* 7.1) and ὁ μὲν γὰρ τύραννος τὸ αὑτῷ συμφέρον σκοπεῖ, ὁ δὲ βασιλεὺς τὸ τῶν ἀρχομένων (Ar. *EN* 1160 b2–3); according to Cic. *Off.* 1.85 Plato laid down this rule for any

96   COMMENTARY

leader: *ut utilitatem civium sic tueantur ut, quaecumque agunt, ad eam rem referant, obliti commodorum suorum*; in a letter to one of his followers Iamblichus formulates it as follows: καὶ γὰρ δὴ καὶ τοῦτό ἐστι τέλος ἄρχοντος σπουδαίου τοὺς ἀρχομένους ποιεῖν εὐδαίμονας (Stob. 4.5.74); defining the decisions made by a king, Themistius says: βασιλέως λέγω βουλήν, ἧς ἔργον τὸ σῴζειν τοὺς ὑπηκόους, ὥσπερ καὶ ἑκάστης ἀρχῆς τὸ σῴζειν ὅτου ἄρχει (*Or.* 13.12, 171 c).

It is impossible to define from which particular source(s) Amm. is drawing, but it it is without any doubt a principle which he supports wholeheartedly. Commenting on the dark days of Valens, he expresses deep regret about this emperor's ignorance of the sound idea that *nihil aliud esse imperium, ut sapientes definiunt, nisi curam salutis alienae* (29.2.18). Alas, Valentinian also failed to treat his subjects as he should have done: *finis enim iusti imperii, ut sapientes docent, utilitas oboedientium aestimatur et salus* (30.8.14). Both phrases demonstrate eloquently how Julian remained 'alive' as a point of reference in the last part of the *Res Gestae*. It should, however, be added that also according to Constantius in his very first speech in the *Res Gestae* the emperor is *alienae custos salutis* (14.10.12).

ad tranquilliora semper, ut nostis, propensior fui It should be noted that *propensior...exter*(*minans*) is only provided by Gelenius. Unfortunate though this is, there is little reason for suspicion; in three other cases *propensior ad* is combined with a comparative in the neutr. pl.: *altiora* (23.5.18, q.v.), *mitiora* (28.1.44), *molliora* (30.6.3), and *minans* cannot be construed. The precise meaning of *tranquilliora* cannot be defined, but the entire phrase obviously expresses Julian's wish to avoid the escalation of conflicts. The phrase *ut nostis* also occurs in 15.8.8, 17.13.28, 20.5.4 (q.v.), *ut nosti* in 18.8.6. It refers to knowledge shared by speaker and audience. The present case stands out in that it does not concern a simple fact, but a guiding principle of the speaker.

licentiam omnem actibus meis exterminans Two other passages in the *Res Gestae* are very helpful to understand the meaning of *licentia* here. In 19.12.18, at the end of the description of a number of treason trials, Amm. says that an emperor should not rejoice in unhappy events, *ne videantur licentia regi subiecti, non potestate*, and in 29.3.1 he gives this verdict on Valentinian: *maiestati fortunae miscenti licentiam gravem.* In both contexts *licentia*, 'licentious behaviour', denotes the same thing as here: the behaviour of a tyrant; see also the note ad 21.16.6. With *actibus meis* Julian aptly refers to his actions: the proof

CHAPTER 3.18   97

of the pudding is in the eating. Fontaine n. 552 suggests that Amm. is implicitly criticizing the reign of Constantius, during which licentious behaviour and corruption were not uncommon and to which Julian put an end; see e.g. 22.4.2.

The clearest parallel of the metaphoric use of *exterminare* in the present text is Hier. *Hom. Orig. in Ier.* 3.2 *Quando exterminatur omnis confusio anima mea.*

rerum corruptricem et morum Attractive though this lapidary phrase is, it is hard to delineate the precise meaning of *rerum* and *morum*. Introducing a long quotation from Ennius' *Annales* (268–86 Sk.) about the qualities required for a friend of a highly placed person, Gellius i.a. notes that the quotation shows *quanta rerum antiquarum morumque veterum ac novorum scientia…esse convenit* (12.4.1). This differs from the present text, but both texts have in common that *res* denotes practical reality and *mores* men's moral behaviour. Here *licentia* causes things to turn out badly and consequently depraves morality. TLL IV 1068.68–75 provides only three other instances of *corruptrix*.

gaudensque abeo sciens V's *adeo* is impossible to explain. Haupt, 1842, 475 therefore conjectured "Gaudensque adeo gestiensque ubicumque u.s.w.", presumably interpreting *adeo* as "what is more" (OLD s.v. 6b), but Julian's 'itching' for dangerous tasks is incongruous. Kellerbauer, 1871, 21 notes that Julian wanted to console those who were present and then asks: "konnte er diesen Zweck besser erreichen als durch die Versicherung, er gehe gern von hinnen, er sterbe freudig?" His plausible reaction is to change *adeo* to *abeo* and to refer to 21.15.3, 22.14.7, 25.3.15 (q.v.) and 26.6.3.

ubicumque me velut imperiosa parens consideratis periculis obiecit res publica The Laws' imaginary rebuke of Socrates in case of 'desertion' in Pl. *Cri.* 50 c sqq. has set the tone for views in which the commonwealth prevails over personal predilections and interests; see e.g. λέληθεν σε ὅτι μητρός τε καὶ πατρὸς καὶ τῶν ἄλλων προγόνων πάντων τιμιώτερόν ἐστιν πατρὶς καὶ σεμνότερον καὶ ἁγιώτερον; (51a7–9, cf. also Pl. *Euthphr.* 2 c, where Socrates says about Meletus: ἔρχεται κατηγορήσων μου ὥσπερ πρὸς μητέρα πρὸς τὴν πόλιν). In his third Oration Julian has this to say about the ideal leader: εἶναι τὴν πατρίδα κοινὴν ἑστίαν καὶ μητέρα, πρεσβυτέραν μὲν καὶ σεμνοτέραν τῶν πατέρων, φιλτέραν δὲ ἀδελφῶν καὶ ξένων καὶ φίλων (89 a). See also *Or.* 4, 246 a. Scheda, 1966, 381 notices a resemblance with Plato's *Crito* (51 b).

The idea is most clearly expressed in what can be regarded as

98   COMMENTARY

Cicero's confession of political faith in *Rep.* 1.8 *Neque enim hac nos patria lege genuit aut educavit* e.q.s.

The 'commonwealth' is exercising its motherly authority (*imperiosa*) in exposing the ruler to dangers which have been examined beforehand (*consideratis*). The verb *considerare* and its cognates imply careful thought: *audacter magis quam considerate* (30.1.5), *concito quam considerato civium assultu perterriti* (31.6.3).

steti fundatus turbines calcare fortuitorum assuefactus The verb *stare* does not necessarily imply firm determination: *cum starent attoniti* (14.7.13), *territi stetere Germani* (27.2.6); this depends entirely on the context: *steterunt…antepilanis hastatisque et ordinum primis velut insolubili muro fundatis* (16.12.20) and *stetit impavidus* (16.12.27) are evidently clearer parallels to the present text. Cf. for *fundatus* 14.9.6 *fundato pectore*, 20.4.15 *mente fundata* (q.v.), 21.12.7 *mentibusque fundatis* (q.v.). As a real soldier and a man who faces his fate – for the theme see §16 of this chapter – Julian stood steadfast. For the 'Stoic' coda of Julian's statement Amm. turns to Solinus: *Heraclitus et Diogenes cynicus nihil umquam de rigore animi remiserunt, calcatisque turbinibus fortuitorum adversus omnem dolorem vel misericordiam uniformi duravere proposito* (1.73). See also the note ad 24.3.9 *mansit immobilis*.

3.19   *nec fateri pudebit* See the first note ad 20.8.9; the present phrase implies that Julian is going to reveal something which one might have expected him to keep to himself.

interiturum me ferro dudum didici fide fatidica praecinente Neither the prediction of the blond young man at Antioch, reported by Zonaras 13.13.29 (see the note ad 25.3.9) nor the oracle quoted in Eun. *fr.* 28.6 contains Julian's death 'by steel'. As Fontaine n. 554 says, this does not mean that Julian's disclosure is improbable. In 21.1.10 *Extis…fatidicis* and 22.12.8 *venas fatidicas Castalii…fontis* the adj. does not pose any problem: the entrails and the springs declare what fate has in store. The present phrase is far more difficult and can perhaps best be understood by taking into account 15.7.8 *fatidicarum sortium fidem* and 23.5.9 *fidem vaticinii Delphici* (q.v.), and assuming that *fide fatidica* here is shorthand for 'a reliable sign about the future given by a divinatory body'. TLL X 2. 440.28sqq. provides a long list of passages in which *praecinere* is "fere i.q. canere, dicere, quae ad futura pertinent". This is also the meaning in 22.12.8 and 25.10.1, whereas its musical meaning occurs in 24.6.10 and 26.3.5. See the note ad 25.3.6 *equestris hasta* about the weapon which inflicted the mortal

CHAPTER 3.19   99

wound. Another prediction is given by Amm. in 23.5.8: a lion, slain by his soldiers and brought to Julian, foretold the coming death of a king. That this king was to be Julian can be surmised from the narrative context in which the offering of the lion is set, namely after the reference to the tomb of Gordian III, which the army had just passed; Gordian was killed on his expedition against the Persians as the result of a conspiracy; 23.5.7 with the notes.

sempiternum veneror numen The same combination of noun and adj. occurs in 17.13.28, 23.5.19 (q.v.) and 31.10.18. See Camus, 1967, 134–6 for Amm.'s henotheistic use of *numen* etc.

quod non clandestinis insidiis nec longa morborum asperitate vel damnatorum fine decedo Julian obviously took the prediction that he would die *ferro* to refer to open battle, otherwise *clandestinis insidiis* would be pointless. Since this phrase also occurs in 16.12.23, 22.11.7 (q.v.), 29.5.7 and 30.1.1, it can be regarded as formulaic and the adj. as pleonastic; it could have been incorporated in Hagendahl, 1924, 202–7. Cf. 16.7.10 *vexatam asperitate morborum*, 28.1.9 *ob diuturnam morborum asperitatem*. The same gen. inversus occurs in *morborum acerbitates* (14.6.23), and *vexatus acerbitate morborum* (28.6.16).

Julian's own father, Iulius Constantius, died in 337 because the sons of Constantine had conspired against him; 25.3.23, q.v.; Jul. *Ep. ad Ath.* 270 c; Lib. *Or.* 18.31; Zos. 2.40.2. Many Roman emperors found their death as a result of machinations against their rule; Amm. mentions Gordian III (23.5.7 q.v.) and Gallus Caesar (14.11.20–3). A well-known example of an emperor who died of a terrible illness is Galerius. According to Lactantius, *mort. pers.* 33–4 he was eaten away from inside by worms while suffering terrible pains. See Meijer, 2004 for the various ways – e.g. through conspiracy, murder, illness, poisoning, (forced) suicide, or in battle – in which Roman emperors found their end.

In 17.1.14 Amm. reports that Julian's detractors ascribed his courageous conduct in all battles to the fact *quod oppetere dimicando gloriose magis optabat quam damnatorum sorte, sicut sperabat, ut frater Gallus occidi.*

in medio cursu florentium gloriarum This may well be a deliberate variation on a common complaint about death: *quare ille in medio cursu raptus est?* (Sen. *Ep.* 93.1), referred to in Sen. *Cons. Pol.* 11.4 *alium in medio cursu vita deseruit.* One might be inclined to think that 'in the midst of glorious success' is even worse, but paradoxically, in Julian's

100   COMMENTARY

eyes this is a boon, since he knows that the gods *quibusdam piissimis mortem tamquam summum praemium persolverunt* (§ 15). The wording of Amm.'s phrase can be compared to two authorial comments on Julian's career (*cursus*) as Caesar and Augustus: he was *bellorum gloriosis cursibus Traiani simillimus* (16.1.4), but by his occasional errors he clouded *gloriarum multiplices cursus* (22.10.6, q.v.). In the present text *florentium* is the most important word: Julian's successes are not merely a memory of the past, death overtakes him when his glory is in full bloom.

hunc merui clarum ex mundo digressum According to TLL V 1.1155.69–70 this is the only occurrence of *digressus* with the meaning 'death'. Amm. uses the verb *digredi* six times in this sense, in three cases combined with *vita* (17.4.14, 29.5.2, 30.1.22), and also in three with *mundo*: 21.14.2 *mundo citius digressurum* (q.v.), 29.1.39 *cum mundo digredi statuisset*, 31.2.22 *fortuitis mortibus mundo digressos*. Julian's thought tallies implicitly with Solon's famous explanation of his refusal to call Croesus truly happy in Hdt. 1.32; cf. especially ἐκεῖνο δὲ τὸ εἴρεό με οὔ κω σε ἐγὼ λέγω, πρὶν τελευτήσαντα καλῶς τὸν αἰῶνα πύθωμαι. The idea that such a judgment could only be passed at the end of a person's life became proverbial; see for this Otto, 1890, 229 (nr. 1141.3) and Bömer ad Ov. *Met.* 3.136.

aequo enim iudicio…cum sit opportunum Julian has steered clear of cowardice and fear when it mattered and this has understandably (*enim*) been rewarded by a glorious departure from life. In fact, cowardice and fear cause a person to long for death or to shrink back from it at the wrong moments. With *cum sit opportunum* Julian returns to the beginning of his speech: *impendio tempestivum*. One fails to understand why in one half of the chiastically structured alternative the ind. is used, in the other the subj. The second case is of course relevant for Julian, and possibly the subj. expresses that for him such an attitude was totally imaginary.

3.20 *vigore virium labente* Julian's physical, not his mental strength begins to fade; so *virium* is not superfluous: cf. *animi vigore collecto* (28.3.1), *vigore animi* (29.1.8).

super imperatore vero creando Cf. 20.8.6 *me creatum Caesarem*, 25.5.1 *super creando principe*. *Epit.* 43.4 also reports that Julian did not want to appoint a successor: *consulto sese de imperio nihil mandare, ne, uti solet in multitudine discrepantibus studiis,† amico ex invidia, reipublicae*

CHAPTER 3.20 101

discordia exercitus periculum pararet. Augustus is said to have done the
same; Tac. *Ann.* 1.13.2. According to Lib. *Or.* 18.273 his friends
begged Julian to appoint a successor, but he left that decision to
the army since he knew nobody as capable for the job as himself;
δεομένων δὲ τῶν φίλων ἀποφῆναι τῆς ἀρχῆς κληρονόμον οὐδένα αὐτῷ
παραπλήσιον ἐγγὺς ὁρῶν ἀφῆκε τῇ στρατιᾷ τὴν ψῆφον. That he would
have appointed Procopius as his successor is no more than a rumour,
as Amm. indicates in 26.6.3: *inter abeuntis anhelitus animae eundem
Iulianum verbo mandasse placere sibi Procopio clavos summae rei gerendae
committi.* For Procopius see the note ad 23.3.2. Lyd. *Mens.* 4.118
makes Julian name Jovian as his successor: Ἰουβιανὸν μὲν αὐτὸς
ψηφισάμενος βασιλεύειν ἐτελεύτα. Amm.'s use of *vero* here betrays
intimate familiarity with the Latin language. Kroon, 1995, 281 sqq.
analyses the function and usage of *vero*, which indicates "the speaker's
personal commitment with regard to" his statement (327). Here
it could be rendered by "you can take my word for that" (Kroon,
1998, 217), which can also imply an adversative connotation. Julian
is adamant in his refusal to name a successor.

There are not many reports of deathbed scenes in which the
dying person names his successor or at least pays serious attention
to him. The most conspicuous is X. *Cyr.* 8.7.11. The *Historia Augusta*
has three examples: *AP* 12.5, *MA* 28.6, *S.* 23.3; *H* 4.8–10 mentions
the contrasting versions of Trajan's last wishes. There are two 'negative' cases in Plutarch's *Lives*: Cato Minor forbidding his son to
engage in politics: πολιτείας ἀπεῖπεν ἅψασθαι τῷ μειρακίῳ (*Cat. Min.*
66.5) and Otho refraining from adopting his nephew Cocceianus
(*Oth.* 16.3). In Paulinus' *Life of Ambrose* the bishop, overhearing a
whispered conversation in which Simplicianus was deemed too old
to succeed him, says: *senex sed bonus* (46.1). Amm. reports that when
the envoys Theolaifus and Aligildus delivered the message of Constantius' death to Julian, they added *quod eum voce suprema successorem
suae fecerit potestatis* (22.2.1). See the note ad loc. and also the notes
ad 21.15.5.

per imprudentiam As in Amm.'s three other instances of *imprudentia*
(14.11.11, 17.13.19, 30.1.8), the word here denotes lack of knowledge, not lack of wisdom; cf. Petr. 79.2 *imprudentia locorum.* In 24.8.2
imprudens may have such a meaning too.

quem habilem reor As appears from TLL VI 2464.54–65, *habilis* when
used of a person rarely occurs without any complement and regarding the present text and 25.5.2 it is stated: "plane i.q. idoneus". In

102   COMMENTARY

Amm.'s two other instances the adj. does have a complement: *ad id negotium* (25.6.14), *ad militiam* (28.5.4).

ad discrimen ultimum V has no preposition with *discrimen ultimum*. Petschenig, 1892, 622 defends *ad* before *discrimen* in these terms: "Doch ist unzweifelhaft *ad* zwischen *o* and *d* ausgefallen". He would have sealed the matter by referring to 14.2.11 *ad discrimen ultimum* and especially to 14.10.4 *ad discrimen trusus est ultimum*.

alumnus autem rei publicae frugi opto bonum post me repperiri rectorem The old-fashioned qualification *frugi*, which denotes that a person is a worthy member of his society (see Cic. *Tusc.* 3.16 on the 'radius' of the term) is still alive in late Latin; Amm. has three other instances: 14.6.5, 16.7.8, 27.3.5. The first of these is a counterpart to the present text: (Roma) *velut frugi parens et prudens et dives Caesaribus tamquam liberis suis regenda patrimonii iura permisit.* Julian is a "besonnener Zögling" (Seyfarth) of her. As is noted ad 20.1.1, *rector* can denote any high authority.

3.21   *Post haec placide dicta* Cf. 16.12.8 (about Constantius) *genuina placiditate sermonis*, 26.7.17 (Procopius) *sermonis placiditate*, 15.8.4 (Constantius) *sermone placido*, 20.7.8 (a bishop) *placido sermone*.

familiares opes iunctioribus velut supremo distribuens stilo Fontaine n. 559 refers to 24.3.5, where Julian protests his lack of personal resources, and concludes that *opes* can only indicate his personal papers, writing material, jewels etc. Apart from undervaluing the rhetoric of Julian's words in 24.3.5, this does not give *opes* its due: this term implies more than some personal belongings. Cf. *iunctioribus proximis* (20.5.10 [q.v.] and 21.14.2). The solutions of the various translators betray their understandable problems with *velut supremo stilo*; "comme s'il rédigeait ses dernières volontés" (Fontaine) and comparable renderings are less satisfactory, since Julian is truly, not 'as if' formulating his will. One should concentrate on *stilo*: 'as if he was using his pen for the last time', an action which he was physically not capable of any more; Rolfe's "as if with the last stroke of his pen" is excellent.

Anatolium quaesivit officiorum magistrum, quem cum beatum fuisse Salutius respondisset praefectus, intellexit occisum Working through his 'list of legatees', Julian arrives at the absent Anatolius; see for him and Anatolius the relevant note ad 25.3.14. Lindenbrog's references to μαϰαϱίτης, supplemented by Brok, are certainly opportune. See

CHAPTER 3.22   103

e.g. Hsch. s.v. μακαρίτης· ὁ τεθνεώς. ὁ μακάριος, Phot. s.v. μακαρίτας
(41): τοὺς τεθνηκότας. οὕτως Μένανδρος (= Koerte *fr.* 871, Kassel and
Austin VI 2, *fr.* 554); see also the app. exeg. ad μακαρίτας (43) in
Theodoridis' edition. Cf. also Jul. *Ep. ad Ath.* 271 a τὸν μακαρίτην
ἀδελφὸν ἐμὸν Γάλλον, 274 b ἡ μακαρῖτις Εὐσεβία. In non-Christian
Latin there are no instances of *beatus* used in such a way. Even Macr.
comm. 1.11.11 *animae beatae ab omni cuiuscumque contagione corporis
liberae caelum possident* and *CE* 432.4 (about a dead son) *Elysios campos
habitans et prata ueatum* are quite far removed from this usage. So it
may well be a Grecism, and this supposition is supported by *intellexit
occisum*, Amm.'s elegant device to help the Roman reader. However,
this does not completely solve the problem: the inf. perf. *fuisse* is very
puzzling and one is tempted to assume that *beatum* is a true participle
here: Anatolius 'had already been made a blessed man'.

† *eletantem* The various solutions proposed to repair V's text either
try to find a noun to contrast with *casum* or some adverb or short
phrase to be a counterpart to *acriter*. Brakman's *letum ante*, modified
by Dufraigne's *letum antea*, printed by Fontaine, apart from the noun
being superfluous, suffers from the fact that *letum* would be a hapax
in Amm., as Fontaine n. 559 admits. The other half of the alternative
is also problematical; *elatus* certainly tallies with Amm.'s vocabulary:
elato animo (21.16.1, cf. 29.5.17), *elatior* is used about Julian in 21.4.7
(q.v.) and 22.9.1; see also the note ad 22.2.2. Yet it sounds somewhat
too 'triumphant' in the immediate context, although one could point
at *exsulto* in § 15. In defence of *laetanter* Kiessling, 1871, 501 refers
to *laetandum esse* in § 15. He might also have mentioned *gaudensque
abeo* in § 18 as a further argument for this reasonable, but still not
fully convincing emendation. Seyfarth's crux cannot be avoided.

et flentes inter haec omnes, qui aderant, auctoritate integra etiam tum   **3.22**
increpabat When Socrates had emptied the cup with the lethal
poison, his friends could no longer restrain their tears, which he
found very disappointing. He reacted by saying that he had sent
the women away precisely for this reason: καὶ γὰρ ἀκήκοα ὅτι ἐν
εὐφημίᾳ χρὴ τελευτᾶν. ἀλλ' ἡσυχίαν τε ἄγετε καὶ καρτερεῖτε (Pl. *Phd.*
117 d). These words made those who were present feel ashamed.
Comparable scenes of tears and words of reproach by the protagonist
can be found in Tac. *Ann.* 15.62 (Seneca) and 16.34 (Thrasea), and
Plut. *Cat. Min.* 69–70. It can be regarded as a structural element
in these texts and, not surprisingly, it is also present in Libanius'
description of Julian's deathbed: ἀπάντων γὰρ τῶν περιεστηκότων εἰς

104 COMMENTARY

θρῆνον πεπτωκότων καὶ οὐδὲ τῶν φιλοσοφούντων δυναμένων καρτερεῖν ἐπετίμα τοῖς τε ἄλλοις καὶ οὐχ ἥκιστα δὴ τούτοις (*Or.* 18.272). Of course, the obvious role of the literary tradition neither proves nor disproves the factual truth of the report.

In his final hour Julian still (*etiam tum*) retained his authority. Brandt, 1999, 349 rightly remarks that *auctoritas* here is "nicht die Autorität des Amtes...sondern die Autorität der Persönlichkeit". Julian dominates until the very end. There is a remarkable likeness between Libanius' ἐπετίμα and *increpabat*; see for this verb the note ad 24.2.15.

humile esse caelo sideribusque conciliatum lugeri principem dicens The adj. *humilis* can be used in a physical or a material sense: *staturae nec procerae nec humilis* (31.14.7), *humilibus...tuguriis* (17.13.12) or denote a low status: 22.9.9 *humilis et privatus*, but it can also have a moral sense, as in Horace's famous *non humilis mulier* (*Carm.* 1.37.32); cf. also e.g. *in rem tam humilem tamque contemptam* (Cic. *Amic.* 32) and especially *Quid autem tam humile ac muliebre est quam consumendum se dolori committere?* (Sen. *Cons. Pol.* 6.2). There are no clear instances of such a usage in Amm.; the present text seems unique in this respect. Moreover, here *humile* has obviously also been chosen as a contrast with the lofty destiny which is awaiting Julian. The idea that the human soul after death heads for an astral destination, either becoming a star (καταστερισμός) or having one as its abode, has a long tradition. In Aristophanes' *Pax* a slave asks Trygaeus on the latter's return from heaven: Οὐκ ἦν ἄρ' οὐδ' ἃ λέγουσι, κατὰ τὸν ἀέρα/ ὡς ἀστέρες γιγνόμεθ', ὅταν τις ἀποθάνῃ; (832–3, see Olson's note ad loc.). In Plato's *Timaeus* the Demiurge διεῖλεν ψυχὰς ἰσαρίθμους τοῖς ἄστροις, ἔνειμεν θ' ἑκάστην πρὸς ἕκαστον (41 d 8-e 1). The idea occurs in real or fictional sepulchral epigrams: αἰθὲρ μὲμ φσυχὰς ὑπεδεχσατο, σόμ[ατα δὲ χθόν (IG I² 945.6 = W. Peek, *Griechische Vers-Inschriften* 20.6), νῦν δὲ θανὼν ἀστέρας οἶκον ἔχει (*AP* 7.64.4 about Diogenes; see Häusle, 1989 and Kay ad Aus. *Epigr.* 54), ἀστὴρ γὰρ γενόμην θεῖος ἀκρεσπέριος ("der früh am Abendhimmel aufgeht", W. Peek, *Griechische Grabgedichte* 304.6), αἰθέρα δ' ὀκταέτης κατιδὼν ἄστροις ἅμα λάμπεις (*ib.* 343.5). In Lucianus' parodic *Vera Historia* 1.29 the travellers arrive in Lychnopolis, μεταξὺ τοῦ Πλείαδων καὶ τοῦ Ὑάδων ἀέρος. Instructive examples can also be found in the *Carmina Latina Epigraphica*, e.g. *sed mea divina non est itura sub umbras/ caelestis anima. mundus me sumpsit et astra,/ corpus habet tellus et saxum nomen inanae* (611.3–5), *sidera me retinent* (1363.1), and especially interesting in view of the present text: *quid o me ad sidera caeli/ ablatum quereris?*

CHAPTER 3.23 105

(1109.15–6). Concerning the origin of such ideas there is no consensus among scholars. Pythagoreanism has been advocated with verve by Cumont and Rougier, and 'astral religion' certainly was strongly present in these circles, but this was also true outside their domain; see Burkert, 1972, 357–68. In any case, as is clear from the quoted phrases, testimonies are provided by diverse sources. Obviously, it had a place within various religious and philosophical convictions.

Julian is sure that his earthly performance has 'commended' him (*conciliatum*) to the heavenly sphere of the stars. Günther, 1888, 43 is puzzled by the part. perf.: Julian is still on earth, "sed evehetur ad sidera". In his view this entails an emendation: *sideribusque conciliandum*. This is a good example of rigid and unfruitful reasoning. The perfect tense is in fact the only possible choice: it is his past which makes him confident, in Libanius' words: τῶν βεβιωμένων αὐτὸν εἰς Μακάρων νήσους ἀγόντων (*Or*. 18.272). At first sight this traditional mythological imagery seems to diverge considerably from the present text. But according to Iamblichus one of the Pythagorean 'akousmata' ran as follows: τί ἐστιν αἱ μακάρων νῆσοι; ἥλιος καὶ σελήνη (*VP* 82), and Servius notes ad Verg. *A*. 5.735: *secundum philosophos elysium est insulae fortunatae…secundum theologos circa lunarem circulum, ubi iam aer purior est: unde ait ipse Vergilius aeris in campis* (cf. also Servius' notes ad *A*. 6.640 and 887). Porphyry had given a comparable explanation of Hom.*Od*. 4.563: Πάλιν αἰνιττόμενος, ὅτι ταῖς τῶν εὐσεβῶς βεβιωκότων ψυχαῖς μετὰ τὴν τελευτὴν οἰκεῖός ἐστι τόπος ὁ περὶ τὴν σελήνην, ὑπεδήλωσεν εἰπών, "ἀλλά σ᾽ ἐς Ἠλύσιον πεδίον καὶ πείρατα γαίης / ἀθάνατοι πέμψουσιν, ὅθι ξανθὸς Ῥαδάμανθυς." Ἠλύσιον μὲν πεδίον εἰκότως προσειπὼν τὴν τῆς σελήνης ἐπιφάνειαν ὑπὸ ἡλίου καταλαμπομένην (Stob. 1.49.61 = 383F. Smith). See for further discussion and material Capelle, 1917; Lattimore, 1942; Cumont, 1949, 142–88; Boyancé, 1952; Nilsson, 1954.

cum Maximo et Prisco philosophis super animorum sublimitate perplexius   **3.23**
disputans Scholars like to refer to the discussion about the immortality of the soul in Pl. *Phd*. 70 b sqq. This is indeed justified, but one should also think of Tac. *Ann*. 15.63.3 and especially 16.34.1 (about Thrasea) *de natura animae et dissociatione spiritus corporisque inquirebat*. Within the direct context *sublimitas* can only refer to the celestial origin and subsequent essence of the human soul. See for *perplexius*, 'in considerable detail', the note ad 21.16.18. Cf. also Julian's own words: Οὐ γὰρ δὴ καὶ ἡμεῖς ἐσμεν τῶν πεπεισμένων τὰς ψυχὰς ἤτοι προαπόλλυσθαι τῶν σωμάτων ἢ συναπόλλυσθαι (*Ep*. 89a, 452 c). For Maximus see the note ad 22.7.3. For Priscus see *PLRE* I, Priscus 5

106   COMMENTARY

and Chrysos, 1980. Although Priscus was a close friend of Julian – the emperor sent him his letters 11–13 – Amm. only mentions him in this passage. Priscus was, according to Eun. *VS* 7.1.10 born in Thesprotia or Molossia; Lib. *Or.* 1.123 only mentions that he was a native of Epirus. As a philosopher he taught in Greece and possibly in Athens; Eun. *VS* 7.1.14; 7.4.4, 12; Lib. *Or.* 12.55. When Julian had become Caesar, he invited Priscus to Gaul (Jul. *Ep.* 13), and when he was Augustus, he invited him to the imperial court in Constantinople (Eun. *VS* 7.4.3–7). Priscus was in Antioch when Julian was preparing the Persian expedition (Lib. *Or.* 14.32, 34; *Ep.* 760), on which he accompanied the emperor (Jul. *Ep.* 96; Eun. *VS* 7.4.9). After the failed campaign, he returned to Antioch; Lib. *Ep.* 1426. He was, together with Maximus, arrested under Valens, but released later and allowed to return to Greece; Eun. *VS* 7.4.11–2. There he was still teaching in 390; Lib. *Ep.* 947. He was still alive in 393 (Lib. *Ep.* 1076) but seems to have died not long afterwards *c.* 395 being over ninety years of age; Eun. *VS* 8.1.11.

hiante latius suffossi lateris vulnere et spiritum tumore cohibente venarum As in the case of the wounding (§6), Amm.'s report on Julian's death is sober and states only the bare facts, which are mentioned in typically medical terms. The verb *hiare* is a medical t.t.; cf. *si vero in carne vulnus est, hiatque* e.q.s. (Cels. 5.26), *si vulnus hiat* (Cels. 7.26). Cf. also Stat. *Silv.* 2.1.4 *vulnus hiat* with Van Dam's note.

Described from a modern medical point of view, the widening of Julian's wound resulted in either valvular pneumothorax or hemorrhagic pericarditis, eventually cardiac tamponade, and possibly a combination of both. A telling symptom is the swelling of the veins in the throat area, followed by inability to breathe. In ancient medicine a direct relationship between respiration and bloodflow is generally assumed. In Galen's view blood is formed in the liver and then flows through the venous system to the various organs. Some of it enters the right side of the heart and then flows through the lungs to its left side. Any blockage in the veins would stifle respiration. In such a view the swollen veins are not so much a symptom as a cause. See Siegel, 1968, 47–56, 78–80, 135–8. Cf. also Furley-Wilkie, 1984.

Basing themselves on the tradition which is mentioned at the end of the note ad *cute bracchii* (25.3.6), viz. that Julian was hit in the abdomen, and on Philostorgius' statement that Oribasius treated Julian intensively for three days (*HE* 7.15: διὰ τριῶν ἡμερῶν), Lascaratos and Voros, 2000 develop a detailed hypothesis concerning the surgical measures which Oribasius may have taken. However,

CHAPTER 3.23 107

Amm.'s version of the events should be preferred. In all probability, he was not one of the *circumstantes* of §3, but, being nearby, he was in a position to gather firsthand information.

epota gelida aqua Scheda, 1966, 382, puts the simple fact of Julian's drinking of ice-cold water in a Socratic setting by comparing it with Socrates' drinking from the poisoned cup. This "Hineininterpretierung" does not have a foundation in Lib. *Or.* 18.272, who was the first to compare Julian's last hours with those of Socrates. Teitler, 2000, 76–8 considers it far more likely that Amm. used either the last moments of the emperor Otho – in particular because of the same wording (*gelida aqua*) – or those of the Persian king Cyrus, or both, as his example. Both rulers are said to have drunk water only moments before they died. In the case of Otho this is reported by Tac. *Hist.* 2.49.2 (*sitim haustu gelidae aquae sedavit*), Suet. *Otho* 11.2 (*sedata siti gelidae aquae potione*) and Plut. *Otho* 17.1 (Ἤδη δε ἑσπέρας οὔσης ἐδίψησε, καὶ πιὼν ὀλίγον ὕδατος). The example of Cyrus comes from Xenophon's *Cyropaedia*, a work with which Amm. was probably well acquainted (see e.g. the note ad 21.9.2). While dying Cyrus drank eagerly: διψῆν δ' ἐδόκει, καὶ ἔπιεν ἡδέως (X. *Cyr.* 8.7.4). These striking resemblances do not rule out that Amm. had Socrates' final moments in mind when writing Julian's deathbed scene, but they make it more likely that he thought of the last moments of Cyrus, and possibly those of Otho. Interesting in this respect is also that especially the combination Socrates – Cyrus was not unfamiliar; already Cicero in his *De Senectute* (78–9) had referred in the same breath to Socrates' discussion of the immortality of the soul (*quae Socrates supremo vitae die de immortalitate animorum disseruisset*) and to Cyrus' last words in the *Cyropaedia* (*apud Xenophontem autem moriens Cyrus maior haec dixit*).

medio noctis horrore See for this phrase the note ad 21.2.2. A similar time is mentioned by *epit.* 43.4 *circa noctis fere medium defecit*. Malalas *Chron.* 13.332, referring to Magnus, reports that Julian died during the night. A different time is mentioned in Pall. *h. Laus.* 4.4: Didymus the Blind had a vision in which he received this message: σήμερον ἑβδόμην ὥραν ἐτελεύτησεν Ἰουλιανός. Soz. *HE* 6.2.7 is less precise about the same event: περὶ τήνδε τὴν ὥραν Ἰουλιανὸν ἀνῃρῆσθαι. Thdt. *HE* 3.24.2 has a comparable story about Iulianus Sabbas, and Malalas *Chron.* 13.333–4 and *Chron. Pasch. a.* 363 about Basil of Caesarea. There are other examples of holy men being informed of the death of a person far away on the very day or even at the exact hour of

108   COMMENTARY

the event. The most famous is the vision of Apollonius of Tyana at Ephesus, in which he witnessed the murder of the emperor Domitian at Rome (Philostr. *VA* 8.26 and D.C. 67.18). See also Athan. *V. Anton.* 60.1–3.

vita facilius est absolutus   In view of the medical details *facilius* is difficult to understand. Hagendahl, 1921, 101 lists *vita absolvi* among the many synonyms for 'to die'. The only other case seems to be Amm. 27.11.1 *Volcacio Rufino absoluto vita.* One cannot help pondering whether in the present context the expression could have some connection with the contents of Servius' note ad *A.* 5.735: *elysium* ἀπὸ τῆς λύσεως, *ab absolutione.*

anno aetatis altero et tricesimo, natus apud Constantinopolim   This passage is one of the indications for Julian's year of birth. There are several other sources which supply information. According to *epit.* 42.12 Julian became Caesar (on 6 Nov. 355) *annos natum fere tres atque viginti.* In his *Ep.* 111, 434 d, written at the end of 362, Julian mentions that until his twentieth year he was a Christian but that for the last twelve years he had venerated the gods. Socrates, *HE* 3.1.8 and Sozomen, *HE* 5.2.9 report that Julian was about eight years of age when his family was killed in 337. A scholiast's note on *Anth. Gr.* 14.148 mentions that Julian celebrated his birthday when he was near Ctesiphon, which was at the end of May or the beginning of June; see the note ad 24.6.3 *utque lassitudini.* Based on this information one can conclude that Julian was born in either 331 or 332. According to Bowersock, 1978, 22 the most likely year of birth is 331; so also Bidez, 1930, 10. *PLRE* I, Iulianus 29, suggests that he was born in May/June 332; also e.g. Browning, 1975, 32. For a discussion in favour of 331, see Bowersock, 1977, 203–4; for a similar one in favour of 332, see Gilliard, 1971. Amm.'s words clearly indicate that Julian died in his thirty-second year, meaning that he was not yet thirty-two; this makes it likely that he was born in 332, possibly in May/June. See Paschoud n. 14 and the note ad 22.5.4 *vixdum adulescens.*

parentis obitu destitutus   Cf. for *destitutus*, 'bereaved', Apul. *Met.* 3.8.3 *parvuli huius in primis annis destituti,* August. *C.D.* 22.8.22 *matris recenti patris eorum obitu destitutae.*

Constanti, quem post fratris Constantini excessum inter complures alios turba consumpsit imperii successorum   See *PLRE* I, Iulius Constantius 7 and

CHAPTER 3.23

Martindale, 1980, 481; Barnes, 1982, 108. Iulius Constantius was the son of Constantius I (Chlorus) and Theodora, and hence half-brother of Constantine the Great. He was married twice; first to Galla, from which marriage Gallus Caesar was born (Lib. *Or.* 18.10) and subsequently to Basilina who gave him Julian; Lib. *Or.* 18.9; cf. e.g. Socr. *HE* 3.1.6–7 and Soz. *HE* 5.2.8. He also had another son who was older than Gallus and Julian; Jul. *Ep. ad Ath.* 270 d. He lived for a while in exile in Toulouse (Aus. *Prof.* 17.11–2) and Corinth (Lib. *Or.* 14.29–31; Jul. *Ep.* 20). He was rehabilitated by Constantine who gave him the title of *patricius* and made him consul in 335 together with Ceionius Rufius Albinus; Bagnall et al., 1987, 204–5. In the same year he was made *nobilissimus*; Zos. 2.39.2. In the strife for the succession of Constantine, Julius Constantius was murdered by the soldiers of Constantine's sons at Constantinople in 337; Jul. *Ep. ad Ath.* 270 c; Lib. *Or.* 18.31; Zos. 2.40.2. See the notes ad 20.8.11 *caritate sanguinis* and 21.16.8 *cunctos sanguine* and add to the literature mentioned there Di Maio-Arnold, 1992. See for sing. *turba* meaning 'riot', 'turmoil' the note ad 20.4.6, and for *consumere* referring to violent death the note ad 20.11.12.

et Basilina matre iam inde a maioribus nobili Cf. *PLRE* I, Basilina. She was the daughter of PPO Iulius Iulianus and the second wife of Iulius Constantius; Lib. *Or.* 18.8–9. She died at a young age, a few months after the birth of Julian; Jul. *Mis.* 352 b. She was a Christian and had donated lands to the church in Ephesus; Pall. *Dial.* 13.169–70; Photius *Bibl.* 96. She seems to have had Arian sympathies; Athan. *Hist. Ar.* 5. In her honour Basilinopolis in Bithynia was named after her by Julian.

The syntactical function of this phrase is unclear because of the author's major change in the structure of the entire sentence. In its basic form this would have been: *natus apud Constantinopolim, patre Constantio et Basilina matre.* However, by introducing a reference to the circumstances of the death of Julian's father Amm. completely altered the second element, without regard for the consequences this had for the third element.

CHAPTER 4

Introduction

After his impressive account of Julian's death in chapter 3, Ammianus brings the history of Julian, who has dominated books 15–25 of his *Res Gestae*, to an end with an elaborate epilogue or elogium, in which he strives to present a balanced judgment of his hero. Other major characters in his work receive the same treatment, the most important being Constantius (21.16) and Valentinian (30.7–9). According to Leo, 1901, 236–40 these sections betray the influence of imperial biography on Ammianus' work, which as a whole belongs firmly to the genre of historiography. However, the categories treated in the two genres are not identical, and it is far more likely that Ammianus took as his model Tacitus, who in his *Annals* inserted comparable accounts of the lives of Augustus (1.9–10) and Tiberius (6.51), to name only the two most famous examples.

The chapter does betray the influence of another genre, viz. the panegyric. The elogia of Constantius, Julian and Valentinian have in common that they consist of a detailed discussion of the *bona* and *vitia* of these emperors, but only in the case of Julian are the *bona* grouped according to the cardinal virtues. As Gaertner, 1968, Classen, 1979 and Blockley, 1975 have shown, this scheme is regularly employed in Greek and Latin panegyrical literature, and explicitly recommended in the treatises of Menander Rhetor on epideictic oratory. Possibly in order to avoid a one-sided emphasis on Julian's philosophical virtues Ammianus has added four subsidiary qualities which characterize the ideal military leader, taken from Cicero's oration *de imperio Gnaei Pompei*. They are: *scientia rei militaris, auctoritas, felicitas* and *liberalitas*. The last quality has been substituted by Ammianus for Cicero's *virtus*, which he had already dealt with under the heading of *fortitudo*. It corresponds to φιλανθρωπία in Greek and deals primarily with the emperor's financial policy. As a result, the section on Julian's *bona* is structured as follows: § 1 introduction, § 2–6 *temperantia* (*castitas*), § 7 *prudentia*, § 8–9 *iustitia*, § 10 *fortitudo*, § 11 *scientia rei militaris* § 12–13 *auctoritas*, § 14 *felicitas*, § 15 *liberalitas*.

The section on Julian's *vitia* is not arranged according to a ready-made scheme. It may be called a recapitulation of the criticisms brought forward in the course of the preceding books, more precisely in the books dealing with Julian's performance as an Augustus, because the exercise of power brings out the qualities of the ruler, as Ammianus remarks in the elogium of Valentinian (30.7.1): *quae potestatis amplitudo monstravit nudare solita semper animorum interna*. Blockley's well known dictum on these criticisms deserves to be quoted once again: "If we set aside Julian's apostasy and his treatment of the Christians, we find in Ammianus' narrative more varied condemnation than in any one ecclesiastical writer" (1975, 77). And one might add that these criticisms do not concern small imperfections or minor decisions, but go to the core of Julian's reign: his religious policy and his record as a lawgiver. In the eyes of Ammianus, Julian's basic flaw was his *nimietas*, his tendancy toward excess, to which he returns time and again, both in the narrative and in the elogium. In this respect Ammianus' evaluation is remarkably similar to that in the *Epitome*, where we read: *Haec* (his good qualities) *minuebat quarundam rerum neglectus modus* (43.7). It manifested itself in his talkativeness, his compulsive divination, his extravagance in sacrificing and in his hankering after popularity. It cannot have been easy for the author to formulate this censure of a beloved emperor and, indeed, he tries repeatedly to mitigate the effect of his own words. He certainly deserves respect for his fair appraisal of Julian's character and deeds.

The relation between the elogium and the narrative of books 15–25 has been studied by Pauw, who concludes (1972, 126) that a considerable number of good qualities, which had been signalled in the narrative, have not been incorporated in the elogium, whereas the negative qualities mentioned there had all been treated explicitly in the preceding books. He gives the plausible explanation that the author was the victim of his self-imposed system and that not all Julian's good qualities could be brought under the heading of the four cardinal virtues.

The *bona* and *vitia* are followed by a section on Julian's *forma*, § 22. This is not just a category imported from imperial biography; it serves as a corollary to the description of Julian's character, since the emperor's physique betrays his nature. To be fully appreciated it must be read side by side with the description of Constantius' *forma* in 21.16.19. In fact, this applies to the elogium as a whole, since it is clearly apparent that Ammianus had Julian's opponent constantly in mind while writing this chapter.

In § 23–27, Ammianus deals with criticisms of the Persian campaign. The section may be compared with 21.16.15, devoted to Constantius' successes in civil wars and failures in his dealings with Sapor,

CHAPTER 4.1

and with the detailed evaluation of Valentinian's political merits in
30.7. Its purport is openly apologetic. It was Constantine, not Julian,
who had provoked the hostilities on the eastern border, and it was
a political necessity for Julian to avenge the defeats inflicted on the
Romans by Sapor. After his splendid victories in Gaul Julian was the
right person to try to restore Rome's authority in the East as well.

As to the final impact of this elogium, Ammianus has chosen his
words and arranged his material in such a fashion, that the reader
cannot but admire Julian's greatness, and deplore his untimely death.
The *bona* are allotted three times as many lines in the Teubner edition
as the *vitia*, and the virtues outnumber the vices 31 to 9, according to
Pauw's reckoning (1972, 177). Still, after the death scene in chapter
3, the opening sections of this elogium are disappointing. It is clear
that Ammianus' gifts as a writer of lively narrative and noble speeches
far surpassed his talent for presenting a balanced synthesis of his,
often conflicting, ideas and feelings about Julian. The section about
the *bona* in particular is written in a somewhat pedantic manner. The
section on *castitas* may serve as an example. It begins and ends with
a factual statement about the emperor's abstinence, and is fleshed
out with two references, one to Plato and one to Bacchylides, which
parade the author's erudition, but are out of proportion as regards
their purpose. The section on *prudentia* on the other hand consists
of an arid enumeration of heterogeneous elements. The writing
becomes more lively and personal, however, in the section on Julian's
shortcomings and above all in the spirited defense of Julian's policies
at the end of the elogium, where Ammianus' pen is no longer guided
by the prescriptions of a rhetorical handbook, but by his personal
convictions.

Vir profecto heroicis connumerandus ingeniis The opening sentence is **4.1**
a direct continuation of the emperor's prosopography in the last
section of the preceding chapter, to which it is attached in the form
of an apposition without a predicate of its own. At the same time
it is a clarion call to carry the reader back to the introduction of
Julian as Caesar in 16.1.3: *quidquid autem narrabitur...ad laudativam
paene materiam pertinebit.* By adding *profecto* Amm. rules out any
doubt, as he tends to do when making a personal comment, 14.6.10
ignorantes profecto maiores suos...non divitiis eluxisse, 14.11.22 *ignorans
profecto Alexandrum Magnum...ita respondisse,* 29.6.7 *evenisset profecto
tunc inexpiabile scelus. Hero(ic)us* is used in 21.2.2 of epic verse (*versus
heroos*); in 22.8.3 it refers to the story of the Iliad (*Ilium heroicis casibus
claram*). These parallels are a clear indication that the adjective

COMMENTARY

implies a comparison to the Homeric heroes, not to a demigod like the seer Mopsus, of whom it is said in 14.8.3 *manes eius heroici dolorum varietati medentur plerumque sospitales.* In Amm. *ingenium* usually refers to a man's character, most often in short descriptions in the form of a gen. qualitatis of the type (Thalassius) *ipse quoque arrogantis ingenii* (14.1.10), sometimes with particular attention to his intellectual gifts, as in 15.2.8 (Julian) *procudendi ingenii causa...ad Graeciam ire permissus est.* In the plural it is used three times "metonymice de hominibus ipsis" (TLL VII 1. 1526.43–80), with the attribute *(prae)celsus*: 15.9.8 *et bardi quidem fortia virorum illustrium facta heroicis composita versibus...ceteris drysidae ingeniis celsiores...despectantes humana pronuntiarunt animas immortales,* 22.15.32 *ad ingenia celsa reiciamus* and 23.6.33 *ad nemorosam quandam venerat solitudinem, cuius tranquillis silentiis praecelsa Brachmanorum ingenia potiuntur,* q.v.

The first attestation of the verb *connumerare* is Gaius *Inst.* 1.3 *populi appellatione universi cives significantur connumeratis etiam patriciis.* As is evident from TLL IV 345.33sqq., the verb is used almost exclusively by jurists and fourth-century Christian authors. In Amm. it is a hapax. It is quite likely that Amm. uses *connumerare* as a calque of συναριθμεῖν, which, according to the TLG, is found over a thousand times, with a marked frequency in fourth-century texts. A highly interesting case in point is the use of this verb in Paeanius' translation of Eutropius' *Breviarium*, in which the phrase *inter divos relatus est* is often rendered with συνηριθμήθη τοῖς θεοῖς. Cf. 7.22.2 (Titus), 8.14.2 (Marcus Aurelius). Also the phrase *meruit inter divos referri,* which is found in 9.15.2 (Aurelianus) and 10.8.2 (Constantinus Magnus) is translated in this way. See Den Boer, 1972, 156–7 on these formulas and Claus, 1999, 520–1 Appendix 2 ("Divinisierung und Konsekration bei Eutrop"). Unfortunately, the text of Paeanius' translation breaks off just before the reign of Julian, but there can be little doubt that Eutropius' statement about Julian: *inter divos relatus est* (10.16.2) was rendered in the same way. Kienast, 1996[2], 324 gives no confirmation from other sources for Julian's consecration, but it must be noted that Amm. gives Julian the predicate *divus* in 26.10.8: *quod divo Iuliano fuit acceptus,* and also that he deplored the fact that Julian had not been buried in Rome among the *divi veteres* (25.10.5). In *Or.* 18.304 Libanius even tells us that after his death a prayer had been addressed to Julian to ask for a blessing and that the prayer had been answered. See for this exceptional form of worship Nock, 1957. In his peroration Libanius addresses Julian as follows: "Ὦ δαιμόνων μὲν τρόφιμε, δαιμόνων δὲ μαθητά, δαιμόνων δὲ πάρεδρε and in the same breath as ὦ θεῶν μὲν ἐπίκουρε, θεῶν δὲ ὁμιλητά" (*Or.* 18.308), to which

CHAPTER 4.1

the church historian Socr. *HE* 3.23.41–2 was to react angrily. There is also the, no doubt fictional, story in Greg. Naz. *Or.* 5.14 that Julian, burning with desire to be deified, attempted to disappear from the earth by drowning himself in the Tigris. If his plan had not been thwarted by the eunuchs, ignorant people would have thought of Julian as a new god: κἂν ἐφάνη τις ἄλλος τοῖς ἀνοήτοις θεὸς νέος ἐξ ἀτυχήματος. According to some scholars, e.g. Wessel, 1948/49 and St. Clair, 1964, the principal figure on the *Apotheosis Diptych* in the British Museum (inv. 57-10-13) should be identified with Julian. See, however, Rumpf, 1955/6, 127–35 and Calza, 1972, 388.

Why did Amm. choose to ignore the subject of Julian's consecration? According to Straub, 1962 (=1972, n. 41) the reason was prudence on the part of Amm.: "Ammianus...legt den Gedanken an die Konsekration Julians...nahe, aber es sieht fast so aus als wolle er, da er ja zur Zeit des Theodosius schreibt, nur andeuten, Julian habe in Tat (*profecto*) die Konsekration verdient, die ihm jedoch offiziell nicht zuerkannt wurde, bzw. nicht mehr nachgerühmt werden durfte." Apart from the fact that this is not what Amm. has actually written, it should be noted that in this respect Amm. does not treat Julian differently from other emperors. The five emperors whose death is reported by Amm., viz. Constantius, Julian, Jovian, Valentinian and Valens, were all consecrated, and in none of these cases did Amm. mention this fact. We must conclude that Amm. did not attach great importance to the consecration. Blockley goes even further and says (1975, 84): "Ammianus appears wholly indifferent to the religious aspect of kingship." As Nock, 1957, 121 observes, "After all, emperors and commoners alike could jest at the whole business", and that is exactly what Julian himself did in *Caes.* 332 d, where Silenus asks Augustus ἦ γὰρ οὐκ ἔπλαττες ἡμῖν, εἶπεν, ὥσπερ ἐκεῖνοι (the puppeteers) τὰς νύμφας, ὦ Σεβαστέ, ὧν ἕνα καὶ πρῶτον τουτονὶ Καίσαρα;

Instead, Amm. compared Julian in all seriousness to the heroes of the past, in accordance with the panegyrical mode, in which such comparisons were *de rigueur*, as i.a. MacCormack, 1976, 39 n. 51, has shown. He had done so before, e.g. 22.12.4 *et haec diu multumque agitantes frustra virum circumlatrabant immobilem occultis iniuriis, ut Pygmaei vel Thiodamas agrestis homo Lindius Herculem* and 24.6.14 *Sonent Hectoreas poetae veteres pugnas, fortitudinem Thessali ducis extollant* e.q.s. According to Barnes, 1998, 147 Amm. "is thinking primarily of Achilles". Barnes moreover suggests that "Constantius and Julian are quarreling like Agamemnon and the hero of the *Iliad*". (p. 144) and that the "concealed image of Achilles...underlies

116 COMMENTARY

the whole of Ammianus' account of Julian" (147). However, as Brandt rightly remarked, "diese überraschende Einsicht wird...mit nicht mehr als drei Stellen gestützt (24,6,9; 14; 25,4,1), die Julian zwar in Bezug setzen zur heroischen Welt der homerischen Helden, jedoch keinerlei Spur einer latenten Parallelisierung Julian – Achill erkennen lassen" (*IJCT* 7 [2001] 442). Amm. compared Julian to heroes, other pagan authors praised the emperor to the skies. Eunapius calls him θειότατος (VS 7.2.12) and θεσπέσιος (VS 7.2.12), and in his history he speaks of his divine excellence (τὸ ἰσομέγεθες τῷ θείῳ, *fr.* 28.1, cf. Blockley's note ad loc.). See further Libanius *Or.* 15.36; 16.35; 18.242, 37.4. Christian authors, of course, were less flattering. Cf. e.g. the invectives against Julian of Gregory of Nazianzus, *Or.* 4 and 5, and Socrates' polemic against Libanius in *HE* 3.23.41–2 mentioned above. This does not mean that some of them did not recognize Julian's talents. Cf. e.g. August. *C.D.* 5.21 (*egregiam indolem*) and Prud. *apoth.* 449–52. For Julian in the eyes of Libanius, Gregory of Nazianzus, Prudentius and Augustine see most recently the articles by Criscuolo, Lugaresi, Palla and Ugenti collected in *Rudiae* 10 (1998). As to Libanius' Julian, cf. also Scholl, 1994; Malosse, 1995; Wiemer, 1995 and Fatouros, 1996, for the Julian of Gregory of Nazianzus Molac, 2001. See for an overview Nesselrath, 2001.

claritudine rerum et coalita maiestate conspicuus The traditional topics *res gestae* and *genus* are only hinted at by Amm. He does not need to expatiate on Julian's illustrious deeds, to which he has already devoted ten books of his history. The fact that he belonged by birth to the imperial family (*a nobilibus cunis*, 16.1.4) must have been an embarrassment rather than an asset to Julian. For *claritudo* cf. 27.2.10 *post claritudinem recte gestorum*, 30.5.4 *ut prosapiae suae claritudo monebat* and see the note ad 23.5.14 *incrementa claritudinis*.

The translation given in the note ad 20.15.2 (*actibus coalitum gloriosis*), viz. "grown fully accustomed to", fits the present phrase less well. Here, as in e.g. 15.3.8 (Rufinum) *ultimorum semper avidum hominem et coalita pravitate famosum* and 27.11.4 (Probus) *magnanimitate coalitus*, the meaning is rather 'innate', 'inborn'. The praise of Julian's 'inborn majesty' comes as a surprise, since Amm. has ventured criticism of his behaviour especially in this respect. See the note ad 22.7.3 (*exsiluit indecore*) and § 18 below.

cum enim sint, ut sapientes definiunt, virtutes quattuor praecipuae The four cardinal virtues, for which see North, 1966 and Pernot, 1993,

CHAPTER 4.1   117

165–73, are enumerated for the first time in Pl. *R.* 427 e, in the order wisdom (σοφία, *prudentia*), courage (ἀνδρεία, *fortitudo*), self-control (σωφροσύνη, *temperantia*), justice (δικαιοσύνη, *iustitia*). Whether Amm. derived his knowledge directly from Plato is, however, a moot point. Fornara, 1992, 426 strikes a note of warning, although he does not mention Plato: "Both in general and in particular…it proves impossible to build the case from his work that Ammianus controlled the standard Greek classics in any meaningful degree". In Latin the locus classicus for this topic is Cic. *Inv.* 2.159, where *prudentia* comes first and *temperantia* last: *habet* (sc. *virtus*) *igitur partes quattuor: pruden-tiam, iustitiam, fortitudinem, temperantiam*; see further Fontaine n. 563, Mähl, 1969 and Becker, 1994.

The *quadriga virtutum* found its way into the handbooks of rhetoric as a convenient guide for the panegyrist. Menander Rhetor, 373, 5–8, gives the following instruction: διαίρει γὰρ ἀπανταχοῦ τὰς πράξεις ὧν ἂν μέλλῃς ἐγκωμιάζειν εἰς τὰς ἀρετὰς (ἀρεταὶ δὲ τέσσαρές εἰσιν· ἀνδρεία, δικαιοσύνη, σωφροσύνη, φρόνησις) and goes on to treat them in this order. Julian himself makes use of the topos in *Or.* 1.10 c τὴν ψυχὴν…πρὸς ἀνδρείαν καὶ δικαιοσύνην καὶ σωφροσύνην καὶ φρόνησιν ἐμμελῶς παρασκευάσει. Gärtner, 1968, argues, no doubt correctly, that Amm. adopted the scheme of the four virtues for the description of Julian's merits from this tradition, and that he intended his praise of Julian as a refutation of the bitter criticisms of Julian's person and policy made by his Christian opponents.

The four cardinal virtues are ascribed to Julian by others. Mamertinus, in his panegyric adressed to Julian on 1 January 362, also mentions them, albeit in a different context and, pace Barnes, 1998, 84 n. 26, in a different order: *Adhibeto tantum tibi gratuitas et paratu facilli-mas comites, iustitiam fortitudinem temperantiam atque prudentiam* (*Pan.* 3.21.4). Libanius, addressing the gods, asks: οὐ σωφρονέστερος μὲν Ἱππολύτου, δίκαιος δὲ κατὰ τὸν Ῥαδάμανθυν, συνετώτερος δὲ Θεμιστοκλέους, ἀνδρειότερος δὲ Βρασίδου; (*Or.* 18.281), while Zonaras, although passing over justice and fortitude, speaks of Julian's wisdom and self-control: ἦν δὲ καὶ παντοδαπῆς σοφίας μετειληχὼς καὶ μάλιστα τῆς περιττοτέρας ('and especially the more eccentric aspects of it'), περὶ τὴν δίαιταν ἐγκράτης, ὥστε καὶ τὰ φυσικὰ ταῦτα διαφυγγάνειν, ἐρυγὰς καὶ τὰς ἐκκρίσεις τὰς διὰ στόματος ('belching and spitting'). ἔλεγε δὲ χρῆναι τὸν φιλόσοφον, εἰ οἷόν τε, μηδὲ ἀναπνεῖν (13.13.27–8). The fact that ἀνδρεία in an anonymous imperial panegyric, fragmentarily preserved on papyrus and named *Paneg. Iul. Imp.* by Guida, 1990, is put at the end of the list of cardinal virtues, just as *fortitudo*

118   COMMENTARY

in Amm., is one of the reasons why Guida, 1990, 75 thinks that the panegyric was dedicated to Julian (note however that Barnes, 1997 argues that the emperor praised may be Constantine rather than Julian).

Throughout the Julianic books Amm. refers to Julian's virtues. In 16.1.4 he uses the following words: *namque incrementis velocibus ita domi forisque colluxit, ut prudentia Vespasiani filius Titus alter aestimaretur, bellorum gloriosis cursibus Traiani simillimus, clemens ut Antoninus, rectae perfectaeque rationis indagine congruens Marco, ad cuius aemulationem actus suos effingebat et mores* and in 22.7.9 he says: *Haec eum curantem et talia commendabat externis nationibus fama ut fortitudine, sobrietate, militaris rei scientia virtutumque omnium incrementis excelsum paulatimque progrediens ambitum oppleverat mundi.*

The attribute *praecipuae* is added to distinguish the cardinal virtues from the additional qualities that will be discussed below. Surprisingly, the TLL X 2 s.v. offers no parallels for the expression *virtutes praecipuae* in this technical sense. Elsewhere Amm. uses *praecipua* for good qualities in contrast to *delicta, vitia* and *probra*: 14.6.25 *aurigarum equorumque praecipua vel delicta scrutantes*, 21.16.1 *Bonorum igitur vitiorumque eius differentia vere servata praecipua prima conveniet expediri*, q.v., and 30.7.4 *inter probra medium et praecipua, quae loco docebimus competenti.*

temperantia, prudentia, iustitia, fortitudo For the usual order in which the cardinal virtues are enumerated see above ad *cum enim*. The present order is unusual, though not without parallel. Lib. *Or.* 18.281, quoted above, also starts with σωφροσύνη and, as Becker, 1994, 16 points out, Ambrose, in his discussion of the virtues, gives *verecundia* pride of place.

eisque accedentes extrinsecus aliae, scientia rei militaris, auctoritas, felicitas atque liberalitas These qualities characterize the *summus imperator* according to Cicero in *Man.* 28: *Ego enim sic existumo in summo imperatore quattuor has res inesse oportere: scientiam rei militaris, virtutem, auctoritatem, felicitatem.* Von Scala, 1898, 148 calls the combination of the cardinal virtues with these qualities "eine Zusammenschweissung von Cic. de off. I, 5, 14 (read 15) mit Cic. de imp. Cn. Pomp. 10,24" and Flach, 1972, 340 n. 39 is of the opinion that Amm. "stümperhaft" knocked together "solche Bildungssplitter". It cannot be denied that this opening section, when compared with the preceding chapter, shows a somewhat wooden and pedantic style. Nevertheless Classen, 1998, 239–40 is right in arguing that "Ammian die einzelnen Teile

CHAPTER 4.1   119

des Juliannekrologs nicht willkürlich aneinandergereiht, sondern
mit größter Sorgfalt ausgewählt und zusammengestellt hat".

Interestingly, the four qualities enumerated in Cic. *Man.* 28 are
still depicted in the *Notitia Dignitatum Or.* p. 101; cf. Berger, 1981,
136–8 and 262–3. Amm. has left out *virtus*, evidently because he
had already used it as a general term for 'virtue'. He substitutes
liberalitas, for which cf. Cic. *Off.* 1.20 *iustitia in qua virtutis splendor
est maximus ex qua viri boni nominantur et huic coniuncta beneficentia
quam eandem vel benignitatem vel liberalitatem appellari licet.* As the more
detailed discussion in section 15 will demonstrate, this applies first
and foremost to the emperor's clemency in financial matters. Indeed,
Julian prided himself on his φιλανθρωπία (see Kabiersch, 1960, 34–
6); this may have compelled Amm. to emphasize this virtue.

As Von Scala noticed, Amm.'s use of *praecipuae* mirrors the Stoic
distinction between primary and subordinate virtues; cf. *SVF* 3.264
Τῶν δ' ἀρετῶν τὰς μὲν εἶναι πρώτας, τὰς δὲ ταῖς πρώταις ὑποτεταγμένας,
πρώτας δὲ τέτταρας εἶναι...τῇ δ' ἀνδρείᾳ (ὑποτάττεσθαι) καρτερίαν,
θαρραλεότητα, μεγαλοψυχίαν, εὐψυχίαν, φιλοπονίαν e.q.s. Amm. seems
to have identified the specific qualities, enumerated in *Man.* 28, with
the Stoic subordinate or secondary virtues. According to Von Scala
the qualification *extrinsecus accedentes* corresponds to the Stoic external goods (such as having good friends) mentioned in D.L. 7.95: Ἔτι
τῶν ἀγαθῶν τὰ μὲν εἶναι περὶ ψυχήν, τὰ δ' ἐκτός. In the same section Diogenes speaks about the ἐπιγεννήματα ('outward accessories') of virtue
(such as happiness). Von Scala is of the opinion that both ἐκτός and
ἐπιγεννήματα are rendered with Amm.'s *extrinsecus accedentes.* In view
of the difference between these notions and the secondary virtues,
this is hard to believe. It seems more probable that Amm. had in
mind a passage like Cic. *Tusc.* 3.36–7, where Cicero addresses Epicurus directly. The four cardinal virtues are reviewed in the order
fortitudo – temperantia – iustitia – prudentia and Cicero asks his opponent à propos of *prudentia: quae si extrinsecus religata pendeat...non
intellego, cur...tanto opere expetenda videatur.* Unfortunately, this does
not help us to choose between *accidentes* (V) and *accedentes*, which
was preferred by Bentley and Wagner, probably on account of *extrinsecus*, which implies direction. Cf., however, August. *C.D.* 1.15 *quae
extrinsecus homini accidunt.*

intento studio coluit omnes ut singulas For *intento studio* see the note
ad 20.9.1 and 27.12.5 *intentiore cura.* Amm. seems to refer to the
Stoic notion of ἀντακολουθία, the connection between the virtues,
expressed in *SVF* 3.295: τὰς δὲ ἀρετὰς λέγουσιν ἀντακολουθεῖν ἀλλή-

120   COMMENTARY

λαις, καὶ τὸν μίαν ἔχοντα πάσας ἔχειν and also in Hier. *ep.* 66.3 (=*SVF* 3.299) *quattuor virtutes describunt Stoici ita sibi invicem nexas et mutuo cohaerentes, ut qui unam non habuerit omnibus careat.* This interpretation presupposes that *ut* is equivalent to *ita – ut*, meaning 'as well as', or rather 'as much as', for which see Szantyr 633 on "Unterdrückung der Korrelativa", who quotes Pl. *As.* 834–5 *agitemus convivium / vino ut sermone suavi.* In Amm. the only parallel would seem to be the v.l. *Histrum ut Aufidum* in 24.3.9, but see the note ad loc. For *colere virtutem (-s)* see TLL III 1678.22 sqq.

4.2   *ita inviolata castitate enituit* After the enumeration of the cardinal virtues in the preceding section we would expect Amm. to start with *temperantia.* For this he substitutes *castitas*, which he defines in section 4 as *temperantiae genus.* It is a marked and remarkable narrowing of the concept of *temperantia*, which, as is evident from Cic. *Off.* 1.93–8, has a bearing on all aspects of human behaviour, not just sexuality. In 16.5.1 Julian's *temperantia* is given a wider scope, and includes his abstinence in matters of food. Julian is said to have lived as if bound by sumptuary laws (*tamquam astrictus sumptuariis legibus*). Classen, 1998, 239 points to a passage in Hier. *in Ephes.* 1.2 (PL 26.494), in which *castitas* has its own place among the main virtues: *in alio iustitia, in alio castitas, in alio temperantia, in alio sapientia, in alio fortitudo.* In an earlier study Classen, 1979, 83 n. 105 had observed that in Latin translations of Origenes σωφροσύνη was regularly translated as *castitas.* These are unmistakable signs (if any were needed) of the predominant importance which Christian authors attached to chastity. Classen supposes that in his elogium Amm. gives pride of place to this acknowledged quality of Julian "um zu verdeutlichen, dass der Apostata, den die Christen so bitter bekämpften und schmähten, gerade die Eigenschaft in hohem Masse besass und pflegte, auf die die Väter der Kirche so grossen Wert legten." In fairness one should add that Amm. also praises the Christian emperors Constantius and Valentinian for their chastity. The former is called *impendio castus* (21.16.6); the latter is said to have been *omni pudicitiae cultu domi castus et foris, nullo contagio conscientiae violatus obscenae* (30.9.2).

Amm. speaks twice of *inviolatus pudor* in connection with the wife of Craugasius: 18.10.3 *certiore iam spe mariti recipiendi et pudoris inviolati mansuri*, 19.9.3 *Uxor vero Craugasii, quae retinens pudorem inviolatum ut matrona nobilis colebatur. Enitere* is used with an abl. complement only here; elsewhere (21.14.5, 24.4.24, 28.6.10, 31.16.8) it is used absolutely.

CHAPTER 4.2   121

ut post amissam coniugem nihil umquam venerium †augis larens The general purport cannot be in doubt: the death of Julian's wife Helena put an end to Julian's sexual activity. None of the proposed emendations, however, is totally convincing. The verbs proposed by different scholars (*attingere, agitare, gustare,*) are not used by Amm. in comparable contexts. Much more convincing is the alternative approach by Walter, 1920, 715, who surmised that the corruption had originated from the abridged form 'aug' for 'augusti', and proposed to read *augusti viserent lares*. A relevant parallel would be Claud. *in Eutr.* 2.62–3 *spado Romuleo succinctus amictu / sedit in Augustis laribus.*

Julian's wife (*PLRE* I, Helena 2) died soon after her husband was proclaimed Augustus in Paris in 360 (cf. the note ad 21.1.5 *Helenae coniugis*; add to the literature cited there Wieber-Scariot, 1999, 231 sqq.; cf. in general for women in Amm. Sabbah, 1992). That Julian's sexual needs were minimal is implicitly expressed in 16.5.4 *Hinc contingebat, ut noctes ad officia divideret tripertita, quietis et publicae rei et Musarum* and explicitly in 16.5.8 *et haec quidem pudicitiae virtutumque sunt signa nocturna.* Cosi, 1986, 69 points to Mamertinus, *Pan.* 3.11.13 *lectulus etiam sine concessis et legitimis voluptatibus Vestalium toris purior* as a parallel. Cf. also Lib. *Or.* 18.179: (after Helena) ἑτέρας δὲ οὔτε πρότερον οὔθ' ὕστερον ἥψατο φύσει...δυνάμενος σωφρονεῖν. Libanius even goes so far as to say that Julian would have remained a virgin, if Hera had not married him to Helena: εἰ μὴ θεσμῷ γάμων ἐζεύχθη παρὰ τῆς Ἥρας, ἐτελεύτα ἂν λογῷ μόνον τὰς ἀνθρώπων μίξεις ἐπιστάμενος (ibid.). During the Persian campaign Julian gave proof of his chastity by refusing even to look at the virgins captured in 'Maozamalcha' and offered to him by the soldiers (24.4.27).

illud advertens, quod Cf. 25.3.15 *illud quoque advertens* and 29.5.24 *Tullianum illud advertens, quod.*

Sophoclen, tragoediarum scriptorem The reference is to Pl. *R.* 329 c: Πῶς, ἔφη, ὦ Σοφόκλεις, ἔχεις πρὸς τἀφροδίσια; ἔτι οἷός τε εἶ γυναικὶ συγγίγνεσθαι; καὶ ὃς Εὐφήμει, ἔφη, ὦ ἄνθρωπε· ἀσμενέστατα μέντοι αὐτὸ ἀπέφυγον, ὥσπερ λυττῶντα τινα καὶ ἄγριον δεσπότην ἀποφυγῶν; in Cicero's version (*Sen.* 47): *cum ex eo quidam...quaereret, utereturne rebus veneriis, 'di meliora', inquit, 'libenter vero istinc sicut ab domino agresti ac furioso profugi'.* See also Plut. *Mor.* 525 a, 788 e, 1094 e and Philostr. *VA* 1.13. Fontaine n. 565 thinks that Amm. follows Plato directly, but note that both Cicero and Amm. avoid the blunt and indiscreet personal question in Plato. Bouffartigue, 1992, 170–1 discusses the range of Julian's reading of Plato.

122   COMMENTARY

4.3 *ut hoc propositum validius confirmaret* For *propositum* see the note ad
20.5.4 *nusquam a proposito.*

recolebat saepe dictum lyrici Bacchylidis, quem legebat iucunde For *recolere*
cf. 25.8.13 *cuius iram metuebant et simultates, recolentes, quae assidue
pertulerit funera.* *Iucunde* 'with pleasure' is found again in 28.1.4
(Phrynichus) *paulisperque iucunde auditus.* There is not a trace of
B. *fr.* 38 Maehler (the Greek text has not come down to us) in
Julian's works, nor is Bacchylides' name mentioned anywhere by
the emperor. There is no compelling reason, however, to doubt the
veracity of Amm.'s statement. Cf. Bouffartigue, 1992, 318.

   "Despite the allusions to Plato and Bacchylides..., the frame
of reference is Christian" (Barnes, 1998, 84). Is it? Objections
against sex on the part of doctors and philosophers are uttered long
before Christianity became the dominant religion in the Roman
empire. Πᾶσα σπέρματος ἔκκρισις ἐπιβλαβής, wrote Soranus in the
second century A.D. (*Gynaec.* 1.30.1), and: βλαβερὰ κατὰ γένος ἡ
συνουσία ('sexual intercourse in itself is harmful', *Gynaec.* 1.32.1).
From Sor. *Gynaec.* 1.30.1 it appears that the question of sexual
continence was a moot point in Soranus' time: τὴν διηνεκῆ παρθενίαν
οἱ μὲν ὑγιεινὴν ἔλεξαν, οἱ δὲ οὐχ ὑγιεινήν, while already in the fourth
century B.C. Epicurus, according to Galenus as cited by Oribasius,
regarded sex as unhealthy: Ἀφροδισίων δὲ κατὰ μὲν Ἐπίκουρον οὐδεμία
χρῆσις ὑγιεινή (Oribasius *Coll. med.* 6.37.1). The fact that Galenus'
citation of Epicurus' words is found in Oribasius' *Collectiones medicae*
seems highly significant. Oribasius, a convinced pagan, wrote this
compilation of excerpts from earlier medical writers at the behest
of Julian (book 6 treats sexuality in chapters 37 and 38). "Comment
oublier la chasteté de Julien, son régime, son ascétisme, en lisant
les textes rassemblés pour lui par Oribase?" (Rousselle, 1983, 16). In
view of the fact that Libanius in *Or.* 16.56 says that Julian in his way of
life did not differ much from Apollonius of Tyana, it is interesting to
note that according to Philostratus the man of Tyana conquered his
sexual urges despite his youth (*VA* 1.13). Philostratus, as was noted
above, refers in *VA* 1.13 to the same saying of Sophocles as is cited
by Amm. See further D.L. 10.118, Porph. *Abst.* 4.20.3 (τὰ ἀφροδίσια
μιαίνει), Iamb. *VP* 31 and cf. Hopfner, 1950 and Delling, 1978.

id asserentis, quod The comparison, in the form in which it is presented by Amm., is muddled. Probably Bacchylides meant to say
that, just as a beautiful face is an ornament to the whole person, so
modesty is an ornament to the man who strives for distinction.

CHAPTER 4.4   123

quam labem...vitavit It has been remarked more than once that Amm. is somewhat careless in his anaphoric expressions, e.g. in the notes ad 23.4.2 *et hac multiplici* and 23.4.5 *ab hac medietate*, but this is a rather extreme case, *labem* being the opposite of Julian's virtuous behaviour described so far.

ut ne suspicione quidem tenus libidinis ullius vel citerioris vitae ministris incusaretur For the use of the dat. auctoris in Amm. see the notes ad 18.4.7 *morantibus* and 22.8.42 *eisque caritates* and cf. 14.1.7 *nullo citerioris vitae ministro praesente.* Although the text in 21.16.6 *ut nec †mare ministro saltem suspicione tenus posset redargui* (q.v.) is corrupt, it is clear, nevertheless, that Amm. said the same with respect to Constantius.

Hoc autem temperantiae genus crescebat in maius iuvante parsimonia   **4.4**
ciborum et somni Amm.'s statements concerning Julian's moderation in eating and sleeping, here and in 16.5.1–4, 21.9.2, 25.2.2–3 (see the notes ad loc.), are confirmed by others: Mamert. *Pan.* 3.14.3 (*nihil somno, nihil epulis, nihil otio tribuit*), Lib. *Or.* 13.44 (τράπεζα δέ σοι μετρία), 12.95, 18.171, 174–5, Greg. Naz. *Or.* 4.71, Zon. 13.13.27. See also Anon. *Paneg. Iul. Imp.* 3.30 sqq., with Guida's note. Mause 1994, 136–40 offers a wealth of parallels for this topos from panegyrical literature. The emperor alludes to his own frugality in *Mis.* 340 b (quoted below ad *namque in pace*), praises it as a characteristic of cynical philosophers in *Or.* 7. 223 c, 226 a, 9. 198 d, 199 d and advises Constantius in *Or.* 1.11 a to put up with very little sleep and scanty food. As Staesche, 1998, 82 notes, referring to Porph. *Abst.* 1.47 and 4.20, Julian's sparing use of food is directly connected with his abstinence in sexualibus.

The pleonastic *crescebat in maius,* which is found only in V, is very rare, but cf. Sen. *Ep.* 89.3 *quicquid in maius crevit, facilius agnoscitur, si discessit in partes.* Elsewhere Amm. uses *parsimonia* exclusively in the phrase *sine (ulla) parsimonia,* e.g. in section 17 below, 25.3.10, q.v. and 29.6.8.

quibus domi forisque tenacius utebatur For the expression *domi forisque* 'at home and in public' see TLL VI 1.1041.57–1042.13. In his pane-gyrical presentation of Julian (16.1.4) Amm. had written *incrementis velocibus ita domi forisque colluxit, ut prudentia Vespasiani filius Titus alter aestimaretur,* and in 30.9.2 Valentinian is called *omni pudicitiae cultu domi castus et foris.* In view of the fact that Amm. proceeds with the divisio *in pace ~ per procinctus,* it seems that he uses the expression as

124 COMMENTARY

more or less equivalent to *domi militiaeque*. *Tenax* has the meaning "close-fisted, niggardly" here (OLD 3).

namque in pace victus eius mensarumque tenuitas erat recte noscentibus admiranda Gellius has provided the model here. Cf. 2.24.1 *parsimonia apud veteres Romanos et victus atque cenarum tenuitas*, which by the way proves *mensarumque* for V's *mensuramque* to be correct. Amm. uses the expression *recte noscentibus* also in 22.9.3 (q.v.) and 27.5.9. Cf. 21.16.12 *utque recte sentientes quidam arbitrabantur* and 23.6.46 *ut recte spectantibus nihil eis videatur ad felicitatem deesse supremam*. The inhabitants of Antioch were certainly not among those who were good judges (*recte noscentibus*), for in their eyes Julian's lifestyle was most objectionable: ἄγρυπνοι νύκτες ἐν στιβάδι, καὶ τροφῇ ἥττων κόρου πικρὸν ἦθος ποῖει καὶ τρυφώσῃ πόλει πολέμιον ("Sleepless nights on a pallet and a diet that is anything rather than surfeiting make my temper harsh and unfriendly to a luxurious city like yours", *Mis.* 340 b, tr. Wright).

velut ad pallium mox reversuri As in earlier days, before Constantius called Julian, *etiamtum palliatum* (15.8.1), away from Athens and made him Caesar in Gaul. For *pallium* as the attire par excellence of Greek philosophers see e.g. the words of Herodes Atticus in Gel. 9.2.4: *'Video' inquit Herodes 'barbam et pallium, philosophum nondum video'* and TLL X.1 135. 17ff., cited in the note ad 22.9.10 *purpureum*, the only other occurrence of *pallium* in Amm. In 16.5.10 Julian is called *philosophus*. According to Libanius, Julian loved philosophy more than did any philosopher (*Or.* 1.118; cf. *Or.* 12.33). In his *Letter to Themistius* 253 a–254 c Julian himself poses more as a philosopher than as a statesman.

per varios autem procinctus stans interdum more militiae cibum brevem vilemque sumere visebatur Amm.'s statement, that Julian on his campaigns (see for *procinctus* the note ad 20.1.3) often took his meal whilst standing, is confirmed by Mamert. *Pan.* 3.11.4 *neque tempus epularum ei qui saepius statarium prandium ad necessitatem humani corporis capiat gaudens castrensi cibo…et poculo fortuito*. This practice was not common in the army. During the Hannibalic war proconsul Ti. Sempronius Gracchus punished some soldiers, who had behaved cowardly, by forcing them to take their meals henceforth whilst standing (Liv. 24.16.13), which implies that others were permitted to do otherwise. The fact that in Spain Scipio Aemilianus, as one of his measures to restore discipline, commanded his soldiers ἀριστᾶν…ἑστῶτας

CHAPTER 4.5

(Plut. *Mor.* 201 c, cf. Polyaen. 8.16.2, *Exc. Polyaen.* 3.8) also suggests that, if ever soldiers were expected to eat whilst standing (cf. [Quint.] Decl. 3.13), this rule was often neglected. In 25.2.2 (q.v.) Amm. gave an example of Julian's habit to eat rather common meals: *imperator, cui non cuppediae ciborum ex regio more, sed sub columellis tabernaculi parcius cenaturo, pultis portio parabatur exigua, etiam munifici fastidienda gregario.* See further Lib. *Or.* 13.29 and 18.216. In this respect Theodosius (if Pacatus is to be believed) was not unlike Julian: *modico et castrensi cibo ieiunia longa solantem (Pan.* 2.13.3).

For *cibum brevem* cf. Hor. *Ep.* 1.14.35 *cena brevis iuvat* and Brink's note ad Hor. *AP* 198 *ille dapes laudet mensae brevis.*

ubi vero exigua dormiendi quiete recreasset corpus laboribus induratum **4.5** For the fact that Julian could do with little sleep see above, ad §4 *Hoc autem temperantiae,* for his ability to endure toil 25.4.10 *Fortitudinem certaminum crebritas ususque bellorum ostendit et patientia frigorum immanium et fervoris.* In this respect he resembled Constantius, who, according to Amm., was also *somno contentus exiguo,* 21.16.6, q.v.

vigiliarum vices et stationum The nouns *vigiliae* and *statio* are found in combination also in 21.8.4 (q.v.) *stationesque nocturnas agerent et vigilias.*

post haec seria ad artes confugiens doctrinarum The same idea is expressed in 16.5.6 *post quae ut ardua et seria terminata ad procudendum ingenium vertebatur.* Note that in both passages Amm. puts *seria* ('public and military duties', as in 20.4.19 *nec agere seria*) in front, "c'est peut-être aussi pour réagir contre l'image trop intellectuelle, et encore plus sophistique que philosophique, de Julien qu'il trouvait chez Libanius" (Sabbah 278 n. 114).

Fontaine eloquently defends the reading *arces...doctrinarum* in V, which is indeed tempting in view of the parallel in 16.5.6 *pabula quaedam animo ad sublimiora scandenti conquirens.* Still, in the final analysis it seems preferable to keep *artes* (Vm3), since, as Fontaine himself points out, *arx* is always used in its literal meaning in Amm. (though with the exception of 21.16.14 *in arce victoris animi*). Moreover, despite the fact that there is no parallel for *artes doctrinarum,* this seems to be an unexceptionable instance of the gen. identitatis or inhaerentiae, for which see Szantyr 63 and the note ad 22.12.7 *caerimoniarum ritus.* As Hagendahl, 1937, 154 has observed "la plupart des substantifs abstraits synonymes qui se rencontrent coordonnés, deux à deux, dans la langue classique, se retrouvent dans le bas

126   COMMENTARY

latin, accouplés de cette façon nouvelle: l'un est le complément de
l'autre." Indeed, coordination of *ars* and *doctrina* is common, e.g.
Cic. *Tusc.* 3.69 *ut omnibus perfectis artibus omni doctrina hominum vita
erudiretur* and Gel. 19.14.1 *doctrinarum...multiformium variarumque
artium...columina.*

4.6   *et si nocturna lumina, inter quae lucubrabat, potuissent voce ulla testari*
The phrase *nocturna lumina* has a poetic ring. Cf. e.g. Verg. *A.* 7.13
urit odoratam nocturna in lumina caedrum. Different types of lamps are
listed in Apul. *Met.* 4.19 *taedis, lucernis, cereis, sebaciis et ceteris nocturni
luminis instrumentis clarescunt tenebrae.* A typical *lucubratio* is evoked
in Quint. *Inst.* 10.3.25 *ideoque lucubrantes silentium noctis et clausum
cubiculum et lumen unum velut tectos maxime teneat* ('let therefore those
who burn the midnight oil be protected, as it were, by the silence of
the night, the privacy of their room, the single lamp'). See for Julian's
activities at night 16.5.4–8 and 25.2.3 with the relevant notes, Jul.
Ep. 4 and 28, Mamert. *Pan.* 3.14.3 (cf. 3.13.3), Lib. *Or.* 1.130, 12.94,
18.157, 175, 178. Cf. also Anon. *Paneg. Iul. Imp.* 10.10 sqq. In Julian's
case there is no need to doubt the assertion of the sources, but, as
Staesche, 1998, 31 rightly remarks, the image of an emperor reading
or, in general, working at night is topical. Cf. e.g. D.Chr. 1.13; Eus. *VC*
4.29; *Pan.* 10.3.4; Jul. *Or.* 1, 11 a, 3, 87 c; Lib. *Or.* 59.144; Them. *Or.*
15. 193 a, 195 b. More examples, especially from juridical sources,
in Hunger, 1964, 95–100.

profecto ostenderant inter hunc et quosdam principes multum interesse   For
the use of the indic. in the apodosis of an irrealis see De Jonge ad
14.3.2. The phrase *voce testari* may well allude to Vergil: *A.* 6.619
magna testatur voce per umbras and 12.580–1 *Aeneas magnaque incusat
voce Latinum / testaturque deos.* According to Fontaine n. 569 Amm.
obliquely criticizes some of Julian's successors, which would give
his remark "quelque valeur d' actualité". Unfortunately, nothing is
known about any activities at night of the emperors after Julian that
would make them qualify. Moreover, the reputation as to *voluptates*
of Valentinian, Valens, Gratian and Theodosius is impeccable. Only
Jovian was *edax...et vino venerique indulgens* (25.10.15). The plural
quosdam does not preclude that Amm. wants his readers to think
of him in particular. For this use of *quidam* see Szantyr 197. It
seems more likely, however, that Amm. had in mind the escapades
of which he accuses Gallus Caesar and Gallienus in 14.1.9, such
as roaming about the inns and streetcorners of the city (cf. HA
Gall. 21.5), which are also attested for Caligula, Nero, Vitellius,

CHAPTER 4.7 127

Lucius Verus, Commodus and Heliogabalus (Suet. *Nero* 26.1; Plin. *Nat.* 13.126; Tac. *Ann.* 13.25.1; D.C. 64.2.1, 80.13.2; HA *V* 4.6, *C* 3.7, with Demandt, 1997², 73–4). Libanius also contrasts Julian's behaviour with that of other emperors: *Or.* 18.179 Ταυτὶ τοῦ μήκους τῶν νύκτῶν ἀπολέλαυκεν ἡμῖν ὁ βασιλεύς, ἑτέροις δὲ ἐν ταῖς τηλικαύταις τῶν Ἀφροδίτης ἐμέλησεν.

quem norant voluptatibus ne ad necessitatem quidem indulsisse naturae At first sight Löfstedt's *quem quidem* for V's *quemquem* is attractive, as it would give the relative clause a causal sense. Amm., however, uses *quidem* only once in a relative clause, and there it is restrictive: 19.12.17 *qui quidem recte sapiat*. Moreover, it would be clumsy to have *quidem* twice in such a short sentence. It seems best therefore to interpret V's *quemquem* as a case of dittography. For other examples in V see Blomgren 145. For the content cf. Mamert. *Pan.* 3.14.3 *ipsa se naturalium necessariarumque rerum usurpatione defrudat; totus commodis publicis vacat.* The terms used by the panegyrist and Amm. call to mind the Epicurean distinction between the desires, as given by Cic. *Fin.* 2.26 *Quo modo autem philosophus loquitur? 'Tria genera cupiditatum, naturales et necessariae, naturales et non necessariae, nec naturales nec necessariae'.* Sexual desire, however, belongs firmly in the second category. Normally, *necessitas naturae* refers to the law(s) of nature, as in Cic. *Sen.* 4 *nihil malum potest videri quod naturae necessitas adferat* or Sen. *Cons. Helv.* 6.8 *ut lex et naturae necessitas ordinavit.* Amm. is probably thinking of the necessity of sexuality for procreation. In that sense Tert. *Pud.* 16.23 speaks of *carnis necessitatem* and Lact. *Inst.* 6.23.4 says (cupiditas venerea) *quam quidam necessitatem dicere maluerunt.* Indeed, Lib. *Or.* 18.181 tells us that the courtiers encouraged Julian to remarry in order to have sons who could succeed to the throne: παρακαλούμενος γὰρ ἐπὶ γάμον παρὰ τῶν ἐπιτηδείων ὅπως παῖδας φυτεύσειε κληρονόμους τῆς ἀρχῆς. Julian refused, however, for fear of begetting a degenerate heir.

Dein prudentiae eius indicia fuere vel plurima In 16.1.4 (quoted ad § 1)   **4.7** Amm. praised Julian as a second Titus as regards *prudentia*. Sabbah 392 well explains the difference between *exempla* ("des actes concrets, particuliers, réprésentatifs") and *indicia* ("des qualités particulières déployées dans des domaines complémentaires"). The remaining part of this section should probably be read as one single period with *praedicabat* as its only main verb.

128   COMMENTARY

armatae rei scientissimus et togatae "Thoroughly skilled in the arts of war and peace" (Rolfe). Menander also brings military expertise under the heading of φρόνησις in 373.11: φρονήσεως γὰρ καὶ τὸ στρατηγεῖν καλῶς ἐν τοῖς πολέμοις. Although Julian had been drawn to the dust of battle *ex academiae quietis umbraculis* and not *e militari tabernaculo* (16.1.5; cf. 16.5.10), he had become a great general, as Amm. i.a. relates in 22.7.9, where *militaris rei scientia* is the equivalent of *armata res* here (cf. *scientia rei militaris* in § 1). In § 11 Amm. uses different words, *castrensium negotiorum scientiam*, but clearly means the same. The meaning of these three expressions should be distinguished from that of *armaturae scientia*, 'management of arms' (cf. 14.11.3 *per multiplicem armaturae scientiam*), which is a less comprehensive characteristic. It is significant that Amm., while praising Julian's knowledge of *armata res*, merely says in Constantius' elogium that the latter was *armaturae pedestris perquam scientissimus* (21.16.7). Apart from the present text *togatus* only occurs in 22.2.4 *armatorum et togatorum agminibus*. For the antithesis *armatae rei...et togatae* cf. *in apparatu vel in ipsis...congressibus proeliorum aut in re civili* in 16.5.9.

The superlative *scientissimus* already occurs in the classical period; Cic. *de Orat.* 1.214 calls M. Scaurus *vir regendae rei publicae scientissimus*. For the opposition *arma(tus) – toga(tus)* cf. [Cic.] *Sal.* 2.7 *an ego tunc falso scripsi cedant arma togae qui togatus armatos et pace bellum oppressi?*

civilitati admodum studens For *civilitas* as an imperial virtue see the note ad 21.16.9 *acrius exsurgens quam civiliter*; for Julian's *civilitas* also Eutropius 10.16.3 *civilis in cunctos* (cf. Scivoletto, 1970) and Mamertinus *Pan.* 3.28.1 *hic...ipse* (dies) *praebuit civilis animi satis clara documenta*. It is above all this quality that, according to Neri, 1984, 4 makes Julian fundamentally different from his predecessor. It gives Amm.'s portrait "una forte coloritura occidentale e romana, per l'accentuazione delle virtù militari e l'insistenza sugli ideali della *civilitas*." For *admodum* see the note ad 21.12.15.

tantum sibi arrogans, quantum a contemptu et insolentia distare existimabat As Seyfarth n. 53 rightly observes, this is taken from V. Max. 3.7 ext. 1. In Valerius, however, *fiducia* is the subject and Amm. has substituted *existimabat* for *satis est*, thereby creating a cursus velox. The purport of the sentence in Valerius is that *fiducia* should be praised if it claims only so much for itself as is enough to provide protection against the insolence and contempt of others. By choosing *existimabat* Amm.

CHAPTER 4.7   129

may hint at the fact that in Julian's case the borderline between *civilitas* and *humilitas* was easily crossed – in § 18 q.v. *Volgi plausibus laetus...cum indignis loqui saepe affectans* he is more outspoken. In this respect, according to Amm., Julian is the opposite of his cousin Constantius, who, although he often asserted that he tried to model his life and character *ad aemulationem civilium principum*, behaved arrogantly, referring to himself sometimes as *Aeternitas mea* and *orbis totius dominus* (15.1.3).

virtute senior quam aetate Cf. Eun. *VS* 7.1.11 ὁ καὶ ἐν μειρακίῳ πρεσβύ-της Ἰουλιανός. "Der *puer senilis* oder *puer senex* ist", according to Curtius, citing many examples, "eine Prägung der heidnischen Spätantike" (1969[7], 109).

studiosus cognitionum omnium On account of what follows, *et indeclinabilis aliquotiens iudex*, these words are sometimes taken as a reference to Julian's "interest in all legal inquiries" (Hamilton; cf. Rolfe: "he gave great attention to the administration of justice", Seyfarth: "Grosse Aufmerksamkeit widmete er dem Rechtswesen", and the note ad 21.12.23 *litesque audiens*; in a juridical sense *cognitio* is found in 29.1.23 *summatibus...quibus cognitiones commissae sunt*). Brok, however, followed by Fontaine n. 572, points to 21.1.7, the introduction to Amm.'s digression on divination, where exactly the same expression is used (*erudito et studioso cognitionum omnium principi*). The context in 21.1.7 leaves no doubt as to its meaning: the words there refer to Julian's various intellectual accomplishments. To assume that this is also the case in the present text is the more attractive because this characteristic of the emperor, though well known and duly mentioned in the catalogue of Julian's merits in book 16 (*ad procudendum ingenium vertebatur* 16.5.6), does not occur elsewhere in the elogium, although it certainly belongs under the heading *prudentia*.

Cf. for Julian's many-sided intellectual interest 16.5.6–8, Eutr. 10.16.3 *Liberalibus disciplinis adprime eruditus, epit.* 43.5 *Fuerat in eo litterarum ac negotiorum ingens scientia, aequaverat philosophos et Graecorum sapientissimos*, Zon. 13.13.27 ἦν δὲ καὶ παντοδάπης σοφίας μετειληχὼς καὶ μάλιστα τῆς περιττοτέρας ('he took an interest in all kinds of wisdom, and especially in its more uncommon aspects'), Lib. *Or.* 15.28, 18.21. Julian himself in *Mis.* 347 a says that he was a man who read widely and in *Ep.* 80 complains that, due to the fact that he was overwhelmed by public business, he had hardly any time to read, although he kept Homer and Plato always close at hand.

130 COMMENTARY

et indeclinabilis aliquotiens iudex For Julian as a judge see the notes ad 21.12.23 *litesque audiens*, 22.9.9 *iudicibus...tristior* and 22.10.1 *iudicialibus causis*. Cf. also Eun. *fr.* 25.1 Ἐπὶ τὸν Ἰουλιανὸν πολλαὶ δίκαι ἐχώρουν, χανδὸν ἐμφορουμένων τῶν ἀνθρώπων τῆς δικαιοσύνης τοῦ κρίνοντος ("because men eagerly enjoyed his fairness as a judge", tr. Blockley). *Indeclinabilis* is an attribute of fate (29.1.34 *indeclinabilis fati*) and justice, cf. also 18.1.2 *erat* (Iulianus) *indeclinabilis iustorum iniustorumque distinctor*.

censor in moribus regendis acerrimus Domitian was the last emperor to bear the title of *censor*. After his reign the title looses its precise meaning and becomes a general term for a (moral) judge. In this sense Valentinian is described in 30.9.1 as *militaris disciplinae censor eximius*. The theme of the *censura morum* is among the favourite fantasies in the *Historia Augusta*, in particular in the Life of the emperor Valerian, chs. 5–6. In *Ep.* 4.29, 4.45, 5.9 and 7.58 Symmachus mentions a discussion in the senate about the reinstatement of the censorship, for which see the notes in Callu's Budé-edition. It may be surmised, therefore, that the censorship was a much discussed topic in the last decades of the fourth century. In the present passage, however, there is no trace of such a debate. Fontaine n. 572 is of the opinion that Amm. refers here to the strict moral demands Julian imposed on priests, and his measures against the luxury at court, as described in 22.4. The measures described there, however, belong rather under the heading *temperantia*. Pauw, 1972, 121 is right in stating that this is one of the very few qualities of Julian not mentioned before in the narrative parts of the *Res Gestae*.

placidus opum contemptor Unlike Valens, *magnarum opum intemperans appetitor* (31.14.5), Julian, who as a good philosopher, heeded Cic. *Parad.* 42–52, was contemptuous of riches. Cf. 24.3.5 *mihi nec facultates...paupertatem honestam* with the notes and Jul. *Ep.* 89 b, 290 c. In his *Letter to the Athenians* (281 b) Julian proudly draws attention to the fact that he did not rob Lupicinus (*PLRE* I, Lupicinus 6) and others of their property, although he was fully entitled to do so (for the circumstances see the note ad 20.9.9 *timebatur Lupicinus*). Cf. further Jul. *Ep.* 26, 415 b, quoted in the note ad 25.4.9 *postremo*. The expression *opum contemptor* is used of Helvidius Priscus in Tac. *Hist.* 4.5.2.

mortalia cuncta despiciens The sentiment may be compared to Cic. *Tusc.* 2.11 *te natura excelsum quendam videlicet et altum et humana despicientem genuit*.

CHAPTER 4.8   131

turpe esse sapienti, cum habeat animum, captare laudes ex corpore In the
speech on his deathbed (25.3.15), Julian had reminded his friends
quantum corpore sit beatior animus. Δεῖ...ὀλιγωρεῖν δὲ πάντη τοῦ σώματος,
he had said earlier, addressing the Cynic philosopher Heraclius (*Or.*
7. 226 c).

Quibus autem iustitiae inclaruit bonis, multa significant On *inclarescere*   **4.8**
see the note ad 24.4.20. People believed, as did Julian himself,
that during his reign the goddess of Justice had returned to earth
(*vetus illa Iustitia...imperante eo reversa ad terras*). Thus Amm. in
22.10.6, although he makes it clear that he does not accept this idea
without qualification (*ni...obnubilaret gloriarum multiplices cursus*). In
the present text, that is in the part of the elogium that deals with
Julian's *bona*, there is no room for criticism. This has to wait till the
discussion of Julian's *vitia*: in § 19 Amm. repeats almost verbatim what
he had said about *Iustitia* in 22.10.6 and, quite appropriately in the
context there, adds some critical remarks of his own (*ni...interdum
ostenderet se dissimilem sui*).

primo quod erat pro rerum hominum distinctione sine crudelitate terribilis
Blomgren, with his usual predilection for the asyndeton bimembre
proposes to keep the reading of V *rerum hominum*. In view of parallels
like Quint. *Inst.* 6.2.13 *ut fluere omnia ex natura rerum hominumque
videantur* and Suet. *Otho* 9.3 *tanto rerum hominumque periculo* it seems
preferable to follow the older Valesius who read *hominumque*. A
good judge not only is *indeclinabilis iustorum iniustorumque distinctor*
(18.1.2), but also "takes into account circumstances and persons"
(Rolfe). What is meant by *distinctio hominum* appears from phrases
like 22.7.8 *sine condicionis discrimine,* 26.10.9 *carnifex enim et unci et
cruentae quaestiones sine discrimine ullo aetatum et dignitatum per fortunas
omnes et ordines grassabantur* or 29.2.2 *sine fortunarum distantia*: Julian
judged people according to their social status. An illustration of
distinctio rerum is Julian's behaviour during the Persian campaign,
when he contented himself *impendentium consideratione difficultatum*
(25.1.9) with a rather mild punishment of the soldiers who had been
accused of running away in battle, or in 362, when the emperor,
Galli similis fratris licet incruentus (22.14.2), dealt firmly but without
the shedding of blood with the rioting inhabitants of Antioch. 'One
might have expected to hear of executions by spear and sword, of
burnings and drownings' (οἴεται τις ἀκοῦσαι...δόρυ καὶ ξίφος καὶ πῦρ
καὶ θάλατταν), Libanius remarked with respect to the latter case, but
nothing of the sort took place (*Or.* 18.195). A little later, Libanius

132   COMMENTARY

continues (*Or.* 18.198), when the city still behaved insubordinately, Julian merely avenged himself by composing an oration (i.e. the *Misopogon*, cf. 22.14.2), as he had done previously in the case of an individual who had acted impudently (i.e. Nilus, *PLRE* I, Nilus 2).

For *terribilis* in the positive sense of 'awe-inspiring' cf. the description of Julian in 15.8.16 *oculos cum venustate terribiles* and 29.5.15 *fulgore signorum et terribili vultu Theodosi praestrictus*. The soldiers hailed Valentinian as their emperor and took him to the palace *ambitiose stipatum iamque terribilem* (26.2.11). The sentence as a whole is found in Eutr. 10.9.4 *exercituique per omne vitae tempus sine gravi crudelitate terribilis* (about Constans).

deinde quod paucorum discrimine vitia cohibebat Perhaps a reference to the punishment of some soldiers during the Persian campaign: *decem...milites ex his, qui fugerant, exauctoratos capitali addixit supplicio* (24.3.2). For *discrimen* 'execution' cf. 26.3.1 *ut veneficos...morte multaret atque ita paucorum discrimine reliquos...formidine parium exturbaret.*

4.9   *ut multa praeteream* One can think of Julian's verdict in the case of a girl who had been raped (16.5.12; cf also 16.5.13), his sovereign treatment of the PPO Galliarum Nebridius (21.5.12, *PLRE* I, Nebridius 1), the way he acted during a lawsuit against a certain woman, related in 22.10.5 and introduced with the words *sufficiet autem pro multis, quae clementer egit in litibus cognoscendis, hoc unum ponere*. Cf. further Jul. *Ep.* 98, 402 a.

constat eum in apertos aliquos inimicos insidiatores suos ita consurrexisse mitissime, ut poenarum asperitatem genuina lenitudine castigaret The prepositional phrase *in...suos*, in which *insidiatores suos* is used predicatively (= *cum sibi insidiarentur*) seems overloaded and inelegant. *Consurgere* normally means 'to rise', c.q. 'to spring to action', as in 17.12.12 *ne ferire foedera simulans in arma repente consurgeret*, 17.13.13 *consurrectum est in perniciem eorum, qui deseruere proelia*, 24.2.12 *exercitus ad fiduciam elatis vocibus in favores principis consurgebat*. Here it is the equivalent of *animadvertere*. One of the two parallels from the *Cod. Theod.* quoted in TLL IV 622.48–52 is 8.5.1 *si eius fuerit dignitatis ut nequaquam in eum deceat tali vigore consurgere*.

Libanius in *Or.* 16.19 says that Julian "allowed those who whetted their swords against him to live" (τοὺς ἀκονήσαντας ἐπ᾽ αὐτὸν ξίφη ζῆν ἀφεὶς tr. Norman; cf. *Or.* 12.85, 18.199–200, *Ep.* 1120.3 with Malosse, 1995, 329–30), and in *Or.* 18.101 that "he had no desire

CHAPTER 4.10   133

to defile his reign with the shedding of blood" (Οὐδενὶ γὰρ αἵματι τὴν βασιλείαν ἐβουλήθη...μολῦναι, tr. Norman). In the latter passage Libanius speaks of the beginning of Julian's rule as Augustus, and indeed, although Julian shortly after the pronunciamiento in Paris had Lupicinus (*PLRE* I, Lupicinus 6) and three other men arrested (they were accused of having openly plotted against him), he did not put them to death (Jul. *Ep. ad Ath.* 281 a; cf. the note ad §7 *placidus opum contemptor*). Julian probably hints at the same incident when he writes in *Ep.* 26, 45 b-c that the philosopher Maximus has the right to know τίνα δὲ τρόπον τὸ τοσοῦτον τῶν ἐπιβουλῶν πλῆθος διαπεφεύγαμεν, κτείναντες οὐδένα, χρήματα οὐδένος ἀφελόμενοι, φυλαξάμενοι δὲ μόνον οὓς ἐλαμβάνομεν ἐπ' αὐτοφώρῳ. Arrested but not executed was also Lucillianus (*PLRE* I, Lucillianus 3), for whom see 21.9.5–10.1 with the notes. Julian declined the offer of some former *agentes in rebus* to point out where his long-time opponent Florentius (*PLRE* I, Florentius 10; cf. the note ad 20.4.2) was hiding (22.7.5). When Theodotus (*PLRE* I, Theodotus 1), who had openly hoped for Julian's death, begged for his life, he was pardoned (22.14.4– 5). Thalassius (*PLRE* I, Thalassius 2) also belonged to the category of Julian's enemies, hated because he had plotted against Julian's brother Gallus. However, when there was an opportunity to ruin Thalassius, Julian did not seize it. Shortly afterwards he was even reconciled with him (22.9.16–7). In view of all this, one almost forgets that Julian sometimes did punish his opponents with death, cf. 22.11.1.

ut poenarum asperitatem genuina lenitudine castigaret Cf. 16.5.13 *delictorum vindictas genuina lenitudine mitigabat.* Artaxerxes displayed the same innate clemency: 30.8.4 *suppliciorum varietates, quas natio semper exercuit cruda, lenitate genuina castigans.* For other instances of c*astigare* in the sense of *cohibere* see TLL III 535.39–56.

Fortitudinem certaminum crebritas ususque bellorum ostendit et patientia **4.10** *frigorum immanium et fervoris* Strictly speaking, only battles, not an abstract quality like experience, can show a man's courage. Kellerbauer, 1873, 131 objected to the "unerträglich lose Satzfügung" and proposed to omit *et* after *ostendit,* thus making *usus bellorum* the object of *ostendit.* It seems preferable, however, to take the two noun phrases as a hendiadys 'the many battles in which he gained his experience in war'. Practical experience in the field is a prerequisite for a good general, cf. Cicero's appraisal of Fonteius in *Font.* 41: *in re militari cum summi consilii et maximi animi, tum vero usu quoque bellorum gerendorum*

134 COMMENTARY

in primis...exercitatus. Amm. mentions the same quality in 16.10.21 *unde misso in locum Marcelli Severo, bellorum usu et maturitate firmato, Ursicinum ad se venire praecepit* and the Halani accepted as their chiefs only men who were *diuturno bellandi usu spectatos* (31.2.25).

Julian's courage is also praised in 17.1.14 and 22.7.9. See further 16.12.3 *ignarus pavendi,* 16.12.28 *animosus contra labores maximos,* 25.4.12 *periculorum socius et laborum.* Sometimes his fortitude came close to recklessness (24.2.14, 24.4.3–4, 24.5.6, 24.6.4, 24.6.15). Among the battles he fought, against Alamanni, Franks and Chamavi as Caesar, against Atthuarian Franks and Persians as Augustus, the battle of Strasbourg (16.12.1 ff.) is the most noticeable.

Before Julian experienced the burning heat of Mesopotamia (see the note ad 25.1.3 *Et cum fatiscerent*), he endured 'the dust of the Alamanni in summer and the frost of Thrace in winter' (*aestate Alamannicum pulverem hieme pruinam Thraciae,* Mamert. *Pan.* 3.13.3). Cf. Anon. *Paneg. Iul. Imp.* 12.29–35, with Guida ad loc., who cites many passages in which endurance of cold and heat is mentioned as a characteristic of good soldiers or generals: X. *Cyr.* 1.6.25, Ephor. *FrGrHist* 70 F 149, D. Chr. *Or.* 3.136, Lucianus *Anach.* 24, Hdn. 3.6.10, Jul. *Or.* 3, 101 d. The Latin locus classicus is Sal. *Cat.* 5.3 *corpus patiens inediae, algoris, vigiliae supra quam quoiquam credibile est.*

cumque corporis munus a milite, ab imperatore vero animi poscitur V reads *fervores quoque corporis.* Petschenig's *fervoris. cumque corporis* makes excellent sense, but concessive *cum* is always followed by a subj. in Amm. Therefore *quamquam* (Kellerbauer, 1873, 131) is preferable. Even better is *et quamquam,* which is found no fewer than 18 times in Amm. Lindenbrog aptly refers to Liv. 44.34.3–4 *militem haec tria curare debere, corpus ut quam validissimum et pernicissimum habeat, arma apta, cibum paratum ad subita imperia; cetera scire de se dis immortalibus et imperatori suo curae esse.* According to Polybius (10.3.7, 10.13.1–2, 10.24.2–3, 10.32.9–11, 10.33.4–5) and Onasander 33, as is noted ad 24.2.14 *omnes aleae casus,* a general should avoid unnecessary risks.

ipse trucem hostem ictu confecit audacter congressus The expression *ictu conficere* is rare; cf. Fron. *Str.* 2.5.41 *cumque admiratus ille quisnam se comitaretur respexisset, aversum uno ictu confecit.* In 24.4.4 we are told that Julian, attacked during a reconnaissance patrol, killed one of the attackers and returned to his camp with the *spolia* of the Persian and of another attacker. It prompted Amm. to compare Julian with T. Manlius Imperiosus Torquatus and M. Valerius Corvus (24.4.5).

CHAPTER 4.11   135

ac nostros cedentes obiecto pectore suo aliquotiens cohibuit solus V's *subiecto*
following *cedentes* is probably a case of dittography. For *obiecto pectore*
compare the description of Scipio during the battle on the Ticinus
in Sil. 4.415–6 *et latum obiectat pectus strictumque minatur / nunc sibi,
nunc trepidis, ni restent, comminus ensem.* Tac. uses the same expression about German women, *Germ.* 8. 1 *memoriae proditur quasdam
acies inclinatas iam et labantes a feminis restitutas constantia precum et
obiectu pectorum.* Although Amm. says that Julian, by obstructing his
soldiers, checked their retreat several times (*aliquotiens*), the only
reference to such an event is in 16.12.40–1 (cf. Lib. *Or.* 18.58).
Amm. reports a similar prowess on the part of the comes Charietto against the Alamans, 27.1.5 *cedentes obiectu corporis...audentius
retinet.*

regnaque furentium Germanorum excindens Verg. *A.* 7.316 *at licet ambo-
rum populos excindere regum,* or *A.* 9.137 *sceleratam exscindere gentem* may
have been in Amm.'s mind. Cf. also 20.4.1 *post Alamanniae quaedam
regna prostrata receptaque oppida Gallicana ante direpta a barbaris et excisa.*
For *furor* as a characteristic of barbarians see Seager 57.

et in pulvere vaporato Persidis For *vaporatus* see the note ad 24.4.17
aestus in meridiem and for *Persidis* the note ad 23.5.16 *non nunc
primitus.*

dimicans inter primos See the note ad *Fortitudinem certaminum* above.

castrensium negotiorum Apart from Plin. *Ep.* 9.25.1 *quereris de turba*   **4.11**
castrensium negotiorum, this expression is found only in Amm., e.g.
26.7.4 *administratio negotiorum castrensium*; TLL III 544.69. Julian's
knowledge of military matters was mentioned already in 25.4.7
(*armatae rei scientissimus,* q.v.) as proof of his *prudentia.*

civitatum oppugnationes et castellorum Amm. may refer in the first place
to the sieges of Pirisabora (24.2.9–22) and 'Maozamalcha' (24.4.6–
24). Cf. also 24.5.7–11.

inter ipsos discriminum vertices This phrase may well have been inspired by expressions Amm. had found in the work of his predecessors: Liv. 6.36.7 *in maiore discrimine domi res vertebantur,* 10.39.7 *quo
maiore discrimine res vertebatur* and Tac. *Ann.* 11.28.2 *sed in eo discrimen
verti.* If so, there is no need to assume a metaphor based on the
meanings of *vertex* 'eddy' or 'top'; cf. the note ad 24.5.11 *quo inter.*

136 COMMENTARY

acies figura multiformi compositae Amm. may be thinking of the *Homerica dispositio* described in 24.6.9 *Hinc imperator catervis peditum infirmis medium inter acies spatium secundum Homericam dispositionem praestituit.* Another example is 25.1.16 *lunari acie sinuatisque lateribus occursuros hosti manipulos instruebat. Componere* as a military t.t. is rare; TLL III 2115.7–29. With *aciem* it is found only in Amm. 27.2.3, 5 and Dict. 2.32 *tum nostri…aciem composuere.*

salubriter et caute castra metata Cf. 24.4.6 *metatis alibi salubrius castris,* q.v. and 24.8.7 *metatis tutius quievimus castris.*

praetenturae stationesque agrariae totis rationibus ordinatae On *praetenturae* see the note ad 21.13.3. *Praetenturae* and *stationes agrariae* are found together in 14.3.2 (q.v.): *praetenturis et stationibus servabantur agrariis* and 31.8.5. In view of Amm.'s insistence on Julian's cautiousness as a military leader, and comparing 16.12.21 *ratione tuta poscente,* 23.5.1 *munimentum tutissimum* and 24.8.7 *metatis tutius quievimus castris,* the reading *tutis,* proposed by Valesius, seems clearly preferable to V's *totis.* The same applies to 26.4.1 and 27.8.9, where V also has a form of *totus.* For *ordinare* cf. 29.5.5 *ad vigilias ordinandas et praetenturas.*

4.12   *auctoritas adeo valuit, ut* The consecutive phrase has the structure (ut) *et…iuberet…et…regeret…allocutusque…minaretur.*

dilectus artissime, dum timetur, ac si periculorum socius et laborum The combination of attachment and respect is well expressed in 17.1.2 *amor enim post documenta flagrantior sequi hortatus est omnis operae conturmalem auctoritate magnificum ducem.* Julian had not fallen short of the expectations formulated by Constantius when he presented him as a new Caesar to the army: *adesto igitur laborum periculorumque particeps* (15.8.13). Cf. also 23.5.19 *imperator et antesignanus* and 24.6.11 *quasi conturmalis strenuus…et rector.* The comparison introduced by *ac si* is subordinated to *dilectus artissime,* a strong expression, found also in Plin. *Ep.* 6.8.1 *hunc ego non ut multi, sed artissime diligo.* For *ac si* as an equivalent of *quasi* see TLL II 1083.76–1084.36. In Amm. cf. § 14 below *ac si quodam caduceo leniente mundano,* 26.9.5 *ut se ac si parentem magis sequerentur* and 30.1.16 *probrosis lacerati conviciis ac si inertes et desides.*

inter concertationes acerrimas In Cicero *concertatio,* regularly followed by *verborum,* means 'wrangling', e.g. *de Orat.* 2.68 *sine ulla serie disputa-*

CHAPTER 4.13   137

tionum et sine ieiuna concertatione verborum, for which cf. 21.16.18 *quae* (discidia) *aluit concertatione verborum.* As TLL IV 24.61–71 shows, in late Latin it is normally used to describe regular fights; see the note ad 21.11.3 *futurae concertationi.*

animadverti iuberet in desides Amm. is thinking of the incident mentioned in 24.3.2 *duo tribunos sacramento solvit ut desides et ignavos; decem vero milites ex his, qui fugerant, exauctoratos capitali addixit supplicio secutus veteres leges.*

et Caesar adhuc sine stipendio regeret militem According to the author it was part of Constantius' tactics to make life difficult for Julian in his capacity as Caesar in Gaul: 17.9.6 *miles exhaustus nec donativum meruit nec stipendium iam inde, ut Iulianus illo est missus.* The result was a mutiny, quelled by Julian *non sine blanditiarum genere vario* (17.10.1).

discessurum ad vitam minaretur privatam, ni tumultuare desistent A reference to Julian's speech to the troops in 24.3.7 *aut certe discedam; nec enim ita vixi, ut non possim aliquando esse privatus.* For the use of the indic. fut. in or. obl. instead of the imperfect subj. compare the note ad 20.8.10 *quod…libens.*

id pro multis nosse sufficiet This is a variation on Amm.'s usual expression *sufficiet unum (pauca) poni (ponere)* found in 18.1.3, 22.9.10, 22.10.5, 29.3.2, 31.14.3.   **4.13**

exhortatum eum suppliciicontione militem Gallicanum Since *supplex* is invariably used of defeated enemies or generally of persons in an inferior position, it is very hard to believe that this is what Amm. wrote. Compare the following examples: 14.7.5 *Antiochensi plebi suppliciter obsecranti,* 16.12.15 *pacem impetraverunt suppliciter obsecrantes,* 22.14.4 *supplici voce vitam precantem et veniam,* 25.9.2 *et haec quidem suppliciter ordo et populus precabatur,* 29.5.17 *suppliciter obsecrantibus veniam animo elato respondit,* 29.5.26 *supplici prece veniam…impetrarunt.* Therefore it is much better to accept Valesius' *simplici,* as Fontaine does. *Simplex* does not mean primarily 'simple', 'easy to understand', but rather 'straightforward', *sine ambagibus.* Cf. Valentinian's speech to the troops in 26.2.7 *proinde pacatis auribus accipite, quaeso, simplicioribus verbis, quod conducere arbitror in commune* and Equitius' report to Valentinian 26.5.10 *simplicibus verbis principem gestorum conscium fecit.* Amm. probably refers to Julian's speech in 23.5.16–23, which

138   COMMENTARY

was enthusiastically greeted by the soldiers, especially by the *numeri Gallicani* (23.5.25).

pruinis assuetum et Rheno As was said in 20.4.4, a promise had been given to these soldiers that they would not be forced to serve beyond the Alps: *qui relictis laribus transrhenanis sub hoc venerant pacto, ne ducerentur ad partes umquam transalpinas.*

peragratis spatiis regionum extentis Thereby, as it were, mirroring Sapor's hostile inroads, 19.11.17 *Mesopotamia relicta post terga per extenta spatia signa moturum.*

per tepentem Assyriam ad usque confinia...Medorum On *tepere* and its derivatives see the note ad 22.15.5 *expressaeque tepore nimio.* For *Assyria* cf. the note ad 23.2.7 *Assyrios.* As to *confinia...Medorum,* in 24.7.3 it was said that, at least in the eyes of Julian, the kingdom of Persia had practically been conquered (*prope iam parta regna Persidis*). The plan to march into the inner parts of the Sasanian empire (24.7.6), however, had to be abandoned soon (24.8.4).

4.14   *Felicitas ita eminuit, ut* On Julian's *felicitas* see the note ad 21.5.9 *fortunatum domitorem.* As Brandt, 1999, 81 rightly says, *felicitas* is a sign of divine assistance. It must be emphasized that Julian's *felicitas* is always mentioned on a par with his virtues. It is his excellence that earned him his success, cf. 16.1.2 *res magnae, quas per Gallias virtute felicitateque correxit.* This is exactly the reason why, in the elogium of Constantius (21.16.12–3), Julian's predecessor is denied this quality. Amm. obviously attached great weight to his assessment of Constantius in this respect, as is shown by the two quotations, from Cicero and Heraclitus, he inserted there. In a similar way the daring metaphor, which follows in the present text, underlines the importance of this part of Julian's elogium. The difference between the elogia of Constantius and Julian in this respect is well brought out by Neri, 1984, 26–8.

ipsis quodammodo cervicibus Fortunae aliquamdiu bonae gubernatricis evectus Several images are evoked by the daring metaphor of the goddess Fortuna bearing Julian on her shoulders, which the association of Fortuna and *fero* may have suggested to the author. Cf. Lyd. *Mens.* 4.7 Φορτοῦναν αὐτὴν (sc. Tyche) ἀπὸ τῆς φορᾶς ἐμφερῶς ὀνομάσαντες. It was a sign of admiration to carry a man on the shoulders, as is evident from Sal. *Hist.* 3.21 *Cn. Pompeii, quem ipsum ubi pertimuere, sublatum in*

CHAPTER 4.14 139

cervices suas, mox dempto metu lacerant, quoted by Fontaine in n. 581, and Cic. *Phil.* 11.24 *tunc vel in caelum vos, si fieri poterit, umeris nostris tollemus.* For *Fortuna* see further the notes ad 23.5.19 *at si fortuna* and 25.9.5 *Fortuna orbis.* Her traditional attributes are the cornucopia in her left arm and the rudder she holds in her right hand; see e.g. *LIMC* VIII 2, 97, pl. 71 and Lichochka, 1997. The rudder symbolizes her function as *gubernatrix,* for which cf. Ter. *Eun.* 1046 *Fortunam conlaudem, quae gubernatrix fuit?* It is also epigraphically attested in *CIL* 13.7792 and 12049. The other attribute is mentioned in 22.9.1, *velut mundanam cornucopiam Fortuna gestans propitia,* q.v. In 27.11.2 we read about Petronius Probus *hunc quasi gemina quaedam, ut fingunt poetae, Fortuna vehens praepetibus pinnis.* Here Fortuna is visualised as a winged creature, as in Plutarch's flight of fancy *fort. Rom.* 317 e–318 a. Cf. also Gaertner, 1968, 513 n. 4.

The word order suggests that *aliquamdiu* qualifies *bonae gubernatricis.* If that is indeed the case, the adverb betrays Amm.'s awareness that *Fortuna orbis Romani* was not Julian's *bona gubernatrix* till the very end. The thought is expressed explicitly in 25.9.7 *Tu hoc loco, Fortuna orbis Romani, merito incusaris, quae…excussa regimenta perito rei gerendae ductori consummando iuveni porrexisti.* Already in 14.11.25 we find a similar complaint directed at Adrasteia: *Haec et huiusmodi quaedam innumerabilia ultrix facinorum impiorum bonorumque praemiatrix aliquotiens operatur Adrastia – atque utinam semper!*

victoriosis cursibus difficultates superstaret immensas Apart from Gel. 4.9.12, who quotes the adjectives *'disciplinosus', 'consiliosus', 'victoriosus'* as neologisms coined by Cato, *victoriosus* is found only here. It is regrettable that Seyfarth, in his Teubner-edition, preferred *superstaret* to *superaret* which he had printed in his bilingual edition. *Superstaret* may be closer to V's *supestaret,* but the fact that *superstare* is always used in its literal meaning 'to stand above', or 'to stand over' renders its use impossible here. There is a note on *superstare* ad 20.6.4.

quoad fuit in terris, quievere nationes omnes immobiles Amm. has a marked predilection for *immobilis,* especially in combination with the verbs *manere* and *stare,* expressing imperturbability. See the note ad 25.3.9 *mansit immobilis.* Amm. may well have had Tacitus in mind: *Ann.* 4.32.2 *immota quippe aut modice lacessita pax.* We find a similar observation in 22.9.1: *dum teneret imperium solus…nec barbarorum quisquam ultra suos exsiluit fines.* Cf. Lib. *Or.* 18.300 οὔτε γὰρ βάρβαρος ὅπλων ἥψατο παρὰ τὰς συνθήκας. In 30.7.5 we read that Alamanni attacked Gaul as soon as word of Julian's death had reached them:

140   COMMENTARY

Gallias...Alamannicis patentes excursibus reviviscentibus erectius cognito principis Iuliani interitu. Cf. Zos. 4.3.4 Τῶν δὲ ὑπὲρ τὸν Ῥῆνον βαρβάρων, ἕως μὲν Ἰουλιανὸς περιῆν, τὸ Ῥωμαίων ὄνομα δεδιότων ἀγαπώντων τε εἰ μηδεὶς αὐτοῖς κατὰ τὴν χώραν μένουσιν ἐνοχλοίη, τῆς τούτου τελευτῆς ἀγγελθείσης ἀπανέστησαν αὐτίκα τῶν οἰκείων ἠθῶν καὶ πρὸς τὸν κατὰ Ῥωμαίων παρεσκευάζοντο πόλεμον.

ac si quodam caduceo leniente mundano The herald's staff is a token of peace, cf. Gel. 10.27.3 *hastam et caduceum, signa duo belli aut pacis.* At the same time it is an attribute of Mercury, and Rike aptly refers to Julian's *Or.* 7. 234 b, where Hermes presents Julian, before he sets out on his mission, with his golden staff. *Mundanus* means 'worldwide', 'universal'. Cf. *velut mundanam cornucopiam* in 22.9.1. This parallel is sufficient to reject Valesius' *mundana.*

4.15   *Liberalitatis eius testimonia plurima sunt et verissima* As was said ad § 1 *eisque accidentes,* Amm. ranges *liberalitas* instead of *fortitudo* among the four additional qualities, in order to pay adequate attention to the virtue Julian prided himself on, his φιλανθρωπία. As Kabiersch, 1960 shows, Julian's φιλανθρωπία is a wide-ranging concept, including basic qualities such as clemency and generosity towards the subjects. In this elogium Amm. concentrates on Julian's generosity in financial matters, especially his tax policy, probably because his short reign and his personal predilection prevented him from implementing other plans, such as an extensive building programme or the organisation of games for the people, for which cf. Mause, 1994, 164–72. Eutropius and Mamertinus also use *liberalis/liberalitas* with respect to Julian, but their emphasis differs from that of Amm. Cf. Eutr. 10.16.3 *In amicos liberalis, sed minus diligens quam tantum principem decuit. Fuerunt enim nonnulli, qui vulnera gloriae eius inferrent* and *Pan.* 3.22.3 *imperatoris nostri posterior liberalitas vincit priorem,* in which passage Mamertinus alludes to the consulate and other honours which Julian bestowed on him. For the concept of *liberalitas* as an imperial virtue see in general Kloft, 1970 and Noreña, 2001, 160–4, for *liberalitas* in Amm. see Brandt, 1999, 34–5, 84–5 and 389–96.

inter quae indicta sunt tributorum admodum levia It seems best to interpret *indicta* as a noun and *tributorum* as a gen. inversus: 'taxes imposed' or a gen. obiectivus 'impositions of taxes'. For *indictum* see TLL VII 1.1159.54–61, where 16.5.15 is quoted *cum constet ubique pauperes inter ipsa indictorum* (so Pithou, V *dictorum,* Seeck *indictionum*)

CHAPTER 4.15   141

exordia solvere universa sine laxamento compelli. The present passage is not quoted under this heading. A similar pattern is e.g. 23.6.42 *oppida vero mediterranea sunt ampliora...inter quae Persepolis est clara et Ardea et Habroatis atque Tragonice.* The meaning would be 'among which are (such as) the very light taxes imposed (by him), c.q. impositions of taxes.' The alternative would be to take *indicta* as a dominant participle, like the following *indultum, remissa, aequata* and *restituta,* and to interpret *tributorum levia* as *levia tributa*: 'the fact that very light taxes were imposed'. This is probably how the TLL interprets it, where this section is mentioned under the heading *indico* (VII 1.1157.76). The syntactical analysis may differ, but the meaning remains the same.

Julian himself boasts in the *Misopogon*: οὐδὲ ηὐξήσαμεν φόρους (365 b), and issued a law in which he stipulates that no tax levy should be made upon the provincials without his knowledge (*Nihil provincialibus indici sine nostra scientia fas est, Cod. Theod.* 11.16.10). Amm. had already referred to this aspect of Julian's reign in books 16–18, dealing with the years in Gaul. Cf. 16.5.14 (Julian attained a 70% reduction of rates), 17.3.1 (*tributi ratiocinia dispensavit*) and 18.1.1 (*Iulianus...haud minore cura provinciarum fortunis multa conducentia disponebat diligenter observans, ne quem tributorum sarcina praegravaret*). Indirectly he praised his hero in 21.16.17 (q.v.), where he says of Constantius: *nec provinciarum indemnitati prospexit, cum multiplicatis tributis et vectigalibus vexarentur.* Eutropius shares Amm.'s view: *In provinciales iustissimus et tributorum, quatenus fieri posset, repressor* (10.16.3), but also points to a drawback of this policy, viz. that Julian neglected the intcrcsts of the treasury: *mediocrem habens aerarii curam* (ibid.). Mamertinus in *Pan.* 3.9.1 states that the Dalmatians and Epirotes found their way back to prosperity only after Julian had relieved them of their oppressive taxation: *levati equorum pretiis enormibus Dalmatae, Epirotae ad incitas* ('extremely') *intolerandi tributi mole depressi providentia, imperator, tua non modo miserias exuerunt, sed ad amplam etiam atque opulentam revixere fortunam,* and in 3.10.2 remarks: *Illud vero cuius miraculi est...quoddam versa vice provinciis pendi tributum, illinc ad universos fluere divitias quo prius undique confluebant* ("What a wonder it is that...by a reversal of the normal way of things, a sort of tribute was paid out to the provinces so that the coffers which previously collected wealth from every quarter were now dispensing it to one and all!", tr. Morgan). Much still had to be done, for, according to Libanius (*Or.* 18.282), Julian hoped that after the Persian expedition he would be able to reduce taxation to the level of old times (ὥστ' αὐτῷ γενέσθαι τὴν εἰσφορὰν εἰς τἀρχαῖα πάλιν ἀπενεγκεῖν).

142 COMMENTARY

A Christian author like Sozomen was less positive and stated that Julian had the Christian populace numbered and subjected to taxes as onerous as those of villages (*HE* 5.4.5 τὸ δὲ πλῆθος τῶν Χριστιανῶν σὺν γυναιξὶ καὶ παισὶ ἀπογράψασθαι καὶ καθάπερ ἐν ταῖς κώμαις φόρους τελεῖν), but Ambrose could not deny that at least some of Julian's fiscal measures were praised by the provinces: *Hoc laudant provinciae Iulianum* (*obit. Valent.* 21) – he himself was of a different opinion: *ille plurima repperit et exhausit omnia* (ibid.) –, while Gregory's reference to φόρων ἄνεσις in *Or.* 4.75, though no doubt sarcastic, is one of the very few utterances in his invectives against Julian that is not totally negative. In view of all this Julian's fiscal policy has often been seen by modern scholars as exemplary and in sharp contrast to that of his predecessors, especially Constantius (see e.g. Ensslin, 1923b, 127 and Andreotti, 1978 (= 1930), 133sqq.; cf. also Frank, 1972, 78–81). Pack, 1986, 61–179, however, shows that this inference needs considerable qualification (the chapter on Julian's "politique financière" in Renucci, 2000, 435–58, published in the same series, is very disappointing indeed).

coronarium indultum Priscianus *gramm.* II 487.1 remarks about the supinum of *indulgere*: *ut 'indulsi indulsum' vel 'indultum', unde Marcellinus rerum gestarum XIIII: tamquam licentia crudelitati indulta* (14.1.4). Priscian is the only Latin author from Antiquity to mention Ammianus. Cf. for *indulgere*, in financial matters "fere i.q. donare, praebere, praestare" (TLL VII 1.1254.45), e.g. *Cod. Theod.* 11.28.1 (a law of Julian) *Excepto auro et argento cuncta reliqua indulgemus* and in general Gaudemet, 1962. The *aurum coronarium* (Amm. does not use the full expression; cf. *coronam* in 25.9.4), was "an offering of gold crowns, in theory voluntary, but long customary, made by the cities of the empire to the emperor on his accession and on the quinquennial celebrations of that event, and also on such festal occasions as triumphs" (Jones 430; Klauser, 1944, reprinted in 1974, is still the best study on this topic; cf. further Ando, 2000, 175–90.). It was an old tax, inherited from the Hellenistic East (cf. Millar, 1977, 140–1), and e.g. mentioned in the *Monumentum Ancyranum*, where Augustus boasts: *Auri coronari pondo triginta et quinque millia municipiis et colonis Italiae conferentibus ad triumphos meos quintum consul remisi, et postea, quotienscumque imperator appellatus sum, aurum coronarium non accepi decernentibus municipiis et colonis aeque benigne adque antea decreverant* (Aug. *Anc.* 21.3; cf. D.C. 51.21.4). Augustus' refusal to accept the *aurum coronarium* apparently set a precedent, for Julian was not the only emperor who is said to have remitted the tax, cf. *P. Fay.* 20 for

CHAPTER 4.15 143

Trajan, Marcus Aurelius and Alexander Severus, HA *H* 6.5, *AP* 4.10 and *AS* 32.5 for Hadrian, Antoninus Pius and, once again, Alexander Severus. Incidentally, *P. Fay.* 20, regarded by some scholars (e.g. Ensslin, 1923b, 129–32, Seston, 1942 and 1943, Renucci, 2000, 142–4) as an edict issued or reissued by Julian, should be ascribed to Alexander Severus (cf. e.g. Moreau, 1964, 37–9 and Pack, 1986, 132–4).

The offering of such crowns to Julian after he had been proclaimed emperor is attested by Eunapius (*fr.* 24): Ὅτι μετὰ τὴν Ἰουλιανοῦ τῆς βασιλείας ἀναγόρευσιν πρεσβεῖαι πανταχόθεν συνέβαινον καὶ στέφανοι πολλοὶ χρυσοῖ οἳ αὐτῷ παρὰ τῶν ἐθνῶν ἀνεκομίζοντο, and Libanius (*Or.* 18.193): Ὁ χρυσὸς δὲ οὗτος ἀνέμνησέ με χρυσῶν στεφάνων οὓς αἱ μὲν πόλεις ἔπεμπον διὰ πρέσβεων ἀλλήλας ὑπερβάλλουσαι τῷ σταθμῷ ("striving to outdo one another in the weight of them", tr. Norman). If Amm. is right in stating that Julian remitted the *aurum coronarium* (and he certainly is, see below), this step apparently was not taken until the embassies, spoken of by Eunapius and Libanius, had set off on their trip.

At first sight Zos. 3.12.2 (about an embassy from Edessa that offered Julian a crown while he stayed in Batnae) and Amm. 23.3.8 (*oblata ex auro corona*, about Saracen princes presenting Julian with a golden crown) also seem to refer to the offering of crown money. However, as was remarked in the note ad 23.2.7 *venit ad Batnas*, "it would seem that Zos. is either simply wrong or his text is faultily transmitted (cf. Paschoud n. 32)", while Amm.'s statement in 23.3.8 is of a different order and refers not to the *aurum coronarium*, but to *annua sollemnia* (cf. the note ad loc.).

Amm.'s *coronarium indultum* has a parallel in Lib. *Or.* 16.19, if indeed, as would seem to be the case (so e.g. Norman ad loc. and Pack, 1986, 135 n. 268 and 329–30 n. 98), Libanius there refers to Julian's remission of the *aurum coronarium* when he says about Julian: ὁ τὴν ἀρχαίαν τοῦ χρυσοῦ φορὰν τοῖς δήμοις ἀνείς. Wiemer, 1995, 289 n. 130 and others assume that Libanius refers to the remission of another tax, viz. the *collatio lustralis* or *chrysargyron* (a tax instituted by Constantine, levied every five years and imposed on *negotiatores*; cf. Jones 431–2), which is the subject of *Cod. Theod.* 12.1.50, issued by Julian on 13 March 362, and spoken of in Jul. *Mis.* 367 d (πολὺ μὲν ἀνῆκα χρυσίον, πολὺ δ' ἀργύριον; cf. *ibid.* 365 b οὐδὲ ἐπεγράψαμεν χρυσίον οὐδὲ ᾐτήσαμεν ἀργύριον with Pack, 1986, 325 ff.).

As to the extent of Julian's remission, according to Lib. *Or.* 18.193 the maximum of the tax was fixed at 70 staters of gold (νομοθετεῖ τὸν στέφανον ἀπὸ στατήρων ἑβδομήκοντα φοιτᾶν), but we

144   COMMENTARY

do not find any mention of this in *Cod. Theod.* 12.13.1, issued by
Julian on 29 April 362. The text of this constitution, "fort curieuse-
ment rédigée" (Lacombrade, 1949, 57), and probably, as so often
(cf. Volterra, 1971 and 1981), only preserved in an abridged form,
makes the crown money once again voluntary (*Aurum coronarium
munus est voluntatis, quod non solum senatoribus, sed ne aliis quidem debet
indici*), but leaves it to the emperor to decide when and where to ask
for it (*Licet quaedam indictionum necessitas postulaverit; sed nostro arbitrio
reservari oportebit*). Cf. for Julian's measure or measures concerning
the *aurum coronarium* ("Es sind offenbar mehrere Gesetze zu diesem
Thema ergangen", Bliembach ad Lib. *Or.* 18.193) in the first place
Pack, 1986, 134 ff.

remissa debita multa diuturnitate congesta There is a discrepancy between Amm.'s words here and his statement in 16.5.15, that Julian
to the very end of his life observed the rule not to cancel fiscal debts,
because he knew that only the rich profited of such cancellations
(*id eum ad usque imperii finem et vitae scimus utiliter observasse, ne per
indulgentias, quas appellant, tributariae rei concederet reliqua. norat enim
hoc facto se aliquid locupletibus additurum, cum constet ubique pauperes
inter ipsa indictorum exordia solvere universa sine laxamento compelli*).
Julian may indeed have been of the opinion articulated by Amm.,
as his words in *Ep.* 73 quoted below suggest, but it was hard to
stick to this rule. The least he could do was to see to it that
no remissions were granted without his personal consent: *Nihil
provincialibus indici sine nostra conscientia fas est neque rursus ex his
quae sunt indicta referri* (*Cod. Theod.* 11.16.10, issued on March 13,
362), but from various sides requests for remission of overdue
taxes reached him. So for example from the Thracians, to whom
he answered in *Ep.* 73 that it was difficult for him, an emperor
with an eye not solely on his own gain or that of a particular city
but on the public prosperity, to grant their request, but that he
nevertheles was willing to do so, as it was his aim to be the source of
wealth for his subjects, and not to collect for the treasury as much
money as possible (ἐπεὶ δὲ ἡμεῖς οὐχ ὅτι πλεῖστα παρὰ τῶν ὑπηκόων
ἀθροίζειν πεποιήμεθα σκοπόν, ἀλλ᾽ ὅτι πλείστων ἀγαθῶν αὐτοῖς αἴτιοι
γίγνεσθαι, τοῦτο καὶ ὑμῖν ἀπολύσει τὰ ὀφλήματα, 428 c). In the rest
of his letter (428 d) Julian adds the proviso that not the whole
sum was to be cancelled. Similar requests no doubt came from the
embassies spoken of by Eun. *fr.* 24 and Lib. *Or.* 18.193 and mentioned
in the previous note – see *Cod. Theod.* 12.13.4 and Synesius, *Or.
de regno* 3 for the connection between the offering of the *aurum*

CHAPTER 4.15   145

coronarium and requests for tax remission; cf. also Jul. *Mis.* 367 c–d. According to Eunapius the Ionians had all their requests granted, the Lydians achieved more than they had asked for: ἐνταῦθα καὶ οἱ τὴν Ἰωνίαν οἰκοῦντες ἔτυχον ὅσων ἐδεήθησαν…Λυδοὶ δὲ καὶ εὐχῆς κρεῖττον ἔπραττον. As to the inhabitants of Antioch, in *Mis.* 365 b Julian writes: πρὸς τοῖς ἐλλείμμασιν ('arrears') ἀνεῖται ('had been remitted') πᾶσι τῶν εἰθισμένων εἰσφορῶν τὸ πέμπτον, in 367 d: ἀνῆκα…φόρους δὲ παμπληθεῖς. Cf. further Lib. *Or.* 18.163 ἐπιβὰς Συρίας χρέα…λύσας ταῖς πόλεσι, *Cod. Theod.* 11.12.2 and 11.28.1 *Excepto auro et argento cuncta reliqua indulgemus* (this law was addressed to the vicar of Africa). For discussion see Ensslin, 1923b, 132–4, Andreotti, 1978, 135–6 and Pack, 1986, 123–4, 331–3.

As in the case of the remission of the *aurum coronarium*, Julian was not the first emperor in Roman history to grant immunity from taxation, nor was he the last. Cf. Millar, 1977, 420ff. and Gaudemet, 1962, passim. Note that in *CIL* 6.967 = *ILS* 309 (about Hadrian, cf. D.C. 69.8.1 and HA *H* 7.6) and *Pan.* 5.10.5 (about Constantine) tax remission is seen, as in the present text, as a sign of the emperor's *liberalitas*.

aequata fisci iurgia cum privatis In TLL I 1020.35–9 this unparalleled use of *aequare* is interpreted as "i.q. placare" on the basis of expressions like Verg. *A.* 5.844 *aequatae spirant aurae* (but see Williams ad loc.). This is followed by Seyfarth who translates "Streitigkeiten zwischen Privatleuten und der Staatskasse beigelegt." For the content of the phrase one might compare 16.12.16 *sedata iurgiorum materia vicinae gentes iam concordabant*. Alternatively *aequare* could be taken to mean *aequo iure tractare* or *perpendere*, as in 22.9.9: *causarum momenta aequo iure perpendens suum cuique tribuebat*. This is how Rolfe seems to understand the phrase: "the impartial treatment of disputes between the privy purse and private persons." Ensslin, 1923b, 27 translates "die Gleichsetzung der Prozesse des Fiskus mit privaten Rechtsstreitigkeiten". It is not clear, however, whether this would mean an improvement for the litigants. While Brok 206 cites without comment the translations of Rolfe and Ensslin, Fontaine n. 585 prefers Rolfe's rendering.

As to *fiscus*, which in Amm. occurs here as well as in 18.5.1 and in 28.4.1, Rolfe's "privy purse" and Seyfarth's "Staatskasse" amount to the same thing, for, as Millar, 1977, 199 notes, "From towards the middle of the third century at any rate, our sources cease to reflect any consciousness of a division between imperial and public revenues; *fiscus* and cognate expressions are applied to all the

146   COMMENTARY

revenues and possessions of the state". See on this in the first place
Delmaire, 1989, 11–3. There is a note on *privatus* ad 25.5.8.

Amm. probably refers to Julian's intervention on behalf of land-
holders who had incurred calamitous losses during the wars in Gaul.
This resulted in a conflict with the praetorian prefect Florentius
(17.3).

vectigalia civitatibus restituta cum fundis Amm.'s statement poses a
number of problems and has, together with the other relevant texts,
provoked much comment (cf. e.g. Ensslin, 1923b, 140–2; Brok
206–7; Liebeschuetz, 1959, 344–7; Jones, 732; Frank, 1972, 79–81;
Lepelley, 1979, 67–72; Bonamente, 1983, 46–59; Ausbüttel, 1988,
65–9; Delmaire, 1989, 641–52; Wiemer, 1995, 102–7). What is the
meaning here of *vectigalia*, and of *fundi*? And, a question which
naturally follows from the foregoing: are *vectigalia* and *fundi* to be
taken as distinct categories, or does the use of *cum* imply a close
relationship between the two concepts? Further, if *vectigalia...cum
fundis* were restored by Julian to the cities, who, then, had taken
them away?

For the answer to these questions other sources, dealing with
the same subject matter, above all the constitutions issued by Julian
himself, may be of some help. Unfortunately, the first and most
important of the relevant laws, *Cod. Theod.* 10.3.1, posted at Constantinople on the ides of March 362, does not clarify the meaning
of the terms used by Amm. It speaks of *possessiones publicae* instead of
vectigalia...cum fundis, which is not very helpful: *Possessiones publicas
civitatibus iubemus restitui.* Nor are the *Historia Acephala* and Libanius as specific as one would wish. In *Hist. Aceph.* 3.1 it is said that by
order of Julian *quae preteritis temporibus illis ablata sunt* should be given
back to 'the gods, the wardens of the temples and the civic treasury'
(*idolis et neochoris et publicae rationi*), while Libanius uses the general
expression κτημάτα when he refers to Julian's attempt to 'amend
the poverty of the cities which had been driven from their old and
lawful possessions, whereby private houses had become great to the
detriment of those of the community' (τὸ ταῖς πόλεσιν ἐπανορθῶσαι
τὴν πενίαν ἐξεληλαμέναις ἀρχαίων τε καὶ δικαίων κτημάτων, ὃ τοὺς μὲν
ἰδίους οἴκους μεγάλους ἐποίησε, τοῖς δὲ κοινοῖς περιέχεεν ἀμορφίαν, Lib.
Or. 13.45, tr. Norman, rev.). On the other hand, from *Cod. Theod.*
15.1.8 (cf. *Cod. Iust.* 8.11.4), 15.1.9 and especially *Cod. Iust.* 11.70.1,
all issued at Antioch later in 362, it can be deduced that Amm.'s *fundi*
probably has the sense, not merely of 'lands', as Rolfe and Hamilton
suggest, but of 'immovable property', 'land with the buildings on

CHAPTER 4.15 147

it', as in Florent. *dig.* 50.16.211 (*'Fundi' appellatione omne aedificium et omnis ager continetur. sed in usu urbana aedificia 'aedes'...dicuntur*; cf. TLL VI 1575.49 et seq.). The cited constitutions read as follows: *Oportuit praetoria iudicum et domos iudiciarias publico iuri atque usui vindicari* (*Cod. Theod.* 15.1.8; *Cod. Iust.* 8.11.4 reads *domos publicas* instead of *domos iudiciarias*), *Conperimus super ergasteria publica, quae ad ius pertinent civitatis, plerosque sibi domos struxisse* (*Cod. Theod.* 15.1.9) and *Pro aedibus, quas nonnulli in solo rei publicae extruxerunt, placitam praestare pensionem cogantur* (*Cod. Iust.* 11.70.1).

As to *vectigalia*, Delmaire, 1989, 275 is certainly right in stating that "tout impôt peut être qualifié de *vectigal*...mais on réserve plutôt ce mot aux impôts indirects et taxes d'utilisation du domaine public". Of course, it is theoretically possible that in the present text "impôts indirects" are meant, like for instance taxes imposed on pimps, harlots and catamites (according to HA *AS* 24.3 Alexander Severus used *lenonum vectigal et meretricum et exoletorum* for the restoration of public buildings in Rome). However, in view of some of the laws of Julian just mentioned it is more likely that Amm. refers to Delmaire's second category, that is, income derived from the lease of public property. *Cod. Theod.* 10.3.1, which, as we saw, opens with the words *Possessiones publicas civitatibus iubemus restitui*, continues as follows: *ita, ut iustis aestimationibus locentur, quo cunctarum possit civitatium reparatio procurari*. And *Cod. Iust.* 11.70.1, just quoted, also speaks of rent (*pensio*) paid for civic possessions. Cf. further *Cod. Theod.* 15.1.10, which deals with the proceeds of illegally obtained public buildings (*Quicumque cuiuslibet ordinis dignitatis aliquod opus publicum quoquo genere obscura interpretatione meruerit, fructu talis beneficii sine aliqua dubitatione privetur*).

In view of all this and taking *cum* in the present text as an indication of a close relationship between the cities' *vectigalia* and their *fundi*, we conclude that with *vectigalia...cum fundis* Amm. must refer to immovable property, both lands and buildings, and the income the cities derived from the lease of this property. We can even go somewhat further. When two other constitutions, preserved in the *Theodosian Code*, are taken into consideration, viz. 5.13.3 and 10.1.8, it is possible to give a more detailed explanation of the *fundi* which Julian restored to the cities: the greater part of them must have consisted of temple lands.

As we have seen, part of the property Julian wanted to restore consisted of *domus, aedes* and *ergasteria* (*Cod. Theod.* 15.1.8, 15.1.9, *Cod. Iust.* 8.11.4, 11.70.1). This is in keeping with the general rule that "most cities...owned a certain number of houses and shops" (Jones, 1979 [= 1940], 246). But shops and houses were not the principal source of a city's income. By far the greatest part of its real estate, as Jones demonstrates (ibid., cf. Jones 732), consisted of lands or, to be more precise, temple lands, i.e. lands in possession of temples but administered by the city. *Cod. Theod.* 5.13.3 and 10.1.8 show that precisely such lands were restored by Julian in 362. In *Cod. Theod.* 5.13.3 we read that in 364 the emperors Valentinian and Valens wanted to reverse Julian's measure with regard to the possessions of temples: *Universa quae ex patrimonio nostro per arbitrium divae memoriae Iuliani in possessionem sunt translata templorum, sollicitudine sinceritatis tuae cum omni iure ad rem privatam nostram redire mandamus* ("All property which was transferred from Our patrimony and placed in possession of temples by the authority of the Emperor Julian of sainted memory, We order to be restored with full legal title to Our privy purse, through the offices of Your Sincerity", tr. Pharr). And *Cod. Theod.* 10.1.8, issued by the same emperors (or, according to some scholars, e.g. Bonamente, 1983, 57 and Wiemer, 1995, 106, by Jovian; but see Delmaire, 1989, 643 and the note ad 25.10.12 *Hinc quoque*), and dealing with parcels of lands and landed estates which are now (*nunc*) the property of temples, evidently also refers to Julian's project: *Universa loca vel praedia, quae nunc in iure templorum sunt quaeque a diversis principibus vendita vel donata sunt retracta, ei patrimonio, quod privatum nostrum est, placuit adgregari* ("It is Our pleasure that all parcels of land and all landed estates which are now the property of temples and which have been sold or donated by various Emperors shall be reclaimed and added to Our private patrimony", tr. Pharr) – note that according to the latter law it was not only one emperor, i.c. Julian, but other emperors as well who had 'sold or donated' land (more on this in the next note). To sum up, what Julian wanted to give back to the cities, as evidenced by the Theodosian Code, was the income the cities had derived in former days from the possession of immovable property, especially houses, shops and temple lands, and the lease of this property.

Some matters still need to be discussed. Firstly, regarding the question who had deprived the cities of the revenues which Julian restored, *Cod. Theod.* 5.13.3 and 10.1.8 once again give a clue. Both constitutions make it clear that with respect to temple lands Julian's successors wanted to return (*redire, retracta*) to the pre-Julianic situation, that is, to the time when temple lands were in the possession of the imperial treasury (*ad rem privatam nostram; ei patrimonio, quod privatum nostrum est*). It was in the reign of

CHAPTER 4.15 149

Constantine that the imperial *fiscus* had begun to profit from the plundering of pagan temples and the confiscation of temple lands (Anon. *de mach. bell.* 2, Jul. *Or.* 7. 228 b, Lib. *Or.* 30.6, 62.8, Soz. *HE* 5.5.3–5; cf. Metzler, 1981, 28–32; Sánchez, 2000, 411–5) and it was under his sons that these practices had continued (Jul. ibid., Amm. 22.4.3, q.v.). Secondly, it is often suggested that not only temple lands, but all the cities' *fundi* had been confiscated by Constantine and/or Constantius. Cf. e.g. Jones 732 with n. 44 on p. 1301: "the confiscation must have taken place in Constantius' last years". However, Wiemer, 1995, 102 sqq. rightly argues that there is no support in the sources for such a supposition. Thirdly, apart from emperors and cities some private persons were also involved in the confiscation c.q. restoration of the *vectigalia…cum fundis*. This can be deduced from Amm.'s addition *absque his, quos velut iure vendidere praeteritae potestates*, which we will now deal with.

absque his, quos velut iure vendidere praeteritae potestates With these words Amm. indicates that Julian's restoration act was not carried out strictly to rule: an exception was made for property sold by 'previous authorities' (for *potestates* in this sense see TLL X 2.318.24–77; here Julian's predecessors seem to be meant, rather than high officials as e.g. in 21.16.2 *cunctae castrenses et ordinariae potestates*, q.v.). The same exception is expressed by the words *inconcusso iure* in *Cod. Theod.* 15.1.9, already partly quoted in the previous note: *Comperimus super ergasteria publica, quae ad ius pertinent civitatis plerasque sibi domos struxisse. Praecipimus ergo eas inconcusso iure qui aedificaverunt, possidere* ("We therefore direct that those persons who built such houses shall possess them with undisturbed right", tr. Pharr). We may think of estates sold under Constantius and Constans, who explicitly stipulated that landholdings bought from the *fiscus* should remain in the possession of the purchasers and their descendants: *Universi cognoscant has possessiones, quas de fisco nostro comparasse noscuntur, nullo a nobis iure retrahi: sed propria firmitate possessas etiam ad posteros suos dominii perpetis durabilitate demitti* (*Cod. Theod.* 5.13.1, February 12, 341). Amm.'s addition in the present text of *velut iure*, 'as if by right' implies that, according to the author, certain transactions might well have been fraudulent. And indeed, some of them certainly were, as can be deduced from the following proviso in a constitution of April 5, 342 (*Cod. Theod.* 12.1.33): *ita ut omni fraude submota si qui venditione simulata praescriptas lege minuat facultates, omne, quod simulata venditione ad alium transtulit, fisci nostri viribus vindicetur* ("Thus all fraud shall be removed, if any person through a pretended sale should decrease

150 COMMENTARY

the amount of property prescribed by law [sc. as a minimum for elegibility to the decurionate], and everything that he transfers to another person under this pretended sale shall be vindicated to the resources of Our fisc", tr. Pharr; see for the interpretation of this law Lehmann, 1984).

Naturally, as a result of Julian's measure legal disputes arose. Libanius in *Ep.* 724.2 describes such a case. He speaks up for a certain Theodulus (not in *PLRE* I), who was accused of having built a villa using misappropriated temple property, and refers approvingly to the very exception Julian had made: Θεόδουλος οὐχ ὕβρει καὶ παροινίᾳ διέσπα τὸ ἱερόν, ἀλλ᾽ ὄντων τῶν πωλούντων ἐώνητο τιθεὶς τὰς τιμάς, πρᾶγμα ποιῶν, ὃ πᾶσιν ἐξῆν τοῖς δυναμένοις ὠνεῖσθαι ("Theodulus didn't pull the temple apart out of arrogance and brutishness, but rather, he bought from the sellers who were at hand, making his payment and doing something that it was possible for anyone to do who could pay the price", tr. Bradbury). A similar case is sketched in Lib. *Ep.* 1364.7: μετέπλασαν νεὼς εἰς οἰκίαν οἱ Θαλασσίου πρᾶγμα ποιοῦντες ἀρέσκον τῷ κρατοῦντι τότε, καὶ οὐκ ἐπαινῶ μέν, ἦν δ᾽ οὖν τῶν τότε τὰ τοιαῦτα νόμων ("The sons of Thalassius [*PLRE* I, Thalassius 2 and Bassianus 2] converted temples into a house: they acted in conformity with the policy adopted by the emperor of the day [i.e. Constantius]. I do not approve of it, but anyway this was legal at the time", tr. Norman). Cf. further Lib. *Ep.* 757, 763, 819, 828, *Or.* 18.126 and, for a different opinion, Soz. *HE* 5.5.5. Libanius is less indulgent as regards Constantius in *Or.* 30.38, accusing him, not of having sold temple property, but of having presented his courtiers with gifts of temples as if he gave them a horse (ἐκεῖνός γε καὶ δῶρα ναοὺς τοῖς ἀμφ᾽ αὑτὸν ἐδίδου καθάπερ ἵππον). Cf. *Or.* 17.7 and 18.23.

quodque numquam augendae pecuniae cupidus fuit, quam cautius apud dominos servari existimabat Although according to Libanius it was easy enough for Julian to increase his possessions, that was not his aim (τὴν μὲν οὐσίαν οὐκ ἐποίει μείζω ῥᾴδιον ὄν, *Or.* 18.18). On the contrary, while for others supreme power resulted in a love of money, Julian gave his possessions away (τῶν γὰρ ἄλλων ὁμοῦ τῇ βασιλείᾳ δεχομένων καὶ χρημάτων ἔρωτα…σὺ μόνος ἐν δυναστείᾳ καταστὰς τῶν πατρῴων ἀπέστης τοῖς γνωρίμοις τῷ μὲν οἰκίαν διδούς, τῷ δὲ ἀνδράποδα, γῆν ἑτέρῳ, χρυσίον ἄλλῳ, *Ep.* 369.8, cf. *Or.* 18.201–2). In this respect he resembled Hadrian (HA *H* 15.1 *Amicos ditavit et quidem non petentes*) and his grandfather Constantius Chlorus, who, according to Eutr. 10.1.2, used to say: *melius publicas opes a privatis haberi quam intra*

CHAPTER 4.16   151

unum claustrum reservari (cf. Eus. *VC* 1.14). Valentinian was cast in a different mould: *Aviditas plus habendi sine honesti pravique differentia et indagandi quaestus varios per alienae vitae naufragia exundavit in hoc principe flagrantius adolescens* (30.8.8).

id aliquotiens praedicans See for cataphoric or preparatory *id* the note ad 22.3.4 *cum id voluminis*. Amm. uses *praedicare* regularly to introduce a sententia: 25.4.7 *id praedicabat turpe esse sapienti, cum habeat animum, captare laudes ex corpore*, 30.8.13 *Lycurgos invenisse praedicabat et Cassios, columina iustitiae prisca*.

Alexandrum Magnum...benivole respondisse For Alexander the Great in Amm. see the notes ad 21.8.3 and 24.4.27 and the literature cited there. The anecdote is found i.a. in Libanius' first *Chria*, 1.5: μὴ ζητήσῃς ἕτερον, φησίν, Ἀλεξάνδρου πλοῦτον. οὗτοι (the friends) γὰρ ἐμοὶ θησαυροί. D.S. 29.29 tells the same story about Ptolemaeus V Epiphanes, who, when asked where he would find money for a military campaign pointed to his friends and answered: Ὁρᾷς τοὺς ἐμοὺς θησαυροὺς περιπατοῦντας. There is an interesting parallel in Julian's own *Caes.* 313 a-b, where Alexander Severus is reproached, because he did not realize ὅσῳ κρεῖττον ἀναλίσκειν ἦν αὐτὰ (τὰ χρήματα) τοῖς φίλοις ἢ θησαυρίζειν. In its proverbial Latin form the sententia is found in Pl. *Truc.* 885 *ubi amici, [esse] ibidem opes* and Quint. *Inst.* 5.11.41: *ubi amici? ubi opes*. Otto, 1890 (1962), 20–1. *Benivole* probably means that Alexander gave a friendly answer to a somewhat impertinent question.

Digestis bonis, quae scire potuimus, nunc ad explicanda eius vitia veniamus, **4.16**
licet dicta sint carptim The opening sentence of the second part of the elogium mirrors that in 21.16.8: *dinumeratis carptim bonis, quae scire potuimus, nunc ad explananda eius vitia veniamus*, q.v. In the case of Constantius the vices far outnumbered the virtues, whereas regarding Julian the section on his virtues is much longer than that on his faults. As was observed in the note ad 21.16.8, it is surprising indeed that the adverb *carptim* is applied to the treatment of those qualities which were less predominant in the two emperors, the good ones of Constantius, the bad ones of Julian. Be that as it may, in view of the, obviously deliberate, parallelism between the two elogia, it is necessary to attribute the same meaning to *carptim* in both passages. That means that the translations of Seyfarth ("wenn sie auch schon hin und wieder genannt worden sind") and Fontaine ("bien que nous en ayons parlé par bribes") must be rejected, since in

historiography *carptim*, 'selectively', is almost a terminus technicus in programmatic statements, cf. Sal. *Cat.* 4.2 *statui res gestas populi Romani carptim, ut quaeque memoria digna videbantur, perscribere*, imitated in 28.1.2 *ac licet ab hoc textu cruento gestorum exquisite narrando iustus me retraheret metus…tamen praesentis temporis modestia fretus carptim, ut quaeque memoria digna sunt, explanabo.* Cf. also 14.4.2 *super quorum moribus licet in actibus principis Marci et postea aliquotiens memini rettulisse, tamen nunc quoque pauca de isdem expediam carptim* and 30.2.8 *quae funera tunc explicari poterunt carptim, si ad ea quoque venerimus.* Rolfe's "although they can be summed up briefly" does more justice to *carptim*, but fails to account for the perfect tense *dicta sint*, as Drexler, 1974, 101 n. 81 rightly remarks. There are parellels for *dicta sint*, such as e.g. Plin. *Nat.* 31.105 *haec de sale dicta sint* and Macr. *Sat.* 1.6.34 *haec eo dicta sint ut aperta ratione constaret* e.q.s., but there the verb refers to what has already been said. The best solution for the present passage has been suggested tentatively by Drexler himself in his note: "es sei denn man wagte zu erklären: 'gesagt sein soll'". In that case the subj. *sint* does not depend on *licet*, which, by the way, is never followed by a perfect subj. in Amm., but has its own adhortative or jussive force. See for a thorough discussion of concessive clauses in Amm. Spevak, 2005. Admittedly this is a rather laboured phrase, and it is tempting to consider as an alternative *dicenda sint*, which is more in agreement with the future tenses in the phrases in Amm. quoted above, and is used regularly in transitional expressions of this type, e.g. Cic. *Tusc.* 4.64 *Sed aegritudini, de qua satis est disputatum, finitimus est metus, de quo pauca dicenda sunt*, Quint. *Inst.* 6.1.2 *quae repetemus quam brevissime dicenda sunt, et, quod Graeco verbo patet, decurrendum per capita*, HA *Gall.* 21.1 *de quibus breviter et pauca dicenda sunt.* While Amm. openly speaks of Julian's *vitia*, Libanius, as is to be expected, only refers to his defects in a veiled way. See for this Malosse, 1995, 335–8.

levioris ingenii, verum hoc instituto rectissimo temperabat emendari se, cum deviaret a fruge bona, permittens The first mention of Julian's *levitas* is 16.7.6, where it is explained as the result of his oriental background: *is* (the eunuch Eutherius) *praepositus cubiculi etiam Iulianum aliquotiens corrigebat Asiaticis coalitum moribus ideoque levem.* Amm. censures Julian's criticism of Constantine as *insulse nimirum et leviter* in 21.10.8, q.v. Even when he was an Augustus Julian's behaviour was at times less than dignified and he is duly taken to task for it by Amm.; cf. especially the scene in the senate of Constantinople 22.7.3 with the notes. In *Mis.* 363 d Julian himself

CHAPTER 4.17   153

admits his προπέτεια. But Amm. hastens to mitigate his criticism by pointing out Julian's willingness to learn and be corrected, illustrated by his respect for the admonitions of Eutherius mentioned above and 22.10.3 *praefectis proximisque permittebat, ut fidenter...monitu opportuno frenarent*. Cf. also 22.11.11 *mitigatus est lenientibus proximis*, Jul. *Ep.* 32, 381 b-c, Eunapius *fr.* 28.2 and Zonaras 13.13.26 (quoted ad 25.4.18 *Volgi plausibus*).

For *institutum* in the sense of "ratio vitae instituta", see TLL VII 1. 1994.39–71. Amm. uses it in the plural for the way of life of a social group: 14.6.24 *haec nobilium sunt instituta*, or nations: 15.11.1 *lingua institutis legibusque discrepantes*. The phrase *bonae frugi* has given rise to prepositional phrases like Cic. *Cael.* 28 *se ad frugem bonam, ut dicitur, recepisse*; cf. TLL VI 1454.63–1455.20; Otto, 1890 (1962), 147. This is the only instance in Amm.

linguae fusioris et admodum raro silentis Thompson, 1947, 82 calls **4.17** this a curious accusation in view of 16.5.9, where Amm. had said that Julian spoke *ornate...et facete*. Indeed, in the section that follows there, some remarks are quoted which show Julian's wit. For a devastating portrait of Julian as an agitated intellectual at the university of Athens see Greg. Naz. *Or.* 5.23. Small wonder that the courtiers in Milan ridiculed the newcomer *appellantes... "loquacem talpam" et "purpuratam simiam" et "litterionem Graecum" et his congruentia plurima* (17.11.1).

praesagiorum sciscitationi nimiae deditus, ut aequiperare videretur in hac parte principem Hadrianum The reading *nimiae*, adopted by Seyfarth in the Teubneriana, is clearly to be preferred to *nimium*, which was printed in his bilingual edition, as it is closer to V's *nimia* and because the adjective occurs with much greater frequency in Amm. than the adverb. In either case the emphasis is on this word, since Amm. is not against divination per se; on the contrary, as the survey of the subject in 21.1.7–14 shows. It is Julian's lack of moderation in this respect which is criticized. The author refers here to his critical description of Julian's behaviour in Antioch, 22.12.7–8, q.v., where the different forms of divination practised by Julian and his entourage are enumerated. Also from this passage stems the comparison with Hadrian, who, like Julian, was guilty of *curiositas* or πολυπραγμοσύνη. See the note ad 22.12.8 *more pacis* and for Hadrian's interest in divination also D.C. 69.11.2, HA *H* 2.8 (with Den Hengst, 2002, 82–3), 16.7, *Ael.* 3.9. Comparisons like these with earlier emperors are a standard element in the *elogia*. For a quick overview see

154   COMMENTARY

Caltabiano, 1989, 55–62. Here again it is revealing to contrast Constantius' elogium with that of Julian. Constantius is compared with Caligula, Domitian, and Commodus for his cruelty (21.16.8, q.v.) and said to be *Marci illius dissimilis principis verecundi* (21.16.11). By contrast Julian is compared with regard to his *vitia* to Hadrian, and is called *Marci illius similis Caesaris* in §17, q.v. For Julian's headstrong attitude towards real experts in the field cf. 25.2.8 with the notes.

superstitiosus magis quam sacrorum legitimus observator   Cf. the similar judgment in the *epit.* 43.7: *cultus numinum superstitiosus.* There can be no doubt that this is a harsh verdict on Julian's religious practices, if only because Amm. has used the same term in the elogium of Julian's enemy Constantius: 21.16.18 *Christianam religionem absolutam et simplicem anili superstitione confundens,* q.v. The precise meaning of *superstitio* is notoriously difficult to pin down. For an overview of the different shades of meaning see Den Boeft (forthcoming) and the studies on *superstitio* and its derivatives quoted there. Three preliminary remarks have to be made. As was said earlier with regard to *carptim,* the deliberate parallelism between the two elogia makes it a priori likely that the term has the same meaning in both passages. Secondly, the statement is a generalization based on Julian's behaviour while in Antioch, as described in 22.12.6–7, and should, preferably, be interpreted with that passage in mind. And thirdly, the words *magis quam sacrorum legitimus observator* must be taken into account for a proper assessment of the meaning of *superstitiosus* here.

What the evaluations of Constantius' and Julian's religiosity have in common seems to be the notion of *pécher par excès*: Constantius was an adherent of the Christian faith, *religionem absolutam et simplicem,* but (instead of staying aloof like Valentinian: *inter religionum diversitates medius stetit nec quemquam inquietavit neque, ut hoc coleretur, imperavit aut illud* 30.9.5) he created confusion and strife by his dabbling in dogmatic subtleties. In the case of Constantius, the notion of excess is expressed by *in qua* (Christiana religio) *scrutanda perplexius quam componenda gravius* (21.16.18). Julian on his part tried to revive the ancient pagan cults, but (instead of staying within the bounds of tradition) he sacrificed extravagantly. The notion of excess is expressed in Julian's case by *aras crebritate nimia perfundebat* (22.12.6) and *augebantur autem caerimoniarum ritus immodice* (22.12.7). This interpretation of *superstitio* as a perverted form of *religio* is in agreement with Marius Victorinus' comment on Cic. *inv.* 2.165, quoted by Den Boeft:

CHAPTER 4.17   155

religio virtus est, inreligiositas vitium; atque religioni vicina, vitium tamen, superstitio nominatur, quae etiam ipsa est vitanda. If this is the correct interpretation of *superstitio* here, it is not so much the object of veneration that is roundly condemned, as the way in which it was venerated and the mentality it betrays.

The phrase *magis quam sacrorum legitimus observator* must again be interpreted against the background of Julian's actions in Antioch, as an explanation of *superstitio*, since *magis quam* is here the equivalent of 'and not'. As is argued there, *legitimus* must mean 'abiding by the rules', so that the phrase is equivalent to: *qui leges observat quae ad sacra pertinent*. This meaning has no literal parallel in the *Res Gestae*, but its content may be compared to 22.10.6 *ni quaedam suo ageret non legum arbitrio*, where Julian's wilfulness as a judge invites criticism. As Neri, 1985, 151-2 has observed, Amm's choice of words may be compared to Lib. *Or.* 12.80, where the orator, whilst probably defending Julian against reproaches from his compatriots, says: οὐ γὰρ νόμων ἀνάγκαις ὑπηρετῶν νῦν μὲν ἔθυσε, νῦν δὲ ἔληξεν...ἀλλ᾽ ἃ τοὺς ἄλλους οἶδε ταῖς νουμηνίαις ἀναθέντας ταῦθ᾽ ἑκάστης ἡμέρας εἶναι πεποίηκεν e.q.s. Neri quotes also Lib. *Or.* 18.128 τὰ μὲν ἀπολωλότα πρὸς ταὐτὸν αὖθις ἄγων, καινὰ δὲ παλαιοῖς προστίθεις, implying that Julian tried to make up for what had been lost by adding new sacrifices to the existing ones. This comes very close indeed to 22.12.7 *cum impensarum amplitudine antehac inusitata*, q.v. By doing so, Julian overstepped the bounds of tradition and, to paraphrase Amm., failed to observe the laws that regulate sacrificing. Amm. evidently condemns this lack of moderation. When Julian does stay within the bounds of tradition, this is explicitly mentioned: 21.2.4 *et ceteris, quae deorum semper fecere cultores*. Another breach of the tradition is signalled by Belayche, 2002, 110: Julian did not confine himself to the role of a magistrate making a sacrifice, but performed menial tasks and appeared in public surrounded by women: *vehens licenter pro sacerdotibus sacra stipatusque mulierculis laetabatur* (22.14.3).

innumeras sine parsimonia pecudes mactans Based on 22.12.7 *cum impensarum multitudine antehac inusitata et gravi.* Julian sacrificed night and day, as he himself admits: ἔθυσα δείλης εἶτ᾽ ὄρθρου βαθέος, ὅπερ εἴωθα ποιεῖν ἐπιεικῶς ἑκάστης ἡμέρας, *Ep.* 98, 401 b, cf. *Ep.* 26, 415 c. The Antiochenes nicknamed him *victimarius*, 'a slaughterer' on account of this, for which see the note ad 22.14.3 *victimarius pro sacricola*. See also 22.12.6 with the relevant notes. It is important to realize that blood sacrifice was not only rejected by the Christians,

156 COMMENTARY

but also severely criticised by important Neoplatonic philosophers, such as Porphyry in his *de abstinentia*. Good accounts of these debates can be found in Bradbury, 1995 and Belayche, 2002.

boves iam defuturos In the terminology of Kroon and Risselada, 1998, 433 *iam* here has counter-presuppositional focus, which means that *iam* "highlights a reference or concept that takes the place of an expected alternative." The unexpected consequence of Marcus' victories will be the extinction of all white bulls.

Marci illius similis Caesaris Amm. is outspoken in his criticism of Julian regarding this issue and the joke about the white bulls that is downright malicious. Still, the emperor is in good company, since it was directed originally against Marcus Aurelius, who was Julian's leading light: 16.1.4 *rectae perfectaeque rationis indagine congruens Marco, ad cuius aemulationem actus suos effingebat et mores.* In conformity with classical usage, Amm. uses *ille* with proper names to indicate that the person is well known, either for his good qualities, as here and in the elogium of Constantius, 21.16.11 *Marci illius dissimilis principis verecundi,* or for his vices, as in 14.1.8 *Maximini truculenti illius imperatoris.* A similar anecdote is told by Seneca with reference to Augustus: *Rufus, vir ordinis senatorii, inter cenam optaverat, ne Caesar salvus rediret ex ea peregrinatione, quam parabat; et adiecerat idem omnes et tauros et vitulos optare (Ben. 3.27).*

οἱ βόες οἱ λευκοὶ Μάρκῳ τῷ Καίσαρι χαίρειν. / ἂν πάλι νικήσῃς, ἄμμες ἀπωλόμεθα As if the bulls were writing a letter to Marcus; cf. e.g. X. *Cyr.* 4.5.27 Κῦρος Κυαξάρῃ χαίρειν (sc. λέγει). For the use of the aorist see Schwyzer-Debrunner II 282, who quotes E. *Med.* 78–9 ἀπωλόμεσθ᾽ ἄρ᾽, εἰ κακὸν προσοίσομεν / νέον παλαιῷ. As to the colour of the victims (see for this in general Radke, 1936, 23 sqq.), in *Ep.* 98, 399 d Julian writes to Libanius that in Beroea he had sacrificed a white bull to Zeus in imperial fashion: ἔθυσα τῷ Διὶ βασιλικῶς ταῦρον λευκόν.

4.18 *Volgi plausibus laetus, laudum ex minimis rebus intemperans appetitor* There is a remarkable correspondence with other sources here: Zonaras 13.13.26 ἦν δ᾽ ἐκεῖνος περὶ δόξαν ἐπτοημένος καὶ ἐπὶ τοῖς τυχοῦσιν ἐπαινεῖσθαι βουλόμενος; cf. *epit.* 43.7 *cupido laudis immodica.* Zonaras' next phrase ἐφ᾽ οἷς δ᾽ ἐσφάλλετο διορθούμενος παρὰ τῶν φίλων οὐκ ἤχθετο closely resembles *emendari se…permittens* in section 16. Cf. further Joh. Antioch. *fr.* 180 δόξης δὲ ἐπιθυμητικῶς τε καὶ ἀκορέστως ἔχων. *Appetitor* is found exclusively in late and Christian

CHAPTER 4.19   157

texts; TLL II 281.50–76. In the elogium of Valentinian the emperor
is called *Magnarum opum intemperans appetitor*, 31.14.5.

popularitatis cupiditate cum indignis loqui saepe affectans Here again, in
the eyes of Amm., Julian goes too far, since *popularitas* may be *civilitati
vicina*, but a *vitium* nonetheless. In this respect Constantius was
decidedly superior: 21.16.1 *imperatoriae auctoritatis coturnum ubique
custodiens popularitatem elato animo contemnebat.* Julian's desire to please
led to measures which are roundly condemned by Amm. See 22.14.1
popularitatis amore vilitati studebat venalium rerum with the note. For
affectare see again the elogium of Constantius, 21.16.4 *doctrinarum
diligens affectator* with the note and 22.7.1 *quod laudabant alii, quidam
ut affectatum et vile carpebant.* A similar disapproval is expressed in
22.7.3 *nimius captator inanis gloriae* and 25.4.7 *tantum sibi adrogans*,
with the notes.

Verum tamen, cum haec essent Amm. interrupts the enumeration of   **4.19**
the *vitia* with a laudatory phrase before continuing his criticism. It
is just possible that *essent* here means 'was (indeed) the case', as in
the expression *sunt ista*. For other instances see OLD s.v. *sum* 8. An
addition of *ita* after *haec* is, however, well worth considering. Cf. the
only other instance of this transitional phrase 30.4.20 *Verum tamen
haec cum ita sint.*

*vetus illa Iustitia...ni quaedam ad arbitrium agens interdum ostenderet se
dissimilem sui* The whole sentence is repeated almost verbatim from
22.10.6, q.v. Cf. for justice as one of Julian's virtues also 25.4.8 with
the notes. In 22.10.6 Amm. had formulated his reservation thus: *ni
quaedam suo ageret non legum arbitrio*, a reproach comparable to *magis
quam sacrorum legitimus auctor* in §17. Amm.'s excuse, that Julian in
some cases had been unlike himself, is an almost touching indication
of his bias in favour of Julian.

namque et iura condidit non molesta The expression *iura condere* is not   **4.20**
found elsewhere in the *Res Gestae*. The closest parallel for *condere* in
a legal context is 28.1.35 *in voluntate* ('will'), *quam condiderat nuper.*
It does, however, occur in juridical literature: Gaius *Inst.*1.7 *responsa
prudentium sunt sententiae et opiniones eorum, quibus permissum est iura
condere.* Cf. also Ov. *Rem.* 465 *et ne forte putes nova me tibi condere iura*
and Liv. 3.33.5 *ad condenda nova iura.* See for Julian as a lawgiver the
notes ad 22.9.2 *Omnibus...dispositis* and 22.10.7 *etiam iura.*

158   COMMENTARY

absolute quaedam iubentia fieri vel arcentia For this use of *absolutus*,
'unambiguous', cf. the notes ad 14.10.13 *veritatis enim absoluta semper
ratio est simplex* and 21.16.18 *Christianam religionem*. The same idea
is expressed by *ambagibus circumcisis* and *liquide* in 22.10.7 *quaedam
correxit in melius ambagibus circumcisis indicantia liquide, quid iuberent
fieri vel vetarent.*

*praeter pauca, inter quae erat illud inclemens, quod docere vetuit magistros
rhetoricos et grammaticos Christianos* Cataphoric *illud* is common in
Amm. Cf. e.g. 14.2.19 *illud tamen clausos vehementer angebat, quod,*
15.12.4 *ut verum illud videatur, quod ait defendens Fonteium Tullius*
and, immediately below *illud...parum ferendum, quod*. For that reason *inclemens* should be taken as the subject complement ("Z.B.
war das Gesetz zu hart", Seyfarth) and not as an attributive adjunct
with *ius* understood, as Fontaine does: "cette fameuse loi impitoy-
able". There are few instances of *inclemens* in Amm., which emphasizes the severity of this criticism: 20.4.13 *fortuna quaedam inclemens,*
cf. 31.8.8 *de te, Fortuna, ut inclementi querebatur et caeca,* the parallel sentence in 22.10.7, quoted below and 27.12.6 *Saporis inclementissimi omnium.* Amm. here repeats almost verbatim what he had
said in 22.10.7, without, however, the strong expression *obruendum perenni silentio: illud autem erat inclemens obruendum perenni silentio, quod arcebat docere magistros rhetoricos et grammaticos ritus Chris-
tiani cultores.* Add to the literature cited in the note ad loc. Dal
Covolo, 1987, Banchich, 1993, Ugenti, 1993 and Wiemer, 1995,
108–10.

ni transissent ad numinum cultum This is Valesius' correction of V's
ne transissent numinum cultu. Instead of *cultum* Rittershusius had
suggested the plural *cultus,* but cf. 22.5.1 *inclinatior erat erga numinum
cultum* (Iulianus). The phrase *numinum cultus* is surprisingly rare, as
TLL IV 1330.50–1331.54 shows, the only parallel being Tac. *Ann.*
3.63.3 *sed cultus numinum utrisque Dianam aut Apollinem venerandi*
("but the divinities' cults in each case consisted of venerating Diana
and Apollo" [Woodman and Martin]).

4.21 *parum ferendum* Cf. 21.10.8 *quod minus erat ferendum, celsa in potestate
crudelem. (Non) ferendum* is found very frequently in Cicero, e.g. *Ver.*
2.4.45 *superbum est enim iudices, et non ferendum.*

quod municipalium ordinum coetibus patiebatur iniuste quosdam annecti
This is repeated from 21.12.23, q.v.: *municipalium ordinum, ad quorum*

CHAPTER 4.22   159

favorem propensior iniuste plures muneribus publicis annectabat (where *annectebat* should be read). In the present passage the accusation is phrased somewhat more mildly: Julian 'suffered' others, the *curiales* presumably, to oblige wealthy persons to join their ranks. For *annectere* see the note ad 21.12.23 *maxime municipalium* and TLL I 779.7–8.

vel peregrinos vel ab his consortiis privilegiis aut origine longe discretos The same categories are distinguished more explicitly in 22.9.12 *licet privilegiis et stipendiorum numero et originis penitus alienae firmitudine communitus*, q.v. For *consortium* cf. the similar complaint in 22.9.8 *alii querentes consortiis se curialium addictos iniuste* and see the notes ad 16.5.11 and 16.10.21. *Longe* looks suspiciously like a stopgap, added to create a cursus planus.

Figura tali situque membrorum General remarks about sections describ-   **4.22**
ing an emperor's *forma* can be found in the notes ad 21.16.19, opening with the same words, where Constantius' outward appearance is discussed. See for the portraits of Julian which are preserved Alföldi, 1978, Lévêque, 1978 and Wegner's contribution to L'Orange-Unger, 1984, 159–64. Coins with the head of the emperor can be found on the relevant plates of Kent, 1978, Kent, 1981 and Carson, 1990. In Antiquity there were also painted pictures to be seen. See for this the remark Julian supposedly addressed to a painter: σύ μοι ἀλλότριον σχῆμα πῶς ἐδίδους, ἑταῖρε; οἷον με εἶδες, τοιοῦτον καὶ γράψον ("Why, my friend, did you give me a form other than my own? Paint me exactly as you saw me", *fr.* 13 Wright), and Sozomen's statement that Julian had himself painted on public pictures in juxtaposition with Zeus or Ares or Hermes, in order that the people might secretly be led to worship the gods when they saluted the emperor (*HE* 5.17.2–4, cf. Greg. Naz. *Or.* 4.80–1).

mediocris erat staturae As Sabbah 421–9 observes in his excellent discussion of Amm.'s knowledge and use of physiognomy, Julian stands in between the short Constantius (16.10.10 *corpus perhumile*) and the lanky Jovian (25.10.14 *vasta proceritate et ardua*). De Baresi, 1990 also refers to physiognomical literature, but is apparently unaware of Sabbah's book. In 22.14.3 Amm. is more outspoken about Julian's short stature: *homo brevis umeros extentans angustos*. Cf. further 22.2.5 *adultum adhuc iuvenem exiguo corpore* and *epit.* 43.6 *usu promptior corporis, quo validus quidem, sed brevis fuit.*

160   COMMENTARY

capillis tamquam pexis et mollibus, hirsuta barba in acutum desinente vestitus There is an almost comical contrast between Julian's well kept smooth hair and his unkempt beard. *Tamquam pexis* probably means that his hair looked as if it was brushed. For the connotation of tidiness cf. by contrast Tac. *Dial.* 20.3 *impexam antiquitatem.* About Julian's beard see the note ad 22.14.3 *barbam prae se ferens hircinam.* A telling parallel for *barba hirsuta* is Ovid's apostrophe to Polyphemus in *Met.* 13.765–6: *iam rigidos pectis rastris, Polypheme capillos / iam libet hirsutam tibi falce recidere barbam.* For *vestire* used of hair cf. Lucr. 5.889 *molli vestit lanugine malas.*

venustate oculorum micantium flagrans, qui mentis eius argutias indicabant The abstract noun followed by a noun in the genitive with an attribute of its own offers an elegant alternative for *oculis venustis et micantibus.* Note, however, that V reads *angustias,* which is defended by Fontaine. The meaning "tourments intérieurs", "soucis anxieux", however, which he ascribes to *angustiae,* does not tally with the panegyrical tone, which Amm. adopts in this section. It could, moreover, easily be mistaken for an insult, cf. e.g. Cic. *Pis.* 24 *magna maiestas consulis; non capiunt angustiae pectoris tui* ("that greatness your narrow mind cannot comprehend", tr. Watts) and Nazarius *Pan.* 4.8.2 *quod magnitudo male crediti muneris extra animi angustias effluebat.* The importance of the eyes when assessing a person is emphasized in 15.8.16 *cuius oculos cum venustate terribiles…contuentes, qui futurus sit, colligebant velut scrutatis veteribus libris.* Cf. also Mamertinus *Pan.* 3.6.4 *micantia sidereis ignibus lumina.* Sabbah 423 n. 68 quotes the Latin translation of Polemo 1.142 Foerster: *si vides oculum umidum neque cavum nec prominentem, nitentem, perlucidum, eum lauda: reperis enim eum intellegentem, docilem, litterarum amantem,* in which *neque cavum nec prominentem* corresponds with *venustate, nitentem* and *perlucidum* with *micantium* and *intellegentem, docilem* with *mentis argutias* in Amm. Julian's eyes are evoked with sadness by Libanius in *Ep.* 1180.1: (ὀφθαλμῶν) κἀκείνων τῶν μεγάλων τε καὶ καλῶν καὶ φοβερῶν, οὓς ζημίαν ἡλίῳ φήσαιμ᾽ ἂν οὐκ ὄντας ἔτι ('and of those great, beautiful and awe-inspiring eyes of his, of which I dare to say that it is a loss to the sun that they are no longer there'). In his note ad loc. Norman rightly calls Julian "a devotee" of Helios. As always, beauty is in the eye of the beholder: Greg. Naz. *Or.* 4.56 refers to τῷ μανιώδει τῶν ὀφθαλμῶν and in his notorious portrait of the youthful Julian (*Or.* 5.23, quoted by Socr. *HE* 3.23.23) he speaks of his ὀφθαλμὸς σοβούμενος καὶ περιφερόμενος καὶ μανικὸν βλέπων ("those darting eyes with their wild gaze", tr. Bowersock). Somville, 2003, 165–6 compares

CHAPTER 4.23   161

this description of Julian's eyes with the emperor's effigy on a hitherto unpublished coin minted at Thessalonica.

liniamentorum recta compage Julian was well built and differed in that respect both from Constantius, who was *ad usque pubem ab ipsis colli confiniis longior, brevissimis cruribus et incurvis* (21.16.19) and from his successor Jovian, who was disproportionally tall (*vasta proceritate et ardua*, 25.10.14, q.v.). Sabbah 427 n. 87 quotes the Latin translation of Polemo 1 268: *Viri audacis hoc signum est: eum vides aequali corpore recta statura.*

viribus valebat et cursu Cf. Mamert. *Pan.* 3.6.4 *cernebant imperatorem longam viam sub gravium armorum onere currentem, properantis anhelitum sine sensu lassitudinis crebriorem, sudorum rivos per fortia colla manantes.*

After the detailed treatment of Julian's personal qualities, Amm. tries to strike a balance when commenting on his political achievements. The purpose of this addendum is clearly apologetic: it begins and ends with a rebuttal of the criticisms brought forward by Julian's opponents (*obtrectatores* and *sunt, qui reprehendant* respectively). The responsibility for the catastrophic war against Persia rests with Constantine, not with Julian, and the humiliations inflicted on the Romans by Sapor simply demanded to be avenged. The gods had withheld the victory Julian deserved, but Amm. invites his readers to remember Julian also for his splendid successes in Gaul. They fully justified the confidence with which Julian set out to restore the eastern border after bringing peace to the West.

obtrectatores Already as a Caesar in Gaul, Julian had his malevo-   **4.23**
lent critics, who ridiculed his achievements (17.11.1). According to Amm., they were driven by envy, like the slanderers of other great men, such as Cimon, Scipio Aemilianus and Pompey (17.11.3–4). They remain anonymous, except for Barbatio, who is called *gloriarum Iuliani pervicax obtrectator* in 16.11.7. Julian's preparations for the Persian campaign met with scepticism, resistance even, as has been mentioned in 22.12.3 *obtrectatores desides et maligni unius corporis permutationem tot ciere turbas intempestivas indignum et perniciosum esse strepebant.* Of course, Julian was aware of these criticisms. In his speech to the troops at the outset of the campaign he defends himself: 23.5.16 *contionari disposui docturus ratione multiplici non nunc primitus, ut maledici mussitant, Romanos penetrasse regna Persidis,* and goes on to enumerate historical precedents.

162 COMMENTARY

novos bellorum tumultus A clear instance of a gen. inversus. The combination of the adjective and the noun phrase is an elegant alternative for *bella nova et tumultuosa*. In the eyes of his opponents the wars are of Julian's making (*novos*) and disruptive (*tumultus*).

ad perniciem rei communis The phrase *ad perniciem* + gen. is found very frequently in Cicero and Livy. Amm.'s model may have been Cic. *Cat.* 1.8 *iam intelleges multo me vigilare acrius ad salutem quam te ad perniciem rei publicae.*

sciant docente veritate perspicue As Sabbah 19 observes, Amm. introduces *veritas*, 'the facts', in passages of special significance, such as prefaces (15.1.1. and 26.1.1) and the sphragis (31.16.9). The present passage belongs in this category. Amm. ends his carefully balanced elogium on an apologetic note. Cf. for Amm.'s repeated insistence on the truth also Blockley, 1975, 96–7, where, however, the present text is not mentioned. The adverb *perspicue* emphasizes that the facts in question are unequivocal, as in 20.2.3 *documenta...perspicue demonstrantia*; TLL X 1.1749.60–9.

non Iulianum, sed Constantinum ardores Parthicos succendisse, cum Metrodori mendaciis avidius acquiescit, ut dudum rettulimus plene Cf. 27.10.3 *cum enim Vithicabius rex...ardores in nos saepe succenderet bellicos.* The text is suspect for two reasons. Amm. seems to use *cum* with present indicative only in a strictly temporal or iterative sense, as e.g. in 15.1.1 *tunc enim laudanda est brevitas, cum...nihil subtrahit cognitioni gestorum* or 15.8.15 *cum hastis clipei feriuntur, irae documentum est et doloris.* As an alternative *dum* should be considered, in the sense which Szantyr 614 calls "koeffektiv" or "kausal". Other instances of this causal overtone in Amm. are e.g. 15.4.11 *dumque elabi properant impediti, corpora nudantes intecta...truncabantur* and 24.4.22 *ut, dum...defensores ultro citroque discurrunt, nec proxima fodientis audiretur ferri tinnitus nec* e.q.s. There seems to be a confusion of *cum* and *dum* also in 18.5.2, where V has *dum...didicisset*, which would be a unique instance of *dum* + coni. pluperfect and for that reason cannot be kept. Two more examples are given by Ehrismann 160–1. The second problem is *avidius* (SBAG), which seems preferable to V's *avidus*, since the adjective invariably has a complement in Amm., normally in the form of a gen., once an infinitive (26.8.14 *provincias...avidas novitatem quandam visere*) and once a prepositional phrase (29.6.3 *Maximinus in omne avidus nefas*). For *acquiescere* in the sense 'to listen to', 'to give credence to' cf. 20.4.4 *Conticuit hisque acquieverat Iulianus potioris*

CHAPTER 4.23   163

arbitrio cuncta concedens and 27.12.17 *Quae imperator doctus...divisioni acquievit Hiberiae.* It seems to be a modernism, frowned upon by Ps. Serg. *gramm* IV 559, 31: *adquiescere aliter in usu nostro est quam esse deberet. cum enim parere nos alicuius desiderio significare volumus aut sententiae, adquiescere nos dicimus*; TLL I 424.42–4. In the Vulgata the verb is used "quinquagies fere hac vi pro graeco ὑπακούω, ἀκούω" (ibid. 54–5).

The contents of 'the lies of Metrodorus' would have remained a mystery, had not the eleventh-century Byzantine compiler Cedrenus lifted a tip of the veil (*Chron.* 1.516–7). The other sources are silent on this topic. *Metrodorus quidam filosofus* is said by Rufinus (*hist.* 10.9) to have visited India *inspiciendorum locorum et orbis perscrutandi gratia.* We find the same information in Socr. *HE* 1.19.3 (Μητρόδωρον, ὅς...τὴν Ἰνδῶν χώραν ἱστόρησεν), but neither Socrates nor Rufinus mentions 'lies' or the connection between Metrodorus and the emperor Constantine which Amm. apparently discussed in a lost book (*ut dudum rettulimus plene*). Nor does Sozomen, who does not even mention Metrodorus' name, pace *PLRE* I, Metrodorus 1 and others. Cedrenus' story runs roughly as follows: Μητρόδωρος τις Περσογενής travelled to India, where he won the respect of the Brahmans. He gained access to their temples and stole many precious stones and pearls. Other jewels he received from the king of the Indians as a present to the Roman emperor. On his return he offered them to Constantine as a gift of his own and said that there would have been more if the Persians had not stolen them on his journey home. Thereupon Constantine wrote a sharp letter to Sapor and demanded the return of the jewels. He received no answer. Διὰ τοῦτο ἐλύθη ἡ εἰρήνη. In the note ad 23.6.85 *super ortu* it has been suggested that the story of Metrodorus may have been the reason why Amm. concluded his long chapter on Persia with a miniature digression on pearls. Whether Cedrenus had direct access to Ammianus' lost books, as e.g. Wagner ("Sine dubio ex Ammiano hauserat Cedrenus") and Fontaine n. 597 think, is doubtful. See for this and other questions concerning Cedrenus' text Warmington, 1981 and Bleckmann, 1991, 359–65.

This is not the first time in Amm. that Constantine the Great is spoken of critically. Cf. 21.10.8 *Tunc et memoriam Constantini...vexavit*, with the note ad loc. (add to the literature cited there Paschoud, 1986, 143–8, Neri, 1992, 188–209 and Warmington, 1999). However, in 22.12.1 (q.v.), when speaking of Julian's plans to punish the Persians for their misdeeds *per sexaginta ferme annos*, Amm. did not refer to the first Christian emperor at all. In the present case

164 COMMENTARY

Amm. is rather unfair. As Matthews 135–6 remarks, "Ammianus' attribution of the collapse of the peace to the 'lies of Metrodorus' must be explained by the convergence of two strong sentiments, his dislike of Constantine and a wish to defend Julian at any cost against his critics; for on any reasonable assessment of the circumstances, the attribution seems trivial and irrelevant". For Constantine and Persia in general see Barceló, 1981, 73–82 and for a systematic investigation into the various versions of Constantine's abortive Persian campaign Fowden, 1994, 146–53. Cf. for Amm.'s use of *Parthi/Parthicus* instead of *Persae/Persicus* 25.1.18 *pulsis…Parthis* and the note ad 23.3.2 *Parthos*.

4.24 *unde caesi ad indignationem exercitus nostri* The text is uncertain. *Unde caesi* is Valesius' brilliant conjecture for V's *vindictae si*, of which he was justifiably proud ("locum pristino nitori restituisse mihi videor"). Gelenius must have found the same reading in the Hersfeldensis, which he made worse by trying to remedy it with the reading *vindictae siti*. Valesius further suggested *ad internecionem* instead of V's *ad indignationem*. That Valesius was on the right track is shown by comparing the present text with 22.12.1, where Amm. discusses Julian's motives to go to war against Persia using the expression *ad internecionem exercitibus nostris saepe deletis*, and Julian's own justification of the enterprise in 23.5.18: *nos vero miseranda recens captarum urbium et inultae caesorum exercituum umbrae et damnorum magnitudines castrorumque amissiones ad haec, quae proposuimus, hortantur*. See Sabbah 484 n. 94 for a more detailed comparison of these three passages. V's *ad indignationem* is kept by all modern editors, despite the fact that no parallel for adverbial use of this phrase is mentioned in TLL I 547.82–551.49, and that Amm. always uses it with an attribute: 17.10.8 *ad indignationem iustam Iulianus erectus*; 24.3.3 *ad indignationem plenam gravitatis erectus*; 25.1.8 *ad indignationem iustam imperator erectus*. There is, in short, ample reason to accept Valesius' emendation.

capti militares aliquotiens numeri As is noted ad 20.1.3 *numerisque* (q.v.), the word *numerus* is a general term covering units of all kinds.

provinciae gravibus impensis exhaustae It is remarkable that Amm. also mentions the indirect consequences of the warfare with Persia for the provinces. Cf. for Amm.'s awareness of the plight of the provincials the notes ad 21.6.6 *vestem armaque* ad fin., 21.16.17 *flagitatorum rapacitas* and 24.3.5 *populatae provinciae*.

CHAPTER 4.25   165

et ad effectum tendentibus minis cuncta petebantur a Persis ad usque Bithynos et litora Propontidis For the expression cf. 15.5.30 *ad effectum tendens consilium.* The opposite seems to be 14.3.4 *absque ullo...effectu.* TLL V 2.133.42 gives no parallels from other authors. In all other instances in Amm. of *tendere ad* except 28.1.31 *tendebat ad usque Probi contemptum,* it means 'to hasten to'. The expression underlines the seriousness of the danger: no empty words, but threats which were meant to be translated into action. See the note on *effectus* ad 17.4.14 *urgens effectus.* The, from a Roman point of view, outrageous Persian claim is formulated in Sapor's letter to Constantius: *ad usque Strymona flumen et Macedonicos fines tenuisse maiores meos antiquitates quoque vestrae testantur* (17.5.5). It was, for that matter, not a new claim. Cf. Ardashir's demand for the restitution of the Achaemenid possessions in D.C. 80.4.1–2.

at in Galliis fervorum tenore gliscente diffusis per nostra Germanis Again **4.25** the text is highly uncertain. In his Teubneriana Seyfarth stays close to V's *vervorum tenore gliscente.* But what could this possibly mean? Earlier, in the bilingual edition, where he had to provide a translation, Seyfarth had accepted the conjectures *barbarorum* and *tumore*, which make perfect sense but show little resemblance to V. All other editors have rejected *tenore.* Rightly so, for it makes no sense and is never used by Amm. None of the solutions offered carries complete conviction. *Bellorum* (G) *fervore gliscente* could be added as a suggestion. For the archaism *gliscere* see the note ad 21.12.4.

Despite these uncertainties it is clear that the opening word *at* marks a sharp opposition, not just between the eastern and western frontier regions of the empire, but above all between the desolate state in which Julian found these regions and the vast improvements he realized in Gaul and hoped to bring about in the East. The distress of Gaul under Constantius, caused inter alia by German invasions, is often mentioned by Amm., e.g. in 14.10.1, 15.5.2, 15.8.1, 13, 19, 16.5.17. Cf. Eutr. 10.14.1 *cum multa oppida barbari expugnassent, alia obsiderent, ubique foeda vastitas esset Romanumque imperium non dubia iam calamitate nutaret,* Mamert. *Pan.* 3.4.1 *Florentissimas quondam antiquissimasque urbes barbari possidebant: Gallorum illa celebrata nobilitas aut ferro occiderat aut immitibus addicta dominis serviebat* and the short survey in Zos. 3.1.1.

iamque Alpibus ad vastandam Italiam perrumpendis In this abl.abs. the gerundive is a kind of future passive participle. For this use of the gerund see the note ad 22.15.3 *mox ostendendis aliis.*

166   COMMENTARY

ubi et praeteritorum recordatio erat acerba et exspectatio tristior impendentium
The neat chiastic phrase is borrowed from Cic. *Brutus* 266 *nam et praeteritorum recordatio est acerba et acerbior exspectatio reliquorum.*

iuvenis iste ad occiduam plagam specie Caesaris missus In 16.1.5 Julian is called *adolescens primaevus*. Cf. the remark ascribed by Zosimus to the empress Eusebia when she discussed with her husband the prospective appointment of Julian to Caesar: Νέος ἐστί (3.1.3). The same qualification νέος is found in Socr. *HE* 3.1.27 and Soz. *HE* 5.2.21. Julian was about 24 years of age when he was appointed Caesar in 355 (see for his birth date the notes ad 20.5.4 *vixdum adulescens* and 25.5.23 *anno aetatis*; cf. also Zos. 3.5.3). In relating his heroic deeds in Gaul, Amm. calls Julian emphatically *iuvenis* in 17.1.1: *Martius iuvenis Rheno post Argentoratensem pugnam otiose fluente securus* and again in 22.2.5 he draws attention to his youth: *somnio enim propius videbatur adultum adhuc iuvenem…post cruentos exitus regum et gentium ab urbe in urbem inopina velocitate transgressum.* With regard to *specie Caesaris*, Julian himself was fully aware of his initially very limited powers. In his *Letter to the Athenians* he writes that he was sent to Gaul not so much as commander of the armies there, but rather to obey the orders of the generals stationed in the region (οὐκ ἄρχοντα μᾶλλον τῶν ἐκεῖσε στρατοπέδων ἢ τοῖς ἐκεῖσε στρατηγοῖς ὑπακούσοντα, 277 d). He adds that Constantius had only chosen him to parade around the dress and image of the emperor he represented (τὸ σχῆμα καὶ τὴν εἰκόνα περιοίσοντι τὴν ἑαυτοῦ· καὶ γάρ τοι καὶ τοῦτο εἴρητο καὶ ἐγέγραπτο, ὅτι τοῖς Γάλλοις οὐ βασιλέα δίδωσιν, ἀλλὰ τὸν τὴν ἑαυτοῦ πρὸς ἐκείνους εἰκόνα κομιοῦντα, 278 a). In his first speech as Augustus Julian reminds the soldiers of this fact: 20.5.4 *vixdum adolescens specie tenus purpuratus, ut nostis, vestrae tutelae nutu caelesti commissus* e.q.s.; cf. Lib. *Or.* 18.42. In 16.11.13, q.v. Amm. refers to the rumour that Julian was sent by Constantius to Gaul not to relieve its distress, but to meet his death. Cf. for this 17.1.14, Eun. *fr.* 14.2, Lib. *Or.* 12.42–4, 18.36, Socr. *HE* 3.1.30, Soz. *HE* 5.2.22.

regesque pro mancipiis agitans ignobilibus One may think of the three *immanissimi reges*, who begged for peace and offered to bear grain on their own shoulders to the Roman troops (17.1.13 *hac fiducia tres immanissimi reges venerunt tandem aliquando iam trepidi* e.q.s.) and of the five kings mentioned in 18.2.18–9 who were granted peace by Julian. Cf. also the rumour reported in 21.9.3 *Iulianum strata per Gallias multitudine regum et gentium…adventare.* In 22.12.2 the memory of his triumphs in Gaul is said to have encouraged Julian to try to do

CHAPTER 4.26   167

the same in Persia: *recalentibus etiamtum regum precibus et regalium, qui vinci magis posse quam supplices manus tendere credebantur.*

quae omnia...cuncta paene mira dictu celeritate correxit Amm. describes Julian's military successes in Gaul, which according to him surpassed many of the valiant achievements of the ancients (*res magnae, quas per Gallias virtute felicitateque correxit, multis veterum factis fortibus praestant*, 16.1.2, cf. 16.1.5), in 16.2.1–4.5, 16.11.1–17.2.4, 17.8.1–10.10, 18.2.1–19. Julian himself dwells on this theme in *Ep. ad Ath.* 278a–280d. Cf. further Lib. *Or.* 12.44–53, 18.37–81, Eun. *fr.* 14.2, 16.2, 17, 18, 19, Zos. 3.3.2–8.1, Mamert. *Pan.* 3.3–4, Eutr. 10.14.1–2, Socr. *HE* 3.1.27–8, Soz. *HE* 5.2.21–2. For modern assessments see e.g. Blockley, 1972, 445–68; Browning, 1976, 79–104, Bowersock, 1978, 33–45. By a curious oversight, Pauw 1972, 134 says that Amm. failed to mention Julian's swiftness in the necrology, on which he had remarked so often in the narrative. He seems to have missed the reference in this section. There is a note on *celeritas* as an imperial virtue ad 21.9.6 (add to the literature cited there Lolli, 1999).

ut orientem pari studio recrearet, adortus est Persas During the Persian   **4.26**
expedition Julian inspired his men with the oath "*sic sub iugum mitteret Persas, ita quassatum recrearet orbem Romanum*" (24.3.9, q.v.). Cf. Cic. *Cat.* 2. 7 *uno mehercule Catilina exhausto relevata mihi et recreata res publica videtur.* See for Julian's further motives to start the war against Persia 22.12.1–2 and 23.5.16–23, with the relevant notes.

triumphum exinde relaturus et cognomentum, si consiliis eius et factis illustribus decreta caelestia congruissent The intention expressed by *relaturus* is also mentioned in 22.12.2: *ornamentis illustrium gloriarum inserere Parthici cognomentum ardebat* (for the *cognomentum* see the note ad 22.9.1 *antegressis*). At the same time, the future participle serves as the apodosis to the *si*-clause: Julian would have won his triumph, if the gods had seconded his plans. This thought is a recurrent theme in Ammianus' description of the Persian campaign: Julian's motives and feats were admirable, whatever the *obtrectatores desides et maligni* (22.12.3) had to say. But they were no guarantee for success. As Julian had said himself in his farewell speech: *tametsi prosperitas simul utilitasque consultorum non ubique concordent, quoniam coeptorum eventus superae sibi vindicant potestates* (25.3.17, q.v.). It is important to note that in this final evaluation Amm. does not refer to Julian's neglect of the many signs and warnings sent by the gods to dissuade him from the invasion of Persia. In that respect Julian certainly had been to

168 COMMENTARY

blame, as has been argued in the Introduction to book 23 on p. x and xi. But one could add that in the last resort even Julian's disregard for the omina was determined by fate *quoniam nulla vis humana vel virtus meruisse umquam potuit, ut quod praescripsit fatalis ordo non fiat* (23.5.5, q.v.).

4.27   *et cum sciamus adeo experimenta quosdam ruere improvidos*   Amm. starts from a well known observation in Sen. *Ben.* 1.10 *adeoque adversus experimenta pertinaces sumus, ut bella victi et naufragi maria repetamus*: people do not learn from their experiences, but stubbornly repeat their mistakes. The only possible interpretation of the text, as transmitted in V and printed by Seyfarth in his Teubneriana, would seem to be: 'although we know that experiences bring certain imprudent people down to such a degree', which makes little sense in itself and is not in accordance with Seneca's dictum. The best emendation seems to be the simple one proposed by Valesius and supported by Kellerbauer, 1873, 132. He restored Seneca's *adversus*, which may easily have dropped out by haplography after *adeoque*. The resulting meaning would be: 'although we know that certain imprudent people rush blindly on against all experience to such a degree.' In that case Amm. substituted the more expressive verb *ruere* for Seneca' s *pertinaces sumus*. Petschenig, 1892, 669 started from the reading *reuere* of V m2. and proposed to read *adeo experimenta quosdam re⟨sp⟩uere*. This makes excellent sense and is very close to the ms. reading. The only reason not to accept his suggestion is that there is no parallel for *respuere* in Amm. To make sure his readers would understand Seneca's point, the author added the prosaic paraphrase *et ad diffultates redeant, quibus succubuere saepissime.*

sunt, qui reprehendant paria repetisse principem ubique victorem   A logical continuation of the sentence would have been: 'the emperor Julian, however, could not be blamed for that, since his successes in Gaul justified the highest expectations.' Eager to expose the folly of Julian's critics, however, Amm. has left out a step in his reasoning, thereby producing a confused sentence.

CHAPTER 5

Introduction

This chapter describes an event of prime importance: the proclamation of Jovian as Julian's successor. It contains a number of details which are not provided in other sources and for this reason it functions as the basic account for modern descriptions. Recently, however, it has more than once been criticized as unreliable and as the overture of a biased and slyly contrived anti-Christian account of Jovian's brief reign. However, if read with an open mind, Ammianus' lively and detailed report is not intrinsically improbable as the perception of an eye-witness and, moreover, not immoderately permeated with personal judgments or innuendoes. In fact, the chapter has only one serious flaw, viz. Ammianus' silence about the identity of the small group of men who managed to exploit the leadership's momentary indecision and to have the imperial power conferred on their favourite Jovian. One can hardly imagine that the author had no idea who these men were, and it is hard not to assume a deliberate concealment.

Ammianus interprets Jovian's elevation as due to 'a particularly blind judgment of Fortuna' (§8), a complaint which he will repeat in his lament on the loss of Nisibis (25.9.7–11), the prime inspiration for his verdict. Things became worse when a Roman defector, out of personal resentment, portrayed Jovian to the Persian king in far more disparaging colours than Ammianus himself in the second half of book 25, and in this way increased the king's confidence.

Nec fuit post haec lamentis aut fletibus locus This contrasts rather **5.1** sharply with the mourning after the death of Constantine, described in Eus. *VC* 4.65 ("in conventionally panegyrical terms", Cameron-Hall, 1999, 343), and of Constantius: *supremis cum gemitu conclamatis excitisque lamentis et luctu* (Amm. 21.15.4). Small wonder, given the fact that when Julian died the Romans were surrounded on all sides by their Persian enemy (*hostibus ex omni latere circumfusis*). To put it in Eunapius' words (*fr.* 28.1): θεωρεῖν ἐξῆν ὡς τὴν ὑπεροχὴν τοῦ κατὰ τὸν βασιλέα πάθους ὁ τοῦ πολέμου φόβος παρὰ πόδας ἑστὼς καταμαραίνων ἀπήμβλυνεν ("one could observe how fear of the enemy, who was at their heels, weakened and dulled the enormous grief they felt for

170   COMMENTARY

their Emperor", tr. Blockley). The next day, for that matter, when everybody had become aware of Julian's death, *in lacrimas effusi sunt omnes et luctum* (25.5.6).

corpore enim curato pro copia rerum et temporis, ut, ubi ipse olim statuerat, conderetur Just before his suicide Nero asked his entourage to take some emergency measures *curando mox cadaveri*, 'to prepare his body for burial' (Suet. *Nero* 49.1). Amm., however, uses the phrase *corpus curare* to denote embalming: *corpore curato defuncti missoque Constantinopolim, ut inter Augustorum reliquias conderetur* (26.1.3), *Post conclamata imperatoris suprema corpusque curatum ad sepulturam, ut missum Constantinopolim inter divorum reliquias humaretur* (30.10.1). In 21.16.20 a specific word is used: *Pollinctum igitur corpus defuncti*. About *pro copia* TLL IV 900.66 notes: "subauditur plerumque 'mediocri'". This is definitely the case in the present text.

Julian had chosen Tarsus as his final resting place: *corpus namque eius illuc relatum exsequiarum humili pompa in suburbano sepultum est, ut ipse mandarat* (23.2.5, q.v.). In 25.9.12 (q.v.) Amm. reports that Procopius travelled to Tarsus with Julian's mortal remains, *ea, ut superstes ille mandarat, humaturus in suburbano Tarsensi*, and in 25.10.5 that Jovian adorned Julian's tomb there, *exornari sepulchrum statuit Iuliani in pomerio situm itineris, quod ad Tauri montis angustias ducit*. Julian's body was later transferred to Constantinople. See for this the note ad 25.10.5.

principio lucis secutae, quae erat quintum kalendas Iulias I.e. 27 June, at dawn. The same date is mentioned in Malalas *Chron.* 13.333: τῇ κζ τοῦ δαισίου τοῦ καί ἰουνίου μηνός, and in Socr. *HE* 3.22.1: τῇ ἑξῆς ἡμέρᾳ (i.e. the day after the day Julian died, which Socrates dates to the 26th: περὶ τὴν ἕκτην καὶ εἰκάδα τοῦ Ἰουνίου μηνός, ἐν τῇ Περσῶν χώρᾳ...τὸν βίον κατέλυσεν, *HE* 3.21.17). Like Socrates the *Chronicon Paschale* a. 363 gives the day of Julian's death as June 26, but then says, apparently by mistake, that Jovian was proclaimed emperor also on 26 June before dawn (μηνὶ τῷ αὐτῷ δαισίῳ πρὸ ς καλανδῶν ἰουλίων πρὸ τοῦ διαφαῦσαι). Cf. further Philost. *HE* 8.1 τῇ ἐπαύριον τοῦ διαφθαρῆναι τὸν ἀποστάτην. Remarkably, the first precise date in book 25 is not the day of Julian's death, but the day on which Jovian was proclaimed emperor.

hostibus ex omni latere circumfusis Apart from Eun. *fr.* 28.1, quoted ad *Nec fuit post haec*, Zosimus points to the army's predicament: ἐν μέσῃ τῇ πολεμίᾳ (3.30.1).

CHAPTER 5.1   171

collecti duces exercitus advocatisque legionum principiis et turmarum super creando principe consultabant In Seyfarth's app. crit. *def. Damsté* is a mistake. In fact, in *Mnemosyne* 58 (1930) 7 Damsté remarks: "Petschenig *collecto...exercitu* scribendum existimat, sed probabilius duco *que* participio *advocatis* male ab aliquo esse affixum". Blomgren 62 rejects both proposals, preferring V's text, the syntax of which, in his view, can be explained in two ways: either *-que* links the part. *collecti* and the abl. abs. *advocatis principiis*, or there is an ellipsis of *sunt* after *collecti.* See Blomgren 70–2 on other instances of such an ellipsis. As to Petschenig's suggestion: this seems to tally less well with *acies ad usque lapidem quartum porrigebatur* in §6.

As more often in Amm. (cf. e.g. 24.4.13 *Victor nomine dux*), *duces* here apparently has a non-technical meaning, 'generals' (for a more specialized use of the word see for instance 24.1.2 *Osdroenae dux Secundinus*). In the next section four of these generals are mentioned by name: Arintheus, Victor, Nevitta and Dagalaifus, all of them probably of barbarian descent (cf. Waas, 1971[2], 87–9, 130–3, 117–9 and 96–7, respectively). See on *legio* above, ad 25.1.7 *eodem die*, on *principia* 'commanding officers' the second part of the note ad 22.3.2 *praesentibus* and on *turma* ad 25.1.3 *ad ultimum*.

Amm.'s account of the events leading up to the election of Jovian (see §4) is fuller in detail than other sources, but it is not without problems. His words here, for instance, seem to imply that only military commanders consulted about the choice of a new emperor (which was necessary because Julian had refrained from naming a successor, 25.3.20; cf. Eun. *fr.* 28.1 ἐν τοῦτο...ᾔδεσαν ὡς αἱρεῖσϑαι ᾐϱοσῆκέν σφισιν ἄϱχοντα). This contrasts with Thdt. *HE* 4.1.1: Μετὰ δὲ τὴν Ἰουλιανοῦ σφαγὴν συνελϑόντες σὺν τοῖς ὑπάρχοις οἱ στρατηγοὶ ἐβουλεύοντο τίνα χρὴ τὴν βασιλείαν παραλαβεῖν, and, perhaps, with the corrresponding passage in Zosimus: Τότε τοίνυν τῶν ἐν τέλει πάντων ἅμα τῷ στρατοπέδῳ συνειλεγμένων βουλὴ προετίϑετο τίνι δέοι παραδοϑῆναι τὴν τῶν ὅλων ἡγεμονίαν (3.30.1). Unfortunately, however, the wording of Zosimus is not entirely unambiguous. Does he refer with τῶν ἐν τέλει and τῷ στρατοπέδῳ to, on the one hand, civil officials and, on the other, military officers, as Von Haehling, 1977, 351 assumes, or to generals and lower ranking military officers, as Paschoud n. 87 seems to suggest? Anyway, Amm.'s words certainly contrast with his own description in 26.1.3 of an in other respects quite similar situation. Then, after the death of Jovian, once again a successor to the throne was needed and both military and civil officials looked around for a new ruler: *potestatum civilium militiaeque rectores...moderatorem quaeritabant diu exploratum et gravem.* One would

172   COMMENTARY

have expected a similar expression in the present case too, unless
all civil officials had actually been excluded from the deliberations
over choosing a successor to Julian. This, however, seems rather
improbable. Of course, the situation after Julian's death, the army
being surrounded on all sides by the enemy, was not the same as
when Valentinian was chosen. But even so, it would have been odd
if the praetorian prefect Salutius (see for him §3) and other *palatini*
(see §2) had not been consulted by Arintheus cum suis.

5.2   *discissique studiis turbulentis* TLL V 1.1315.64–9 lists *cum plebe discissa*
(22.5.3), *discissis votorum studiis* (28.4.31) and the present text as
cases in which *discissus* is "i.q. divisus, discors".

Arintheus et Victor et e palatio Constanti residui Arintheus (*PLRE* I,
Arinthaeus) and Victor (*PLRE* I, Victor 4) had served prominently
and loyally under Julian during the Persian campaign (see for
Arintheus 24.1.2, q.v., and 7.2, for Victor 24.1.2, q.v., 4.13, 4.31,
6.4 and 6.13). However, their career must have begun under Constantius, (Arintheus was in 355 *tribunus*, cf. 15.4.10; Victor's career
before 362–363 is unknown), whom they presumably had followed
to the East. Apparently they enjoyed the confidence of Constantius'
former *palatini* and were still seen to be more Constantius' men than
Julian's. Both continued their career under Jovian and, after the
latter's death, under Valentinian and Valens. See for *palatium* the
note ad 20.4.11 *ad comitatum*. As is noted ad 20.4.6, Amm. often uses
residuus as a synonym of *reliquus*, but here it is more likely that it
denotes 'those who still remained'. Some other examples of *residuus
e(x)*: *ex veteribus discordiis residui motus erant* (Liv. 39.48.5), *subolem
ex illis residuam fovet* (Sen. *Cons. Marc.* 16.8), *si quae residua ex priore
tempore manebant* (Suet. *Cal.* 15.6).
    For Julian's purge of Constantius' court clique see 22.4. Among
the court officials referred to may have been the *primicerius notariorum*
Iovianus (see for him ad §3 *quae dum ambiguntur*), who at any rate
was a member of the *consistorium* in virtue of his office (cf. Teitler,
1985, 35 with n. 27 on p. 234).

de parte sua quendam habilem scrutabantur See for *habilis*, 'suitable',
the note ad 25.3.20 *quem habilem reor*. As is noted ad 20.3.3 *scrutatores*,
Amm. often uses the verb *scrutari*. Normally it means either 'to
investigate' (e.g. 15.1.1 *veritatem scrutari*) or 'to search' (e.g. 24.1.13
frutecta squalida vallesque scrutabatur). See also the note ad 21.16.8
hanc sine fine scrutando. In the present text, however, it apparently

CHAPTER 5.3   173

expresses that they racked their brains trying to think of the right candidate.

Nevitta et Dagalaifus proceresque Gallorum Nevitta (*PLRE* I, Nevitta) was one of the consuls of 362 (21.10.8, q.v.) and Dagalaifus (*PLRE* I, Dagalaifus + A. Lippold in *Gnomon* 46[1974] 272) had been appointed *comes domesticorum* by Julian in 361 (21.8.1, q.v.). Like Arintheus and Victor, both had won their spurs during Julian's Persian campaign (24.1.2, q.v. and 4.13). They had been brought along by Julian from the West, which may be the reason why the 'leaders of the Gauls' sided with them. As to *proceres Gallorum*, was the PPO Salutius perhaps one of them? He at any rate hailed from Gaul (Jul. *Or.* 4, 252 a). While Dagalaifus continued to serve under Jovian and later under Valentinian and Gratian, Nevitta is not heard of any more, unless in 25.7.13 (q.v.) *Nevitta* should be read instead of *Nemota*.

ex commilitio suo quaeritabant In the list in TLL III 1882.44–50 this occurs as a case in which *commilitium* is the equivalent of "ii qui commilitant". Perhaps there is a deliberate contrast with *e palatio Constanti*, in view of the author's clear dislike of the *Palatina cohors* (18.5.4 [q.v], 19.12.16). The intensivum *quaeritabant* expresses the same urge as *scrutabantur*.

quae dum ambiguntur Neither the nominee(s) for the throne proposed by Arintheus and his associates are known, nor the choice of Nevitta cum suis, and it is only in 25.8.18, q.v., that we hear of the candidacy, supported by only a few, of the *primicerius notariorum* Iovianus (*PLRE* I, Iovianus 1): *Iuliano perempto ipse quoque nominatus a paucis ut imperio dignus.* This namesake of the future emperor Jovian had distinguished himself by bravery at the siege of the city of 'Maozamalcha' (24.4.23, 25.8.18). Which criteria a possible successor had to meet is equally obscure. Did religion play a part? We do not know. We only know that, of the *duces exercitus* who tried to find a suitable candidate, Victor and Arintheus were Christians (the latter at any rate on his deathbed in 378, when he received baptism), and it is likely that their opponents Nevitta and Dagalaifus were pagans (cf. Von Haehling, 1978, 249–50 [Nevitta], 253 [Dagalaifus], 256–7 [Victor], 258–9 [Arintheus]).

nulla variante sententia itum est voluntate omnium in Salutium The translators interpret *nulla variante sententia* in two ways; Seyfarth

174 COMMENTARY

("niemand änderte seine Ansicht") and Selem ("senza che nessuno si opponesse") may serve as representatives. The latter category can i.a. adduce *Valentinianus nulla discordante sententia...electus est* (26.1.5) as a telling parallel and OLD s.v. 4b. On the other hand, this rendering involves a pleonasm in view of *voluntate omnium*. Seyfarth's translation is based on the assumption that *variare* does not express lack of consensus here, as in e.g. *variantesque geographi* (22.15.4, q.v.), but means "to waver" (OLD s.v. 5b); no one showed any sign of giving in. In this interpretation the comma after *ambiguntur* should rather be put after *sententia*. It would bring out more clearly that Salutius was a compromise candidate. See for *itum est* the note ad 24.7.1. In the present text *in Salutium* is not shorthand for *in sententiam Saluti*: it obviously means that the deadlock was resolved by a unanimous decision to nominate Salutius.

The *praefectus praetorio* Saturninius Secundus Salutius (*PLRE* I, Secundus 3) was a man of importance, who, for instance, had presided over the judicial commission at Chalcedon (22.3.1) and had been present at Julian's deathbed (25.3.21). A pious pagan, he was respected by pagans (cf. Lib. *Or.* 18.182) and Christians alike (cf. Greg. Naz. *Or.* 4.91). His office was, in Eunapius' words (*VS* 10.6.3), a magistracy which, though lacking the imperial purple, exercised imperial power (ἡ δὲ ἀρχὴ βασιλεία ἐστὶν ἀπόρφυρος), while Socrates (*HE* 2.16.2) speaks of the PPO as 'second after the emperor' (δεύτερος δὲ μετὰ βασιλέα χρηματίζει), cf. Demandt, 1989, 245–6; for literature on the praetorian prefecture see the note ad 25.3.14 *Salutius*. It is therefore not surprising that Salutius was offered the imperial throne to overcome the deadlock, pace Von Haehling, 1977, 350 (see below), following Straub, 1964, 216 n. 60.

Zosimus' words in 3.36.1 are strikingly similar to those of Amm. (πάντων δὲ ἡ ψῆφος εἰς ἕνα συνήει Σαλούστιον τὸν τῆς αὐλῆς ὕπαρχον), as are those of Zonaras in 13.14.16 (καὶ οἱ μὲν τόνδε, οἱ δὲ τόνδε ὠνόμαζον, οἱ πλείους δ' ἐπὶ τῷ Σαλουστίῳ ὑπάρχῳ τῷ πραιτωρίων τυγχάνοντι ὡμοφώνησαν). However, both Zosimus and Zonaras assign the nomination of Salutius to a date in 364, after the death of Jovian, and not, as Amm. does, to the day after Julian died in 363. How should we resolve this discrepancy? Is Zosimus (and in his wake Zonaras) wrong? So e.g. Dillemann, 1961, 145, who accuses Zosimus of many errors and lists the present case as one of his distortions. We have seen, however, that Dillemann is often unduly hard on Zosimus (cf. e.g. the notes ad 25.1.4 *qua ex regione*, 25.1.5 *extremos*, 25.1.10 *Progressi*). Or are Zosimus and Zonaras right and is Amm. mistaken? But Amm. was present in 363, although, admittedly, probably not at

CHAPTER 5.3 175

the deliberations of the *duces exercitus* and the *legionum principia et turmarum*. Did Amm. make a mistake, or is he perhaps, as Von Haehling, 1977, 350 ff. suggests, deliberately misdating Salutius' nomination to discredit Jovian? This is a serious accusation. Von Haehling's stand deserves therefore a full analysis, the more so because his article, according to Matthews 508 n. 5, "is by far the most convincing attempt to interpret the events within a religious dimension, and does justice to Ammianus' manner of writing as well as to the possible motives of individual actors". Barnes, 1998, 139 goes even further: "Raban von Haehling...has demonstrated how utterly tendentious, and hence how unreliable, his (= Ammianus') account in fact is".

Von Haehling's main arguments as to the text under discussion are the following. 1) It is "unvorstellbar und widerspricht dem Herkommen, daß der bislang höchste Zivilbeamte diese schwierige militärische Aufgabe übernehmen sollte" (350, cf. 354). Von Haehling does not, however, question the fact that another civil official, the *primicerius notariorum* Iovianus, was also a candidate for the throne (351; see for Iovianus above, the note ad *quae dum ambiguntur*). Neither does he reject Zosimus' and Zonaras' statement that Salutius – though still a "Zivilbeamte" – was nominated in 364, after Jovian's death (353 n. 41). It should also be noted that Procopius, proclaimed emperor in 365 (see for him below, the note ad *si Mesopotamiam videre*), was a (former) *tribunus et notarius*. Add to this the fact that Salutius' eminence was beyond dispute and one can very well imagine that Salutius was asked to ascend the throne (so rightly Neri, 1985, 157 n. 19). 2) Does it not arouse suspicion, Von Haehling asks, that the choice which fell on Salutius was unanimous (*voluntate omnium*)? Was he not one of the *proceres Gallorum* (see above, the note ad §2 *Nevitta*) and therefore biased with regard to the question of succession (351)? Suspicion is certainly legitimate, but, firstly, one should not forget that the earlier discussion had brought no solution (*quae dum ambiguntur, nulla variante sententia*), and, secondly, that, even if Salutius was one of the *proceres Gallorum*, it is not a foregone conclusion that he was already at the outset the candidate of Nevitta cum suis. A deadlock had occurred, and it was only then that all united behind the generally respected Salutius. 3) After Jovian had been chosen as successor to Julian, Salutius continued to serve as praetorian prefect under the new emperor, who sent him later in the year, together with Arintheus, to negotiate with the Persians (25.7.7). This embassy would have been impossible, according to Von Haehling, if, as Amm. asserts, Salutius had been offered the throne: "Diese Mission setzt ein Vertrauensverhältnis voraus, das nicht hätte beste-

176 COMMENTARY

hen können, wenn der als nachtragend gekennzeichnete Kaiser in Salutius seinen Rivalen erkannt hätte" (351). Not a very strong argument. Moreover, Von Haehling is not consistent in his reasoning. He accepts, as we have seen, Zosimus' and Zonaras' report that Salutius was offered the throne in 364, after Jovian's death and before Valentinian's succession to the throne. But he does not see Salutius as Valentinian's rival, although Salutius continued to serve under Valentinian, albeit with an intermission. 4) Von Haehling's argumentum e silentio is not convincing either: "Der nicht gerade verschwiegene Libanius hätte einer solch unerwarteten Erhöhung seines Freundes Salutius sicherlich Erwähnung getan" (353).

There is one other possibility to resolve the disagreement between the accounts of our sources, viz. that Salutius was offered the throne twice, in 363, as Amm. reports, and in 364, as Zosimus and Zonaras relate. This option is preferred by e.g. Paschoud n. 105; Neri, 1985, 153 sqq.; Vanderspoel, 1995, 149 and Lenski, 2000, 495. Rightly, it would seem.

eoque causante morbos et senectutem Cf. for *causari*, 'to mention something as an excuse for not taking a particular action', *Sabinus inhabilem labori et audaciae valetudinem causabatur* (Tac. *Hist.* 3.59.3), *causatusque capitis acrem dolorem* (Apul. *Met.* 3.13), *morbosque diu causatus* (Amm. 14.7.10). Libanius' *Ep.* 1298, 1428 and 1429 are addressed to Salutius and confirm that Salutius was not in good health (the correspondence between the PPO and Libanius started shortly after Julian's death). Although Salutius' age in 363 is not known, he probably was a *senex*, since he already had been *praeses provinciae Aquitanicae*, *magister memoriae* and *proconsul Africae* (*CIL* 6.1764 = *ILS* 1255), presumably under Constans, before he was assigned as an adviser to Julian after the latter was appointed Caesar in Gaul in 355 (Jul. *Ep. ad Ath.* 281 d, Zos. 3.2.2). Moreover, Libanius in *Or.* 12.43 compares him to Phoenix, Achilles' fatherly friend (Norman's translation "the Phoenician" is surely wrong; cf. Lib. *Or.* 15.8). There is therefore little reason to follow Von Haehling, 1977, 352, who states that Amm.'s "Formulierung…erkennen läßt, daß die von Salutius vorgebrachten Gründe nur einen Vorwand darstellten". He argues that old age and illness were more often used as an excuse (e.g. D.C. 73.1.4–5, Hdn. 2.3.3, HA *DI* 8.3), so that Amm. may well have been influenced by reports of this type. Moreover, Salutius apparently was not too old or too sick to become PPO a second time in November 365. With the help of such arguments wellnigh any fact reported by whichever author can be reasoned away.

CHAPTER 5.3   177

Once again the similarity between Amm. and the corresponding passages in Zosimus and Zonaras is noticeable (Zos. 3.36.1 τοῦ δὲ τὸ γῆρας προϊσχομένου καὶ διὰ τοῦτο φήσαντος οὐχ οἷός τε ἔσεσθαι πεπονηκόσιν ἀρκέσειν τοῖς πράγμασι, Zon. 13.14.16 ὁ δ' ἀπηνήνατο, τὸ γῆρας εἰς παραίτησιν προβαλόμενος). However, there are also some differences. Only Amm. speaks of Salutius' illness, while Zosimus and Zonaras declare that Salutius' son was offered the throne after his father had refused, but that the father declined this, arguing that the boy was too young. The fact that these divergencies exist corroborates the idea expressed in the note above that there were indeed two attempts to make Salutius emperor.

honoratior aliquis miles advertens destinatius reluctantem The long list in TLL VI 2949.25 sqq. shows that *honoratus* is a t.t., the precise demarcation of which is difficult to define. As in Amm.'s two other instances in which the comparative is used about soldiers (14.10.7 *quibus erat honoratioris militis cura commissa*, 31.12.1 *honoratiores alii*), it is obvious that here too a high-ranking officer is concerned. "Perhaps Ammianus himself", Gibbon suggested in one of his footnotes (III, 518 n. 104 in Bury's edition of 1897). Some scholars considered the idea attractive, e.g. Brakman, 1919, 108 (referring to the νεανίσκος in X. *An.* 2.4.19, who is sometimes identified with Xenophon himself), Fontaine n. 608 and Von Haehling, 1977, 354 ("so wird die gesamte Passage als Einschub einer subjektiven Meinungsaußerung Ammians entlarvt"). However, Cart, 1868, 19 already objected that Amm., who was always keen enough to record his own activities (as in the case of his escape from Amida, 18.8.1 sqq.), would not have concealed his identity here. Moreover, as Thompson, 1947, 12 points out, Amm. was scarcely of a high enough rank to have been among those who discussed the choice of a new emperor. See further Demandt, 1965, 43 with n. 118 and Matthews 183–4 with n. 6 on p. 508.

Clearly, speculations about the identity of the anonymous officer are bound to lead nowhere. It is more fruitful to concentrate on the form, the contents and the purpose of the remark, which the author presumably regards as worthwhile. From TLL V 1.761.59–63 it appears that Amm. idiosyncratically uses *destinate* as a synonym of *pertinaciter*. See also the note ad 17.2.2 *destinatis*. As was noted ad 20.4.8, *reluctari* usually occurs in contexts of stubborn resistance. The *honoratior miles* drew the lucid conclusion that it was impossible to persuade Salutius.

178   COMMENTARY

"et quid ageretis", ait, "si id bellum vobis curandum commisisset absens, ut saepe factum est, imperator? nonne posthabitis ceteris militem instantibus aerumnis eriperetis?" Two rhetorical techniques are combined here, an irrealis and a rhetorical question, in order to convince the assembly that the absence of an emperor and commander does not imply any changes concerning the urgent priorities of the moment. Moreover, Amm. has spiced up the soldier's intervention with an idiomatic nicety: the use of *et* at the beginning of the first question. This expresses a certain degree of indignation or resentment; see TLL V 2.890.68 sqq. and Szantyr 480. Another fine example in Amm. is 27.7.7: in a fit of anger Valentinian has ordered the execution of three decurions in a number of cities. The prefect Florentius then reacts with these words: *"et quid agitur", ait "si oppidum aliquod curiales non habuit tantos?"*

As appears in TLL II 1835.49–50, *bellum curare* does not occur often: Liv. 2.48.8 *vos alia bella curate* and 7.26.10 *bellum maritimum curare*, and Hor. *Carm.* 4.5.27–8 *quis ferae/ bellum curet Hiberiae?* are the other examples. With *vobis* and the second person plural *ageretis*, *eriperetis* and *agite* the officer addresses the generals and their staff. This probably implies that he himself did not belong to the highest echelons of the army. Amazingly, Barnes, 1998, 140 assumes that these words were addressed to Salutius: "A soldier of high rank thereupon upbraided him".

id nunc agite "Zur Einführung der tatsächlichen Wirklichkeit nach einem Irrealis dient gewöhnlich *nunc, nunc vero*" (Kühner-Stegmann 2.299, cf. OLD s.v. 11). The speaker, however, breaks out of this usual pattern by calling for exactly the action which they would have taken in the hypothetical situation of the irrealis. First things first!

si Mesopotamiam videre licuerit, utriusque exercitus consociata suffragia legitimum principem declarabunt Amm.'s use of *videre* is a sign of his familiarity with idiomatic niceties of the Latin language: here the verb means "to live to see" (OLD s.v. 11c), as e.g. in Cic. *de Orat.* 3.8 *Non vidit flagrantem bello Italiam, non ardentem invidia senatum*; see Leeman-Pinkster ad loc.

As was observed ad 23.2.7 *unde contractis copiis* (q.v.), in Amm. the term *Mesopotamia* usually denotes the Roman province of that name, with its capital Nisibis, and not 'all the land between the rivers Euphrates and Tigris'. This is also the case here. The *miles* argues that a new emperor should not be chosen while the army was still surrounded by the enemy, but only after they had reached Roman

CHAPTER 5.4 179

territory safe and sound. There they were to be united with the army corps which Julian, after the division of his forces at an early stage of his campaign, had put under the command of Procopius and Sebastianus (23.3.5 *triginta milia lectorum militum eidem commisit Procopio iuncto ad parilem potestatem Sebastiano comite ex duce Aegypti*) who actually met the main force some time later (25.8.16 *Profecti exinde Thilsaphata venimus, ubi Sebastianus atque Procopius cum tribunis principiisque militum sibi ad tuendam Mesopotamiam commissorum…occurrerunt*). Undoubtedly Amm.'s *miles* refers to this army corps (so e.g. Solari, 1933, 331 and Fontaine n. 608), pace Brok 216, who thinks that with *utriusque exercitus* the armies of the western and eastern parts of the empire are meant.

The expression *legitimus princeps* also occurs in 15.8.21, 19.12.17, 26.9.10, 27.5.1, 30.10.1; cf. also *imperator legitime declaratus* (30.10.5). "The legitimacy is very important for Amm." (De Jonge ad 19.12.17). E.g. Solari, 1933, 331–2 and Neri, 1985, 159–63 propose that one should regard the phrase here as a veiled allusion to an attempt to push forward the said Procopius (*PLRE* I, Procopius 4 + A. Lippold in *Gnomon* 46 [1974] 270) as another candidate for the throne. This is an attractive suggestion. In 23.3.2 (q.v.) Amm. had transmitted the story that Julian, in Carrhae, had appointed Procopius as his successor in case he himself should die during the campaign. As Amm. there indicates (*dicitur* and *nullo arbitrorum admisso*, cf. 26.6.2 *obscurior fama*), this story was based on rumours. It is probably not true, and it is at any rate incompatible with Amm.'s statement in 25.3.20 that Julian had refrained from nominating a successor. However, it is quite understandable that the story was launched: Procopius' ambition to ascend the throne became manifest in 365 when he was proclaimed emperor (cf. 25.9.13, 26.5.8, 26.6.12 sqq.). That this man was also named as a possible successor to the throne in 363 is quite feasible.

Inter has exiguas ad tantam rem moras Amm. wants to prevent his readers from jumping to the conclusion that far too much time was wasted by the heated discussion about various candidates. In fact the time used (*moras*) was brief (*exiguas*) in proportion to (OLD s.v. *ad* 35b) the huge importance of the matter. Gelenius' version of the text is therefore perfectly in order, in contrast to the ill-advised *adtonitorum* of Petschenig, 1891, 353. It is true that Amm. has other cases of *attonitus* (see the note ad 23.5.3 *populo venustate attonito*), but here it is the wrong term: they certainly were not 'dumbfounded', but quarrelling *studiis turbulentis* (§2). Socr. *HE* 3.22.1 (μηδὲν ὑπερθέμενοι τῇ ἑξῆς ἡμέρᾳ ἀναδεικνύουσι βασιλέα

5.4

180   COMMENTARY

'Ιοβιανόν) and Greg. Naz. *Or.* 5.15 (Διαδεξάμενος δὲ τὴν βασιλείαν εὐθὺς μετ' ἐκεῖνον sc. Iovianus) also stress the rapid course of events after Julian's death.

nondum pensatis sententiis tumultuantibus paucis, ut in rebus extremis saepe est factum, Iovianus eligitur imperator A phrase quoted ad 21.12.20 *aequitate pensata* probably expresses well what Amm. intends to convey in the first three words: Liv. 22.51.3 *ad consilium pensandum temporis opus esse.* Whether *tumultuantibus paucis* is a dat. auctoris (see the note ad 23.5.11 *sed calcabantur*) or, far more likely, as will be argued below in a detailed analysis, an abl. abs., the few men who caused a rowdy scene (see for *tumultuare* the note ad 22.10.5 *hoc factum*) are held responsible by Amm. He refrains, however, from disclosing their identity. Since it is difficult to imagine that he did not know it, his silence seems deliberate.

The phrase *ut in rebus extremis saepe est factum* is reminiscent of Sal. *Hist.* 3.95 *uti solet in extremis rebus.* See for other expressions denoting a crisis (*in rebus extremis*) the note ad 14.2.6 *ex necessitate ultima.* In the present text the phrase presumably refers to the numerous usurpations in the lost books of the *Res Gestae.*

The election of Jovian (PLRE I, Iovianus 3) as depicted by Amm. and other authors has led to different interpretations. One of the impediments to a proper assessment of the event is the fact that no report is as detailed as Amm.'s about the events between Julian's death and Jovian's accession. Most of the sources, Christian and pagan alike, are very concise indeed, and in their brevity often hide more than they reveal, as some scholars have argued. By its sheer length therefore Amm.'s account was given preference in much of the scholarly literature, until Von Haehling's article of 1977 cast a doubt on Amm.'s veracity. Although his arguments were largely refuted by Neri, 1985, Von Haehling still finds followers (see above, the note ad 25.5.3 *nulla variante sententia*), and, whatever its cogency, the virtue of his article is that it started an interesting discussion (the participants include Wirth, 1984, 355–8; Matthews 183–5; Carrasco Serrano, 1995, 178–9; Vanderspoel, 1995, 138–44; Barnes, 1998, 140–2; Heather, 1999, 105–8; Lenski, 2000). Yet it would seem that Amm.'s representation of what happened is intrinsically plausible and correct, which does not mean that it is altogether clear and as complete as one should wish.

Before scrutinizing Amm.'s version, an outline will be given of what the parallel sources have to say. Although there are some differences between them, one thing is clear: unlike Amm. all other

CHAPTER 5.4   181

sources give the impression that Jovian's accession was undisputed. Only Zos. 3.30.1 and Thdt. *HE* 4.1.1, cited in the note ad *collecti duces* in §3, at least hint that there was some discussion. Of those who suggest that the succession passed off smoothly, John the Lydian surpasses all others. According to him it was Julian who, on his deathbed, had decided the issue beforehand by nominating Jovian (Ἰουβιανὸν μὲν αὐτὸς ψηφισάμενος βασιλεύειν ἐτελεύτα sc. Iulianus, Lyd. *Mens.* 4.118) – an incredible story, and in flat contradiction of Amm. 25.3.20 *super imperatore vero creando caute reticeo* (q.v.). Zosimus states that Jovian was proclaimed emperor by common consent (ψήφῳ κοινῇ βασιλεὺς Ἰοβιανὸς ἀναδείκνυται, 3.30.1), leaving it to modern commentators to decide what precisely is meant by ψήφῳ κοινῇ. This point will be discussed more fully below. It should be noted here, however, that stricto sensu Zosimus' ἀναδείκνυται is not the equivalent of Amm.'s *eligitur*. With *eligitur* Amm. refers to the first stage in the process of choosing a new emperor, the '*electio*' (see for the various stages, '*electio*', '*commendatio*', '*acclamatio*', most recently Heim, 1990), while Zosimus' ἀναδείκνυται evidently alludes to the last, the '*acclamatio*', which in Amm.'s account is narrated in §5 and 6. Zonaras, who apparently borrows from Zosimus the puzzling expression ψήφῳ κοινῇ, is in this respect closer to Amm., for his προυκέκριτο must refer to the election: ψήφῳ κοινῇ Ἰοβιανὸς εἰς τὴν αὐταρχίαν προυκέκριτο (13.14.1). A unanimous vote for Jovian is also reported by Themistius in the oration which he held in the presence of the new emperor at Ancyra on 1 January 364. Themistius is more specific than Zonaras. He speaks of ψηφηφόροι καὶ στρατιῶται who made Jovian emperor "giving their votes among the swords and among the spears, an unsolicited judgement, an unpremeditated election...in an assembly beyond our borders, outside Roman territory" (οἱ δὲ ἡμέτεροι ψηφηφόροι καὶ στρατιῶται...ἀπέφηναν κληρονόμον τῆς ἁλουργίδος ['the imperial purple']...ἐν τοῖς ξίφεσιν, ἐν τοῖς δόρασι φέροντες τὰς ψήφους, ἀπαράκλητον γνώμην, ἀκατασκεύαστον χειροτονίαν...ἐν ἐκκλησίᾳ ὑπερορίῳ, ἔξω τῆς Ῥωμαίων γῆς, *Or.* 5. 65 c–d, tr. Moncur). When Eutropius, another contemporary and a participant in the Persian expedition at that, mentions Jovian's election, he says that it took place 'with the consent of the army': *Iovianus...ad obtinendum imperium consensu exercitus lectus est* (10.17.1; cf. κοινῇ συνθήκῃ τοῦ στρατοπέδου παραλαμβάνει τὴν βασιλείαν Ἰοβιανός, Soz. *HE* 6.3.1). Some later authors go a step further and relate that it was the army itself which wanted Jovian as emperor (τούτων δὲ περὶ τούτων βουλευομένων, ἡ στρατιὰ συναθροισθεῖσα κατὰ ταὐτὸν Ἰοβιανὸν ἐξῄτησε βασιλέα, Thdt. *HE* 4.1.2; καὶ εὐθέως ὁ στρατὸς...ἀπῆλθαν ἐν

182 COMMENTARY

τῷ παπυλεῶνι ('tent') Ἰοβιανοῦ...καὶ ἀγνοοῦντος αὐτοῦ τὰ τῆς τελευτῆς Ἰουλιανοῦ, ἤγαγον αὐτὸν εἰς τὸν βασιλικὸν παπυλεῶνα...καὶ...συνέχοντες αὐτὸν ἀνηγόρευσαν βασιλέα, *Chron. Pasch.* a. 363; Καὶ διαδέχεται τὴν Ῥωμαικὴν βασιλείαν ψήφῳ τοῦ παντὸς στρατεύματος Ἰωβιανός, Photius 484 b). To sum up, the parallel sources all state that Jovian was elected without much ado, but they differ as to the question how the election came about: at Julian's behest (John the Lydian), by the army (Theodoret, the *Chronicon Paschale*, Photius), with the consent of the army (Eutropius and Sozomen), by common consent (Zosimus and Zonaras) or by the army and the ψηφηφόροι (Themistius). How these reports relate to Ammianus' account must now be considered.

When we turn to Amm.'s narrative, it should first of all be stressed again that, according to him, the succession was much disputed (25.5.1–3). As we have seen, only Zosimus and Theodoret confirm that there was some discussion as to who would be Julian's successor; nevertheless, the silence of the other sources should not deter us from accepting this as a fact. Whatever Jovian's merits (see below, the note ad *paternis meritis mediocriter commendabilis*), he was not an obvious candidate for the throne and there were other candidates, as we have already seen (see the notes ad §3). Under these circumstances, while the issue was not yet settled and the various opinions still had to be weighed (*nondum pensatis sententiis*, τούτων δὲ περὶ τούτων βουλευομένων, Thdt. *HE* 4.1.2), Jovian was elected *tumultuantibus paucis*. These words immediately raise some questions. Who were these *pauci*? What is the grammatical structure of the sentence? To start with the grammar, is *tumultuantibus paucis* a dat. auctoris? Was, in other words, the election of the new emperor de facto taken out of the hands of Arintheus cum suis (cf. 25.5.2) 'by a few men who caused a rowdy scene', thus presenting their superiors with a fait accompli? Or is *tumultuantibus paucis* to be taken as an abl. abs.? If so, does Amm. with these words want to express the cause which induced the army commanders (and probably other officials; cf. the note ad *collecti duces* in § 1) to decide the issue, or does he merely want to indicate that Jovian's election took place under troubled circumstances? In view of the context the last mentioned possibility can be ruled out. It would seem that in any case the *pauci* are held responsible by Amm. As to the choice between a dat. auctoris and an abl. abs., a comparison with the defector's version of the scene in 25.5.8 (q.v.), where there can be no doubt about the case of *turbine concitato calonum*, suggests that *tumultuantibus paucis* in the present text is also best taken as an abl. abs.: 'Jovian was elected when (or: because) a few men caused a rowdy scene'.

CHAPTER 5.4   183

This interpretation does not, of course, answer the question of the identity of the men who caused the tumult. Moreover, it raises another question: if not by the *pauci*, by whom then was Jovian elected? To begin with the first problem, the *pauci* of this section are disparagingly termed *calones*, 'camp followers', by the traitor in 25.5.8. That clearly does not tally with the facts. They must have been military men, presumably officers. The deserter's words should not be taken literally. The man was at odds with Jovian (*cum novo dissidens principe etiamtum privato*) and Amm. deliberately puts insulting terms into his mouth (see the note ad loc.). It seems a reasonable assumption therefore that the so-called *calones* of 25.5.8 and the *pauci* of the present text were soldiers. "Illyrian soldiers" perhaps? (cf. Vanderspoel, 1995, 141, referring to Soraci, 1968, 23). Or "Christian guardsmen" (so Lenski, 2000, 502)? We can only guess, but it seems indeed likely that they had served under the father of Jovian (see for him below, the note ad *Varroniani*) and/or were colleagues of Jovian himself. It is difficult to imagine that Amm. did not know who they were, but, alas, he does not tell. What he does tell, however, is not implausible and moreover suggests the answer to the remaining question: it is quite understandable that some soldiers thought that the deliberations of Arintheus cum suis took too long, that they became unruly and that this caused their superiors finally to make up their minds and elect Jovian. In the section under discussion Amm. does not deem it necessary to say explicitly by whom Jovian was elected. His vagueness is no doubt deliberate and reinforces the impression that Jovian's election came as a considerable surprise. However, from what Amm. says in the first three sections of this chapter it can be deduced that according to him Jovian was elected by Arintheus, Victor, Nevitta e tutti quanti (cf. the note ad §1 *collecti duces*). There is no need, therefore, to question the legitimacy of the procedure (as do e.g. Von Haehling, 1977, 351 n. 31 and Lenski, 2000, 492); cf. Kolb, 2001, 94: "Er [= Amm.] bestreitet Iovian nicht die Rechtmäßigkeit seines Kaisertums".

The over-simplified accounts of Theodoret, the *Chronicon Paschale* and Photius, quoted above, cannot be reconciled with Amm.'s representation of Jovian's election, if thus interpreted, and should be rejected: Jovian was not elected 'by the army' (so rightly Weber, 2000, 164 against Vanderspoel, 1995, 141). The absurd version of Lydus can also be ruled out. As to the other sources, the greater part 1) seems to contaminate the various stages in the process of electing a new emperor and 2) leaves out all that could be seen to

184   COMMENTARY

be discrediting Jovian. To begin with Eutropius' formulaic statement that Jovian was elected *consensu exercitus* (cf. *consensu militum* in 9.2.1, 10.10.2 and 10.15.1): the election proper by the principal leaders and its approval by the army are here apparently taken together. Further, in Eutropius' account there is not a word about unruly soldiers. Neither does he say anything about disagreements among the leaders who elected Jovian, nor that there had been other candidates. Eutropius himself took part in the Persian campaign (*cui expeditioni ego quoque interfui*, 10.16.1) and one may suspect that he knew more. However, he altogether omits to mention the unflattering circumstances of Jovian's election and confines himself to the final and undeniable outcome: Jovian's election was accepted by the army. He is telling the truth, to be sure, but not the whole truth. Eutropius may be excused for this brevity. He was, after all, the author of a *Breviarium*. The Christian Sozomen, who followed in his wake, had other reasons to be brief. He was glad that the reign of the Apostate had ended and that a Christian had been offered the throne. Why then bother about unpleasant details? The same holds good for Zonaras. He also obscures the fact that Jovian's election was by no means without problems. However, instead of *consensu exercitus* (Eutropius) or κοινῇ συνθήκῃ τοῦ στρατοπέδου (Sozomen), he says that Jovian was elected ψήφῳ κοινῇ, 'with common consent'. This would imply that according to him not only the soldiers approved of the choice of Jovian, but others as well. Is this a veiled reference to Arintheus cum suis (cf. Wirth, 1984, 357 n. 22: "sowohl auf Consistorium wie Heer zu beziehen")? Is Zonaras suggesting, not only that the whole army supported Jovian, but that the leaders who elected him were unanimous as well? If so, he even more than Eutropius and Sozomen perpetrates contamination. By altering Zosimus' ψήφῳ κοινῇ βασιλεὺς Ἰοβιανὸς ἀναδείκνυται into ψήφῳ κοινῇ Ἰοβιανὸς εἰς τὴν αὐταρχίαν προυκέκριτο, Zonaras merges the stages of '*electio*' and '*acclamatio*' into one (unlike Zosimus himself, whose report is confined to the acclamation). The accounts of all these authors are equally brief. Themistius, to whom we come now, has a bit more to say in the oration which celebrated Jovian's accession to the consulship, but in his speech, which was held in the presence of the emperor, there was of course no room for unpleasant details. It is not surprising, therefore, that Themistius, when referring to Jovian's election, sketches a rosy picture in which, for instance, any mention of soldiers causing a rowdy scene is lacking. He does mention soldiers, but makes them work together harmoniously with ψηφηφόροι to get Jovian elected. As to these ψηφηφόροι, this is a clear reference to

CHAPTER 5.4   185

Arintheus cum suis (even a tendentious and flattering representation of the facts may contain some true elements).

domesticorum ordinis primus Jovian will have been *primicerius domesticorum*, that is, the *domesticus* who by seniority ranked first among his colleagues. See for *domestici* the note ad 20.4.21 *tribuni*. The technical term for his rank is found in Hier. *Chron.* a. 363 *ex primicerio domesticorum* and Jord. *Rom.* 305 (Amm. uses *primicerius* only once, in 18.3.5, where one Valentinus is called *ex primicerio protectorum tribunus*). Jovian must have been *primicerius domesticorum* and not *comes domesticorum*, 'commander of the *domestici*' (pace Malalas *Chron.* 13.333 Ἰοβιανοῦ, κόμητος τῶν δομεστίκων and the author of *Chron. Pasch.* a. 363), for that post was still occupied by Dagalaifus (cf. for him the note ad 25.5.2). Malalas and the author of the Chron. Pasch. may have been misled by the fact that both Jovian's father Varronianus and his father-in-law Lucillianus had been *comes* (see for them the notes ad 25.5.4 *paternis meritis* and 25.8.9 *Lucillianum*). Nor was Jovian *tribunus militum*, as Socr. *HE* 3.22.2 (χιλίαρχος ὤν) and Zon. 13.14.1 (τότε χιλιαρχῶν) assume. Eutr. 10.17.1 simply says *domesticus militabat*, which, though not very accurate, is at least not wrong. The same holds good for Them. *Or.* 5.66 b (ἐξεστράτευσας...αἰχμοφόρος). A *primicerius domesticorum* at the time of Julian's death, Jovian had risen in rank since the last time he was mentioned by Amm. *(etiamtum protector domesticus*, 21.16.20, q.v.). For the fact that the *signifer* of 25.5.8 calls him *adhuc protectorem* see the note ad loc.

paternis meritis mediocriter commendabilis Amm. expresses his reservations about Jovian's capability in a dignified manner. Jovian is recommended on the grounds of his father's distinguished career, just like Valentinian: *Cuius* (i.e. his father's) *meritis Valentinianus ab ineunte adulescentia commendabilis* (30.7.4), but note a) the absence of *mediocriter*; this adverb is in principle a vox media, but, as is noted in TLL VIII 565.70–1, in many cases "magis respicitur defectus summitatis vel perfectionis", as a synonym of *modice*, b) the sequel of the text in 30.7.4: *contextu suarum quoque suffragante virtutum*, "l'ensemble de ses qualités personnelles lui valant aussi les suffrages" (Sabbah). Frank, 1967 discusses the use of *commendabilis* elsewhere in Amm. (it occurs also in 19.1.10, 29.2.16, 30.7.4 and 31.13.18), and concludes that the term denotes "a new kind of hereditary status" (1967, 310), which is rather questionable.

About Jovian's personal qualities Amm. has nothing to report at this crucial moment. Only in his lament on the surrender of

186 COMMENTARY

Nisibis to the Persians (25.9.7–11), which he calls *indignum imperio facinus* (§8), does Amm. pass a clearer judgment. He blames the lady Fortuna for handing the helm of the ship of state to a man, *quem nullis ante actae vitae insignibus in huiusmodi negotiis cognitum nec vituperari est aequum nec laudari (25.9.7)*. Eutropius 10.17.1 shares Amm.'s view that Jovian benefited from his father's reputation: *commendatione patris militibus magis quam sua notior*, as do Eun. *fr.* 29.1 ἄνθρωπος οὐ δι᾽ ἀρετὴν οἰκείαν, ἀλλὰ διὰ τὴν τοῦ πατρὸς δόξαν ἐς τοσοῦτον ἀρχῆς προελθών and Joh. Antioch. *fr.* 181 τῇ τοῦ πατρὸς μᾶλλον ἤπερ τῇ οἰκείᾳ δόξῃ τοῖς περὶ τὸ στρατόπεδον ἔγνωστο. Cf. also Them. *Or.* 5.65 b σοι πατρῴας μὲν ἀρετῆς ἕνεκεν ὠφλισκάνετο καὶ πρὶν ἡ βασιλεία.

Nevertheless, the new emperor was by no means a nobody: when still *protector domesticus* he had fulfilled the honorific duty of escorting the coffin of Constantius to Constantinople, 21.16.20. Theodoret even calls Jovian remarkably distinguished and for many reasons well known (ἐπίσημον δὲ ἄνδρα καὶ περιφανῆ καὶ πολλῶν ἕνεκα γνώριμον, *HE* 4.1.2).

erat enim Varroniani notissimi comitis filius haud dudum post depositum militiae munus ad tranquilliora vitae digressi Amm.'s designation of Jovian's father Varronianus as *comes* poses a problem. Is this term here used as shorthand for *comes rei militaris*, a title which was "selten in dieser Vollständigkeit gebraucht" (Seeck, 1901, 662; cf. the note ad 20.4.18 *postea comes*) and which "seems to have been given to officers commanding groups of *comitatenses*, ranging from substantial army corps to a couple of regiments, allocated to a special task or assigned to a particular area" (Jones 124)? Or had Varronianus been *comes domesticorum*, that is, commander of the corps of guards to which his son also belonged?

Scholars most often opt for the latter solution (cf. e.g. Hoffmann, 1969, 312, *PLRE* I, Varronianus 1, Paschoud n. 87 and Lenski, 2000, 507), pointing to the only ancient author who is specific about Varronianus' function, Zos. 3.30.1 Βαρρωνιανοῦ τοῦ τῶν δομεστίκων ἡγουμένου τάγματος παῖς (Zon. 13.14.1 merely says, like Amm., that Jovian's father had been *comes*: υἱὸς Βαρωνιανοῦ χρηματίσαντος κόμητος). Dillemann, 1961, 145, however, rejects Zosimus' testimony rather curtly and without taking into account the difference between a *primicerius* and a *comes domesticorum*: "c'est Iovien et non son père qui était chef des Domestici". Woods follows Dillemann in deeming it most unsafe to place great reliance on Zosimus, but, unlike the French scholar, he offers an alternative interpretation. According to him "Varronianus ended his career as a *comes* in

CHAPTER 5.5   187

command of the *Ioviani*" (1995a, 43). Now, we know from Amm.
25.5.8 *Iovianorum...quos Varronianus rexerat dudum* that Varronianus
indeed had once been in charge of the legion of that name ("il
avait d'abord été *signifer* des *Ioviani*" in Paschoud n. 87 is a slip).
The common interpretation of Varronianus' career, based on both
Amm. and Zos., takes this into account and offers the following
reconstruction: Varronianus first served some years with the Ioviani
(as *tribunus*, presumably), was then promoted to the post of *comes
domesticorum* (under Constantius), kept this position until Dagalaifus
replaced him (under Julian) and shortly afterwards retired. Woods
on the other hand, rejecting Zosimus' statement, argues for "a longstanding association with the Ioviani, from as early as 331 to the time
of his retirement shortly before 363. He never gained a more senior
position such as *comes domesticorum*" (1995a, 44).

It is evident that Zos. 3.30.1 is crucial for the question under discussion. Pace Dillemann and Woods there seems to be no reason not
to accept his words as essentially correct. Although Zosimus, instead
of saying that Jovian was the son of the *comes domesticorum* Varronianus (Βαρρωνιανοῦ τοῦ τῶν δομεστίκων ἡγουμένου τάγματος), ought to
have said that Jovian was the son of a former *comes domesticorum*, since
Dagalaifus held this position at the time (this is the main argument
of Woods, 1995a, 43), it would seem that this is a minor inaccu-
racy and no reason to reject the passage as a whole. Together with
Amm.'s remark in 25.5.8 *Iovianorum...quos Varronianus rexerat dudum*
and his designation of Varronianus here as *comes*, Zosimus' words
make good sense. It seems best therefore to stick to the communis
opinio and assume that Amm.'s *comes* in the present text stands for
comes domesticorum.

Cf. for *ad tranquilliora vitae digressi* 14.6.4 *ad tranquilliora vitae
discessit* and 26.7.1 *ad pacatiora iam vitae discesserant*. As is noted ad
20.2.5 *digredi*, Amm.'s less flowery expressions for retirement are
digredi or *discedere ad* (or *in*) *otium*.

et confestim indumentis circumdatus principalibus subitoque productus e   **5.5**
tabernaculo Here Jovian is still the Patiens of the swift action of his
supporters, who, without any delay, present their favourite in official attire. This may have caused some problems. In the necrology
Amm. reports concerning Jovian's great height, presumably somewhat hyperbolically, that the emperor's measurements were such,
*ut diu nullum indumentum regium ad mensuram eius aptum invenire-
tur* (25.10.14). The purple robe was donned in 'legal' cases: 15.8.10
(Constantius about Julian) *eum...amictu principali velabo* (q.v.), 26.2.3

188　　　　　　　　　COMMENTARY

(Valentinian presenting himself to the army) *principali habitu circumdatus et corona*, but this also happened at real or alleged usurpations: 20.4.22 (about Julian) *fulgentem eum augusto habitu* (q.v.), 26.7.10, 29.2.9. See for *productus* the note ad 21.5.7 *producturo*.

While Amm. only mentions Jovian's investiture with the imperial clothing, Zosimus, no doubt correctly, speaks of another part of the crowning ceremony (cf. for this the note ad 20.4.17 *iubebatur diadema*): Ἰοβιανὸς δὲ τὴν ἁλουργίδα ἐνδὺς καὶ τὸ διάδημα περιθέμενος (3.30.2). Malalas *Chron.* 13.334 also refers to the diadem and says that it was offered to Jovian by the army: στεφθεὶς ὑπὸ τοῦ στρατοῦ. Since this ὑπὸ τοῦ στρατοῦ is rather vague and Malalas, in the case of Valentinian's coronation, states that it was the praetorian prefect Salutius who crowned Valentinian (ἐστέφθη βασιλεὺς ὑπὸ Σαλουστίου τοῦ ἐπάρχου τοῦ πραιτωρίων, *Chron.* 13.337), Rosen's suggestion (1978, 438 n. 52) is not implausible: Salutius, the man to whom in all probability the crown was offered both in 363 and 364 (cf. the note ad 25.5.3 *nulla variante*), "hat wohl auch Jovian investiert und gekrönt".

per agmina iam discurrebat proficisci parantia The situation now developed at a rapid pace: Jovian, having become the Agens himself, had 'already' swung into action, making his presence felt among the troops which were getting ready to resume their march. Jovian's imperial power was an accomplished fact. See for *discurrere* denoting the commander's restless activity the note ad 24.6.9 *per prima*.

5.6 *et quoniam acies ad usque lapidem quartum porrigebatur* As is noted ad 20.9.3 *acies*, this term does not always denote an army in battle array, but can also simply mean 'army'. Here Fontaine even renders "l'armée en marche". See for *lapis*, 'milestone', the note ad 17.1.8. The distance implies a considerably more compact order than in 24.1.3 *ut decimo paene lapide postremi dispararentur a signiferis primis*.

antesignani clamare quosdam Iovianum audientes Augustum eadem multo maius sonabant See the note ad 20.4.14 *Augustum Iulianum*. From afar the men in the vanguard heard their fellow-soldiers shouting 'Iovianus Augustus' and with a loud voice repeated what they thought they heard. The verb *sonare* here means 'to utter' and is accompanied by a word denoting the contents of the uttering (see OLD s.v. 8b).

gentilitate enim prope perciti nominis, quod una littera discernebat, Iulianum recreatum arbitrati sunt deduci magnis favoribus, ut solebat Those read-

CHAPTER 5.6   189

ers, who might be surprised by Jovian's unexpected popularity, are now informed about the reality hidden behind *eadem*. It was a pure case of misunderstanding: the similarity of the names 'Julian' and 'Jovian', especially when heard at a distance, was the cause of the remarkable enthusiasm. Translators obviously and understandably do not know how to handle *prope*, either neglecting it or somehow combining it with *gentilitate* (e.g. Caltabiano's "quasi affinità"), which is impossible. As it stands, it can only mean that their emotions of joy were 'nearly' roused, i.e. they very soon found out the truth. See for Amm.'s predilection for *percitus* the notes ad 20.11.5, 21.3.1 and 21.9.5. In his 'historical' note ad 14.1.1 *gentilitateque etiamtum Constantii nominis* De Jonge suggests that *gentilitas nominis* and similar phrases in 14.9.4, 23.6.55, 31.2.13 and the present text mean "Namensübereinstimmung". This is confirmed by TLL VI 2.1873.21 sqq. The 'one letter' concerns the consonants, the vowels -o- and -u- sounding much the same.

They thought that Julian had 'recovered' from his wound. Cf. for this meaning of *recreari* 27.6.4 *remediis multiplicibus recreatus*, Tac. *Ann.* 2.69.2 *ubi recreatum accepit*. Cf. for *deducere*, 'to escort' a general or an emperor 23.2.4 *cumque eum profecturum deduceret multitudo promiscua*, 28.3.9 *favore omnium ad usque fretum deductus*. TLL VI 1.386.39 sqq. provides a long list of instances in which *favor* is "i.q. actio, qua favor ostenditur": applause, acclamations and the like. The singular is usual, but there are some examples of the plur., e.g. Amm. 24.1.12, where the army *elatis vocibus in favores principis consurgebat*. Cf. further 16.10.13 *in palatium receptus favore multiplici*, 29.5.56 *aetatum ordinumque omnium celebrabili favore susceptus*.

verum cum incurvus ille visus et longior adventaret, suspicati, quod acciderat, in lacrimas effusi sunt omnes et luctum In all its straightforwardness, this part of the report is excellent. They saw that the figure in purple, who was approaching them, had quite a tall stature and a stooping deportment. Evidently, this was not Julian, who *mediocris erat staturae* (25.4.22, cf. also 22.14.3 *homo brevis*) and moved like a macho: *grandiaque incedens* (*ib.*, q.v.), and they inferred 'what had happened', viz. that Julian had died and a successor had been nominated. There are not many instances of *longus*, 'tall', in Latin literature, and this is the only one in Amm., since 21.16.20 is a different case. In the necrology Amm. describes Jovian as *vasta proceritate et ardua* (25.10.14). The slightly bizarre scene ends in tears, which can be regarded as a final tribute to Julian. See for similar cases of 'Synonymenhäufung' with alliteration Hagendahl, 1924, 165, who

190   COMMENTARY

refers to *lamentis et luctu* (21.15.4 and 25.9.5) and *ad luctus et lamenta progressus* (18.3.1), and to Wölfflin, 1886, 448–9.

Whereas *effundere lacrimas* (or *fletus*) occurs quite often (see TLL V 2.216.83–217.13), *effundi ad* (or *in*) *lacrimas* is far less common. The first case seems to be Liv. 44.31.13 *ad preces lacrimasque effusus*. Tacitus has more examples, e.g. *in lacrimas effusi* (*Hist.* 2.45.3) and *effusi in lacrimas* (*Ann.* 3.23.1); see also *Ann.* 1.11.3 and 4.8.2. Servius auctus notes ad Verg. *A.* 2.651 *effusi lacrimas: pro effusi in lacrimas.*

5.7   As will appear clearly in §8, Amm. does not at all approve of the sudden elevation of Jovian. However, this does not prevent him from giving vent to his irritation at the hindsight verdicts of armchair critics, who fail to understand that in the thick of things decisions, whatever their quality, simply have to be made. Two metaphors and a comparison lend a hybrid character to his outpourings.

quodsi gravis quidam aequitatis spectator in ultimo rerum spiritu factum criminatur improvide   In contrast to other editors Seyfarth prints *quodsi* as one word, the only instance in his edition. If this is right, it expresses that the conditional clause is closely connected with the preceding text; see Kühner-Stegmann 2.321, Szantyr 571. Alternatively, printing *quod si* would imply that *quod* is the subject in an a.c.i.-construction, *factum* (*esse*) being the predicate. This entails the problem that *quod* could only refer to the immediately preceding sentence, whereas it should refer to the contents of §4 and 5. Seyfarth's decision may well be right, but it does not eliminate all difficulties; *factum* now means 'that which had been done' and the precise function of *improvide* is less clear. Nearly all translators combine it with *factum*, which is syntactically somewhat forced. Only Rolfe regards it as qualifying *criminatur*: "with undue haste", and TLL.VII 700.7–8 agrees by comparing the present text with August. *adult. coniug.* 1.26.33 *improvidius quam cautius iudicare.*

As is noted ad 21.12.20 *exploratius spectato*, Amm. often uses the verb *spectare* with the meaning 'to examine'. Such a meaning also suits his instances of the nomen agentis (21.16.9 [q.v.], 24.5.11, 27.5.8, and indeed the present text); cf. OLD s.v. 2: "scrutinizer". It is not easy to delineate what is denoted by *aequitatis*. In the present text the usual meaning 'justice' is not entirely satisfactory; it rather seems to indicate 'reasonableness': the imaginary serious critic examines whether a particular action was 'reasonable'. The juridical metaphor implied in *spectator* comes out more clearly in *criminatur*, quite a strong term.

CHAPTER 5.7   191

Among the translators only Fontaine and Hamilton try to bring out the hyperbolic metaphor *in ultimo...spiritu* with "en une conjoncture où l'Empire rendait le dernier souffle" and "when the army was at its last gasp", respectively. The main problem is, of course, the vagueness of *rerum*, which Latin literary language allows, whereas translators are bound to be more explicit. In any case, Amm.'s metaphor turns the tables on any critics who fail to realize that the 'patient' was at death's door.

nauticos idem iustius incusabit Amm. now introduces the trite image of steering a ship (in stormy weather), which in ancient literature is often used metaphorically, allegorically and in comparisons, as in the present case. One of the oldest and most famous instances is Pl. *R.* 488 b–489 a; cf. also Cic. *Rep.* 1.11, *Sest.* 20, Quint. *Inst.* 8.6.44, Amm. 21.13.10 *utque cautus navigandi magister clavos pro fluctuum motibus erigens vel inclinans* (q.v.). See for other examples in Greek literature Van Nes, 1963, 122–8.

See for *nauticus* used as a noun the note ad 16.12.51 *nautici*. This occurs already a number of times in Livy, e.g. 29.25.5 *nauticos C. Laelius...continuit*, 39.26.4 *quos portus mercatores aut nautici petant*. In all probability, *idem* is nom. masc. Verbs like *incusare* can be construed with two accusatives, "Wenn das sächliche Objekt durch den Akkusativ eines neutralen Pronomens...ausgedrückt wird" (Kühner-Stegmann 1.303; cf. Ter. *Ph.* 914 *quae tute dudum coram me incusaveras*), but in the case of *incusare* this is a rarity. There are no examples in Amm.

si amisso perito navigandi magistro saevientibus flabris et mari clavos regendae navis cuilibet periculi socio commiserunt On the basis of the erased *s* in V Petschenig, 1891, 353 has proposed *si*, which has also been accepted by Clark and Fontaine. Earlier editions print *quod*. See for the nautical sense of *magister* TLL VIII 80.64 sqq. Here it is a synonym of *gubernator*, as in Verg. *A.* 5.176–7 *ipse magister/ hortaturque viros clavumque ad litora torquet* (with Williams' note), Ov. *Ars* 1.6 *Tiphys in Haemonia puppe magister erat.* Amm.'s only instance of *flabrum* is here used as a synonym of *ventus*; cf. *graviter spirantibus...flabris* (Lucr. 6.428) and *cum...flabra saeviant* (Sol. 27.39). The combination of *socius* and *periculi* (or -*orum*) also occurs in 16.12.6, 16.12.41, 24.2.15, 25.4.12, 27.6.9. The vital point of the comparison is *cuilibet*, 'any comrade in danger, whoever he may be': the first phrase of the next section will emphasize this.

192   COMMENTARY

5.8 *his ita caeco quodam iudicio fortunae peractis* Fortune's blindness was
proverbial. Otto, 1890, 141–2 lists a number of important passages.
See also the additions in Häussler, 1968, 103, 164 and 236. A
remarkable instance is the apostrophe in Amm. 31.8.8 *de te Fortuna ut
inclementi querebatur et caeca*, which also shows that in the present text it
would be preferable to print *Fortunae*. See the note ad 20.4.13 *fortuna
quaedam* for the use of *quidam* intensifying the sense of the preceding
adj.: in this case Fortune's judgment had been 'exceedingly' myopic.
See for *fortuna* Naudé, 1964, and the relevant notes ad 20.4.13 and
23.5.19, and cf. the explicit accusation in 25.9.7 with the note ad loc.

Iovianorum signifer, quos Varronianus rexerat dudum…discessit ad Persas
Libanius presumably refers to the same man when he says τῷ μὲν
δὴ Πέρσῃ παρ᾽ αὐτομόλου τινὸς μαθεῖν ὑπῆρξεν ἐν ὅτῳ εἴη τύχης (*Or.
1.134*). Amm. 25.6.6 implies that the *signifer* was not the only one
who informed the Persians of Julian's death: *audierant enim ipsi quoque
referentibus transfugis…Iulianum…cecidisse.* As to the function of the
deserter, Vegetius at one time seems to suggest that in the late
Roman army *signiferi* were no longer in existence, but had been
replaced by *draconarii (mil. 2.7.5 Signiferi qui signa portant, quos nunc
draconarios vocant)*. Elsewhere, however, he distinguishes *draconarii*
from *signiferi (mil. 1.20.7)*, as does Amm. (cf. the note ad 24.3.1
unum rapuisse; see also 25.1.8 *ademptis signis* and Müller, 1905, 609–
12). Amm. mentions a *draconarius* in 20.4.18 and *signiferi*, apart
from the present text, in 15.8.13, 16.12.18, 16.12.70 and 24.1.3.
Together with *aquiliferi* (this term not in Amm., but see *aquila* in
15.8.4, 16.12.12, 17.13.25, 18.2.17, 20.5.1, 26.2.11, 26.7.17, 27.6.9,
28.5.3 and cf. Veg. *mil.* 2.13.1) *draconarii* and *signiferi* ranked "über
und außer den Mannschaftsgraden" (Demandt, 1989, 261), but
below officers. During the Principate *signiferi* themselves "had a
hierarchy: a *principalis*, adjutants and *discentes*" (Le Bohec, 1994,
49), but nothing of this is known as regards Late Antiquity. Among
their duties was the keeping of the regimental savings bank. *Et ideo
signiferi non solum fideles sed etiam litterati homines eligebantur* (Veg. *mil.*
2.20.7). For Varronianus' rank when he was in charge of the Ioviani
see above, ad §4 *erat enim*, for the legion of Ioviani the note ad
22.3.2 *praesentibus Iovianorum*. See also Woods, 1995a, 1995b and
1998b, whose views, however, are open to question.

*cum novo dissidens principe etiamtum privato ut patris eius obtrectator moles-
tus periculum ex inimico metuens iam communia supergresso* With these
words Amm. succinctly describes the background to the anonymous

CHAPTER 5.8

signifer's desertion to the Persians. Amm. first stipulates that the man had been on bad terms with Jovian even before the latter became emperor, in other words, when Jovian still was a *privatus* (TLL X 2.1391.4sqq. "aetate imperatoria privati vocantur omnes praeter ipsum principem"; cf. Béranger, 1985 and Demandt, 1997², 27–9). He then says that the origin of this quarrel was the fact that the man had annoyed and slandered Jovian's father, who had once been his commanding officer. See for *obtrectator* the note ad 20.2.1 *obtrectatores*. In 29.5.23 and 31.7.5 such nasty people are styled *malivoli*, which has prompted Fontaine to conjecture *malevolus* here instead of Haupt's *molestus*. However, that is much nearer V's *mobeatus* and, pace Fontaine, it gives an excellent sense: the man made a nuisance of himself by making disparaging remarks about the commander of his unit. Finally, Amm. refers to the standard-bearer's fear for his life, now that his long-time enemy Jovian had achieved a position which easily would enable him to punish his opponent: Jovian had gone beyond what he had in common with his personal enemy (*iam communia supergresso*; cf. for this the contrast in 14.11.20 between *regiis indumentis and paludamento communi*). All in all, although this is not an illogical explanation, it is a rather summary one. It does not satisfy David Woods: "This passage...fails to explain the nature or origin of this quarrel" (1995a, 42). Woods thinks that "the passion of Bonosus and Maximilianus provides the background to an event described by Ammianus Marcellinus which seems quite unintelligible otherwise" (1995a, 50).

The Latin *passio ss. Bonosi et Maximiliani militum de numero Herculianorum Seniorum* (BHL 1427) purports to describe the martyrdom of two unknown standard-bearers, now called Bonosus and Maximilianus (§1sqq.), then Jovianus and Hercolianus (§5), who, having refused to remove from their *labarum* the chi-rho symbol, had to stand trial before the *comes* Iulianus, Julian's uncle and namesake (see for him the note ad 25.6.3). Woods concedes that there are some extremely unlikely details in the *passio* (p. 26 and 38: the *praefectus* Secundus, seeing that an attempt to burn Bonosus and Maximilianus alive had failed, ordered some pagan priests to be subjected to the same ordeal, which of course proved fatal to them), chronological problems (p. 28 and 39) and inventions of the author (p. 51). Moreover, "it contains very little which is not explicable as the work of a clever forger" (p. 38). Nevertheless, "the passion was not necessarily a complete fiction" (p. 36). Or rather, precisely its connection with Amm. 25.5.8 "is the strongest single argument in favour of accepting the passion as a valuable historical source" (p. 50). Unfortunately, in his attempt to prove his case Woods piles one speculation on top of another. 1) No mention is made of Jovian anywhere in the *passio*, but, according to Woods, "it would have been most surprising if the martyrs had not enjoyed the support of a wide network of friends...and among the friends who rallied to the cause of Bonosus and Maximilianus, the name of Jovian, the son of their former commander Varronianus, was surely prominent" (p. 45). 2) So, "Jovian had opposed the removal, and execution, of the former standard-bearer of the *Ioviani*, Bonosus" (p. 46). 3) "And in so doing he had stood in the way of Bonosus' replacement who was eager to advance his career, the anonymous standard-bearer whose desertion is recorded by Ammianus" (ibid.). 4) "One wonders whether Bonosus' replacement...had in fact stirred up the whole controversy to begin with by making complaints about the behaviour of Bonosus to officials such as the *comes* Julian" (ibid.). Pace Barnes, 1998, 52, this chain of hypotheses has not produced a plausible description of the course of events; in fact, a convincing description can only be based on clear and reliable evidence.

docet Saporem iam propinquantem exstincto, quem verebatur, turbine concitato calonum ad umbram imperii Iovianum adhuc protectorem ascitum, inertem quendam et mollem In 25.1.1 Amm. mentioned some facts indicating *adesse regis copias*, the present text explicitly states the king's personal approach. Is *exstincto, quem verebatur* the reason for Sapor moving nearer, or part of what the man told the king? The translators are unanimous in choosing the latter possibility, and the sentence structure backs them up. The advantage of the former solution would consist in making it more comprehensible that Sapor (see for him the note ad 20.6.1 *truculentus rex*) was 'already' coming nearer: he must have heard very soon about Julian's death and wanted to seize his opportunity. Moreover, one cannot very well imagine a defector telling the Persian king: "the man whom you feared is dead". Nevertheless, in spite of the lacuna in §9 that section squares far better with the assumption that it was the deserter who told Sapor that Julian had died. Consequently, *quem verebatur* should be taken as authorial and not as reproducing the man's words.

The defector fully lives up to this reputation as an *obtrectator*. Amm. has a great liking for the figurative use of *turbo*; see the note ad 21.13.14. In the present text it denotes revolutionary action, as in 18.3.1 *turbo novarum exoritur rerum* (q.v.); in fact, *turbine concitato* is a stronger phrase than *tumultuantibus paucis* in §4. However, the

CHAPTER 5.9   195

deserter adds that the storm had not been caused by proper soldiers, but by mere *calones*. See on them the notes ad 18.8.10 and 23.2.8; their low status comes out clearly in the deprecatory phrase about the Persian infantry: *iussa faciunt ut calones* (23.6.83, q.v.). A phrase in the speech of M. Philippus in Sallust's *Historiae*, in which mud is slung at a political opponent, is quite comparable to the present text: *tunc erat Lepidus latro cum calonibus et paucis sicariis* (Sal. *Hist.* 1.67.7). See for *protectorem* the note ad 21.16.20 *Iovianus etiamtum protector domesticus*. This is the only correct piece of information which the defector provides and it is not even complete: 25.5.4 *domesticorum ordinis primus* shows that Jovian had risen in the regiment's hierarchy. See the note ad 20.4.22 *asciti* for Amm.'s use of *asciscere*. For the present text phrases like *Iulianum...in societatem imperii asciscere cogitabat* (15.8.1) and *ascito in collegium trabeae Sallustio* (23.1.1) are relevant. However, the difference is that Jovian's imperial power is no more than an *umbra*, a "faint resemblance" (Courtney ad Juv. 14.109). Its use here is distinctly akin to Tac. *Ann.* 15.6.4 *pro umbra regis*, "statt eines Phantoms von König" (Koestermann). The present text differs from Aus. *Caes.* 80 Green (about Vitellius) *umbra tamen brevis imperii*, since that phrase concerns the brevity of Vitellius' reign, whereas here the lack of substance is meant. Cf. also 21.16.21 *imperium quidem, sed et cassum et umbratile* (q.v.). The defector ends with a characterization which is highly insulting to a soldier, and which is not shared by the author himself in the rest of book 25.

Amm. has done his best to convey that the biased information, provided by a defector with personal grudges, is a caricature, but such exertions are obviously wasted on Lenski, 2000, 494, who has this to say about *turbine concitato calonum*: "Ammianus, reporting through the persona of a third party."

hoc ille audito, quod semper trepidis votis...et inopina prosperitate elatus   **5.9**
Presumably, *hoc* refers to the defector's entire report, including Julian's death, which Sapor had always eagerly longed for; *trepidis* here denotes anxious eagerness rather than fear, as in Aus. *Eph.* 3.79 *maesto trepidantia vota reatu*. Neither Clark nor Seyfarth puts faith in the various proposals to fill the evident lacuna after *votis*. Perhaps Fontaine's *concepisset* might have persuaded them: it makes use of *et* and it is well supported by the parallel in 26.7.16 *ne votis quidem concipere ausus est*. The subj. can be explained as expressing Sapor's feeling rather than being a remark of the author.

See for *elatus* the note ad 21.4.7 *Hoc casu elatior* and Seager 43–4, who regards the present instance as a case of overreaction,

196 COMMENTARY

which is debatable. In any case Amm.'s main purpose seems to be to emphasize the effects of the deserter's treachery on the king's morale.

multitudine ex regio equitatu adiuncta his, qui dimicavere nobiscum, celeri disposuit gradu agminis nostri invadi terga postremi Amm.'s statement is more realistic than that of Themistius, according to whom the Persians threw aside their weapons as soon as they heard that Jovian had been proclaimed emperor (*Or.* 5.66 a, τὰ ὅπλα ῥίψαντες, ἐπειδὴ τῆς ἀναρρήσεως ᾔσθοντο). The phrase *celeri gradu* (or *gradu celeri*) occurs seven times in Amm., in some cases in the literal sense of a quick march (20.11.19 *legiones procinctae celeri gradu venerunt*), in others more generally ('at high speed'), as in 20.9.4 *Leonam...ad Iulianum pergere celeri statuit gradu*. See for *disponere*, 'to decide', with a.c.i. the note ad 16.11.4 *rite disposita*. Curiously, the sequel of the text does not specifically mention an attack on the Roman rearguard.

CHAPTER 6

Introduction

After the death of Julian and the election of his successor Jovian, the Roman army has to move on in order to reach Roman territory and to find food, which was already in desperately short supply when Julian was still in command (25.2.1 *nos...inedia cruciabat iam non ferenda*). At the end of ch. 5 Ammianus had written that Sapor, elated at the fall of his formidable opponent, personally took part in the pursuit of the Romans. In chapter 6 he is absent, and the focus is exclusively on the Roman side.

Several skirmishes take place that follow a similar pattern. First the Persians create disorder in the Roman ranks, but, as soon as a regular battle starts the Romans prove stronger than their opponents. Finally the Persians avoid open battle altogether, restricting themselves to brief attacks on the advancing army and withdrawing at an agonizingly slow pace when the Romans make a stand against them. Nevertheless they manage to inflict serious damage. Three officers fall in battle (§3) and are given an improvised burial, like the one for the magister officiorum Anatolius, who was found dead near the fortress of Sumere (§4). Moreover, the Roman army is forced to march more slowly, until it practically comes to a standstill during four whole days (§11). No wonder this harassment drives the soldiers to distraction and to acts of despair. They cross the Tigris when the water level is exceptionally high and before proper preparations have been made.

As the morale of the Roman army deteriorates, the Persians grow more confident. When the Roman army sets up camp in a narrow valley (§5–6), the Persians attack from the surrounding slopes with weapons and words. They sneer at the Romans and accuse them of murdering their own outstanding leader. It is only in this indirect way that Ammianus shows he is aware of the rumour, that Julian had been killed by a soldier belonging to his own troops. Even if this is only an idle rumour, as Ammianus insists it is, it is still a slur on the memory of the emperor, who had said on his deathbed *non clandestinis insidiis...decedo, sed...hunc merui clarum ex mundo digressum* (25.3.19). After this terrible insult Persian horsemen even dare to force their way into the camp and reach the tent of the emperor before they are beaten back.

198   COMMENTARY

All in all, the predicament of the Roman army is brought out vividly. Ammianus refrains from openly criticizing the new commander – indeed, Jovian's resistance to the demand of the soldiers to cross the Tigris is eminently reasonable – still, it is clear that Jovian lacks the natural authority of his predecessor, as Ammianus intimates by his choice of words and phrases like *exorabat* (§12) and *cum haec saepe congeminando refragaretur in cassum* (§13).

The report of Ammianus is much more detailed than the parallel account in Zosimus (3.30.4–5), who jumps from the battle, in which the three officers fall, to the four days, during which the army is practically brought to a standstill, leaving out the events at three encampments (the narrow valley §5–6, Charcha §8 and Dura on the Tigris §9). Nor does Zosimus mention the attacks of the Saracens and their particular hostility against the Romans, created by the disdain with which Julian had treated them (§9–10).

The chapter ends on a more positive note. The German and Gaulish swimmers, who receive permission to cross the Tigris by night, manage to do so and kill the Persian guards on the other side of the river. This only increases the desire on the part of the remaining soldiers to cross immediately. This success also prepares the reader for the next chapter, in which Ammianus, totally unexpectedly, describes the despondency of king Sapor.

6.1 *Quae dum ultro citroque ordinantur* For the shades of meaning of *ordinare* see the note ad 20.9.8 *Anatolium ordinavit*. With these words Amm. recapitulates the preceding chapter, i.e. the election of Jovian, and Sapor's preparations for an attack. *Ultro citroque* must mean 'on both sides'. In all other instances in Amm. *ultro citroque* is combined either with *discurrere* (ten times) or *dicere/dictare* (five times); see the notes ad 18.6.3 and 21.12.4.

hostiis pro Ioviano…extisque inspectis For Jovian see the notes ad 21.16.20 and 25.5.4, and for his Christian convictions and religious tolerance the note ad 25.10.15 *Christianae legis*. Because of his broad-mindedness in religious affairs it is not surprising that Jovian allowed the inspection of the entrails of sacrificial victims; for *extis inspectis* cf. 26.1.5 *extis Romae inspectis*. Moreover, the interpretation of prodigies continued also under Christian emperors and was only condemned officially by Theodosius; see the note ad 23.5.10 *Etrusci*.

pronuntiatum est As is evident from TLL X 2.1925.5 sqq., *pronuntiare* is a t.t. in divination. Cf. Cic. *Div.* 2.117 *Quid tam divinum autem quam*

CHAPTER 6.2   199

adflatus e terra mentem ita movens ut eam providam rerum futurarum efficiat, ut ea non modo cernat multo ante, sed etiam numero versuque pronuntiet? and Suet. *Jul.* 61 *cum haruspices* (equum) *imperium orbis terrae significare domino pronuntiassent.*

si intra vallum remansisset I.e. the camp to which Julian was taken after he was mortally wounded (25.3.7 *relatus in castra*) and where he eventually died. The day after Julian's death, i.e. 27 June, was spent on deliberations about the succession. The Roman army left this camp on the morning of 28 June. As was related in 25.5.5–6, the soldiers were ready to march, and their marching formation already extended over a distance of four miles, when they heard that Jovian had been made emperor.

ut cogitabat The verb has the meaning 'to have in mind, plan', cf. 21.7.6 *incertum, quonam erumpere cogitantes* and Cic. *Att.* 5.15.3 *inde ad Taurum* (ire) *cogitabam*; TLL III 1469.29 sqq.

superiorem vero fore profectum Amm. uses *superior* 'victorious' again in 25.7.5 *quos omnibus paene proeliis pars Romana superior gravius quassabat in dies* and 31.15.13 *pari modo res Romana superior stetit.* Cf. Caes. *Gal.* 5.15.1 *essedarii...cum equitatu nostro in itinere conflixerunt, ita tamen ut nostri omnibus partibus superiores fuerint.*

egredi iam coeptantes See Chausserie-Laprée, 1969, 497–517 on this **6.2** use of *iam*, which prepares the reader for an important development in the narrative. As the table on p. 513 shows, the combination of this "*iam* de préparation" with a present participle is rare. Normally it is combined with indicative imperfect or pluperfect. For a more general discussion of the particle *iam* see Kroon & Risselada, 2003.

adoriuntur nos elephantis praeviis Persae This Persian attack took place on 28 June. Contrary to Amm. (cf. below 25.6.4), Zos. 3.30.2 reports that the battle took place when the Romans had reached the fort of Suma: ἐπεὶ δὲ εἰς Σοῦμα τὸ φρούριον ἦλθεν, ἐπιπεσοῦσα ἡ Περσῶν ἵππος τοῖς ἀμφ' αὐτόν, ἐλέφαντάς τε οὐκ ὀλίγους ἐπαγαγοῦσα, τοὺς κατὰ τὸ δεξιὸν κέρας ἐκάκουν· ἐτετάχατο δὲ ἐν τούτῳ Ἰοβιανοὶ καὶ Ἑρκουλιανοί ('after he had reached the fortress of Suma, the Persian cavalry attacked him (Jovian) and his men. They brought a large number of elephants into the battle and inflicted harm on the men on the right flank. There the Ioviani and the Herculiani were stationed.') For elephants see the notes ad 24.6.8 and 25.1.14, 15. The position

200   COMMENTARY

of the elephants in the line of battle is not altogether clear. Here they
apparently go in front of the Sasanian soldiers; see also 25.3.11 and
the note ad loc. In 25.1.14, however, the archers go in front followed
by the elephants: *post hos* (sc. the archers) *elephantorum fulgentium
formidandam speciem.*

ad quorum faetorem inaccessum terribilemque Guenther, 1888, 44 proposed to read *faetorem accessumque terribilem* on the basis of V's *fraetum
inaccessumque terribilem. Faetorem* is decidedly better than *fremitum*, the
reading of EBAG, since TLL VI 1278.75–1279.25 gives no other
instances of *fremitus* for the trumpeting of elephants, which Amm.
calls *stridor* in 19.7.6, 25.1.14 and 25.3.4, where also their revolting
smell is mentioned. See Drijvers, 2005. Cf. also Flor. 1.18.8 (elephanti) *quorum cum magnitudine tum deformitate et novo odore simul ac
stridore consternati equi.* However, *accessus* in Amm. seems to denote
accessibility rather than actual approach: 24.4.10 *accessus undique
rupibus amfractu celsiore discissis flexuosisque excessibus ob periculum anceps
adeundi copiam denegabat,* 29.1.20 *erat enim expositus accessu insidi-
antium.* In conformity with classical Latin, Amm. uses *incessus* for a
specific way of walking: 16.12.7 *pedestres copiae lentis incessibus educun-
tur,* 17.10.3 *vultus incessusque supplicem indicabat.* Valentinian's *incessus* even changed during his fits of anger: 29.3.2 *ut irascentis saepe
vox et vultus, incessus mutaretur et color.* For that reason *faetorem incessumque terribilem* seems better. Heraeus preferred to keep V's *inaccessum*, which is indeed attractive, since Amm. uses *inaccessus* both
in its literal meaning, as in 23.6.62 *inter has nationes paene ob asperitatem nimiam inaccessas,* and figuratively about the unrivalled beauty
of Constantinople: 31.16.7 *inaccessas pulchritudines urbis* (cf. Macr.
Sat. 5.17.7 *Pindarum, quem Flaccus imitationi inaccessum fatetur*). As
a consequence, however, Heraeus had to transfer *-que* to follow *terribilem*. All things considered, leaving *-que* in its place and reading
incessumque seems the most economical solution to the problem.

equis inter initia turbatis et viris Also according to Zos. 3.30.2–3 the
Romans, including the wing where the Ioviani and Herculiani were
positioned, were initially overwhelmed by the elephants' strength,
and many Roman soldiers fell whilst fleeing: Τὸ μὲν οὖν πρῶτον ὑπὸ
τῆς τῶν ἐλεφάντων ἀλκῆς ἐβιάζοντο, καὶ πολλοὶ φεύγοντες ἔπεσον.

Ioviani et Herculiani See for these legions the note ad 22.3.2. Also
mentioned by Zos. 3.30.2 (see lemma above). For legions in general
see the note ad 25.1.7 *eodem die.*

CHAPTER 6.3

occisis beluis paucis Liv. uses *belua* for the elephant in 27.49.2: *ea celerrima via mortis in tantae molis belua inventa erat...primusque id Hasdrubal instituerat.* This phrase is imitated and modified in 25.1.15 *exploratum est enim aliquando ab Hasdrubale Hannibalis fratre ita citius vitam huiusmodi adimi beluarum.* For the various ways in which war elephants could be eliminated, see the note ad 25.3.5 *beluarum.* Zos. 3.30.3 has a different story. The Persians, when driving the Romans back, reached a higher ground where there happened to be Roman baggage carriers. These latter joined the battle and fired from above on the Persians; some elephants were wounded and ran away in pain, causing chaos within the Persian cavalry ranks, whilst others were killed; ἐπελαυνόντων δὲ αὐτοῖς τῶν Περσῶν πρὸς τῇ ἵππῳ καὶ τοὺς ἐλέφαντας, ἦλθον εἴς τι χωρίον ἄναντες, ἐν ᾧ τοὺς τῶν Ῥωμαίων σκευοφόρους ἔτυχεν εἶναι· ("but, when the Persians rode their elephants as well as their horses against them, they came to the rising ground, where the Roman bagage carriers were"; tr. Ridley). τούτων δὲ συνεπιλαβόντων αὐτοῖς τοῦ κινδύνου καὶ ἐξ ὑπερδεξίου τοὺς Πέρσας ἀκοντιζόντων, ἐτρώθησάν τινες τῶν ἐλεφάντων, καὶ ᾗπερ ἦν ἔθος αὐτοῖς, ἔφυγον ὀδυνώμενοι μετὰ βρυχηθμοῦ καὶ τὴν ἵππον ἅπασαν συνετάραξαν, ὥστ᾽ ἐν τῇ φυγῇ καὶ ἐλέφαντας ὑπὸ τῶν στρατιωτῶν κατασφαγῆναι καὶ πολλοὺς ἐν αὐτῇ τῇ μάχῃ πεσεῖν.

catafractis equitibus For *catafracti* see the note ad 25.1.12 *erant autem.*

legiones Ioviorum atque Victorum The *Iovii* and *Victores* were elite troops **6.3** belonging to the *auxilia palatina*; they were of western origin and seem often to have operated together: 26.7.13 *agmina duo praeire iussisset, quibus nomina sunt Iovii atque Victores*; 27.8.7 *unde cum consecuti Batavi venissent et Heruli Ioviique et Victores*; Hoffmann I 156–7. See for the Iovii also Drew-Bear, 1977 and Scharf, 1991. The *Victores* are also mentioned in 24.4.23 (q.v.), as well as by Zos. 3.22.4. They belonged to the *numeri Gallicani* referred to in 23.5.25 and were brought to the East by Julian; Brok 253; Fontaine n. 400. The *Iovii* are mentioned in *Not. Dign. Occ.* 5.168, 184, 212; 7.16, 42, 76 and the *Victores* in *Not. Dign. Occ.* 5.185, 212; 7.17, 27, 126, 154 (cf. 48) as well as in *Not. Dign. Or.* 5.63. It seems that Amm. did not distinguish carefully between the various units – legions, auxiliaries, *comitatenses* etc. – of the Roman army. Possibly for that reason he refers to the Iovii and Victores as legions, whereas the *Not. Dign.* calls them *auxilia* (*palatina*), unless, as Vogler, 1995, 391 suggests in the case of the *Victores*, they were legions in Amm.'s time and later became *auxilia*.

202   COMMENTARY

cum hostium plebe non parva For *plebs* referring to the common
soldiers cf. 16.12.34 *ne, si quid contigisset adversum, deserta miserabili
plebe facilem discedendi copiam repperirent.* The only parallels in other
authors seem to be Luc. 6.144 *Scaeva viro nomen: castrorum in plebe
merebat* and Tac. *Hist.* 4.70.4 *plebes omissis armis per agros palatur.* See
on *plebs* the note ad 20.6.6 *ad quam.*

in laevo proelio Not "on our left wing" (Rolfe, Hamilton), "al fian-
co sinistro" (Selem), for which Amm. uses the expression *laevum,*
c.q. *sinistrum cornu* (16.12.21, 16.12.24, 16.12.37, 24.1.2, 25.3.4,
31.7.12, 31.12.12, 31.13.2), but rather 'in this inauspicious battle',
the adjective being explained by the death of the three eminent
officers mentioned immediately after this phrase. Elsewhere Amm.
uses *laevus* for a divine power leading man to perdition: 14.11.12 *his
illecebris ad meliorum exspectationem erectus egressusque Antiochia numine
laevo ductante,* 31.4.9 *quasi laevo quodam numine deligente.*

Iulianus et Macrobius et Maximus Zos. 3.30.4 Ἀπέθανον δὲ καὶ Ῥωμαίων
τρεῖς λοχαγοὶ γενναίως ἀγωνισάμενοι, Ἰουλιανὸς καὶ Μαξιμιανὸς καὶ
Μακρόβιος. These men are otherwise unknown. *PLRE* I, Iulianus 13,
Macrobius 2, Maximus 18. Woods, 1995, 52–3 argues that the author
of BHL 1427 (see for this passio the note ad 25.5.8) has confused
the emperor Julian's maternal uncle Iulianus (*PLRE* I, Iulianus 12)
with the Iulianus of the present text, and that the latter was a *comes*
of the Ioviani and Herculiani. Both suggestions are unsound and
should be rejected.

legionum tribuni, quae tunc primas exercitus obtinebant This is the only
instance of *primae* (sc. partes) in the sense of 'the chief position'
in Amm. As TLL s.v. *prior* X 2.1355.72 sqq. shows, the expression is
normally used of persons. It is a favourite with Cicero. A well known
example is *de Orat.* 3.213 *huic* (actioni) *primas dedisse Demosthenes dicitur, cum rogaretur quid in dicendo esset primum, huic secundas huic tertias.*
Other authors use the expression sparingly, e.g. Tac. *Ann.* 14.21.4
eloquentiae primas nemo tulit, sed victorem esse Caesarem pronuntiatum.
The present sentence would seem to imply that there was a hierarchy of legions, but it is not clear from other sources which legions
held the highest rank in the army. The only legions to which Amm.
refers by name in the context of the Persian campaign are the Ioviani
and the Herculiani. For the status of the Iovii and the Victores, also
mentioned by Amm., see the note ad *legiones Ioviorum* above. For
tribunes see the notes ad 23.3.9 and 24.3.1 *paucissimos.* The word is

CHAPTER 6.4   203

a generic term for military officers who commanded the soldiers in battle. Hierarchy among tribunes depended on the importance of the troops they commanded.

ut rerum angustiae permiserunt On restrictive *ut* see the note ad **6.4** 21.10.5 *His ut.* Amm. uses *angustiae* both literally, as in 15.5.29 *angustias Alpium perrumpere Cottiarum* and figuratively, as here and 25.3.17 *cum in umbram et angustias amendarer*, q.v. *Rerum angustiae* is a good example of the gen. inversus.

prope confinia noctis Cf. 25.1.11 *prope lucis confinia immensa Persarum apparuit multitudo* with the note. The word *confinium* is strikingly explained in Ov. *Met.* 4.399–401 *iamque dies exactus erat tempusque subibat, / quod tu nec tenebras nec posses dicere lucem, / sed cum luce tamen dubiae confinia noctis.*

castellum Sumere nomine Sumere, called Σοῦμα by Zos. 3.30.2, is identified with modern Samarra; see the note ad 25.3.2 *invasa subito*; Paschoud n. 88; Talbert, 2000, Map 91, E3; see also the note ad 25.2.1. It is situated on the right bank of the Tigris some 150 km from Ctesiphon, and several km north of the site where the battle had taken place in which Julian was mortally wounded. See also Northedge et al., 1990.

citis passibus This phrase is found only in Amm., who uses it no fewer than eight times. The singular occurs in Ov. *Fast.* 2.741 *inde cito passu petitur Lucretia* and twice in Silius (8.126 and 17.530).

iacens Anatolii corpus est agnitum Two actions are implied by *est agnitum*: a body was found and recognized as that of Anatolius. *Inventum* (BG) looks suspiciously like a simplification. For *iacens* 'lying on the ground' cf. e.g. 15.4.12 *multique cum equis interfecti iacentes etiamtum eorum dorsis videbantur innexi.* Zos. 3.30.4 relates that while the Romans were searching for bodies after the battle with the Persians they also found that of Anatolius, which they gave as honourable a burial as possible in the circumstances: διερευνώμενοι δὲ τοὺς κειμένους, καὶ ἐν τούτοις εὑρόντες τὸ Ἀνατολίου σῶμα, ταφῆς ἠξίωσαν ἧς ὁ καιρὸς ἐδίδου, πολεμίων πανταχόθεν ἐπικειμένων. In 25.3.14 Amm. had related that Anatolius had been killed on the same day that Julian received his fatal wound. In this battle Anatolius and other Roman soldiers, provoked by an attack of a Persian contingent, may have pursued the Persians, or were put to flight by them (Zos. 3.29.4) in

204   COMMENTARY

the direction of Sumere, in the neighbourhood of which Anatolius
found his death; see the relevant notes ad loc. For Anatolius see
further the note ad 20.9.8 *libellis antea respondentem.*

quod tumultuaria opera terrae mandatum est The actions of this day
are characterized by haste and improvisation. The election of Jovian
was rushed through (*his caeco quodam iudicio fortunae peractis*, 25.5.8).
The burial of Iulianus, Macrobius and Maximus was a hurried affair
(*ut rerum angustiae permiserunt*). The same applies to the burial
of Anatolius. For *tumultuarius* cf. 17.1.11 *munimentum…tumultuario
studio reparatum est* and 24.2.18 *His raptim ac tumultuarie agitatis.*

milites…quos in munimentum †vaccatum confugisse rettulimus The author refers back to 25.3.14, q.v.: *palatini quidam militesque per multa
discrimina occupato castelli vicini praesidio post diem denique tertium iungi
exercitui potuerunt.* As was remarked ad loc., there is in itself no
reason to change the adjective *vicini*, which is perfectly natural in the
context. Kellerbauer, however, conjectured *vacui* in order to bring
that passage into line with the present one, where he proposes to
read *vacuum* for V's *vaccatum.* In view of Amm.'s explicit reference,
Kellerbauer was certainly right in postulating a correspondence
between the two passages and it would be surprising if Amm. at this
point added the new information that the fort was undefended. For
that reason it is also highly unlikely that *Vaccatum* was the name of the
castellum, as Matthews 185 thinks. Petschenig's *vacuatum* is closer to
V's *vaccatum,* but the verb is not found in Amm., who does write 17.2.1
vacua praesidiis loca vastantes, 27.10.1 *Mogontiacum praesidiis vacuam
cum expeditis ad latrocinandum latenter irrepsit,* and 31.6.4 *suadensque,
ut populandas opimas regiones et uberes absque discrimine ullo vacuas
praesidiis etiamtum adorerentur.* In 25.3.14 Amm. had related that
Roman soldiers and some court officials – among whom undoubtedly
Anatolius – had succeeded in capturing a stronghold. According to
Zos. 3.29.4 the Persians where the ones who chased the Romans in
the direction of the fortress.

6.5 *Secuto deinde die* I.e. 29 June; see the note on chronology.

pro captu locorum reperta †est in valle castra ponuntur The sentence
would be perfectly understandable without the words *reperta est.*
Of the different attempts to remedy the text none is really convincing. Petschenig, 1891, 742 *reperta convalle* and Fontaine's *reperta
angusta valle* both deserve consideration. The prepositional phrase

CHAPTER 6.5   205

pro captu + gen. is found ten times in Amm., but rarely in other authors. Cf. Vell. 2.104.3 *pro captu mediocritatis adiutor fui*, Maur. 1286 *pro captu lectoris habent sua fata libelli*. See De Jonge's note ad 14.11.4. Its meaning is 'as well as...allowed'.

Presumably the Roman army had camped the night of 28–29 June at Sumere, left the following morning for another day's march, and pitched camp at the end of the day.

velut murali ambitu circumclausa For comparable descriptions cf. 24.5.2 *extentum spatium et rotundum loricae ambitu circumclausum* (the King's hunting-grounds) and 15.11.3 *post circumclausum ambitu insulari Parisiorum castellum* (l'Île de la Cité). The slopes surrounding the valley offer protection, as walls might do; cf. *e saltibus* in the next section. Veg. *mil.* 1.22.2 mentions that care should be taken lest mountains and high ground near the camp might become dangerous if taken by the enemy: *Cavendum etiam, ne mons sit vicinus aut altior locus, qui ab adversariis captus possit officere.*

praeter unum exitum eundemque patentem For *idem* "introducing a sb. or an adj. as a further attribute of the same subj." (OLD s.v. 8) there are no parallels in Amm., but cf. Cic. *Phil.* 10.16 *certissimi idemque acerrimi Caesaris actorum patroni*; Plin. *Nat.* 37.80 *minimum iidemque plurimum ab iis differunt opali*; TLL VII 2.191.68–192.20. Opposite this exit was probably the *porta praetoria*, for which see the note ad 25.6.7 *ausi denique.*

undique in modum mucronum praeacutis sudibus fixis On *sudes* see the note ad 24.5.12 *vallum tamen*. The phrase is modeled on Caes. *Gal.* 5.18.3 *ripa autem erat acutis sudibus praefixisque munita.* It seems best to take the abl. abs. *sudibus fixis* as indicating the attendant circumstances of pitching the camp, rather than as the means by which the camp was surrounded as if by a wall.

In case of serious enemy threat Veg. *mil.* 1.24.2–4 advises to fortify the camp with a proper fosse and a stockade of stakes made of very strong wood which the soldiers are accustomed to carry with them: *Sed ubi vis acrior imminet hostium, tunc legitima fossa ambitum convenit munire castrorum ita, ut duodecim pedes lata sit et alta sub linea, sicut appellant, pedes novem. Supra autem saepibus hinc inde factis, quae de fossa levata fuerit terra, congeritur et crescit in altum quattuor pedes. Sic fit, ut sit tredecim pedibus alta et duodecim lata; supra quam sudes de lignis fortissimis, quas milites portare consueverant, praefiguntur.* In 1.21.3 Vegetius observes that the knowledge of building camps with lines

206   COMMENTARY

of fosses and a stockade had disappeared, but according to Milner,
1996, 23 n. 3 this is rhetorical exaggeration. On marching camps,
see Southern and Dixon, 1996, 132–3.

6.6 *hocque viso* This phrase is rarely found in classical authors; among
the few examples in the BTL are Ov. *Ars* 2.615 *In medio passimque coit
pecus: hoc quoque viso / avertit vultus nempe puella suos* and Suet. *Otho*
10.1 *hoc viso proclamasse eum aiebat, non amplius se in periculum talis
tamque bene meritos coniecturum.* Amm. uses it also in 25.1.2, 26.9.8
and 31.7.10. *Quo viso* occurs more frequently. Among the eighteen
instances in the BTL six are from Amm.

e saltibus nos hostes diversitate telorum et verbis turpibus incessebant For the
gen. inversus with *diversitas* cf. e.g. 30.9.5 *inter religionum diversitates
medius stetit* and see the note ad 22.4.5 *ambitiosa ornatarum*. Normally
verba turpia would refer to taunts of a sexual nature, as in Cic. *de
Orat.* 2.242 *praestet idem* (orator) *ingenuitatem et ruborem suum verborum
turpitudine et rerum obscenitate vitanda* ("the orator must give proof
of his own good manners and modesty by avoiding dishonourable
words and obscene subjects", tr. May-Wisse) and Gel. 1.5.1 *turpibus
indignisque in eum verbis non temperatum, quin parum vir et ore quoque
polluto diceretur* ("they did not refrain from applying to him foul and
shameful epithets, alleging that he was no man and was even guilty
of unnatural vice", tr. Rolfe) As the following *ut*-clause shows, this
is not the case here. With the sentence as a whole compare 17.11.1
virtutes eius (Iuliani) *obruere verbis impudentibus conabantur ut segnem
incessentes et timidum et umbratilem.*

ut perfidos et lectissimi principis peremptores This is a startling detail.
Amm. shows awareness of the rumour that Julian had been killed
by one of his own men, but he puts this embarassing version in the
mouth of the Persian enemies instead of presenting it in the report
of Julian's death, where he limits himself to saying that the emperor
was wounded *incertum unde* (that is, if we accept Haupt's addition
of *unde!*). See for the various traditions as to who might have killed
Julian, the note ad loc. Sabbah 413 argues persuasively that "le sens
de la solidarité militaire et de l'honneur romain" have induced the
historian to arrange the information in this way. One might add
that Amm. insists upon the unreliability of the rumour. The Persians
heard it from the defectors (in all probability the standard bearer
of the Ioviani who fled to the Persians after Jovian had become
emperor, 25.5.8), who were naturally inclined to compromise their

CHAPTER 6.6   207

former comrades-in-arms; therefore he hastens to call the rumour *incertus*. Amm.'s words imply that the Persians, too, were uncertain as to who killed Julian.

The words *lectissimi principis* also merit attention. Is this a case of embedded focalisation, in other words, are these the words the Persians actually used, as the use of *ut* seems to imply, or does Amm. attribute his own opinion to the enemy? Amm. certainly has a tendency to do so. A good example is to be found in the scene on the battlefield just before Julian is fatally wounded as described in 25.3.6. His *candidati* shout that Julian must avoid the mass of fugitives *tamquam ruinam male compositi culminis* "as he would the collapse of a badly built roof" (Hamilton). As it is inconceivable that the guards in their warning cry would make such an elaborate comparison, we must suppose that Amm. puts these words into their mouths to refer to the omen mentioned in 23.2.8 (see the note ad 25.3.6). Still, in the present passage it is quite conceivable that the Persians used these words sarcastically, if only to remind the Romans of their loss, and by implication to denigrate Julian's successor, who had been qualified by the standard bearer as *inertem quendam et mollem* (25.5.8).

audierant enim ipsi quoque referentibus transfugis rumore iactato incerto Iulianum telo cecidisse Romano Too much information is crammed into this one sentence, with the result that it has become less than transparent. *Ipsi quoque* contrasts the Persians with the Romans, which is a highly casual way of saying that the latter too knew this rumour. The varia lectio *ipsis...referentibus* does not make sense, for who else could have passed this information to the enemy? Strictly speaking the AcI *Iulianum...cecidisse* depends on *audierant*, which would present the information as an established fact, but Amm. only wants to convey to his readers, that a rumour of this nature existed.

The syntactical status of *rumore iactato incerto* is not easy to establish. At first sight one takes it as an abl. abs. The content of the rumour would then be expressed by the AcI, depending apo koinou on *audierant* and on *rumore iactato*: 'since, (or after) an unconfirmed rumour had been dispersed (to this effect).' Alternatively, *rumore* could be taken as an instrumental abl. with *audierant*. That, however, would turn both *iactato* and *incerto* into attributes, unconnected at that: 'by an unconfirmed rumour that was spread.' This seems very unattractive and the word order *iactato incerto* seems to rule it out.

Rumores in Amm. are not false by definition. He distinguishes true rumours: 18.4.7 *novi motus rumoribus densis audiuntur et certis,*

208   COMMENTARY

29.5.19 *Quae cum rumores veri distulissent et crebri,* false ones, as in
26.6.3 *falsoque rumore disperso* and unconfirmed rumours, as in the
present passage and in 15.5.4 *ut iactavere rumores incerti,* 16.11.13 *illud
tamen rumore tenus ubique iactabatur,* 18.4.2 *Et cum haec primo rumores,
dein nuntii certi perferrent.*

6.7   *ausi denique inter haec equitum cunei porta perrupta praetoria prope ipsum
tabernaculum principis advenire* Although there are many instances of
audere followed by *venire,* the combination with *advenire* is unique
in the BTL, which is not surprising, since the action of *advenire* is
uncontrolled by the Agens. In the present sentence the Persians
show their daring by forcing their way through the main gate of the
camp, so that the sentence is equivalent to *ausi perrumpere portam
praetoriam…advenerunt.* Blomgren 79, who gives a list of parallels, in
which the present sentence is missing, remarks: "Ammianus haud ita
raro necessariam orationis partem, quam per verbum finitum expres-
sam malueris, participio sive coniuncto sive absoluto comprehendit."
Denique marks this attack as the ultimate proof of their increased
confidence, which was already manifest in their other actions (*inter
haec*).

   Cuneus has the general meaning of a troop of soldiers. Amm.
uses the word both for Roman and, as here, enemy cavalry (16.11.5,
17.2.1, 24.5.5, 27.1.1 (*cuneatim*), 28.5.6, 31.16.5); for contingents of
soldiers (23.5.8, 25.1.17, 27.2.4, 9.6, 29.6.16, 31.11.4); for military
formations (17.12.9, 18.8.9, 19.13.1, 20.11.6; in the last text Seyfarth's *contis consertis* is, as is argued in the note ad loc., to be read as
cuneis confertis). In 15.7.4 Amm. uses the word to designate a group of
rioters (*tumultuantium…cuneorum*). See the notes ad 20.11.6, 23.5.8
and 24.2.14 (*cuneatim*). Cf. Brok 75–6 and Nicasie, 1998, 110–2.

   The *porta praetoria* was the main gate of a Roman military camp.
According to Veg. *mil.* 1.23.2, it should either face east or in the
direction which faces the enemy; when the army is on the march,
the gate should face the direction in which the army proceeds:
*Porta autem, quae appellatur praetoria, aut orientem spectare debet aut
illum locum, qui ad hostes respicit aut, si iter agitur, illam partem debet
adtendere, ad quam est profecturus exercitus.* The gate gave access to
the *praetorium,* the tent of the commanding general – in this case the
Roman emperor himself –, by way of the *cardo maximus.* J. *BJ* 3.79–84
gives a description of a Roman army camp, which was constructed
according to a set pattern and laid out like a city bisected by two
streets leading to four gates. In the centre of the camp were the
general's quarters.

CHAPTER 6.8 209

The Persian threat must have been immense, or the Roman weakness great, for the Persian cavalry to be able to enter the fortified Roman camp. For *tabernaculum* see the note ad 24.1.11 *ita confuderat*.

Egressi exinde proxima nocte Charcham occupavimus locum I.e. the night **6.8** of 30 June; see the note on chronology. *Proxima nocte* is best taken with *occupavimus*. Herzfeld's suggestion (1948, 67), that the army marched during the night because of the heat during the daytime is rightly doubted by Brok 219–20 who has difficulty believing that the army marched through enemy territory in the dark of night. Amm. switches here to the first person plural and he continues in this way until section 11 of this chapter. Herzfeld, 1948, 67 identifies Charcha with Karkh Fairuz, also called Karkh Samarra, some 11 km north of Samarra. Charra on *Tab. Peut.* X 5 is probably the same place, see Dillemann, 1962, 319–21 and Talbert, 2000, Map 91, E3. Neither the stop at Charcha nor that at Dura (25.6.9) is mentioned by Zosimus. Amm. mentions another Charcha in 18.10.1, q.v.

ideo tuti, quod This must refer to the march rather than the halting-place itself, since the irrigation channel mentioned in this section would not have offered enough space for a camp. Moreover, Amm. uses the term *agmina*, 'troops on the march.'

riparum aggeribus humana manu instructis, ne Saraceni deinceps Assyriam persultarent Brok suggests that the Roman army marched through an old irrigation canal which ran parallel to the Tigris; the dykes along this canal offered the Romans protection from Persian attacks. The combination *agger ripae* has an epic ring, cf. e.g. Verg. *A.* 7.106 *gramineo ripae religavit ab aggere classem*, Stat. *Theb.* 6.274 *laevus harundineae recubans super aggere ripae.* With regard to the motive for building these mounds or dykes Amm. is probably mistaken. It is more likely that they were part of the irrigation system which once was used in the region of Charcha. See Brok 220 and Fontaine n. 625, both referring to Herzfeld, 1948. For the Saracens see the notes ad 22.15.2 *Scenitas*, 23.3.8 *Saracenarum*, 25.1.3 *hinc recedentibus*. Assyria is Amm.'s designation for either the Persian province of Assyria, east of the river Tigris (23.6.14, 15, 23), or the Persian territory between Euphrates and Tigris (24.1.1). Here the former is meant. See also the note ad 23.2.7 *Assyrios. Persultare* is regularly used of barbarians overrunning the Roman provinces; see the note ad 20.5.4 *cladis immensitas.*

210   COMMENTARY

6.9 *cumque hinc kalendis Iuliis stadiis triginta confectis civitatem nomine Duram adventaremus* Amm. uses both Greek and Roman designations for distances; see the note ad 24.2.3. A stade is about 200 m., so thirty stades is some 6 km; a short distance for a day's march. The use of *adventare* with an acc. of direction is also found in classical authors; TLL I 836.48–58. In Amm. it is the rule; see the note ad 21.12.22.

The city is Dura on the Tigris, not to be confused with Dura (Europos) on the Euphrates mentioned by Amm. in 23.5.8 (q.v.) and 24.1.5 (q.v.). Although it is impossible to establish the precise location of Dura (on the Tigris) due to insufficient data, as Oppenheimer, 1983, 118–9 rightly observes, attempts have been made to identify it with Dur Arabya and Imam Dur; Dillemann, 1962, 303, n. 1; Paschoud n. 89; Fontaine n. 626. Dura is even indicated in Talbert, 2000, Map 91, E3, but at a much greater distance from Charcha than the 6 km (30 stades) Amm. mentions.

fatigatis iumentis vectores eorum novissimi pedibus incedentes For *iumentum* 'horse' see the note ad 16.12.22 *latere forato*. Amm. uses the word *vector* four times. In 16.12.51 and 17.1.7 it refers to passengers and soldiers travelling in ships; in 17.12.2, as in this passage, it designates horsemen.

a Saracena multitudine circumsaepti For Saracens see the note ad 25.6.8 and the references there. On *circumsaeptus* see the note ad 20.11.6 *fixis tentoriis*.

ni expeditiores turmae nostrorum opem laborantibus attulissent On this use of "*ni* de rupture" (Chausserie-Laprée, 1969, 636–7) see the note ad 20.11.18 *et Persae*. Amm.'s choice of moods in the irrealis is discussed by Hassenstein 39 and De Jonge ad 14.3.2. For *turma* see the note ad 25.1.3 *ad ultimum*. The adj. *expeditiores* contrasts these *turmae* with the men walking beside their tired horses.

6.10 *hos autem Saracenos ideo patiebamur infestos* The emphasis is on the adj.: 'we suffered from the hostility of these Saracenes.' Supposedly they had earlier fought on the Roman side (see 23.3.8, q.v.).

salaria muneraque plurima a Iuliano ad similitudinem praeteriti temporis accipere vetiti This is the only occurrence of *salaria* in Amm. For a comparable use of *vetare* cf. HA *AS* 26.3 *senatores, si fenerarentur, usuras accipere primo vetuit.* The Saracenes seem to have become dissatisfied

CHAPTER 6.11   211

because by order of Julian they had received little or no pay and remuneration for their military assistance, in contrast to the time of Constantius.

solum audierant Petschenig, 1891, 742 compared phrases like 15.5.25 *id aptius videbatur, ut,* 16.7.9 *praeter id solum, quod,* and 16.12.56 *id observatum est, ut* and therefore suggested to add cataphoric ⟨*id*⟩ before *solum*; rightly, it seems. See for cataphoric or preparatory *id* the note ad 22.3.4 *cum id.*

imperatorem bellicosum et vigilantem ferrum habere, non aurum For *bellicosus* as a positive quality see the note ad 20.1.2 *bellicosum sane.* Fontaine n. 627 considers Amm.'s words an authentic representation of what Julian had said. To sustain his argument Fontaine refers to 24.3.4, q.v., where Julian criticizes his predecessors for buying peace from barbarians with gold (*auro quietem a barbaris redemptare*). The Saracens, however, were paid for military assistance and not for keeping the peace. Amm. may have been inspired by V. Max. 6.4. ext.1, who reports that the inhabitants of the Lusitanian city of Cinginnia refused to buy their liberty from D. Brutus for money: *propemodum uno ore legatis Bruti respondit* (Cinginnia) *ferrum sibi a maioribus, quo urbem tuerentur, non aurum, quo libertatem ab imperatore avaro emerent, relictum.*

in hoc loco Persarum obstinatione tritum est quadriduum 2–5 July; see the **6.11** note on chronology and Paschoud n. 89. If *in hoc loco* is interpreted strictly as referring to Dura, this would mean that the Roman army tried several times to march on, but each time was forced to return to its camp. It is hard to imagine that Amm. would have left such a return unmentioned. Alternatively, the words may be taken to refer more loosely to the region around Dura, as Paschoud, following Dillemann, does. In that case *tritum est quadriduum* means that the Romans, despite their efforts, made little progress. Zosimus, quoted below ad *nam progredientes,* only tells us that after Sumere the Roman army marched on for four days while being harassed by the enemy, who pursued them, but fled whenever the Romans turned on them. Therefore, as soon as they had the opportunity, the Romans decided to cross the Tigris. For the next bit of geographical information we have to wait until 25.7.8, q.v., where we are told that after these four days, the army was a hundred miles away from Corduene: *Corduenae, uberis regionis et nostrae, ex eo loco, in quo haec agebantur, centesimo lapide disparatae.*

212   COMMENTARY

nam progredientes nos sequebantur crebris lacessitionibus retrahentes; cum staremus ut pugnaturi, gradum sensim referentes moris diuturnis excruciabant In 19.3.1 we find Ursicinus urging his superior Sabinianus to harass the Persians, who are laying siege to Amida, in the same way: (ut) *lacessitionibus crebris occuparent obsidioni fortiter adhaerentes.* For *stare* in the pregnant sense 'standing firm (in battle)' see OLD s.v. 3. The expression *gradum/pedem sensim referre* is also found in Liv. 8.8.11, 22.29.5 and 30.18.12 *sed donec stetit ante signa Mago, gradum sensim referentes ordines et tenorem pugnae servabant.* The angry frustration of the Romans at these delaying tactics of the Persians is powerfully expressed by the verb *excruciare*, which is normally used of torture: 15.3.11 *excruciatique tormentis,* 29.1.44 *omnique laniena* (butchery) *excruciato.*

These are the usual and efficient tactics of the Persians; they attacked the marching Roman army on the march with small contingents, and avoided, where possible, open battle. We find a very similar description of the tactics of the Persians along with the same indication of time (four days) in Zosimus, who continues, after mentioning the fortress Sumere, with the following passage: ἡμέρας δὲ τέσσαρας προελθόντες καὶ πανταχόθεν ὑπὸ τῶν πολεμίων ἐνοχλούμενοι, διωκόντων μὲν ἐπὰν ὁδεύοντας ἴδοιεν, φευγόντων δὲ ὁπότε αὐτοῖς ἀντεπίοιεν Ῥωμαῖοι, γενομένης τινὸς εὐρυχωρίας ('opportunity') αὐτοῖς τὸν Τίγριν περαιωθῆναι διέγνωσαν (3.30.4). Since it is hardly conceivable that the passages in Zosimus and Ammianus do not refer to the same series of events, we may surmise that Zosimus' εὐρυχωρία presented itself in the place mentioned in 25.7.8. His report suggests that the decision to cross the Tigris there was made by Jovian and his generals. This is in glaring contrast with Amm., who reports that the emperor and generals were reluctant to cross the Tigris, but were forced to do so by the soldiers.

ut solent extrema metuentibus etiam ficta placere The phrase *extrema metuere* is less usual than one would expect. In fact the BTL has only three examples: Suet. *Cal.* 54.2 *multaque et extrema metuentis,* *Vesp.* 4.4 *extrema metuenti* and Dict. 2.29 *perterritum senem atque extrema metuentem.* With *timere* there is only one instance: Sil. 8.353 *quippe extrema simul gentique urbique timebant.*

fama circumlata fines haud procul limitum esse nostrorum Elsewhere in Amm. *fama* is the subject of verbs like *vulgare* (14.2.20), *diffundere* (14.10.14), *augere* (15.3.6), *loqui* (28.1.30). With the present phrase cf. 31.6.1 *Hoc gestorum textu circumlato. Fines limitum* is a fine example

CHAPTER 6.12

of the gen. identitatis; see the note ad 22.12.7 *caerimoniarum ritus*. There is a note on *limes* ad 23.3.4 *vicino limite*; (add to the literature cited there Zuckerman, 1998), where it is said that *limes* can indicate the borderline as well as the border region. Probably the latter is meant here.

exercitus vociferans immodeste dari sibi copiam transeundi Tigridis flagitabat The soldiers had become desperate and mutinous, and wanted to reach Roman territory as soon as possible by crossing the Tigris. As appears from the next sections, Jovian and his generals were opposed to this but had to make some concessions to the wish of their soldiers. Crump, 1975, 79 has the interesting observation that the reason why Amm.'s description of the crossing of the Tigris and the accompanying incidents is so elaborate is that it clearly demonstrates the demoralization of the once formidable invading army. The disintegration of the Roman army must have made a great impression on Amm. It is impossible to establish where exactly the boundary line between Roman and Persian territory was, since the Romans had a completey different concept of territory from the modern one. The Roman empire was not thought of as a territorial entity and territorial limits of the empire are rarely mentioned in ancient sources, and then only in a vague manner; see Isaac, 1998[2], 394 ff.

The soldiers overstep the mark interfering with the decision making at this crucial point. Amm.'s indignation is conveyed by *immodeste*, for which cf. 30.3.5, where it is used of barbarians who fail to show due respect for the Roman emperor: *immodestis gestibus murmureque barbarico tandem sedato* and Suet. *Aug.* 24.2 *immodeste missionem postulantes…exauctorauit*. For *vociferari* cf. the similar situation in 24.8.2: *super rerum summa consultabatur…cum reverti debere per loca, quae venimus, plebs vociferaretur imprudens, resistebat intentius princeps*. For *flagitare* with AcI cf. 17.13.1 *ocius signa transferri utilitas publica flagitabat* and see TLL VI 845.3–15.

quibus oppositus cum rectoribus imperator The participle is used reflexively, as in 25.8.9 *ut Lucillianum…properare Mediolanum urgerent…, si casus novi quidam exsurgerent, opponendum* ('to offer resistance') and 31.13.6 *magno animorum robore oppositi incumbentibus*. For *rector* see the notes ad 20.1.1, 20.5.7 and 20.11.20 *refectus…excitus*.

6.12

tumentemque iam canis exortu sideris amnem I.e. the constellation of stars of which the Canicula, also known as Sirius or Dog Star, was

214   COMMENTARY

the brightest; Cic. *N.D.* 2.114; Vitr. 9.5.2; Verg. *G.* 1.218, 2.353; Hor. *S.* 1.7.25; *Ep.* 1.10.16; Ov. *Fast.* 4.904; Plin. *Nat.* 18.285. The rise of the Dog Star introduced the summer heat in the month of July. The melting of snow and ice on the mountains in Armenia and the Zagros mountains caused the Tigris to flood, which resulted in strong currents. It is to be noted that the Tigris reaches its maximum height at the end of April and the beginning of May, but is liable to sudden flooding later in the year; see the note ad 24.6.7 *scutis...proni.*

This is the only instance of *tumere* in its literal sense in Amm. Everywhere else the verb is used of human arrogance. The phrase has a poetic ring, cf. e.g. Verg. *A.* 8.86–7 *Thybris ea fluvium, quam longa est, nocte tumentem / leniit* and Luc. 6.272 *sic pleno Padus ore tumens super aggere tutas / excurrit ripas.*

ne se periculosis committerent gurgitibus, exorabat A similar phrase is found in 16.12.55 *ne hostem avidius sequens nostrorum quisquam se gurgitibus committeret verticosis,* 17.13.15 *amnis vicini se commisere gurgitibus.* The fact that the emperor is begging his soldiers demonstrates how badly discipline has been affected.

hostiles manus hinc inde margines superfusi fluminis occupasse For the asyndeton *hinc inde* see the note ad 20.6.5. Here it may mean 'on both sides', *margines* referring to the two banks of the Tigris. This is how all translators interpret it. Alternatively, *hinc inde* may mean 'here and there', 'in many places'. In that case the plural *margines* would refer to different points on the opposite bank. For the latter meaning cf. e.g. 17.3.5, where Julian is pleading for the long-suffering provincials of Gaul: *rescripsit gratandum esse, si provincialis hinc inde vastatus saltem sollemnia praebeat* and 31.7.13 (quisque) *ritu grandinis undique volitantibus telis oppetebat et gladiis et sequebantur equites hinc inde fugientium occipitia...praecidentes.* For *margines* in the sense of 'different points on the bank' cf. 16.12.56 *ut marginibus insistentes confoderent telorum varietate Germanos,* 19.11.4 *exercitu diffuso per Histri fluminis margines barbaros observabat* and 24.6.5 *signum sibi datum nostros, quod margines iam tenerent, ut mandatum est, erexisse proclamans.* In view of section 14, where we are told that the advance party kills Persian guards after crossing the river, the latter interpretation is more likely to be correct.

6.13   *sed cum haec saepe congeminando refragaretur in cassum* For *refragari* see the note ad 16.12.5 *nullo refragante* and for the archaism *in cassum* Fesser 43.

CHAPTER 6.14   215

milesque conclamans magno contentionis fragore minaretur extrema See
the note ad 20.4.17 *maximoque contentionis fragore*, where a very similar
situation of near mutiny is described. There, as here, the soldiers
actually threaten to kill the emperor.

*id impetratur aegerrime, ut mixti cum arctois armatis Galli amnem primi
omnium penetrarent* V's text *id imperator aegerrimae ut mixti cum areto
isarmaris* has been emended by different scholars. Kellerbauer's
impetratur is closer to the ms reading than Valesius' *impetratum*. The
historic present, however, is used sparingly by Amm. and reserved for
salient points in the narrative, as is shown in Kroon & Rose, 1996,
78 and 87. For that reason Valesius' *impetratum* seems marginally
better. Although this is not stated explicitly, we must assume that the
soldiers wring the concession from the emperor, and not vice versa,
since the second *ut*-clause states the purpose he wanted to achieve
by his decision. The word *isarmaris* has been emended to *Sarmatis*,
Germanis and *armatis*. The first option is excluded, pace Češka, by a
comparison with 25.8.1 where we read that the soldiers who crossed
the Tigris were *rapti a Saracenis vel Persis, quos, ut diximus paulo ante,
exturbavere Germani*. Since Amm. nowhere has two names of peoples in
juxtaposition, *armatis* ('soldiers') is better than *Germanis*. For *armatus*
and *penetrare* see the notes ad 20.4.22 and 21.13.2 respectively.
The Germans were considered experienced swimmers as appears
from 16.12.57 and other sources mentioned in the note ad 24.6.7
scutis...proni. To these sources may be added Tac. *Hist.* 2.35.1, 4.66.2
and 5.14.2, where the ability of Germans to swim across wide rivers
is likewise mentioned.

ut his magnitudine fluentorum abreptis residuorum pertinacia frangeretur
See the note ad 22.8.30 *undarum magnitudo* and for *residui* 'those left
behind' the note ad 25.5.2 *Arintheus et Victor*.

aut, si id perfecissent innocui, transitus fidentior temptaretur On active
and passive *innocuus* see the note ad 20.7.2 *abscessit innoxius*. On
fidenter indicating justified confidence see the note ad 20.8.19.
The predicative use of *fidentior* is surprising, for although adjectives
denoting emotions tend to favour predicative use (Szantyr 172),
Amm. uses *fidentius* no fewer than fourteen times.

electique sunt ad id negotium habiles Their number is given in 25.7.3:   **6.14**
quingenti viri transgressi tumidum flumen. According to Zos. 3.30.5 the
whole Roman army crossed the river, whereas Amm. 25.8.2–3 reports

216   COMMENTARY

that the main force went across only after the peace-treaty with the
Persians had been concluded. See the note ad 21.6.8 *damna negotiis*
for *negotium* as the equivalent of *res.*

*qui maxima prae ceteris flumina transmeare in regionibus genuinis...sunt
instituti* The prepositional phrase *prae ceteris* is found almost exclusively in Gellius, Apuleius, the HA and Amm. (28.1.19 *ea tempestate
prae ceteris notus*, 28.2.12 *prae ceteris hostibus Saxones timentur ut repen-
tini*). TLL X 2.375.57–69 gives a few parallels for the pleonastic
combination with a superlative, e.g. August. *C.D.* 21.8 *stella prae ceteris
magnitudine ac splendore notissima.* For *genuinus* 'native' see the note
ad 22.8.26 *Hypanis fluvius.* The regions Amm. refers to are northern
Gaul and Germany with their great rivers like the Rhine, the Meuse
and the Moselle.

cum latendi copiam nocturna qúïes dáret The phrase is repeated in
29.5.34 *quoniam latendi copiam nocturna quies dedit.*

tamquam e transenna simul emissi "They shot off in a body like men at
the start of a race" (Hamilton). For the meaning of *transenna* see the
note ad 20.11.22 *ictus varii.* In this passage it means the rope that
holds runners back before the start of a race.

Persarumque conculcatis pluribus et truncatis These are violent terms,
betraying the simultaneous exasperation and relief on the part of the
soldiers, who have been toyed with by the Persians for such a long
time. For *conculcare* cf. the lynching scene in 14.7.6 *calcibus incessens
et pugnis conculcans seminecem laniatu miserando discerpsit.*

quos loca servare dispositos securitas placido vinxerat somno The metaphor is surprisingly rare. Amm. probably borrowed it from Liv. 5.44.7
nisi vinctos somno velut pecudes trucidandos tradidero. Ennius *Ann.* 2 Sk.
has *somno leni placidoque revinctus.* Note that in both cases *somnus* is the
Agens, whereas in the phrase under discussion *somno* is an ablative
of instrument.

efficacis audaciae signum elatis manibus contortisque sagulis ostendebant
In 14.8.5 the name of Nicator Seleucus is explained as follows:
efficaciae impetrabilis rex, ut indicat cognomentum. The emphasis is on
the adjective *efficacis*: the soldiers triumphantly signal the success of
their derring-do. Cf. 18.6.13 *porrecto extentius brachio et summitatibus
sagi contortis elatius adesse hostes signo solito demonstrabam*, q.v. See also

CHAPTER 6.15   217

the note ad 25.3.6 *diffluxisse trepidos.* Vegetius, who has a chapter on military signs, distinguishes three types of signals: voiced, semi-voiced signs, and mute. There is a variety of mute signs, i.a. those made by hands and clothes: *praeterea manu aliquid vel flagello more barbarico vel certe mota, qua utitur, veste significat*; *mil.* 3.5.9. See Kubitschek, 1923, 2325 ff. *Sagulum* is the diminutive of *sagum,* the normal designation for a military cloak (Caes. *Civ.* 1.75.3, *Gal.* 5.42.3, Cic. *Fam.* 7.10.2, Liv. 10.30.10). *Sagulum* also occurs in 14.4.3 (about Saracens) and *sagum* in 18.6.13, 19.5.5 (about Persians) and 29.5.48. Amm. uses *contorquere* in two meanings, 'to roll up', 'twist', as here and in his scathing description of the prancing Maximinus in 28.1.13 *ideoque pedes huc et illuc exsultando contorquens saltare, non incedere videbatur.* More frequently the meaning is 'to hurl', as in 17.7.3 *velut numine summo fatales contorquente manubias* and 20.7.4 *telum nemo contorsit.*

ardens ad transitum miles Prepositional phrases with *ad* are extremely rare after *ardere/ardescere.* To the few examples in TLL II 486.46– 9 may be added Sen. *Contr.* 7, pr. 4 *memini admiratione Hermagorae stupentem ad imitationem eius ardescere.* Other instances in Amm. are 26.5.12 *ardens ad redeundum eius impetus* and 27.3.12 *Damasus et Ursinus supra humanum modum ad rapiendam episcopi sedem ardentes.*

6.15

utribus e caesorum animalium coriis coagmentare pontes architecti promit- tébant The engineers (for *architectu*s see the note ad 24.4.28 *nostrae partis*) promise to build platforms (*pontes*), kept afloat on inflated leather bags, and joined together to form a pontoon bridge. For this meaning of *pons* cf. Plin. *Nat.* 6.176 (Arabes) *bubulos utres binos inster- nentes ponte piraticam exercent.* A similar technique is used in 24.3.11, q.v. The preposition *e*, which is lacking in V, has been added by Gelenius, rightly it seems. Fontaine defends the reading of V as an instance of the abl. materiae without a preposition, but here we do not have the singular *corio* 'of leather', but the plural *coriis* 'skins'. Petschenig, 1891, 730 thought the attributive adjunct as a whole "von unerträglicher Plattheit", but Sallustius did not think it otiose to write *ex coriis utres uti fierent, curabat* (*Jug.* 91.1). The description in Zos. 3.30.5 is very similar: Ἀσκοὺς τοίνυν ἀλλήλοις συνδήσαντες καὶ ζεύγματα τρόπον τινὰ διὰ τούτων κατασκευάσαντες ἐποχούμενοί τε τούτοις διέβησαν. For the present infinitive after *promittere* see the note ad 22.7.5 *promittentes latebras* and for the cursus velox Harmon 212 n. 2.

CHAPTER 7

Introduction

In chapter six Ammianus had concentrated on the difficulties of the situation in which the new emperor and the Roman army found themselves. The scorched earth policy of the Persians left them without provisions. Although the army had the upper hand in regular battles, it was constantly harassed by the Persian forces, whose delaying tactics slowed down its march northwards along the Tigris. Morale was low and Jovian had problems establishing his authority.

Chapter seven comes as a surprise to the reader, who is led to expect that Jovian's opponent, king Sapor, will be full of confidence because of the plight of the Romans. But on the contrary, in §1–3 the Persian king is portrayed as worried by the superior force of the Roman army and the losses inflicted on his own people. In particular the successful crossing of the Tigris by 500 Roman soldiers had come as a shock to Sapor.

These considerations serve to explain why the Persians decide to start peace negotiations, even though the Roman engineers have failed to build a bridge across the Tigris, as they had promised to do, and the hunger is getting worse every day (§4). In §5 Ammianus ascribes this development to the protection which heaven granted to the Roman side and insists once again on the despondency of the Persians. But when the Persians actually propose peace terms, their despondency has suddenly disappeared. In his infinite clemency Sapor is willing, they say, to allow the Romans an unopposed withdrawal, if the emperor complies with his terms. Four long days of complicated negotiations follow (§7), during which the starving army has to wait passively. Ammianus complains about this waste of time. Jovian should have used these days to advance in the direction of Corduene, which would have improved his bargaining position (§8).

The precise demands of Sapor are stated in the next section (§9). He claims the restoration of all the losses the Sasanids had suffered in the treaty of 298/9: five *regiones Transtigritanae*, three border towns, Nisibis, Singara and Castra Maurorum, and fifteen forts. Ammianus is very outspoken in his comments on these terms: under no circumstances should Jovian have accepted them. The

220 COMMENTARY

emperor, however, does just that. According to Ammianus, the reason is that Jovian's courtiers had exploited his fear that Procopius might become a usurper to make him accept Sapor's demands without opposition or delay (§ 10–11). Apart from the shameful surrender of these important regions and border cities, the Romans also agree not to support their old ally, king Arsaces of Armenia, against future attacks from the Persians, which results in the capture of Arsaces and the annexation of a large part of Armenia (§ 12).

In the concluding sections (§ 13–14) Ammianus reports that highly placed Romans and Persians were exchanged as hostages to guarantee the peace, adding that the treaty was to be valid for thirty years and that it was confirmed by solemn oaths. It was decided to follow another route to Roman territory, because the terrain along the Tigris was heavy going.

Ammianus' account of the peace treaty between Sapor and Jovian is not entirely convincing. There is a discrepancy between the worrying situation, in which the Roman army finds itself, and the despondency ascribed to Sapor; this in turn is belied by the king's arrogance and the exacting demands he makes during the actual negotiations. Ammianus' presentation of the events seems to be dictated by his wish to blame Jovian for a treaty that, in his eyes, amounted to a disgraceful capitulation. By insisting on the superiority of the Roman army, Ammianus conveys the impression that the concessions Jovian made, among which the surrender of Nisibis was especially outrageous, were out of all proportion compared to the actual strength of the opposing armies. Apart from this error of judgment, Jovian, according to Ammianus, made the tactical mistake of getting bogged down in lengthy negotiations at a time when he should have used every hour to get closer to Roman territory. To make things worse, Ammianus states that Jovian's motives were dishonourable. Instead of giving priority to the interests of his subjects, his actions are said to be dictated by his fear for his own position and his haste to anticipate a possible usurpation by Procopius. There is no reason to believe that the author paints this bleak picture of the emperor's behaviour because of his personal animosity towards Jovian. Rather, by emphasising the inadequacy of Jovian as a leader during these critical days Ammianus ignores the fact that Jovian had taken over power in an almost desperate situation, for which his predecessor Julian was responsible.

7.1 *Quae dum vanis conatibus agitabantur* The wording may have been inspired by Liv. 7.7.8 *postquam equestris pugna effectu quam conatibus*

CHAPTER 7.1   221

vanior erat. The reading of V *agitabantur* has been corrected by Vm2 to *agitantur.* Petschenig, 1892, 681 doubted whether the correction was really by Vm2 and proposed to return to V's original reading on the grounds that *dum* + indic. impf. does occur in the *RG*, although Amm. prefers the classical construction of *dum* 'while' with present indicative. Petschenig mentioned 17.3.1 and 19.11.12 as parallels, to which may be added 28.1.13 *dum studebat* and 31.12.8 *dum necessaria parabantur ad decernendum.* Nevertheless, it seems decidedly better to accept the correction, since everywhere else Amm. uses *dum* with *agere / agitare* either in the present ind. or, in a small minority of cases, in the subjunctive impf., for which see the note ad 20.6.1. Moreover *conátibus agitántur* is a regular cursus velox. See further Pighi, 1935, 89–90 for phrases expressing contemporaneity.

As a rule opening phrases like this one summarize the content of a preceding chapter or passage. In this case, however, *vani conatus* anticipates the failure of the engineers' efforts to construct a pontoon bridge, mentioned in section four. This new setback makes the transition in the narrative from the Romans with their manifold problems to Sapor, who is portrayed as no longer exultant (25.5.9 *inopina prosperitate elatus*), but as deeply worried (25.7.2 *ob quae reputabat multa et formidanda*) even more striking.

rex Sapor et procul absens et, cum prope venisset Cf. 25.5.8 *Saporem iam propinquantem* with the note. Wagner ad loc. rightly links *procul* with *exploratores* and *propinquantem* with *perfugae.*

exploratorum perfugarumque veris vocibus Note the insistence on the veracity of the reports Sapor receives. Amm. is fully aware of the fact that the emphasis on the resilience of the Roman army will come as a surprise to the reader. The combination of *exploratores* and *perfugae* can also be found in 20.4.1 (q.v.) and 21.7.7. Cf. further 21.13.4 *speculatores vero et transfugae* with the note, and see in general now Ezov, 2000.

fortia facta nostrorum, foedas suorum strages The words have a solemn ring; cf. Verg. *A.* 1.641 *fortia facta patrum* and Sal. *Jug.* 85.4 *maiorum fortia facta.* Amm. may be referring to the outcome of the battle of Maranga in particular (25.1.19): *In hoc proelio Persarum maior, ut dictum est, apparuit strages, nostrorum admodum levis.* Cf. further 25.6.2, 6.7 and 6.14. For the wording cf. Liv. 22.51.5 *ad spolia legenda foedamque etiam hostibus spectandam stragem.*

222   COMMENTARY

elephantos, quod numquam se regnante meminerat, interfectos As has been
reported in 25.3.4–5 and 25.6.2–3. See for elephants also 25.1.14–5
(q.v.). The structure of the relative clause is similar to 23.1.1 *quod
post Diocletianum et Aristobulum nullus meminerat gestum.* See the note
ad 20.10.2 *nullum ad* on the effect of αὔξησις in phrases of this type.
This should suffice to reject G's *quot*, apart from the fact that Amm.
uses that word only twice, in 14.6.6 *per omnes tamen quot orae sunt
partesque terrarum*, a quotation from Cic. *Balb.* 9, and 14.11.33.

exercitumque Romanum continuis laboribus induratum This is a variation
on 14.2.14 *legiones bellicis sudoribus induratae.* The army is like its
former commander Julian, of whom we read 25.4.5 *corpus laboribus
induratum.*

gloriosi rectoris The adjective is another instance of authorial intrusion in a passage recording the thoughts of one of the characters.
The only other emperor to receive this epithet is Claudius II Gothicus
(31.5.17).

non saluti suae, ut memorabat, consulere, sed vindictae The only possible
subject for singular *memorabat* would be Sapor himself, which does
not make sense (Seyfarth's "wie er meinte" is inadmissible). Therefore either *memorabant* or *memorabatur* must be read here. The question remains whether the Agens is to be supplied from the context or
whether it is indefinite. Fontaine prefers the former, supposing the
exploratores perfugaeque to be the source of the information. This is
highly unlikely, since their information emphasizes the confidence
of the Roman army. The alternative is to leave the identity of the
informers in the dark. This is how Petschenig, 1891, 730 interprets
this passage, naming "Höflinge und Schmeichler" as the possible
source in question. For the expression *saluti consulere* 'to save one's
life', cf. 29.5.36 *digressu celeri consulturus saluti.* It is especially frequent
in Cicero, e.g. *Fam.* 15.1.6 *utinam saluti nostrae consulere possimus! dig-
nitati certe consulemus.* With regard to the Roman thirst for revenge
we are reminded of the soldiers' reaction to Julian's death: 25.3.10
*incredibile dictu est, quo quantoque ardore miles ad vindictam ira et dolore
ferventior involabat.*

aut victoria summa aut morte memorabili The phrase *victoria summa* is
extremely rare. In fact, the only example in the BTL is Liv. *per.* 115
*summam victoriam cum magno discrimine ad Mundam urbem consecutus
est.* It is tempting to substitute the expression *summa victoriae,* ' final

CHAPTER 7.2 223

victory', which occurs in Caes. *Civ.* 1.82.3, *Gal.* 7.21.3, Liv. *per.* 19 and
98 and Veg. *mil.* 3.1.2, but the corresponding phrase *morte memorabili*
makes this unlikely.

ob quae reputabat multa et formidanda The 'many alarming consid- **7.2**
erations' are elaborated in the three participial clauses *expertus, sciens* and *comperiens.* Compare the description of Sapor in a similar
predicament, 19.9.9 *profundo tamen animi graviter aestuabat reputans
in obsidionalibus malis saepe luctuosas se pertulisse iacturas.* For the substantivized adjectives cf. 15.12.3 *multa contempturus et formidanda* and
29.5.2 *multa ciebat et formidanda.*

diffusum abunde militem per provincias Apart from the expeditionary
force which Julian had mobilized, perhaps more than 100,000 men
(cf. the note ad 23.3.5 *triginta milia*), there were of course more
troops quartered in the eastern provinces of the Roman empire.
Jones 683 estimates their grand total at 352,000. Cf. e.g. Demandt,
1989, 256 and Nicasie, 1997, 74–6, but note the latter's remark on
p. 75: "It is impossible to compute the total size of the late Roman
army with any degree of certainty".

levi tessera colligi posse expertus 'That troops could easily be sum-
moned'. Vegetius defined the *tessera* as follows: *tessera autem dicitur
praeceptum ducis, quo vel ad aliquod opus vel ad bellum movetur exercitus*
(*mil.* 2.7.5); see the note ad 21.5.13. *Levi tessera* is a daring variation
on one of Amm.'s favourite expressions, *levi negotio*, on which see the
note ad 20.10.2 *superavit negotio* and TLL VII 2.1210.16–9.

*sciens populum suum post amissam maximam plebem ultimis terroribus
deformatum* This is the first time that Amm. mentions the effects of
Julian's campaign on Sapor's subjects. After the preceding chapters,
with their emphasis on the hardships the Romans had to endure,
this comes as a bit of a surprise, but it is entirely consistent with
his earlier declarations of Roman superiority whenever it came to a
regular battle. We may think in particular of the outcome of the battle
of Maranga (25.1.19), quoted above ad *fortia facta*, and of the battle
in which Julian fell (25.3.13 *quinquaginta tum Persarum optimates et
satrapae cum plebe maxima ceciderunt*). Note the opposition between
populus, the entire population, and *plebs*, the common soldiers, for
which see the note ad 25.6.3 *cum hostium.*
    Amm. uses very strong language here. For *ultimis terroribus* cf. Liv.
26.41.12 *adde ultimum terrorem ac pavorem, castra Punica inter Anienem*

224 COMMENTARY

ac moenia Romana posita. The present use of *deformare* is brought under the heading "i.q. foedare" in TLL V 1.371.39.

simul comperiens in Mesopotamia relictum haud multo minorem exercitum Blomgren 35 defends the asyndeton, pointing to 18.6.2 as a parallel: *memores, quod...simul metuentes saluti,* which is convincing enough. In spite of *simul,* the action of the present participle *comperiens* should not be interpreted as being strictly contemporaneous with the action of the main verb *reputabat,* since Sapor must have known for a long time that the army corps under the command of Sebastianus and Procopius was advancing along the West bank of the Tigris (cf. 23.3.5, 25.8.7 and 25.8.16). See Szantyr 387: "Das Spätlatein findet in dem Part. Praes. ein bequemes Mittel, das fehlende Part. Perf. Akt. zu ersetzen." The sequence *expertus – sciens – comperiens* means that Sapor takes into account experience and knowledge as well as military intelligence. See for the size of the army left in Mesopotamia the note ad 23.3.5 *triginta milia.* As to *haud multo minorem,* Amm.'s wording is rightly explained by Rolfe: "i.e. than the one which had invaded Persia".

7.3 *quae super omnia hebetarunt eius anxiam mentem, uno parique natatu quingenti viri transgressi tumidum flumen incolumes* The preposition *super* is rarely followed by an accusative in Amm., except in its spatial meaning 'over' and in phrases describing a cumulative effect, such as 14.11.16 *aliis super alias urgentibus litteris* or 31.10.12 *urgentibus aliis super alios nuntiis.* The present phrase is the only instance of postponed *super.* Presumably Amm. followed Tac. *Hist.* 3.26.3 *quae super cuncta terrebat* (sc. duces) *ipsorum miles periculi quam morae patientior,* which is also similar in that the subject is a noun with a dominant attribute ('the fact that their own soldiers were more willing to endure danger than delay') just as is the case here ('the fact that 500 men had crossed unharmed'). Seyfarth added a comma after *mentem,* probably because he failed to see that *super* is in postposition, as his translation suggests ("Was seinen ängstlichen Sinn aber mehr als alles andere lähmte, war die Tatsache, dass"). This is clearly impossible, so the comma should go.

For *hebetare* see the note ad 20.11.11 *clausorum hebetaverat.* One gets the impression that Amm. wanted to substitute a more expressive verb for Tacitus' *terrebat. Uno parique natatu* is a variation on *uno parique ardore,* which is found four times in Amm.; see the note ad 20.4.17. Amm. is the only author to use the combination *uno parique.* The noun *natatus* is used by Amm. of animals: 23.6.52 (tigers) and

CHAPTER 7.4   225

24.1.5 (deer). It is a rare noun, found in poets like Statius, Ausonius (*Mosella*) and Claudian.

One wonders why the successful crossing of the Tigris (cf. 25.6. 13–4) had this effect on Sapor. Was he not pleased to see his enemies on the run? The answer is probably that he preferred to starve them in his own territory in order to obtain the greatest concessions from them, rather than seeing them escape to safety. In the eyes of Sapor the crossing of the Tigris has indeed the effect on the soldiers envisaged in 25.6.13 (ut) *si id perfecissent innocui, transitus fidentior temptaretur.*

custodibusque confossis reliquos consortes suos ad similem fiduciam concitasse Amm. switches from the personal construction *hebetarunt mentem viri transgressi…incolumes* to an infinitive construction, as if he had written e.g. *nuntius hebetavit mentem.* Several critics have been of the opinion that this is inadmissible and have proposed different remedies. Hagendahl, 1921, 127 however, gives an excellent parallel in Amm. for such an anacoluthon: 25.9.9 *numquam enim ab urbis ortu inveniri potest annalibus replicatis, ut arbitror, terrarum pars ulla nostrarum ab imperatore vel consule hosti concessa, sed ne ob recepta quidem, quae direpta sunt, verum ob amplificata regna triumphales glorias fuisse delatas,* q.v.

Haec inter…absumi This complicated sentence is syntactically flawed, **7.4** since the second part of the *cum*-clause, which is expected after *neque,* takes the form of an abl. abs. instead of a finite verb. A further complication is, that the two participle constructions are uncoordinated, which makes it necessary to subordinate *absumptis omnibus* to *acto miserabiliter biduo,* the former explaining why the two days were passed in misery.

cum neque pontes compaginari paterentur undae torrentes For *compaginare* see the note ad 21.12.9 *quos ante compaginarant.* It is used six times for the construction of bridges, but these bridges do not all belong to the same type. In 16.11.8 *septem a Barbatione petierat naves ex his, quas velut transiturus amnem ad compaginandos paraverat pontes* and 23.3.9 *totidemque* (naves) *ad compaginandos necessariae pontes* ship bridges are evidently meant. In the present case we have to think of the pontoon bridge promised by the engineers in 25.6.15. One might wonder why the engineers did not make use of the ships kept apart especially for this purpose, when the rest of the fleet was destroyed (24.7.4 *praeter minores duodecim, quas profuturas pangendis pontibus disposuit vehi carpentis*), but already in 24.7.8, q.v., we have been told that

226 COMMENTARY

these were no longer available: *nec contabulandi pontis erat facultas amissis navibus temere.*

et absumptis omnibus, quae mandi poterant, utilibus ullis acto miserabiliter biduo Since a collocation of *omnis* and *ullus* without an intervening negation or a preposition like *sine* seems impossible, the text as transmitted in V cannot be kept. Heraeus' addition of *sine* before *utilibus* is simple and attractive in view of the fact that of the 68 occurrences of *ullus* no fewer than 31 are part of a prepositional phrase with *sine*. Petschenig's deletion of *ullis* ("als Dittographie von *utilibus* zu streichen", 1892, 519), however, seems preferable for two reasons. *Utilia* is used substantivally for a whole range of useful things, such as means of transport (17.4.13 *dum translationi pararentur utilia*), siege material (21.11.3 *futurae concertationi praeparabant utilia*) and food, as in 27.9.7 *ad victum utilia* and 31.8.1 *cunctis utilibus ad vivendum in civitates validas comportatis*. In the present passage the relative clause *quae mandi poterant* makes it clear that food is meant, after which a general statement that the Romans were deprived of all *utilia* makes little sense. Moreover, Petschenig provides a convincing paleographical explanation of the corruption. As to *biduo*, 6–7 July must be meant (cf. the note on chronology).

furebat inedia iraque percitus miles To what terrible excesses hunger can lead has been described in 14.7.6, where the populace of Antioch *famis et furoris impulsu* lynches Theophilus, the governor of Syria. In this book Amm. "repeats like an incantation" (Matthews 186) the soldiers' sufferings caused by hunger, cf. the notes ad 25.2.1 *inedia cruciabat* and 25.7.7 *dies quattuor*. Normally, *furor* is mentioned as a characteristic of barbarians, see Seager 57. For *percitus* see ad 25.5.6.

ferro properans quam fame ignavissimo genere mortis absumi As TLL X 2.1982.70 sqq. shows, *properare* is often used of emotions, meaning 'to be eager'. Cf. 19.7.1 *omnes oppetere gloriose iam properabant aut ruina urbis animis litasse caesorum* and 25.1.2 *hocque viso accensum properantem congredi militem...prohibuit imperator.* The idea that a death from starvation is especially miserable goes as far back as Hom. *Od.* 12.342 λιμῷ δ' οἴκτιστον θανέειν καὶ πότμον ἐπισπεῖν. Amm., who in 17.9.4 uses almost the same words (*fame ignavissimo mortis genere tabescentes*), probably follows Sal. *Hist.* 2.98.1 *fame, miserruma omnium morte.*

7.5 *erat tamen pro nobis aeternum dei caeléstis númen* The opening sections of this chapter, which emphasized Sapor's despondency, anticipate

CHAPTER 7.5   227

this statement. Just when things are at their worst, the Persian initiative to enter into negotiations offers the prospect of salvation. For comparable phrases expressing Amm.'s belief in divine guidance see Camus, 1967, 134–6, who notes that Amm. uses *deus* and *numen* indiscriminately, and that this is the only place where *numen* and *deus* are combined "dans une expression redondante". It is this redundancy that gives the sentence its solemn ring. Theodoret, Rufinus and John Chrysostom, of course, praise the God of the Christians as the saviour of the army, which was now led by a Christian emperor, when they say: παραυτίκα γὰρ τὴν οἰκείαν ἔδειξε προμήθειαν ὁ τῶν ὅλων θεὸς καὶ τὴν φαινομένην ἔλυσεν ἀπορίαν (Thdt. *HE* 4.2.2), *denique statim adfuit ei divina clementia* (Rufin. *hist.* 11.1), τοῦ Θεοῦ...νεύσαντος (Chrys. *Laud. Paul.* 4.6).

Note that there is no regular cursus here. Hagendahl, 1921, 42 pointed to the parellel *caelitis dei favore* in 16.12.13 and wondered whether *caélitis númen* should be written. But, as Hagendahl himself observes, *caelestis* is the more usual form in Amm. For the combination with *numen* cf. 19.1.4, 26.1.5, 27.6.8 and 31.16.4.

et Persae praeter sperata priores super fundanda pace oratores Surenam et optimatem alium mittunt Amm. evidently interprets the initiative taken by the Persians (*praetor sperata priores*) as a sign of weakness on their part, and as the consequence of the proven superiority of the Romans in battle. In view of the sequel it is likely that these overtures are merely another example of the delaying tactics employed by the Persians, who are, of course, aware that time is working for them and against the Romans. *Praeter sperata* is a variation, found only in Amm., on the more familiar *praeter spem*; TLL X 2.997.46–73. Cf. *contraque omnem spem* in Rufin. *hist.* 11.1 on the same subject matter. Zosimus too presents the Persian initiative as a welcome surprise, 3.31.1 Καίπερ οὖν ἐν τούτοις ὄντι τῷ στρατοπέδῳ περὶ φιλίας ὅμως ἐποιοῦντο λόγους οἱ Πέρσαι, σουρήναν τε καὶ ἄλλους τῶν ἐν δυνάμει παρ' αὐτοῖς ὄντων ἐκπέμψαντες. Note that he, unlike Amm., speaks of more than one negotiator apart from the Surena (see for the latter the note ad 24.2.4 and for *optimas* the notes ad 20.6.3 *per optimates* and 21.13.4 *praeter optimates*). Malalas *Chron.* 13.335 (quoted in the note ad 25.7.5 *animos ipsi*) only mentions the Surena, as does the *Chron. Pasch.* a. 363. Cf. further Thdt. *HE* 4.2.2 τὴν γὰρ τούτου (i.e. Jovian's) βασιλείαν ὁ Περσῶν μεμαθηκὼς βασιλεὺς πρέσβεις ἀπέστειλεν ὑπὲρ εἰρήνης πρεσβευσομένους, Rufin. *hist.* 11.1 *subito emissos a barbaris oratores adesse vident pacemque deposcere* and Lyd. *Mag.* 3.52.3, who

228   COMMENTARY

speaks of 'the most outstanding of the Persians' as their ambassadors (Περσῶν τοῖς ἐξοχωτάτοις).

Apart from HA *S* 22.4 *non solum victor sed etiam in aeternum pace fundata* Amm. is the only author to use the expression *pacem fundare*, cf. 16.10.21 *libratisque diu super pace consiliis, quam fundari posse cum Persis Musonianus rettulerat* and 18.7.7 *quasi fundata cum mortuis pace*; TLL VI 1560.65–6. *Orator* in the sense of *legatus* is an archaism, for which see Fesser 53. Cf. e.g. Sal. *Jug.* 108.1 *praemissus ab Iugurtha, postquam Sullam adcitum audierat, orator et subdole speculatum Bocchi consilia.* Amm. writes it in 14.10.14, 17.1.12, 27.12.9, 29.5.8, 31.4.1 and even uses *orare* in the sense of 'to speak' in 17.12.9 and 19.12.12, q.v.; cf. Hagendahl, 1921, 105 n. 1.

animos ipsi quoque despondentes For the expression cf. 26.7.13 *atrocitate nuntii Valens perculsus...eo usque desponderat animum, ut.* It is found in all periods of Latin, e.g. Pl. *Merc.* 614 *Quaeso hercle, animum ne desponde* and Liv. 31.22.5 *despondentibus iam animos sociis spem ingentem attulerant.* Also according to Malalas *Chron.* 13.335, the Persian king acted out of fear: ὁ δὲ βασιλεὺς Περσῶν Σαββουραρσάκιος μαθὼν τὴν τοῦ βασιλέως Ἰουλιανοῦ τελευτήν, φόβῳ πολλῷ συνεχόμενος ἐκ τῆς Περσαρμενίας χώρας πρεσβευτὴν ἐξέπεμψεν, αἰτῶν περὶ εἰρήνης καὶ δεόμενος ἕνα τῶν μεγιστάνων αὐτοῦ ὀνόματι Σουρραεινᾶν πρὸς τὸν βασιλέα Ῥωμαίων. *Chron. Pasch.* a. 363 is, as usual, almost identical, apart from the fact that we read there: μήπω μαθὼν τὴν τοῦ βασιλέως Ἰουλιανοῦ τελευτήν. Cf. further Greg. Naz. *Or.* 5.15, quoted in the note ad §6 *condiciones.* According to Ruf. Fest. 29 the Persians acted out of respect for Rome: *tanta reverentia Romani nominis fuit, ut a Persis prius de pace sermo haberetur, ac reduci confectus inedia exercitus sineretur.*

quos...pars Romana superior gravius quassabat in dies In view of the harsh demands made by the Persians, as Amm. will report in the next section, this must be an overstatement. Eutr. 10.17.1 (*uno a Persis atque altero proelio victus*, sc. Jovian) depicts the situation more gloomily. For *pars Romana* cf. 30.2.2 *remotisque inde partis Romanae praesidiis* and V. Max. 1.8.1 *Castor ac Pollux Romanarum partium propugnatores.* In 24.3.9 Julian is quoted as saying *"sic sub iugum mitteret Persas, ita quassatum recrearet orbem Romanum".* Cf. Exup. 7.42 (Sertorio) *qui tunc Romanum armis quassabat imperium.*

7.6 *condiciones autem ferebant difficiles et perplexas* The two adjectives are quite distinct. The peace terms are both difficult to carry out and

CHAPTER 7.6   229

deliberately obscure. *Perplexus* is the opposite of *simplex* or *apertus*, and has the connotation of wiliness, as the following parallels show 15.5.10 *ut doceret aperte, quae vellet, non ita perplexe*, Liv. 34.57.6 *ex iis Menippus ignorare se dixit quidnam perplexi sua legatio haberet, cum simpliciter ad amicitiam petendam iungendamque societatem venisset*, Liv. 35.14.12 *perplexum Punico astu responsum*. For the combination cf. Quint. *Inst.* 11.1.63 *adeo in causa difficili atque perplexa nihil prius intuendum credidit, quam quid deceret*.

Ruf. Fest. 29 speaks in the matter under discussion of conditions, which cost the Romans dearly *condicionibus (quod numquam antea accidit) dispendiosis*. Greg. Naz. *Or.* 5.15 on the one hand says that the Persians refrained from grasping all they could because of their customary moderation or out of fear (τῇ νίκῃ μετριάζοντες – καὶ γὰρ νόμος οὗτος αὐτοῖς εἰδέναι μετρεῖν εὐπραγίαν – ἤ τι δείσαντες ἄλλο τῶν λεγομένων) and therefore proposed unexpectedly lenient conditions (εἰς συμβάσεις ἐτράποντο καὶ ταύτας ἀδοκήτους οὕτω καὶ φιλανθρώπους), but on the other hand calls the result dishonourable and unworthy of Rome's strength (συνθήκαις...αἰσχραῖς τε καὶ ἀναξίαις τῆς Ῥωμαίων χειρός).

fingentes humanorum respectu reliquias exercitus redire sinere clementissimum regem Here the wording, with its condescending emphasis on the clemency of Sapor and the deplorable state of the 'remnants' of the Roman army, clearly reflects the attitude of the Persians. The epithet *clementissimus* is in marked contrast to the authorial qualification *truculentus rex ille Persarum* in 20.6.1, q.v. Sapor is presented by Amm. as a harsh and cruel ruler, even when he pretends to be lenient (18.10.4 *lenitudinem profecto in tempore simulans, ut omnes, quos antehac diritate crudelitateque terrebat, sponte sua metu remoto venirent*; 27.12.6 *motum Saporis inclementissimi omnium*). Sapor's most often mentioned characteristic is rage (19.1.6 *orantibus potissimis ducibus, ne profusus in iram a gloriosis descisceret coeptis*; 20.7.3 *ira tamen tum sequestrata*; 20.7.8 *efferata vesania regis obstante*; 20.7.11 *rabies regis*; 27.12.11: *Sapor ultra hominem efferatus*).

The phrase *humanorum respectu* has no exact parallel, although Liv. 29.9.5 *sine respectu non maiestatis modo sed etiam humanitatis in legatum impetum...faciunt* comes close. *Humanorum* belongs under the heading "neutr. pro subst." in TLL VI 3094.73–83. The meaning is clear: Sapor allows the Romans to return home for humanitarian reasons. The hypocritical nature of this clemency is made explicit in 25.8.1 *pax specie humanitatis indulta*.

230　　　　　　　　　　　　COMMENTARY

si, quae iubet, impleverit cum primatibus Caesar Brok interprets the reference to the *primates* as a sign that Sapor had little confidence in Jovian's authority and points to 30.2.3, where Sapor, in a dispute with Valens about the terms of the peace treaty, appeals to the Roman co-signatories: *asseverarat enim non posse semina radicitus amputari discordiarum, nisi intervenissent conscii pacis foederatae cum Ioviano.* For *primas* see the note ad 24.7.1 *Digesto itaque.* As to *Caesar*, there are two passages in Amm. where this term without further qualification refers to the reigning emperor, the present text and 24.2.21. Cf. Béranger, 1976, 55–6.

7.7　*contra hos cum Salutio praefecto mittitur Arintheus* Lib. *Or.* 24.20 names Victor instead of Arintheus and says that there were other envoys as well (Βίκτωρα καὶ Σαλούστιον καὶ τοὺς ἄλλους τοὺς ὑπὲρ τῆς εἰρήνης πρεσβεύοντας), presumably, as Norman ad loc. argues, because he combined the mission of Salutius and Arintheus on the one hand, and that of Nemota and Victor, mentioned by Amm. in 25.7.13, on the other. Lyd. *Mag.* 3.52.3 only speaks of Salutius, Malalas *Chron.* 13.335 and *Chron. Pasch.* a. 363 only of Arintheus. The Arabic historian al-Tabari has yet another version: "While Jovinianus (Jovian) was quite willing to go to Shapur, none of his commanders favoured this intention. He, however, insisted and came to Shapur, with eighty of the most respected men in the camp and in the whole army, and wearing the crown" (*Annales* p. 843 Barth-Nöldeke, tr. al-Issa and Dance, quoted in Greatrex-Lieu, 2002, 9). However, they are all wrong. Zos. 3.31.1 confirms Amm.'s report that Σαλούστιος i.e. Salutius (cf. for the confusion between Secundus Salutius and Flavius Sallustius the note ad 22.3.1 *Brevi deinde*) and Arintheus were sent (στείλαντός τε Σαλούστιον τὸν τῆς αὐλῆς ὕπαρχον καὶ Ἀρινθαῖον σὺν τούτῳ) and there is no need to doubt this. Salutius is mentioned four times in this book, apart from the present text in 25.3.14 (q.v.), 25.3.21 and 25.5.3 (q.v.), Arintheus thrice, cf. 25.5.2 (q.v.) and 25.10.9.

dum deliberatur examinatius, quid finiri deberet The adverb ('weighing every word') is rare; TLL V 2. 1170. 23–33. The only other instance of the comparative form is 30.3.2 *quibus ille, ut cunctatorem decuerat ducem, examinatius lectis. Finiri* is the reading of V. It seems at least defensible, in view of the parallels quoted in TLL VI 783.68–784.8, e.g. Liv. 3.13. 8 *vades dari placuit…quot darentur, permissum tribunis est. decem finierunt* 39.17.1 *diem se certam finituros,* V. Max. 5.3.1a *tanti namque poena finita est.* Although Malalas *Chron.* 13.335 and

CHAPTER 7.8   231

Chron. Pasch. a. 363 state that Jovian had handed the whole matter to Arintheus and would sanction whatever peace terms his ambassador brought back, this does not seem likely. From 25.7.10 it appears that Jovian had to be persuaded to accept the terms. Cf. Blockley, 1992, 27.

dies quattuor sunt evoluti inedia cruciabiles et omni supplicio tristiores As Amm. tells us in 25.2.1, already before Julian died on the battlefield the Romans suffered from hunger: *commeatibus nos destitutos inedia cruciabat iam non ferenda.* The troops are more acutely aware of it during periods of rest (*indutiae* in ch. 2, waiting for the bridge to be built in section 4 above, awaiting the outcome of the negotiations here). In Libanius' version everything started to go wrong only after Julian's death. The Persians realized that Roman morale was broken and cleverly exploited their longing for peace: Lib. *Or.* 18.277 πρῶτον μὲν γὰρ οὐκ ἤνεγκαν οὓς πρότερον ἤλαυνον, ἔπειτα δὲ δελεασθέντες εἰρήνης ὀνόματι...πάντες ἐβόων δέχεσθαι καὶ στέργειν, καὶ πρῶτος ὁ βασιλεύων εἵλκετο. λαβὼν δὲ αὐτοὺς πρὸς τὴν ἡσυχίαν ὡρμηκότας ὁ Μῆδος διῆγε, διέτριβεν ἐρωτῶν, ἀποκρινόμενος, τοῦτο δεχόμενος, ἕτερον ἀναβαλλόμενος, ἐν πλήθει πρεσβειῶν ἀναλίσκων αὐτοῖς τὴν τροφήν ("in the first place, they did not stand up to those whom they previously used to put to flight: secondly, ensnared by this word 'peace'...they all demanded its acceptance without demur, and the new emperor was the first to be taken in by it. The Persians found them hankering after peace and dillied and dallied with question and answer, accepting this point, deferring that, and exhausting their supplies with a string of parleys." tr. Norman). Cf. further Futr. 10.17.1 (*exercitu quoque inopia laborante*), Zos. 3.30.5 (προσέτι ἐνδείᾳ τροφῆς πιεζόμενοι), Socr. *HE* 3.22.6 (τῶν στρατιωτῶν λιμῷ φθειρομένων), Soz. *HE* 6.3.2 (καμνούσης τε τῆς στρατιᾶς ἐνδείᾳ τῶν ἐπιτηδείων). Rufin. *hist.* 11.1 and Thdt. *HE* 4.2.2, quoted ad 25.8.1 *pax specie*, are also relevant.

As to *dies quattuor* (Malalas *Chron.* 13.335 speaks of ἡμέρας τρεῖς, as does *Chron. Pasch.* a. 363), 8–11 July must be meant (cf. the note on chronology).

quo temporis spatio, antequam hi mitterentur, si exabusus princeps paulatim **7.8**
terris hostilibus excessisset, profecto venisset ad praesidia Corduenae, uberis regionis et nostrae, ex eo loco, in quo haec agebantur, centesimo lapide disparatae The relative phrase *quo temporis spatio* can only refer back to the *dies quattuor* just mentioned, during which Salutius and Arintheus negotiated with Sapor. For that reason the interpretation by Matthews 186 is wrong: "In Ammianus' opinion, the emperor

232   COMMENTARY

could have taken advantage of the time wasted before the Roman envoys were sent (this must mean while the attempts were being made to construct the bridges)". The temporal phrase *antequam hi mitterentur* is subordinated to *si exabusus...excessisset*, and a correct paraphrase would be: 'if Jovian had made good use of these four days by marching on in the direction of Corduene and only then had sent his delegates to negotiate with Sapor' (the Romans would have been in a stronger bargaining position). In classical prose the subj. *mitterentur* would have expressed the idea of purpose on the part of the Agens, i.e. Jovian. In Amm., however, with one exception, *antequam* is always used with the subjunctive (see the note ad 20.9.5 *antequam sciretur*), so that no conclusion can be drawn from his use of this mood. The conjunction *si* occupies the seventh position in this sentence, which is an extreme case of traiectio, for which see Kühner-Stegmann II 614–5. Traiectio of *si* occurs more often in relative clauses, e.g. 23.4.9 *hoc genere operis, si fuerit exserto vigore discussum.* The present case is highly revealing in that the author focuses in this way on the words *antequam hi mitterentur*. Jovian should have used these days *before* sending the envoys to Sapor. The addition of *paulatim* makes it clear that Amm. is thinking of a gradual withdrawal from Persian territory, not of reaching Corduene within four days, which would have been wellnigh impossible even in the best of circumstances, let alone for a demoralized and hungry army, bound to be unremittingly attacked by the enemy. Amm. only claims that the army would finally have made it to Corduene, if it had used the wasted days to march on (cf. Badian, 1977, 107–8). Incidentally, to go to Corduene had been the emperor Julian's original plan (cf. 24.8.5 *sedit...sententia, ut...Corduenam arriperemus*).

As to *praesidia*, in Amm. the plural always refers to 'forts', 'military strongholds' (TLL X 2.891.63: "pertinet ad locum copiis munitum, sc. de stationibus, castellis, castris sim."), as a synonym of *castra praesidiaria* (23.3.7) and *munimenta praesidiaria* (25.9.12). There is one exception: 15.2.9 *sed accidebat nonnumquam, ut opulenti pulsantes praesidia potiorum* e.q.s., where the plural is necessary, because the help is provided by different persons. Therefore the translations by Rolfe ("he could surely have reached the protection of Corduena"), and Seyfarth ("in den Schutz Corduenes") have to be rejected. For *nostrae* in *uberis regionis et nostrae* see the note ad *quinque regiones* in § 9.

The form *exabusus* (V) is unique and has for that reason been tampered with more or less drastically, by modern editors. Löfstedt, 1911, 94, however, defends it convincingly as an example of what he calls "Dekomposition", the tendency in Late Latin to make composita

CHAPTER 7.9   233

yet more expressive by adding a second prefix. Other instances
of this phenomenon in Amm. are, according to him, 29.2.21 *post
inconvolutos multiplices casus*, 29.6.1 *Quadorum natio mota est diu inexcita
repentino* and 30.1.6 *apparitoris, qui portam tuebatur, indicio impercitus*
(Seyfarth reads *percitus*).

ex eo loco, in quo haec agebantur, centesimo lapide disparatae For similar
designations of distance cf. 24.1.3 *ut decimo paene lapide postremi
dispararentur a signiferis primis*, q.v. and the note ad 24.5.3 *quo loco*.
The distance to Corduene was not, as Amm. alleges, 'only a hundred
miles' (i.e. some 150 km), but, as is often observed (e.g. by Brok 222),
nearer to two hundred miles. The topographical error is surprising,
for Amm. knew the region rather well (cf. 18.6.20 and Matthews 48–
57). His complaint about the waste of time and the missed chances
may have been prompted by his memory of the anger and frustration
he had experienced during these fateful days. In all probability Amm.
intentionally shortens the distance in order to censure Jovian even
more for not choosing the route his illustrious predecessor had opted
for.

Petebat autem réx obstinátius, ut ipse aiebat, sua dudum a Maximiano erepta,   **7.9**
ut docebat autem negotium, pro redemptione nostra The comparative
obstinatius is chosen to produce a cursus tardus. *Obstinatio* and its
derivatives can denote commendable determination, but negative
occurrences predominate; see the note ad 20.4.8, Bitter 153–4
and Seager 29–31, 40–1. According to Amm., Sapor was adamant
in his refusal to accept the losses Persia had suffered as a result
of the treaty of 298/9 (for the date see Barnes, 1982, 63), after
the defeat of his grandfather Narses against C. Galerius Valerius
Maximianus (see for the latter the notes ad 22.4.8 and 23.5.11;
he is also mentioned in 25.10.2). The Persian king had already
incorporated this in the letter to Constantius which Amm. 'quotes'
in 17.5.3–8: *ideoque Armeniam recuperare cum Mesopotamia debeo avo
meo composita fraude praereptam* (17.5.6). Faced with a refusal on the
part of Constantius' envoys to accept an agreement on such terms
(*amicitiae foedus sub hac lege firmari debere asseverantes, ne super turbando
Armeniae vel Mesopotamiae statu quidquam moveretur*, 17.14.1), Sapor
was unwilling to compromise: 17.14.2 *cum obstinatissimum regem nisi
harum regionum dominio sibi adiudicato obdurescentem ad suscipiendam
cernerent pacem, negotio redierunt infecto.*
   The opposition *ut ipse aiebat* versus *ut docebat negotium* can be
explained as follows: during the negotiations Sapor only insisted on

234 COMMENTARY

his alleged historical rights, but the unspoken threat was, that the Roman army was *de facto* taken hostage and would not be allowed to return unless Sapor's demands were met. It is tempting to interpret *negotium*, for which see the note ad 21.6.8 *damna negotiis*, as 'the facts', 'reality', in the sense of classical *res*, but among the numerous occurrences of this noun in Amm. there is no clear parallel for such a meaning. Therefore Rolfe and Fontaine rightly take *negotium* to refer to the negotiations between the two parties.

Although, according to Amm., Sapor insisted on the retrocession of the lands Galerius had taken and although Amm. depicts Jovian as complying with this (*sine cunctatione tradidit omnia, quae petebantur*, 25.7.11), what Sapor actually obtained was less than what Narses had lost, as a comparison of the terms of the treaty of 298/9 with those of the peace of 363 shows (more on this in the following note). See e.g. Blockley, 1984, 29, 35; Wirth, 1984, 364, Winter, 1989, 557, Blockley, 1992, 26–7, Winter-Dignas, 2001, 157–8. Cf. for both treaties also Chrysos, 1976, 25–32 and Chrysos, 1993.

Mazzarino, 1971, 71 n. 62 has pointed to *pro redemptione nostra* as a parallel for a phrase in the *Res Gestae Divi Saporis* where it is stated that the Romans after the death of Gordian, for which see the note ad 23.5.7 *cuius actus*, had to pay 500.000 denarii τῶν ψυχῶν αὐτῶν ἀντίτειμ', 'an exchange for their lives', that is to say as a ransom to let them return unharmed.

quinque regiones Transtigritanas: Arzanenam et Moxoenam et Zabdicenam itidemque Rehimenam et Corduenam Libanius in *Or.* 18.278 speaks in general terms of the surrender of πόλεις καὶ χώρας καὶ ἔθνη, as do Eutr. 10.17.1 (*nonnulla imperii Romani parte tradita*) and Soz. *HE* 6.3.2 (παραδούς τινα Πέρσαις τῶν πρότερον Ῥωμαίοις ὑποτελῶν). Zos. 3.31.1 is more specific, giving a list of ceded territories which on the whole comes close to that of Amm.: συνεδόκει δὲ Ῥωμαίους τοῦ τε Ζαβδικηνῶν ἔθνους ἐκστῆναι τοῖς Πέρσαις, ἔτι δὲ Καρδουηνῶν καὶ Ῥημηνῶν καὶ Ζαληνῶν. The differences (Moxoena is missing in Zosimus, instead of Arzanena we find Zalene, Rehimena is differently spelled), though food for thought for 'Quellenforscher' (cf. Klein, 1914, 127–8 and Klotz, 1916, 504), are slight and, given Zosimus' notorious carelessness (cf. Paschoud n. 91), not very surprising. It seems best therefore to prefer the number and names in Amm.'s list to those of Zos., the more so because we find the five regions mentioned by Amm. as "dioceses in the same constellation in the signatures of the synod of the patriarch Isaak in 410" (Winter, 1989, 563 n. 8).

CHAPTER 7.9   235

As the note ad 21.6.7 *ad Transtigritanos* stated, there has been considerable discussion as to the number and extent of the *regiones Transtigritanae* (add to the literature cited there Chaumont, 1969, 119–26, Adontz, 1970, 25–37, Blockley, 1984, Winter, 1989, Grattarola, 1989 and Winter-Dignas, 2001, 150–5). "Non sono identificate in modo del tutto preciso sulla carta" (Grattarola, 1989, 415; maps can be found in the editions of Paschoud and Fontaine, Grattarola, 1989, 416 and Winter-Dignas, 2001, 150). One of the problems is the fact that not all of these regions seem to have been *Transtigritanae* in the strict sense: Zabdicena, with on its territory Bezabde (cf. 20.7.1), stretched out on both banks of the river (cf. already Valesius and see Paschoud n. 91, Blockley, 1992, 27; for Zabdicena in general Treidler, 1972), as did perhaps Rehimena (cf. the divergent views on this matter listed by Grattarola, 1989, 429 n. 91; see further Fontaine n. 646, Blockley, 1984, 41 n. 19 and Winter, 1989, 556 with n. 10). Rehimena, for that matter, is only mentioned by Amm. and Zosimus. As to the other regions, in their case the adj. *transtigritanus* seems to be appropriate. Arzanena is the most western region of those mentioned by Amm., to be found east of the river Nymphius, modern Batman Suyu (Brok 224 is certainly wrong in situating Arzanena to the west of this river; cf. Dillemann, 1962, 121–3; for Arzanene in the sixth century see Whitby, 1983). There are notes on Moxoena and Corduena ad 23.3.5.

The five regions mentioned by Amm. all extended to the east of the river Nymphius. This implies that in 363 some of the regions taken from the Persians by Galerius, were left in Roman hands, viz. Ingilene and Sophene, both to the west of the Nymphius – one wonders whether Amm. omitted to mention this fact through ignorance or intentionally. That these territories had been ceded to Rome in 298/9 is stated by Petrus Patricius *fr.* 14, our main source for the treaty of 298/9, who mentions as one of the terms ὥστε κατὰ τὸ ἀνατολικὸν κλίμα τὴν Ἰντηληνὴν (rectius Ἰγγηληνὴν, cf. *Cod. Iust.* 1.29.5) μετὰ Σοφηνῆς καὶ Ἀρζανηνὴν μετὰ Καρδουηνῶν καὶ Ζαβδικηνῆς Ῥωμαίους ἔχειν (for more information concerning the total number of these regions, nine, not five, according to some scholars, cf. e.g. Adontz, 1970, 35–6, Blockley, 1984, 32, Winter, 1989, 557, Grattarola, 1989, 417–8; see also the commentary on the translations of Patricius' fragment in Dodgeon-Lieu, 1991, 133 and Winter-Dignas, 2001, 146–7).

When in 298/9 Ingilene, Sophene and the other principalities mentioned came under Roman control, they were apparently expected to provide the Roman army with troops (cf. 19.9.2 *Transti-*

236   COMMENTARY

gritanis...contruncatis, with De Jonge's note, 20.7.1 *cum sagittariis pluribus Zabdicenis* and *Not. Dign. Or.* 36.34, where an *ala quintadecima Flavia Corduenorum* is mentioned), and to accept the establishment of Roman fortifications in their territory (cf. 25.7.8 *praesidia Corduenae* and 25.7.9 *cum castellis quindecim*), but they were not incorporated into the Roman empire as provinces. The *regiones Transtigritanae* remained autonomous, comparable to the *civitates foederatae liberae et immunes* of former times (Garsoïan, 1971, 344), and kept their local chiefs: *vitaxae*, *reges* and *satrapae*, cf. 23.6.14 and in general, Adontz, 1970, 25–37 and Winter, 1989, 560. Amm.'s wording here is an indication of this in that he simply speaks of *regiones* and does not add a qualification like the one in 14.8.12 *has quoque regiones...Pompeius...in provinciae speciem delata iuris dictione formavit.* Elsewhere Amm. employs the word *gentes* instead of *regiones* for the principalities on the other side of the Tigris (18.9.2). Likewise Festus, speaking on two occasions of the treaty of 298/9, now uses *gens*, now *regio* (*pace facta Mesopotamia est restituta et supra ripas Tigridis limes est reformatus, ita ut quinque gentium trans Tigridem constitutarum dicionem adsequeremur*, Ruf. Fest. 14, and *Mesopotamiam cum Transtigritanis regionibus reddiderunt*, id. 25). Cf. Zosimus' ἔθνους in 3.31.1, with Paschoud n. 91.

   One of the terms of the treaty of 298/9 was that the Tigris would be the frontier between Persia and the Romans (Petr. Patr. *fr.* 14 τὸν Τίγριν ποταμὸν ἑκατέρας πολιτείας ὁροθέσιον εἶναι). At least nominally this remained so (cf. Amm. 18.5.3 and Jul. *Or.* 1.22 b-c) until Jovian, by the treaty of 363, ceded parts of Mesopotamia to Sapor (see the next note). However, the years between 298/9 and 363 saw some changes in the status quo. After hostilities had been resumed under Constantius the Persians for instance were able to capture Amida (19.8), Singara (20.6) and Bezabde (20.7). Such discrepancies between the de iure and the de facto situation (for which see e.g. Dillemann, 1962, 220) must also have occurred in the *regiones Transtigritanae*, as the case of Corduene makes clear. In 18.6.20 Amm., speaking of the year 359, says that at that time this region *obtemperabat potestati Persarum*, but in 25.7.8 he says that Corduene was under Roman control again (*Corduenae, uberis regionis et nostrae*). Unless Amm.'s *et nostrae* is an exaggeration, this was presumably the result of the activities of Procopius and Sebastianus in that area (cf. 23.3.5).

   Not mentioned by any other author is the story told by Lyd. *Mag.* 3.51.6–52.4 that in the treaty of 363 Romans and Persians agreed to share the costs of building a fortress near the Caspian Gates in

CHAPTER 7.9   237

order to block barbarian invasions. Though accepted as historical by
e.g. Frézouls, 1981, 217 and Clauss, 1998, 816, it is most probably
anachronistic and, as e.g. Chrysos, 1976, 30 and Blockley, 1984, 37
argue, should be rejected.

cum castellis quindecim et Nisibin et Singaram et Castra Maurorum Zos.
3.31.1 omits to mention Singara and Castra Maurorum, but he
refers to Nisibis and mentions the same number of forts as Amm.
He, moreover, adds that these strongholds should be surrendered
to the Persians with everything and everyone included, but that
the Romans were permitted to remove the inhabitants of Nisibis
(see on this the note ad §11 *difficile hoc*): πρὸς τούτοις καὶ ἐπὶ
πᾶσιν τῶν περὶ αὐτὰ φρουρίων, ὄντων τὸν ἀριθμὸν πεντεκαίδεκα, μετὰ
τῶν οἰκητόρων καὶ κτημάτων καὶ ζῴων καὶ πάσης ἀποσκευῆς, Νίσιβιν
δὲ παραδοῦναι δίχα τῶν ἐνοικούντων· ἐδόκει γὰρ τούτους, ἔνθα ἂν
δόξειε Ῥωμαίοις, μετοικισθῆναι. Cf. Lib. *Or.* 24.9 πόλις ἡ ἐπὶ τοῖς ὁρίοις
(i.e. Nisibis)...φρούρια πολλὰ καὶ καρτερά, Philost. *HE* 8.1 τῆς τε
Νισίβεως αὐτῷ (sc. the Persian king) ὑπεκστὰς (sc. Jovian) καὶ τῶν
φρουρίων ὅσα Ῥωμαίοις ἐπὶ Πέρσας ἄχρι τῆς Ἀρμενίας οἰονεὶ τεῖχος
προὐβέβλητο. In Zon. 13.14.5 there is no reference to the forts, but
the cession of Nisibis and Singara is mentioned: τῆς γὰρ Νισίβεως καὶ
Σιγγάρας, πόλεων περιφανῶν, ἐξέστη αὐτοῖς, μετοικίσας τοὺς κατοίκους
τῶν πόλεων. Cf. further Ruf. Fest. 29 (ut) *Nisibis et pars Mesopotamiae
traderetur*, Eun. *fr.* 29.1, Socr. *HE* 3.22.7, Hier. *Chron.* a. 364, Oros.
hist. 7.31.2, Malalas *Chron.* 13.336, *Chron. Pasch.* a. 363.

The location of the fifteen forts has provoked discussion (cf. e.g.
Blockley, 1984, 44 n. 41, Giattarola, 1989, 429–30 and Chrysos,
1993, 176). Dillemann's suggestion on that subject (1962, 220,
accepted by Paschoud n. 91) should be rejected. He takes *cum
castellis quindecim* with wat follows ("c'est le *cum castellis quindecim*
qu'il faut séparer de *Corduenam* puisqu'il se rattache à *Nisibin* et à la
Mésopotamie") and wants us to believe that Nisibis, Singara et Castra
Maurorum are to be included in the number of the fifteen forts.
This is impossible. The words *cum castellis quindecim* certainly belong
to what precedes. They are to be taken either with *Corduenam* alone,
which would imply that not only the *praesidia* of 25.7.8, but all fifteen
of the forts are to be found in Corduene (so e.g. Toumanoff, 1963,
181 n. 142), or Amm. means that the fifteen *castella* were scattered
over all five *regiones Transtigritanae*. In view of Zosimus' περὶ αὐτά,
Philostorgius' ἄχρι τῆς Ἀρμενίας and Amm.'s *munimenta praesidiaria
cum regionibus* in 25.9.12 the latter option seems preferable. Since,
as we have seen in the previous note, some of the so-called *regiones*

238   COMMENTARY

Transtigritanae were on both sides of the Tigris, the *castella* could also have been on either side. "Attempts to locate them more precisely...are wasted effort" (Blockley, 1992, 184 n. 26, referring to Honigmann, 1935, 6, Toumanoff, 1963, 181 and Dillemann, 1962, 219–20). See however Lightfoot, 1986.

The restitution of Nisibis (modern Nusaybin), mentioned in all the sources cited, is painted in dramatic terms by Amm. in chapter 9. It had an enormous impact on public opinion (cf. Turcan, 1966 and the note ad §13 *Quo ignobili*) and must have been of special significance for Sapor, who had more than once tried to capture this important city (cf. the notes ad 20.7.1 *memor*, 25.1.15 *acceptae apud* and 25.9.3 *Iovianum inter*). Its possession brought economic profits as well as strategic advantages (in 25.8.14 Amm. calls Nisibis *orientis firmissimum claustrum*, cf. *provinciarum muro* in 25.9.3). In the treaty of 298/9 it had been stipulated that Nisibis should be the only place where commercial transactions between Romans and Persians could take place (Petr. Patr. *fr.* 14 εἶναι δὲ τόπον τῶν συναλλαγμάτων Νίσιβιν) and its loss "eliminated the Roman monopoly of the income from the trans-border trade" (Blockley, 1984, 36; cf. Winter-Dignas, 2001, 158–9). See for the doubtful story that Nisibis was only handed over to the Persians for a fixed period, the note ad 25.7.14 *foederata itaque*.

The surrender to Sapor of Singara, modern Beled-Singar, *sine incolis* at that (25.7.11, q.v., Zos. 3.31.1), causes surprise. Amm. had described the capture of this city by the Persians and the deportation of its citizens and garrison in chapter 6 of book 20 (for literature see the note ad 20.6.1 *oppugnandam*). Moreover, in 20.7.1 he had related that Sapor had destroyed Singara (this is apparently overlooked by Blockley, 1984, 45 n. 44 and 1992, 28 with n. 33). There is no indication that the Romans regained and rebuilt Singara in the meantime. What use then was it to the Persian king to obtain in 363 a city he had already taken and demolished in 360? The answer to this question is suggested by, among others, Paschoud n. 91, Fontaine n. 647 and Chrysos, 1993, 178: the treaty of 363 between Sapor and Jovian confirmed in some respects de iure what was already a reality de facto. The alternative would be that we have to assume that the Romans did recapture Singara, although this has not been recorded.

Castra Maurorum is also mentioned by Amm. in 18.6.9. Its location is not known, but see the suggestions of Dillemann, 1962, 31, 104, 212–4, who identifies it with Rhabdium or Rhabdius, known from Procop. *Aed.* 2.4.1, which could be Qal'at el Hatem; Oates, 1968, 77, who wants to locate it in the area just to the west of the Tigris around Tell Hugna or Tell al-Hawa and, more convincing than

CHAPTER 7.10   239

the others, Ball, 1989, opting for Seh Qubba, on top of a high bluff
overlooking the Tigris about 90 km north-west of Mosul.

munimentum pérquäm opportúnum For *perquam* see the notes ad 20.6.9
intervallo perquam and 20.7.16 *munimenti perquam.* See for *opportunum*
the note ad 20.9.1 *opportunam urbem.*

et cum pugnari deciens expediret, ne horum quidquam dederetur Amm.'s **7.10**
disapproval of the treaty that Jovian is about to sign, is expressed
succinctly in section 13: *Quo ignobili decreto firmato* (q.v). Libanius is
less explicit, but his sarcastic choice of words leaves no doubt about
his feelings in the matter, *Or.* 18.278 (Sapor) τότε δὴ τὸν κουφότατον
ᾔτει μισθόν, πόλεις καὶ χώρας καὶ ἔθνη, τὰ τείχη τῆς Ῥωμαίων ἀσφαλείας.
Zosimus inserts at this point in his narrative a long digression (3.32)
about the question whether the Romans had ever before given up
part of their territory (cf. the introductory note ad 25.9.9–11). The
answer, of course, is negative.

adulatorum globus instabat timido principi History repeats itself; cf.
14.11.2 *versabilium adulatorum refragantibus globis* and 18.4.2 where a
timid Constantius is being pressurized by his courtiers: *Comitatensis
fabrica...imperatori suspicaci ac timido intendebat Ursicinum velut vultus
Gorgonei torvitatem.* That eunuchs were among these flatterers, as
Turcan, 1966, 877 suggests, is a mere guess. For *instare* 'to press
hard' cf. 16.6.1 *instabatque ei strepens immania comes Verissimus nomine.*

Procopii metuendum subserens nomen Jovian's fear of Procopius is not
wholly unfounded, since there were rumours that Julian had wanted
him as his successor, 23.3.2 *dicitur...paludamentum purpureum propin-
quo suo tradidisse Procopio mandasseque arripere fidentius principatum, si
se interisse didicerit apud Parthos.* Jovian's anxiety about his position
is also expressed in 25.8.9 *quod magis metuebatur,* 25.9.2 *alia metuens*
and 25.9.8 *dum extimescit aemulum potestatis* (q.v.). The verb *subserere,*
lit. 'to insert (below)' is extremely rare, but is used eleven times by
Amm., mostly in the meaning of 'to add', as in 16.7.4 *Res monuit super
hoc eodem Eutherio pauca subserere.*

*eumque affirmans, si redit cognito Iuliani interitu cum intacto milite, quem
regebat, novas res nullo renitente facile moliturum* Gelenius probably
misinterpreted *si redit* as referring to Jovian and consequently introduced the 'Verschlimmbesserung' *nisi rediret* (it is possible, however,
that he read *rediret* in the Hersfeldensis!). If we take Procopius as the

240 COMMENTARY

subject of *redi(re)t*, we have to supply 'from Mesopotamia'. In that case *cognito Iuliani interitu* may well be a reference to *si se interisse didicerit* quoted above, and moreover *cum intacto milite*, if applied to Procopius' troops (cf. 25.7.2 *in Mesopotamia relictum haud multo minorem exercitum*), would be in stark contrast to the sorry state of Jovian's army. Procopius' actual return is reported in 25.8.16, while we hear in 25.8.7 that his army had plenty of provisions. The present indicative is in itself perfectly acceptable. See the note ad 20.4.12 *ubi potestas*. As is the case there, the use of *redit* could be intended to present the phrase as a direct quotation. As is noted ad 20.8.3 *circumspectis itaque* the expression *res novae* is used of Procopius also in 17.14.3 and 26.5.8. For *reniti* see the note ad 20.4.18 *si reniti*.

7.11 *hac perniciosa verborum ille assiduitate nimia succensus* For a list of instances of the gen. inversus see Blomgren 170–1. Amm. exploits to the full the opportunity provided by this use of the gen. to accumulate adjectives. In this way he manages to qualify the words of Jovian's advisers in one noun phrase as fatal (*perniciosa*) and constantly repeated (*nimia assiduitate*). See the note ad 22.4.5 *ambitiosa ornatarum*. There is therefore no reason to read *nimium* instead of V's *nimia*, as Fontaine, followed by Greatrex-Lieu, 2002, 248 n. 11, has proposed. For *succendere* used of emotions cf. 24.4.20 (*ira et dolore*), 26.6.6 (*cupiditate*) and 26.9.7 (*alacritate*).

sine cunctatione tradidit omnia, quae petebantur Casual remarks like *sine cunctatione* contribute to the unfavourable impression of Jovian which Amm. wants to convey to his readers. Libanius in *Or.* 18.278 also relates that Jovian complied with all Sapor's wishes: ὁ δὲ ἐπένευέ τε καὶ παντὸς ἀφίστατο καὶ δεινὸν οὐδὲν ἐδόκει ("made no bones about it", tr. Norman). Cf. further Lib. *Or.* 1.134. Actually, as is explained in the note 25.7.9 *quinque regiones*, this was not the case: "doch scheint Šāpūr II. 363 letzlich zu einigen Zugeständnissen bereit gewesen zu sein" (Winter-Dignas, 2001, 158).

difficile hoc adeptus, ut Nisibis et Singara sine incolis transirent in iura Persarum The preceding *sine cunctatione tradidit* seems to contradict *difficile…adeptus*. Both statements, however, aim at damaging Jovian's reputation. He was too compliant in his dealings with Sapor, and it was difficult for him to obtain even a minor concession. Zon. 13.14.5, quoted ad §9 *cum castellis*, also relates that the Romans were allowed to remove the inhabitants of Nisibis and Singara. Zos. 3.31.1 only speaks of the Nisibenes, as do *Art. Pass.* 70 and Malalas *Chron.*

CHAPTER 7.12   241

13.336 (δοῦναι Ῥωμαίους Πέρσαις πᾶσαν τὴν ἐπαρχίαν τὴν λεγομένην Μυγδονίαν καὶ τὴν μητρόπολιν αὐτῆς τὴν λεγομένην Νιζτίβιος γυμνὴν σὺν τείχεσι μόνοις ἄνευ ἀνδρῶν τῶν οἰκούντων αὐτήν), the latter followed, with minor differences, by *Chron. Pasch.* a. 363. For Singara see the note ad 25.7.9 *cum castellis.* In 360 that city had been treated with less consideration. After it had been taken by the Persians the Roman garrison had been deported together with the inhabitants (20.6.7–8).

In V *ut* before *Nisibis* is missing. There are quite a few instances in V where a subjunctive is found in final and consecutive clauses not introduced by *ut.* Cf. Blomgren 158–9 and De Jonge ad 15.6.3 *causam enim,* who adduces i.a. the following examples: 20.5.9 *obsecravere Petulantes et Celtae, recturi, quas placuisset, provincias mitterentur* and 26.1.11 *effectum est, ad unum distinctumque exitum circumversio cursus annui revoluta nec vaga sit nec incerta.* However, the other two clauses depending on *adipisci* (27.9.8 and 28.5.2) are introduced by *ut,* so it seems preferable to follow G in this case, pace Fontaine n. 651. The omission in V can easily be explained by haplography. Both Baehrens, 1912, 349 and Pighi, 1935, 110 defend V's *transirent iura Persarum* as an instance of the accusative of direction, but 25.8.14 *constabat enim orbem eoum in dicionem potuisse transire Persidis* makes this unlikely. A comparable expression is HA *T* 30.3 (Zenobia) *vix denique ab Aureliano victa et triumphata concessit in iura Romana.*

a munimentis vero alienandis reverti ad nostra praesidia Romana permitterentur The *munimenta* are identical with the *castella quindecim* mentioned in section 9. The verb *alienare* is found only here. It is the t.t. for the conveyance of territories; TLL I 1564.41–8. Cf. Liv. 25.36.15 *exercitus amissi et alienata provincia et publica...clades.*

As Petschenig, 1892, 682 explains clearly, the transition from the cities to the forts, expressed by *vero,* emphasizes the different ways in which their inhabitants are treated. The citizens of Nisibis, Singara and, presumably, Castra Maurorum are free to leave, whereas only the Roman garrisons of the fifteen forts are allowed to withdraw to Roman territory. Zos. 3.31.1 reports explicitly that the *munimenta* had to be ceded to the Persians μετὰ τῶν οἰκητόρων καὶ κτημάτων καὶ ζῴων καὶ πάσης ἀποσκευῆς. For *ad nostra* cf. 20.4.4 *barbari militares saepe sub eiusmodi legibus assueti transire ad nostra* with the note, where the present passage should be added. For the use of infinitives after *permittere* see the note ad 24.1.14 *inflammari permisit.*

quibus exitiale aliud accessit et impium What Amm. says about the status **7.12** of Armenia as a result of the peace of 363 is, as Seager, 1996, 275–6

242 COMMENTARY

rightly observes, "manifestly not a statement of the content of a clause of the treaty, but rather a highly emotional comment on a clause the terms of which he unfortunately does not see fit to reproduce". It is rather difficult to reconstruct what precisely was agreed between Sapor and Jovian (see, apart from Seager, Chrysos, 1976, 32–6, Blockley, 1984, 36–7, Blockley, 1992, 28–9 and Chrysos, 1993, 182–3), the more so because the other sources are not very useful. Zosimus alleges that the Persians received the greater part of Armenia, while they conceded only a small part to the Romans (Προσαφείλοντο δὲ καὶ Ἀρμενίας τὸ πολὺ μέρος οἱ Πέρσαι, βραχύ τι ταύτης Ῥωμαίοις ἔχειν ἐνδόντες, 3.31.2), but, as Paschoud n. 91 points out, he apparently confuses the situation of 363 with that of a quarter of a century later. Libanius' lapidary statement in *Or.* 24.9 that Ἀρμενία πᾶσα was surrendered (cf. *Or.* 1.134), is also evidently anachronistic (so rightly Wirth, 1984, 366). Only in the *Epic Histories* attributed to P'awstos Buzand we find a passage which offers a parallel to Amm.'s words (see the next note). The clause pertaining to Arsaces is *exitiale* in that it offered the Persians later (*postea*) the opportunity to seize a considerable part of Armenia; it is *impium* in the sense that the Romans promise to betray a loyal ally. The consequences are spelled out chiastically in the last sentence of this section.

ne...Arsaci poscenti contra Persas ferretur auxilium, amico nobis semper et fido In 20.11.1, q.v., the first mention of Arsaces in the extant books, the king is called upon *ut nobis amicus esse perseveraretet fidus.* In 21.6.8 Constantius sends him precious gifts, to assure his loyalty towards Rome. At the beginning of the Persian campaign, Julian asks Arsaces to await his orders (23.2.2), which are detailed in 23.3.5. In 24.7.8, q.v., we are told that Arsaces, together with Sebastianus and Procopius fails to turn up in time to bring assistance to Julian's main force, for reasons probably explained in the lacuna in 24.7.3, for which see the note ad *hinc opulenta.* The last time Arsaces was mentioned was in 24.8.6.

quod ratione gemina cogitatum est For the expression cf. 31.3.8 (after lengthy deliberations a majority of the Goths decided to settle in Thrace): *cogitavit Thraciae receptaculum gemina ratione sibi conveniens.*

ut puniretur homo, qui Chiliocomum mandatu vastaverat principis The order had been given by Julian, who told Arsaces, Sebastianus and Procopius to join him in Assyria *per Corduenam et Moxoenam Chiliocomo*

CHAPTER 7.12   243

uberi Mediae tractu partibusque aliis praestricto cursu vastatis (23.3.5, q.v.). *Homo* seems to be used here "anaphorice vel demonstrative" (TLL VI 2882.14), without any connotation of scorn or contempt, as is so often the case, also in Amm., e.g. 22.14.3 (Julian) *ridebatur enim ut Cercops homo brevis umeros extentans angustos* or 27.3.5 (Lampadius) *homo indignanter admodum sustinens, si, etiam cum spueret, non laudaretur.*

et remaneret occasio, per quam subinde licenter invaderetur Armenia The regular meaning of *subinde* in Amm. is 'repeatedly'. Here, however, it is used in the sense of 'in the future', 'from then on', as in 16.7.7. It is used in a comparable context in 21.3.4, where Constantius writes to king Vadomar *ut tamquam rupto concordiae pacto subinde collimitia sibi vicina vexaret.* There, as here, the breach of friendly relations with the Romans, real or pretended, results in a different pattern of behaviour for the future. For that reason the paraphrase given ad loc., viz. 'from time to time' should be corrected. The following *postea* refers to the precise moment when the Persians took the opportunity to attack Arsaces. For Amm.'s frequent use of *licenter / licentius* 'at will', see the note ad 20.10.2 *inquietorum hominum.* Amm. returns to the Armenian question in 26.4.6 (*Persarum rex manus Armeniis iniectabat eos in suam dicionem ex integro vocare vi nimia properans)* and 27.12.1 (*Rex vero Persidis, longaevus ille Sapor…iniectabat Armeniae manum, ut eam…dicioni iungeret suae*), when discussing the years 365 and 368, respectively. See on this the literature cited above. Incidentally, Amm.'s words in 26.4.6 and 27.12.1 clearly show, that Zosimus and Libanius are wrong in stating that already in 363 the greater part, or even all, of Armenia was surrendered to the Persians. At the time Armenia must still have been at least nominally an autonomous kingdom, independent from both Rome and Persia. More to the point seems Ps. P'awstos Buzand 4.21: "And I (sc. Jovian) am withdrawing from the middle country of Armenia. If you will be able to overcome and subject them, I shall not support them" (tr. Greenwood, quoted in Greatrex-Lieu, 2002, 5), which is more or less what Amm. says here ("this is one of the rare points at which Armenian and classical sources explicitly confirm each other", Garsoïan, 1989, 292 n. 5). It amounts to the concession on the part of Jovian to abstain from military intervention in Armenia, even if Persia should invade the country.

unde postea contigit, ut vivus caperetur idem Arsáces As Clark observes in the preface to his edition, p. vii, "Graeca vocabula fere ubique

244 COMMENTARY

Graecum retinent accentum." Cf. e.g. 17.7.11 *sýringas appellámus* and 25.10.1 *Antióchiam vénimus.* The story of Arsaces' capture and execution is told in 27.12.3. For anaphoric *idem* see the note ad 20.4.5 *cum isdem.*

et Armeniae maximum latus Medis conterminans et Artaxata inter dissensiones et turbamenta raperent Parthi The collocation of *dissensiones et turbamenta* is not found elsewhere. *Dissensio* is as common as *turbamentum* is rare. Amm. probably found it in Sal. *Hist. 1.55.25 turbamenta rei publicae atque exitia* and/or Tac. *Hist.* 1.23.1 *quaeque alia turbamenta volgi.* See also 26.7.8 *in publicis turbamentis.* In Amm.'s account of the struggle over Armenia in 27.12 Artaxata is not mentioned. This city, modern Artašat, on the left bank of the Araxes some thirty kilometers south-east of Erivan, was the ancient capital of Armenia, founded according to the tradition by the Armenian Artaxas on Hannibal's advice (Str. 11.14.6, 528–9C, Plut. *Luc.* 31.3). For Amm.'s use of *Parth*i instead of *Persae* see the note ad 23.3.2.

7.13 *Quo ignobili decreto firmato* It is not the first time that Amm. expresses his indignation concerning the peace of 363 (cf. 25.7.10), nor the last (cf. 25.9.7–8, 27.12.1), but the way in which he expresses himself here is especially revealing. Before speaking of *pax*, as in the next section, he calls the treaty between Sapor and Jovian a *decretum*, i.e. a formal decision of a magistrate (for which cf. e.g. 22.5.2 *planis absolutisque decretis* with the note), seemingly in an effort to lay the blame for this despicable (*ignobili*) peace wholly on Jovian. The choice of the adjective *ignobilis* is also most unusual. The only real parallels quoted in the TLL are Eutr. 4.17.1 *Q. Pompeius deinde consul, a Numantinis...superatus, pacem ignobilem fecit* and 10.17.1 (Jovian) *pacem cum Sapore, necessariam quidem, sed ignobilem, fecit.* Although Eutropius, like Amm., calls the peace despicable, he adds that Jovian had no other choice but to accept its terms. This is definitely not Amm.'s opinion (cf. 25.7.10 *et cum pugnari deciens expediret, ne horum quidquam dederetur*), but we do find Eutropius' point of view expressed in some other sources: Socr. *HE* 3.22.6 αἱ συνθῆκαι δὲ πρὸς μὲν τὴν δόξαν Ῥωμαίων ἦσαν ἀπρεπεῖς, πρὸς δὲ τὸν καιρὸν ἀναγκαῖαι, Oros. *hist.* 7.31 *foedus cum Sapore Persarum rege etsi parum putant dignum, satis tamen necessarium pepigit*; cf. also Zon. 13.14.4. Note, however, the fine distinction. While the pagan Eutropius says that he found the peace *necessariam quidem, sed ignobilem*, the Christian authors just quoted reverse the order ('unbecoming, but necessary'), which is without question a milder way of putting it

CHAPTER 7.13   245

(Turcan, 1966, 885). Their presentation is in accordance with the overall image of the Christian Jovian in most Christian sources: he has a priori more goodwill than his pagan predecessor. Greg. Naz. *Or.* 5.15, for example, deems the conditions of the peace treaty to be as scandalous and unworthy of Rome's strength as does Amm. (συνθήκαις...αἰσχραῖς τε καὶ ἀναξίαις τῆς Ῥωμαίων χειρός), but he does not blame Jovian, for, according to him, it was all Julian's fault. Soz. *HE* 6.3.2 tries to whitewash Jovian in another way. He refrains from commenting on the merits of the peace treaty, and merely states that the emperor was compelled by necessity to come to terms with the Persians: ἀναγκαῖον εἶδεν εἰς συμβάσεις ἐλθεῖν. Likewise Hier. *Chron.* a. 364: *rerum necessitate compulsus.* However, while more often than not an author's religion has a bearing on the way he views Jovian's agreement with Sapor, this is not always the case. The Christian historian Agathias, for instance, is rather severe in his judgment. Although pleading Jovian's difficult position in a strange and hostile country in mitigation, he does not withhold criticism and calls the truce shameful, outrageous and still in his own time (i.e. in the sixth century) detrimental to the Roman state: ξυνθήκας...ἀγεννεῖς καὶ ἀσχήμονας καὶ ὁποίας μέχρι καὶ νῦν τῇ Ῥωμαίων λυμαίνεσθαι πολιτείᾳ (4.25.7). The pagan Themistius on the other hand was able to see the treaty in a favourable light (*Or.* 5.69 b) and argued that it brought economic profits (*Or.* 8.114 c).

The reason for Amm. to call the peace despicable is twofold. There is on the one hand the fact that Rome for the first time since time immemorial ceded territory to a foreign state: *numquam enim ab urbis ortu inveniri potest annalibus replicatis, ut arbitror, terrarum pars ulla nostrarum ab imperatore vel consule hosti concessa* (25.9.9). This is also the implicit criticism of the greater part of the ancient authors just quoted and it is explicitly stressed by Eutr. 10.17.2–3, Ruf. Fest. 29.2 and Zos. 3.32 (cf. the note ad 25.9.9 *numquam enim*). But perhaps even more objectionable in Amm.'s eyes was Jovian's haste to retreat from hostile territory because of his fear of potential usurpers. Amm. refers to this fear for the first time in 25.7.10 (*adulatorum globus instabat timido principi Procopii metuendum subserens nomen eumque affirmans...novas res nullo renitente facile moliturum*), but returns to it time and again (cf. 25.8.9 *quod magis metuebatur*, 25.9.2 *alia metuens* and 25.9.8 *extimescit aemulum potestatis*). Parallels for this are found in Eutr. 10.17.3 and Ruf. Fest. 29.2, quoted in the note ad 25.9.8 *dum extimescit.*

As we have seen, the greater part of the ancient sources for the peace of 363, pagan and Christian alike, describe its terms

246   COMMENTARY

as disgraceful. On this point they are in agreement with Amm.,
although only a few share Amm.'s view that Jovian was to blame for
his haste to sign a peace treaty because he feared rivals to the throne.
Some authors put forward extenuating circumstances and say that
the newly chosen emperor had no other choice. Libanius maintains
that Jovian's decision to accept an unfavourable peace was forced
upon him by the gods (καταναγκασθῆναι, *Or.* 24.9). This, however,
should by no means be understood as an excuse, since it is the direct
consequence of the anger of the gods which Jovian had incurred.
Amm. is the only author who explicitly states that Jovian would have
done better to fight ten battles than give up any of the territories
actually ceded (25.7.10). Incidentally, he nowhere says that Jovian's
religious conviction had anything to do with his behaviour during
the peace negotiations.

   In modern scholarly literature the settlement of 363 has often
been condemned as "schmählich" (Seeck, 1923[4], 364), "déshono-
rant" (Piganiol-Chastagnol, 1972[2], 163), "humiliating and expensive" (Ferrill, 1986, 56). Jovian's reign, writes Marié, 1989, 179, "a
laissé comme seul souvenir la honteuse paix conclue pour trente ans
avec la Perse". This is hardly fair. Jovian, as e.g. Wirth, 1984, 358–61
and Winter-Dignas, 2001, 159–60 argue, deserves more understanding. Under the circumstances he accomplished all that was possible.
Moreover, the peace of 363 created for a long period a 'balance of
power' on the eastern frontier, disturbed only by troubles in Armenia.

ne quid committeretur per indutias contrarium pactis During the truce the
terms of the treaty, such as the handing over of Nisibis, wil have to be
put into effect. Thus the *indutiae* (see on this term the note ad 25.2.1
post quae) seem to be a transition period between the hostilities and
a true peace. *Per indutias* is found in classical historians, e.g. Sal. *Cat.*
51.6 *quom saepe Carthaginienses et in pace et per indutias multa nefaria
facinora fecissent* and Liv. 38.2.14 *per indutias sepeliendi caesos potestas
facta est.* In Amm. there are six instances of the expression, one of
them metaphorical: 14.11.17 *per indutias naturae conquiescentis.* For
contrarium pactis cf. 26.1.6 *ne quid nouaretur contrarium placitis.*

   According to Zos. 3.31.2 the peace treaty was ratified in writing, which seems quite plausible. He adds that there were certain clauses in the agreement which granted the Romans a safe
retreat: ἐπὶ τούτοις αἱ σπονδαὶ γεγονυῖαι καὶ γραμματίοις ἑκατέρωθεν
ἐπισφραγισθεῖσαι δεδώκασι Ῥωμαίοις εὐρυχωρίαν τῆς οἴκαδε ἐπανόδου,
κατὰ μηδὲν τὰ Περσῶν διαφθείρουσιν ὅρια, μήτε αὐτοῖς ὑπὸ Περσικῆς
ἐπιβουλευομένοις ἐνέδρας. See on this the note ad 25.8.4 *a conatu.*

CHAPTER 7.13 247

obsidatus specie viri celebres altrinsecus dantur The noun *obsidatus* occurs only in Amm., who has – *sorte* in 17.12.16 and 18.6.20, – *pignore* in 16.12.25 and 17.12.21. *Specie* suggests that the dignitaries mentioned did not have the formal status of hostages, but that their presence was meant to ensure that the terms of the treaty were kept. Amm. does not use *celeber* of persons elsewhere; it is altogether rare, e.g. Celsus 7 pr. *Gorgias quoque et Sostratus et Heron et Apollonii duo et Ammonius Alexandrinus, multique alii celebres viri, singuli quaedam repererunt.* As to *altrinsecus* ('on both sides'; cf. the note ad 20.7.11), this word and the explanation which follows (*Nemota...non obscuri*) clearly indicate that an exchange took place. It is a feature of a new pattern in the history of diplomatic relations between Rome and the rest of the world. In earlier periods Rome took hostages, she did not give them. See on this Lee, 1991.

Nemota et Victor ex parte nostrorum et Bellovaedius, insignium numerorum tribuni The tribunes Nemota (*PLRE* I, Nemota), Victor (*PLRE* I, Victor 3) and Bellovaedius (*PLRE* I, Bellovaedius) are not mentioned in any other source, and the names Nemota and Bellovaedius are actually totally unknown. This, plus the fact that on the Roman side there were three, on the Persian side four hostages (who, moreover, were higher in rank than their Roman colleagues) has raised doubts about the soundness of the text – although Seyfarth in his bilingual edition acknowledged the issue (1986[3], 252 n. 107), he printed in the Teubneriana the text as given here.

Some scholars tried to solve at least one of the problems by assuming, in the wake of Heraeus, a lacuna behind *Nemota* in which the name of the fourth Roman hostage could have been written (so e.g. Rolfe). However, in that case the discrepancy between the rank of the Roman *tribuni* on the one hand and of the Persian *optimates* on the other still remains. Now, Gelenius has *Nevita* instead of V's *Nemota*. If this indeed was what Gelenius found in the Hersfeldensis, and if we read *Nevitta et Victor ex parte nostrorum, et ⟨NN⟩ et Bellovaedius, insignium numerorum tribuni*, another problem would be solved: Nevitta, a former consul (21.10.8, q.v.) and Victor (*PLRE* I, Victor 4, magister equitum, presumably, not *PLRE* I, Victor 3, a tribune; note that Nevitta and the magister equitum Victor both in 24.1.2 and 24.4.13 are mentioned in one and the same section) were certainly equal in rank to the Persian noble Bineses cum suis.

The reading *Nevitta* instead of *Nemota* seems quite plausible (it is defended by Fontaine n. 654 and accepted by e.g. Paschoud n. 92 and Greatrex-Lieu, 2002, 248 n. 13). What about *Bellovaedius*? This

248   COMMENTARY

name is not certain either. V has *bello vae clius*, E *bellovedius*, SBA *Bel-
lonedius*. Fontaine ingeniously proposed to read *bello incliti* (*Nevitta
et Victor ex parte nostrorum, et bello incliti insignium numerorum tribuni*),
which has the advantage that one does not have to assume a lacuna
behind Nevitta. But in all probability Gelenius' *Mellobaudes* is also
taken from the Hersfeldensis and should be regarded as the correct reading. It is true that *PLRE* I has no entry for Mellobaudes,
but Merobaudes and Mallobaudes are common names. For *numerus*
see the note ad 20.1.3, for *tribunus* ad 23.3.9 and 24.3.1 *paucissimos*.

*ex parte vero diversa Bineses e numero nobilium optimatum tresque alii
satrapae non obscuri* We meet Bineses again in 25.9.1, where Amm.
relates his raising of the Persian flag on the citadel of Nisibis. He
should have been mentioned in *PLRE* I, as Baldwin, 1976, 119 rightly
notes. According to Justi, 1895, 68 the Persian means: "a man who
wields a far-reaching lance". Malalas *Chron.* 13.336 and *Chron. Pasch.*
a. 363 are in accordance with Amm.'s statement in the present text
in calling Bineses a σατράπης – they call him Iunius (Ἰούνιος), while
Ephrem says he was a 'Magian' (*HcJul.* 3.1). For *optimas* see ad 20.6.3
per optimates and 21.13.4 *praeter optimates*. There is a note on *satrapa*
ad 25.3.13 *quinquaginta*.

7.14   *foederata itaque pace annorum triginta* For the wording see the notes
ad 24.2.21 *pace foederata* (add to the parallels quoted there 26.4.6
post Iouiani excessum, cum quo foedera firmarat et pacem) and 25.8.4
post firmatam pacem et foedera. Zosimus confirms that the peace was
made for thirty years: αὐτοῖς πρὸς ἀλλήλους ἐγίνοντο μὲν τριακοντούτεις
σπονδαί (3.31.1), as do Socr. *HE* 4.2.4, Soz. *HE* 6.7.10, Thdt. *HE*
4.2.3 and Philost. *HE* 8.1. Curiously, Rufin. *hist.* 11.1 speaks of
29 years: *in viginti et novem annos pace composita*. It is i.a. with reference to the time span that Amm. describes Sapor's invasion of
Armenia in 365 as unjust in 26.4.6: *Persarum rex manus Armeniis
iniectabat…sed iniuste, causando, quod post Iouiani excessum, cum quo
foedera firmarat et pacem, nihil obstare debebit, quo minus* eqs. (cf. 27.12.1
calcata fide sub Iouiano pactorum). According to Ps. Joshua the Stylite
(*Chron.* 7) a special clause of the treaty of 363 pertained to Nisibis: the city would be handed over to the Persians for only one
hundred and twenty years and would revert to Rome after that.
The *Julian Romance* (220.23–4) has a similar version, but speaks
of a period of a hundred years. The historicity of these statements
in Syriac is, pace Lieu, 1989², 96 and Chrysos, 1993, 186–8, more

CHAPTER 7.14 249

than doubtful. Cf. in the first place Luther, 1997, 99–101 and see further e.g. Blockley, 1992, 29 and Winter-Dignas, 2001, 158–9.

"The introduction of a time span for the treaty...appears to have been an innovation" (Blockley, 1992, 29; cf. Chrysos, 1976, 30). Some see the agreement between Sapor and Jovian as an advantage for the Persians, who could consolidate their gains during the thirty years period (so Blockley, ibid.). Others believe that "es Jovian trotz der hoffnungslosen Lage, in der er sich befand, gelungen ist, die Gültigkeitsdauer des abzuschließenden Vertrages zu beschränken, was, wenn auch zunächst ohne handfeste Folgen, für die Römer vorteilhaft war" (Chrysos, 1993, 187). Perhaps the truth lies somewhere in the middle. As Schulz, 1993, 102 argues, the time span betrays the fact that the agreement was a compromise.

For the presumably fictitious story about a clause in the treaty concerning the fortification of the Caspian Gates see the note ad 25.7.9 *quinque regiones*. The contention of Marié, 1989, 180 that in the treaty it was i.a. stipulated that the Romans had to pay "une indemnité de guerre" is not supported by the sources. Von Gall, 1990, 56–9 argues, perhaps rightly, that the so-called Sapor-cameo in the Parisian Bibliothèque Nationale (see pl. 9 in Winter-Dignas, 2001, 100) does not, as is commonly thought, represent Sapor I and Valerian, but refers to the treaty between Sapor II and Jovian.

eaque iuris iurandi religionibus consecrata For *iuris iurandi religio* see the note ad 25.9.4, where the remark is made that *religio* expresses the sacred character of the oath and therefore the impossibility of transgressing it. We find the confirmation of agreements with oaths not only in cases of an apparently oral character (cf. 17.1.13, 17.10.7, 17.12.21 and 30.3.5), but also when written documents were involved, as in the cases described by Procop. *Vand.* 2.11.4, *Goth.* 1.6.26, 2.25.21, 3.9.20 and, seemingly, in the present case (cf. the note ad § 13 *ne quid*). See on this Lee, 1993, 36 and for the Byzantine period in general Miller, 1971, 71–5. Time and again (cf. 25.9.2, 4, 8) Amm. makes Jovian insist that his oath prevents him from doing anything for the Nisibenes, whose misery is lamented in 25.8.13–4 and 25.9. It is difficult to imagine how Jovian could have acted differently. Still, Amm. refuses to accept this justification of Jovian's conduct, and suggests that the emperor's real motive was his wish to consolidate his power. See for this the note ad 25.9.2 *sed ventis*.

reversi itineribus aliis The word *aliis* must be seen in relation to what is said in § 8: instead of heading for Corduene, as Amm. would have

250   COMMENTARY

liked, Jovian chose to return by another route (which first of all meant that the Tigris had to be crossed, 25.8.2).

quoniam loca contigua flumini ut confragosa vitabantur et aspera, potus inopia premebamur et cibi Chapter 7 ends in a minor key. Referring to things to come Amm. stresses the fact that, though the peace treaty was signed, the army's acute hardship was not over. Since the route chosen by Jovian avoided the terrain near the Tigris because it was rough and uneven, the soldiers on their way to Ur (25.8.7) via Hatra (25.8.5) had to march through dry regions with hardly any water and almost nothing to eat (25.8.6), so that once again (cf. 25.4.4, 25.7.4 and 25.7.7 with the notes), the whole army, Amm. himself included (*premebamur*), suffered from lack of food and drink. On the route taken by the army see section 4 of the next chapter. The adjective *confragosus* ('rough') is a favourite of Livy. Amm. uses it four times, once in a metaphorical sense: 28.1.39 *quod in variis et confragosis actibus vitae plerumque contingit.*

CHAPTER 8

Introduction

Various subjects are dealt with in this chapter, which may be typified as slightly incoherent. The thread running through the chapter is the army's march to Nisibis from Dura, where it had stayed while the peace negotiations with the Persians, described in chapter 7, were going on. The army's arrival in Dura had been mentioned in 25.6.9. Unfortunately, Ammianus only gives a few indications about the route the army took to reach Nisibis, so that an exact reconstruction is not possible. Also, the time it took the army to march from Dura to Nisibis can only be guessed at. As in the previous chapter, Ammianus emphasizes the army's lack of provisions and the threat of starvation; even the peace treaty with the Persians had not put an end to the hardships the Roman army suffered. Another important topic concerns Jovian's efforts to secure his authority.

The chapter opens with the crossing of the Tigris by the entire army (§ 1–3). After an attempt by the Persians to harass the retreating Roman army by also crossing the Tigris had been thwarted (§ 4), the Romans managed with swift and forced marches – Ammianus does not mention how many – to reach Hatra (§ 5). There followed a six-day march to Ur through a barren plain where no water and food were available; water had to be brought along, and camels and pack-animals had to be slaughtered to feed the soldiers (§ 6). At Ur new provisions were supplied by Cassianus, the *dux Mesopotamiae*, and the tribune Mauricius; however, these provisions brought only a temporary relief (§ 7). At this point Ammianus interrupts his account of the march to report that Jovian sent the *notarius* Procopius and the tribune Memoridus to Illyricum and Gaul to announce the death of Julian and to give instructions to Lucillianus, the emperor's father-in-law. Jovian assigned Lucillianus to attend to possible difficulties in connection with the change over of power and to replace officials who had supported Julian by those loyal to Jovian. Moreover, the messengers were ordered to present the conclusion of the Persian campaign as a success (§ 8–12). Before returning to the army's march, Ammianus relates that a rumour had reached Nisibis that the city was to be surrendered to Sapor (§ 13–14). From Ur the army, still afflicted by hunger (§ 15), marched via Thilsaphata –

252   COMMENTARY

where it was joined by the generals Sebastianus and Procopius, who
had been commissioned by Julian to defend Mesopotamia (§16)
– to Nisibis. Jovian pitched camp outside the walls and refused to
enter the city (§17). The chapter ends (§18) with an elaborate
account of the liquidation of the *notarius* Iovianus, who after Julian's
death had been mentioned as a possible successor to the throne, and
was therefore considered by Jovian as a threat to his position. This
ruthless liquidation of his namesake, as well as the measures taken by
Jovian to gain support in the West, demonstrates the determination
of the new emperor to consolidate his power.

8.1 *pax specie humanitatis indulta* According to Amm. feigned feelings
of humanity, as referred to in 25.7.6, induced Sapor to allow what
was left of the Roman army to return home (see for the different
meanings of *species* in Amm. De Jonge ad 17.4.7 *specie quadrata* and
18.2.2 *legationis specie*). Greg. Naz. *Or.* 5.15 is less sceptical about
the Persian humanity: εἰ μὲν οὖν μὴ Πέρσαι...εἰς συμβάσεις ἐτράποντο,
καὶ ταύτας ἀδοκήτους οὕτω καὶ φιλανθρώπους, 'if the Persians had
not chosen to negotiate peace, and that on such unexpectedly
humane terms' (the defeat of the Roman army would have been
total). Rufin. *hist.* 11.1 reports that envoys, sent by the Persians to
negotiate peace, promised to sell food and other provisions to the
Roman army: *subito emissos a barbaris oratores adesse vident pacemque
deposcere, exercitui quoque inedia consumpto cibos ceteraque necessaria in
mercimoniis polliceri omnique humanitate nostrorum temeritatem emendare*
("they [the Romans] suddenly saw envoys approaching from the
barbarians who sued for peace, who promised to sell food and other
provisions to the army, which was prostrate from famine, and who
with unbounded kindness corrected the rashness of our people"; tr.
Amidon). Rufinus ascribes the Persian kindness towards the starving
Roman soldiers to God's mercy. Thdt. *HE* 4.2.2 also states that Sapor,
when informed about Jovian's accession, sent envoys to negotiate
peace and despatched provisions for the Roman troops: εἶτα τροφὰς
τοῖς στρατιώταις ἐξέπεμψε, καὶ ἀγορὰν αὐτοῖς ἐν τῇ ἐρήμῳ γενέσθαι
προσέταξε. However, as Paschoud n. 92 observes, it is unlikely that the
Persians provided the Roman army with food; presumably Rufinus
and Theodoret represent a hagiographical tradition favourable to
Jovian.

The only quotation from Amm. in Antiquity concerns the form
indultus as perfect participle of *indulgere*: Prisc. *gramm* II.487.1: *ut
indulsi indulsum vel indultum, unde Marcellinus rerum gestarum XIV
tamquam licentia crudelitati indulta* (14.1.4).

CHAPTER 8.1   253

fame ad usque spiritum lacerati postremum The phrase *ad usque spiritum postremum* is unique. Amm. may have been inspired by expressions like Cic. *Ver.* 5.118 *filiorum suorum postremum spiritum ore excipere* and *Pan.* 2.36.2 *postremum spiritum in admiratione nominis tui...fundebant*; TLL X 2.214.61–2. *Lacerare fame* is found already in Pac. *trag.* 158 *te...lacerabo fame* and in Ov. *Met.* 8.784 *pestifera lacerare Fame*, where Fames is personified.

latenter progressi The threat of starvation had apparently driven some soldiers to leave the main body of the army in order to find a way to reach Roman territory on their own initiative by crossing the river Tigris. *Latenter* occurs in two isolated instances from the classical period (Cic. *Top.* 63, Ov. *Pont.* 3.6.60). Only Apuleius and Ammianus use it frequently (10 and 18 times respectively).

gurgite fluminis absorbebantur Harmon 185–6 discusses cases like this, where the possibility of a one-word clausula (*ábsorbebántur*) must be taken into consideration. He argues that Amm. avoided such endings, and interprets the rare instances as the result of textual corruption. In the present case he proposes to read *flúminis sorbebántur*, which would result in a normal cursus velox. He compares 18.7.5 *fluminibus mersi sorbentur*. V's *adorbibantur*, however, definitely suggests a derivational compound, and there is a parallel for *absorbere* in 17.7.13: (qui) *terrarum partes absorbent*. Consequently, it seems wisest to accept the slight irregularity.

rapti a Saracenis vel Persis, quos, ut diximus paulo ante, exturbavere Germani Amm. had reported in 25.6.13–4, q.v., and 25.7.3 that 500 experienced swimmers from northern regions had crossed the Tigris and killed a considerable number of Persians who were posted on the opposite riverbank. The wording here rather suggests that these soldiers had driven all the Persians away, which is evidently not the case. For Saracens see the note ad 25.6.8 and the references there. *Persae* is Amm.'s general designation for the inhabitants of the Sasanid Empire; see the note ad 23.3.2 *Parthos*.

longius amendati sunt venundandi TLL I 1880.12 states that from the fourth century onward *amendare* takes the meaning 'to hide'. That meaning is indeed found in Amm., e.g. in 17.7.2 *amendato solis splendore nec contigua vel apposita cernebantur*. Here, however, as in 16.12.15 *barbari longius amendati* and 30.10.3 *Sebastianum...longius amendavit*, the verb has its original meaning 'to send away'. For the

254   COMMENTARY

gerundive *venundandi* used as a part. fut. pass. see the note ad 20.2.4 *opitulari.*

8.2 *ubi vero transeundi amnis aperte signum dedere bucinae concrepantes* In contrast to what Amm. had reported in the previous paragraph, in this and the following sections he describes the 'official' crossing of the Tigris by the Roman army, the contrast being marked by the opposition *latenter – aperte.* Amm. shows a special interest in the crossing of great rivers; see 16.11.9, 12.57, 17.13.15, 24.6.7, 25.6.14, 30.1.8–9, 31.4.5, 5.3. For the role of the *bucina* and other musical instruments in the army see the notes ad 20.7.6 *hinc inde,* 24.4.14 *clangore Martio* and 24.5.9 *sed ubi.* The sound of the *bucina* wakes the soldiers and signals the beginning of special manoeuvres, as here.

immane quo quantoque ardore Cf. i.a. 15.8.15 *immane quo quantoque gaudio* and 25.3.10 *incredibile dictu est, quo quantoque ardore* and 30.3.4 *immane quo quantoque flatu.* Wirz, 1887, 632 points to Sal. *Hist.* 2.44 *immane quantum animi exarsere* as the model for this expression. Cf. also Tac. *Hist.* 3.62.1 *et Flavianus exercitus immane quantum ⟨aucto⟩ animo exitium Valentis ut finem belli accepit.* See the note ad 23.6.78.

temere rapiendo momenta periculorum The reading *temere* is practically certain, as it is close to V and suits the context perfectly. For the sentence as a whole cf. 18.7.7 *inter rapienda momenta periculorum communium.* In his note ad loc. De Jonge argues convincingly that in this phrase *momentum* has the meaning 'shift', 'change', for which see TLL VIII 1393.79sqq. *Momenta periculorum* would then be an instance of the gen. inversus 'the (swiftly) changing dangers'. This seems to be totally Amm.'s own phrase. Probably more common expressions like *momento fortunae* and *momento rerum* provided the basis for this idiomatic development.

semet quisque reliquis omnibus anteponens "Alius alium occupans, retrudens" (Wagner). This is another proof that the discipline of the army was crumbling, cf. the note ad 25.6.12 *ne se.*

ratibus Cf. 14.2.10 *contextis ratibus* used by the Isaurians to cross the river Melas. Amm. uses the word *ratis* again in 31.4.5 and 31.5.3 in his description of the crossing of the Danube by the Thervingi and Greuthingi.

CHAPTER 8.3 255

iumenta retinentes hinc inde natantia For *hinc inde* see the note ad 25.6.12 *hostiles manus.* Here it is best taken as 'left and right'. The soldiers, sitting or lying on their improvised rafts, hold their horses by the reins and use them as outboard motors.

utribus For *utres,* leather bags or bladders filled with air or hay, see the note ad 24.3.11 *constratis ponticulis.*

diversa...versantes Apart from rafts, horses, inflated bladders or bags and shields (16.11.9, 12.57, 24.6.7, q.v.) were used to cross rivers. In 30.1.9 Amm. relates that bladders functioned as a support for beds on which the Euphrates was crossed. For *versare* 'to ponder' cf. e.g. Verg. *A.* 11.550–1 *omnia secum / versanti subito vix haec sententia sedit.*

in necessitatis abrupto The same expression is found in 30.1.8. In 16.18.6 Amm. writes *in abrupto necessitatis.*

obliquis meatibus penetrabant See the note ad 24.2.8 *equites vero* and for *penetrare* ad 21.13.2 *nam si.*

imperator ipse brevibus lembis, quos post exustam classem docuimus reman- **8.3** *sisse, cum paucis transvectus* The order seems to be that the emperor crossed first, together with a small retinue (*cum paucis*). After him 'all of us', probably meaning 'the rest of the staff', went across (*dum omnes conveheremur*). Finally all the soldiers (*universi*) reached the opposite bank of the Tigris. The *breves lembi* are identical to the twelve *naves minores* that survived the burning of the fleet; see the note ad 24.7.5 *duodecim tantummodo.*

ultro citroque discurrere For the expression see the note ad 25.6.1 *Quae dum.*

dum omnes conveheremur Note that Amm.'s personal involvement in the events, as shown by his use of the first person plural, comes again to the fore in the context of a river-crossing. For Amm.'s special interest in naval matters see the note ad 24.6.1 *Ventum est.*

universi praeter mersos ad ulteriores venimus margines Brok detects a note of bitter sarcasm in the words *praeter mersos.* This does not sit well with the gratitude for the escape from danger expressed in the words that follow, so that it is better to take *praeter mersos* as a strictly

256 COMMENTARY

factual observation. Fontaine n. 659 seems unaware that Brok had noticed the surprising juxtaposition *universi praeter mersos* ("il est, en tout cas, curieux que les éditeurs n'aient jamais été intrigués par cette singularité du texte"). He rightly rejects any irreverent interpretation. However, his tentative explanation, that Amm. intimates that those who had drowned did not deserve the *favor superi numinis* is far from convincing. It is difficult to imagine that Amm. would have expressed an idea of such grave implications in so casual a manner. For the plural *margines* see the note ad 25.6.12 *hostiles manus.*

favore superi numinis Amm. uses *numen* in a henotheistic way, often adding adjectives such as *magnum, supernum, superum, summum, perpetuum* and *sempiternum*; Camus, 1967, 134–6; Rike, 1987, 31–4.

discrimine per difficiles casus extracti For *extrahere* in the meaning *liberare* see the note ad 17.13.12 *extractae*. Amm. uses the verb always with a separative abl. For other constructions (prep. phrases with *a* and *ex* or dative) see TLL V 2.2069.72–84.

8.4 *Dum nos pendentium aerumnarum opprimit timor* Those scholars who defend V's *pendentium* do so on the ground that the use of simplex pro composito is a typical feature of Late Latin. This is undoubtedly correct, but the individual *usus* of Amm. should be decisive. As it happens, he never writes *pendere* in the sense of *impendere*, whereas *impendere* referring to future dangers is found no fewer than sixteen times. See the note ad 20.8.15 *ne…desperatione* and cf. e.g. 29.5.54 *impendentis aerumnae terrore*. For *aerumna* see the note ad 20.7.7. The soldiers may have felt relieved after the perilous crossing of the Tigris, but they know they are far from safe. They have a long way to go before reaching friendly territory and food is still desperately short.

procursatorum For *procursatores* see the note ad 23.3.4 *agmina et commeatus* and cf. Lee, 1993, 171. Amm.'s information differs slightly from that of Zosimus. Whereas Amm. reports in this section that the Persians intended to attack the Romans after the conclusion of the treaty, but had to give up this plan, Zosimus tells us that according to the truce the Romans were allowed to march home and would not be harassed anymore by the Persians; Zos. 3.31.2 ἐπὶ τούτοις αἱ σπονδαὶ γεγονυῖαι καὶ γραμματίοις ἑκατέρωθεν ἐπισφραγισθεῖσαι δεδώκασι Ῥωμαίοις εὐρυχωρίαν τῆς οἴκαδε ἐπανόδου, κατὰ μηδὲν τὰ Περσῶν διαφθείρουσιν ὅρια, μήτε αὐτοῖς ὑπὸ Περσικῆς ἐπιβουλευομένοις ἐνέδρας ('The truce, concluded on these terms and confirmed by contracts on

CHAPTER 8.5   257

both sides, allowed the Romans to march home, provided that they
would destroy nothing in Persian territory, as they would not be the
victims of Persian ambush'). Zos. 3.33.1 reports that Jovian, although
the Roman army could march safely, lost many men on his return
to Roman territory because of the difficulty of the terrain and the
lack of water: Τῆς δὲ πρὸς Πέρσας γενομένης εἰρήνης ὃν διεξήλθομεν
τρόπον, Ἰοβιανὸς ὁ βασιλεὺς μετὰ ἀδείας ἐπανιὼν ἅμα τῷ στρατοπέδῳ
καὶ πολλαῖς περιπεσὼν δυσχωρίαις καὶ τόποις ἀνύδροις, πολλούς τε τῆς
στρατιᾶς ἀποβαλὼν ἐν τῇ διὰ τῆς πολεμίας παρόδῳ ('When peace was
made with Persia on the terms I have mentioned, Jovian undertook
the return in all safety with his army, but lost many of his men on the
march through enemy country because he was beset by the difficulty
of the terrain and lack of water').

pontem iungere Cf. 18.2.9 *ne...pons cum multorum discrimine iungeretur.*
This expression, 'to make by joining', (OLD s.v. 5) refers to pontoon
bridges, as is the case in Tac. *Ann.* 13.7.1 (Nero) *pontes per amnem
Euphraten iungi...mandat. Ponte iungere,* which is far more frequent in
classical authors, is not found in Amm.

post firmatam pacem et foedera Like *a conatu nefario* below, the fulsome
phrase, for which see the note ad 25.7.13 *Quo ignobili,* expresses
indignation about the perfidious nature of the Persians.

sopitis belli turbinibus The metaphor is probably inspired by examples
such as Lucr. 1.29–30 *effice ut interea fera moenera militiai...sopita
quiescant.* For *turbo* see the note ad 21.13.14 *turbinibus excitis* and
cf. Flor. 3.5.5 *subitus turbo Pontici belli.*

incuriosius gradientes In 23.5.21 (q.v.) Julian had emphasized how
important it was for soldiers to stick together during the marches; if
they did not, they would be an easy prey for the enemy.

a conatu nefario destiterunt The phrase, with which cf. 14.7.17 *nefariis
...conatibus* and 23.1.7 *intempestivo conatu desistere,* is probably taken
from Cic. *Cat.* 1.11 *compressi conatus tuos nefarios.* The Persian attempt
to attack the Romans is called *nefarius,* because it is in violation of the
treaty; cf. the note ad 25.7.13 *ne quid* and Zos. 3.31.1, just quoted.

itineribus magnis The same expression occurs in 15.5.24, 26.7.3, and   **8.5**
29.5.17; *magnis itineribus* in 28.1.54 and 28.6.16. See the note ad
20.8.21 *venit ad.* After having been delayed near Dura and after Jovian

258   COMMENTARY

had concluded a peace treaty with Sapor, the army resumed its march
to Roman territory. Amm. nor other sources contain indications
about the route the army took from Dura to Hatra. According to
Dillemann, 1962, 304–5 the army crossed the Tigris north of Dura
– possibly at Tikrit, which Dillemann locates some 18 km north of
Dura – and marched along the right bank of the Tigris up to Gibrata;
from there the Romans marched in north-western direction through
a desert area to Hatra. Dillemann, 1962, figs. 25 and 28 suggests that
the army may have followed the route depicted on *Tab. Peut.* X 4–5.
It is also possible that the army followed a caravan route which had
water wells at stopping places; a possible caravan route was explored
by Alois Musil at the beginning of the twentieth century; Musil, 1927,
60. It is hard to say anything about the distance Dura-Hatra because
the precise location of Dura is not known (see the note ad 25.6.9
civitatem) and the exact route to Hatra can only be guessed at. Stein,
in Gregory-Kennedy, 1985, 84 mentions a distance of 110 miles, but
he thought that the army travelled in a straight line. Assuming that
the army followed a caravan route it is probable that the distance
was greater; a caravan route is dictated by the presence of water wells
and it is unlikely that these were located in a straight line. The route
may have been longer than Stein's 110 miles; Brok, 227, followed by
Fontaine n. 662, suggests 250 km. Since the distance Dura-Hatra can
only be guessed the number of days it took to get from Dura to Hatra
is also uncertain. The army arrived at Dura on 1 July (25.6.9) and was
delayed in the neighbourhood of Dura for four days due to attacks
by the Persians. The attempt to build pontoon bridges to cross the
Tigris took two days (25.6.15 and 25.7.4), i.e. 6 and 7 July. Then the
negotiations with Sapor began, which, according to Amm. 25.7.7,
lasted four days, from 8 to 11 July. Taking into consideration that
the preparations for crossing the Tigris as well as the crossing not far
north of Dura took some time, it may be inferred that the Roman
army had reached the right bank of the river by 16 July. Assuming
that the army marched some 18 km per day in the difficult desert
circumstances and that the distance was some 250 km, the journey
took 14 days, so that the army arrived at Hatra on July 30; cf. Brok
229.

Hatram I.e. al-Hadr in modern Iraq, some 80 km south of Mosul
and some 50 km west of Assur. The city, which had nomadic begin-
nings, flourished between *c.* A.D. 90–241 as a semi-independent city
between Rome and Parthia and was ruled by monarchs. Around
240–241 it was destroyed by Sapor I; Millar, 1993, 150–1. The city

CHAPTER 8.5   259

had a circular form and was surrounded by a moat and a wall of
some 6 km. Excavations, which started in 1951, clearly indicate that
Hatra had been a prosperous city; remains of temples, streets, house
tombs, statues as well as many inscriptions in Aramaic have been
found. The city owed its prosperity mainly to trade and commerce.
Hatra's culture was in every respect a mix: its religion was syncretistic
– Semitic with Mesopotamian and Graeco-Roman elements – and
its material culture shows Parthian and Graeco-Roman influences;
Drijvers, 1977, 803–37; Colledge, 1977, passim; Isaac, 1992, 152–6;
Millar, 1993, 494–5; Gawlikowski, 1994; Hauser, 1998. Hatra had
been a crucial halting place for armies marching from Singara to
Ctesiphon or vice versa. It also had great economic significance for
the trade between the Roman Empire and the East. The importance
of Hatra for the Romans is manifested by the presence (until 238) of
a Roman military unit, the *cohors IX Maurorum Gordiana*; Isaac, 1992,
154.

*quod eruendum adorti temporibus variis Traianus et Severus principes
bellicosi* For the construction of *adoriri* with predicative gerundive
cf. 20.6.1 *oppugnandam adoritur Singaram* (q.v.), 21.12.13 *portarum
obices effringendas adorti.* The classical construction is with an infinitive: Tac. *Agr.* 25.3 *oppugnare ultro castellum adorti.* For the Parthian
campaigns of Trajan and Septimius Severus see the note ad 23.5.17.
In 116–117, after the capture of Ctesiphon by Trajan, uprisings broke
out in Mesopotamia including Hatra. In 117 Trajan laid siege to the
city but was unable to conquer it; D.C. 68.31. In 198–199 Septimius
Severus made two attempts to conquer Hatra; both sieges, however,
were unsuccessful and the Romans suffered heavy losses; Hdn. 3.9.3–
8; D.C. 75.10.1, 76.11.1. Severus besieged Hatra because its ruler
Barsemias had supported the emperor's rival Pescennius Niger by
sending him a contingent of archers; Hdn. 3.1.3, 9.1. The chronology of Severus' campaign and the sieges of Hatra is not quite clear;
see Drijvers, 1977, 817. *Bellicosus* is considered a positive quality; see
the note ad 20.1.2 *bellicosum sane.*

ut in eorum actibus has quoque digessimus partes I.e. in the lost books
that dealt with the reigns of Trajan and Septimius Severus. For *actibus,*
which Amm. frequently uses to refer to the events in the reigns
of earlier emperors, see the note ad 21.8.1 *cuius in actibus.* It is
difficult to decide whether *partes* refers to earlier parts of Ammianus'
own narrative or to geographical regions. Fontaine chooses the
former interpretation ("nous avons également relaté cet épisode

260 COMMENTARY

en retraçant leurs faits et gestes"), for which cf. 31.5.10 *Et quoniam ad has partes post multiplices ventum est actus.* On the other hand, *partes* 'regions' is very common in Amm. (and, for that matter, in Late Latin generally, as Löfstedt, 1911, 245 observes). See De Jonge ad 18.4.2. If *partes* is taken in this geographical sense, the meaning becomes: 'as we have told in the history of Trajan and Severus, when we also dealt with these regions.'

8.6   *cognito* For the abl. abs. without a nominal ablative see the note ad 20.5.1 *edictoque, ut.* This is the only case in Amm. where the participle is followed by an AcI. For examples from the classical period see Kühner-Stegmann I 778–9, e.g. Liv. 37.13.5 *cognito hostium naves ad Aethaliam stare.*

per porrectam planitiem ad usque lapidem septuagensimum Cf. 14.2.12 *planitie porrecta.* The model is Tac. *Ann.* 1.64.4 *porrigebatur planities,* 13.38.3 *pars in planitiem porrigebatur.* The seventy miles roughly correspond to the distance between Hatra and Ur, if indeed the *castellum* of that name, mentioned in §7, can be identified with Zagura.

nec aquam inveniri posse praeter salsam et faetidam The water was salty because of the saline content of the waters of the Tigris, Euphrates and their tributaries, which regularly flooded the land; Oates, 1968, 4; Brok 229.

nec ad victum aliquid nisi "In nachklassischer Zeit erweitert *aliquis* sein Gebiet sowohl durch Verdrängung von *quis* hinter *ne, num…* als durch Eindringen in negative und negativische Sätze"; Szantyr 195.

abrotonum et absinthium et dracontium aliaque herbarum genera ut tristissima Plin. *Nat.* 21.160–2 gives a description of *abrotonus, -um* (southernwood). It is efficacious against e.g. poisoning by snakes (see also Luc. 9.921), scorpions and spiders, and against constipation and coughing; see further Schmidt, 1905, Stemplinger, 1950, André, 1985, 113. For *absinthius, -um* (wormwood) see the elaborate description by Plin. *Nat.* 27.45–52, and Schuster, 1958; André, 1985, 1. *Dracontium* (dragonwort) is described by Plin. *Nat.* 24.142; André, 1985, 90–1. The use of *ut* is problematic. It has been compared to Greek ὡς with superlative, but unlike ὡς in such cases, *ut* does not seem to denote the highest possible degree. There are, moreover, no parallels for this use of *ut* in Amm. Guenther's *vel* is at first

CHAPTER 8.7   261

sight very attractive, since V's compendium for *vel* is almost indistinguishable from *ut*. Amm., however, never uses *vel* 'quite' with a superlative. More daring conjectures like Cornelissen's *infestissima* or Petschenig's *austerissima* are misguided, since *tristis* is 'le mot juste', cf. Ov. *Pont.* 3.1.23 *tristia per vacuos horrent absinthia campos.* All in all, it seems best to accept Gelenius' *genera tristissima* as the reading of the Hersfeldensis and *ut* as a mistake introduced by V.

vasa, quae portabantur The verb *portare* is almost a t.t. where food and drink are concerned as part of the soldiers' standard equipment, cf. 17.9.3 *miles expensis, quae portabat, nusquam repperiens victum.*

mactatis camelis iumentisque aliis alimenta quaesita sunt licet noxia This is the first time that Amm. refers to camels as pack animals in connection with the Persian expedition. He uses the word *camelus* in five other places: 14.4.3, 22.11.10, 23.6.56, 28.6.5, 29.5.55. They and the other beasts of burden were slaughtered while the army was in Hatra. Cf. Hdt. 3.25 for the eating of pack animals by the army of Cambyses. Another comparable case is mentioned by Curt. 9.10.13 who reports that Alexander's Macedonian soldiers were driven by hunger to eat their pack animals and even their horses. Although camel and horse meat can be eaten, the soldiers were evidently not used to this kind of food and fell ill: *quippe insalubrium ciborum noxii suci* ('the harmful juices of this unwholesome food'), *ad hoc itineris labor et aegritudo animi vulgaverant morbos.* For *noxius* used in this sense cf. also Plin. *Nat.* 22.99 *noxii erunt fungi, qui in coquendo duriores fient.*

via sex dierum emensa In these six days (presumably 3–8 August) the   **8.7**
army marched some seventy miles (see §6) from Hatra to Ur. For the passive use of *emensus* see the note ad 22.13.3 *medietate noctis.*

solacia necessitatis extremae Cf. 18.7.2 *magno necessitatis ducente solacio,* where, however, *necessitatis* is gen. explicativus. With the present use of *solacium* with objective gen. cf. Seneca's complaint about decadent ladies nibbling ice-creams *Ep.* 95.21 *nivem rodunt, solacium stomachi aestuantis.*

dux Mesopotamiae Cassianus For *dux* see the notes ad 21.16.2, 22.16. 6, 24.4.13, 25.1.2. In Amm. Mesopotamia usually denotes, as in this passage, the Roman province of that name and not the land between Euphrates and Tigris; see the note ad 23.2.7 *unde contractis.* For Cas-

262   COMMENTARY

sianus see *PLRE* I, Cassianus. Amm. is the only source that provides information about him. He was already *dux Mesopotamiae* in 356, when Strategius Musonianus took counsel with him on the plans of Sapor, who was raiding Roman territory (16.9.1–2). He had a leading role in the scorched earth strategy when Sapor invaded Mesopotamia in 359 (18.7.3). It is possible that Cassianus laid down his office as *dux Mesopotamiae* in 363, when, as a consequence of Jovian's peace treaty with Sapor, much of the province of Mesopotamia, including Nisibis, was handed over to the Persians; 25.7.9 with note. Brok 229 suggests that Cassianus may have been Amm.'s source for the story about Craugasius (18.10, 19.9.3–8), the curialis of Nisibis, who defected to Persia.

tribunus Mauricius pridem ob hoc missus For Mauricius see *PLRE* I, Mauricius 1. It seems that Mauricius was sent by Jovian – possibly already before the army had arrived in Hatra – to Cassianus to bring the supplies of the army of Procopius and Sebastianus, and that the two of them journeyed together (from Nisibis?) to Ur. Zosimus has fewer and slightly different details; he reports (3.33.1) that Mauricius was sent by Jovian to bring food from Nisibis and to come back as far as possible to meet the Roman army with the fresh supplies: Ἰοβιανὸς...Μαυρίκιον μὲν τῶν λοχαγῶν ἕνα τροφὴν ἐκ Νισίβιος ἀγαγεῖν ἐκέλευε τῷ στρατοπέδῳ, ἀπαντῆσαί ⟨τε⟩ μετὰ ταύτης ὡς ἂν οἷός τε ᾖ πορρωτάτω; Paschoud n. 97. For *tribunus* see the notes ad 22.11.2 *Romanus quin etiam*, 23.3.9 *tribuno Constantiniano*, and 24.3.1 *paucissimos trucidasse*.

Ur nomine Persicum...castellum The exact location of this stronghold is difficult to establish. Various suggestions have been put forward. Rolfe's explanatory note 3 that it was the Ur of the Chaldaeans should be rejected, since this Ur was in South-Babylonia. Brok 230 does not specify a precise location but rejects, as does Dillemann, 1962, 309–10, the identification with modern Jaddalah proposed by Stein, 1985, 84. The latter was only 30 km away from Hatra, and therefore too short a distance for a march of six days; moreover, Jaddalah is too far to the east. Following Dussaud, 1927, 497 Brok suggests that Ur is on the route as shown on *Tab. Peut.* X 5: Sirgora (Singara) – Zogarra (Tell Uzga) – Dicat – Ad Herculem – Hatris (Hatra). Dillemann, 1962, 310–2, followed by Fontaine n. 664, identifies Ur with Zagura, close to the modern village of Ain Sinu; see also Oates, 1968, 79 and Talbert, 2000, Map 89, E4. This was on the route to the north and was indeed some 70 miles, i.e. some 105 km, from

CHAPTER 8.8   263

Hatra, and thus corresponds well with a march of six days. See also
Dillemann, 1962, 149, fig. XVIII. Paschoud n. 97, where it is said that
Dillemann places Ur close to Singara, is correct, although Zagura was
further to the east of Singara than one might infer from this remark.
If Ur is indeed to be identified with Zagura, then it used to be a
Roman stronghold – barracks and a *castellum* have been excavated
(Oates, 1968, 79–92; Isaac, 1992, 256) – before it became a Persian
fort.

quos relictus cum Procopio et Sebastiano exercitus parcius victitans conser-
varat This army of 30.000 men under the command of Procopius
and Sebastianus was left by Julian on the right bank of the Tigris
in order to keep Sapor occupied in northern Mesopotamia, and
to prevent a Persian attack from the north on the main body of
Julian's army. They were also to join forces with the Armenian king
Arsaces. See 23.3.5 and the relevant notes there, as well as the note
ad 25.5.3 *si Mesopotamiam*. It is noticeable that Amm. never criticises
Procopius and Sebastianus for not turning up when they were badly
needed, i.e. when the main force was in the vicinity of Ctesiphon. On
the contrary, the words *parcius victitans* are an unmistakable compli-
ment.

Procopius alter notarius et Memoridus militaris tribunus These two men   **8.8**
are also mentioned in 25.10.6 *ubi ei reversi Procopius notarius et Memo-*
ridus tribunus occurrunt. Amm. deliberately added *alter* to distinguish
this Procopius from the Procopius mentioned in the previous section, who was Julian's kinsman and the later usurper. Zos. 3.35.2
thinks they are one and the same person; Paschoud n. 103. The
mistake is understandable since the latter Procopius had also been
notarius for a long time, cf. 26.6.1 *notarius diu perspicaciter militans et*
tribunus; 17.14.3 *Procopius tunc notarius.* See for the Procopius in this
passage *PLRE* I, Procopius 3 and Teitler, 1985, 162. For *notarius* consult the note ad 20.4.2 *Decentium tribunum.* Memoridus is unknown,
apart from Amm.'s two references to him. For *tribunus* see the note
tribunus Mauricius in the previous section.

ad tractus Illyricos mittuntur et Galliarum nuntiaturi Iuliani mortem
et Iovianum post eius obitum ad culmen augustum evectum Cf. Zos.
3.33.1 κατὰ δὲ τὴν Ἰταλίαν ἄλλους ἐξέπεμπε, τὴν Ἰουλιανοῦ τελευτὴν καὶ
τὴν ἀνάρρησιν τὴν οἰκείαν ἀπαγγελοῦντας and 3.35.1 τοῖς ἐν Παιονίᾳ
στρατοπέδοις Λουκιλλιανόν, ὄντα κηδεστὴν αὐτῷ, καὶ Προκόπιον καὶ
Οὐαλεντινιανόν, ὃς μετὰ ταῦτα γέγονε βασιλεύς, ἐξαπέστειλε, τήν τε Ἰου-

264   COMMENTARY

λιανοῦ τελευτὴν ἀπαγγελοῦντας, καὶ ὅτι περ εἴη μετ᾽ αὐτὸν αὐτοκράτωρ προβεβλημένος. The coordination of *Iuliani mortem* and *Iovianum... evectum* suggests that the participle phrase serves as a noun clause ('the fact that Jovian was raised to the purple'). The alternative explanation is, of course, that *Iovianum...evectum* is AcI with ellipsis of *esse*, which in view of the fact that *nuntiare* is a verbum dicendi seems preferable. For *evehere ad culmen* see the note ad 20.8.21 *eum ad*.

8.9 *Lucillianum, socerum suum* Cf. Zos. 3.35.1 Λουκιλλιανόν, ὄντα κηδεστὴν αὐτῷ and Symm. *Or.* 1.4. See for Lucillianus *PLRE* I, Lucillianus 3. He was a loyal supporter of Constantius both against Gallus (14.11.14) and Julian (21.9.5). According to Zos. 2.45.2, 3.8.2 in 350 Constantius gave him the command in the war against the Persians and he defended Nisibis against the attacks of Sapor; cf. for Zosimus' erroneous dating of the latter event to 359 Paschoud's note 19 ad 3.8.2. Lucillianus, who had been *comes domesticorum* under Gallus Caesar (14.11.14) before he became *comes et magister equitum* in Illyricum – for this function see the note ad 21.9.5 *rem curabat* – was removed from this latter position by Julian in 361 (21.9.6–8; 21.10.1) and replaced by Iovinus (22.3.1). In 359 he was sent as an envoy to Sapor to negotiate a peace treaty (17.14.3). His career having been cut short by Julian, he retired in Sirmium where he had also been stationed as *comes et magister equitum*, and continued to live there; it may have been his hometown. He was killed in a soldiers' mutiny at Rheims in 363; 25.10.7 and notes ad loc. His daughter Charito was married to Jovian; Zon. 13.14; *PLRE* I, Charito.

post depositum militiae munus digressum ad otium For the use of the so-called ab urbe condita-construction as a feature of 'Roman bureaucratese' see the note ad 22.2.2 *post exemptos*. For *digredi / discedere ad otium* see the note ad 20.2.5 *digredi iussit*.

apud Sirmium The preposition is used as in 25.3.23 *natus apud Constantinopolim;* cf. the note ad 14.11.21 *apud Antiochiam*. For this important city in Late Antiquity see the note ad 21.9.5 *agensque apud Sirmium*.

oblatis magisterii equitum et peditum codicillis See for the functions of *magister equitum* and *magister peditum* the notes ad 20.1.2 *ire...Lupicinum* and 20.2.1 *peditum magistrum*. In the fourth century there came into being, apart from the imperial *magister equitum* and *magister peditum* – called *in praesenti* or *praesentalis* (Jones 124–5) – also

CHAPTER 8.9   265

regional *magistri.* These regional *magistri* commanded both infantry and cavalry: "the *magistri* led mixed commands, consisting of both infantry and cavalry; thus, in practice, there was no strict separation between the two branches of the army"; Nicasie, 1998, 78; see also Brok 231; Jones 124–5, 174–8, 191–2. Presumably, Lucillianus' nomination as *magister equitum et peditum* did not differ from his previous position, i.e. that of (*comes et*) *magister equitum*; see the note ad 21.9.5 *rem curabat.*

It is not known with certainty who was *magister peditum praesentalis* during Jovian's reign but it was probably Victor; see the notes ad 24.1.2 *agmina vero* and 25.5.2 *Arintheus.* The *magister equitum praesentalis* was most probably Dagalaifus, as may be inferred from 26.1.6, 4.1, 5.2; see for him also the notes ad 24.1.2 *agmina vero* and 25.5.2 *Nevitta.* As *magister equitum per Orientem* Jovian nominated Lupicinus (26.5.2), Iovinus was *magister equitum per Gallias* but soon to be replaced by Malarichus (25.8.11; cf. 26.5.2).

A *codicillus* was an imperial letter by which the emperor could adlect people to the equestrian order or the senate as well as appoint them to magistracies; see in general Jones 530–2 and Millar, 1977, 288–90, 296, 305–6, 311. In Late Antiquity *codicilli* consisted of two hinged ivory plaques, the outside of which had a portrait of the emperor. *Codicilli* were important *insignia* for a magistrate since they proclaimed the legitimacy of his acts and showed that his position depended on the emperor; see TLL III 1408.73–1409.31 and Kelly, 1998, 152.

properare Mediolanum urgerent res firmaturum ancipites et, quod magis metuebatur, si casus novi quidam exsurgerent, opponendum A similar juxtaposition of the future participle and the gerundive is found in 26.9.5 *destituendo iam et casuro.* There *destituendo* is passive, whereas in the present text *opponendum* is used reflexively: *qui se opponeret,* as in 25.6.12 *quibus oppositus…imperator;* cf. TLL IX 2.763. 51–5. With regard to *magis,* Viansino acutely observes that in Amm. the adverb is used "comparativa vi saepe omissa", e.g. in 25.1.14 *ad quorum stridorem…magis equi terrebantur.* Instances from other authors are grouped in TLL VIII 56.70–57.35.

It was only logical that Lucillianus should travel to Milan immediately after his new appointment. Not only was Milan an important imperial residence in Late Antiquity (see Krautheimer, 1983, 68–92; Lavizzari Pedrazzini, 1990), it was also the seat of the *praefectus praetorio Italiae, Illyrici et Africae*; Lucillianus' military command was to be exercised in the territory of this praetorian prefect, who at the time

266 COMMENTARY

was Claudius Mamertinus (*PLRE* I, Mamertinus 2). Mamertinus had been a great supporter of Julian's regime and a favourite of the late emperor, who made him consul in 362; 21.10.8, 21.12.25, 22.3.1, 22.7.1; see also the note ad 21.8.1 *Mamertino*. There was therefore an added reason for Lucillianus to travel to Milan: Mamertinus might well be ill-disposed towards the new emperor, and it was feared that he might organise opposition against Jovian. Jovian's fears, however, were unfounded, as appears from the fact that Mamertinus remained in office.

8.10 *quibus imperator secretiores addiderat litteras Lucillianum itidem monens, ut* V reads *quibus per secretiores*, Gelenius has only *quibus secretiores*. Petschenig 1892, 519 proposed to emend *per* to *super*, but although *addere super* is not uncommon in Latin, there is no parallel for it in Amm. Heraeus' *imperator* is even less attractive, since Amm. starts his account of the letter with the words *quibus id mandaverat princeps*. A different term for the same Agens, viz. *imperator*, would be without parallel and is indeed completely redundant. Finally, Fontaine defends the reading of V, interpreting *per litteras* as an instrumental adjunct, which, again, is not in conformity with Amm.'s *usus*. Moreover, his suggestion that the following *ut* depends both on *addiderat* and *monens* is strained and not supported by 21.13.3 *addebatque monendo saepius et scribendo, ut*, where the *ut*-clause depends solely on *addebat, monendo et scribendo* describing the ways in which Constantius made his wishes known. All in all, it seems again advisable to accept Gelenius' reading as representing the text of the Hersfeldensis and to ignore V's *per* altogether. The scribe may have misread the first syllable of *secretiores*, noticed his mistake and proceeded to write the correct form. For *itidem* see the note ad 21.9.4 *eodem ictu*.

There are some interesting parallels to the procedure followed here by Jovian. In 20.8.18 Julian is said to have added a secret letter to his official one, which was intended to be read out aloud in the presence of Constantius: *His litteris iunctas secretiores alias Constantio offerendas clanculo misit obiurgatorias et mordaces* and in 31.12.9 we read that the Christian envoy of Fritigern did exactly the same: *praeter haec idem Christianus ut conscius arcanorum et fidus secretas alias eiusdem regis obtulit litteras*. In HA *Gd* 10.6 a secret addendum to a letter is to be delivered by word of mouth: *fictae sunt litterae Maximini...et missi cum quaestore milites, qui eas ferrent, addentes quaedam praeter litteras secreto esse dicenda*.

CHAPTER 8.11   267

quosdam lectos Among them the tribunes Seniauchus and Valentinianus, the later emperor; 25.10.6 (q.v.) *Lucillianus Mediolanum ingressus cum Seniaucho et Valentiniano tribunis.*

adminiculis eorum usurus pro incidentium captu negotiorum There is a note on *adminiculum* ad 24.7.8. For substantivized incidentia see the note ad 21.2.3 *animo tranquillo* and for the phrase *pro captu* the note ad 25.6.5.

prudentique consilio Malarichum, ex familiaribus negotiis agentem etiam **8.11**
tum in Italia Amm. frequently uses the ablative of manner with *consilio*; see the note ad 20.7.1 *Nisibin prudenti.* For *ex familiaribus negotiis*, ' for private business', see the note ad 22.7.6 *ex negotio.* In view of Jovian's insecure position (*nutantem adhuc statum*, at the end of this section) Amm. apparently considers it a sensible policy to replace Iovinus with Malarichus, as he explains in the second part of this section. Malarichus had been *gentilium rector* (15.5.6), i.e. tribune of the *schola Gentilium*; see for this *schola* the note ad 20.2.5 *Gentilium.* He defended (in 355) his fellow-countryman Silvanus against the court intrigues, arguing that *homines dicatos imperio* ought not to become the victims of cliques and wiles; 15.5.6 with De Jonge's note, 15.5.9, 10, 11. It is not known when he retired, but the life of leisure apparently suited him since he declined Jovian's offer to become *magister armorum per Gallias* in succession to Iovinus; 25.10.6 *Malarichus recusavit suscipere magisterium.* PLRE I, Malarichus.

Iovino PLRE I, Flavius Iovinus 6. See for him the note ad 21.8.3. Iovinus had been a great supporter of Julian which, apart from the fact that he was a distinguished general and therefore a possible threat to Jovian, may have been another reason for Jovian to replace him as *magister armorum per Gallias.* As Brok 232 notes, it was important for the new emperor to gain a foothold in Gaul: Julian had been popular in Gaul and several officials there had favoured him – not only Iovinus but also Sallustius, who had been praetorian prefect of Gaul and was consul in 363; 23.1.1 with note *Sallustio* and the note ad 21.8.1 *Germaniano.* Lucillianus may have felt sweet revenge when he saw Iovinus replaced, whose appointment as *magister equitum per Illyricum* had moved him out of that office (see the note above ad 25.8.9). At least at the end of his life Iovinus was a Christian, as appears from CIL 13.3256. According to Fontaine n. 671 he converted in 365–7; cf. Piétri, 1970, 452 who thinks his conversion should be dated after

268   COMMENTARY

367, and Von Haehling, 1978, 250–1 who places his conversion in
the reign of Jovian.

armorum magistro Amm., who is not always precise in his military
designations, uses this title often for *magister equitum*; see the note
ad 20.1.2 *ire...Lupícinum plácuit*. For examples: 15.5.24, 36 (Ursicinus), cf. 15.13.3; 16.7.3 (Marcellus), cf. 16.4.3; 20.1.2 (Lupicinus),
cf. 20.4.6; 20.9.5 (Gomoarius); 21.8.1 (Nevitta), cf. 21.8.3; 26.5.2
(Iovinus); 29.6.3 (Aequitius).

gemina utilitate praespeculata Apart from a dubious place in Suetonius (*Jul.* 58.1) and one in the sixth century author Rusticius (*c.
aceph.* p. 1233b) this is the only instance of *praespeculari*; TLL X
2.895.72 sqq.

dux meriti celsioris ideoque suspectus For *dux* see the note ad 25.8.7.
The qualification given to Iovinus does not imply that Jovian is hostile
to merit. Having been one of Julian's most trusted collaborators and
holding a powerful position, Iovinus is potentially a rival for the
throne. In a similar situation, after Valentinian had been chosen
as emperor, the order was given *ne potioris quisquam auctoritatis vel
suspectus altiora conari procederet postridie mane*, where *suspectus* is used
in the same sense (26.2.1). Cf. 26.6.3 *novaque exinde coeptare suspectum.*
Amm. uses *suspectus* also in an active sense, e.g. in 16.12.27 *stetit
impavidus suspectiorque de obscuris*, q.v.

abiret e medio Iovinus is given the opportunity to retreat silently from
power. For *e medio* see TLL VIII 595.56–68.

homo inferioris spei ad sublimiora provectus Amm. dislikes such sudden
promotions. Cf. 20.2.5 *Agilone ad eius locum immodico saltu promoto.*
For *inferior spes* cf. 20.11.11 *spes nostrorum.*

auctoris sui nutantem adhuc statum In a similar way Constantius is
called the *auctor* of Gallus, because he had given him the rank of
Caesar: 14.1.1 *ausurus hostilia in auctorem suae felicitatis ut videbatur.*
Julian, also raised to the purple by Constantius, is pointedly reminded
of his obligations by the senate of Rome: *auctori tuo reverentiam
rogamus* (21.10.7). For more examples see TLL II 1198. 38 sqq.
For *status nutans* cf. 16.12.12 *statum nutantium rerum...divina remedia
repararunt* and HA *MB* 17.9 *ita ego precor, ut in eo statu vobis rem p.
servent, in quo eam vos adhuc nutantem collocaritis.*

CHAPTER 8.12   269

iussum est...perrecturis I.e. to the *notarius* Procopius and the military   **8.12**
tribune Memoridus (25.8.8).

extollere seriem gestorum in melius This is the first occurrence of the
expression *series gestorum*, which is found only in the later books of
Amm. (25.8.15, 27.9.3, 28.1.22, 29.1.4, 29.3.1) and in Claud. *Cons.
Stil.* 1.139. *Extollere in melius* is found only in Amm. The failure of
the Persian expedition and the probably necessary but humiliating
peace treaty – Eutropius (10.17.1): *pacem cum Sapore, necessariam
quidem, sed ignobilem fecit* – were definitely not helpful to Jovian's
endeavours to secure his position as emperor. The conclusion of
the Persian campaign was therefore to be presented in a favourable
way. This is clearly shown in Jovian's coinage which was struck as
from mid-August in Antioch and other mints. Some coin-types have
the legends VICTORIA ROMANORUM and VICTORIA AUGUSTA,
evidently to announce the Persian campaign as a success and to
present the new emperor in a positive way. It was undoubtedly one
of the tasks of the messengers Procopius and Memoridus to take
care that these coin-types with the portrait of Jovian were struck. See
Ehling, 1996.

procinctum Parthicum For *procinctus*, 'campaign', see the note ad
20.1.3 *festinaret ocius*. For *Parthicus* see the note ad *Parthos* in 23.3.2.

additisque festinando itineri noctibus...remeare velociter The word order
strongly suggests that *itineri festinando* is the dative complement with
additis, rather than a final dative on its own: 'adding the nights
to the journey which had to be made with great speed'. Contrast
itinere festinato in section 17 about a journey that was completed.
Procopius and Memoridus left from Ur (25.8.8) around 12 August
and returned with their reports to the emperor when the latter was
in Tyana (25.10.6) at the end of November. This means that their
journey took nearly four months. They must have used the usual
route via Antioch to Constantinople and from there to Sirmium and
subsequently to Milan. Brok 233 and Fontaine n. 673 assume that
they went all the way to Reims, but this is nowhere mentioned. Maybe
they did not go further than Milan from where Lucillianus may have
taken over from them. Of the latter it is known that he travelled
to Reims (25.10.6). If Procopius and Memoridus travelled all the
way to Reims they covered some 7800 km in total: Ur-Antioch 700
km, Antioch-Constantinople 1100 km, Constantinople-Milan 1800
km, Milan-Reims 800 km, Reims-Tyana 3400 km. If they did not go

270 COMMENTARY

further than Milan the total distance was some 6200 km: Ur-Milan 3600 km, Milan-Tyana 2600 km; Brok 233.

provinciarum militiaeque rectoribus insinuare novi principis scripta V has *insinuarent*. In itself such a switch from the infinitive to the subjunctive far removed from the main verb *iussum est* would be grammatically incorrect, but perfectly understandable, which is why Blomgren 63–4 wants to keep it. The author, however, goes on to write *remeare*, which proves that he has not lost sight of the construction he had chosen. The word *rector* is used by Amm. in a very general way. It denotes all kinds of high officials and officers, and even a Caesar as in 20.1.1, q.v.

omniumque sententiis occultius sciscitatis Apparently one of the assignments given by Jovian to Procopius and Memoridus was to probe the sentiments of provincial governors and military commanders towards his regime.

ut comperto, quid in longinquis agatur, principatus corroborandi matura consilia quaerantur et cauta For the abl. abs. without a nominal subject see the note ad *cognito* in 25.8.6. Again Amm. emphasizes Jovian's insecure position, as at the end of 25.8.11 *nutantem adhuc statum*.

8.13 *Hos tabellarios fama praegrediens index tristiorum casuum velocissima per provincias volitabat et gentes* It is worth considering whether *tabellarios* should not be taken predicatively. Jovian wanted his two messengers to monitor the information about the Persian campaign. But, as it turned out, *fama* was faster and more truthful. For winged Fama cf. 18.6.3 *credimus (neque enim dubium est) per aerios tramites famam praepetem volitare* and Stat. *Theb.* 9.32–3 *Fama per Aonium rapido vaga murmure campum / spargitur in turmas, solito pernicior index*. The rumour spread amongst the Roman provincials and peoples living outside the Empire. Mommsen, 1889, 216, n. 2: "Im gewöhnlichen Sprachgebrauch...sind die *gentiles* wie die *barbari* die nicht Reichsangehörigen Ausländer, wie zum Beispiel Ammian 25,8,13 *provinciae et gentes* setzt für das Inland und das Ausland." See for rumours spreading in situations of war, Chauvot, 1988, especially pp. 132–5 where the mission of Procopius and Memoridus is discussed from that point of view. In particular rumours which were newsworthy, as the peace treaty with the Persians no doubt was, spread rapidly; Lee, 1993, 153–5.

CHAPTER 8.14 271

maximeque omnium Nisibenos acerbo dolore perculsit Amm. prepares the way here for the highly charged description of the plight of the Nisibenes in the next chapter. The phrase *dolore percellere* is peculiar to Ammianus, cf. 16.12.3 *qui ignarus pavendi nec ira nec dolore perculsus,* 28.1.49, and 29.5.46.

Sapori…cuius iram metuebant et simultates Whereas *ira* normally means 'a spurt of anger', *simultas,* or rather *simultates,* denotes the resulting hostility; cf. Ov. *Am.* 1.8.82 *saepe simultates ira morata facit.* Not surprisingly, from a Persian point of view he is called *clementissimum regem* in 25.7.6, q.v.

recolentes, quae assidue pertulerit funera eam saepe oppugnare conatus For Sapor's vain attempts to conquer the city see the note ad 25.1.15 *acceptae apud.* With a rare slip of the pen Seyfarth translates "welche Leiden er ihnen beständig gebracht hatte." *Perferre* has its normal meaning 'to suffer'.

orbem eoum A reference to the eastern provinces of the Roman **8.14** Empire; see the note ad 20.3.1 *per eoos tractus.*

haec civitas For references concerning Nisibis see the notes ad 20.6.9 and 25.1.15.

habili situ Amm. seems to be the only author who uses *habilis* in the sense of 'strategic'; TLL VI.2464.4–6.

miseri tamen…firmissimum claustrum In spite of the rumours, the Nisibenes still had a slight but in the end futile hope that since their city was a strong bulwark against the Persians, it would not be surrendered by Jovian. Cf. 25.9.2–4.

constringerentur The Nisibenes are prey to a 'strangling' fear. Cf. *cura constrictus* in 20.4.19 with the note.

hac scilicet velut suopte motu vel exoratus For the explicative use of *scilicet* cf. e.g. 17.10.9 *condicione difficili premebatur hac scilicet, ut* and 31.7.6 *id scilicet praestruentes, ut.* Note that in both cases the next clause is introduced by *ut,* which supports Löfstedt's *ut vel.* As a matter of fact, the scribe of V seems to be slightly dyslectic; cf. in this same chapter *brevis* instead of *verbis* (§ 12) and *perclusit* instead of *perculsit* (§ 13); therefore a misreading of this type would not be out of character.

272 COMMENTARY

The problem remains that both after *ut* and after *velut* the indic. fut *retinebit* would be without parallel in Amm. Such a use of the indic. fut. in oratio obliqua is, on the contrary, very common after *quod*. For that reason Gelenius' *quod vel* seems preferable. Cf. 14.11.6 *quae licet ambigeret metuens saepe cruentum, spe tamen, quod eum lenire poterit ut germanum, profecta* and 30.1.4 *odio Papae speque, quod revertetur.*

orientis firmissimum claustrum For *oriens*, probably referring here to the *dioecesis Orientis*, see the note ad 20.1.1 *per Illyricum.* There is a note on *claustrum* ad 20.11.24 *quod munimentum.* Cf. also the note ad 25.9.3 *Iovianum inter.*

8.15 In this section Amm. returns to his report on the army's march through the desert from the moment the food had been delivered by Cassianus and Mauricius in Ur (*quos advectos praediximus,* 25.8.7). Apparently the supplies were far from sufficient for the march from Ur to Nisibis; therefore once again the soldiers had to slaughter pack-animals.

Dum gestorum seriem ubique rumores diffunditant varii So much for Jovian's efforts to give a unanimously positive account of the Persian campaign, as mentioned in section 12 *verbis diffundere concinentibus.*

quos advectos praediximus Sc. by Cassianus and Mauricius (25.8.7). Rolfe's "which (as we have said) we had brought with us" is therefore incorrect.

in corpora sua necessitas erat humana vertenda A thinly veiled allusion to cannibalism. In his account of Cambyses' expedition to Ethiopia, quoted ad section 6, Hdt. 3.25 had related that the Persian soldiers resorted to this. V. Max. 7.6.2–3 ext. has the story that during the sieges of Numantia and Calagurris the inhabitants ate their fellow citizens. In Caes. *Gal.* 7.77.12 Critognatus exhorts the Alesians to do the same. The phrase *necessitas humana* must be understood as 'human need'. The soldiers, being only human, had no alternative but to turn to their own kind for food. Fontaine's translation "la nécessité aurait contraint les hommes à se tourner vers les cadavres des leurs" is fine; Rolfe's "to resort to human bodies" is misleading. The idea is expressed more clearly in Sen. *Contr* 9.4.5 *Necessitas magnum humanae imbecillitatis patrocinium est* with a reference to the Saguntines who killed their own fathers during the siege.

CHAPTER 8.16   273

ut et armorum pleraque proicerentur et sarcinarum Cf. Lib. *Or.* 18.280
οὗτοί γε τὰ ὅπλα ῥίψαντες ἐκείνοις ἔχειν…ἐπανῄεσαν ('our men returned, having thrown their weapons away for the enemy to keep').
After eating their pack animals (cf. the note ad §6 *mactatis camelis*),
Alexander's soldiers did the same: Curt. 9.10.12 *Et cum deessent,*
quae sarcinas veherent, spolia de hostibus, propter quae ultima Orientis
peragraverant, cremabant incendio.

atroci tabuimus fame Cf. 17.9.4 *fame ignauissimo mortis genere tabescentes*
and Apul. *Met.* 6.32 *inediae diutinae letali fame tabescet.*

ut, si usquam modius unus farinae fuisset repertus, quod ráro contígerat,
aureis decem mutaretur ut minus For the iterative subjunctive after *si*
see the note ad 21.16.8 *si affectatae.* For *(n)usquam* see the notes ad
20.4.11 and 22.14.2. *Contigerat* is a good example of a pluperfect
instead of a perfect for metrical reasons. The *modius* is the Roman
corn-measure and is the equivalent of 8.75 lt. Ten gold pieces for a
modius of grain was an extravagant price as appears from 28.1.18
where it is said that in a time of food shortage Hymetius, the
proconsul of Africa, sold ten *modii* to the needy for one gold piece:
denis modiis singulis solidis indigentibus venumdatis, that is to say for one
percent of the price mentioned here. In Anon. Vales. 11.53 we read
that during the siege of Ravenna by Theoderic the price of a bushel
went up to six *solidi*: *et factum est usque ad sex solidos modius tritici,*
while Anon. Vales. 12.73 reports that during the reign of Theoderic
one could buy 60 bushels for one gold piece: *Sexaginta modios tritici*
in solidum ipsius tempore emerunt. The *aureus* or *solidus aureus* was
introduced by Constantine and consisted of 4.55 gr. of gold; Jones
107–9 and the note ad 20.4.18 *quinos omnibus.* The context suggests
that *ut minus* must be taken to mean 'at a bargain'. There are
no parallels for this expression. Petschenig, 1892, 519 ingeniously
suggested *ut medimnus,* 'as if it was a *medimnus*', adding "dies gibt
den guten Sinn, dass der Preis des Getreides auf das Sechsfache
des gewöhnlichen gestiegen war." Fontaine rightly mentions this
conjecture in his apparatus criticus.

Profecti exinde Since Ur is the last place mentioned by Amm. (§7),   **8.16**
we must assume the army set out from there, pace Dillemann, 1962,
311 who thinks Singara (not mentioned by Amm.) is meant. *Exinde*
may either be taken as an adverb of time or of place. The army had to
march 106 Roman miles (*c.* 160 km) from Ur to Nisibis, according
to the distances given by *Tab. Peut.* X 4–5. It would have taken some

274 COMMENTARY

eight days to complete this stretch. If, as suggested in the note ad 25.8.7 *sex dierum*, the army arrived in Ur on 8 August, it may have continued its march on 11 or 12 August to reach Nisibis by 19 August.

Thilsaphata This place should probably be identified with Thebetha or Thebitha, as Dillemann, 1962, 311–2 suggests. Identification with a modern site is difficult; according to Oates, 1968, 79 and fig. 5 it was situated perhaps south-west or south of Nisibis in the neighbourhood of Tell Brak on the Wadi al-Radd; cf. Talbert, 2000, Map 89, C4. It seems to have been a rather large place, since Trajan besieged it; Arr. *Parth.* fr. 11. According to *Tab. Peut.* X 4 Thebetha was on the route from Ur/Zagura to Nisibis and 33 Roman miles away from that city. Presumably the Roman army followed the route as indicated on the Peutinger Table: Zagura (Ur)-Singara-Baba-Thebetha-Nisibis. A possible reason why Amm. does not mention Singara is that this city had recently been destroyed by the Persians. See the note ad 25.7.9 *cum castellis.*

Sebastianus atque Procopius See for them the notes ad 23.3.5 and 23.3.2 respectively, as well as the note ad §7 *quos relictos* above and 25.5.3 *si Mesopotamiam*. At this time Procopius apparently did not yet fear for his life. According to Amm. it was the liquidation of the *notarius* Iovianus – see §18 below – which made Procopius aware that his life was also in danger; subsequently he went into hiding: *e medio se conspectu discrevit maxime post Ioviani territus necem, notariorum omnium primi, quem Iuliano perempto veluti dignum imperio paucis militibus nominatum novaque exinde coeptare suspectum cruciabiliter didicerat interfectum* (26.6.3). In 25.9.13, q.v., Amm. reports that Procopius, after having fulfilled his mission to bury Julian at Tarsus, disappeared, to turn up again in Constantinople in the purple: *qui ad exsequendum profectus confestim corpore sepulto discessit nec inveniri usquam potuit studio quaesitus ingenti, nisi quod multo postea apud Constantinopolim visus est subito purpuratus.*

tribunis principiisque militum For *tribunus* see the notes ad 22.11.2 *Romanus quin etiam*, 23.3.9 *tribuno Constantiniano*, and 24.3.1 *paucissimos trucidasse*. For *principia*, 'commanding officers', see the note ad 22.3.2 *praesentibus*.

ad tuendam Mesopotamiam The original assignment was slightly different. The army under the command of Sebastianus and Procopius was to stay on the right bank of the Tigris river in order to keep

CHAPTER 8.17 275

Sapor occupied in northern Mesopotamia, and later to join forces with Arsaces; 23.3.5 with relevant notes.

ut poscebat sollemnitas For *sollemnis* and its derivatives see the note ad 20.4.9 *et sollemniter*. One may conclude from these words that there existed a kind of protocol for such meetings between generals and their commander-in-chief, but Amm. does not give any details.

et sequebantur benigne suscepti In the note ad 25.1.6 *in hac* it is stated that Amm. regularly pays attention to the way in which envoys, embassies and other visitors are received by the emperor, and that this says something about their standing. This is probably also the case here. The fact that Sebastianus and Procopius receive a friendly welcome implies that it was not held against them that they had not been able to join the main force of the army. We may suppose that the two generals were greeted with a kiss, cf. 22.9.13 *osculo susceptum rectorem provinciae* and 29.5.16 *susceptusque cum osculo*.

post quae itinere festinato Nisibi cupide visa extra urbem stativa castra posuit princeps Nisibis was 33 Roman miles, i.e. some 50 km, away from Thilsaphata/Thebetha; *Tab. Peut.* X 4. The journey may have taken the army two or three days. Note the poignant detail *cupide visa*. The soldiers had longed for the safety of Nisibis, which makes it only more distressing that the city was to pass into the hands of the enemy. According to Eun. *fr.* 29.1 Jovian remained near Nisibis only for two days (but see the note ad 25.9.12 *Proinde extractis*), using up all the city's resources without a kind word or a good deed for the inhabitants. Zos. 3.33.2 confirms that Jovian did not enter the city but encamped outside its walls: Μόλις δὲ σὺν πολλῇ κακοπαθείᾳ τῇ Νισίβει πλησιάσας ἐπιστῆναι μὲν οὐκ ἤθελε τῇ πόλει τοῖς πολεμίοις ἐκδεδομένῃ, καταλύσας δὲ ἔν τινι πρὸ τῆς πύλης ὑπαίθρῳ. Malalas *Chron.* 13.336 has the same information: Καὶ καταφθάσας ὁ βασιλεὺς Ἰοβιανὸς τὸ Νιζτίβιος ('after reaching the region of Nisibis') πόλιν οὐκ εἰσῆλθεν ἐν αὐτῇ, ἀλλ' ἔξω τῶν τειχέων κατεσκήνωσεν. Ephrem Syrus, inhabitant of Nisibis, reports that he saw the corpse of Julian, when the Roman army camped near his native city; *HcJul.* 3.1–2.

8.17

enixe 'Earnestly', a hapax in Amm. It is used frequently only by Livy.

ut ingressus palatio more succederet principum In view of the fact that *palatio* must be taken with *succederet*, it is better not to take *ingressus palatio* as an independent colon.

276   COMMENTARY

erubescens…urbem…tradi Although *erubescens* denotes the feeling of Jovian, the opinion is unmistakably that of the author himself, with his insistence on the shameful submission to Sapor.

8.18 In the last section Ammianus gives a detailed report of a particularly despicable act of Jovian. He had his namesake, the notary Iovianus, killed, thrown into a well and pelted to death with stones. The story illustrates Jovian's obsessive fear of losing the throne to a rival. It was his fear of another possible rival, Procopius, which, according to Amm., had driven Jovian to accept the surrender of i.a. Nisibis. This liquidation made Procopius decide to go into hiding: *e medio se conspectu discrevit maxime post Ioviani territus necem…quem…cruciabiliter didicerat interfectum*, 26.6.3. Sabbah 354–9 discusses the contrast between Amm.'s account of Jovian's short reign and that of Themistius in *Or.* 5. According to the panegyrist, Jovian had no difficulty in consolidating his power, because nobody was against him and because Jovian did not fear anybody as being more suitable than himself to reign: αἴτιον δέ, ὅτι μήτε δύσνουν τινὰ ὑπειλήφεις μήτε ἐδεδίεις ὡς ἀξιώτερον. (*Or.* 5.66 d).

Iovianus, primus inter notarios omnes See for this Iovianus and his function the note ad 24.4.23. He is also mentioned in 26.6.3 *Ioviani…notariorum omnium primi*.

quem in obsidione civitatis Maozamalchae per cuniculum docuimus evasisse cum aliis See for this 24.4.21–4 with the relevant notes. The fact that the *notarius* had been decorated by Julian as a war hero (*enituerunt hi, qui fecere fortissime, obsidionalibus coronis donati et pro contione laudati veterum more*, 24.4.24) is an indictment of Jovian. For Maozamalcha see the note ad 24.4.2 *cumque Maozamalcha venisset*.

praeceps actus in puteum siccum obrutus est saxorum multitudine superiacta After Alexander's death his wife Roxane got rid of her rivals in the same way, Plut. *Alex.* 77.6 τοὺς νεκροὺς εἰς τὸ φρέαρ κατέβαλε καὶ συνέχωσεν. The Macedonian king Archelaos killed his young brother, a possible rival for the throne, εἰς φρέαρ ἐμβαλὼν καὶ ἀποπνίξας, Pl. *Grg.* 471 c.

Iuliano perempto ipse quoque nominatus a paucis ut imperio dignus Iovianus may have been mentioned as a possible successor during the deliberations after Julian's death; 25.5.3 and the note *quae dum*. Fontaine n. 681 calls the liquidation of Iovianus "un acte d'intimida-

CHAPTER 8.18   277

tion envers le parti favorable à Julien." According to Sabbah 355
n. 33 Amm. deliberately used the words *ipse quoque nominatus a
paucis* to malign Jovian, who was also elected by only a few; he
argues convincingly that Amm. alludes here to 25.5.4 *tumultuantibus
paucis…Iovianus eligitur imperator.*

*nec post creatum Iovianum egit modeste, sed susurrans super negotio quaedam
audiebatur* It seems best to take *nec* in the sense of *ne quidem*; the
following clause then explains in what respect Iovianus failed to
change his tune. For *susurrare* see the note ad 20.8.11 *susurrantes
perniciosa*, where it is said that in Amm. whispering has almost always
a negative connotation. *Super negotio* is the equivalent of classical *ea
de re;* see the note ad 21.6.8 *damna negotiis.*

invitabatque ad convivia subinde militares One is reminded of Julian,
who on the eve of his pronunciamiento invited the officers who were
to leave for the eastern provinces at his table: 20.4.13 *ad conuiuium
proceribus corrogatis petere iure, si quid in promptu esset, edixit.* The fact
that Iovianus did this repeatedly (see for *subinde* the note ad 23.1.7)
could not fail to raise suspicion. The word *militares* is, as in this
passage, sometimes used by Amm. to refer to military officers; 14.5.3
militarium vel honoratorum; 15.5.12, 6.1 *consistorianis atque militaribus;*
21.16.3 *ut militarium aliquis ad civilia regenda transiret.* In general the
word means military men, those belonging to the army; 14.5.6, 7.15;
15.2.5, 3.1; 16.8.13; 20.4.4 (q.v.); 21.16.1; 26.7.1; 29.1.15.

CHAPTER 9

Introduction

Apart from the last two sections this chapter is concerned with an event which obviously was a very painful thorn in the author's flesh, viz. the actual surrender of Nisibis and the concomitant forced exile of its inhabitants.

In § 1–6 Ammianus describes the course of events. Many details tally with the report in Zos. 3.33.2–34.2, but, as the convenient synopsis in Klein, 1914, 130–1 clearly shows, Ammianus leaves out some facts, and his chronological order is slightly, but markedly different. There is every reason to assume that Ammianus' arrangement of the available evidence is due to his wish to compose a tightly structured and moving episode, culminating in the heartbreaking scenes of the exiles leaving the city in which they had been born and bred. Two allusions to the second book of the *Aeneid* bring the similarity with the Trojans' plight to the reader's notice.

Having roused the reader's sympathy, perhaps even his indignation at the loss of Nisibis, Ammianus has paved the way for a complaint against the lady Fortuna, who brought an inexperienced man to supreme power, a man who turned his attention primarily to the dangers posed by his potential rival Procopius, and who therefore was in a hurry to return from Persia. This entailed a surrender of territory, which was shamefully un-Roman, as anyone familiar with Roman history ought to know. The same history teaches that Roman authorities never hesitated to violate ignominious treaties which they had been forced to conclude. Jovian would have been fully justified in following their examples.

The final two sections (§ 12–13) contain brief and matter-of-fact information about Procopius taking care of Julian's burial, and his subsequent disappearance from sight.

Postridie I.e. the day after Jovian had made his camp outside Nisibis **9.1** and ordered the execution of the *notarius* Iovianus (25.8.17–8). Cf. τῇ ὑστεραίᾳ in Zos. 3.33.2.

Bineses, unus ex Persis, quem inter alios excellere diximus Amm. refers to 25.7.13 (q.v.), where he mentions *Bineses e numero nobilium optimatum*

280 COMMENTARY

as one of the four Persian hostages given to the Romans after the conclusion of the treaty with Sapor. Cf. for *excellere*, without any mention of a particular form of excellence, denoting a high status 17.12.12 *inter optimates excellens.*

mandata regis complere festinans Since Amm. never uses *rex* to denote a Roman emperor and, moreover, often refers to Sapor simply as *rex*, there can be no doubt that the latter's 'directives' are meant here. For Roman imperial *mandata* see the note ad 21.7.4 *mandatorum* and Marotta, 1991. Cf. 18.7.4 *imperatis sine mora completis.* As De Jonge notes ad loc., this meaning of *complere* ('to carry out') is by no means common. Examples can be found in TLL III 2096.33–42.

What orders Sapor gave to Bineses before he and the other hostages were exchanged is not explicitly stated, but implied in what follows: *promissa flagitabat instanter* and *gentis suae signum ab arce extulit summa.* Zosimus does not mention Bineses, but refers to the Persians' demands in 3.34.1: Περσῶν παραλαβεῖν κατὰ τὰς σπονδὰς ἐθελόντων τά τε ἔθνη καὶ τὰ φρούρια καὶ τὴν πόλιν.

promissa flagitabat Viz. the immediate surrender of Nisibis (25.7.11, cf. 25.8.13, 8.17). Cf. for the expression Cic. *Fam.* 3.11.4 *cum tua promissa per litteras flagitabam.*

et principe permittente Romano civitatem ingressus gentis suae signum ab arce extulit summa In the reports of Malalas and the *Chronicon Paschale* the same fact is related. In their versions, however, the name 'Bineses' has inexplicably become 'Iunius', the *arx* of Nisibis is merely 'one of the towers', and the parallel to Amm.'s *principe permittente* is slightly different in that it was not 'by permission' of Jovian, but 'at his command' that the banner was affixed: ἔλαβεν μεθ' ἑαυτοῦ ὁ βασιλεὺς Ἰοβιανὸς ἕνα τῶν σατραπῶν Περσῶν…ὀνόματι Ἰούνιον, εἰς τὸ παραλαβεῖν τὴν ἐπαρχίαν ('province') καὶ τὴν μητρόπολιν αὐτῆς. καὶ καταφθάσας ὁ αὐτὸς βασιλεὺς Ἰοβιανὸς τὴν Νισιβέων πόλιν οὐκ εἰσῆλθεν ἐν αὐτῇ, ἀλλ' ἔξω τῶν τειχῶν ἔστη. ὁ δὲ Ἰούνιος ὁ τῶν Περσῶν σατράπης ἐπελθὼν ἐν τῇ πόλει κατὰ κέλευσιν τοῦ βασιλέως εἰς ἕνα τῶν πύργων σημεῖον Περσικὸν ἐπέθηκε (*Chron. Pasch.* a. 363, cf. Malalas *Chron.* 13.336). See on this also the next note.

Cf. for *signum*, 'banner', 16.12.39 (q.v.) *purpureum signum draconis summitati hastae longioris aptatum.* Persian standards and banners are already attested for the Achaemenid period (Hdt. 9.59, X. *Cyr.* 6.3.4, 8.5.13). See Ackerman, 1939, 2767–72. According to Xenophon the standard of Cyrus the Great and other Persian kings

CHAPTER 9.1   281

was a golden eagle with outspread wings mounted upon a long shaft
(ἦν δὲ αὐτῷ τὸ σημεῖον ἀετὸς χρυσοῦς ἐπὶ δόρατος μακροῦ ἀνατεταμένος.
καὶ νῦν δ' ἔτι τοῦτο τὸ σημεῖον τῷ Περσῶν βασιλεῖ διαμένει, X. *Cyr.* 7.1.4,
An. 1.10.12; cf. Curt. 3.3.16). This changed later. At Persepolis some
audience scenes in the Throne Hall and among the Treasury Reliefs
include depictions of soldiers carrying square plaques on poles, while
the famous Alexander Mosaic from the Casa del Fauno in Pompeii,
now in the museum of Naples, shows, albeit 'per interpretationem
Romanam', the royal standard of Darius III. References in Shahbazi,
1996, who further notes: "Four Sasanian banners are represented in
sculptured scenes" (Shahbazi, 1996, 314 with pl. xxvi).

V's *submigratione* poses a problem. To assume the existence of a
noun *submigratio*, attested nowhere else, is hazardous; textual critics
have therefore concluded that *sub* should be detached and emended
to an appropriate word. Müller and Cornelissen try to salvage *sub* with
subitam and *sublime* respectively. Both solutions are, paleographically
speaking, possible, but *subitus* is the wrong word. The forced emi-
gration was not 'unexpected'; an adj. or adv. meaning 'immediate'
would have been appropriate. Although *sublime* (Cornelissen, 1886,
304) is not impossible, a clear parallel is lacking and it does not
result in a normal cursus. That is precisely the advantage of Clark's
summa, accepted by Seyfarth and Fontaine, which, having lost *-ma* by
haplography, could end up as *sub*.

In his *Carm. Nis.* 21 "scheint Ephraem von der Auslieferung noch
nichts zu wissen" (Beck ad 21.14 "Siehe die Kunde vom neuen König
usw."). In *HcJul.* 3, however, Nisibis' surrender is clearly present: "the
banner which was sent from the East wind the Magian took and
fastened on the tower" (3.1), "There I saw a foul sight, the banner
of the captor, which was fixed on the tower" (3.3) in J.M. Lieu's
translation (Lieu, 1989², 117–8).

migrationem e patria civibus nuntians luctuosam This is in accordance
with the proviso, *ut Nisibis et Singara sine incolis transirent in iura
Persarum* (25.7.11, q.v.). See for Amm.'s use of *luctuosus* and *luctificus*
the note ad 14.5.2 *victoriam luctuosam.* The raising of the flag was
apparently one of the orders Bineses had received from Sapor, "so
that a flag might point out for spectators that the city was the slave of
the lords of that banner" (Ephr. *HcJul.* 3.1, tr. Lieu). Amm.'s words
imply that the flag was raised and Nisibis evacuated on Sapor's order:
the Persian king gave the orders (*mandata regis*), Bineses carried them
out, and the Roman emperor could only comply (*principe permittente*).
The relevant passages of Malalas and the *Chronicon Paschale* do not

282   COMMENTARY

unequivocally refer to Sapor's part in the procedure. They do not
contradict Amm., but their wording suggests that Jovian was in
control: τοῦ βασιλέως Ῥωμαίων κελεύσαντος τοὺς πολίτας πάντας σὺν
πᾶσι τοῖς διαφέρουσιν αὐτοῖς ἕως ἑνὸς ἐξελθεῖν ('to leave the city to the
last man with all their property'), Malalas *Chron.* 13.336, cf. *Chron.
Pasch.* a. 363 (= Malalas, except for the addition of εὐθέως before
ἐξελθεῖν).

9.2 *et vertere solum extemplo omnes praecepti manus tendentes flentesque orabant,
ne imponeretur sibi necessitas abscedendi* The corresponding passage in
Zosimus reads thus: (Jovian listened to supplications) πάντων ὅσοι
κατὰ τὴν πόλιν ἦσαν ἐκλιπαρούντων μὴ προέσθαι σφᾶς μηδὲ εἰς πεῖραν
καταστῆσαι βαρβάρων ἠθῶν, τοσούτων ἐτῶν ἑκόντας τοῖς Ῥωμαίων νό-
μοις ἐντεθραμμένους (3.33.2). See for *vertere solum*, 'to migrate as
an exile', the last note ad 22.15.9. Personal passive constructions
are increasingly used in later Latin; see the notes ad 20.2.5 *nec
patefieri…permissis*, 20.4.6 *mitti praeceptis* and 24.1.14 *inflammari permisit.* In the present text the Agens is not mentioned, presumably
because Amm. focuses above all on the Patientes. Nevertheless, *imperatore…declinante* at the end of the section seems to suggest that Jovian
was the Agens.

        Referring to 20.4.15 *manus tendens oransque* and 31.15.9 *manus
tendentes orantesque*, Günther, 1891, 69 proposed to add *flentes*; this
proposal was also accepted by Clark and Fontaine, and can indeed
be defended as repairing a case of haplography.

*ad defendendos penates se solos sufficere sine alimentis publicis affirmantes
et milite* In Amm. the *ordo et populus* of Nisibis utter these words
(cf. *et haec quidem suppliciter ordo et populus precabatur* at the end
of this section). In Zosimus' version such sayings are put into the
mouth of a certain Σαβῖνος (see for him §3), who added them to
the supplications of the people: προσετίθει τοῖς παρὰ τοῦ πλήθους εἰς
ἱκεσίαν προσενεχθεῖσιν ὡς οὔτε δαπάνης εἰς τὴν πρὸς Πέρσας δεήσονται
μάχην οὔτε ἐπικουρίας ἐπεισάκτου ('an auxiliary force brought in from
outside'), δυνήσονται δὲ αὐτοὶ σώμασιν οἰκείοις καὶ δαπανήμασι τὸν
ἐπαχθησόμενον αὐτοῖς ἀποκρούσασθαι πόλεμον (3.33.4).

satis confisi affuturam iustitiam pro genitali sede dimicaturis Clark, Seyfarth and Viansino all print *iustitiam*, but Fontaine's *Iustitiam* is more
plausible. As is noted ad 23.5.17 *veluti librante*, Amm. likes to person-
ify justice, and there is no clear reason not to add the present text
to Seyfarth's eleven instances of *Iustitia*, as is advocated by Brandt,

CHAPTER 9.2

1999, 276; cf. also the note ad 25.5.8 *his ita* about *fortuna*. See for *genitalis*, 'native', the last note ad 22.8.19.

ut experti sunt saepe As in 337, 346 and 350 (cf. the note ad 25.1.15 *acceptae*). Ironically, in 350 Jovian's father-in-law Lucillianus had played an important part in defending the city (see the note ad 25.8.9 *Lucillianum*). In 25.8.14 and 25.9.8 Amm. also refers to the glorious past of Nisibis. There is, of course, no reference to the time when Nisibis, favouring the Persian cause, was captured and destroyed by Odaenathus (Zos. 1.39.1).

In classical prose the indicative would identify this as an authorial remark, but in Amm. it also occurs in subordinate clauses of oratio obliqua; see the second part of the note ad 21.5.11 *cuius beneficiis*.

ordo et populus See the note ad 22.9.4 *ordo squalens*.

sed ventis loquebantur in cassum imperatore, ut fingebat alia metuens, periurii piacula declinante Cf. 15.5.8 *ventis tamen loquebatur incassum*, where the same pleonasm occurs. Otto, 1890, nr. 1865 has a long list of instances in which *ventus* has a comparable proverbial sense. With *alia metuens* Amm. means Jovian's anxiety about his position; cf. *Procopii metuendum...nomen* (25.7.10), *quod magis metuebatur* (25.8.9) and *extimescit aemulum potestatis* (25.9.8). Amm.'s allegation that Jovian's wish to avoid the guilt of perjury was just make-believe, is repeated in 25.9.4 (*iuris iurandi religionem principe destinatius praetendente*) and 25.9.8 (*amictu periurii fugiendi*). See the notes ad loc. Zosimus also relates Jovian's reluctance to violate the agreement with the Persians, as do Malalas (*Chron.* 13.336) and, almost in the same words, the *Chronicon Paschale* a. 363 (ὀμωμοκέναι γὰρ ἔφασκεν καὶ μὴ βούλεσθαι δόξαν ἐπιόρκου παρὰ πᾶσιν ἔχειν). In 3.33.5 Zosimus refrains from commenting: Τοῦ δὲ εἰπόντος (sc. Jovian) οὐδὲν οἷόν τε τῶν συντεθειμένων παραβαθῆναι. However, the use of προίσχετο in 3.33.4 ὁ βασιλεὺς...τὰ συντεθειμένα προίσχετο perhaps suggests that Zosimus (or his source) had doubts about Jovian's motives as well (cf. LSJ s.v. προίσχω II "metaph. in Med.: to put forward as a pretext, allege"). So Brok 235. Paschoud n. 99 "Ammien seul parle de l'hypocrisie de Jovien" is only correct in that Amm. states this far more explicitly (*fingebat*).

In 25.7.14 (q.v.) Amm. says that the peace, concluded by Sapor and Jovian, had been consecrated by solemn oaths (*pace...iuris iurandi religionibus consecrata*). Anyone believing in the maxim οὐδενὶ τρόπῳ παραβατέον τὸν πρὸς τοὺς πολεμίους ὅρκον (Pseudo-Mauricius

284 COMMENTARY

Tacticus *Str.* 8.1.36) would have thought Jovian to be tied hand and foot. But Amm. was of another opinion, as is clear from his wording here (cf. 25.9.4 and 25.9.8) and his argument in 25.9.11, where he points to examples from the past. According to him a Roman commander should give preference to Rome's interest over anything else. He nowhere sets forth this view more clearly than in 28.5.4–7. After having related first that some Saxons in Gaul were ambushed by the Romans and killed to the last man although a truce had been made (*pactis indutiis*), he adds: *ac licet iustus quidam arbiter rerum factum incusabit perfidum et deforme, pensato tamen negotio non feret indigne manum latronum exitialem tandem copia data consumptam* (28.5.7). This did not preclude the author from judging Rome's enemies according to strict standards. Cf. e.g. Amm.'s *calcata fide sub Ioviano pactorum* when Sapor invaded Armenia (27.12.1).

See for *piaculum* as a synonym of *nefas* or *scelus* the long list of examples in TLL X 1.2071.31 sqq. and the note ad 23.6.35 *eratque piaculum*. The genitive *periurii* can be explained as explicative or as possessive ('belonging to'). Amm. has a predilection for *declinare*, 'to avoid'; *ut Martis ambigua declinentur* (14.10.14) and *haec aliaque pudenda declinant* (23.6.79) are comparable to the present text.

9.3 *tum Sabinus fortuna et genere inter municipes clarus ore volubili replicabat* Cf. for Sabinus, who is not included in *PLRE* I, Zos. 3.33.4, where he is called τοῦ βουλευτικοῦ προεστὼς καταλόγου. He is not mentioned elsewhere, but in the versions of Malalas and the *Chronicon Paschale* we find a man called Silvanus, described both as *comes* and *curialis*, playing the role of Sabinus: καὶ ἐξελθὼν πρὸς αὐτὸν Σιλουανός, κόμης τὴν ἀξίαν καὶ πολιτευόμενος τῆς αὐτῆς πόλεως, προσέπεσεν τῷ βασιλεῖ, δεόμενος μὴ παραδοῦναι τὴν πόλιν Πέρσαις (*Chron. Pasch.* a. 363, cf. Malalas *Chron.* 13.336). Apparently these authors mistakenly lumped together the Sabinus of the present text and the Silvanus of §4 (q.v.). Whether we should accept the assertion that Silvanus/Sabinus held the function of *comes* is disputed. Barnes, 1974, 230 does not exclude the possibility ("the man could have held the rank of *comes*"), but it is more likely that Paschoud n. 99 is right in stating that "Sabinus…n'était certainement pas en possession de la dignité de *comes*", for the combination *comes* and *curialis* would be rather odd.

See for *volubilis*, '(swiftly) rotating', either in a literal sense or metaphorically, the notes ad 20.11.26 *supinantur volubiliter* and 22.1.1 *Dum haec* respectively. In the present text, however, the adj. is almost a rhetorical t.t.; cf. 17.9.3 *verborum volubilitate conspicui, Rhet.*

CHAPTER 9.3

Her. 3.14.25 *vim volubilem orationis*, Cic. *Or.* 53 *flumen aliis verborum volubilitasque cordi est*, Macr. *Sat.* 7.9.9 *vestri oris nota volubilitas*. These various examples show that *volubili(ta)s* denotes a swift fluency of speech. In the notes on *replicare* ad 14.7.5 and 16.12.3 it is stated that Amm. never uses this verb in a legal sense. Strictly speaking this is true, but in the present case it is undeniably used figuratively in this sense. Heumann-Seckel provide this meaning s.v. *replicare*: "gegen die vom Beklagten vorgeschützten exceptio eine Gegenrede vorschützen." Jovian's '*exceptio*' was that he pleaded the impossibility of perjury, but the 'prosecutor' Sabinus now counters with a persuasive comparison with Constantius. That notorious loser of external wars (see the notes ad 21.1.2 *utrumque formidabat* and 21.16.15 *Ut...fuit*) never gave up Nisibis!

Constantium immani crudescente bellorum materia superatum a Persis interdum The verb *crudescere* is not attested before Vergil, who uses it twice in a context of warfare: *A.* 7.788 *effuso crudescunt sanguine pugnae* (Fordyce's "grew bloodier" is based on the assumption of a hidden etymological link, *crudus* being the adj. corresponding to *cruor*), *A.* 11.833 *crudescit pugna*. Perhaps Amm. is alluding to these phrases. Among the translators of the present passage only Selem and Fontaine try to bring out the metaphor in *immani crudescente bellorum materia* with "mentre infuriavano immani le fiamme delle guerre" and "au moment où le monstrueux brasier des guerres faisait rage". Presumably, they take *materia* to mean 'fuel'; cf. 19.4.2 *ignis materies*, 24.6.5 *materia, qua alitur ignis*. However, the present case could be a worn out metaphor, with *materia* as the equivalent of *causa* (see the relevant notes ad 19.11.3 and 20.4.15). In both interpretations *crudescere* poses a problem; TLL IV 1232.51sqq. suggests the meaning "invalescere, crudeliorem vel saeviorem fieri" (cf. Servius' explanation of *crudescit* in *A.* 11.833: *crudelior fit caede multorum*). This is far easier to understand in 19.2.6 *confestimque lacrimabilis belli turbo crudescit* (q.v.), where *turbo* refers to actual warfare. Perhaps in the present text *immani* should be taken with the predicate: 'when the reason for warfare grew to enormous proportions'.

Probably, Amm. himself would have been happy to say that Constantius was always beaten by the Persians, but in Sabinus' mouth he found this less opportune and so he wrote *interdum*, of which Paschoud n. 99 approves: "le *interdum* d'Amm. est plus juste", viz. than Zosimus' Κωνστάντιον μὲν τρεῖς Περσικοὺς πολέμους ἀναδεξάμενον καὶ ἐν πᾶσιν ἐλαττωθέντα (3.33.3). For Constantius and

286 COMMENTARY

his Persian wars see Blockley, 1989, the note ad 21.1.2, Paschoud's n. 19 ad Zos. 3.8.2 and, for all the sources in translation, Dodgeon-Lieu, 1991, 164–230.

deductumque postremo per fugam cum paucis ad Hibitam stationem intutam The story is only found in Amm. According to Dillemann, 1961, 109–10 *Hibita*, a name not mentioned elsewhere, is to be identified with *Thebeta*, which in its turn is probably to be identified with the *Thilsaphata* of 25.8.16 (q.v.): "Ammien montre ainsi, qu'...il n'a pas compris qu'il désignait le même lieu...par deux noms transcrits ou prononcés de manière différente". Blockley, 1989, 475 n. 60 convincingly dates the events described here to the time before 348.

In his edition Fontaine steers a bold, but lonely course. Basing himself on the total obscurity of Hibita, he prints *fugam cum paucis adhibitam ⟨in⟩ stationem intutam*, which poses two problems: *adhibere* with 'flight' as direct object, and the insertion of *in*. The latter could be accepted as repairing a loss by haplography, but there are no parallels for the expression *adhibere fugam*; Cic. *de Orat.* 2.294 *adhibere quandam in dicendo speciem atque pompam et pugnae similem fugam* describes the use of a rhetorical technique, when one has to 'retreat' during an argument.

panis frusto vixisse precario ab anu quadam agresti porrecto This must have been hard even for a man who *in vita parca et sobria edendi potandique moderatione valetudinem...retinuit firmam* (21.16.5, q.v.). Although not at all often, a 'lump of bread' does appear from time to time in Roman literature. The first instance is Cato about a corrupt politician: *frusto panis conduci potest* ('he can be hired'), *vel uti taceat vel uti loquatur* (Gel. 1.15.10 = Cato, *fr.* 40.2 Jordan = 112 Malcovati); in Sen. *Ep.* 18.10 *frustum hordeacei panis* is typical of a frugal diet; Juv. 14.128 goes one better about a miser, who eats *mucida caerulei panis...frusta* ("crusts of stale bread, blue with mould", tr. P. Green); in Apul. *Met.* 6.11 Venus goes to sleep *frusto cibarii panis ei* (i.e. Psyche) *proiecto*. The only other example in Amm. is 31.6.5 about Gothic slaves who had been sold *vino exili vel panis frustis*. In all these instances *frustum panis* represents the bare minimum of food. In the present text it is used for the *amplificatio* of a pathetic scene: Constantius has fled with a handful of men to an undefended fort, "where he lived on a crust of bread begged from an old woman" (Hamilton). So he was down and out, yet he never gave up Nisibis. Cf. the contrast noted by Zos. 3.33.3: αὐτὸν δὲ (i.e. Jovianus) μηδεμιᾶς τοιαύτης ἐπικειμένης ἀνάγκης τοῖς πολεμίοις τὴν πόλιν ἐκδοῦναι καὶ δεῖξαι

CHAPTER 9.3 287

Ῥωμαίοις ἡμέραν ἦν οὔπω τεθέανται, περιδεῖν ἀναγκαζομένοις πόλιν τοσαύτην καὶ χώραν πολεμίοις ἐκδιδομένην.

Iovianum inter exordia principatus provinciarum muro cessisse, cuius obice iam inde a vetustate innoxiae permanserunt Amm. has an idiosyncratic liking for the phrase *inter exordia*, using it fifteen times, i.a. 21.1.4 *inter exordia principatus* (q.v.), 21.16.8 *inter imperandi exordia*, 27.7.4 *inter imperitandi exordia*. Jovian is urged to regard Nisibis as "the barrier protecting his provinces" (Hamilton); cf. the phrase *orientis firmissimum claustrum* (25.8.14, q.v.). This wall or barrier is an obstacle for any enemy. The word *obex* figures in a variety of expressions, literally or metaphorically; it consists of shields in 16.12.36 (q.v.), of city gates (21.12.13, 24.5.2, 31.16.4) or walls (31.10.13). In 31.9.1 it denotes a person; it can be either a man-made obstacle (19.8.2) or a natural one (31.8.5 *undarum obicibus ruptis*). Here it is said to have safeguarded the security of the provinces from time immemorial. Cf. the comparable phrases in Zos. 3.33.5 πολλάκις οἱ ἀπὸ τῆς πόλεως ἐδεήθησαν ἱκετεύοντες μὴ στερηθῆναι τὴν Ῥωμαίων ἀρχὴν τοῦ προτειχίσματος, Ephr. *HcJul.* 2.18 'the shield of the cities' and Chrys. *pan. Bab.* 2.123 ὥσπερ τεῖχος...ἀρραγές.

The phrase *iam inde a vetustate innoxiae* (cf. Eun. *fr.* 29.1 Νίσιβιν... πάλαι Ῥωμαίοις οὖσαν κατήκοον and Zos. 3.33.2, quoted ad §2 *et vertere*) is a rhetorical hyperbole, quite functionally used in the circumstances. The earliest contacts with Rome date from the first century B.C., when Lucullus' troops took the city (cf. 25.9.8 *iam inde a Mithridatici regni temporibus*, with the note), but the Roman occupation then and under Trajan (D.C. 68.23.2, cf. 68.30.2) was only temporary. It was probably in the second century A.D., after Lucius Verus' successful campaign in Mesopotamia, that Nisibis first became a Roman city (the evidence for this, however, is only indirect, see Sturm, 1937, 735). The city was made a *colonia* by Septimius Severus (D.C. 36.6.2, 75.3.2; cf. Millar, 1990, 38–9). In the turbulent third century, however, and especially after the Sasanians had replaced the Arsacids, it was often lost, recaptured and lost again (cf. e.g. HA *Gd.* 26.6, 27.6, *Gall.* 10.3, 12.1, *T* 15.3, Zos. 1.39.1). In 298 Nisibis once more became Roman ("though how long it had been lost seems quite unclear", Millar, 1993, 178), as a result of the campaigns against the Persian king Narses (cf. the notes ad 23.5.11 *Maximiano* and 25.7.9 *Petebat*). From then onwards it remained under Roman rule until 363, so that in actual fact Nisibis was Roman for little more than half a century. To put it into the words of Ps. Joshua the Stylite, author of a chronicle

288   COMMENTARY

in Syriac: "In 609 (= 297/298 A.D.) the Romans ⟨plundered⟩ the city of Nisibis, and it was under their control for sixty-five years" (*Chronicle* 7, tr. Trombley-Watt; cf. the commentary of Luther, 1997, 96–101).

9.4 *cumque nihil promoveretur* TLL X 2.1896.17sqq. lists this instance of *promovere* as an example of the verb expressing "effectum quendam..., ut significetur i.q. proficere". Even an eminent citizen, a gifted speaker at that, who pulled out all the rhetorical stops, failed to make headway. Cf. Zos. 3.34.1 Ἐπεὶ δ' ἤνυον πλέον οὐδέν (but note the different order of events in Zosimus' account).

iuris iurandi religionem principe destinatius praetendente Burkert, 1997, 35 lucidly summarizes the advantages of one of the most remarkable and useful achievements of ancient religions, the oath, which functions in agreements on all levels: "Immer geht es darum, Lüge und Betrug auszuschalten, was die Sprache von sich aus nicht zu leisten vermag". Cic. *Off.* 3.104 formulates the Roman view: *est enim ius iurandum affirmatio religiosa.* It testifies to a degree of civilization which is not available to barbarians; in defending Fonteius against accusations by Gauls, Cicero (*Font.* 30) asks the rhetorical question: *An vero istas nationes religione iuris iurandi...commoveri arbitramini?* The Pythagoreans venerated the τετϱακτύς so much, *ut ex eo et iuris iurandi religionem sibi fecerint* (Macr. *comm.* 1.6.41). The present text refers to 25.7.14 (pace) *iuris iurandi religionibus consecrata.* In all these cases *religio* expresses the sacred character of the oath, and therefore the impossibility of transgressing it. Remarkably, however, both the inhabitants and the author are expecting just this from Jovian. Although *destinate* and *praetendere* can both be used as neutral terms (see the notes ad 25.5.3 and 23.5.11 respectively), in view of *ut fingebat alia metuens* (§2) and *amictu periurii fugiendi* (§8) they can only be interpreted in a negative sense here. The implication is therefore that breaking the oath would have been perfectly honorable. In §11 history will provide the arguments.

cum oblatam ei coronam aliquamdiu recusans coactus denique suscepisset Amm.'s order of events differs markedly from the scene which is reported by Zos. 3.33.2–4, which begins with the offering of crowns and moreover does not mention Jovian's reluctance to accept these: τῇ ὑστεϱαίᾳ στεφάνους ἅμα καὶ ἱκεσίας ἐδέχετο. In Amm.'s version it comes at the very end, as an incident during which Jovian loses his patience.

CHAPTER 9.4   289

With *coronam* Amm. must refer to the *aurum coronarium*, the
'crown-gold' (cf. Klauser, 1974, 300 n. 68) and not, pace TLL IV.2
984.16–21 and Viansino, 1985, I, 332 s.v. B, to the crown worn as
a sign of imperial rank as for instance in 26.2.3 *principali habitu circumdatus et corona* and 27.6.11 *corona indumentisque supremae fortunae
ornatum* – it was of course not up to Nisibis, or any other city, to invest
Jovian with the paraphernalia of emperorship. Amm. points to the
fact that the city of Nisibis (just like other cities, cf. the next note)
discharged itself of the customary, only in theory voluntary, duty of
offering gold crowns to an emperor at his accession (see for this the
note ad 25.4.15 *coronarium indultum*). A different matter is the way in
which the Nisibenes performed this duty. Klauser, 1974, 292 notes
that the *aurum coronarium* originally was paid "in goldenen Kränzen
von mehr oder weniger hohem Gewicht, daneben auch in anderen
kostbaren Gegenständen und nur ersatzweise in Geld; später war
die Geldzahlung wohl das Gewöhnlichere". From the context here
it would seem that not money, but a real golden crown was offered
(or, if Zosimus is right, more than one). Jovian must have felt the
embarrassing character of this offer, but in the end he saw no way to
refuse and so he accepted the crown(s).

*Silvanus quidam causarum defensor confidentius exclamavit: "ita", inquit,
"imperator, a civitatibus residuis coroneris."* The explicit mention of
Silvanus' profession (see *Cod. Theod.* 2.12.6 for the combination
defensor causarum) may simply be due to the historian's wish to
provide precise information, when he has this at his disposal, but
there are three reasons for considering another intention: 1. whereas
Sabinus is pictured as an eloquent aristocrat, Silvanus is obviously
placed much lower on the social scale, 2. *confidentius exclamavit*: see
for the most often unfavourable meaning of *confidenter* the note ad
20.4.18 *capiti Iuliani*; the man had the gall to shout loudly during the
ceremony, 3. Amm.'s personal aversion to lawyers in the eastern part
of the empire, which later found such a clear expression in the satiric
digression in 30.4.3–22. One may tentatively conclude that Amm.
contrasts the distinguished gentleman Sabinus with the vulgar blab
Silvanus, and therefore reject Frakes' proposal to see in Silvanus not
a lawyer (so the communis opinio, cf. e.g. *PLRE* I, Silvanus 4), but a
"hidden *defensor civitatis*" (Frakes, 1992, 528–9, cf. Frakes, 2001, 83).
For the person called 'Silvanus' by Malalas and the *Chronicon Paschale*
(apparently a mistake for 'Sabinus'), see the note ad §3 *Sabinus*.
   Is *residuus* here, as often, merely a synonym of *reliquus*: 'the other
cities' (thus Selem and Rolfe) or does it retain its full original mean-

290 COMMENTARY

ing 'still remaining' (see the note ad 25.5.2), as in the translations of Fontaine, Seyfarth, Hamilton and Caltabiano? Jovian's exasperation shows that he in any case understood it in the latter sense, and so Silvanus' inopportune remark only hastened the proceedings. We know from Eun. *fr.* 31 and Lib. *Ep.* 1436, 1439 that embassies from other cities, bearing gold crowns for Jovian, were on their way.

quo verbo exasperatus intra triduum omnes iussit excedere moenibus Singular *verbum* denoting a statement consisting of more words does not occur frequently. Sal. *Jug.* 11.7 *quod verbum in pectus Iugurthae altius quam quisquam ratus erat descendit* and Amm. 29.3.6 *subagresti verbo pius responderat imperator* are clear parallels, as appears from the respective contexts. Amm.'s only other instance of *exasperare* is *exasperati militis* (20.11.31, q.v.). Surveys of the outbursts of imperial anger in the *Res Gestae* can be found in Seager 34–5 and Brandt, 1999, 169 n. 270.

Zosimus also relates that Jovian was angry (ἀναχωρήσαντος σὺν ὀργῇ τοῦ βασιλέως, 3.34.1), but, unlike Amm., he does not say why. On the other hand, we owe to him the statement that the greater part of the inhabitants of Nisibis went to Amida, and that the other victims of Jovian's agreement with the Persians either fled or surrendered unconditionally: οἱ μὲν τῶν ἐθνῶν καὶ τῶν φρουρίων οἰκήτορες, εἰ μὴ λάθρα φυγεῖν ἠδυνήθησαν, ἐνέδοσαν τοῖς Πέρσαις πράττειν εἰς αὐτοὺς ὅ τι βούλοιντο, Νισιβηνοὶ δὲ ἀνακωχῆς ('delay'; = Amm.'s *intra triduum*?) εἰς τὸ μεταστῆναι τυχόντες, οἱ μὲν πολλοὶ καὶ σχεδὸν ἅπαντες εἰς τὴν Ἀμίδαν ἀπανέστησαν, ὀλίγοι δὲ ἑτέρας κατῴκησαν πόλεις (3.34.1). In Malalas' report of the departure of the Nisibenes the following detail concerning their new home is recorded: καὶ τειχίσας πόλιν ἔξω τοῦ τείχους τῆς πόλεως Ἀμίδης, καλέσας τὴν κώμην Νισίβεως, ἐκεῖ πάντας τοὺς ἐκ τῆς Μυγδονίας χώρας οἰκεῖν ἐποίησε (sc. Jovian) καὶ Σιλουανὸν τὸν πολιτευόμενον (*Chron.* 13.336, cf. *Chron. Pasch.* a. 363 and Chrysos, 1976, 27 n. 15). The poet Ephrem, as Lieu, 1989², 99 points out, referring to *Hist. S. Ephr.* 10, col. 26 Lamy, was one of those who went to Amida, where he had some maternal relatives. But Ephrem, who later moved from Amida to Edessa, did not leave Nisibis immediately. At first he remained in the city, seeing to his surprise that Sapor showed himself full of respect for Christianity (cf. *HcJul.* 2.22–3, 27).

What Sapor did to replace the inhabitants of Nisibis after they had left the city is not recorded in the classical sources. The Arabic historian al-Tabari, however, relates that the Persian king "had twelve thousand people of good family from Istakhr, Ispahan and other

CHAPTER 9.4   291

regions of his land sent to Nesibin and settled them there" (*Annales* p. 843 Barth-Nöldeke, tr. al-Issa and Dance, quoted in Dodgeon-Lieu, 1991, 294). Although Tabari's account of the contacts between Sapor and Jovian is rather distorted, this detail may be true. Julian in *Or.* 1.27 a–b, speaking of one of Sapor's attempts to take Nisibis, already mentioned the plans of the Persians to bring in colonists to the cities they had captured: διενοοῦντο γὰρ ὡς καὶ τὰς πόλεις καθέξοντες καὶ τῆς χώρας ἤδη κρατήσαντες κληρούχους ἡμῖν ἐπάξουσι ("for it was their intention to reduce our cities and, once masters of the country, to bring in colonists in spite of us", tr. Wright; cf. Lieu, 1986, 498 and Teixidor, 1995, 504).

The impact of the forced migration on Nisibis' position as a centre of Syriac Christianity may have been more limited than one might expect. "De fait, ni la population transférée depuis les régions orientales de l'empire ne dut être tellement nombreuse, ni le départ des habitants si massif, car le syriaque continua à être la langue parlée et écrite de la ville après la retraite romaine" (Teixidor, 1995, 505; there is hardly any direct information about Christianity in Nisibis for the second half of the fourth century, as the relevant pages of Vööbus, 1965 and Fiey, 1977 make clear). It is also possible that some of the inhabitants of Nisibis returned to the city they first were forced to leave. However, it is wrong to see with Seeck, 1923[4], IV, 365 an indication for this in Ephr. *HcJul.* 2.26. In the passage referred to ("The Just one, whose wrath is powerful, mixed with anger his compassion in that he did not send us into captivity or expel us, he made us dwell in our land", tr. J.M. Lieu), Ephrem only implies that the Nisibenes were allowed to go to another part of Roman territory and were not like, for instance, the populace of Singara in 360, deported to the remotest parts of Persia (20.6.7, q.v.). Cf. S.N.C. Lieu's note ad loc. and Sturm, 1937, 749. For deportations see the note ad 24.1.9 *reliqui vero* (add to the literature cited there Kettenhofen, 1996 and Winter-Dignas, 2001, 257–67).

detestantes rerum praesentium statum Jovian's anger is matched by the emotions of Nisibis' citizens: *detestari* is a strong term, as appears e.g. from the famous phrase *Quidam detestantes ut venena doctrinas* (28.4.14) in the second satire on Roman society; cf. also 31.6.3, where it is reported that the Goths, stationed at Hadrianopolis, were being treated badly *laceratique ad ultimum detestatione atque conviciis.* The phrase *rerum praesentium status* also occurs in 18.7.10 and 21.2.3; cf. also 15.5.25 *pro statu rei praesentis.*

292 COMMENTARY

9.5 In sections 5 and 6 the episode reaches its climax in an impression-istic description of the piteous scenes which took place, when the inhabitants of Nisibis were forced to leave their city. Two clear allusions to the second book of the *Aeneid* invite the reader to compare Nisibis' plight with the fall of Troy.

Appositis itaque compulsoribus mortem, si qui distulerit egredi, minitantibus In 22.6.1 (q.v.) and 27.12.7 *compulsor* is a t.t. in the field of taxation, but here it is obviously a general term denoting 'a person who is constraining'. See the note ad 22.16.23 *erubescit* for *si qui* as the equivalent of *quicumque*, and cf. also the note ad 22.9.10 *qui esset* for the use of interrogative and indefinite *qui* and *quis*. Threatening those who were slow in departing with death is a breathtaking detail, not present in other sources.

moenia permixta sunt lamentis et luctu This seems a clear parallel of Zos. 3.34.2 πάντα δὲ ἦν οἰμωγῆς καὶ θρήνων μεστά, but that phrase concerns the situation in the entire region, not only in Nisibis. More important, however, is the fact that Amm. is undeniably alluding to Verg. *A.* 2.298 *diverso interea miscentur moenia luctu*. TLL X 1.1540.40 (see also 1544.21–2) regards *permiscere* here as almost a synonym of *implere*. This is correct, provided the connotation of confusion is not forgotten. See for the combination *lamentis et luctu* the relevant notes ad 18.3.1 and 21.15.4 and cf. for the entire scene Chrys. *pan. Bab.* 2.123.

per omnia civitatis membra See for *membra* denoting the parts of a town the note ad 20.6.7 *cuncta oppidi membra*.

cum laceraret crines matrona, exsul fuganda laribus, in quibus nata erat et educata, orbataque mater liberis vel coniuge viduata procul ab eorum manibus pelleretur et turba flebilis postes penatium amplexa vel limina lacrimabat Amm. now focuses on the emotions of the married women and the widows, using the singular for some vivid vignettes, without violating the standards laid down by Polybius in his attack (2.56) on the historian Phylarchus' predilection for pathetic scenes of wailing women. In despair or sorrow women often damaged or tore apart their hairdo. There are quite a few examples in Ovid's *Metamorphoses*, e.g. 11.682–3 *nec crines solvere curat,/ scindit*, 13.534 *albentes lacerata comas* (see Bömer ad loc.); cf. also Verg. *A.* 9.478 *scissa comam* and 12.870 *infelix crinis scindit Iuturna solutos* and see further TLL VII 2.825.50sqq.; *fuganda* is one of Amm.'s many examples of

CHAPTER 9.6 293

the gerundivum functioning as a part. fut. pass.; see the note ad 20.2.4 *opitulari* and Szantyr 394.

Possibly, *in quibus nata erat et educata* is meant to allude to Livy's description of the deportation of Alba Longa's populace to Rome in ch. 29 of the first book of *Ab urbe condita*; §4 contains these words *cum larem ac penates tectaque in quibus natus quisque educatusque essent relinquentes exirent.* See Tränkle, 1962, 24 n. 8a and Eigler, 2003, 188. However, the verbs in question are more often paired, and in Liv. 5.54.3 and 42.34.2 similar phrases occur in a different context. In contrast to 31.6.7 *raptae sunt matres et viduatae maritis coniuges ante oculos caesis*, viz. by the Goths, in the present text women who had earlier lost their children or husbands are meant.

TLL VI 1.890.49–60 provides a list of cases in which *flebilis* is the equivalent of "flens vel ad flendum pronus"; cf. Ov. *Met.* 14.748–9 *qua flebilis/ ibat pompa* (see Börner ad loc.), Apul. *Met.* 3.8 *quaedam mulier…lacrimosa et flebilis* (see Van der Paardt ad loc.). The second Vergilian allusion in this section is to *A.* 2.489–90 *tum pavidae tectis matres ingentibus errant/ amplexaeque tenent postis atque oscula figunt*; cf. also *A.* 3.351 *Scaeaeque amplector limina portae.*

See for the curious change of modus in *laceraretur…pelleretur…lacrimabat* the end of the note ad 25.3.10 *aestus calescens.*

For the final phase of his description Amm. widens the view to a general picture, in which the Nisibenes are seen fleeing in all directions with only a small part of their belongings. Two instances of *enim* appeal to the reader's empathy. **9.6**

exin variae complentur viae, qua quisque poterat dilabentium The translators treat *dilabentium* as the complement of *complentur*, which is indeed the most likely syntactical structure of the sentence. See for the gen. with verbs of 'filling' Kühner-Stegmann 1.467 and Szantyr 82.

properando enim multi furabantur opes proprias See for the abl. gerundii as the equivalent of the part. praes. the note ad 20.4.22 *diu tacendo.* Note the powerful paradox to describe the predicament of Nisibis' exiles: they had been put in such a difficult situation that they could only hurriedly 'smuggle away their own possessions'.

hanc enim reliquerunt peniuria iumentorum The Roman army could not be of assistance in this predicament, since many of their pack animals had been consumed for want of food (25.8.6, 25.8.15).

294   COMMENTARY

9.7 *Tu hoc loco, Fortuna orbis Romani, merito incusaris* With his sensitive
sketch of the misery which had hit Nisibis' inhabitants Amm. has
laid the foundation for his indictment of the accountable authority.
Surprisingly, this is not primarily the new emperor, but the divine
personification of the historical course of the Roman empire. The
word *fortuna* occurs more than a hundred times in the *Res Gestae*; in a
comparatively small minority of the cases Seyfarth prints it as *Fortuna*.
The criteria are not fully clear. Why *Fortunae saevientes procellae*
(14.1.1) and *Fortunae aliquamdiu bonae gubernatricis* (25.4.14), but
si affuisset fortuna flatu tandem secundo (16.1.1) and *fortuna versabilis*
(23.5.19)? See on fortune's role in the *Res Gestae* Ensslin, 1923,
69–77, Naudé, 1964, Camus, 1967, 177–84, Matthews 427, Marié,
1989 and the notes ad 20.4.13, 23.5.19 and 25.4.14. It is hard, if
not impossible, to define this role, since it essentially defies and
baffles human scrutiny. In adversity man is inclined to complain, like
e.g. Procopius: *ut in arduis necessitatibus solet, cum Fortuna expostulabat
luctuosa et gravi* (26.9.9). In the present case the author would have
expected the Fortuna of the Roman empire to take better care of her
domain. Whereas Livy often used the phrase *fortuna populi Romani*,
Amm., as a writer of imperial times, has substituted the Roman
people by the Roman world. The phrase *orbis Romanus* is often used
by other fourth-century historians, Eutropius, Aurelius Victor, the
Historia Augusta, and it occurs fourteen times in the *Res Gestae*. See
the notes ad 22.9.1 and 23.5.19, and consult Vogt, 1929 for the
history of the concept.

As to *hoc loco*, Zosimus in 3.32 also felt the need to interrupt his
narrative (§ 1 εἰς τοῦτο τῆς ἱστορίας ἀφιγμένῳ) for a digression on the
significance of the treaty of 363 (see below, ad § 9), but, unlike Amm.,
he put it not after but before his sketch of the events at Nisibis.

*quae difflantibus procellis rem publicam excussa regimenta perito rei gerendae
ductori consummando iuveni porrexisti* Strictly speaking, *difflare* means
"to scatter by blowing" (OLD s.v.), but here it rather seems to express
that the storms were driving the ship of the commonwealth 'off
course'. No doubt *regimenta*, the 'poetical' variant of *regimina*, denotes
the steering-oar, which had been knocked out of the hands of a
leader who knew how to deal with the task in hand. In contrast to
this experience Jovian's training had not been completed yet. The
verb *consummare* is often used in a comparable sense by Quintilian.
In the present text *consummando* is the counterpart of *perito* (cf. Ruf.
Fest. 29.2 *in imperio rudis*). Seyfarth's "einem schon vom Tode ge-
zeichneten jungen Mann" is based on an entirely different meaning

CHAPTER 9.8   295

of the verb and does not fit the context at all. The term *iuveni* only
serves to emphasize the contrast; in actual fact Jovian was the same
age as Julian. However, the latter had already won his spurs in Gaul
(cf. 25.4.25 *quae omnia iuvenis iste ad occiduam plagam specie Caesaris
missus…cuncta paene mira dictu celeritate correxit*, with the notes). See
for *ductor* the note ad 25.1.2 *Machameus*.

*quem nullis ante actae vitae insignibus in huiusmodi negotiis cognitum nec
vituperari est aequum nec laudari* Fontaine's rendering of *nullis…insig-
nibus* must be correct: "par aucune action remarquable dans sa vie
antérieure"; Caltabiano's translation is similar. It is, however, very
difficult to find any parallels for *insignia*, 'significant feats'; 18.6.22
multisque victoriarum insignibus nobilis would come near, if *victoriarum*
is interpreted as a gen. explicativus or identitatis.

Praise and blame are the gist of epideictic rhetoric: *Demonstra-
tivum est quod tribuitur in alicuius certae personae laudem vel vitupera-
tionem* (*Rhet. Her.* 1.2), *constat laude et vituperatione* (Quint. *Inst.* 3.7.1),
τῶν δὴ ἐπιδεικτικῶν τὸ μὲν ψόγος, τὸ δὲ ἔπαινος (Men. Rh. 331.15).
But praise and blame also often crop up in philosophical discussions
about determinism and free will. The adversaries of determinism ask:
πῶς ἔτ᾽ ἂν εὐλόγως οἱ μὲν εἶεν ἐν ἐπαίνοις, οἱ δὲ ἐν ψόγοις; (Alex. Aphr.
Fat. 16, p. 187.26–7 Bruns), and the consequences of determinism
are clear: εἰ γὰρ εἵμαρται τόνδε τινὰ ἀγαθὸν εἶναι καὶ τόνδε φαῦλον,
οὔθ᾽ οὗτος ἀπόδεκτος οὐδὲ ἐκεῖνος μεμπτέος (Just. 1 *apol.* 43.2). See
further the survey in Amand, 1945. It is not possible to define from
which tradition Amm.'s remark ultimately derives. The combination of praise and blame also occurs in 15.5.38, 22.10.4, 29.5.23.
Glossing over Jovian's shortcomings has a hidden implication: with
a slight variation of a wellknown saying one could say: "qui excuse,
accuse".

illud tamen ad medullas usque bonorum pervenit In contrast to Amm.'s   **9.8**
two other instances of *medullae* (16.8.12, 30.4.13) *medullae* here
denotes the seat of emotions, the 'heart'; cf. *mihi haeres in medullis*
(Cic. *Fam.* 15.16.2), *hoc si quis in medullas demiserit* (Sen. *Tranq.*
11.8). Amm.'s three instances of the adv. *medullitus* (14.1.9, 15.2.3,
30.8.10) have a comparable meaning. Cf. for *boni*, 'decent people',
'law abiding citizens', 15.5.8 *inimicus bonorum omnium diuturnus et
gravis*, 19.12.17 *propugnatoris bonorum et defensoris* (q.v.), 27.6.9 *faciet,
ut sciant se boni intellegi*, 30.4.4 *ad usque bonorum extulit odium*. The
cursus planus brings out that *pervenit* is in the perfect tense.

296 COMMENTARY

dum extimescit aemulum potestatis Cf. *alia metuens* in § 2. The same criticism is expressed by Eutropius (*Sed dum aemulum imperii veretur, intra Orientem residens gloriae parum consuluit*, 10.17.3, cf. Ruf. Fest. 29.2 *cupidior regni quam gloriae*), who, according to Valesius, may have been Amm.'s model: "Eutropium imitatus videtur Marcellinus". Paschoud, 1975, 188–201 argues for a more complicated interdependence of Amm., Eutropius and others in these matters. See for this below, ad § 9. The *aemulus* in question must be Procopius (cf. 25.7.10) rather than Jovian's namesake Iovianus (cf. 25.5.18), Procopius being the more intimidating of the two possible rivals (cf. the note ad 25.5.3 *si Mesopotamiam*).

dumque in animo Gallias et Illyricum versat quosdam saepe sublimiora coeptasse This fear of Jovian has already been mentioned in 25.8.8–11. Valesius' suggestion to introduce *per* before *Gallias* has been accepted by Clark and Fontaine, but Seyfarth follows Blomgren 40, who regards *quosdam...coeptasse* as an asyndetically added explanation. Neither solution results in a fully satisfactory structure of the sentence. See the note ad 20.4.6 *perque varias curas* for the various ways in which Amm. uses the verb *versare*, 'to turn over in the mind'. The meaning of *sublimiora* is determined by its context. In 16.5.6 *animo ad sublimiora scandenti* Julian's love of lofty thoughts is expressed; 25.8.11 *ad sublimiora provectus* denotes promotion, but 19.12.12 *temptandi sublimiora* (causa) refers to forbidden ambitions. A similar meaning is required for the present text. Some recent examples of usurpers in the West: Magnentius, Silvanus, Julian in Gaul (A.D. 350, 355 and 360), and Vetranio in Illyricum (350).

famam adventus sui praevenire festinans indignum imperio facinus amictu periurii fugiendi commisit The phrase at the beginning may have been borrowed from Liv. 8.30.12 *non tamen praevenire famam adventus sui potuit*, but see Oakley ad loc. for some comparable phrases; as to Amm., cf. 14.2.9 *ut motus sui rumores celeritate nimia praevenirent*, 18.2.14 *sollicitarum gentium opinione praeventa* (q.v.), 18.6.3 *fama celeritate praeventa*, 25.8.13 *Hos tabellarios fama praegrediens*. See also the note ad 21.9.6 *ut fax* about Julian's speed of action and on such speed as an imperial virtue. Jovian's eagerness to rush on can be regarded as its caricatural contrast.

Does *indignum imperio* mean "unworthy of an emperor" (Rolfe, Hamilton, Selem, Caltabiano) or "indigne de l'empire" (Fontaine, Seyfarth)? The latter is perhaps not impossible for Amm.'s usage: cf. e.g. *addidit quaedam imperio* (16.10.2), *Romano imperio iuncta est*

CHAPTER 9.9–11   297

(22.16.6, about Egypt), although it should be noted that these instances are primarily concerned with geography. In view of the context, which focuses on Jovian's conduct, it is more likely that his imperial dignity is at stake. Cf. Sal. *Hist.* 2.70.2, where the author reports that the extravagant private behaviour of the proconsul Q. Caecilius Metellus Pius harmed his reputation, *maxime apud veteres et sanctos viros superba illa, gravia, indigna Romano imperio aestimantis* ("especially in the estimation of men of the old Roman type, men of irreproachable character who judged such an attitude as arrogant, unsupportable, and unworthy of the authority of Rome", tr. McGushin). The proconsul Metellus failed to be a worthy representative of Roman authority in Spain. In a different way Jovian also went astray and in his case it was the imperial authority which was damaged; cf. also *cum imperio congruens* (20.8.17), *non esse imperatorium* (22.7.5) and *imperio dignus* (25.8.18). See for the assessment of Jovian's conduct, 25.7.13 *Quo ignobili decreto firmato* (q.v.).

Referring to 19.11.4 *amicitiae velamento* (q.v.), Wagner interprets *amictu* as *praetextu*. This is no doubt right (cf. 25.9.2 *ut fingebat*, 25.9.4 *principe...praetendente*), but remarkable: from TLL I 1901.47–50 it appears that this meaning of *amictus* is very rare.

Nisibi prodita, quae iam inde a Mithridatici regni temporibus, ne oriens a Persis occuparetur, viribus restitit maximis The adj. *Mithridaticus* occurs only here in Amm.; *Mithridates*, i.e. Mithridates VI Eupator (120–63 B.C.), is, apart from the present text, mentioned in 16.7.9, 16.12.41, 23.6.56 and 29.5.33.

During the third Mithridatic war Roman soldiers, led by L. Licinius Lucullus (see for him the note ad 23.5.16 *ut Lucullum*), captured Nisibis (Plut. *Luc.* 32.3–4, cf. 36.7; D.C. 36.6.1–8.1). However, as is explained in the note ad 25.9.3 *Iovianum inter*, Amm. greatly simplifies the history of this city in the Roman period. His allegation, that Nisibis ever since the time of king Mithridates had struggled with all its might to prevent the Persian occupation of the East (see for *oriens* the note ad 20.1.1), is a gross exaggeration. In Zos. 3.32.2 Lucullus' successes are also mentioned.

A brief excursion into the history of the Roman republic intends to show the unprecedented character of Jovian's concessions. A similar aside, with some of the same *exempla* as given by Amm., can be found in Eutr. 10.17.2–3. Ruf. Fest. 29.2 is much shorter and refrains from giving *exempla*, but he also stresses the uniqueness of what happened (*quod numquam antea accidit*) as a result of the peace treaty of 363, as

9.9–11

298 COMMENTARY

does Zosimus (3.32). In a rather lenghty digression Zosimus refers to Lucullus, Pompey, Crassus and Marc Antony (3.32.2–3), but, unlike Amm. and Eutropius, he leaves out examples derived from Roman republican history of old. Instead, he refers to the imperial period, mentioning Gordian III, Philippus Arabs and Valerian (3.32.4–5). Paschoud, 1975, 188–201 discusses Zosimus' chapter and its connection with the other sources mentioned. He argues inter alia that all these digressions ultimately go back to the work of Nicomachus Flavianus and that "Ammien suit sans doute de très près Nicomaque en reprenant peut-être intégralement ses exempla" (p. 198). Since the work of Nicomachus Flavianus is completely lost, it is hard to substantiate this view. However, the theory of a common source for all the digressions is no doubt right.

9.9 *numquam enim ab urbis ortu inveniri potest annalibus replicatis, ut arbitror, terrarum pars ulla nostrarum ab imperatore vel consule hosti concessa* With *enim* Amm. seems to appeal to the reader's understanding of Nisibis' enduring tenacity: such staunchness is totally normal for a Roman stronghold, as anyone with a decent knowledge of Roman history ought to know. The restriction implied in *ut arbitror* (see for this especially the very last section of the *Res Gestae*, where it also tones down *numquam*) is meant to protect the author against the accusation of flagrantly tampering with historical evidence. See for *replicare*, 'to unroll', the note ad 20.9.6 *replicatoque volumine*.

With *ab urbis ortu* Amm. prepares his readers for examples taken from five or more centuries ago. The expression is remarkably rare, the only parallels seem to be Cic. *Tusc.* 4.1 *a primo urbis ortu*, HA *Car.* 2.1 *ab ortu urbis*; cf., however, also Serv. *A.* 1.272 *usque ad urbis Romae ortum* and ad 1.267. As to the contents of §9 and 10, obviously Amm., in unrolling 'the historical evidence', stopped at V. Max. 2.8.4–5, strictly speaking not an annalistic source. Cf. Eutr. 10.17.1–2 *Qui* (i.e. Jovian)...*pacem cum Sapore...fecit multatus finibus ac nonnulla imperii Romani parte tradita. Quod ante eum annis mille centum et duobus de viginti fere, ex quo Romanum imperium conditum erat, numquam accidit* and Ruf. Fest. 29.2 *condicionibus (quod numquam antea accidit) dispendiosis Romanae rei publicae inpositis ut Nisibis et pars Mesopotamiae traderetur.* Zosimus, in his digression, is more circumstantial. He first raises a question, viz. 'if ever the Romans had had to yield to others what they had obtained before or, in other words, if ever they had endured the sight of an enemy getting what once had been in Rome's possession' (εἴ ποτε Ῥωμαῖοι τῶν αὐτοῖς τι κτηθέντων ἑτέροις ὑπέστησαν παραδοῦναι, ἢ ὅλως ἕτερον ἔχειν τι τῶν ὑπὸ τὴν

CHAPTER 9.9 299

ἐπικράτειαν αὐτῶν ἅπαξ γενομένων ἠνέσχοντο, 3.32.1). In his decidedly negative answer, in which he restricts himself to the history of the East, he argues that, after the conquests of Lucullus and Pompey (3.32.2), Rome never lost any territory, not after Crassus' crushing defeat (3.32.3), not after Mark Antony's careless actions (ibid.), not after the death of Gordian III and the disgraceful peace concluded by Gordian's successor Philippus (3.32.4), and, finally, not even after the humiliating capture of Valerian (οὐδὲ οὕτω Πέρσαις ἄδειαν δέδωκεν ὑφ' ἑαυτοῖς τὰ χωρία ταῦτα ποιήσασθαι, 3.32.5). It was only after Julian's death that the Romans had to abandon part of their territory: Μόνη δὲ ἡ Ἰουλιανοῦ τοῦ αὐτοκράτορος τελευτὴ πρὸς τὴν τούτων ἀπώλειαν ἤρκεσεν (3.32.6).

Paschoud, 1975, 193–4 sees a difference between the accounts of Ammianus, Eutropius and Festus on the one hand and Zosimus on the other: "Zosime omet une précision importante: ces derniers, explicitement (Eutrope) ou implicitement (Festus et Ammien), parlent de cessions territoriales *à la suite d'un accord*, alors que Zosime parle de cessions territoriales en général, ce qui rend tout son raisonnement non pertinent". However, the restriction, italicized by Paschoud, cannot be upheld. Like Zosimus, the three Roman authors mentioned simply state that Rome had never before accepted the surrender of part of its territory. In this they exaggerate, of course, as Casaubonus (see Wagner's note ad loc.) already argued, pointing to Hadrian's evacuation of Mesopotamia, Assyria and Greater Armenia (cf. e.g. Eutr. 8.6.2 and HA *H* 5.3, 9.1), Aurelian's abandonment of Trans-Danubian Dacia (cf. HA *A* 39.7) and Diocletian's surrender of part of Egypt (cf. Procop. *Pers.* 1.19.29).

sed ne ob recepta quidem, quae direpta sunt, verum ob amplificata regna triumphales glorias fuisse delatas Having availed himself of a nom. c. inf. construction in the first part of the sentence, Amm. construes the second part as if something like *annales veteres ostendunt* had preceded. V. Max. 2.8 deals with the *ius triumphandi*. In §4 we find *cautum erat ut pro aucto imperio, non pro reciperatis quae populi Romani fuissent triumphus decerneretur*, precisely the same restriction as worded by Amm. There are no other testimonia for such a restrictive provision, and Mommsen, 1887[3], I, 133. n. 1 explains that Valerius Maximus makes a mistake here. No triumph could be awarded for "die Überwindung aufständischer Bürger" and that was the case at Capua and Fregellae, to which Amm. refers in the next section.

Amm.'s use of *regna* to denote Roman territory in the present text and in 26.1.12 *nondum extentis fusius regnis* is remarkable. The clearest

300 COMMENTARY

parallel is Lucr. 3.836–7 *in dubioque fuere utrorum ad regna cadendum/ omnibus humanis esset terraque marique.* Kenney ad loc. interprets *regna* as "territorial empire rather than 'rule' in the abstract".

9.10 *unde Publio Scipioni ob recuperatas Hispanias, Fulvio Capua post diuturna certamina superata et Opimio post diversos exitus proeliorum Fregellanis tunc internecivis hostibus ad deditionem compulsis triumphi sunt denegati* V. Max. 2.8.4–5 is the source for the contents of this section. In 2.8.5 Valerius Maximus remarks that neither Scipio *ob reciperatas Hispanias* nor M. Marcellus *ob captas Syracusas* was awarded a triumph, *quod ad eas res gerendas sine ullo erant missi magistratu.* This wellknown rule (cf. e.g. Liv. 28.38.4 *magis temptata est triumphi spes quam petita pertinaciter, quia neminem ad eam diem triumphasse, qui sine magistratu res gessisset, constabat* and Plut. *Pomp.* 14.1 διὸ καὶ Σκιπίων ὁ πρῶτος ἀπὸ μειζόνων καὶ κρειττόνων ἀγώνων, ἐν Ἰβηρίᾳ Καρχηδονίων κρατήσας, οὐκ ᾔτησε θρίαμβον· ὕπατος γὰρ οὐκ ἦν οὐδὲ στρατηγός, with Mommsen, 1887³, 126ff.) was of no use to Amm. and neither was Marcellus' feat. The recovery of Spain by Publius Scipio took place in 210–206 (cf. Scullard, 1970, 39–108). This Scipio, i.e. P. Cornelius Scipio Africanus Maior, is called *superior* in 21.14.5 and 15.10.10 (pace Brok 237 the *Africanus* of 24.4.27 is Scipio Minor, not Scipio Maior). Apart from Amm. and Valerius Maximus it is related by Liv. 28.38.4 (quoted above), 31.20.4 and D.C. 17.57.56 (cf. Plut. *Pomp.* 14.1) that Scipio was refused a triumph. Broughton, 1951, 299 among others argues that there also was another tradition: "according to Polybius (11.33.7) and Appian (*Ib.* 38…) he received one. Perhaps he celebrated an *ovatio*". This is only correct as far as Appian is concerned: καὶ Σκιπίων…ἐθριάμβευεν. Polybius merely says that Scipio took home a splendid victory: κάλλιστον θρίαμβον καὶ καλλίστην νίκην τῇ πατρίδι κατάγων.

In 2.8.4 Valerius Maximus reports that *Q. Fulvius, qui Capua capta, et L. Opimius, qui Fregellanis ad deditionem compulsis* asked permission to hold a triumph, met with a refusal. Cf. the note ad 25.9.9 *sed ne.* For the other sources concerning these events see Broughton, 1951, 274; 1986, 95 (Fulvius) and 1951, 510; 1986, 152 (Opimius). In 212 B.C. consul Q. Fulvius Flaccus laid siege to Capua, which had been won over to Hannibal's side after the battle of Cannae, and in 211 starved this city to surrender (cf. Von Ungern-Sternberg, 1975, 77–124). The Latin colony of Fregellae revolted in 125 B.C., for what cause is unknown. It was conquered and totally destroyed by L. Opimius, then praetor, after one of its citizens had betrayed the city to Rome. Near its site the Roman colony of Fabrateria Nova was

CHAPTER 9.11 301

founded. Cf. Conole, 1981 and Rawson, 1998. See for *internecivus*, 'murderous', the last note ad 20.4.10.

id etiam memoriae nos veteres docent in extremis casibus icta cum dedecore **9.11**
foedera, postquam partes verbis iuravere conceptis, repetitione bellorum ilico
dissoluta See for preparatory *id* in general the note ad 22.3.4 *cum id voluminis*, and for *id* preparing a statement in the a.c.i. Kühner-Stegmann 1.625; *etiam* adds the contents of §11 to those of §9–10. Cf. for *memoriae*, 'records', 22.16.14 *ut priscae memoriae tradunt*, Gel. 4.6.1 *ita in veteribus memoriis scriptum legimus*. The phrase *in extremis casibus* expresses that the humiliating treaties in question were perhaps understandable in the circumstances, but nevertheless could not be accepted; see for similar phrases to denote a crisis the note ad 14.2.6 *ex necessitate ultima*. See for *verbis conceptis* the notes ad 21.5.10 *gladiis* and 23.6.35 *conceptis*. The phrase is by no means otiose: Amm. emphasizes that even treaties which were concluded in accordance with official rules proved ephemeral.

This is Amm.'s only instance of *repetitio*, which in late Latin is more commonly used by grammarians to indicate a stylistic device. Curiously, *ilico*, for which Amm. has a predilection, does not figure in the list of archaic adverbs in Fesser 42–9; in late Latin it almost exclusively occurs in grammarians.

ut temporibus priscis apud Furcas Caudinas sub iugum legionibus missis in Samnio et per Albinum in Numidia sceleste pace excogitata et auctore turpiter pactionis festinatae Mancino dedito Numantinis The three ignominious events of the republican period are often referred to as black pages in Roman history, but seldom together. The Caudine Forks (321 B.C.) and Numantia (137 B.C.) are combined in Quint. *Inst.* 3.8.3 *foedus Numantinum iugumque Caudinum*, Tac. *Ann.* 15.13.2 *provisis exemplis Caudinae Numantiaeque ⟨pacis⟩*, Flor. 1.34.7 *non minus Numantini quam Caudini illius foederis flagrans ignominia aut pudore.* Amm. himself refers to these disasters in 14.11.32 (q.v.) *eadem* (sc. Fortuna) *Mancinum post imperium dedidit Numantinis, Samnitum atrocitati Veturium.* However, as Lindenbrog noted, the most telling parallel of the present text is Eutr. 10.17.2 *Quin etiam legiones nostrae ita et apud Caudium per Pontium Telesinum et in Hispania apud Numantiam et in Numidia sub iugum missae sunt ut nihil tamen finium traderetur. Ea pacis conditio* (Eutropius means Jovian's peace treaty) *non penitus reprehendenda foret, si foederis necessitatem tum cum integrum fuit mutare voluisset, sicut a Romanis omnibus his bellis quae commemoravi factum est. Nam et Samnitibus et Numantinis et Numidis confestim bella inlata sunt neque pax*

302 COMMENTARY

rata fuit. The line of thought is similar to Amm.'s. The difference in wording may point to a common source rather than to the supposition that Amm. was directly inspired by Eutropius or vice versa. Matthews 187 draws attention to the fact that the examples from the Roman Republic are meaningless, since in those days "agreements reached by commanders in the field might be disavowed by a senate that was the ultimate arbiter of the making and breaking of war and treaties." In 363 A.D. the only authority in such matters was held by the emperor.

The sources for the disaster of the Caudine Forks, to be found in the valley between Arienzo and Arpaia (cf. Sommella, 1967, 49–64 and Horsfall, 1982), are listed by Broughton, 1951, 150–1. After the Roman army under the consuls T. Veturius Calvinus and Sp. Postumius Albinus in 321 B.C. had been trapped by Samnites and forced to capitulate *non, ut vulgo credunt Claudiusque etiam scribit, foedere pax Caudina, sed per sponsionem facta est* (Liv. 9.5.2, but see for a critical assessment Crawford, 1973 and Urso, 1997). Both consuls abdicated. Another Sp. Postumius Albinus and his brother Aulus were responsible for a similar disaster in 110 B.C. After an ineffectual campaign in Numidia against Jugurtha consul Sp. Albinus left for Rome to hold the elections, leaving his brother and legate Aulus in charge of the troops. Jugurtha forced Aulus to surrender, spared the lives of the Roman soldiers, but made them march in a single file under a yoke of spears (cf. Broughton, 1951, 543). Sp. Albinus was sent into exile (cf. Hayne, 1981). The fate of consul C. Hostilius Mancinus, Amm.'s third example, was more deplorable, although "Mancinus himself does not seem to have considered his misfortune a dishonour" (Wikander, 1976, 99; cf. also Rosenstein, 1986). In 137 B.C., when surrounded by the Numantines in Spain, he saved his army by signing a treaty, although the senate refused to ratify it. Instead, Mancinus was handed over to the Spaniards, naked and in chains. Cf. for the sources Broughton, 1951, 484, 486; 1986, 103–4.

As was noted at the same phrase in 20.6.9, *temporibus priscis* denotes days long past. As in the case of *memoriae veteres*, the modern reader should be aware of the ancients' awe for the normative past. It is significant that Amm. has no phrase comparable with Eutropius' *neque pax rata fuit*, which is the vital part of the historical parallel. Perhaps Amm. realized that it was of no use in the case of a treaty concluded by the emperor himself. In its stead he avails himself of the adverbs *sceleste* and *turpiter* to emphasize the anomaly of the agreements and their likeness to Jovian's treaty, by which the reader

CHAPTER 9.12 303

is invited to conclude that the emperor would have been perfectly justified in breaking his oath.

Proinde extractis civibus After the short digression in sections 7–11 **9.12** Amm. returns to his narrative. For *proinde* see the note ad 24.6.4 *Proinde cunctis*. See the list of examples of *extrahere* in the note ad 17.1.7 *extractisque captivis* as illustrating the implication of force; but see the note ad 25.8.3 *discrimine*. Nisibis' citizens were "arrachées à leur cité" (Fontaine). If Eun. *fr.* 29.1 is to be believed, Jovian stayed near Nisibis only for two days, i.e. 20–21 August. If not (the handing over of the city may have taken more time) Jovian left Nisibis a couple of days later.

missoque tribuno Constantio One should not rule out that Seeck, 1906, 112 and *PLRE* I Constantius 2 are right in assuming that this tribune (see for the function of tribune the notes ad 23.3.9 and 24.3.1) was the man, who became closely acquainted with Libanius during Julian's stay in Antioch in 362–363, and to whom Libanius wrote *Ep.* 803, expressing wonder ὅτι δὴ φύσιν Ἑρμῇ προσήκουσαν ἐνεβίβασας εἰς στρατιώτου βίον. But of course, Constantius was a rather common name.

qui munimenta praesidiaria cum regionibus Persicis optimatibus assignaret I.e. the fortifications and border districts mentioned in 25.7.9. For *munimenta praesidiaria* see De Jonge ad 18.7.10 *castra duo praesidiaria*, for *optimates* denoting the aristocracy of foreign people the note ad 20.6.3 *per optimates*. Cf. also 25.7.13 *Bineses e numero nobilium optimatum*.

cum Iuliani supremis Procopius mittitur ea, ut superstes ille mandarat, humaturus in suburbano Tarsensi See for *suprema*, 'mortal remains', the note ad 22.11.10 *ne collectis supremis*. In 25.10.5 Amm. speaks of Julian's *suprema et cineres*, for which expression see the note ad loc. Procopius was "a relative, probably on the mother's side, of the Emperor Julian" (*PLRE* I, Procopius 4; cf. Austin, 1972, 189–91), and this may well have been the reason why he was chosen to escort Julian's remains to Tarsus or had volunteered for it. Obviously this was a honourable task. In 361 Jovian himself, then still a *protector domesticus*, had escorted Constantius to his final resting-place (21.16.20). Apart from the present text, Procopius is mentioned in this book in 25.7.10, 25.8.7 and 25.8.16. See for him also the notes ad 17.14.3 *Procopius* and 25.5.3 *si Mesopotamiam*.

304 COMMENTARY

Although Philostorgius says it was Merobaudes (*PLRE* I, Merobaudes 2) who escorted the corpse for burial (τὸν δὲ νεκρὸν Ἰουλιανοῦ Μεροβαύδης καὶ οἱ σὺν αὐτῷ ἐν Κιλικίᾳ κομίσαντες, *HE* 8.1), there is no reason to doubt the truth of the report of Amm., who, after all, was an eyewitness. Either Philostorgius is wrong, or his words are to be taken as giving additional information. Neither Procopius nor Merobaudes is mentioned by Zosimus, although in 3.34.3–4 he does speak of a division of the army: παρεγένοντο μὲν τῶν στρατιωτῶν ὅσοι τὴν δορυφορίαν εἶχον εἰς τὴν Ἀντιόχειαν ἅμα τῷ βασιλεῖ, εἵπετο δὲ καὶ ὁ στρατὸς ἅπας τῷ Ἰουλιανοῦ σώματι. Καὶ τοῦτο μὲν εἰς Κιλικίαν ἀπενεχθὲν ἔν τινι Ταρσοῦ προαστείῳ βασιλικῇ ταφῇ παρεδίδοτο. Cf. Zon. 13.13.23 τὸ δὲ σῶμα αὐτοῦ ἡ στρατιὰ εἰς Ταρσὸν τῆς Κιλικίας κομίσασα ἔθαψεν ἐν προαστείῳ τῆς πόλεως. Zosimus' words may be regarded as supplementing Amm.'s report. His *Antiochiam venimus* in 25.10.1 can refer to the arrival (παρεγένοντο) of Jovian and his guards, among whom Ammianus himself. In the meantime the army accompanied (εἵπετο) Julian's body; the imperfect tense indicates the background of the event expressed by the aorist παρεγένοντο. When they had reached a suburb of Tarsus, the body was immediately buried there: as is expressed by the imperfect tense παρεδίδοτο after the aorist participle ἀπενεχθέν. See Rijksbaron, 2002³, 11–2 and 7. Cf. also Paschoud's translation and his notes 101 and 102.

See for Amm.'s use of *superstes* as a synonym of *vivus* the note ad 21.7.5 *eo enim superstite* and for Julian's orders the note ad 25.5.1 *corpore enim curato*. His wish to be buried in Tarsus is discussed in the note ad 25.10.5 *exornari sepulchrum*. The present text, which makes it unambiguously clear that, according to Amm., Julian wanted Tarsus as his burial place, is overlooked by Arce, 1984, 182–3. Starting from 23.2.5 Arce argues that Julian after his campaign merely wanted to go to Tarsus to stay there for a while, and that he had no clear wish to be buried there: one should in 23.2.5 (*corpus namque eius illuc relatum exsequiarum humili pompa in suburbano sepultum est, ut ipse mandarat*) take the words *ut ipse mandarat* with *exsequiarum humili pompa*, and not with *in suburbano*. The present text, however, falsifies this interpretation.

9.13 *qui ad exsequendum profectus* It is slightly surprising that Amm. uses the gerund and not the gerundive, as in 16.11.6 *ad exsequendum id*; cf. also 16.4.5 *ad exsequenda plurima*, 28.1.44 *ad haec fortiter exsequenda*. Perhaps, Amm. uses *exsequi* in the present text as a rare t.t.: "i.q. sequi cum aliquis ad sepulturam effertur" (TLL V 2.1850.12–20), but even in that case the verb is normally accompanied by a Patiens.

CHAPTER 9.13　　　　305

confestim corpore sepulto discessit　In 26.6.3 Amm. explains why Procopius deemed it wise to disappear: *veritus, ne ex hac causa* (i.e. because of the rumour that Julian on his deathbed had declared him his successor) *indemnatus occideretur, e medio se conspectu discrevit maxime post Ioviani territus necem, notariorum omnium primi, quem Iuliano perempto veluti dignum imperio paucis militibus nominatum novaque exinde coeptare suspectum cruciabiliter didicerat interfectum* (cf. for the death of the *notarius* Iovianus 25.8.18). As to *corpore sepulto*, in 23.2.5 Amm. had noted that Julian was buried with simple rites (*exsequiarum humili pompa*). According to the satiric description in Greg. Naz. *Or.* 5.18, however, the burial resembled a burlesque and was accompanied by comic actors and fluteplayers, while Julian's burial place (adorned some time later by Jovian, cf. 25.10.5) was a τέμενος ἄτιμον καὶ τάφος ἐξάγιστος καὶ ναὸς ἀπόπτυστος καὶ οὐδὲ θεατὸς εὐσεβῶν ὄψεσι. In a later oration Gregory even maintains that the burial in Tarsus was accompanied by an earthquake, as if the earth refused to receive Julian's body (*Or.* 21.33, cf. Greg. Naz. *Carm.* 1 [*In laudem virginitatis*, PG 37.557]).

nec inveniri usquam potuit studio quaesitus ingenti　Adverbial phrases consisting of *studio* with an adj. (e.g. *agilis, flagrans, impensior, pervigil, velox*) abound in the *Res Gestae*; the combination with *ingens* also occurs in 14.2.20, 17.8.1, 21.4.6, 25.8.11. See further the note ad 20.9.1 *nec minore studio*. Cf. for *quaerere*, 'to look for a person in order to collar him', 14.7.18 *aequisoni his* ("men of the same name", tr. Rolfe) *magna quaerebantur industria*, 19.9.2 *sollicita quaerebantur industria*, Tac. *Ann.* 12.18.2 *terra marique Romanis per tot annos quaesitus*. Procopius himself was fully aware that he figured on the list of wanted persons: *se quaeri industria didicerat magna* (26.6.4). Cf. Lib. *Or.* 24.13 καὶ δεδιὼς καὶ κρυπτόμενος καὶ ἀεὶ ληφθήσεσθαι προσδοκῶν. Zosimus says nothing of the sort, on the contrary. He has the unlikely story that Procopius, immediately after Jovian's accession, gave the new emperor the imperial robe he himself had been given by Julian (cf. for this rumour Amm. 23.3.2 with the relevant note) and then was allowed to retire to his family estates in Cappadocian Caesarea (4.4.3).

nisi quod multo postea apud Constantinopolim visus est subito purpuratus　Normally *nisi quod* introduces an exception to a general statement: 'apart from the fact that' (see Szantyr 587). Some examples in Amm.: 16.3.1 *nec civitas ulla visitur nec castellum, nisi quod apud Confluentes…Rigomagum oppidum est*, 22.15.2 *Aegyptum gentem omnium*

306   COMMENTARY

vetustissimam, nisi quod super antiquitate certat cum Scythis. In the present
text *nisi quod* actually does not introduce an exception, but rather
a contrast: the investigators could not find him anywhere, but he
suddenly appeared in the eastern capital. Alternatively, one could
assume that Amm. silently shifts from purely passive *inveniri* in the
main clause to a deponential meaning, as a synonym of *apparere*
(TLL VII 2.144.7 sqq.). The date vaguely referred to is September 28,
365 (*Cons. Const.* a. 365). It was a caricatural appearance according
to the report in Amm. 26.6.15. See for *purpuratus* the long note ad
20.5.4 *specie tenus*, and note the author's clever placing of the word
as an ἀπροσδόκητον at the end of the statement.

CHAPTER 10

Introduction

From a purely factual point of view the last chapter of book 25 and, more importantly, of what many regard as the first version of the *Res Gestae*, reports on the second half of Jovian's short reign, viz. his stay at Antioch and the subsequent journey westward in the direction of Constantinople, which ended prematurely some 180 km west of Ancyra, at Dadastana, where the emperor died. In comparison with the description of the first half of his reign, this report stands out by its brevity and the impressionistic selection of the evidence. It contains very few vivid descriptions with the exception of the wailing sounds of protest of Jovian's baby son during the installation ceremony of the consuls of 364 at Ancyra. The succinct brevity has its counterpart in the repeatedly emphasized speed of Jovian's westbound march. Various expressions used at significant moments of this journey testify to this, and they finally culminate in §12 in an amazing phrase, which reveals that all the time fate had been driving him on. The ancient reader, who had no maps at his disposal and perhaps only a rudimentary idea of the time such a journey would take, must have gained the impression that the period at Antioch plus the voyage took no more than a few weeks, at most a month, whereas in reality the chapter describes a period of four months.

Apart from its brevity and speed the chapter is characterized by the repeated occurrence of omina. This even prompts a short digression on comets and in general creates an atmosphere within which Jovian's death is continually foreshadowed. The various signs are wasted on the emperor himself, who seems to have had no inkling of the impending disaster, but the importance of such signs did not escape the author, who, after the obligatory, but remarkably short necrology of Julian's successor, ends book 25 with Jovian's father's wrong interpretation of a dream. Modern readers may be puzzled by this, but for ancient historians in general, and for Ammianus in particular, signs and warnings about the future and man's failure to interpret these correctly are a decisive factor in history. Man's inadequate assessment of the signs, which blinds his insight, is a feature of history's course. Ammianus expected his readers to have reached this lucid conclusion on the basis of his historiography.

308   COMMENTARY

10.1 *His hoc modo peractis discursisque itineribus Antiochiam venimus* Comparable formulaic phrases with *peractis* occur in 16.12.67, 17.10.10, 21.8.1, 23.6.9, 25.5.8. See for *discurrere*, 'to speed along or through', the notes ad 20.6.2 *per turres* and 21.12.3 *discursis Thraciis*. It is the first of a series of phrases in this chapter which express Jovian's haste while travelling westward; see Sabbah 357 n. 43.

Amm. had left off his description of the Roman retreat when Jovian had arrived at Nisibis (25.8.17). Although Jovian's route from Nisibis to Antioch is not described by Amm., it is known that he travelled via Edessa where he issued *Cod. Theod.* 7.4.9 on 27 September. It is likely that from Nisibis he went to Edessa via Ammodios, Macharta and Antoninopolis and from Edessa via Batnae, Hierapolis, Beroia and Litarba to Antioch; for this route see Talbert, 2000, Maps 89 and 67. Jovian's route from Batnae to Antioch was also taken by Julian – in the opposite direction – when he set out on his Persian campaign; see Note on Chronology, Bk. 23, xv–xvii. Although by using the word *discurrere* Amm. gives the impression that Jovian travelled with great haste, an impression also given by Zos. 3.34.3 (Ἰοβιανοῦ δὲ σπουδῇ τὰς πόλεις διαδραμόντος), Jovian may actually have taken his time to make the journey from Nisibis to Antioch, a distance of *c.* 450 km. It is not known when Jovian left Nisibis, where he had arrived on 19 August (see the note ad 25.8.16 *Profecti exinde*). Assuming that the handing over of the city to the Persians may have taken a few days – Eun. *fr.* 29.1 mentions two days – Jovian perhaps left again on *c.* 23 August. He arrived at Antioch sometime in the first half of October (see the note ad 25.10.4 *Moratum*). Hence he took some forty to fifty days to travel from Nisibis to Antioch. Wirth, 1984, 369 may therefore be right ("Bei seinem Rückmarsch nach Antiochia liess Jovian sich alle Zeit"), unless we assume that Jovian stayed longer at Nisibis than suggested here. This was a slow pace indeed, especially if Zosimus (3.34.3) is correct in reporting that the emperor only travelled with his guards and that the army accompanied Julian's remains to Tarsus; see the note ad 25.9.12 *cum Iuliani.* Contrary to Zosimus' information (*ibid.*) that Jovian marched quickly through the cities, the emperor may have spent some time in several of the cities he passed. In Edessa he seems to have had a meeting with two Arian bishops from Lydia, Arrianus (*PLRE* I, Arrianus) and Candidus (*PLRE* I, Candidus 1), who were distant relatives and who, apparently, intended to plead for the Arian cause: Philost. *HE* 8.4–7. In Hierapolis he may have had a meeting with the orthodox Alexandrian bishop Athanasius; *Hist. Aceph.* 4.4 (Athanasius) *occurrit navigio ad imperatorem Iovianum*; see Martin's notes 95–99 in

CHAPTER 10.1

SC 317; Barnard, 1989, 385; Barnes, 1993, 159–60; Martin, 1996, 572–89. According to Seeck, 1906, 414 and 1916, 2010 a certain Strategius of Ancyra held an oration to congratulate Jovian on his accession and to deliver a golden crown either when the emperor was on his way to Antioch, or when he had arrived there. Seeck bases this on Lib. *Ep.* 1436, which he dates to October 363; cf. also Lib. *Ep.* 1119. Remarkably, this Strategius is not mentioned in the *PLRE*. Jovian's slow travelling pace may also be explained by the fact that he had to take all kinds of administrative decisions en route. Christian authors emphasize his measures concerning the faith and the church, such as the recalling of bishops and prelates from exile, the restoration of churches of Nicene conviction, the closing of temples and banning of sacrifices, as well as the reconfirmation of the Nicene doctrine; Rufin. *hist.* 11.1; Socr. *HE* 3.24–5; Soz. *HE* 6.3–5; Thdt. *HE* 4.2–4.

For Antioch see the note ad 22.9.14; add to the literature mentioned there Kondoleon, 2000. *Venimus* is the last instance in book 25 of the first person plural. At first sight it is tempting to assume that Amm. remained at Antioch when the emperor left, the more so because of the fragmentary character of the report on Jovian's voyage until his death at Dadastana. However, there are other cases where the author gives an 'impressionistic' account of events witnessed by himself; chapters 7 and 8 of book 24 are a clear example. Moreover, both the detailed information about official reports on the situation in Gaul in §6–10 and the vignette of Jovian's young son wailing in protest against being carried in the *sella curulis* on January 1, 364 (§11) seem to bear the stamp of an eyewitness account.

per continuos dies velut offenso numine multa visebantur et dira Cf. for *per continuos dies* Pl. *Mil.* 741 *ubi dies decem continuos siet*, Liv. 27.42.9 *insequentibus continuis diebus aliquot*, Plin. *Nat.* 9.180 *eademque hora per aliquot dies continuos*, Amm. 22.9.10 *eadem diebus continuis replicans*. Obviously, in these phrases *continuus* means 'successive' (without any interruption). The phrase *offenso numine* also occurs in Ov. *Tr.* 5.10.52 (cf. also *Pont.* 2.2.28 *offensi numinis*), but Amm. uses singular *numen* here, as more often, in a general henotheistic sense; see Ensslin, 1923, 48 ff., Camus, 1967, 134 ff., Rike, 1987, 31–4 and the notes ad 21.2.5 *sollemniter* and 21.13.14 *favore numinis*. The author's slightly tentative *velut* is followed by the explicit divinatory t.t. *dirus*, 'boding ill'; see the long list of examples of this meaning in TLL V 1.1268.67 sqq. and cf. 22.8.3 and 29.1.29 *diris auspiciis*.

310   COMMENTARY

quorum eventus fore luctificos gnari rerum prodigialium praecinebant See
for *eventus* as a divinatory t.t. the note ad 22.1.2 *nuntiavit eventus.*
Amm.'s use of the adjectives *luctificus* and *luctuosus* is dealt with in
the note ad 14.5.2 *victoriam luctuosam.* According to Fontaine n. 698
and Montero, 1991, 124 *gnari rerum prodigialium rerum* denotes the
Etruscan haruspices, but 23.5.10 *Etrusci tamen haruspices, qui comita-*
bantur gnaros prodigalium rerum clearly shows that this identification
is unlikely. Rather, it seems that 'the experts in the field of prodigies'
belong to the emperor's direct entourage and that, if necessary, they
can avail themselves of the 'technical' support of the haruspices, as
in 25.2.7 *Etrusci haruspices accersiti consultique* (q.v.).

10.2   *Maximiani statua Caesaris, quae locata est in vestibulo regiae* See for
C. Galerius Valerius Maximianus the notes ad 22.4.8 and 23.5.11; he
is also mentioned in 25.7.9. In 305 Maximianus had been elevated to
the status of Augustus, but Amm. is right in referring to him as Caesar
here, since during the tetrarchy the palace was the residence of the
eastern Caesar. It was the "best known of Diocletian's buildings at
Antioch" (Downey, 1963, 117) situated on the island in the Orontes.
See for a short description Lib. *Or.* 11.205–6 with the notes of
Fatouros and Krischer, and for a clear map of Antioch and the
representation of the palace on a mosaic Kondoleon, 2000, XV and
114 respectively. It had been Gallus' residence (14.1.6, 14.7.4 and
10).

amisit repente sphaeram aeream formatam in speciem poli Cf. 21.14.1,
where it is related that Constantius dreamt that his father held
out a fair child to him which he put in his lap. Then the child
shook from him *sphaeram, quam ipse dextra manu gestabat* (q.v.). This
could only signify *permutationem temporum.* In the present text this
implication is left to the reader. Discussing the present passage, Kolb,
2001, 252 suggests that the statue was "nicht zufällig diejenige des
Persersiegers Galerius", a clear contrast with Jovian, who surrendered
Roman territory to the enemy. After initial setbacks Maximianus
overwhelmingly defeated the Persian king Narses, when he was still
a Caesar. Presumably, *sphaeram* concerns the round shape of the
object, in which the outlines of the globe had been fitted (*formatam*
in speciem poli). Valesius refers to a passage in a sermon of Basilius,
the fifth-century bishop of Seleucia: χεῖρα δὲ τῷ σφαιροειδεῖ σχήματι
τοῦ κόσμου τὸν κύκλον τοῖς δακτύλοις φέρειν νομιζομένην (PG 85, 37A).
Most modern readers will be reminded of the often photographed
statue of a late-antique emperor ('il Colosso') at Barletta or of the

CHAPTER 10.2   311

colossal bronze statue of Constantine which once stood in Rome. The globe, a hand and the head of the latter statue are now in the Capitoline Museums in Rome (not to be confused with the remains of a marble statue of the emperor in the courtyard of the same museums). For the globe as a symbol of power, see Schramm, 1958, 12–9; Kolb, 2001, 52–4.

et cum horrendo stridore sonuerunt in consistorio trabes Amm. uses *stridor* to denote the gnashing of teeth (16.12.13, 30.6.6), the shrill sound produced by human beings (17.13.10 *horrendo stridore*, 31.13.4), the trumpeting of elephants (19.7.6, 25.1.14, 25.3.14; see also the note ad 25.6.1 *ad quorum*) and the sound of ballistas being wound up (24.4.16, q.v.). The common element in the various instances is "a high-pitched sound" (OLD s.v.); the most famous example is perhaps *stridorque rudentum* (Verg. *A.* 1.87). One can imagine those who heard the squeaking sound of the beams in the 'room where the consistory met', getting the creeps. Weiss, 1975, 6–18, i.a. referring to Amm.'s use of verbs like *ingredi* (15.5.18, 25.10.10), *admittere in* (14.7.11, 16.7.2), *intromittere in* (28.1.25, 30.6.2), argues that the term *consistorium*, the first instances of which occur in Tertullian, in late antiquity primarily denotes a specific room in an imperial palace. See also Leumann 301 on the use of the suffixes *-torium* and *-sorium* for "Bezeichnungen von Aufenthalts-räumen". TLL IV 473.11–38 lists the cases in Amm. mentioned above as instances of *consistorium* denoting the emperor's council. In the present text, however, *consistorium* undoubtedly means a room or a hall, presumably during a meeting of the council. See the note ad 20.4.22 *asciti in consistorium* and Demandt, 1989, 231–2.

et visa sunt interdiu sidera cometarum This is the climax of the three omina, which is also made clear by the various characteristic elements: Maximianus' statue lost its globe 'without warning' (comparable instances of *repente* are 23.1.5 and 23.5.14), the sound of the beams made the members of the consistory 'shiver', a comet now appears 'in broad daylight': nobody could fail to see it; this is Amm.'s only instance of *interdiu*. The significance of the appearance of comets was clear: *inter quae sidus cometes effulsit, de quo vulgi opinio est, tamquam mutationem regis portendat* (Tac. *Ann.* 14.22.1); cf. also Luc. 1.529 *terris mutantem regna cometen*, Stat. *Theb.* 1.708 *quae mutent sceptra cometae*, Suet. *Nero* 36.1 *stella crinita, quae summis potestatibus exitium portendere vulgo putatur.*

312   COMMENTARY

In the *Res Gestae* there is only one other example of a comet: *ruinas fortunarum indicantia celsarum arsere crinita sidera cometarum, quorum originem supra docuimus* (30.5.16). In both these cases *cometarum* is best explained as a gen. identitatis. With *sidera* Amm. implicitly chooses a position in the field of theories: comets are real heavenly bodies. On the other hand, his use of the plural deviates from normal Latin usage and tallies better with other views. Only the comet of the present text has been listed in Kronk, 1999, 65–6. A Chinese source reports that a comet was seen in the evening sky from August 26 until September 23. Kronk adds Amm. 25.10.2–3 in Rolfe's translation as the second source. The date, however, poses a problem. According to the plausible conjecture of Seeck, 1919, 84 and 213, *Cod. Theod.* 7.4.9 shows that Jovian was still in Edessa on September 27. He must have arrived in Antioch before October 22 in view of *Cod. Theod.* 10.19.2, but even if one bears in mind that the dates mentioned are not absolutely certain, one has to assume some post-dating by Amm. This is more obvious in 30.5.16, where the appearance of a comet is reported as taking place shortly before Valentinian's death on November 17, 375. However, as can be found in Kronk, 1999, 66–7, according to Chinese sources Halley's comet was seen in March-April 374. See also Barrett, 1978, 103–4. In this case Kronk has wrongly refrained from quoting Amm.: the latter's dating was prompted by the wish to place the comet's appearance near the date of Valentinian's death. This is comparable to Demandt's findings concerning the dating of eclipses in ancient reports. See especially the summary of the various types of adaptation in Demandt, 1970, 507.

super quorum natura ratiocinantes physici variant This introduces the brief digression in §3. See for an analysis of Amm.'s scientific digressions and especially for the compatibility of explanations from the viewpoint of 'natural' sciences and religious or theological interpretations Den Hengst, 1992: "subjects like *divinatio* and the role of the *genius*" can be regarded as "just as scientific" as earthquakes and eclipses. Fögen, 1997, 152–6 is less satisfactory in this respect. In late Latin *ratiocinari* and its cognates almost exclusively occur as technical rhetorical terms in handbooks. Macrobius' *Commentary* is an exception: *quibus syllogismis de immortalitate animae diversi sectatores Platonis ratiocinati sint oportet aperiri* (2.13.9), *Aristotelica ratiocinatio* (2.14.22). Such a usage is more akin to Amm., whose only other instance is 21.1.12 *ratiocinantes*.

CHAPTER 10.3   313

The Ancients failed to develop a satisfactory scientific theory about   **10.3**
comets. Sen. *Nat.* 7.25.3 regards this failure as entirely understandable: *Quid ergo miramur cometas, tam rarum mundi spectaculum, non
teneri legibus certis nec initia illorum finesque notescere, quorum ex ingentibus intervallis recursus est?* Surveys of the theories which had been
developed can be found in Aristotle, *Metereologica* 1.6–7 (342 b 25–
345 a 10) and Seneca, *Naturales Quaestiones*, book 7. Amm.'s overview
does not contain any clear indication that he used either of these two
or a brief survey like that of Aetius, reconstructed in Diels, 1958[3],
366–7. Moreover, the succinct character of his information makes
it wellnigh impossible to identify the various anonymous theories
which are summarized: in the brief catalogue of the various explanations he had come across Amm. refrains from mentioning any
names of specific authorities. See on this Den Hengst, 1992, 42–3.
The most authoritative twentieth-century scholarly survey is Gundel,
1922. Von Scala, 1898, 127–8 mentions some doxographic parallels
with the present section.

*quidam enim eos hoc nomine ideo existimant appellari, quod tortos ignes
spargunt ut crines in unum stellis multiplicibus congregatis* Amm.'s first
group of *physici* is said to take its name as a starting point for their
explanation: κομήτης, *crinitus* ('wearing long hair'); cf. 30.5.16 *crinita
sidera cometarum*, Plin. *Nat.* 2.89 *cometas Graeci vocant, nostri crinitas.*
Amm. complicates the customary explanation by *tortos ignes...ut
crines.* Fontaine assumes that the comparison is with hair knotted
into a chignon and translates: "des flammes torsadées comme des
cheveux"; cf. also Viansino's "fuochi attorcigliati". However, the
phrase *torti crines* usually denotes curly hair, either natural, e.g. Man.
4.722 *et Syriam produnt torti per tempora crines*, Tac. *Agr.* 11.2 (cf. also
Mart. 4.42 *tortas...comas*), or frizzled, as in Man. 5.146 *tortos in fluctum
ponere crines* ("they will set their locks in waves of curls", tr. Goold);
cf. also Ov. *Ars* 2.304 and see Van Mal-Maeder ad Apul. *Met.* 2.19
pueri calamistrati. Caltabiano possibly refers to frizzling with "fiamme
ondulate come capelli". Amm.'s other instances of *torquere* either
concern the shooting of missiles or, in the majority of cases, torture.
The present text may, however, be his only example of *torquere* with
the meaning 'to twine', as in Mart. *Sp.* 3.9 *crinibus in nodum tortis* (v.l.
torti) venere Sugambri. This would imply that Fontaine's rendering is
correct and that Amm.'s etymology of *cometes* does not focus on the
length of the comets' tail, but on its compactness.
     The descriptive phrase *in unum stellis multiplicibus congregatis* is
comparable to the view ascribed to Anaxagoras and Democritus by

314   COMMENTARY

Aristotle: εἶναι τοὺς κομήτας σύμφασιν ('conjunction') τῶν πλανήτων ἀστέρων, ὅταν διὰ τὸ πλησίον ἐλθεῖν δοξῶσι θιγγάνειν ἀλλήλων (342 b 28–9), and the one which Seneca ascribes to 'some ancient authorities': *cum ex stellis errantibus altera se alteri applicuit, confuso in unum duarum lumine facies longioris sideris redditur (Nat. 7.12.1).* However, neither of these two descriptions is explicitly connected with the term 'comet' as such. Moreover, Amm.'s *multiplicibus* also differs from this view.

alii eos arbitrantur ex halitu sicciore terrarum ignescere paulatim in sublimiora surgentes As Brok notes, this is reminiscent of the first part of Arist. *Mete.* 1.7 about the ἀναθυμίασιν ξηρᾶν καὶ θερμήν, 'hot and dry exhalation' (344 a 10) underneath the circular movement of the heavens and being carried along with it. When this exhalation and the air around it catch fire, in some cases shooting stars arise, and in specific circumstances ἀστὴρ τοῦτο γίγνεται κομήτης (344 a 20–1). This has been further developed by the Stoa: *Placet ergo nostris cometas...denso aere creari* (Sen. *Nat.* 7.21.1); cf. also D.L. 7.152 κομήτας...πυρὰ εἶναι ὑφεστῶτα ('that have come into being') πάχους ἀέρος εἰς τὸν αἰθερώδη τόπον ἀνεχθέντος. Seneca himself will have nothing to do with this Stoic view: *Non enim existimo cometen subitaneum ignem sed inter aeterna opera naturae (Nat.* 7.22.1). See for the Ancients' ideas about exhalations the note ad 20.11.26 *halitus terrae* and Fritscher, 2000, 91.

quidam...currentesque radios solis densiore nube obiecta degredi ad inferiora prohibitos splendore infuso corpori crasso lucem velut stellis distinctam mortali conspectu monstrare In spite of *eos*, referring to *cometarum* in § 2, the first two theories in Amm.'s list, strictly speaking, deny an independent existence as celestial bodies to the comets. This is even more evident in this third case, in which they are no more than an interplay between sunlight and a very dense cloud. This explanation is quite similar to that of meteors in 25.2.6 *vel certe radiorum flammas iniectas nubibus densis acri scintillare contactu* (q.v.) and of the rainbow theory in 20.11.29 (q.v.).

V's *currentesque* poses a problem, which Gelenius, followed by Rolfe and Viansino, has solved by leaving out *que*. Fontaine follows another track in boldly expanding *que* into *usquequaque*. The loss of another present participle before *currentesque* seems more likely: *descendentes* might, tentatively, be suggested. However, Seyfarth wisely follows Clark's decision to print a lacuna. Both *velut stellis distinctam* and *mortali conspectu* emphasize that the interpretation of the phe-

CHAPTER 10.3   315

nomenon is based on faulty human observation. See for this 20.3.12 with the relevant notes.

sedit quorundam opinioni hanc speciem tunc apparere, cum erecta solito celsius nubes aeternorum ignium vicinitate colluceat At this point Amm.'s survey becomes quite puzzling. The view which is described in the present text only differs from its immediate predecessor in that not a thick cloud, but a high one produces a comparable effect. Is it perhaps a mere appendix or a parenthesis, with *hanc speciem...apparere* taking up *mortali conspectu monstrare*? In that case a different punctuation would be needed. On the other hand, *sedit quorundam opinioni* seems too solemn for a secondary addition. Von Scala refers to the opinion ascribed to Heraclides Ponticus: νέφος μετάρσιον ὑπὸ μεταρσίου φωτὸς καταυγαζόμενον (p. 366.29–31 Diels = *fr.* 116 Wehrli). The phrase *erecta solito celsius nubes* also occurs in 20.3.6 in the digression on eclipses, but with an entirely different function; cf. the note ad loc. and the note ad 20.11.29 *altius delatae*.

See for similar phrases with *sedere* and their Vergilian ring the notes ad 14.1.5 *sedet* and 24.8.5 *sedit tamen*. The abl. comparationis *solito* is not rare in Latin, but Amm. is remarkably fond of it. See the notes ad 14.6.9 *solito* and 20.8.8 *solito*. His pen has turned it into a hackneyed phrase.

vel certe stellas esse quasdam ceteris similes, quarum ortus obitusque, quibus sint temporibus praestituti, humanis mentibus ignorari This is an instance of Amm.'s curious use of *vel certe* to express the "loaded alternative", dealt with in the note ad 25.2.6 *vel certe*. It is the only view which assumes that comets are celestial bodies in their own right. Arist. *Mete.* 342 b 30–3 ascribes it to the Pythagoreans: ἕνα λέγουσιν αὐτὸν εἶναι τῶν πλανήτων ἀστέρων, ἀλλὰ διὰ πολλοῦ τε χρόνου τὴν φαντασίαν αὐτοῦ εἶναι καὶ τὴν ὑπερβολὴν ἐπὶ μικρόν ("that a comet is one of the planets, but that it appears only at long intervals and does not rise far above the horizon", tr. H.D.P. Lee); cf. also Aetius p. 366.6–10 Diels. According to Seneca, Apollonius of Myndus held a comparable view: *proprium sidus cometae est, sicut solis ac lunae* (*Nat.* 7.17.1), *ceterum non est illi palam cursus; altiora mundi secat et tunc demum apparet cum in imum cursus sui venit* (*Nat.* 7.17.2).

The essential word in Amm.'s all too brief summary of the view in question is *praestituti*: in contrast to the various other theories, which explain the phenomenon in a similar way, its regularity is assumed, although man's intellect has as yet not been able to map it out. In Amm. the verb *praestituere* usually concerns a human

316   COMMENTARY

appointment or decision: 17.1.13 *ad praestitutum usque diem* (q.v.),
17.4.10 *litterarum numerus praestitutus*, but in a few cases he has in
mind the laws of nature: in 22.15.6 the flooding of the Nile takes
place *anni temporibus…praestitutis* and in the digression on the pearls
these are said to be *permixtione roris anni tempore praestituto conceptae*
(23.6.85).

plura alia de cometis apud peritos mundanae rationis sunt lecta The author
has only presented a small part of his wide reading on the subject;
lecta reminds of the phrase *visa vel lecta quaedam* (22.8.1). The term
ratio here denotes the "law (of nature)" (OLD s.v. 12a): see for this
Bailey's note ad Lucr. 1.51. The only other passage in which it is
combined with *mundanus* is Mart. Cap. 8.815. Cf., however, 23.6.33
rationes mundani motus et siderum.

quae digerere nunc vetat aliorsum oratio properans See for *digerere*, 'to set
out in orderly fashion', the examples in the note ad 17.8.3 *negotio
plene digesto*, and for formulas used to conclude a digression the note
ad 22.8.48 *prolati aliquantorsum longius*.

10.4 *Moratum paulisper Antiochiae principem curarumque ponderibus diversis
afflictum exeundi mira cupiditas agitabat* The length of Jovian's stay at
Antioch cannot be determined exactly. From Seeck's reading of *Cod.
Theod.* 7.4.9 (see above the note ad §2 *et visa sunt*) it appears that
on September 27 he was still at Edessa, some 250 km. from Antioch;
Cod. Theod. 11.20.1 (November 12) places him at Mopsuestia, on the
road to Tarsus; on October 22 he was still at Antioch (*Cod. Theod.*
10.19.2). Therefore one may assume that he spent the best part of
October at Antioch and left at the beginning of November after a
far shorter stay than Julian's six months (before July 28, 362 until
March 5, 363). Amm.'s *paulisper* tallies with this.
     The complex variety of different tasks made heavy demands on
an emperor's competence and mental strength: *distractusque in sol-
licitudines varias* (20.1.1), *distrahebatur multiformibus curis* (22.10.1),
accidentium varietatem sollicita mente praecipiens (23.1.2). These three
phrases are about Julian, who proved equal to any occasion, in contrast to Jovian, who was 'knocked down' by the sheer 'weight' of his
responsibilities. Cf. for the metaphorical use of *pondus* 14.7.20 *atro-
cium criminum ponderibus*, 14.11.1 *curarum abiectis ponderibus aliis*, Luc.
9.951 *cetera curarum proiecit pondera*, Stat. *Theb.* 4.38–9 *aeger/ pondere
curarum*. Apart from the normal burden of an emperor Jovian had to
cope with a host of ecclesiastical problems, which are not mentioned

CHAPTER 10.4 317

at all by Amm., such as the rehabilitation of Athanasius, who had travelled to Hierapolis to meet him, and the schismatic situation at Antioch; see for these matters Barnes, 1993, 159–60 and the note ad 25.10.1 *His hoc modo*. He was also worried by the uncertainty as to whether his emperorship would be accepted in the western part of the empire. Moreover, if Eunapius' report (*fr.* 29) on his stay at Antioch, preserved in *Suda* I 401, can be relied upon, he, like Julian (see 22.14.2–3 with the notes), had become the object of the local populace's sarcastic wit: οἱ δὲ Ἀντιοχεῖς ἠγανάκτησαν κατὰ τοῦ βασιλέως. This irritation resulted in all sorts of pamphlets and nasty remarks, like ἤλυθες ἐκ πολέμου, ὡς ὤφελες αὐτοῦ' ὀλέσθαι. When she saw that Jovian was a tall and handsome man, an old lady exclaimed: ὅσον μῆκος καὶ βάθος ἡ μωρία, 'I had not realized that folly could rise or fall to such proportions!', and a visit to the hippodrome turned into a most unpleasant experience for the emperor. See the text in Blockley, 1983, 46. Small wonder that Jovian could not wait to leave the city. Cf. for *mirus* denoting extraordinary proportions *mira inventorum sese varietate dispendens* (15.3.4, about Paulus Catena), *arte mira* (24.1.3, about Pyrrhus' shrewd tactics), *mira velocitate* (29.5.13, about a military action of Theodosius senior); in combination with *cupiditas* the adj. also occurs in Tac. *Dial.* 2.1, Plin. *Nat.* 7.10, 25.98.

proinde nec iumento parcens nec militi flagrante hieme die profectus signis, ut dictum est, vetantibus plurimis Jovian probably left Antioch at the beginning of November, a somewhat surprising time to start a journey into the heartland of Asia Minor, although 'in the dead of winter' is exaggerated. V's *flagrante hieme die* seems impossible and Petschenig's easy correction *hieme media* (1892, 519) is plausible enough in view of e.g. Liv. 37.8.6 *media ferme hieme*, Plin. *Nat.* 27.23 *incipit a media hieme* and above all *epit.* 44.4 (about Jovian) *hieme aspera mediaque Constantinopolim accelerans*. However, both Clark and Seyfarth follow Heraeus' advice to print V's text. Only Seyfarth's translation is available to offer a sort of explanation, but, to put it mildly, "an einem Tag mitten im tiefsten Winter" is not particularly convincing, the less so since this seems to combine V with Petschenig. For *flagrante* see the notes ad 21.12.23 *nec privatorum* on *in tempore ita flagranti* and 24.4.24 *in congressu flagranti*. In combination with *hieme* it seems to result in an extravagant metaphor, but perhaps there is a reasonable explanation: in 27.12.12 one finds the expression *sidere flagrante brumali*, for which Wagner refers to 16.12.15 *sidere urente brumali*. In this phrase *urente* denotes the scorching effect of cold and frost (cf. OLD s.v. 4c). If Amm. regarded *urere* and *flagrare* as synonyms in all

318 COMMENTARY

circumstances, this might be the background to his bold phrase in the present text. Both the Suda and Johannes Antiochenus fr. 181 have χειμῶνος ὄντος to denote the time of Jovian's departure, but the latter has the curious detail that the emperor did not leave Antioch of his own free will: Σαλούστιος…τὸν Ἰοβιανὸν μὴ βουλόμενον παρώρμησεν ὁδοιπορῆσαι, καὶ ταῦτα χειμῶνος ὄντος, ἐπὶ Κιλικίαν καὶ Γαλατίαν. Wirth, 1984, 384 denies that Jovian's haste was excessive. In his view the emperor's aim was "die Armee kampfbereit im Frühjahr an den potentiellen Gegner bringen zu können." For Jovian's route from Antioch to Dadastana, where he died, see French, 1981, esp. Map 2.

If *signis…vetantibus plurimis* is an adverbial adjunct with *profectus*, it is difficult to explain. The signs of §2 have no specific relation to the departure from Antioch, and if the phrase rather determines *Tarsum…introiit*, the problem remains.

Tarsum urbem Cilicum nobilem introiit, cuius originem docuimus supra Only Zonaras 13.14.10 ἐξ Ἀντιοχείας δὲ εἰς Ταρσὸν γεγονώς joins Amm. in explicitly mentioning Jovian's arrival at Tarsus, which should be dated after November 12, the date of *Cod. Theod.* 11.20.1, issued at Mopsuestia. Amm.'s *supra* refers to 14.8.3 (q.v.). Tarsus is a usual stopping place on the route from Antioch to western Asia Minor; French, 1981, 27 and Map 2. Although Amm. does not say so, Constantinople must have been Jovian's destination; Zos. 3.35.3: Ἐξορμήσαντι δὲ τῆς Ἀντιοχείας Ἰοβιανῷ καὶ ἐχομένῳ τῆς ἐπὶ Κωνσταντινούπολιν ὁδοῦ. For Tarsus and Cilicia see the notes ad 21.15.2, 22.9.13 and 23.2.5.

10.5 *exornari sepulchrum statuit Iuliani in pomerio situm itineris, quod ad Tauri montis angustias ducit* Julian's burial had already taken place (25.9.13 [Procopius] *corpore sepulto discessit*), in a plain style (23.2.5 *exsequiarum humili pompa*), but now Jovian has his tomb properly furnished. Perhaps this implied an inscription, either the one reported by Zos. 3.34.4

Ἰουλιανὸς μετὰ Τίγριν ἀγάρροον ἐνθάδε κεῖται,
ἀμφότερον βασιλεύς τ' ἀγαθὸς κρατερός τ' αἰχμητής,

which is also incorporated in the *Anthologia Graeca* (7.747) and ascribed to Libanius, or the one in Zon. 13.13.24:

Κύδνῳ ἐπ' ἀργυρόεντι ἀπ' Εὐφρήταο ῥοάων
Περσίδος ἐκ γαίης ἀτελευτήτῳ ἐπὶ ἔργῳ
κινήσας στρατιὴν τόδ' Ἰουλιανὸς λάχε σῆμα,
ἀμφότερον βασιλεύς τ' ἀγαθὸς κρατερός τ' αἰχμητής.

CHAPTER 10.5   319

"Ces deux morceaux, faits de fragments homériques, sont fort suspects" (Paschoud n. 102). There is, indeed, some reason for doubt, but not primarily because of the allusions to Homer. These do not seem unfitting for a man who was quite familiar with Homer and often quoted him at first hand (see Bouffartigue, 1992, 134–56), and who, on the day of his inauguration as Caesar, whispered *Iliad* 5.83 to himself (Amm. 15.8.17). For the adornment of Julian's tomb cf. Gregory of Nazianzus' sneering remark in his *Or.* 5.18 cited in the note ad 25.9.13 *confestim*. Libanius (*Or.* 24.10) refers to the concern which Valentinian and Valens pretended to have shown for Julian's tomb and their intention to make it into a magnificent memorial.

Julian's grave was *in suburbano* (23.2.5), ἔν τινι Ταρσοῦ προαστείῳ (Zos. 3.34.4), ἐν προαστείῳ τῆς πόλεως (Zon. 13.13.23). Amm.'s only other instance of *pomerium* is 14.6.22 in the satirical digression on Roman society. Perhaps he found this classical term more apt than *suburbanum*, when writing about Julian's tomb; combined with *itineris* it seems to denote 'the extramural (or "suburban") part of the road'. From Tarsus to the Cilician Gate is about 40 km. Julian had arrived there less than sixteen months before (22.9.13), and on November 3, 361 Constantius had died at Mobsucrenae, halfway between Tarsus and the Gate (21.15.2–3, q.v.). One wonders whether Julian's decision to substitute Antioch by Tarsus (see the note ad 23.2.5 *disposuisse enim*) and his wish to be buried there has anything to do with the fact that Constantius' death near the city implied the beginning of his own rise to supreme power as the sole Augustus. He may also have regarded Constantinople as a through and through Christian city, which dampened his love for the city of his birth: *natus enim illic diligebat eam ut genitalem patriam et colebat* (22.8.2, q.v.). However, according to Zon. 13.13.25 his remains were eventually brought there: ὕστερον δὲ ἀνεκομίσθη εἰς τὴν βασιλίδα τῶν πόλεων. See for a scholarly discussion about the date of this transfer, the precise place allotted to Julian's remains and the possible identification of his sarcophagus Downey, 1959; Grierson, 1962; Mango, 1962; Di Maio, 1978; Arce, 1984; Arce, 1988; Kelly, 2003, 591 ff.

Philostorgius *HE* 8.1 adds another detail about the site of Julian's grave in the suburb of Tarsus: ἀντικρὺ τοῦ τάφου ὃς τὰ Μαξιμίνου συνεῖχεν ὀστᾶ..., λεωφόρου μόνης ἀπ' ἀλλήλων τὰς θήκας αὐτῶν διατειχιζούσης, 'where only the highway divided their tombs from one another'. Maximinus Daia died at Tarsus in the summer of 313 (Eutr. 10.4.4). Philostorgius' information may have been inspired by the wish to bring the graves of two dangerous enemies of the Christian

320 COMMENTARY

faith together. In a note ad Greg. Naz. *Or.* 5.18 Bernardi suggests
that the presence of Maximinus' grave "n'ait pas déplu à Julien".

*cuius suprema et cineres, si qui tunc iuste consuleret, non Cydnus videre
deberet* In his eagerness to convey the idea that Julian ought to have
been buried at Rome, Amm. confuses two sentence patterns. In the
present text *si qui tunc iuste consuleret* is superfluous: the sentence
would be complete and indeed fully clear without this clause: not
the Cydnus, but the Tiber should be the river on the banks of which
Julian was laid to rest. Amm., however, wanted to bring in human
responsibility and thus the irrealis became at least partially one of the
past, with *deberet* as the superfluous element: 'if proper measures had
been taken at the time, not the Cydnus, but the Tiber would have
become the setting of Julian's mausoleum.' See for the imperfect
tense in the irrealis of the past, "besonders wenn Zeitpartikeln wie
tum die Vergangenheitsbedeutung stützen", Szantyr 332–3.

The combination *suprema et cineres* is an instance of 'Synonymenhäufung': see for *suprema*, 'mortal remains', the notes ad 22.11.10
ne collectis and 25.9.12 *cum Iuliani*. OLD s.v. *cinis* 4 notes that when
this word denotes "the condition of the body after death", it does
not necessarily imply cremation. There is no description of Julian's
funeral extant, but the vague references to it in the sources do not
contain any indication of a cremation.

quamvis gratissimus amnis et liquidus Amm. hastens to profess his
adherence to the laudatory tradition concerning Tarsus' river. Ruge,
1924 provides a catalogue of references. Some examples: *lucide Cydne*
(Ov. *Ars* 3.203), *aquae liquore conspicuus Tarson interfluit* (V. Max. 3.8
ext. 6), ψυχρός τε ἐστι καὶ τὸ ὕδωρ καθαρός (Arr. *An.* 2.4.7). Amm.
surpasses even such praise by an allusion to Vergil's phrase about the
Tiber: *caelo gratissimus amnis* (*A.* 8.64).

*sed ad perpetuandam gloriam recte factorum praeterlambere Tiberis interse-
cans urbem aeternam divorumque veterum monumenta praestringens* TLL
X 2.1029.36–40 has only two instances of *praeterlambere*, the present
one and 17.2.2 *Mosa fluvius praeterlambit*, which inspired Valesius to
print *praeterlambere* here for V's *praeter labuerit*. Modern editors follow
in his tracks. No doubt Amm. alludes to Vergil's famous *vel quae,
Tiberine, videbis/ funera, cum tumulum praeterlabere recentem* (*A.* 6.873–
4). If Valesius' correction of V is right, Amm.'s slight variation of
the verb would be a singular example of 'aemulatio'. The correction
may, however, be questioned. The verb *praeterlabi* occurs five times in

CHAPTER 10.6   321

Amm.: in 15.11.16, 17.13.4, 21.12.8 and 28.2.2 as a present participle, but 22.8.4 *praeterlabitur* shows that Amm. was fully aware that it is a deponens and therefore Accursius' *praeterlabere* cannot be envisaged; Gelenius' *praeterlaberetur* deserves to be seriously considered. If anything, it is nearer to V's *praeter lab(u)erit*, and, moreover, as has been pointed out in the preceding note, the entire sentence is a hybrid in any case; *praeterlaberetur* itself would make excellent sense with *si...consuleret*. With all due respect for Valesius, in the present text Gelenius should be preferred.

Cf. 29.6.17 *Tiberis, qui media intersecans moenia*; the verb is used about the Ganges in 23.6.13 and 31.2.16. See for the 'eternal city', a phrase occurring fifteen times in the *Res Gestae*, the note ad 21.12.24 *urbi praefecit*. Its occurrence in the present text is entirely functional: Rome's eternal existence would be the best guarantee for the continuity of Julian's glory. This is Amm.'s only instance of *perpetuare*, a verb which is attested almost exclusively in late Latin.

As in 26.10.8 *divo Iuliano*, 28.1.11 and 30.10.1, *divus* denotes a deified emperor. The memorials to these emperors, mentioned by Amm., are the mausolea of Augustus and Hadrian. In both monuments other members of the imperial family and, indeed, other emperors had been buried. Nerva was the last emperor to be buried in Augustus' mausoleum: *Cuius corpus...in sepulcro Augusti sepultum est* (*epit.* 12.12); see further Macciocca, 1996. See for epigraphic and literary evidence about burials in Hadrian's mausoleum Jordan-Huelsen, 1907, 663–4.

Amm.'s complaint that eternal Rome, where the Roman emperors of the past lay buried, ought to have provided the resting place for Julian too, contrasts remarkably and, presumably, deliberately with a comparable lament of Libanius at the end of his 'funeral oration': εἶχε δ' ἂν δικαιότερον τὸ τῆς Ἀκαδημίας πλησίον τοῦ Πλάτωνος ὥστ' αὐτῷ παρὰ τῶν ἀεὶ νέων τε καὶ διδασκάλων ἃ καὶ τῷ Πλάτωνι τελεῖσθαι, "it ought more properly to have been in the Academy next to Plato's tomb, so that he too might receive the honours paid to Plato by each successive generation of students and teachers" (*Or.* 18.306, tr. A.F. Norman). This contrast is an excellent illustration of the divergent opinions held by the soldier who had become a Roman historian and the Hellenic rhetor about their common hero. See Tränkle, 1962, 31.

extentis itineribus venit oppidum Cappadociae Tyana The adverbial adjunct may have been borrowed from Liv. 30.19.1 *itineribus extentis*. The adj. *magnus* is more often used in this phrase, both by Livy

     10.6

322 COMMENTARY

and Amm. See for the occurrence of other adjectives and participles the note ad 20.8.21 *venit ad Constantium*. In the present text *extentis itineribus* is one of the phrases depicting Jovian's haste while travelling westward. See for the different function of 22.8.27 *itineribus...extensis* the note ad loc. From Tarsus to Tyana is a distance of well over 100 km with the Cilician Gate as the main obstacle. It must have been quite exacting to cover this distance in haste during the second half of November. However, four centuries earlier Cicero had left Tarsus on January 5 (Cic. *Att.* 5.21.7) with a similar destination.

The word order after *venit* deviates from the usual pattern: cf. 14.11.19 *venit Poetovionem oppidum Noricorum*, 22.9.3 *Nicomediam venit, urbem antehac inclutam*. See for Tyana Berges-Nollé, 2000, who on p. 399 print an English translation of parts of §4–6. This is only the second place where Amm. mentions Tyana; the other one is 23.6.19 (q.v).

ubi ei reversi Procopius. notarius et Memoridus tribunus occurrunt See on Procopius and Memoridus and their mission the notes ad 25.8.8–11. All in all, their journey had taken some four months.

gestorumque aperiunt textum hinc, ut ordo poscebat, exorsi See the note ad 20.4.11 *quo textu* for the two meanings of *textus* in Amm. In combination with *gestorum* it also occurs in 20.8.11, 26.7.2, 27.12.11, 28.1.2, 31.6.1, with the meaning 'train of events'. See the notes ad 21.3.2 *negotium* and 22.8.37 *ut ordo* for the use of *poscere* or *postulare* expressing an inherent necessity. In the present text *ut ordo poscebat* at first sight might seem superfluous, but to assume this would be a mistake: in fact, with this phrase Amm. states explicitly that the subsequent report about the order of events is the correct one, in contrast to any other version. Zosimus' report on Lucillianus' fate in 3.35.1–2 belongs to such an unreliable tradition.

Lucillianus Mediolanum ingressus cum Seniaucho et Valentiniano tribunis See on Lucillianus the notes ad 14.11.14 *Lucillianus*, 21.9.5 *rem curabat* and 25.8.9, on Seniauchus the long note ad 15.4.10 (he was one of the three tribunes who led a Roman recovery after victories of the Alamanni in Raetia: *Seniauchus, qui equestrem turmam Comitum tuebatur*), on Valentinianus *PLRE* I, Flavius Valentinianus 7. For Milan see the note ad 25.8.9 *properare Mediolanum*.

Malarichus See for him the note ad 25.8.11, where he is mentioned as the intended successor to the post of *magister equitum per Gallias*.

CHAPTER 10.7   323

effuso cursu petierat Remos See for *effuso cursu* the notes ad 19.11.11 *equo veloci* and 22.7.3 *effuso cursu*. In earlier times *Remi* denoted the tribe, their main town being called Durocortorum. Since the late third century A.D. this name became obsolete and gradually the town came to be called *Remi*; it was the official residence of the *magister equitum per Gallias*. For this reason Lucillianus made haste to get there: he wanted this important post. See for a historical survey of 'Remi' Keune, 1920. Amm. refers to Rheims (Remi), the capital of Gallia Belgica II, in 15.11.10 (q.v.), 16.2.8, 16.11.1, 17.2.1, 26.5.14. For Rheims see Wightman, 1985, *passim* and Berthelot and Neiss, 1994, 56–7 ('Reims au Bas-Empire').

In Zos. 3.35.2 Lucillianus' speedy visit to northern Gaul is absent; Sirmium is the place where Jovian's father was murdered.

Zos. 3.35.2 reports that Lucillianus was killed by Batavi at Sirmium,   **10.7** because he brought the bad news of Julian's death. Evidently Zosimus has confused Lucillianus' place of residence – Sirmium – with the town where he met his death – Rheims. According to *Not. Dign. Occ.* V 186; VII 72, 167, 169 Batavi were stationed in Gaul and not in Illyricum. Paschoud n. 103 has explained well how obviously wrong Zosimus' report is. He might have added that Amm. warned against such a version by his *ut ordo poscebat* (§6, q.v.). The present section briefly summarizes the main events during Lucillianus' ill-timed adventure in northern Gaul.

et tamquam in alto gentis silentio The noun expresses "peaceful conditions" (OLD s.v. 6) and the absence of any particular risks: *dum undique altum esset silentium* (28.2.5), *alto externorum silentio* (30.4.1); cf. Tac. *Hist.* 3.47.1 *Nec ceterae nationes silebant*. With *tamquam* Lucillianus' (wrong) assessment of the situation is expressed.

extra calcem, ut dicitur, procurrebat The present text and 21.1.14 are the only places where this proverb occurs. In 21.1.14 it is used as a formula to conclude the digression on divination; see the note ad loc. Here it expresses that Lucillianus 'ran past the line' where his mission ought to have finished.

et intempestive As will appear from the sequel of the text, Lucillianus had every reason to suspect the administration of embezzlement, but his excessive zeal testified to a fatal lack of tact; see the note ad 22.7.3 *per ostentationem* for the meaning and connotations of *intempestivus*.

324   COMMENTARY

parum etiamtum firmatis omnibus This was the real state of affairs, in contrast to Lucillianus' perception, introduced by *tamquam*.

...ex actuario ratiociniis scrutandis incubuit Clark is undoubtedly right in assuming a lacuna here. Five of the rare instances of *incumbere* with a gerundive construction occur in Amm.: apart from the present text 14.11.1, 17.12.4 *populandis* (q.v.), 26.3.5, 31.8.6; see TLL VII 1074.14–8. In V's version of the present text this construction leaves *ex actuario* floating in thin air.

One of the idiosyncracies of Amm.'s language is his frequent use of *ex* meaning 'former' with terms denoting military and political posts. From TLL V 2.1102.10sqq. it appears that such a use occurs primarily in late Latin official texts. See for *actuarius*, 'regimental quartermaster', the note ad 20.5.9 *pro actuariis*. These functionaries were corrupt, but served the interests of the soldiers, so that Lucillianus was treading on dangerous ground by 'devoting his energy to an investigation of the military administration'; see for the range of the term *ratiocinium* the note ad *circa ratiocinia* (18.5.1).

qui fraudum conscius et noxarum ad militaria signa confugit Lucillianus' suspicion proved fully justified, but he was thwarted by the culprit's flight to the barracks, where his popularity would guarantee his safety. Cf. the phrase *noxarum conscientia* in 15.8.2, 16.12.61 and 21.15.4 (q.v.). The idea occurs more often in Latin literature; some examples: Cic. *Pis.* 44 *infrenatum conscientia scelerum et fraudum suarum*, Sal. *Hist.* 1.77.7 *scelerum conscientia exagitati*, 2.87 D *conscientia noxarum*, Stat. *Theb.* 12.548 *dirae nec conscia noxae*.

finxitque Iuliano superstite in res novas quendam medium surrexisse See for *superstes* as a synonym of *vivus* the note ad 21.7.5 *eo enim*. Fontaine's "un homme de rien" and Hamilton's "a nobody" for *quendam medium* would suit the context, but they go too far in their interpretation of *medius*, which simply cannot denote any extreme. TLL VIII 590.23 explains *quendam medium* as "hominem mediocrem, sc. haud magni ingenii". Caltabiano's "un mediocre individuo" is a prudent rendering.

cuius fallaciis turbo militaris acerrime concitus Lucillianum et Seniauchum occidit As to *cuius*, Blomgren 145 lists this as one of the cases in which "haud sine aliqua ambiguitate" a relative does not refer to an immediately preceding person or thing, but to an earlier one, in this case *ex actuario*. In the majority of its occurrences in the *Res Gestae* the

CHAPTER 10.8   325

word *turbo* has a metaphorical meaning. As in *militaris turbo* (17.12.6, q.v.), the adj. replaces a genitive, probably a gen. inversus, so that the phrase in fact denotes 'rioting soldiers, who had been vehemently stirred up' (*acerrime concitus*). According to Zos. 3.35.2 Batavi, who were charged with the duty to guard Sirmium, killed Lucillianus, because he brought the bad news of Julian's death. Paschoud n. 103 suggests that 'Batavi' may be the only correct element in this version. See on the Batavi the note ad 20.1.3 *Heruli scilicet*.

Valentinianum enim paulo postea principem trepidum et, quo confugeret, ambigentem Primitivus hospes tutius amendarat Cf. Zos. 3.35.1: Οὐαλεντινιανόν, ὃς μετὰ ταῦτα γέγονε βασιλεύς. Valentinian's second appearance in the *Res Gestae* is even less glorious than the first one in 16.11.6. With *enim* the author wants the reader to understand that the fact that Valentinian is not mentioned as a victim implies that he had escaped the danger. The present text reports how that came about. When he panicked, he had been safely removed from the spot by his host Primitivus, a man about whom any further information is lacking; he has not been listed in *PLRE*. See for *tutius* the note ad 20.5.1 *saeptusque tutius*; here the comparative is clearly used to create a cursus velox. As is noted ad 20.2.4 *amendata didicit*, the verb *amendare* is a strong term, implying complete disappearance; cf. also Julian's use of it regarding his exile at Macellum: *cum in umbram et angustias amendarer* (25.3.17).

The almost casual addition *paulo postea principem* is actually the second, clearer announcement of Jovian's approaching death after the vaguer indications of the omina in § 2. In little more than three months, on February 25 or 26, 364 Valentinian would be hailed as Augustus (26.2.3).

his ita tristibus See for *ita* qualifying an adj. with reference to a preceding statement the note ad 20.11.5 *quod dictum*.   **10.8**

missos a Iovino milites Iovinus, the magister equitum in Gaul, appears a number of times in the *Res Gestae*. See the notes ad 21.8.3, his first appearance, and 25.8.11.

quos capita scholarum ordo castrensis appellat It is difficult, if not impossible, to provide a fully satisfactory explanation of this phrase. No doubt this is an instance of sermo castrensis; see the note ad 21.16.21 *ut ipsi*. It is, however, not easy to pinpoint the precise meaning of *ordo castrensis*. See the note ad 20.5.7 *ut autem* for the

326   COMMENTARY

various meanings of *ordo* in Amm. In the present text it denotes either
the hierarchical military order (cf. Caltabiano's "gerarchia militare")
or the military part of society (cf. Fontaine's "les milieux des camps"
and Viansino's "la classe militare", and see also the note ad 21.6.6
omnisque ordo). The phrase *capita scholarum* is even more difficult. As
to *caput*, the modern reader who is used to terms like 'head', 'Haupt',
'chef', 'capo', 'jefe' indicating official functions, should realize that
in antiquity *caput* could indeed mean "homo princeps vel auctor
alicuius rei" (TLL III 421.38 sqq.), "leading person" (OLD s.v. 14
a), but in the cited examples it somehow retains its metaphorical
character, and clear cases where there is a crossover to an official use
are scarce.

   In the note ad loc. (136) of his bilingual edition Seyfarth
expresses his adherence to the explanation of *scholarum* by Müller,
1905, 599–600, who argues that *scholae* here means "die bei den
einzelnen Truppenkörpern vorhandenen Bureaus". He i.a. refers to
Veg. *mil.* 2.19.1 *in legionibus plures scholae sunt*, rendered by Milner as
"there are several administrative departments in the legions", and,
wrongly it seems, to *Cod. Theod.* 11.16.4 *officiorum capita*. However,
all Amm.'s other instances of *schola* concern the *scholae palatinae*; see
the notes ad 14.7.9 *solisque scholis* and 20.2.5 *Gentilium Scutariorum*.
Moreover, it would be confusing if in the present text administrative
units are meant, since in the immediate sequel, at the beginning
of the next section a *schola Scutariorum* appears. To conclude, the
expression *capita scholarum* refers to the leading officers of the *scholae
palatinae*.

nuntiantes aequo animo Ioviani imperium amplecti exercitum Gallicanum
As Nicasie, 1998, 47 and note 24, shows, members of the *scholae*
"often were entrusted with special secret missions, both diplomatic
and military". No doubt it was a pleasing message that Jovian's emperorship was accepted by the army in Gaul, although it is difficult to
define its attitude with due precision. The translators vary between
"the army in Gaul cordially welcomed Jovian as emperor" (Hamilton)
and "dass das gallische Heer die Übernahme der Kaiserherrschaft
durch Jovian wohlwollend aufnahm" (Seyfarth). The reader might
be inclined to assume that *amplecti*, when used figuratively, implies
eagerness or enthusiasm: Liv. 28.41.6 *etsi magis partam quam speratam
gloriam amplecteris*, Tac. *Ann.* 15.59.3: after the betrayal of his conspiracy some participants urged Piso to act bravely: *quanto laudabilius
periturum, dum amplectitur rem publicam*. However, not all the examples
listed in TLL I 1993.41–67 have this connotation. Amm.'s two other

CHAPTER 10.9   327

instances are 17.5.2: on being informed that Constantius was asking
for peace, Sapor *pacis amplectitur nomen*, 17.12.15: when they were
invited to hand over hostages as a guaranty for preserving peace, the
Sarmatians *gratanter amplexi sunt*. In the latter case *gratanter* describes
their attitude, which may be compared to the function of *aequo animo*
in the present text. This phrase, which occurs so often in classical
Latin, is attested far more scarcely in late Latin. Amm.'s only other
instance is 21.6.9: when Constantius ordered the prefect Helpidius
to torture a prisoner, he asked *aequo animo abrogari sibi potestatem*.
In this passage *aequo animo* obviously has its normal meaning "with
calmness" (OLD s.v. *aequus* 8). Regarding the present text it may be
concluded that a cautious rendering after the manner of Seyfarth
does most justice to Amm.'s words.

    Not. Dign. Occ. VII 64–110 has a list of the various troops based in
Gaul who were under the supreme command of the *magister equitum
Galliarum*.

Quibus compertis Valentiniano, qui cum isdem redierat, regenda Scutariorum   **10.9**
secunda committitur schola   Other examples of the formulaic abl. abs.
are 17.1.4, 27.5.2, 27.8.2, 28.6.8, 31.10.6. Matthews 77 explains
that Valentinian's late promotion to a prestigious post – he was now
forty-two – is due to mishaps in his career. In 357 he had even
been dismissed from military service, as Amm. reports in 16.11.6–7.
See for the Scutarii the note ad 20.2.5 *Gentilium Scutariorum*; add
to the literature mentioned there Nicasie, 1998, 45–8. Although
a perceptive reader will have no difficulty in understanding that
anaphoric *isdem* refers to the men mentioned at the beginning
of §6, Viansino wisely follows Selem in making this explicit in his
translation: "tornato con Procopio e Memorido".

*Vitalianus domesticorum consortio iungitur, Herulorum e numero miles, qui
multo postea auctus comitis dignitate male rem per Illyricum gessit*   Whereas
it is immediately clear that Valentinian's appointment as tribunus of
the Scutarii fully deserved to be reported, the importance of the
enrolment of a soldier belonging to one of the auxiliary units in a
schola domesticorum is less obvious. For modern students of the late
Roman military system it is a precious piece of information about the
composition of the *scholae domesticorum*, but it is unlikely that this was
Amm.'s purpose. It is tempting to assume that he did not relish out-
siders being admitted to these ranks. Sabbah 203 n. 133 avails himself of stronger terms: "cette intrusion d'un *gregarius*, appartenant
à un corps d'auxiliaires barbares, dut lui paraître particulièrement

328   COMMENTARY

choquante et indue." The contrast between the factual *Herulorum e numero miles* and the almost solemn *domesticorum consortio* cannot be overlooked; cf. 23.1.6 *e sacerdotum consortio*, 26.6.1 *adiunctus consortio comitum*, and see TLL IV 488.32 sqq. for other examples of *consortium* as a synonym of *societas*. In 16.10.21 Amm. refers to his own regiment with *e consortio nostro*. See for the Heruli the note ad 20.1.3 *Herulis* and for *numerus* as a general term for all sorts of units the note ad 20.1.3 *numerisque*.

Vitalianus was later promoted to the rank of *comes*; see for *augere* in phrases denoting promotion the note ad 20.11.7 *dignitatibus augendos*. In the rank of *comes* he took a leaf out of the book of a certain Maurus, *postea comes, qui rem male gessit apud Succorum angustias* (20.14.18, q.v.). Maurus was a soldier of the Petulantes, also an auxiliary unit. As to Vitalianus' failure in Illyricum, Zos. 4.34.1 briefly hints at his lack of competence, when Gratian sent him there in 380: Γρατιανὸς ὁ βασιλεὺς ἐκπέμπει τοῖς κατὰ τὸ Ἰλλυριῶν κλῖμα στρατιωτικοῖς τάγμασι στρατηγὸν Βιταλιανόν, ἄνδρα πεπονηκόσι τοῖς πράγμασι κατ' οὐδὲν ἀρκέσαι δυνάμενον. There is no further evidence about the man. Amm. mentions a Vitalianus in 26.7.15, but the words used there clearly imply that this was another person. See further Ensslin, 1931, 133 and *PLRE* I, Vitalianus 3. He may have been of Germanic descent considering his service with the Heruli; Waas, 1971, 113.

mittitur in Gallias Arintheus ferens litteras ad Iovinum This emphasizes the great value which Jovian attached to Iovinus' loyalty. The general Arintheus was one of the most distinguished members of the emperor's entourage who had been a loyal servant of both Constantius and Julian. These qualities must have induced Jovian to charge him with this crucial mission. See the notes ad 15.4.10 *tribuni* and 24.1.2 *Arintheo*, and for Iovinus the note ad 25.8.11.

ut constanter ageret suum obtinens locum Because Malarichus declined the offer to become *magister armorum per Gallias* (25.10.6), Jovian retained Iovinus in that office. Iovinus had been a loyal supporter of Julian but had presumably gained Jovian's confidence by his behaviour in response to the soldiers' uprising against Lucillianus c.s.; he seems to have suppressed this revolt. He is now urged to continue in the course he had chosen, viz. loyal acceptance of the new emperor. Some translators assume that *constanter* refers to firmness, e.g. Fontaine's "faire preuve de fermeté", but it is more likely that it means 'consistently'. TLL IX 2.285.68 interprets the present text as a case in which *locum obtinere* is used "aut de statu, condicione, aut de

CHAPTER 10.10

329

gradu", with Cic. *Quinct.* 43 *ne locum suum...obtineat* and *Dig.* 50.2.2 *pr. Locum suum...non obtinebit* as parallels. Cf. also OLD s.v. *obtineo* 7 and Amm. 19.13.2 *eo diu provinciam obtinente* (q.v.).

cuique mandatum est, ut animadverteretur in concitorem tumultus auctoresque seditionis ad comitatum vincti transmitterentur Clark preferred Gelenius' *eique*, but Seyfarth has been persuaded by Blomgren's defence of the sentence's somewhat anomalous construction (Blomgren 64) and therefore adheres to V's *cuique*. His argument can be strengthened by the following reflection. In §9 and 10 the main actions are reported in the historic present: *committitur, iungitur, mittitur, iubentur*. The perfect tense *mandatum est* would, therefore, be less appropriate in a main clause here. Blomgren also notes the variation of active and passive predicates in *ageret* and *animadverteretur...transmitterentur*. This is, however, entirely functional: *ageret* appeals to Iovinus' personal attitude and the other two predicates focus on the measures that have to be taken. Jovian's orders imply a careful distinction between the *ex auctuario* and the ringleaders in the barracks at Rheims. The latter took advantage of the commotion stirred by the former quartermaster and started a mutiny. Amm. may have borrowed *concitor*, which occurs eight times in the *Res Gestae*, from Livy or Tacitus, in whose works a few instances can be found.

post quae, ut videbatur expedire, disposita The reader might be inclined   **10.10** to regard *ut videbatur* as an instance of dramatic irony: Jovian thought that these measures were profitable, but his death would soon prove that all was in vain. However, in other cases *videbatur* does not have such a connotation at all. When in 20.9.8 Julian made some appointments, *ut sibi utile videbatur et tutum*, there is no suggestion that he was mistaken; in 26.1.5 Valentinian is urged to hasten to Nicaea to accept the emperorship, *quia...hoc e re publica videbatur*: it is unlikely that Amm. means to say that this was in fact not the case. The present phrase is quite similar to 21.9.1 *Quibus ita, ut videbatur, apte dispositis*: Julian's measures were no doubt apt. See for *disponere*, 'to decide', the note ad 20.4.9 *disposuit*.

apud Aspona Galatiae municipium breve Gallicani militis visa principia After Tyana (§6) Aspona, modern Sarihüyük, is the next place name in Amm.'s report; Talbert, 2000, Map 63, C2. For Galatia see the note ad 22.9.5 *ad Gallograeciae fines*. Thirty years earlier a pilgrim from Bordeaux had traveled in the other direction. When the various distances between the mansiones on the route from Aspona to Tyana

330   COMMENTARY

which he mentions are added up, the sum total is 180 Roman miles; the distance between Aspona and Ancyra can be calculated as 96 km (*Itin. Burdig.* 575.5–12). The latter number is almost equal to *Itin. Anton. Aug.* 143, but the former is 19.5 km more than in *Itin. Anton. Aug.* 144.1–145.2. The meeting at Aspona with the officers of the Gallic army took place about December 10, it would seem. See for *brevis*, 'small', the note ad 23.6.16 *si avicula*. Aspona was situated near the river Halys.

Unfortunately, the precise date of the meeting at Aspona cannot be ascertained. When he travelled from Tyana to Aspona, Jovian must have passed (Colonia Claudia) Archelais, some 130 km southeast of Aspona. Seeck, 1919, 70 suggests that both the date and place of *Cod. Theod.* 15.1.10, which according to the manuscripts was issued at Aquilea on December 7, 362, should be emended and changed to Archelais and December 7, 363 respectively. This bold suggestion is not convincing, because it implies a remarkable so-called *post consulatum* date, which in the *Codex Theodosianus* is rarely attested so late in the following year, and then only with the explicit mention *post consulatum*; see Ensslin, 1923b, 141 n. 1. Obviously retaining Dec. 7, 362 as date, Pharr ad loc. suggests Antioch instead of Aquilea.

Clark and Seyfarth both accept Heraeus' emendation *visa principia*, but Fontaine prefers V's *visi principi* and corrects V's *militis* in *milites*. This is indeed nearer to V and the dat. auctoris occurs more often in Amm.: see the note ad 18.4.7 *morantibus*, and add 20.3.10, 22.8.24 and 42. Moreover, *ingressique* would agree with *milites*. Nevertheless, Heraeus' solution is more attractive, in that *principia* can clearly refer to *capita* in §8. See for *principia* denoting 'commanding officers' the second part of the note ad 22.3.2 *praesentibus*. In this case *ingressique* can be regarded as an easily understandable instance of constructio ad sensum. If this interpretation is correct, *Gallicani militis...principia* is a slightly loose shorthand for 'the officers of the *scholae*, who on this mission represented the soldiers in Gaul'.

10.11 *Et cum introisset Ancyram imperator* If the plausible correction of the date, proposed by Seeck, 1919, 84 is right, *Cod. Iust.* 1.40.5 was published at Ancyra on December 28, 363. Jovian therefore arrived in the capital of Galatia before that date. See the note ad 22.9.8 *Ancyram rediit* about Julian's stay there two and a half years earlier. Ancyra, the provincial capital of Galatia, was founded in the early Augustan period; Mitchell, 1993, vol. 1, 86 ff. See for Ancyra in Late Antiquity Foss, 1977 and 1985 and Mitchell, 1993, vol. 2, 91–5.

CHAPTER 10.11   331

paratis ad pompam pro tempore necessariis consulatum iniit In spite of
the haste which Amm. describes as a significant characteristic of
Jovian's journey to the West, when he entered his consulship on
January 1, 364, he was still nearly 500 km from Constantinople. In
the final section of his speech on that occasion (*Or.* 5.11, 70 c–d)
Themistius expresses the metropole's regret not to be able to witness
the ceremony. How gladly would she have welcomed the likeness of
Constantine the Great! At Ancyra the infrastructure for organizing
such a prestigious event must have left something to be desired, but
obviously the essential preparations could be made, albeit 'as the
circumstances allowed'; see the note ad 24.3.8 *pro tempore*.

Amazingly, Socr. *HE* 3.26.3 describes Themistius as holding his
speech at Dadastana and later repeating it at Constantinople. See
Vanderspoel, 1995, 138 n. 15.

adhibito in societatem trabeae Varroniano filio suo admodum parvulo See
the note ad 22.7.1 *cum Mamertini* for Amm.'s various expressions to
denote the appointment of consuls, among which are the phrases
about the colleague in the consulship of an emperor. Amm. emphasizes the very young age of Jovian's son, and in the sequel of the
text he will make this more vivid by *vagitus*, which expresses the typical wailing of babies. It is justified to conclude from Them. *Or.* 5.3
(65 a) υἱέως τῆς πατρῴας ἁλουργίδος ἡλικιώτου, 'equal in age to his
father's purple robe', that the child was still in its first year. He is
called *infans etiamtum* in 25.10.17. See further Hartke, 1951, 222
n. 2, Vanderspoel, 1995, 153, *PLRE* I, Varronianus 2.

Curiously, Philost. *HE* 8.8 mentions Varronianus as one of two
sons See for technical data about Jovian's consulate Bagnall c.s.,
1987, 262–3.

*cuius vagitus pertinaciter reluctantis, ne in curuli sella veheretur ex more, id,
quod mox accidit, portendebat* To most readers the eyewitness account
of Jovian's baby son loudly expressing his aversion to being carried in
a sella curulis, will be quite recognizable and convincing, but in the
eyes of Heather, 1999, 108 "literary invention may have intruded".
He does not add any specific argument, but in a note ad loc. he
refers to the fact that Themistius did not mention the boy's distress.
Heather seems to think that the envoy from Constantinople delivered his speech whilst the two new consuls were being carried in their
official seats. If there is a problem here, it is solved by Sabbah's observation that Amm. and Themistius have each chosen an element of
the baby's conduct "au service d'un symbolisme contraire" (Sabbah

332   COMMENTARY

359). The characteristic wailing of very young children is expressed
by *vagitus*; a famous example is *lupam…ad puerilem vagitum cursum
flexisse* (Liv. 1.4.6). There are no other examples of *reluctari, ne*, but
it can easily be recognized as a picturesque alternative for *recusare ne*
or *resistere ne*: one sees the little boy trying to wriggle out of that nasty
chair.

See for the new consuls being carried to the ceremony Claudius
Mamertinus' thrilled report about his own experience: Julian *paene
intra ipsas palatinae domus valvas lecticas consulares iussit inferri*, made
the consuls sit in these chairs and then preceded them on foot
(*Pan.* 3.30.2); in the case of Honorius' fourth consulship *iam trabeam
Bellona gerit parmamque removit/ et galeam sacras umeris vectura curules*
(Claud. *IV Cons. Hon.* 12–3; cf. also 569–70 and 584). Johannes
Lydus notes: καθέδρα (σέλλαν αὐτὴν ἐκεῖνοι καλοῦσιν) ἐξ ἐλέφαντος,
ἐφ' ᾗ καθήμενον τὸν ὕπατον οἱ πολῖται σχίδακας ὑπομήκεις ὑποβαλόντες
('having put long poles underneath') ἔφερον προιόντα (*Mag.* 1.32).
Amm. regards it as a normal custom: *ex more*. See further the relevant
part of the note ad 22.7.1 *humilior*, Delbrück, 1929, 63–4, Lippold,
1957, 400, Meslin, 1970, 56, Antès ad Cor. *Iust.* 4.107, and above all
Göll, 1859, 601–2.

Amm. does not explain why the wails of little Varronianus were
a portent of his father's death. Did the tears announce mourning or
does the author allude to the age-old feeling that ceremonies may
not be disturbed by unappropriate sounds?

10.12 *Hinc quoque Iovianum celeri gradu praescriptus vitae finiendae dies exegit*
The chapter's various phrases expressing Jovian's haste culminate in
a daring personification of his dying day, which drives him on, away
from Ancyra. The structure of the sentence makes this perfectly clear:
Jovian is the Patiens and fate is the Agens, in the fine sense of the
word. This differs markedly from the beginning of §4, where Jovian
is also the Patiens, but in that case his own *exeundi mira cupiditas* was
the active principle. Now the truth becomes clear. The fact that it was
fate all along which hurried him on is simply, but subtly, expressed
by *quoque*.

Regrettably, it is impossible to calculate the length of his stay at
Ancyra. *Cod. Theod.* 13.3.6 of January 11, 364 mentions no place, and
Seeck's proposal to emend the place where *Cod. Theod.* 10.1.8 was
issued on February 4, 364 from Milan to Mnizos, *c.* 70 (*Itin. Burdig.*
575) or *c.* 78 (*Itin. Anton. Aug.* 142.4–143.1) km west of Ancyra is
disputable. It seems more probable that Milan is correct, but that the
date should be February 4, 365. See Vanderspoel, 1995, 150 n. 67.

CHAPTER 10.13   333

Other instances in which Amm. uses *praescribere* in an expression denoting decisions of fate are 15.3.3 *praescriptum fatorum ordinem*, 25.3.9 *praescripta...sorte*, 29.1.32 *praescribente fatali necessitate*, 30.6.6 *ultimae necessitatis adesse praescripta*. From TLL X 2.825.56–66 it appears that this usage is quite rare.

cum enim venisset Dadastanam, qui locus Bithyniam distinguit et Galatas, exanimatus inventus est Dadastana is 167.5 (*Itin. Burdig.* 574.5–575.4) or 187.5 (*Itin. Anton. Aug.* 142) km west of Ancyra. Cf. for *distinguere* denoting topographical demarcation 18.2.15 *terminales lapides Romanorum et Burgundiorum confinia distinguebant*, 22.8.2 *a Thessalo mari distingunt Aegaeum.* Socr. *HE* 3.26.1 and Thdt. *HE* 4.5.1 also report that Dadastana was on the border of Galatia and Bithynia. According to Zon. 13.14.10 it was a day's journey away from Ancyra, but that cannot be right considering the distances given by the *Itin. Burd.* and the *Itin. Anton. Aug.*; see Talbert, 2000, Map 86, B3. Zos. 3.35.3 reports that Jovian suddenly became ill and died there: νόσος αἰφνιδίως ἐνσκήψασα τῆς Βιθυνίας ἐν Δαδαστάνοις ἐπήγαγε τοῦ βίου τὸ τέλος αὐτῷ.

The date of Jovian's death was *tertio decimo Kal. Mart.* (Eutr. 10.18.2), τῇ ἑπτακαιδεκάτῃ τοῦ Φεβρουαρίου μηνός (Socr. *HE* 3.26.5). *Chron. Pasch.* a. 364 has February 19. The detail *nocte* is implicitly paralleled by Zon. 13.14.12 κατέδραθε, 'he fell asleep' (in a recently whitewashed room); *inventus est* means that nobody was present when he died, a huge contrast with Julian's deathbed, as described in 25.3.15–23.

super cuius obitu dubietates emersere complures The late Latin noun *dubietas* does not occur frequently and the plural is rare. It is not clear what Amm. wants to express: "doubtful points" (Rolfe), "conflicting accounts" (Hamilton) or simply "dubbi" (Caltabiano)? In fact, only one doubt prevailed, viz. whether Jovian's death was natural, and this led to a number or suppositions or speculations. Hence the plural.

fertur enim recenti calce cubiculi illiti ferre odorem noxium nequivisse vel   **10.13**
extuberato capite perisse succensione prunarum immensa These possible causes are also mentioned by Eutr. 10.8.1, Soz. *HE* 6.6.1, Philost. *HE* 8.8, Zon. 13.14.12. Perhaps more interesting than these parallels is the fact, already noted by Lindenbrog, that in 87 B.C. Q. Lutatius Catulus committed suicide in this manner: see Vell. 2.22.4, V. Max. 9.12.4, Plut. *Mar.* 44.5, App. *BC* 1.74. Evidently such a cause of death

334 COMMENTARY

was deemed possible, which is not surprising in view of Gal. *De usu respirationis* 4.3 πῶς οὖν, φασίν, ἔν τε τοῖς Χαρωνίοις βαράθροις ("in Charonian pits" [tr. Furley and Wilkie], i.e. caverns full of poisonous vapors) καὶ τοῖς νεωστὶ κεχρισμένοις οἴκοις τιτάνῳ ('newly whitewashed houses') καὶ πρὸς τῆς ἐσβεσμένων ἀνθράκων ὀσμῆς πνιγόμεθα ("we are stifled"); Galenus differs from the other authors in that not the heat of the coalfire, but the smell, when the fire is quenched, causes stifling; nevertheless, it is clear that the two causes described in the lemma were not totally unfounded fictions, but part of existing medical lore. Julian had once been in danger of losing his life in this way. During an unexpectedly severe winter in Paris he refused to use the heating system of his bedroom, but finally had his attendants bring in πῦρ κεκαυμένον ("fire that had burned down", tr. Wright) καὶ⟨ἄνθρακας⟩ (or ⟨δάλους⟩) λαμπροὺς ἀποθέσθαι παντελῶς μετρίους ('in a very moderate number'). This brought out steam from the walls and: ἐδέησα...ἀποπνιγῆναι. He was taken out of the room and on the orders of his doctors threw up the food he had eaten (Jul. *Mis.* 7, 341 b-d).

TLL V 2.2090.55–64 provides a small list of instances, among which the present text, of *extuberari* as a synonym of *intumescere*. Whereas the verb *succendere* is already current in classical Latin, late Latin *succensio* is rare.

aut certe ex colluvione ciborum avida cruditate distentus See the notes ad 25.2.6 and 25.10.3 *vel certe* for this curious use of *aut* or *vel certe*, which introduces the most probable cause of Jovian's death, viz. indigestion as a result of excessive eating. Amm.'s description is humiliating: Jovian had 'greedily' (*avida* is best explained as an enallage) swallowed a "heterogeneous mass" (OLD s.v. *colluvio* 1) of food and this caused (*ex*) him to be 'gorged with indigestion'. As is pointed out in the note ad 24.4.21 *pervigili cura distento*, the past participle *distentus* can derive from either *distinere* or *distendere*. Amm. has examples of both, but the present one undeniably belongs to *distendere* and, more specifically, is an instance of *distentus* as a t.t. in the domain of gluttony. In this respect Jovian is not in enviable company: cf. Enn. *Ann.* 321 Sk. about the Cyclops' belly: *carnibus humanis distentus*; in Sen. *Ep.* 47.2 the wealthy man *ingenti aviditate onerat distentum ventrem*; according to Suet. *Cl.* 33.1 (Claudius) *nec temere umquam* ("scarcely ever", tr. Hurley) *triclinio abscessit nisi distentus ac madens*; Amm. himself characterizes Julian's soldiers at Antioch as *carnis distentiore sagina victitantes* (22.12.6, q.v.). With his bold *cruditate distentus* Amm. surpasses these phrases, even in comparison with *cruditate pressus exspiravit* (*epit.* 20.9

CHAPTER 10.13   335

about Septimius Severus). The supposition that Jovian's death was caused by indigestion can also be found in Eutr. 10.18.1 (*nimia cruditate*), Socr. *HE* 3.26.4 (τῷ τῆς ἐμφράξεως νοσήματι συσχεθείς), Soz. *HE* 6.6.1 (ἀφειδέστερον δειπνήσας), *epit.* 44.4 (in combination with the freshly whitewashed room), Hier. *Chron.* a. 364 (in combination with the smell of charcoal), Zon. 13.14.12 (Zonaras, in fact, combines Amm.'s three possibilities). Eun. *fr.* 29 (= *Suda* I 401) mentions a poisoned mushroom, as does Zonaras 13.14.12. Zosimus' 'sudden illness' (3.35.3) is the least specific of all the sources. See for these Bleckmann, 1992, 393–4.

decessit autem anno tricensimo aetatis et tertio This tallies with other authors who mention his age, with one exception: *annos gerens proxime quadraginta* (*epit.* 44.4). Zos. 3.35.3 reports that he reigned for eight months (μῆνας μὲν ὀκτὼ βασιλεύσαντι) as does Soz. *HE* 6.6.1. According to Philost. *HE* 8.8 he had ruled only six months. Jovian had ruled exactly seven months and twenty-one days (27 June 363 – 17 February 364). According to Zon. 13.14.23 he was buried in Constantinople ἐν τῷ τῶν ἁγίων ἀποστόλων...ναῷ. See for this the literature mentioned near the end of the note ad 25.10.5 *exornari sepulchrum*. Eutr. 10.18.2 reports Jovian's apotheosis: *inter divos relatus est*, which tallies with the title *divus* allotted to him, i.a. in CIL 6.1729 and 6.32422 (ILS 1254 and 4938 respectively).

cumque huic et Aemiliano Scipioni vitae exitus similis evenisset, super neutrius morte quaestionem comperimus agitatam P. Cornelius Scipio Aemilianus Africanus (185 or 184–129) is also mentioned in 17.11.3, 23.5.20, 24.2.16, always in the context of his military feats; see the notes ad loc. His sudden death caused quite a fuss and many sources suggest foul play; see the list in Pease's note ad Cic. *N.D.* 3.80. However, no judicial investigation was held: *nulla quaestio decreta a senatu est* (Cic. *Mil.* 16), *de morte tamen eius nulla quaestio acta* (Liv. *per.* 59), *mortis punitorem in foro non repperit* (V. Max. 5.3.2d). In a mutilated fragment of Laelius' funeral oration the word *morbo* occurs, which might suggest that he regarded Aemilianus' death as natural, "but whether he really believed this or was trying to avoid some scandal it is impossible to say" (Astin, 1967, 241).

See for the phrase *quaestionem agitare* the note ad 22.13.2 *quaestiones agitari*. Brok follows Wagner in assuming that the comparison with Aemilianus' death implies that Amm. is suggesting that Jovian had been murdered. This is not a good idea: Amm. has already strongly suggested indigestion as the cause. What surprises him is

336   COMMENTARY

the absence of a proper investigation into the sudden deaths of the
two most important political leaders of their respective times.

10.14–15 In contrast to the extensive necrologies of Constantius (21.16)
and Julian (25.4) Jovian receives only a very brief elogium, which,
remarkably, begins with a description of his physical appearance. For
Amm. the brevity of his reign and his undeveloped qualities did not
warrant a longer survey of Jovian's personality. Neither is there any
room for his origins or his marriage. In fact, Jovian's wife is nowhere
mentioned by Amm. Other sources also hardly refer to her and her
name is not mentioned before Zon. 13.14.25 in regard to her tomb
in Constantinople: συνετάφη καὶ ἡ γυνὴ αὐτοῦ Χαριτώ.

10.14 *Incedebat autem motu corporis gravi* The necrology is marked as a new
discourse topic by *autem*; see for this Kroon, 1995, 261–2. Ancient
readers familiar with physiognomy would have been surprised at
Wagner's "non sine dignitate" or Hamilton's "dignified gait", for
they would have associated Amm.'s phrase with the ideas which Pol.
Phgn. p. 262 bears testimony to: *si natura eius gravi incessu et lento est,
ei ingenium hebes et difficultatem discendi tribuas.*

vultu laetissimo Here one can hardly imagine any dark physiognomic
connotations. In fact *Physiogn.* 37, a chapter which emphasizes that
not all cheerful eyes can be praised, detects a perfectly admirable
character, *ubi totius vultus aperta atque absoluta laetitia fuerit.* Cf. also
laetus ingenio (*epit.* 44.3).

oculis caesiis Jovian shared this with Nero (Suet. *Nero* 51.1). Eyes of
this color, grey-blue (OLD), were not admired; see Lucr. 4.1161 for a
list of cases in which men glorify the beauty of a woman they love: *cae-
sia Palladium*, a blue-eyed woman (is regarded as) "Athena's image"
(Bailey), and Apul. *Met.* 2.2 in Byrrhena's portrait of Lucius: *oculi cae-
sii quidem, sed vigiles*; see Van Mal-Maeder ad loc., who adds that i.a.
the present text belongs to the class of "occurrences dépourvues de
toute nuance péjorative". This overlooks the physiognomic point of
view: *glaucus in oculo color defectum humanitatis et indolis rigorem indicat*
(Pol. *Phgn.* p. 246).

vasta proceritate et ardua For this aspect of the description of Jovian's
physique Amm. borrows a phrase from Claudius Quadrigarius in *fr.*
12, preserved in Gel. 9.11: the leader of the Gauls, who became the
adversary of Valerius Corvinus, was *vasta et ardua proceritate.* In the

CHAPTER 10.14   337

note ad 15.2.9 *tamquam inrita* De Jonge draws attention to the fact that Amm. adapts the word order to the pattern he is fond of. Jovian's huge stature puts him in the class of the rioter Petrus Valvomeres: *vasti corporis* (15.7.4) and the emperor Vitellius: *erat enim in eo enormis proceritas* (Suet. *Vit.* 17.2). True manly beauty is represented by Lucius' *inenormis proceritas* (Apul. *Met.* 2.2 with Van Mal-Maeder's note). Amm.'s brief description in 25.5.6 is also quite unflattering: *incurvus...et longior*. See also Thdt. *HE* 4.1.2 σῶμα...μέγιστον εἶχε.

indumentum regium ad mensuram eius aptum See the note ad 22.9.10 *"purpureum sibi"* and cf. *indumentum regale* (14.7.20 and 14.9.7) and *confestim indumentis circumdatus principalibus* (25.5.5). For *ad mensuram* consult the relevant note ad 21.12.6.

et aemulari malebat Constantium Wagner asks: "quam Iulianum?", but this question may be unnecessary: TLL VIII 202.82–203.38 registers a large number of cases in which *malle* is used "vi comparativi prorsus evanida" as a synonym of *velle*. See, however, the next note. Fontaine n. 727 construes a threefold antithesis in the immediate sequence of the text between likenesses and differences in comparison to Constantius, and then concludes that Amm. indirectly presents Jovian as falling short even of Constantius, whom he does not think highly of. This construction, which entails a change of punctuation is not convincing, since the various contrasts are rather disparate.

agens seria quaedam aliquotiens post meridiem iocarique palam cum proximis assuetus These two habits of Constantius are not mentioned in the extant part of the *Res Gestae*. As is noted ad 20.4.19 *nec agere, seria* denotes public and military duties. In 25.4.5 Amm. reports that Julian used to rise early to fulfil his duties and then *post haec seria* turned to his studies. Jovian's love of food, wine and sex will not have led to early morning activities and he could not be styled a bookworm (§ 15 *mediocriter eruditus*), so that it is not surprising to find him still at work in the afternoon. Although one can intuitively imagine Jovian exchanging jokes (*iocari*) with the members of the consistorium (see for *proximis* the note ad 22.7.8 *suadentibus proximis*), it is more difficult to envisage him doing this in imitation of Constantius, *imperatoriae auctoritatis coturnum ubique custodiens* (21.16.1, q.v.). Concerning Jovian's general conduct Eutr. 10.17.3 is quite favourable: *vir alias neque iners neque imprudens*. In his dealings with other people he was *civilitati propior et natura admodum liberalis* (Eutr. 10.18.2).

338   COMMENTARY

10.15 *Christianae legis itidem studiosus et nonnumquam honorificus* Jovian's
Christian conviction is mentioned here for the first time; it has never
cropped up before. This must be a problem for scholars who detect
an anti-christian bias in Amm.'s description of Jovian's behaviour
and the way in which he coped with the precarious situation of the
Roman army during its retreat from Persia. Such a bias could have
manifested itself easily at various points in the report, but there are
simply no signs of it. Jovian belonged to the homoousian branch
within Christianity; Socr. *HE* 3.22, 24–6; Soz. *HE* 6.3–5; Thdt. *HE*
4.1–4. His religious allegiance finds i.a. expression in the Christian
symbols of the ChiRho monogram, the labarum or representations
of the Cross on coins; *RIC* VIII, 1981, pl. 8, no. 328; pl. 13, no. 510;
pl. 18., no. 112; pl. 20, no. 229; pl. 21, no. 107.

See for *Christiana lex* denoting the Christian religion the relevant
note ad 15.7.6 and TLL VII 2.1245.68–78. In late Latin *itidem* often
has a much weakened copulative sense; see Blomgren 34. Here,
however, it has its full force: 'like Constantius' Jovian was a convinced
Christian. The adj. *studiosus* denotes considerable involvement; cf.
studioso cognitionum omnium principi (21.1.7) and the similar phrase
in 25.4.7. The enthusiastic phrases in some Christian texts may,
therefore, well be less guilty of overstatement than one might be
inclined to think: ἀνὴρ ἐπιφανὴς τά τε ἄλλα καὶ τὴν εὐσέβειαν (Greg.
Naz. *Or.* 5.15), χριστιανικώτατος καὶ θεοφιλέστατος (*Artemii Passio* 70),
ἦν δὲ χριστιανὸς πάνυ (Malalas *Chron.* 13.334). This did not, however,
preclude pagan rituals at the start of his emperorship: see the note
ad *hostiis pro Ioviano* (25.6.1).

In all probability, *honorificus* here implies material support, as
in CIL 9.1685 in honour of a *patronus coloniae: largissimo adque
honorificentissimo viro,* and in *epit.* 48.9 about Theodosius: *in omnes
homines honorificus.* Amm. may i.a. refer to Jovian's restoration of
several privileges and subsidies, which Julian had abolished, to the
churches; see for this Soz. *HE* 6.3.4, Philost. *HE* 8.5, Thdt. *HE* 4.4.1.
Cod. Theod. 13.3.6 revokes Julian's notorious ban on the participation
of Christian teachers in the educational system. See the notes ad
22.10.7 *Illud autem* and 25.4.20 *inter quae.* As to his general attitude
in religious matters, Socr. *HE* 3.24.5 reports that τὰ ἱερὰ τῶν Ἑλλήνων
πάντα ἀπεκλείετο, and there are also a few passages in Theodoret
in which repressive measures against pagan religious practices are
hinted at: *HE* 4.24.3 (σβεσθεῖσαν ἐξαπατήν), 5.21.2 (τὴν τῶν εἰδώλων
ἐκώλυσε θεραπείαν). In the absence of any reflection of this in the
Codex Theodosianus the very broad terms of these brief pieces of
information do not inspire trust in their veracity. The only measure

CHAPTER 10.15   339

disadvantageous for pagan cults is *Cod. Theod.* 10.1.8, referred to above in the note ad *Hinc quoque* (§12): landed property, awarded to temples, has to be returned *ei patrimonio, quod privatum nostrum est.* Another pro-christian law ascribed to Jovian is *Cod. Theod.* 9.25.2 on penalties for the corruption of virgins and widows who had dedicated themselves to the Christian God. It was issued on 19 February 364, two days after Jovian's death.

In the second half of his speech in Ancyra on January 1, 364 (*Or.* 5) Themistius assumes that Jovian adopts a neutral stance of tolerance. See the analysis in Dagron, 1968, 163–86 and Daly, 1971. There is no evidence of any laws or practical measures in this vein, but, as Dagron says, "Thémistius félicite Jovien pour les qualités dont il devrait faire preuve" (175). He seems therefore not to have repressed the old cults, and favoured the virtues of religious toleration, as also Vanderspoel, 1995, 148–54 and Heather-Moncur, 2001, 154–8 argue. Occasionally a temple seems to have been burned down; Socr. *HE* 3.24.5, Lib. *Or.* 18.287, IG IX.1 271; Eun. *fr.* 29.1 refers to the destruction of a temple built by Hadrian and made into a library by Julian. However, there was no legal persecution of pagans or the destruction of sanctuaries, and pagan practices and sacrifices could continue as Libanius clearly states in his *Oration for the Temples* (*Or.* 30.7). Jovian's Christianity did also not prevent him from maintaining good relationships with the philosophers Maximus and Priscus (Eun. *VS* 7.4.11 ὅ τε Ἰοβιανὸς ἐβασίλευσε καὶ τιμῶν τοὺς ἄνδρας διετέλεσεν), Julian's advisers; Socr. *HE* 3.26.1–2. For Jovian's attitude in religious matters, see also Wirth, 1984, 373–84.

Two improbable stories concerning Jovian's Christianity circulated. Socrates (*HE* 3.22.1–2) and Eunapius (*fr.* 29.1) report that Jovian, when a military tribune, was given the option by Julian of either sacrificing or resigning his rank in the army; however, when Jovian chose to lay down his commission, Julian, pressed by the urgency of war, did retain him. Socrates (*HE* 3.22.2) and others also relate that Jovian declined becoming emperor because, being a Christian, he did not want to command an army consisting of pagans. Thereupon the soldiers replied that they were also Christians; Rufin. *hist.* 11.1; Soz. *HE* 6.3.1; Thdt. *HE* 4.1.4–6; Zon. 13.14.2–4.

mediocriter eruditus magisque benivolus et perpensius, ut apparebat ex paucis, quos promoverat iudices, electurus See for *mediocriter* the note ad 25.5.4 *paternis meritis.* Jovian's intellectual accomplishments left something to be desired; according to Eun. *fr.* 29 he was even ἄγευστος παιδευσέως. In any case, he lagged far behind Julian and

340   COMMENTARY

was more or less on the same level as Constantius; see 21.16.4 with
the notes. Zonaras 13.14.20 is more positive: γραμμάτων οὐκ ἄπειρος,
and according to *epit.* 44.3 he was even *litterarum studiosus*. In his
speech on January 1, 364 Themistius mentions that Jovian appreciated eloquence and philosophy (*Or.* 5.63). However, he surpassed
Constantius (*magis*) in kindness, and would have been as careful
regarding promotions as that emperor used to be: 21.16.3 *examina-
tor meritorum nonnumquam subscruposus* etc. (q.v.). Unfortunately, it is
impossible to know which 'few' nominations gave rise to this expec-
tation. Them. *Or.* 5.6 (67 a-b) also speaks well of Jovian's staffing
policy and human resource management. Cf. for *perpensius* 22.6.4
cura perpensiore (q.v.). See for *iudex*, 'civil official', the note ad 20.5.7
civilis, and for *promovere*, 'to advance (a person) to higher function',
the notes ad 20.2.5 *immodico saltu* and 20.9.5 *praefectum praetorio*.

*edax tamen et vino venerique indulgens, quae vitia imperiali verecundia
forsitan correxisset* As appears from 21.16.5–6, in these respects
Jovian was the absolute opposite of the abstemious and chaste
Constantius. Zonaras 13.14.20 agrees with Amm.: οἴνου δ' ἥττητο
καὶ ἀφροδισίων. Lib. *Or.* 18.279 had already alluded to these habits
of Jovian. Eun. *fr.* 29 ascribes ῥᾳθυμίαν ("sluggishness") to Jovian.
However, Amm. thinks that he would have been able to mend
his ways 'by the attitude of restraint and avoidance of disgraceful
conduct, which emperorship could not but entail'. Such a meaning
of *verecundia* or *verecundus* is not common in the *Res Gestae*, where
these words usually denote some form of fearful respect. As to the
idea expressed by Amm., one is irresistibly reminded of the story
about the young aristocratic debauchee C. Valerius Flaccus, whom
the pontifex maximus in 209 B.C. forced to become flamen Dialis.
As soon as he received this priesthood, he *ita repente exuit antiquos
mores ut nemo tota iuventute haberetur prior* (Liv. 27.8.6).

10.16–17 Many modern readers will be surprised that book 25, and, according to many, the entire first version of the *Res Gestae*, ends with a
minor piece of information about a dream of Jovian's father, which
hardly deserves to be mentioned. The phrase *convenerat iam referre
a notioribus pedem* (26.1.1) can also be interpreted as implying that
Amm. never intended book 25 to be the final book of his *Res Gestae*. Even in that case one might have expected some formal closure,
since he had begun his 'Julianic' series of books with an introductory
section (15.1.1) and will start book 26 with a comparable statement.
It should, however, be noted that carefully written prefaces are a fea-

CHAPTER 10.16 341

ture of ancient biography and historiography, but that short sections
of closure, and certainly fully developed epilogues, are less common.
Lucian, who is exceptional in formulating some precepts for composing prefaces in historical works (*Conscr. Hist.* 53–4), does not pay
any attention to forms of closure. Of course, this lack of theory does
not imply the absence of short sections of closure. These can e.g. be
found in Xenophon, Polybius, Eutropius, in the later biographies of
the *Historia Augusta* and indeed at the definite end of the *Res Gestae*, Amm.'s sphragis in 31.16.9. Nevertheless, composing a formal
ending of a historical work does not seem to have been regarded as
a necessity, witness the case of Herodotus. In the second place, the
information will not have been insignificant in the eyes of ancient
readers, who were familiar with the important role of omina and
warning, or predicting, dreams. The former abound in the *Res Gestae*, the latter are less numerous. Julian dreamed about Constantius'
approaching death (21.1.6), Valentinian about the tasks required
from an emperor (26.1.7). These announcements were evidently
clear enough, and they testified to the reliability of dreams (21.1.12
rata fides et indubitabilis), but at times human interpretation goes
astray: *ni ratiocinantes coniectura fallerentur interdum* (21.1.12). Jovian's
father Varronianus was an example of this: his interpretation of his
dream was mistaken. Amm.'s original readers will have recognized it
as a general phenomenon. Man wants to know what the future has in
store and he is informed about this by signs and dreams, but he does
not always succeed in interpreting these correctly. This is undoubtedly one of the messages of the *Res Gestae* and, on reflection, not an
unimportant one, but one which could function as a worthy end of
Amm.'s history.

dicebatur autem Varronianus pater eius monitu cuiusdam somnii dudum **10.16**
praescisse, quod evenit The imperfect *dicebatur*, presumably in a general sense, refers to the period of Jovian's emperorship: 'it was said at
the time'. See for *autem* the note ad *Incedebat autem* (25.10.14); § 16–
17 should, of course, have been printed as a separate paragraph. See
for Varronianus the note ad 25.5.4 *erat enim*. Cf. for *monitu…somnii*
Plin. *Ep.* 3.5.4 and Suet. *Aug.* 91.1 *somnio monitus*, HA *AP* 3.5 *somnio
saepe monitus est*. At least Julian's reign must be implied by *dudum*.
The sequel of the text makes clear what is meant by the cryptic *quod
evenit*, viz. Jovian's rise to imperial power. Weber, 2000, 164–5 refers
to another dream of Varronianus, reported in *epit.* 44.2: *Eius patri,
cum liberos crebros amitteret, praeceptum somnio est, eum, qui iam instante
uxoris partu edendus foret, diceret Iovianum.*

342 COMMENTARY

idque duobus amicis commisisse fidissimis illo adiecto, quod ipsi quoque deferetur trabea consularis Amm. adds that Varronianus informed his two friends, in order to explain how he himself knew about the dream; cf. Ensslin, 1923, 14. Weber, 2000, 120 n. 148 refers to Eus. *VC* 1.30: after his famous dream about the cross Constantine ἅμα δ' ἡμέρᾳ διαναστὰς τοῖς φίλοις ἐξηγόρευε τὸ ἀπόρρητον. These friends were utterly reliable, otherwise Varronianus and his son would have been in severe danger during Julian's reign. Afterwards it was safe to tell others, and therefore the story reached the author. The usual expression is *consulatum deferre*: Cic. *Att.* 7.26.2 *cui noster alterum consulatum deferret*, Gel. 4.8.4 *adnixus est Fabricius uti Rufino consulatus deferretur*. Amm. has turned the phrase into a concrete image, since that was what Varronianus had actually dreamed. The *trabea* was originally the ceremonial dress of the equestrian order and of certain Roman priests, before it became the official robe of the consuls in imperial times. In Late Antiquity *trabeatus* is equivalent to *consularis*; Claud. *In Ruf.* 1.243; Symm. *Ep.* 9.112. See further the notes ad 21.10.8 *eum aperte* and 23.1.1 *ascito*.

audita enim filii celsiore fortuna, antequam eum videret, fatali praeventus est morte See for *celsiore fortuna* denoting the imperial dignity the note ad 20.10.1 on the same expression. Cf. for *fatali...morte*, 'natural death', Vell. 2.48.6, Eutr. 1.11.4 *fataliter mortuus est*, and *fato obiit* (Tac. *Ann.* 6.10.3 and 14.62.4). Instances of *mors* as the Agens of *praevenire* are Suet. *Iul.* 44.4 *Talia agentem atque meditantem mors praevenit*, *Tit.* 10.1 *morte praeventus est*, Apul. *Met.* 10.11 *morte praeventus est* (with Zimmerman's note), HA *P* 15.7 *mors eum praevenit*.

10.17 *et quia huic nomini amplissimum magistratum portendi per quietem praedictum est seni* In classical Latin *quoniam*-clauses usually precede the main clause, whilst *quia*-clauses tend to follow. This is the result of the different functions of the two conjunctions: *quoniam* begins with establishing a factual state of affairs, with due consequences for what is stated in the main clause, *quia* adds the causal background of an event reported in the preceding main clause. See for this Fugier, 1989, Bolkestein, 1991, Mellet, 1995. Roca Alamá, 1997 argues that in Amm. *quia* has often become the equivalent of *quoniam*, preceding the main clause in the majority of its occurrences. This is further emphasized by Amm.'s predilection for beginning sentences with *et quia*. In the present text the author registers the fact that the consulate was predicted to 'Varronianus' and then notes that, when this proved not to refer to the grandfather, the prediction obviously

CHAPTER 10.17   343

meant the grandson of the same name. Events were not steered by
human reflections, but by fate, and since this was the basis of the
prediction, it had to be correct.

Weber, 2000, 165–6 assumes that this causal clause expresses the
reflections of Jovian and his advisers which persuaded them to confer
the consulate on Jovian's baby son, but there is nothing in the text
which points in this direction. On the contrary, in §16 Amm. had
explicitly stated that only two close friends knew about Varronianus'
dream. Moreover, the view advocated above in the introductory note
to §16 and 17 implies that these sections are a 'symbolic' closure of
book 25 and indeed of the entire sequence of books (15–25) about
Julian.

See for *per quietem*, 'in a dream', the note on this expression
ad 20.5.10. Valesius notes that outside the sphere of dreams Them.
Or. 5.3 (65 a) refers to the same interchange of grandfather and
grandson with ὁδὶ ('this baby boy') δὲ ὕπατος, ἐφ' ἕτερον τῆς ὁρμῆς
γεγενημένης.

BIBLIOGRAPHY

This is not an exhaustive or selective list of handbooks, monographs and articles pertaining to the study of Ammianus Marcellinus. It only registers all publications referred to in the commentary after the manner described in section 3 of the *Legenda*. *RE*-articles are cited after the date of the second 'Halbband'.

Ackerman, P., 'Standards, Banners, and Badges', in: A.U. Pope and P. Ackerman (eds.), *A Survey of Persian Art. From Prehistoric Times to the Present*, III, London-New York 1939, 2766–2782.

Adontz, N., *Armenia in the Period of Justinian. The Political Conditions based on the* Naxarar *System* (translated with partial revisions, a bibliographical note and appendices by N.G. Garsoïan), Lisbon 1970.

Agozzino, T., and G. Piovene, *Ammiano Marcellino, Giuliano e il paganesimo morente. Antologia delle storie*, Turin 1972.

Alföldi, A., 'Some Portraits of Julianus Apostata', *AJA* 66 (1962) 403–405 = 'Einige Porträts des Kaisers Julian Apostata', in: R. Klein (ed.), *Julian Apostata*, Darmstadt 1978, 298–304, cited as Alföldi, 1978.

Allan, J.W., 'Armor', *EncIr* 2 (1987) 483–489.

Amand, D., *Fatalisme et liberté dans l'antiquité grecque. Recherches sur la survivance de l'argumentation morale antifataliste de Carnéade chez les philosophes grecs et les théologiens chrétiens des quatre premiers siècles*, Louvain 1945.

Ando, C., *Imperial Ideology and Provincial Loyalty in the Roman Empire*, Berkeley-Los Angeles-London 2000.

André, J., *Les noms de plantes dans la Rome antique*, Paris 1985.

Andreotti, A., 'L'opera legislativa ed amministrativa dell'imperatore Giuliano', *NRS* 14 (1930) 236–273 = 'Kaiser Julians Gesetzgebung und Verwaltung', in: R. Klein (ed.), *Julian Apostata*, Darmstadt 1978, 130–190, cited as Andreotti, 1978.

Arce, J., 'La tumba del emperador Juliano', *Lucentum* 3 (1984) 181–191.

Arce, J., *Funus imperatorum: los funerales de los emperadores romanos*, Madrid 1988.

Arnold, W.H., see M. Di Maio.

Astin, A.E., *Scipio Aemilianus*, Oxford 1967.

Ausbüttel, F.M., *Die Verwaltung der Städte und Provinzen im spätantiken Italien* (Europäische Hochschulschriften, Reihe 3; Geschichte und ihre Hilfswissenschaften 343), Frankfurt am Main 1988.

Austin, N.J.E., 'A Usurper's Claim to Legitimacy. Procopius in A.D. 365/6', *RSA* 2 (1972) 187–194.

Azarpay, G., 'The Role of Mithra in the Investiture and Triumph of Šāpūr II', *IA* 17 (1982) 182–187.

Babuin, A., 'Standards and Insignia of Byzantium', *Byzantion* 71 (2001) 5–59.

346 BIBLIOGRAPHY

Badian, E., 'Gibbon on War', in: P. Ducrey (ed.), *Gibbon et Rome à la lumière de l'historiographie moderne* (Publications de la Faculté des Lettres de l'Université de Lausanne 22) Geneva 1977, 103–130.

Baehrens, W.A., 'Beiträge zur lateinischen Syntax', *Philologus* Suppl. 12 (1912) 233–556.

Bagnall, R.S., A. Cameron, S.R. Schwartz and K.A. Worp, *Consuls of the Later Roman Empire*, Atlanta 1987.

Baldwin, B., 'Some Addenda to the Prosopography of the Later Roman Empire', *Historia* 25 (1976) 118–121.

Baldwin, B., 'Gregory Nazianzenus, Ammianus, *scurrae*, and the Historia Augusta', *Gymnasium* 93 (1986) 178–180.

Ball, W., 'Seh Qubba, a Roman Frontier Post in Northern Iraq', in: D.H. French and C.S. Lightfoot (eds.), *The Eastern Frontier of the Roman Empire* (Proceedings of a Colloquium held at Ankara in September 1988, BAR Intern. Ser. 553[i]), Oxford 1989, 7–18.

Banchich, Th., 'Julian's School Laws: *Cod. Theod.* 13.5.5 and *Ep.* 42', *AncW* 24 (1993) 5–14.

Barlow, J., and P. Brennan, '*Tribuni scholarum palatinarum* c. A.D. 353–364: Ammianus Marcellinus and the *Notitia Dignitatum*', *CQ* 51 (2001) 237–254.

Barceló, P.A., *Roms auswärtige Beziehungen unter der Constantinischen Dynastie (306–363)*, Regensburg 1981.

Baresi, L. de, 'Il ritratto di Giuliano in Ammiano Marcellino 25.4.22', in: I. Lana (ed.), *La storiografia latina del IV secolo D.C.*, Turin 1990, 192–197.

Barnard, L.W., 'Athanasius and the Emperor Jovian', *Studia Patristica* 21 (1989) 384–389.

Barnes, T.D., 'Another forty missing persons (AD 260–395)', *Phoenix* 28 (1974) 224–233.

Barnes, T.D., *The New Empire of Diocletian and Constantine*, Cambridge Mass. 1982.

Barnes, T.D., 'Constantine and the Christians of Persia', *JRS* 75 (1985) 126–136.

Barnes, T.D., *Athanasius and Constantius. Theology and Politics in the Constantinian Empire*, Cambridge Mass. 1993.

Barnes, T.D., 'Julian or Constantine? Observations on a Fragmentary Imperial Panegyric', in: B. Kramer e.a. (eds.), *Akten des 21. Internationalen Papyrologenkongresses*, Berlin 1995, I (*Archiv für Papyrusforschung*, Beiheft 3), Leipzig 1997, 67–70.

Barnes, T.D., *Ammianus Marcellinus and the Representation of Historical Reality*, Ithaca-London 1998.

Barrett, A.A., 'Observations of Comets in Greek and Roman Sources before 410', *Journal of the Royal Astronomical Society of Canada* 72 (1978) 81–106.

Becker, M., *Die Kardinaltugenden bei Cicero und Ambrosius: De officiis* (Diss. Münster 1992), Basel 1994.

Belayche, N., 'Sacrifice and Theory of Sacrifice during the "Pagan Reaction": Julian the Emperor', in: A.I. Baumgarten (ed.), *Sacrifice in Religious Experience*, Leiden-Boston-Cologne 2002, 101–126.

BIBLIOGRAPHY

Béranger, J., 'La terminologie impériale. Une application à Ammien Marcellin', *Mélanges d'histoire ancienne et d'archéologie offerts à Paul Collart*, Lausanne 1976, 47–60.

Béranger, J., 'Le *privatus* dans l'histoire Auguste et dans la tradition historique', *BHAC* 1982/1983, Bonn 1985, 21–55.

Berger, P.C., *The Insignia of the Notitia Dignitatum*, New York-London 1981.

Berges, D., and J. Nollé, *Tyana. Archäologisch-historische Untersuchungen zum südwestlichen Kappadokien* (Inschriften griechischer Städte aus Kleinasien 55.1–2), Bonn 2000.

Berthelot, F., and R. Neiss, 'Reims antique et médiéval', *Archéologia* 300 (1994) 50–57.

BHL, *Bibliotheca Hagiographica Latina antiquae et mediae aetatis*, I–II, ediderunt socii Bollandiani (Subsidia hagiographica 6), Brussels 1898–1901 (repr. 1992).

Bidez, J., *L'empereur Julien, Oeuvres complètes*, I.2, *Lettres et fragments*, Paris 1972³.

Bishop, M.C., and J.C.N. Coulston, *Roman Military Equipment. From the Punic Wars to the Fall of Rome*, London 1993.

Bitter, N., *Kampfschilderungen bei Ammianus Marcellinus*, Bonn 1976.

Bivar, A.D.H., 'Cavalry Equipment and Tactics on the Euphrates Frontier', *DOP* 26 (1972) 271–291.

Bleckmann, B., 'Die Chronik des Johannes Zonaras und eine pagane Quelle zur Geschichte Konstantins', *Historia* 40 (1991) 343–365.

Bleckmann, B., *Die Reichskrise des III. Jahrhunderts in der spätantiken und byzantinischen Geschichtsschreibung. Untersuchungen zu den nachdionischen Quellen der Chronik des Johannes Zonaras*, Munich 1992.

Bliembach, E., *Libanius, Oratio 18 (Epitaphios). Kommentar (§§ 111–308)*, Diss. Würzburg 1976.

Blockley, R.C., 'Constantius Gallus and Julian as Caesars of Constantius II', *Latomus* 31 (1972) 433–468.

Blockley, R.C., *Ammianus Marcellinus. A Study of his Historiography and Political Thought*, Brussels 1975.

Blockley, R.C., *The Fragmentary Classicising Historians of the Later Roman Empire, Eunapius, Olympiodorus, Priscus and Malchus*, II, Text, Translation and Historiographical Notes, Liverpool 1983.

Blockley, R.C., 'The Roman-Persian Peace Treaties of A.D. 299 and 363', *Florilegium* 6 (1984) 28–49.

Blockley, R.C., 'Constantius II and Persia', in: C. Deroux (ed.), *Studies in Latin Literature and Roman History* V, Brussels 1989, 465–490.

Blockley, R.C., *East Roman Foreign Policy. Formation and Conduct from Diocletian to Anastasius*, Leeds 1992.

Blockley, R.C., 'Ammianus Marcellinus's Use of *Exempla*', *Florilegium* 13 (1994) 53–64.

Blomgren, S., *De sermone Ammiani Marcellini quaestiones variae*, Uppsala 1937.

Boeft, J. den, *Calcidius on Demons (commentarius ch. 127–136)*, Leiden 1977.

Boeft, J. den, 'Ammianus graecissans?', in: J. den Boeft, D. den Hengst and

348 BIBLIOGRAPHY

H.C. Teitler (eds.), *Cognitio Gestorum. The Historiographic Art of Ammianus Marcellinus*, Amsterdam 1992, 9–18.

Boeft, J. den, 'Ammianus Marcellinus' Judgment of Julian's Piety', (forthcoming).

Boer, W. den, *Some Minor Roman Historians*, Leiden 1972.

Bolkestein, A.M., 'Causally Related Predications and the Choice between parataxis and hypotaxis in Latin', in: R. Coleman (ed.), *New Studies in Latin Linguistics*, Amsterdam 1991, 427–451.

Bonamente, G., 'Le città nella politica di Giuliano l'Apostata', *AFLM* 16 (1983) 33–96.

Bonamente, G., 'Il canone dei divi e la Historia Augusta', in: G. Bonamente and N. Duval (eds.), *Historiae Augustae Colloquium Parisinum*, Macerata 1991, 59–82.

Bouffartigue, J., *L'Empereur Julien et la culture de son temps*, Paris 1992.

Bowersock, G.W., 'Gibbon and Julian', in: P. Ducrey (ed.), *Gibbon et Rome à la lumière de l'historiographie moderne* (Publications de la Faculté des Lettres de l'Université de Lausanne 22), Geneva 1977, 191–213.

Bowersock, G.W., *Julian the Apostate*, Cambridge Mass.-London 1978.

Bowersock, G.W., *Fiction as History. Nero to Julian*, Berkeley-Los Angeles-London 1994.

Boyancé, P., 'La religion astrale de Platon à Cicéron', *REG* 65 (1952) 312–350.

Bradbury, S., 'Julian's Pagan Revival and the Decline of Blood Sacrifice', *Phoenix* 49 (1995) 331–356.

Bradbury, S., *Selected Letters of Libanius from the Age of Constantius and Julian* (Translated Texts for Historians 41), Liverpool 2004.

Brakman, C., 'Ammianea', *Mnemosyne* 47 (1919) 100–110.

Brandt, A., *Moralische Werte in den Res gestae des Ammianus Marcellinus* (Hypomnemata 122), Göttingen 1999.

Brennan, P., see J. Barlow.

Briquel, D., *Chrétiens et haruspices: la religion étrusque, dernier rempart du paganisme romain*, Paris 1998.

Brok, M.F.A., *De Perzische expeditie van keizer Julianus volgens Ammianus Marcellinus*, Groningen 1959.

Broughton, T.R.S., *The Magistrates of the Roman Republic* I–II, New York 1951–1952; III, Atlanta 1986.

Browning, R., *The Emperor Julian*, Berkeley-Los Angeles 1976.

BTL-2, P. Tombeur (ed.), *Bibliotheca Teubneriana Latina*, Munich-Turnhout 2002.

Burgess, R.W., 'The Dates of the First Siege of Nisibis and the Death of James of Nisibis', *Byzantion* 69 (1999) 7–17.

Burkert, W., *Lore and Science in Ancient Pythagoreanism*, Cambridge Mass. 1972.

Burkert, W., 'Fitness oder Opium? Die Fragestellung der Soziobiologie im Bereich alter Religionen', in: F. Stolz (ed.), *Homo naturaliter religiosus. Gehört Religion notwendig zum Mensch-Sein?* (Studia religiosa Helvetica: Jahrbuch 3), Bern 1997, 13–38.

BIBLIOGRAPHY

349

Caltabiano, M., *Ammiano Marcellino. Storie*, Milan 1989.

Caltabiano, M., 'Giuliano imperatore nelle Res Gestae di Ammiano Marcellino: tra panegirico e storia', in: *Giuliano imperatore, le sue idee, i suoi amici, i suoi avversari*, Atti del convegno internazionale di studi Lecce 10–12 Dicembre 1998 (= *Rudiae* 10), Lecce 1998, 335–355.

Calza, R., *Iconografia Romana Imperiale da Carausio a Giuliano (287–363 d.C.)*, Rome 1972.

Cameron, Av., and S.G. Hall, *Eusebius. Life of Constantine*. Introduction, translation and commentary, Oxford 1999.

Camus, P.-M., *Ammien Marcellin. Témoin des courants culturels et religieux à la fin du IVe siècle*, Paris 1967.

Capelle, P., *De luna, stellis, lacteo orbe animarum sedibus*, Diss. Halle 1917.

Carrasco Serrano, G., 'El retrato amianeo del emperador Joviano', *Fortunatae* 7 (1995) 177–185.

Carson, R.A.G., *Coins of the Roman Empire*, London-New York 1990.

Cart, G.A., *Quaestiones Ammianeae*, Diss. Berlin 1868.

Češka, J., 'Ad Ammiani Marcellini libros XXII–XXXI a W. Seyfarth novissime editos adnotationes criticae', *Eirene* 12 (1974) 87–110.

Češka, J., 'Julians Nichtbeachtung der bösen Vorzeichen bei Ammianus Marcellinus XXIII 1,7 und XXV 2,8', *LF* 106 (1983) 169–173.

Chaumont, M.-L., *Recherches sur l'histoire d'Arménie de l'avènement des Sassanides à la conversion du royaume*, Paris 1969.

Chausserie-Laprée, J.-P., *L'expression narrative chez les historiens latins. Histoire d'un style*, Paris 1969.

Chauvot, A., 'Guerre et diffusion des nouvelles au bas empire', *Ktèma* 13 (1988) 125–135.

Christensen, A., *L'Iran sous les Sassanides*, Copenhagen 1944² (repr. Osnabrück 1971).

Chrysos, E., 'Some Aspects of Roman-Persian Legal Relations', ΚΛΗΡΟΝΟ-ΜΙΑ 8 (1976) 1–60.

Chrysos, E., 'Ο ΗΠΕΙΡΩΤΗΣ ΦΙΛΟΣΟΦΟΣ ΠΡΙΣΚΟΣ', *Parnassos* 22 (1980) 449–461.

Chrysos, E., 'Räumung und Aufgabe von Reichsterritorien. Der Vertrag von 363', *BJ* 193 (1993) 165–202.

Clark, C.U., *Ammiani Marcellini rerum gestarum libri qui supersunt*, Berlin 1910–1915 (repr. 1963).

Classen, C.J., 'Der platonisch-stoische Kanon der Kardinaltugenden bei Philon, Clemens Alexandrinus und Origenes', in: A.M. Ritter (ed.), *Kerygma und Logos. Beiträge zu den geistesgeschichtlichen Beziehungen zwischen Antike und Christentum. Festschrift für Carl Andresen zum 70. Geburtstag*, Göttingen 1979, 68–88.

Classen, C.J., 'Griechisches und Römisches bei Ammianus Marcellinus', in: C.J. Classen, *Zur Literatur und Gesellschaft der Römer*, Stuttgart 1998, 215–241.

Clauss, M., 'Iovianus', *RAC* 18 (1998) 811–820.

Clauss, M., *Kaiser und Gott. Herrscherkult im römischen Reich*, Stuttgart-Leipzig 1999.

350 BIBLIOGRAPHY

Colledge, M.A.R., *Parthian Art*, London 1977.

Conole, P., 'Allied Disaffection and the Revolt of Fregellae', *Antichthon* 15 (1981) 129–140.

Cornelissen, J.J., 'Ad Ammianum Marcellinum adversaria critica', *Mnemosyne* 14 (1886) 234–304.

Cosi, D.M., *Casta Mater Idaea. Giuliano l'Apostata e l'etica della sessualità*, Venice 1986.

Coulston, J.C.N., 'Roman, Parthian and Sassanid Tactical Developments', in: Ph. Freeman and D.L. Kennedy (eds.), *The Defence of the Roman and Byzantine East*, 2 vols. (BAR International Series 297), Oxford 1986, 59–75.

Coulston, J.C.N., 'Later Roman Armour, 3rd–6th Centuries A.D.', *JRMES* 1 (1990) 139–160.

Coulston, J.C.N., see also M.C. Bishop.

Covolo, E. dal, 'La paideia anticristiana dell' imperatore Giuliano. A proposito dell' editto del 17 giugno 362', in: S. Felici (ed.), *Crescita dell' uomo nella catechesi dei padri (età postnicena)* (Convegno di studi e di aggiornamento Fac. Lett. crist. e class. PIAL, Roma 20–21 marzo 1987), Rome 1987, 73–85.

Crawford, M.H., '*Foedus* and *sponsio*', *PBSR* 41 (1973) 1–7.

Criscuolo, U., '*Virtutes Iuliani*', in: G. Germano (ed.), *Classicità, Medioevo e Umanesimo. Studi in onore di Salvatore Monti*, Naples 1996, 259–274.

Criscuolo, U., 'Giuliano nell'epitafio di Libanio', in: *Giuliano imperatore, le sue idee, i suoi amici, i suoi avversari*, Atti del convegno internazionale di studi Lecce 10–12 Dicembre 1998 (= *Rudiae* 10), Lecce 1998, 267–291.

Crump, G.A., *Ammianus Marcellinus as a Military Historian* (Historia Einzelschriften 27), Wiesbaden 1975.

Cumont, F., *Lux perpetua*, Paris 1949.

Curtius, E.R., *Europäische Literatur und lateinisches Mittelalter*, Bern-Munich 1969[7] and 1978[9].

Dagron, G., *L'Empire romain d'Orient au IVe siècle et les traditions politiques de l'hellénisme. Le témoignage de Thémistius* (Centre de recherche d'histoire et civilisation byzantines. Travaux et Mémoires 3), Paris 1968.

Daly, L.J., 'Themistius' Plea for Religious Tolerance', *GRBS* 12 (1971) 65–79.

Damsté, P.H., 'Ad Ammianum Marcellinum', *Mnemosyne* 58 (1930) 1–12.

Daremberg, C., E. Saglio and E. Pottier, *Dictionnaire des Antiquités Grecques et Romaines*, Paris 1877–1919.

Davies, R.W., 'The Roman Military Diet', in: R.W. Davies, *Service in the Roman Army*, ed. by D. Breeze and V.A. Maxfield, Edinburgh 1989, 187–206.

Debrunner, A., see E. Schwyzer.

Delbrück, R., *Die Consulardiptychen und verwandte Denkmäler*, I, Berlin 1929.

Delling, G., 'Geschlechtsverkehr', *RAC* 10 (1978) 812–829.

Delmaire, R., *Largesses sacrées et res privata. L'Aerarium impérial et son administration du IVe au VIe siècle*, Rome 1989.

Demandt, A., 'Verformungstendenzen in der Überlieferung antiker Sonnen- und Mondfinsternisse', *Akad. d. Wiss. u. Lit. in Mainz, Abh. d. Geistes-u. Sozialwiss. Kl.* 7 (1970) 469–527.

Demandt, A., *Die Spätantike. Römische Geschichte von Diocletian bis Justinian 284–565 n. Chr.*, Munich 1989.

Demandt, A., *Das Privatleben der römischen Kaiser*, Munich 1997[2].

Diels, H., *Doxographi Graeci*, Berlin 1958[3].

Dignas, B., see E. Winter.

Dillemann, L., 'Ammien Marcellin et les pays de l'Euphrate et du Tigre', *Syria* 38 (1961) 87–158.

Dillemann, L., *Haute Mésopotamie Orientale et Pays Adjacents*. Contribution à la géographie historique de la région, du Ve s. avant l'ère chrétienne au VIe s. de cette ère, Paris 1962.

Di Maio, M., 'The Transfer of the Remains of the Emperor Julian from Tarsus to Constantinople', *Byzantion* 48 (1978) 43–50.

Di Maio, M., and W.H. Arnold, '*Per vim, per caedem, per bellum*: a Study of Murder and Ecclesiastical Politics in the Year 337 AD', *Byzantion* 62 (1992) 158–211.

Dixon, K.R., see P. Southern.

Dodgeon, M.H., and S.N.C. Lieu, *The Roman Eastern Frontier and the Persian Wars (AD 226–363). A Documentary History*, London-New York 1991 (repr. 1994).

Downey, G., 'The Tombs of the Byzantine Emperors at the Church of the Holy Apostles in Constantinople', *JHS* 79 (1959) 27–51.

Downey, G., *Ancient Antioch*, Princeton 1963.

Drew-Bear, T., 'A Fourth-Century Latin Soldiers's Epitaph at Nakolea', *HSCP* 81 (1977) 257–274.

Drexler, H., *Ammianstudien*, Hildesheim-New York 1974.

Drijvers, H.J.W., 'Hatra, Palmyra und Edessa. Die Städte der syrisch-mesopotamischen Wüste in politischer, kulturgeschichtlicher und religionsgeschichtlicher Beleuchtung', *ANRW* 2.8 (1977) 799–906.

Drijvers, J.W., 'Ammianus' Image of Sasanian Society', in: J. Wiesehöfer and Ph. Huyse (eds.), *Ērān und Anērān. Beiträge zu den Beziehungen zwischen Ost und West in sasanidischer Zeit*, Stuttgart (forthcoming).

Drummen, M., and J. Meeus, 'De perihelische opposities van Mars', *Sterrengids 2003*, Utrecht 2003, 106–107.

Dussaud, R., *Topographie historique de la Syrie antique et médiévale*, Paris 1927.

Edwards, J., 'The Irony of Hannibal's Elephants', *Latomus* 60 (2001) 900–905.

Ehling, K., 'Der Ausgang des Perserfeldzuges in der Münzpropaganda des Jovian', *Klio* 78 (1996) 186–191.

Ehrismann, H., *De temporum et modorum usu Ammianeo*, Diss. Strasbourg 1886.

Eigler, U., Lectiones vetustatis. *Römische Literatur und Geschichte in der lateinischen Literatur der Spätantike* (Zetemata 115), Munich 2003.

Elton, H., *Warfare in Roman Europe, AD 350–425*, Oxford 1996.

Ensslin, W., *Zur Geschichtsschreibung und Weltanschauung des Ammianus Marcellinus* (Klio-Beiheft 16), Leipzig 1923 (repr. Aalen 1971), cited as Ensslin, 1923a.

Ensslin, W., 'Kaiser Julians Gesetzgebungswerk und Reichsverwaltung', *Klio* 18 (1923) 104–199, cited as Ensslin, 1923b.

352   BIBLIOGRAPHY

Ensslin, W., 'Macameus', *RE* 14 (1930) 93.

Ensslin, W., 'Zum Heermeisteramt des spätrömischen Reiches, II. Die *magistri miiitum* des 4. Jahrhunderts', *Klio* 24 (1931) 102–147.

Ezov, A., 'Reconnaissance and Intelligence in the Roman Art of War Writing in the Imperial Period', in: C. Deroux (ed.), *Studies in Latin Literature and Roman History* X, Brussels 2000, 299–317.

Falkner, R., see A. Northedge.

Fatouros, G., and T. Krischer, *Libanios, Antiochikos (or. XI): zur heidnischen Renaissance in der Spätantike*, Vienna-Berlin 1992.

Fatouros, G., 'Julian und Christus: Gegenapologetik bei Libanios?', *Historia* 45 (1996) 114–122.

Ferrill, A., *The Fall of the Roman Empire. The Military Explanation*, London 1986.

Fesser, H., *Sprachliche Beobachtungen zu Ammianus Marcellinus*, Diss. Breslau 1932.

Fiey, J.-M., *Nisibe, métropole syriaque orientale et ses suffragants des origines à nos jours*, Louvain 1977.

Flach, D., 'Von Tacitus zu Ammian', *Historia* 21 (1972) 333–350.

Fletcher, G.B.A., 'Ammianea', *AJPh* 58 (1937) 392–402.

Fögen, M.Th., *Die Enteignung der Wahrsager. Studien zum kaiserlichen Wissensmonopol in der Spätantike*, Frankfurt am Main 1997.

Fontaine, J., 'L'affaire Priscillien ou l'ère des nouveaux Catilina. Observations sur le Sallustianisme de Sulpicius Sévère', in: P.T. Brannan (ed.), *Classica et Iberica. A Festschrift in Honor of Joseph M.F. Marique*, Worcester Mass. 1975, 355–392.

Fontaine, J., *Ammien Marcellin, Histoire* IV *(Livres XXIII–XXV)*, 2 vols., Paris 1977.

Fontaine, J., 'Un cliché de la spiritualité antique tardive: *stetit immobilis*', in: G. Wirth (ed.), *Romanitas-Christianitas*. Untersuchungen zur Geschichte und Literatur der römischen Kaiserzeit Johannes Straub zum 70. Geburtstag am 18. Oktober 1982 gewidmet, Berlin-New York 1982, 528–552.

Fornara, C.W., 'Studies in Ammianus Marcellinus, II: Ammianus' Knowledge and Use of Greek and Latin Literature', *Historia* 41 (1992) 420–438.

Foss, C., 'Late Antique and Byzantine Ankara', *DOP* 31 (1977) 27–87.

Foss, C., 'Ankyra', *RAC* Suppl. 3 (1985) 448–465.

Fowden, G., 'The Last Days of Constantine: Oppositional Versions and their Influence', *JRS* 84 (1994) 146–170.

Frakes, R.M., 'Some Hidden *Defensores Civitatum* in the *Res Gestae* of Ammianus Marcellinus', *ZRG* 109 (1992) 526–532.

Frakes, R.M., Contra Potentium Iniurias: *The* Defensor Civitatis *and Late Roman Justice*, Munich 2001.

Frank, R.I., '*Commendabiles* in Ammianus', *AJPh* 88 (1967) 309–318.

Frank, R.I., 'Ammianus on Roman Taxation', *AJPh* 93 (1972) 69–86.

French, D.H., *Roman Roads and Milestones of Asia Minor*, BAR Intern. Ser. 105 fasc. 1: The Pilgrim's Road, Oxford 1981.

Frézouls, E., 'Les fluctuations de la frontière orientale de l'empire Romain',

BIBLIOGRAPHY 353

in: *La géographie administrative et politique d'Alexandre à Mahomet* (Actes du Colloque de Strasbourg 14–16 juin 1979), Leiden 1981, 177–225.

Fritscher, B., 'Meteorologie, II Klassische Antike', *DNP* 8 (2000) 89–93.

Fugier, H., '*Quod, quia, quoniam* et leurs effets textuels chez Cicéron', in: G. Calboli (ed.), *Subordination and Other Topics in Latin*, Amsterdam 1989, 91–119.

Furley, D.J., and J.S. Wilkie, *Galen on Respiration and the Arteries. De usu respirationis, An in arteriis natura sanguis contineatur, De usu pulsuum & De causis respirationis*, Princeton 1984.

Gall, H. von, *Das Reiterkampfbild in der iranischen und iranisch beeinflussten Kunst parthischer und sasanidischer Zeit* (Teheraner Forschungen 6), Berlin 1990.

Garsoïan, N.G., 'Armenia in the Fourth Century. An Attempt to Re-define the Concepts "Armenia" and "Loyalty"', *REArm* 8 (1971) 341–352.

Garsoïan, N.G., *The Epic Histories (Buzandaran Patmut'iwnk')* (Harvard Armenian Texts and Studies 8), Cambridge Mass. 1989.

Gärtner, H., 'Einige Überlegungen zur kaiserzeitlichen Panegyrik und zu Ammians Charakteristik des Kaisers Julian', *Ak. d. Wiss. u. Lit. in Mainz, Abh. d. Geistes- u. Sozialwiss. Kl.* 1968, 10, Mainz 1968, 497–529.

Gatier, P.-L., 'Romains et Saracènes: deux forteresses de l'Antiquité tardive dans des documents méconnus', *Topoi* 9 (1999) 209–218.

Gaudemet, J., *Indulgentia principis* (Università degli Studi di Trieste, Conferenze Romanistiche VI), Trieste 1962.

Gawlikowski, M., 'A Fortress in Mesopotamia: Hatra', in: E. Dabrowa (ed.), *The Roman and Byzantine Army in the East*, Krakow 1994, 47–56.

Geffcken, J., *Kaiser Julianus*, Leipzig 1914.

Germino, E., *Scuola e Cultura nella legislazione di Giuliano l'Apostata* (Pubbl. d. Fac. d. Giurisprudenza d. Seconda Università di Napoli 27), Naples 2004.

Gignoux, Ph., *Noms propres sassanides en moyen-Perse épigraphique* (= M. Mayrhofer and R. Schmitt [eds.], *Iranisches Personennamenbuch* II.2), Vienna 1986.

Gilbert, O., *Die meteorologischen Theorien des griechischen Altertums*, Leipzig 1907 (repr. Hildesheim 1967).

Gilliard, F.D., 'The Birth-Date of Julian the Apostate', *CSCA* 4 (1971) 147–151 (= 'Das Geburtsdatum von Julian Apostata', in: R. Klein (ed.), *Julian Apostata*, Darmstadt 1978, 448–454.

Goffin, E., *Oppositions of Mars 0-3010* (Memoir I of the Vereniging voor Sterrenkunde), Brussels 1976.

Göll, H., 'Über den *processus consularis* der Kaiserzeit', *Philologus* 14 (1859) 586–612.

Grattarola, P., 'Le satrapie Romane da Diocleziano a Giovano', in: A. Garzya (ed.), *Metodologie della Ricerca sulla Tarda Antichità* (Atti del Primo Convegno dell' Associazione di Studi Tardoantichi), Naples 1989, 415–433.

Greatrex, G., and S.N.C. Lieu, *The Roman Eastern Frontier and the Persian Wars II, AD 363–630. A Narrative Sourcebook*, London-New York 2002.

Gregory, S., and D. Kennedy (eds.), *Sir Aurel Stein's Limes Report. The full text of M.A. Stein's unpublished Limes Report (his aerial and ground*

354 BIBLIOGRAPHY

reconnaissances in Iraq and Transjordan in 1938–1939) edited and with a commentary and bibliography (BAR Internat. Ser. 272), Oxford 1985.

Grierson, Ph., 'The Tombs and Obits of the Byzantine Emperors (337–1042): with an Additional Note by Cyril Mango and Ihor Ševčenko', *DOP* 16 (1962) 1–63.

Grosse, R., 'Lorica', *RE* 13 (1927) 1444–1449.

Guida, A., *Un anonimo panegirico per l'imperatore Giuliano* (*Anon*. Paneg. Iul. Imp.) (Accademia Toscana di Scienze e Lettere, Studi 107), Florence 1990.

Gundel, W., 'Kometen', *RE* 11 (1922) 1143–1193.

Gundel, W., 'Sternschnuppen', *RE* 3A (1929) 2439–2446.

Günther, O., *Quaestiones Ammianeae criticae*, Diss. Göttingen 1888.

Günther, O., 'Zur Textkritik des Ammianus Marcellinus', *Philologus* 50 (1891) 65–73.

Gutsfeld, A., 'Der Prätorianerpräfekt und der kaiserliche Hof im 4. Jahrhundert n. Chr.', in: A. Winterling (ed.), *Comitatus. Beiträge zur Erforschung des spätantiken Kaiserhofes*, Berlin 1998, 75–102.

Haack, M.-L., '*Haruspices* publics et privés: tentative d'une distinction', *REA* 104 (2002) 111–133.

Haehling, R. von, 'Ammians Darstellung der Thronbesteigung Jovians im Lichte der heidnisch-christlichen Auseinandersetzung', in: A. Lippold and N. Himmelmann (eds.), *Bonner Festgabe Johannes Straub zum 65. Geburtstag am 18. Oktober 1977 dargebracht von Kollegen und Schülern* (*BJ*, Beiheft 39), Bonn 1977, 347–358.

Haehling, R. von, *Die Religionszugehörigkeit der hohen Amtsträger des Römischen Reiches seit Constantins I. Alleinherrschaft bis zum Ende der Theodosianischen Dynastie* (Antiquitas, Reihe 3, Band 23), Bonn 1978.

Hagendahl, H., *Studia Ammianea*, Diss. Uppsala 1921.

Hagendahl, H., 'Zu Ammianus Marcellinus', *Strena Philologica Upsaliensis* (Festschrift Persson), Uppsala 1922, 74–90.

Hagendahl, H., 'De abundantia sermonis Ammianei', *Eranos* 22 (1924) 161–216.

Hagendahl, H., *La prose métrique d'Arnobe. Contribution à la connaissance de la prose littéraire de l'empire*, Göteborg 1937.

Hahn, I., 'Der Tod Julians des Abtrunnigen', *Klio* 53 (1960) 225–232.

Harmon, A.M., *The Clausula in Ammianus Marcellinus* (Transactions of the Connecticut Academy of Arts and Science 16), New Haven 1910, 117–245.

Hartke, W., *Römische Kinderkaiser. Eine Strukturanalyse römischen Denkens und Dasein*, Berlin 1951 (repr. Darmstadt 1972).

Hassenstein, G., *De syntaxi Ammiani Marcellini*, Diss. Königsberg 1877.

Haupt, M., e.a., 'Zur Kritik und Erklärung der klassischen Texte', *RhM* 1 (1842) 447–478.

Hauser, S.R., 'Hatra und das Königreich der Araber', in: J. Wiesehöfer (ed.), *Das Partherreich und seine Zeugnisse / The Arsacid Empire: Sources and Documentation* (Historia Einzelschriften 122), Stuttgart 1998, 493–528.

BIBLIOGRAPHY

355

Häusle, H., *Sag mir, o Hund, wo der Hund begraben liegt. Das Grabepigramm für Diogenes von Sinope; eine komparative literarisch-epigraphische Studie zu Epigrammen auf theriophore Namensträger* (Spudasmata 44), Hildesheim 1989.

Häussler, R., *Nachträge zu A. Otto, Sprichwörter und sprichwörtliche Redensarten der Römer*, Darmstadt 1968.

Hayne, L., 'The Condemnation of Sp. Postumius Albinus (Cos. 110)', *AClass* 24 (1981) 61–70.

Heather, P., 'Ammianus on Jovian: History and Literature', in: J.W. Drijvers and E.D. Hunt (eds.), *The Late Roman World and its Historian'*, London-New York 1999, 105–116.

Heather, P., and D. Moncur, *Politics, Philosophy, and Empire in the Fourth Century. Select Orations of Themistius* (Translated Texts for Historians 36), Liverpool 2001.

Heim, F., '*Vox exercitus, vox dei.* La désignation de l'empereur charismatique au IVe siècle', *REL* 68 (1990) 160–172.

Hengst, D. den, 'The scientific digressions in Ammianus' *Res Gestae'*, in: J. den Boeft, D. den Hengst and H.C. Teitler (eds.), *Cognitio Gestorum. The Historiographic Art of Ammianus Marcellinus*, Amsterdam 1992, 39–46.

Hengst, D. den, 'L'empereur et les sortilèges. Literaire orakels in de *Historia Augusta'*, in: J.H. Blok, J.-J. Flinterman, L. de Ligt (eds.), *Tesserae Romanae. Opstellen aangeboden aan Hans Teitler* (Utrechtse Historische Cahiers 23.1), Hilversum 2002, 80–93.

Hermann, J., *Observationes criticae Ammianeae*, Diss. Bonn 1865.

Herzfeld, E., *Geschichte der Stadt Samarra* (= *Die Ausgrabungen von Samarra* VI), Hamburg 1948.

Heumann, H.G., and E. Seckel, *Handlexikon zu den Quellen des römischen Rechts*, Graz 1958[10], cited as Heumann-Seckel.

Hoffmann, D., *Das spätrömische Bewegungsheer und die Notitia Dignitatum*, 2 vols., Düsseldorf 1969–1970.

Hofmann, J.B., and A. Szantyr, *Lateinische Syntax und Stilistik*, Munich 1965 (repr. 1972), cited as Szantyr.

Honigmann, E., *Die Ostgrenze des byzantinischen Reiches von 363 bis 1071 nach griechischen, arabischen, syrischen und armenischen Quellen*, Brussels 1935.

Hopfner, Th., 'Abstinenz', *RAC* 1 (1950) 41–44.

Horsfall, N., 'The Caudine Forks: Topography and Illusion', *PBSR* 50 (1982) 45–52.

Huelsen, C., see H. Jordan.

Hug, A., 'Puls', *RE* 23 (1959) 1971.

Hunger, H., *Prooimion. Elemente der byzantinischen Kaiseridee in den Arengen der Urkunden* (Wiener Byzantinische Studien 1),Vienna 1964.

Hunt, E.D., 'Julian', in: Av. Cameron and P. Garnsey (eds.), *The Cambridge Ancient History* XIII. The Late Empire, A.D. 337–425, Cambridge 1998, 44–77.

Isaac, B., *The Limits of Empire. The Roman Army in the East*, Oxford 1992 (revised ed.).

Isaac, B., see A. Oppenheimer.

Johann, H.-Th., *Trauer und Trost. Eine quellen- und strukturanalytische Untersuchung der philosophischen Trostschriften über den Tod*, Munich 1968.

Jones, A.H.M., *The Greek City. From Alexander to Justinian*, Oxford 1940 (repr. 1979).

Jones, A.H.M., *The Later Roman Empire (284–602). A Social Economic and Administrative Survey*, Oxford 1964 (repr. 1986).

Jonge, P. de, *Sprachlicher und Historischer Kommentar zu Ammianus Marcellinus c.q. Philological and Historical Commentary on Ammianus Marcellinus* XIV–XIX, Groningen 1935–1982.

Jordan, H., and C. Huelsen, *Topographie der Stadt Rom im Altertum* I–IV, Berlin 1878–1907 (repr. 1970).

Justi, F., *Iranisches Namenbuch*, Marburg 1895 (repr. Hildesheim-New York 1963).

Kabiersch, J., *Untersuchungen zum Begriff der Philanthropia bei dem Kaiser Julian*, Wiesbaden 1960.

Kaegi, W.E., 'Challenges to late Roman and Byzantine Military Operations in Iraq (4th–9th Centuries)', *Klio* 73 (1991) 586–594.

Kawerau, P., *Die Chronik von Arbela* (CSCO, SS 199), Leuven 1985.

Kellerbauer, A., 'Kritische Kleinigkeiten (zu Ammianus Marcellinus)', *Blätter für das Bayerische Gymnasialschulwesen* 7 (1871) 11–24; 9 (1873) 81–91, 127–141.

Kelly, Chr., 'Emperors, government and bureaucracy', in Av. Cameron and P. Garnsey (eds.), *The Cambridge Ancient History* XIII. The Late Empire, A.D. 337–425, Cambridge 1998, 138–183.

Kelly, G., 'The New Rome and the Old: Ammianus Marcellinus' Silence on Constantinople', *CQ* 53 (2003) 588–607.

Kennedy, D., see S. Gregory.

Kent, J.P.C., 'An Introduction to the Coinage of Julian the Apostate (A.D. 360–363)', *NC* 19 (1959) 109–117 = 'Eine Einführung in die Münzprägung des Julian Apostata (360–363)', in: R. Klein (ed.), *Julian Apostata*, Darmstadt 1978, 256–269, cited as Kent, 1978.

Kent, J.P.C., *The Roman Imperial Coinage* VIII, The Family of Constantine I, A.D. 337–364, London 1981.

Kessler, K., 'Nisibis', *DNP* 8 (2000) 962–963.

Kettenhofen, E., 'Deportations, II. In the Parthian and Sasanian Periods', *EncIr* 7 (1996) 297–308.

Keune, J.B., 'Remi', *RE* 1A (1920) 587–594.

Kiessling, A., 'anz. v. Ammianus Marcellinus rec. F. Eyssenhardt', *Fleckeisens Jbb.* 17 [105] (1871) 481–504.

Klauser, Th., '*Aurum coronarium*', *MDAI(R)* 59 (1944) 129–153 (repr. in Th. Klauser, *Gesammelte Arbeiten zur Liturgiegeschichte, Kirchengeschichte und christliche Archäologie*, ed. E. Dassmann, Münster 1974, 292–309).

Kloft, H., *Liberalitas principis. Herkunft und Bedeutung. Studien zur Prinzipatsideologie*, Cologne 1970.

Klotz, A., 'Die Quellen Ammians in der Darstellung von Julians Perserzug', *RhM* 71 (1916) 461–506.

BIBLIOGRAPHY   357

Kolb, F., *Herrscherideologie in der Spätantike*, Berlin 2001.

Kondoleon, Chr. (ed.), *Antioch. The Lost Ancient City*, Princeton 2000.

Krautheimer, R., *Three Christian Capitals. Topography and Politics*, Berkeley-Los Angeles-London 1983.

Krischer, T., see G. Fatouros.

Kromayer, J., and G. Veith, *Heerwesen und Kriegführung der Griechen und Römer*, Munich 1928 (repr. 1963).

Kronk, G.W., *Cometography. A Catalog of Comets* I: Ancient-1799, Cambridge 1999.

Kroon, C.H.M., 'Causal Connectors in Latin: the Discourse Function of *nam, enim, igitur* and *ergo*', 5 *Colloque linguistique*, Louvain 1989, 231–243.

Kroon, C.H.M., *Discourse Particles in Latin. A Study of* nam, enim, autem, vero, *and* at, Amsterdam 1995.

Kroon, C.H.M., and P. Rose, '*Atrociter corruptus*? The use of "narrative" tenses in Ammianus Marcellinus' *Res Gestae*', in: R. Risselada, J.R. de Jong and A.M. Bolkestein (eds.), *On Latin. Linguistic and Literary Studies in Honour of Harm Pinkster*, Amsterdam 1996, 71–89.

Kroon, C.H.M., 'A Framework for the Description of Latin Discourse Markers', *Journal of Pragmatics* 30 (1998) 205–223.

Kroon, C.H.M., and R. Risselada, 'The Discourse Functions of *iam*', *Estudios de lingüística latina* (Actas del IX Coloquio Internacional de Lingüística Latina) I, Madrid 1998, 429–445.

Kroon, C.H.M., and R. Risselada, 'Phasality, Polarity, Focality: A Feature Analysis of the Latin Particle *iam*', in: T. van der Woude, A. Foolen and P. van de Craene (eds.), *Particles* (*Belgian Journal of Linguistics* 16 [2002]), Amsterdam 2003, 65–78.

Krüger, P., 'Jacob von Nisibis in syrischer und armenischer Überlieferung', *Le Muséon* 81 (1968) 161–179.

Krylová, B., 'Die Partikeln *ergo* und *igitur* bei Ammianus Marcellinus. Ein textologischer Beitrag zur Diskussion um Ammians Sprachkompetenz', in: G. Thome, J. Holzhausen, S. Anzinger (eds.), *Es hat sich viel ereignet, Gutes wie Böses. Lateinische Geschichtsschreibung der Spät- und Nachantike*, Munich 2001, 57–79.

Kubitschek, W., 'Signa (militaria)', *RE* 2A (1923) 2325–2347.

Kühner, R., and C. Stegmann, *Ausführliche Grammatik der lateinischen Sprache* II, *Satzlehre*, 2 vols., Hannover 1955⁴, 1976⁵.

Lacombrade, Chr., 'Notes sur l' 'aurum coronarium', *REA* 51 (1949) 54–59.

Langen, P., *Emendationes Ammianeae*, Gymn.-Progr. Düren 1867, 3–23.

Lascaratos, J., and D. Voros, 'Fatal Wounding of the Byzantine Emperor Julian the Apostate (361–363 A.D.): Approach to the Contribution of Ancient Surgery', *World Journal of Surgery* 24 (2000) 615–619.

Lattimore, R., *Themes in Greek and Latin Epitaphs* (Illinois Stud. in Lang. & Lit. 28,1–2), Urbana 1942.

Lavizzari Pedrazzini, M.P., *Milano: capitale dell' impero romano, 286–402 d.C.*, Milan 1990.

Le Bohec, Y., *The Imperial Roman Army*, London 1994 (first published in French, 1989).

Lecker, M., see A. Oppenheimer.

Lee, A.D., 'The Role of Hostages in Roman Diplomacy with Sasanian Persia', *Historia* 40 (1991) 366–374.

Lee, A.D., *Information and Frontiers. Roman Foreign Relations in Late Antiquity*, Cambridge 1993.

Lehmann, H., 'Grenzen der Mehrfachbesteuerung in der Spätantike. Zur Auslegung von CT 12, 1, 33', *Historia* 33 (1984) 378–384.

Lenski, N., 'The Election of Jovian and the Role of the Late Imperial Guards', *Klio* 82 (2000) 492–515.

Leo, F., *Die griechisch-römische Biographie nach ihrer literarischen Form*, Leipzig 1901.

Lepelley, C., *Les cités de l'Afrique romaine au bas-empire, I, La permanence d'une civilisation municipale*, Paris 1979.

Lévêque, P., 'De nouveaux portraits de l'empereur Julien', *Latomus* 22 (1963) 74–78 = 'Neue Porträts des Kaisers Julian', in: R. Klein (ed.), *Julian Apostata*, Darmstadt 1978, 305–317, cited as Lévêque, 1978.

Lewandowski, I., 'Les déesses Fortune, Adrastie-Némésis et Justice dans les *Res gestae* d'Ammien Marcellin', in: E. Delruelle and V. Pirenne-Delforge (eds.), *Κῆποι. De la religion à la philosophie*. Mélanges offerts à André Motte, Liège 2001, 297–307.

Lichocka, B., *L'iconographie de Fortuna dans l'empire romain (Ier siècle avant n.è. – IVe siècle de n.è.)* (Travaux du Centre d'Archéologie méditerranéenne de l'Académie Polonaise des Sciences) 29, Warszawa 1997.

Liebeschuetz, W., 'The Finances of Antioch in the Fourth Century', *ByzZ* 52 (1959) 344–356.

Lieu, S.N.C., 'Captives, Refugees and Exiles: A Study of Cross-Frontier Civilian Movements and Contacts between Rome and Persia from Valerian to Jovian', in: Ph. Freeman and D.L. Kennedy (eds.), *The Defence of the Roman and Byzantine East*, 2 vols. (BAR International Series 297), Oxford 1986, 475–505.

Lieu, S.N.C. (ed.), *The Emperor Julian. Panegyric and Polemic. Claudius Mamertinus, John Chrysostom, Ephrem the Syrian* (Translated Texts for Historians 2), Liverpool 1989².

Lieu, S.N.C., see also M.H. Dodgeon and G. Greatrex.

Lightfoot, C.S., 'Tilli. A late Roman *equites* fort on the Tigris?', in: P. Freeman and D. Kennedy (eds.), *The Defence of the Roman and Byzantine East* (BAR Intern. Ser. 297), Oxford 1986, 509–529.

Lightfoot, C.S., 'Facts and Fiction – The Third Siege of Nisibis', *Historia* 37 (1988) 105–125.

LIMC, *Lexicon Iconographicum Mythologiae Classicae*, Zurich-Munich 1981–1999.

Lippold, A., '*Consul*', *RAC* 3 (1957) 390–404.

Löfstedt, E., *Philologischer Kommentar zur* Peregrinatio Aetheriae. *Untersuchungen zur Geschichte der lateinischen Sprache*, Uppsala 1911.

Lolli, M., 'La "celeritas principis" fra tattica militare e necessità politica nei "Panegyrici Latini"', *Latomus* 58 (1999) 620–625.

L'Orange, H.P., and R. Unger, *Das spätantike Herrscherbild von Diokletian bis zu den Konstantin-Söhnen, 284–361 n. Chr.*, mit einem Nachtrag von M. Wegner: Die Bildnisse der Frauen und des Julian, Berlin 1984.

Lugaresi, L., 'Giuliano imperatore e Gregorio di Nazianzo: contiguità culturale e contraposizione ideologica nel confronta ellenismo e cristianesimo', in: *Giuliano imperatore, le sue idee, i suoi amici, i suoi avversari*, Atti del convegno internazionale di studi Lecce 10–12 Dicembre 1998 (= *Rudiae* 10), Lecce 1998, 293–334.

Luther, A., *Die syrische Chronik des Josua Stylites* (Untersuchungen zur antiken Literatur und Geschichte 49), Berlin-New York 1997.

Macciocca, M., '*Mausoleum Augusti*: Le sepolture', in: E.M. Steinby (ed.), *Lexicon Topographicum Urbis Romae* III, Rome 1996, 237–239.

MacCormack, S., 'Latin Prose Panegyrics. Tradition and Discontinuity in the Later Roman Empire', *REAug* 22 (1976) 29–77.

MacDonald, D., 'Another Representation of the Sasanid Triumph over Julian', *JNG* 28/29 (1978–1979) 31–33.

MacMullen, R., 'How Big was the Roman Imperial Army?', *Klio* 62 (1980) 451–460.

MacMullen, R., 'Tax-Pressure in the Roman Empire', *Latomus* 46 (1987) 737–754.

Madvig, J.N., *Adversaria critica ad scriptores Graecos et Latinos* III, Haunia (Copenhagen) 1884.

Mähl, S., *Quadriga Virtutum. Die Kardinaltugenden in der Geistesgeschichte der Karolingerzeit* (Archiv f. Kulturgeschichte, Beih. 9; Diss. Hamburg 1965/66), Cologne 1969.

Malosse, P.-L., 'Rhétorique et psychologie antiques: éloge des vertus et critiques obliques dans le portrait de l'Empereur Julien par Libanius', *Ktèma* 20 (1995) 319–338.

Malosse, P.-L., 'Vie et mort de l'empereur Julien, par Libanios', *QS* 24 nr. 48 (1998) 43–68.

Mango, C., 'Three Imperial Byzantine Sarcophagi discovered in 1750', *DOP* 16 (1962) 397–402.

Marié, M.-A., 'Virtus et Fortuna chez Ammien Marcellin. La responsabilité des dieux et des hommes dans l'abandon de Nisibe et la défaite d'Andrinople (*Res Gestae* XXV, 9 et XXXI)', *REL* 67 (1989) 179–119.

Maróth, M., 'Le siège de Nisibe en 350 ap. J.-Ch. d'après des sources syriennes', *AAntHung* 27 (1979) 239–243.

Marotta, V., *Mandata Principum*, Turin 1991.

Martin, A., *Athanase d'Alexandrie et l'Église d'Égypte au IVe siècle (328–373)* (Collection de l'École française de Rome 216), Paris 1996.

Martindale, J.R., 'Prosopography of the Later Roman Empire: addenda et corrigenda to volume I', *Historia* 29 (1980) 474–497.

Matthews, J.F., *The Roman Empire of Ammianus*, London 1989.

Mause, M., *Die Darstellung des Kaisers in der lateinischen Panegyrik* (Palingenesia 50), Stuttgart 1994.

Maxfield, V.A., *The Military Decorations of the Roman Army*, London 1981.

Mazzarino, S., *L'impero romano*, Rome 1962^2.

Mazzarino, S., 'La tradizione sulle guerre tra Shābuhr I e l'impero Romano: prospettiva e deformazione storica, *AAntHung* 19 (1971) 59–82.

Meeus, J., see M. Drummen.

Meijer, F.J.A.M., *Emperors Don't Die in Bed*, London 2004.

Mellet, S., '*Quando, quia, quod, quoniam*: analyse énonciative et syntaxique des conjonctions de cause en latin', in: D. Longrée (ed.), *DE VSV. Études de syntaxe latine offertes en hommage à Marius Lavency*, Louvain-la-Neuve 1995, 211–228.

Meslin, M., *La fête des Kalendes de janvier dans l'empire romain. Étude d'un rituel de Nouvel An* (Collection Latomus 115), Brussels 1970.

Metzler, D., 'Ökonomische Aspekte des Religionswandels in der Spätantike: die Enteignung der heidnischen Tempel seit Konstantin', *Hephaistos* 3 (1981) 27–40.

Meulder, M., 'Julien l' Apostat contre les Parthes: un guerrier impie', *Byzantion* 61 (1991) 458–495.

Meurig Davies, E.L.B., 'Elephant Tactics: Amm. Marc. 25.1.14; Sil. 9.581–583; Lucr. 2.537–539', *CQ* 45 (1951) 153–155.

Michael, H., *De Ammiani Marcellini studiis Ciceronianis*, Diss. Breslau 1874.

Migl, J., *Die Ordnung der Ämter. Prätorianerpräfektur und Vikariat in der Regionalverwaltung des Römischen Reiches von Konstantin bis zur Valentinianischen Dynastie* (Europäische Hochschulschriften, Reihe 3, Geschichte und ihre Hilfswissenschaften 623), Frankfurt am Main 1994.

Millar, F., *The Emperor in the Roman World (31 BC – AD 337)*, London 1977 (repr. 1992).

Millar, F., 'The Roman *Coloniae* of the Near East: a Study of Cultural Relations', in: H. Solin and M. Kajava (eds.), *Roman Eastern Policy and Other Studies in Roman History* (Commentationes Humanarum Litterarum 91), Helsinki 1990, 7–58.

Millar, F., *The Roman Near East, 31 BC – AD 337*, Cambridge Mass. 1993.

Miller, D.A., 'Byzantine Treaties and Treaty-Making: 500–1025', *Byzantinoslavica* 32 (1971) 56–76.

Milner, N.P., *Vegetius: Epitome of Military Science* (Translated Texts for Historians 16), Liverpool 1993 (1996^2).

Mitchell, S., *Anatolia. Land, Men, and Gods in Asia Minor*, 2 vols., Oxford 1993.

Molac, Ph., 'L'image de Julien l'Apostat chez Saint Grégoire de Nazianze', *BLE* 102 (2001) 39–48.

Mommsen, Th., *Römisches Staatsrecht*, I and II.1, Leipzig 1887^3.

Mommsen, Th., 'Das römische Militärwesen seit Diocletian', *Hermes* 24 (1889) 195–279 (= *Gesammelte Schriften* 6, Berlin 1910, 206–283).

Moncur, D., see P. Heather.

Montero, S., *Política y adivinación en el Bajo Impero Romano: emperadores y harúspices (193 D.C. – 408 D.C.)*, (Collection Latomus 211), Brussels 1991.

Moreau, J., 'Krise und Verfall. Das dritte Jahrhundert n. Chr. als historisches Problem', *Heidelb. Jahrb.* 5 (1961) 128–142 (repr. in J. Moreau, *Scripta Minora*, ed. W. Schmitthenner, Heidelberg 1964, 26–41), cited as Moreau, 1964.

BIBLIOGRAPHY 361

Moro, M., 'I prefetti del pretorio degli anni 355–363: indagine proso-pografica, funzioni, rapporti con gli imperatori', in: G. Crifò and S. Giglio (eds.), *Atti dell' Accademia Romanistica Costantiniana. XI Convegno Internazionale in onore di Felix B.J. Wubbe*, Naples 1996, 369–376.

Müller, A., 'Militaria aus Ammianus Marcellinus', *Philologus* 64 (1905) 573–632.

Münzer, F., 'Claudius 220 (M. Claudius Marcellus)', *RE* 3 (1899) 2738–2755.

Münzer, F., 'Sergius 40 (M. Sergius Silus)', *RE* 2A (1923) 1719–1720.

Münzer, F., 'Siccius 3 (L. Siccius Dentatus)', *RE* 2A (1923) 2189–2190.

Naudé, C.P.T., 'Fortuna in Ammianus Marcellinus', *AClass* 7 (1964) 70–88.

Neiss, R., see F. Berthelot.

Neri, V., *Costanzo, Giuliano e l' ideale del Civilis Princeps' nelle storie di Ammiano Marcellino* (Studi Bizantini e Slavi 1), Rome 1984.

Neri, V., *Ammiano e il Cristianesimo. Religione e politica nelle 'Res Gestae' di Ammiano Marcellino*, Bologna 1985.

Neri, V., 'Ammiano Marcellino e l' elezione di Valentiniano', *RSA* 15 (1985) 153–182.

Neri, V., *Medius princeps. Storia e immagine di Costantino nella storiografia latina pagana*, Bologna 1992.

Nes, D. van, *Die maritime Bildersprache des Aischylos*, Diss. Utrecht 1963.

Nesselrath, H.-G., 'Kaiserlicher Held und Christenfeind: Julian Apostata im Urteil des späteren 4. und des 5. Jahrhunderts n. Chr.', in: B. Bäbler and H.G. Nesselrath (eds.), *Die Welt des Sokrates von Konstantinopel. Studien zu Politik, Religion und Kultur im späten 4. und frühen 5. Jh. n. Chr. zu Ehren von Christoph Schäublin*, Munich-Leipzig, 2001, 15–43.

Neue, F., *Formenlehre der lateinische Sprache*. Dritte, sehr vermehrte Auflage von C. Wagener, Leipzig 1892–1905 (repr. Hildesheim 1985).

Neufeld, E., 'Insects as Warfare Agents in the Ancient Middle East', *Orientalia* 49 (1980) 30–57.

Nicasie, M.J., *Twilight of Empire. The Roman Army from the Reign of Diocletian until the Battle of Adrianople*, Amsterdam 1998.

Nicholson, O.P., 'Taq-i Bostan, Mithras and Julian the Apostate, an Irony', *IA* 18 (1983) 177–178.

Nilsson, M.P., 'Die astrale Unsterblichkeit und die kosmische Mystik', *Numen* 1 (1954) 106–119.

Nock, A.D., 'Deification and Julian', *JRS* 47 (1957) 115–123 (= A.D. Nock, *Essays on Religion and the Ancient World* II, Oxford 1972, 833–846).

Nollé, J., see D. Berges.

Noreña, C.F., 'The Communication of the Emperor's Virtues', *JRS* 91 (2001) 146–168.

North, H.F., 'Canons and Hierarchies of the Cardinal Virtues in Greek and Latin Literature', in: L. Wallach (ed.), *The Classical Tradition. Literary and Historical Studies in Honor of Harry Caplan*, Ithaca 1966, 165–183.

Northedge, A., T.J. Wilkinson and R. Falkner, 'Survey and Excavations at Sāmarrā 1989', *Iraq* 52 (1990) 121–147.

Oates, D., *Studies in the Ancient History of Northern Iraq*, London 1968.

BIBLIOGRAPHY

Oppenheimer, A., in collaboration with B. Isaac and M. Lecker, *Babylonia Judaica in the Talmudic Period*, Wiesbaden 1983.

Otto, A., *Die Sprichwörter und sprichwörtlichen Redensarten der Römer*, Leipzig 1890 (repr. Hildesheim 1962).

Pack, E., *Städte und Steuern in der Politik Julians. Untersuchungen zu den Quellen eines Kaiserbildes* (Collection Latomus 194), Brussels 1986.

Palla, R., 'Perfidus ille deo, quamvis non perfidus orbi: l'imperatore Giuliano nei versi di Prudenzio', in: *Giuliano imperatore, le sue idee, i suoi amici, i suoi avversari*, Atti del convegno internazionale di studi Lecce 10–12 Dicembre 1998 (= *Rudiae* 10), Lecce 1998, 357–371.

Paschoud, F., *Cinq Études sur Zosime*, Paris 1975.

Paschoud, F., Zosime, *Histoire Nouvelle* II.1 *(Livre III)*, Paris 1979.

Paschoud, F., 'Justice et providence chez Ammien Marcellin', *Studi Tardoantichi* 1 (1986) 139–161.

Pauw, D.A., *Karaktertekening by Ammianus Marcellinus*, Diss. Leiden 1972.

Pauw, D.A., 'Methods of Character Portrayal in the *Res Gestae* of Ammianus Marcellinus', *AClass* 20 (1977) 181–198.

Pauw, D.A., 'Ammianus Marcellinus and Ancient Historiography, Biography and Character Portrayal', *AClass* 22 (1979) 115–129.

Peeters, P., 'La légende de saint Jacques de Nisibe', *AB* 38 (1920) 285–373.

Pernot, L., *La rhétorique de l'éloge dans le monde gréco-romain*, Paris 1993.

Petschenig, M., 'Zu Ammianus Marcellinus', *ALL* 6 (1889) 268–269.

Petschenig, M., 'Bemerkungen zum Texte des Ammianus Marcellinus', *Philologus* 50 (1891) 336–354; 51 (1892) 519–529, 680–691.

Petschenig, M., 'Zu Ammian', *Philologus* 50 (1891) 742; 51 (1892) 64, 265, 283, 360, 622, 669, 734.

Piétri, L., 'La conversion en Belgique seconde d'un ancien officier de l'armée de Julien, Jovin', *Revue du Nord* 52 (1970) 443–453.

Pighi, G.B., *Studia Ammianea. Annotationes criticae et grammaticae in Ammianum Marcellinum*, Milan 1935.

Piovene, G., see T. Agozzino.

PLRE I, *The Prosopography of the Later Roman Empire, I, A.D. 260–395*, A.H.M. Jones, J.R. Martindale and J. Morris (eds.), Cambridge 1971.

PLRE III, *The Prosopography of the Later Roman Empire, III, A.D. 527–641*, 2 vols. (A and B), J.R. Martindale (ed.), Cambridge 1992.

Radke, G., *Die Bedeutung der weißen und der schwarzen Farbe in Kult und Brauch der Griechen und Römer* (Diss. Berlin), Jena 1936.

Rawson, E., 'Fregellae: Fall and Survival', in: F. Coarelli and P.G. Monti (eds.), *Fregellae. 1. Le fonti, la storia, il territorio*, Rome 1998, 71–76.

Renucci, P., *Les idées politiques et le gouvernement de l'empereur Julien* (Collection Latomus 259), Brussels 2000.

RIC, see J.P.C. Kent.

Ridley, R.T., 'Notes on Julian's Persian expedition (363)', *Historia* 22 (1973) 317–330.

Rijksbaron, A., *The Syntax and Semantics of the Verb in Classical Greek. An Introduction*, Amsterdam 2002³.

BIBLIOGRAPHY 363

Rike, R.L., *Apex Omnium. Religion in the Res Gestae of Ammianus*, Berkeley-Los Angeles-London 1987.

Risselada, R., see C.H.M. Kroon.

Robinson, H.R., *The Armour of Imperial Rome*, New York 1975.

Roca Alamá, M.J., '*Quod, quia, quoniam* en Amiano Marcelino', *Fortunatae* 9 (1997) 237–251.

Rolfe, J.C., *Ammianus Marcellinus*, with an English translation, 3 vols., London-Cambridge Mass. 1935–1939 (repr. 1971–1972).

Rose, P., see C.H.M. Kroon.

Rosen, K., 'Beobachtungen zur Erhebung Julians, 360–361 n. Chr.', *AClass* 12 (1969) 121–149 = R. Klein (ed.), *Julian Apostata*, Darmstadt 1978, 409–447, cited as Rosen, 1978.

Rosenstein, N., '*Imperatores Victi*: The Case of C. Hostilius Mancinus', *ClAnt* 5 (1986) 230–252.

Rougier, L., *La religion astrale des Pythagoriciens*, Paris 1959.

Rousselle, A., *Porneia. De la maîtrise du corps à la privation sensorielle, II–IV siècles de l'ère chrétienne*, Paris 1983.

Ruge, W., 'Kydnos', *RE* Suppl. 4 (1924) 1124.

Rumpf, A., 'Römische historische Reliefs', *BJ* 155/156 (1955/56) 112–135.

Sabbah, G., *La méthode d'Ammien Marcellin. Recherches sur la construction du discours historique dans les* Res Gestae, Paris 1978.

Sabbah, G., 'Présences féminines dans *l'histoire* d'Ammien Marcellin. Les rôles politiques', in: J. den Boeft, D. den Hengst and H.C. Teitler (eds.), *Cognitio Gestorum. The Historiographic Art of Ammianus Marcellinus*, Amsterdam 1992, 91–105.

Salazar, C.F., *The Treatment of War Wounds in Graeco-Roman Antiquity* (Studies in Ancient Medicine 21), Leiden 2000.

Sánchez, B. Enjuto, 'Las disposiciones judiciales de Constantino y Juliano a propósito de las tierras de los templos paganos', *Gerión* 18 (2000) 407–423.

Scala, R. von, 'Doxographische und stoische Reste bei Ammianus Marcellinus', in: *Festgaben zu Ehren Max Büdingers*, Innsbruck 1898, 117–150.

Scharf, R., '*Seniores-iuniores* und die Heeresteilung des Jahres 364', *ZPE* 89 (1991) 265–272.

Scharf, R., *Comites und comitiva primi ordinis* (Ak. d. Wiss. u. d. Lit., Mainz, Abh. d. Geistes- u. Sozialwiss. Kl., 1994, 8), Stuttgart 1994.

Scheda, G., 'Die Todesstunde Kaiser Julians', *Historia* 15 (1966) 380–384 = R. Klein (ed.), *Julian Apostata*, Darmstadt 1978, 381–386.

Schippmann, K., *Grundzüge der Geschichte des sasanidischen Reiches*, Darmstadt 1990.

Schlumberger, J., *Die Epitome de Caesaribus. Untersuchungen zur heidnischen Geschichtsschreibung des 4. Jahrhunderts n. Chr.* (Vestigia 18), Munich 1974.

Schmidt, M.C.P., 'Eberraute', *RE* 5 (1905) 1894–1895.

Schmidt, W., *De ultimis morientium verbis*, Marburg 1914.

Scholl, R., *Historische Beiträge zu den julianischen reden des Libanios*, Stuttgart 1994.

Schramm, P.E., *Sphaira, Globus, Reichsapfel. Wanderung und Wandlung eines*

*Herrschaftszeichens von Caesar bis zu Elisabeth II. Ein Beitrag zum 'Nachleben'
der Antike*, Stuttgart 1958.

Schulz, R., *Die Entwicklung des römischen Völkerrechts im vierten und fünften
Jahrhundert n. Chr.* (Hermes Einzelschriften 61), Stuttgart 1993.

Schuster, M., 'Wermut', *RE* 8A (1958) 1553–1558.

Schwyzer, E., and A. Debrunner, *Griechische Grammatik* II, Munich 1975[4],
cited as Schwyzer-Debrunner.

Scivoletto, N., 'La *civilitas* del IV secolo e il significato del *Breviarium* di
Eutropio', *GIF* 22 (1970) 14–45.

Scullard, H.H., *Scipio Africanus: Soldier and Politician*, London 1970.

Scullard, H.H., *The Elephant in the Greek and Roman World*, London 1974.

Seager, R., *Ammianus Marcellinus. Seven Studies in his Language and Thought*,
Columbia 1986.

Seager, R., 'Ammianus and the Status of Armenia in the Peace of 363',
Chiron 26 (1996) 275–284.

Seager, R., 'Perceptions of Eastern Frontier Policy in Ammianus, Libanius,
and Julian (337–363)', *CQ* 47 (1997) 253–268.

Seckel, E., see H.G. Heuman.

Seeck, O., '*Candidatus* 4', *RE* 3 (1899) 1468–1469.

Seeck, O., '*Comes rei militaris*', *RE* 4 (1901) 662–664.

Seeck, O., *Die Briefe des Libanius zeitlich geordnet*, Leipzig 1906 (repr. Hildesheim 1967).

Seeck, O., 'Iovianus 1', *RE* 9 (1916) 2006–2011.

Seeck, O., *Regesten der Kaiser und Päpste für die Jahre 311 bis 476 n. Chr. Vorarbeit
zu einer Prosopographie der christlichen Kaiserzeit*, Stuttgart 1919 (repr. 1964).

Seeck, O., *Geschichte des Untergangs der antiken Welt*, 6 vols., Stuttgart 1920–
1923[2-4].

Selem, A., 'Ammiano XXV, 2, 8', *Athenaeum* 51 (1973) 399–402.

Seston, W., 'Notes critiques sur l'Histoire Auguste, I. Julien et l'or coronaire',
REA 44 (1942) 224–233 (repr. in W. Seston, *Scripta varia. Mélanges d'
histoire Romaine, de droit, d' épigraphie et d' histoire du Christianisme*, Rome
1980, 509–518).

Seston, W., 'Notes critiques sur l'Histoire Auguste, I. Julien et l' 'aurum
coronarium'. Addendum', *REA* 45 (1943) 49–60 (repr. in W. Seston,
*Scripta varia. Mélanges d' histoire Romaine, de droit, d' épigraphie et d' histoire
du Christianisme*, Rome 1980, 519–522).

Seston, W., 'Feldzeichen', *RAC* 7 (1969) 689–711 (repr. in W. Seston,
*Scripta Varia. Mélanges d'histoire Romaine, de droit, d'épigraphie et d'histoire
du Christianisme*, Rome 1980, 263–281).

Shahbazi, A.S., 'Derafš', *EncIr* 7 (1996) 312–315.

Siegel, R.E., *Galen's System of Physiology and Medicine. An Analysis of his Doctrines
and Observations on Bloodflow, Respiration, Humors and Internal Diseases*,
Basel-New York 1968.

Solari, A., 'La elezione di Gioviano', *Klio* 26 (1933) 330–335.

Sommella, P., *Antichi campi di battaglia in Italia. Contributi all' identificazione
topografica di alcune battaglie d' età repubblicana* (Quaderni dell'Istituto di
Topografia Antica della Università di Roma 3), Rome 1967.

BIBLIOGRAPHY

Somville, P., 'Portrait physique de l'Empereur Julien', *AC* 72 (2003) 161–166.

Southern, P., and K.R. Dixon, *The Late Roman Army*, London 1996.

Spevak, O., *La concession en Latin*, Brussels 2005.

Staesche, M., *Das Privatleben der römischen Kaiser in der Spätantike. Studien zur Personen- und Kulturgeschichte der späten Kaiserzeit*, Bern-Frankfurt am Main 1998.

St. Clair, A., 'The Apotheosis Diptych', *The Art Bulletin* 46 (1964) 205–211.

Stein, M.A., 'The trade route past Hatra', in: S. Gregory and D. Kennedy (eds.), *Sir Aurel Stein's Limes Report*. The full text of M.A. Stein's unpublished *Limes Report* (his aerial and ground reconnaissances in Iraq and Transjordan in 1938–1939) edited and with a commentary and bibliography (BAR Internat. Ser. 272), Oxford 1985, 57–67.

Stein, M.A., 'The routes to Hatra in Peutinger's Tabula and Jovian's retreat', in: S. Gregory and D. Kennedy (eds.), *Sir Aurel Stein's Limes Report*. The full text of M.A. Stein's unpublished *Limes Report* (his aerial and ground reconnaissances in Iraq and Transjordan in 1938–1939) edited and with a commentary and bibliography (BAR Internat. Ser. 272), Oxford 1985, 79–85.

Stemplinger, E., 'Abrotonon', *RAC* 1 (1950) 28.

Stephenson, I.P., *Roman Infantry Equipment. The Later Empire*, Stroud 1999.

Straub, J.A., *Vom Herrscherideal in der Spätantike*, Stuttgart 1939 (repr. Darmstadt 1964).

Straub, J.A., 'Die Himmelfahrt des Julianus Apostata', *Gymnasium* 69 (1962) 310–326 = J. Straub, *Regeneratio Imperii. Aufsätze über Roms Kaisertum und Reich im Spiegel der heidnischen und christlichen Publizistik*, Darmstadt 1972, 159–177.

Streck, M., 'Hucumbra', *RE* 8 (1913) 2517–2518.

Sturm, J., 'Nisibis', *RE* 17 (1937) 714–757.

Szantyr, A., see J.B. Hofmann.

Taisne, A.M., 'Ammien Marcellin, successeur de Tacite dans la description de la mort de Julien (H., XXV, I–V)', in: R. Chevallier and R. Poignault (eds.), *Présence de Tacite. Hommage au professeur G. Radke*, Tours 1992, 243–256.

Talbert, R.J.A. (ed.), *Barrington Atlas of the Greek and Roman World*, Princeton 2000.

Teitler, H.C., *Notarii and Exceptores. An Inquiry into Role and Significance of Shorthand Writers in the Imperial and Ecclesiastical Bureaucracy of the Roman Empire (from the Early Principate to c. 450 A.D.)*, Amsterdam 1985.

Teitler, H.C., 'Julian's Death-bed and Literary Convention', in: Caroline Kroon and Daan den Hengst (eds.), *Ultima Aetas. Time, Tense and Transience in the Ancient World. Studies in Honour of Jan den Boeft*, Amsterdam 2000, 71–80.

Teixidor, J., 'Conséquences politiques et culturelles de la victoire sassanide à Nisibe', in: E. Frézouls and A. Jacquemin (eds.), *Les relations internationales*, Paris 1995, 499–510.

Thompson, E.A., *The Historical Work of Ammianus Marcellinus*, Cambridge 1947 (repr. Groningen 1969).

BIBLIOGRAPHY

TLG, *Thesaurus Linguae Graecae*, University of California at Irvine, 2000.

Tombeur, P., see BTL-2.

Tomlin, R.S.O., 'The Legions in the Late Empire', in: R.J. Brewer (ed.), *Roman Fortresses and their Legions. Papers in Honour of George C. Boon*, London-Cardiff 2000, 159–181.

Toumanoff, C., *Studies in Christian Caucasian History*, Georgetown 1963.

Tränkle, H., 'Ammianus Marcellinus als römischer Geschichtsschreiber', *Antike und Abendland* 11 (1962) 21–33.

Trombley, F.R., and Watt, J.W., *The Chronicle of Pseudo-Joshua the Stylite* (Translated Texts for Historians 32), Liverpool 2000.

Trümpelmann, L., 'Triumph über Julian Apostata', *JNG* 25 (1975) 107–111 + Tafel 16–19.

Turcan, R., 'L'abandon de Nisibe et l'opinion publique', in: R. Chevallier (ed.), *Mélanges d'Archéologie et d'Histoire offerts à André Piganiol* II, Paris 1966, 875–890.

Ugenti, V., 'Tertulliano, Giuliano e l'insegnamento delle lettere classiche', *Rudiae* 5 (1993) 153–159.

Ugenti, V., 'La figura di Giuliano in Ambrogio e Agostino', in: *Giuliano imperatore, le sue idee, i suoi amici, i suoi avversari*, Atti del convegno internazionale di studi Lecce 10–12 Dicembre 1998 (= *Rudiae* 10), Lecce 1998, 373–386.

Ungern-Sternberg, J. von, *Capua im Zweiten Punischen Krieg. Untersuchungen zur römischen Annalistik* (Vestigia 23), Munich 1975.

Urso, G., 'Le Forche Caudine, "media via" tra vendetta e perdono', in: M. Sordi (ed.), *Amnisti, perdono e vendetta nel mondo antico*, Milan 1997, 237–251.

Vanderspoel, J., *Themistius and the Imperial Court. Oratory, Civic Duty, and Paideia from Constantius to Theodosius*, Ann Arbor 1995.

Viansino, J., *Ammiani Marcellini rerum gestarum Lexicon*, 2 vols., Hildesheim-Zurich-New York 1985.

Vogler, Ch., 'Les officiers de l'armée romaine dans l'oeuvre d'Ammien Marcellin', in: Y. Le Bohec (ed.), *La hiérarchie (Rangordnung) de l'armée sous le haut-empire*, Paris 1995, 389–404.

Vogt, J., *Orbis Romanus. Zur Terminologie des römischen Imperialismus* (Philosophie und Geschichte 22), Tübingen 1929.

Volterra, E., 'Il problema del testo delle costituzioni imperiali', *La critica del testo* (Atti del secondo congresso internazionale della Società Italiana di storia del Diritto II), Florence 1971, 821–1097.

Volterra, E., 'Sul Contenuto del Codice Teodosiano', *BIDR* 84 (1981) 85–124.

Vööbus, A., *History of the School of Edessa*, Louvain 1965.

Voros, D., see J. Lascaratos.

Waas, M., *Germanen im römischen Dienst im 4. Jh. n. Chr.*, Bonn 1971^2.

Wagner, J.A., *Ammiani Marcellini quae supersunt*, cum notis integris Frid. Lindenbrogii, Henr. et Hadr. Valesiorum et Iac. Gronovii, quibus Thom. Reinesii quasdam et suas adiecit, editionem absolvit Car. Gottl. Aug. Erfurdt, 3 vols., Leipzig 1808 (repr. in 2 vols., Hildesheim 1975).

BIBLIOGRAPHY 367

Walter, F., 'Zu Ammianus Marcellinus', *BPhW* 33 (1913) 94, 541–542, 1162.
Walter, F., 'Zu Ammianus Marcellinus', *BPhW* 40 (1920) 715.
Waltz, R., 'Autour d'un texte de Sénèque (*Nat. Quaest.* IV, praef. 17)', *REL* 17 (1939) 292–308.
Warmington, B.H., 'Ammianus Marcellinus and the Lies of Metrodorus', *CQ* 31 (1981) 464–468.
Warmington, B.H., 'Some Constantinian References in Ammianus', in: J.W. Drijvers and E.D. Hunt (eds.), *The Late Roman World and its Historian*, London-New York 1999, 166–177.
Weber, G., *Kaiser, Träume und Visionen in Prinzipat und Spätantike* (Historia Einzelschriften 143), Stuttgart 2000.
Weiss, P.B., *Consistorium und Comites Consistoriani. Untersuchungen zur Hofbeamtenschaft des 4. Jahrhunderts n.Chr. auf prosopographischer Grundlage*, Würzburg 1975.
Wessel, K., 'Eine Gruppe oberitalischer Elfenbeinarbeiten', *JDAI* 63/64 (1948/49) 111–160.
Whitby, M., 'Arzanene in the late Sixth Century', in: S. Mitchell (ed.), *Armies and Frontiers in Roman and Byzantine Anatolia* (BAR Intern. Ser. 156), London 1983, 205–218.
Wieber-Scariot, A., *Zwischen Polemik und Panegyrik. Frauen des Kaiserhauses und Herrscherinnen des Ostens in den* Res gestae *des Ammianus Marcellinus* (Bochumer Altertumswissenschaftliches Colloquium 41), Trier 1999.
Wiemer, H.-U., *Libanios und Julian. Studien zum Verhältnis von Rhetorik und Politik im vierten Jahrhundert n. Chr.*, Munich 1995.
Wiesehöfer, J., *Das antike Persien. Von 550 v. Chr. bis 650 n. Chr.*, Munich 1994.
Wightman, E.M., *Gallia Belgica*, London 1985.
Wikander, Ö, 'Caius Hostilius Mancinus and the *foedus Numantinum*', *ORom* 11 (1976) 85–104.
Wilkie, J.S., see D.J. Furley.
Wilkinson, T.J., see A. Northedge.
Winter, E., 'On the Regulation of the Eastern Frontier of the Roman Empire in 298', in: D.H. French and C.S. Lightfoot (eds.), *The Eastern Frontier of the Roman Empire.* Proceedings of a Colloquium held at Ankara in September 1988 (BAR Internat. Ser. 553, 2 vols.), Oxford 1989, II, 555–571.
Winter, E., and B. Dignas, *Rom und das Perserreich. Zwei Weltmächte zwischen Konfrontation und Koexistenz*, Berlin 2001.
Wirth, G., 'Jovian. Kaiser und Karikatur', in: E. Dassmann and K. Thraede (eds.), *Vivarium. Festschrift Theodor Klauser zum 90. Geburtstag* (*JbAC*, Ergänzungsband 11), Münster 1984, 353–384.
Wirz, H., 'Ammians Beziehungen zu seinen Vorbildern, Cicero, Sallustius, Livius, Tacitus', *Philologus* 36 (1877) 627–636.
Wittchow, F., *Exemplarisches Erzählen bei Ammianus Marcellinus. Episode, Exemplum, Anekdote* (Beiträge zur Altertumskunde 144), Munich-Leipzig 2001.
Wölfflin, E., 'Zur Alliteration und zum Reime', *ALL* 3 (1886) 443–457.
Woods, D., 'Ammianus Marcellinus and the Deaths of Bonosus and Maximilianus', *Hagiographica* 2 (1995) 25–55, cited as Woods, 1995a.

Woods, D., 'Julian, Arbogastes, and the *signa* of the *Ioviani* and *Herculiani*', *JRMES* 6 (1995) 61–68, cited as Woods, 1995b.

Woods, D., 'Maurus, Mavia, and Ammianus', *Mnemosyne* 51 (1998) 325–336, cited as Woods, 1998a.

Woods, D., 'Valens, Valentinian I, and the *Ioviani Cornuti*', in: C. Deroux (ed.), *Studies in Latin Literature and Roman History* IX, Brussels 1998, 462–486, cited as Woods, 1998b.

Yar-Shater, E., 'Were the Sasanians Heirs to the Achaemenids?', in: *Atti del Convegno Internazionale sul tema: La Persia nel Medioevo* (Acc. Naz. dei Lincei, Quaderno 160), Rome 1971, 517–533.

Zuckerman, C., '*Constantiniani – Constantiniaci* from Pylai. A Rejoinder', *Tyche* 13 (1998) 255–258.

Zuckerman, C., 'Sur le dispositif frontalier en Arménie, le "limes" et son évolution sous le Bas-Empire', *Historia* 47 (1998) 108–128.

INDICES

I. *Lexical (Latin)*

abire e vita: 88
abrotonum: 260
abruptus: 255
absinthium: 260
absolutus: 158
absorbere: 253
ac si: 136
accendere: 4
accessus: 200
acies: 188
acquiescere: 162
actuarius: 324
actus: 259
adipisci: 241
adminiculum: 267
admodum: 128
adoreus: 83
adulta nocte: 47
advenire: 208
aequare: 145
aequitas: 190
aequo animo: 327
aer: 52
aereus: 25
aerumna: 256
aestus: 7
aetherius: 50
affectare: 157
agger: 209
agmen: 6
ala: 10
alacritas: 16, 78
alienare: 241
aliquis: 260
altitudo: 45
altrinsecus: 59, 247
amendare: 92, 253, 325
amplecti: 326
angustiae: 92, 160, 203
anima: 94

animadvertere: 132
animosus: 79
animus: 94
annectere: 159
antesignanus: 62
apparitor: 85
appetitor: 156
apponere: 18
aptare: 24
architectus: 217
arguere: 18
armatura: 64
armatus: 215
arx: 125
asciscere: 195
attenuare: 20
attonitus: 179
attritus: 52
auctor: 268
auctoritas: 104
audere: 208
augere: 328
aulaeum: 46
autem: 336
avidus: 162
beare: 103
bellicosus: 211, 259
belua: 201
bene: 91
bona fide: 89
bonae frugi: 153
boni: 295
brattea: 24
brevis: 4, 125, 330
bucina: 254
cadere: 49
caelestis: 47, 227
caelitus: 49
calescere: 78
calo: 183, 195

370 INDICES

camelus: 261
captivus: 18
caput: 326
carptim: 151
castitas: 120
caterva: 23
causari: 176
cautus: 54
celeber: 247
celeri gradu: 196
celsus: 114
censio hastaria: 17
centuria: 63
Christiana lex: 338
cinis: 320
circumsaepire: 210
citus: 203
claritudo: 116
claustrum: 272
clemens: 229
clipeus: 73
coalitus: 116
codicillus: 265
cogere agmen: 13
cogitare: 199
cognitio: 129
colere: 120
columella: 42
commendabilis: 185
commilitium: 173
compages: 23
compaginare: 225
componere: 136
compulsor: 292
concertatio: 136
conciliare: 105
concipere: 301
concitor: 329
conculcare: 216
condere: 157
confinium: 21, 203
conflictus: 34
confragosus: 250
congruus: 11
connumerare: 114
considerare: 98
consiliarius: 85

consilium: 267
consortium: 159, 328
constans: 328
constringere: 271
consumere: 109
consummare: 294
consurgere: 132
contemptor: 130
continuus: 309
contorquere: 217
contrarius: 246
contus: 25
cornu: 63, 84
cornucopia: 46
corpus: 52
correctio: 19
corruptrix: 97
crista: 79
crudescere: 285
culmen: 46, 264
cuneus: 208
cuppedia(e): 42
curare: 170
cutis: 71
decernere: 33, 64
declinare: 284
decretum: 244
deducere: 189
defensor: 289
deferre: 342
defluere: 94
deformare: 84
delabi: 49
demissus: 88
denique: 208
densetus: 33
depulsorius: 47
destinare: 41, 288
destinate: 177
destitutus: 108
detestari: 291
difflare: 294
diffluere: 65
digerere: 316
digredi: 100, 187
dii caelestes: 90
dirus: 309

INDICES

371

discedere: 187
discessus: 84
discissus: 172
discrimen: 132
discurrere: 188, 255, 308
disponere: 18, 196, 329
dissensio: 244
distentus: 334
distinguere: 333
divaricatus: 27
divus: 114, 321
dolor: 77
domi forisque: 123
dracontium: 260
dubietas: 333
ductor: 5, 18, 295
dux: 84, 171, 261
e(x): 217
e medio: 268
effectus: 165
effundere, -i: 190
effundere: 66
effuso cursu: 323
effusus: 34
elatus: 195
eligere: 181
eminere: 37
enim: 19, 76, 293, 298, 325
enitere: 120
enixe: 275
ergo: 36
etiamtum: 61
evehere: 264
eventus: 310
exabuti: 232
examinatus: 230
exauctorare: 78
excellere: 280
excidere: 71
excruciare: 212
excursator: 5
exinde: 273
exitialis: 242
exsequi: 304
exsilire: 64
exsultare: 89
exterminare: 97

extollere: 269
extrahere: 256, 303
extremus: 212
extuberari: 334
exuere: 18
exuviae: 14
facilis: 108
faetor: 200
fama: 212, 270
fatalis: 342
fatidicus: 98
fatiscere, -i: 7
favor: 189
ferratus: 23
ferre suppetias: 62
ferre: 158
fidenter: 215
fiducia: 35
firmiter: 60
fiscus: 145
flabrum: 191
flagitare: 32, 213
flammeus: 36
flebilis: 293
flectere: 2
foederare: 248
fortuna: 342
frugi: 102
frustum: 286
fulgere: 28
fulgor: 2
fundare: 98
fundus: 146
furor: 226
genitalis: 283
gens: 236
gentiles: 270
gentilitas: 189
genuinus: 216
gliscere: 165
globus: 63
gloriosus: 222
gradum referre: 212
habilis: 101, 172, 271
habitus: 50
hebetare: 224
hero(ic)us: 113

372 INDICES

hiare: 106
hiatus: 28
hinc inde: 214, 255
homo: 243
honoratus: 177
honorificus: 338
horrere: 59
humanus: 229
humilis: 104
humilitas: 129
iacere: 203
iam: 41, 156, 199
idem: 205
igitur: 36
ignobilis: 244
ilico: 301
imbratteare: 24
immaculatus: 93
immanis: 254
immemor: 65
immensus: 21
immobilis: 74, 139
immodestus: 213
impendere: 256
impendio: 88
imperium: 296
impius: 242
imprudentia: 101
imus: 42
in cassum: 214
inaccessus: 200
incertum unde: 67
incessus: 200
incidentia: 267
inclarescere: 3, 131
inclemens: 158
inclinare: 35
increpare: 104
incumbere: 324
incusare: 191
indeclinabilis: 130
indicere: 140
indictum: 140
indulgere: 142, 252
indutiae: 39, 40, 246
ingenium: 114
innectere: 9

inniti: 9
innocuus: 215
insidias struere: 59
insignia: 295
instare: 239
institutum: 153
intellegere: 13
intempestivus: 323
intento studio: 119
inter exordia: 287
interfector: 6
interficere: 6
internecivus: 301
invenire: 306
involare: 76
ira: 66, 77, 271
ire: 174
irruere: 9
ita: 325
itidem: 266, 338
iucundus: 122
iudex: 340
iumentum: 71, 210
iunctura: 23
iungere: 86
labi: 49
lacerare: 253
laevus: 202
lamentum: 292
lapis: 188
lassare: 36
latenter: 253
laxus: 60
legitimus: 155, 179
levis: 223
liberalitas: 119
licenter: 243
licentia: 96
limes: 213
locus: 328
longus: 189
lorica: 3
luctificus: 281, 310
luctuosus: 281, 310
luctus: 292
lucubratio: 126
lugubris: 33

INDICES

lumina: 2
lunaris: 32
macula: 83
magis quam: 155
magis: 265
magister: 29, 191
magniloquentia: 81
magnus: 321
malle: 337
mamma: 27
mandatum: 280
manipulus: 32
manubriatus: 29
margo: 214, 256
materia, -es: 285
mederi: 41
medicina: 72
medimnus: 273
mediocriter: 185, 339
medius: 324
medulla: 295
membrum: 292
memoria: 301
mensura: 337
migrare: 52
militares: 277
ministerium: 44
mirus: 317
Mithridaticus: 297
moderamen: 19
modius: 273
moles: 13
momentum: 254
monstrare: 50
mos: 97
multitudo: 21
mundanus: 140
munifex: 44
natatus: 224
nauticus: 191
nec: 277
necessitas: 272
negotio levi: 13
negotium: 234, 267, 277
nisi quod: 305
nisus: 33
nitor: 49

non ferendus: 41
noster: 232, 241
noxa: 324
noxius: 261
numen: 47, 99, 227, 256, 309
numerus: 15, 164, 248, 328
nusquam: 273
obex: 287
obsidatus: 247
obstinatio: 233
obstinatus: 78
obtrectator: 193
obumbrare: 83
offundere: 78
opportunus: 239
ops: 102
optimas: 227, 247, 248, 303
optimates: 81
orare: 228
orator: 228
orbis Romanus: 294
orbis: 271
ordinare: 136, 198
ordo: 326
oriens: 272
pacem fundare: 228
palatium: 172
pallescere: 7
pallium: 124
parma: 74
pars Romana: 228
pars: 7, 260
parsimonia: 123
Parthi/Parthicus: 164
Parthi: 36
Parthicus: 63, 269
patulus: 13
pedem referre: 212
pendere: 256
penetrare: 215, 255
peragere: 308
percellere: 271
percitus: 189
permiscere: 292
pernicies: 162
perpensius: 340
perpetuare: 321

374 INDICES

perplexus: 229
perquam: 239
perspicuus: 162
persultare: 209
piaculum: 284
planities: 260
plebs: 42, 202, 223
pollingere: 170
pomerium: 319
pondus: 316
pone versus: 35
ponte(m) iungere: 257
popularitas: 157
porrectus: 50
porrigere: 260
portare: 261
poscere/postulare: 322
postulare: 44
potestas: 95
prae ceteris: 216
praecelsus: 114
praeceps: 85
praecinere: 98
praecipuus: 118
praedicare: 151
praescribere: 76, 333
praesidium: 232
praespeculari: 268
praestituere: 315
praestringere: 27
praetendere: 288
praetentura: 136
praeter sperata: 227
praeterlambere: 320
praetorium: 208
praevalere: 27
primae: 202
primas: 230
principatus: 92
principium: 171, 274, 330
priscus: 302
privatus: 193
pro captu: 205, 267
pro tempore: 331
procinctus: 124, 269
procursator: 256
producere: 188

profanus: 50
profecto: 113
proinde: 303
promovere: 288, 340
pronuntiare: 198
properare: 226
propositum: 122
protrudere: 33
provolvere: 71
proximus: 337
prudentia: 129
pugnax: 37
puls: 43
purpuratus: 306
quadratus: 60
quaerere: 11, 305
quaestio: 335
quidem: 1, 127
quies: 343
quodsi: 190
quoniam: 95, 342
ratio: 316
ratiocinari: 312
ratis: 254
recolere: 122
recreare: 189
recte: 124
rector: 102, 213, 270
refragari: 214
regimentum: 294
regnum: 299
religio: 249
reluctari: 177, 332
remissus: 34
removere: 18
remunerare,-i: 14
reniti: 240
repedare: 9
repente: 311
repetitio: 301
replicare: 285
repulsa: 7
res novae: 240
res: 97, 191, 234
residuus: 172, 289
respectus: 62
retinaculum: 25

INDICES

375

rex: 280
ruere in: 79
ruere: 168
sagulum: 217
sagum: 217
salaria: 210
saluti consulere: 222
satietas: 11, 80
satrapa: 248
scientia: 55
scientissimus: 128
scilicet: 271
scire: 91
scrutari: 172
scutum: 73
sedatius: 12
sedere: 315
sempiternus: 83, 99
series gestorum: 269
serius: 125
sidus: 2
signa inferre: 32
signifer: 192
signum: 17, 280
simplex: 137
simultas: 271
sine (ulla) parsimonia: 79
sinuatus: 32
solacium: 261
solere: 2
solidus: 24, 273
solitum: 315
sollemnis: 275
sollemniter: 33
solvere: 18
sonare: 188
sors: 76
species: 252
spectare: 190
spes: 268
sphaera: 310
spiculum: 27
spiritus: 72
squalere: 46
stabilis: 59
stadium: 20
stare: 98, 212

stridor: 200, 311
stringere: 91
studiosus: 338
studium: 305
subinde: 243, 277
sublimis: 296
sublimitas: 105
subserere: 239
subsidiarius: 10
suburbanum: 319
succendere: 240
succensio: 334
succinctus: 65
succumbere: 91
sudes: 205
sufficere: 50, 137
suffrago: 65
sui securus: 44
superfundere: 64
superior: 199
superstare: 139
superstes: 304, 324
superstitiosus: 154
supervenire: 13
supplex: 137
suprema: 303, 320
supremitas: 24
suspectus: 268
suspensus: 44
sustinere: 13
susurrare: 277
tabernaculum: 209
tamquam: 93, 323
tempus: 12
tenax: 124
tendere: 165
tenebrosus: 80
tentorium: 36
tepere: 138
terebrare: 31
terribilis: 132
tessera: 223
testari: 126
textus: 322
thorax: 3
togatus: 128
torquere: 313

376 INDICES

trabea: 342
trabeatus: 342
tractus: 21
tranquillus: 96, 187
transenna: 216
transtigritanus: 235
trepidus: 195
tribunus: 18, 263, 274
tristis: 261
tumere: 214
tumultuare: 180
tumultuarius: 204
turba: 109
turbamentum: 244
turbo: 194, 257, 325
turma: 7, 210
tutus: 325
uaeritare: 173
uia: 342
ullus: 226
ultro citroque: 198, 255
umbra: 195
usquam: 273
ut: 260
uter: 255
vacuus: 204

vagitus: 331
vaporatus: 135
vectigal: 146
vector: 210
vel certe: 51, 315, 334
verbum: 290
verecundia: 118
vero: 101, 241
versare: 255, 296
vertere solum: 282
vestire: 160
vetare: 210
vexillatio: 18
viare: 59
vicinus: 204
victimarius: 155
victoria summa: 222
victoriosus: 139
videre: 178
videri: 329
villa: 10
vis: 32
vita absolvi: 108
volitare: 64
volubilis: 284

II. *Lexical (Greek)*

ἀλεξίκακος: 47
ἀναδείκνυμι: 181
ἀντακολουθία: 119
ἀπόκρουσις: 50
δαίμων: 46
διαΐσσων: 49
ἔθνος: 236
ἐπιγέννημα: 119

φιλανθρωπία: 119, 140
καταστερισμός: 104
μακαρίτης: 102
πολυπραγμοσύνη: 153
σατράπης: 248
συναριθμεῖν: 114
σωφροσύνη: 120
ὡς with superlative: 260

III. *Syntax and Style*

abl. abs. without a nominal subject:
260, 270
abl. abs., agreement with Head:
11
abl. gerundii and part. praes.: 35,
293
abl. materiae: 217

abl. of the comparative ending on
-i: 20
abstractum pro concreto: 44, 72
accentuation of Greek words: 244
active and passive: 329
adoriri, constructions with: 259
aliae, fem. sing: 18

INDICES

aliquis, quis, quisquam: 260
allegory: 191
alliteration: 43
amplificatio: 286
anacolouthon: 51, 225
anaphoric pronouns: 1, 52, 123
anaphoric huiusmodi: 31
anaphoric idem: 244, 327
antequam
  with subjunctive: 232
apo koinou: 207
asyndeton: 95, 131, 214, 224
αὔξησις: 222
combination of modes: 78, 293
composita with a second prefix:
  233
consecutio temporum: 91
contamination: 95
cum
  concessivum: 134
  inversum: 67
  with present indicative: 162
cursus: 42, 74, 77, 128, 217, 221,
  227, 233, 295, 325
dat. auctoris: 123, 180, 330
dum
  causal: 162
  with ind. or coni: 221
  with present indicative: 41
emensus, passive: 261
et
  at the beginning of a question:
  178
ex meaning 'former': 324
expressions for daybreak: 53
'figura etymologica': 88
formulaic expressions: 99
gen. identitatis: 24, 83, 125, 213
gen. inhaerentiae: 125
gen. inversus: 19, 45, 64, 78, 99,
  162, 203, 206, 240, 254, 325
gen. part: 64
gen. with verbs of 'filling': 293
gerundive as part. fut. pass.: 165,
  254, 265, 293
Grecisms: 103
hendiadys: 133

hic
  in opening phrases: 1
historic present: 215
horrere
  with direct object: 59
hyperbaton: 80
hyperbole: 287
iam 'de préparation': 199
igitur, discourse function of -: 36
ille
  with proper names: 156
imperfect and perfect: 73
imperfect tense in past irrealis: 320
ind. and subj., use of -: 100
indic. fut. instead of imperfect
  subj.: 54, 137
inf. praes. after promittere: 217
infinitives after permittere: 241
interjection o: 88
irrealis as a rhetorical means: 178
iterative subjunctive after si: 273
metaphor: 7, 18, 48, 94, 135,
  138, 190, 191, 216, 257, 316,
  326
metus, metonymical use of -: 62
moods used in the irrealis: 126,
  210
ni
  'de rupture': 210
nunc (vero)
  following an irrealis: 178
one-word clausula: 253
opening phrases: 221
orare
  with personal object: 54
parenthesis: 89, 94
passive participle used reflexively:
  213
personal passive constructions: 282
pluperfect and perfect: 273
poetic plural: 7
polyptoton: 34
praes. historicum: 329
preparatory id: 151, 211, 301
preparatory illud: 158
qui
  and quis: 292

378 INDICES

quia
-clauses: 342
quidam: 126
quidam, aliquis
and quisquam: 2, 45
quidam
intensifying: 192
quoniam
-clauses: 342
rapere
with dat: 79
relative clause, structure of -: 222
relative pronoun, distance from
antecedent: 79
rhetorical question: 178
'Roman bureaucratese': 264
sentence patterns: 1
sermo castrensis: 325
si, traiectio of -: 232
si qui

as the equivalent of quicumque:
292
simplex pro composito: 256
subjunctive in final and consecutive
clauses without ut: 241
substantivized adjectives: 223
super
postponed -: 224
with acc: 224
Synonymenhäufung: 88, 91, 189,
320
ut
equivalent to ita-ut: 120
restrictive: 203
with superlative: 260
verb, agreement with subject: 21
verbs with two possible
constructions: 78
vitare, ne: 54

IV. *Geographical Names*

Accete: 20, 21
Ad Herculem: 262
Amida: 236, 290
Ammodios: 308
Ancyra: 330
Antioch: 75, 131, 226, 269, 303,
308–310, 316, 317, 330
Antoninopolis: 308
Aquilea: 330
Araxes: 244
Armenia: 220, 241–244, 246, 248
Artaxata: 244
Arzanena: 234, 235
Asia: 76
Aspona: 329
Assyria: 138, 209, 242
Barsaphthae: 2, 8
Basilinopolis: 109
Batnae: 308
Beroia: 308
Bethlehem: 11
Bezabde: 235, 236
Boubios: 75
Calagurris: 272

Capua: 300
Caspian Gates: 236, 249
Castra Maurorum: 219, 237, 238,
241
Caudine Forks: 301
Cercusium: 5
Charcha/Charra: 209
Cilician Gate: 322
Cinginnia: 211
Constantinople: 170, 186, 269,
274
Corduene: 4, 219, 232, 233,
235–237, 249
Ctesiphon: 203, 259, 263
Dadastana: 331
Dicat: 262
Douros: 4, 5
Dura: 209, 210, 251, 257, 258
Dura Europos: 210
Durocortorum: 323
Ecbatana: 76
Edessa: 290, 308
Euphrates: 178, 209, 210
Fregellae: 300

INDICES

379

Galatia: 329
Hadrianopolis: 291
Halys: 330
Hatra: 250, 251, 258–263
Hibita: 286
Hierapolis: 308
Hucumbra/Symbra: 8, 10, 11
Ingilene: 235
Litarba: 308
Macellum: 92
Macharta: 308
Mantinea: 72
Maozamalcha: 135, 173, 276
Maranga: 12, 21, 36, 39, 40, 223
Mediolanium: 265, 266, 269, 322
Melas: 254
Mesopotamia: 178, 224, 233,
    236, 240, 252, 259, 261–263,
    275
Milan: 269, 270
Mnizos: 332
Mobsucrenae: 319
Mopsuestia: 316, 318
Moxoena: 234, 235
Munda: 45
Nisbara: 10
Nischanadalbe: 10
Nisibis: 29, 30, 169, 178, 186,
    219, 220, 237, 238, 240,
    241, 246, 248, 251, 252, 262,
    264, 271–276, 287, 289, 291,
    308
Numantia: 272, 301
Nymphius: 235

Persepolis: 281
Phrygia: 61, 75, 76, 82
Pirisabora: 135
Ra(s)sia: 76
Radia: 76
Ravenna: 273
regiones Transtigritanae: 219,
    234–238
Rehimena: 234, 235
Samarra: 61, 75
Singara: 219, 236–238, 240, 241,
    259, 262, 263, 273, 274,
    291
Sirmium: 264, 269, 323, 325
Sophene: 235
Sumere: 61, 76, 84, 85, 197,
    203–205, 211, 212
Symbra: 10
Tarsus: 170, 274, 303, 316, 318
Thilsaphata: 251, 274, 275, 286
Ticinus: 135
Tigris: 4, 10, 11, 59, 84, 115, 178,
    197, 198, 203, 209–215, 219,
    220, 224, 225, 236, 238, 239,
    250, 251
Toummara: 40, 58
Tyana: 269, 270, 322, 329
'Ukbara: 11
Ur: 250, 251, 260–263, 269, 270,
    272–274
Zabdicena: 235
Zagros: 214
Zalene: 234
Zogarra: 262

V. Names of Persons/Peoples

Achilles: 176
Adaces: 13–15
Alamanni: 134
Alexander Severus: 143, 151
Alexander: 44, 151, 261, 273, 276
Aligildus: 101
Anatolius: 84, 88, 102, 103, 197,
    203, 204
Anaxagoras: 50
Apollonius of Tyana: 108, 122

Arintheus: 171–173, 175, 182–185,
    230, 231, 328
Aristotle: 51, 52
Arrianus: 308
Arsaces: 220, 242–244, 263, 275
Athanasius: 308
Augustus: 45, 49, 101
Balchobaudes: 65
Barbatio: 161
Barsemias: 259

380 INDICES

Basilina: 109
Basilius of Caesarea: 107
Batavi: 323
Bellovaedius: 247
Bineses: 247, 248, 279
Bonosus: 193, 194
Caligula: 126
Callistus: 69
Cambyses: 76, 261, 272
Candidus: 308
Cassianus: 251, 261, 262, 272
Cato: 87, 91, 101
Ceionius Rufius Albinus: 109
Charietto: 135
Charito: 264
Chilo: 92
Claudius II Gothicus: 222
Cleobis and Biton: 90
Cocceianus: 101
Commodus: 127
Constans: 132, 149, 176
Constantine: 99, 109, 149, 163
Constantius Chlorus: 109, 150
Constantius tribunus: 303
Craugasius: 262
Croesus: 100
Cyrus: 107
Dagalaifus: 171, 173, 185, 187, 265
Dalmatians: 141
Didymus the Blind: 107
Domitian: 130
Epaminondas: 58, 72, 73
Ephrem: 290
Epimetheus: 50
Epirotae: 141
Eusebius: 75
Eustathius: 14
Eutherius: 152
Eutychianus: 76
Felix: 74
Flavius Sallustius: 230, 267
Florentius: 133, 178
Fortuna: 186
Franks: 134
Fritigern: 266
Fulvius, Q. – Flaccus: 300
Galerius: 99, 233–235

Galla: 109
Gallienus: 126
Gallus: 99, 109, 126, 133, 264, 268
Germanicus: 49
Gordianus III: 99, 234, 298
Goths: 291
Gratian: 173
Gratianus: 126
Hadrianus: 43, 54
Halani: 134
Hannibal: 31, 244
Hasdrubal: 31
Helena: 121
Heliogabalus: 127
Helpidius: 327
Herakleios: 90
Herodes Atticus: 124
Hormisdas: 84
Hostilius, C. – Mancinus: 302
Huns: 48
Hymetius: 273
Iovianus (notarius): 173, 175, 252, 274, 276, 279, 296, 305
Iovinus: 264, 265, 267, 268, 325, 328
Isaurians: 254
Iugurtha: 302
Iulianus Sabbas: 107
Iulianus, Julian's uncle: 74, 202
Iulius Constantius: 99, 108, 109
Iulius Iulianus: 109
Iunius: 248
Iustitia: 157
Jovian: *passim*
Julian: *passim*
Julius Caesar: 45
L. Sergius Catilina: 83
Leonas: 14
Libanius: 303
Lucillianus: 14, 133, 251, 264–267, 269, 283, 322, 323, 328
Lucius Verus: 127, 287
Lucullus, L. Licinius: 297
Lupicinus: 130, 133, 265, 268
Lutatius, Q. – Catulus: 333
Mac(h)ameus: 5, 8
Macrobius: 202, 204

INDICES

381

Macrones: 38
Magnentius: 296
Magnus: 107
Malarichus: 265, 267, 322, 328
Mallobaudes: 248
Mamertinus: 117, 266
Manlius Torquatus: 134
Marcellus: 82
Marcus Aurelius: 156
Mauricius: 251, 262, 272
Maurus: 5, 6, 8, 328
Maximianus: 310
Maximilianus: 193, 194
Maximinus Daia: 319
Maximus: 88, 105, 133, 202, 204, 339
Meletus: 97
Mellobaudes: 248
Memoridus: 251, 263, 269, 270, 322
Merena: 22, 81
Merobaudes: 248, 304
Metellus, Q. Caecilius – Pius: 297
Metrodorus: 51, 163
Mithridates VI Eupator: 297
Mopsus: 114
Narses: 14, 233, 234, 287, 310
Natuspardo: 83
Nebridius: 132
'Nemota': 230, 247
Nero: 126
Nevitta: 171, 173, 175, 183, 247, 248
Nicator Seleucus: 216
Nicomachus Flavianus: 298
Nilus: 132
Nisus and Euryalus: 6
Nohodares: 81
Occius: 15
Opimius: 300
Oribasius: 72, 88
Otho: 87, 101, 107
Parthicus: 63
Persae: 253
Pescennius Niger: 259
Petronius Probus: 139
Philippus Arabs: 298

Phoenix: 176
Phosphorius: 85
Postumius, A. – Albinus: 302
Postumius, Sp. – Albinus: 302
Primitivus: 325
Priscus: 88, 105, 339
Procopius (the later usurpator): 14, 101, 170, 175, 179, 220, 224, 236, 239, 240, 242, 251, 252, 262, 263, 269, 274–276, 296, 303, 305
Procopius (notarius): 270, 322
Prometheus: 50
Prosper: 14
Ptolemaeus V Epiphanes: 151
Remi: 323
Roxane: 276
Sabinianus: 212
Sabinus: 284, 289
Salutius: 85, 88, 102, 172–178, 188, 230, 231
Sapor I: 11, 258
Sapor II: *passim*
Saracens: 9, 68, 198, 209–211, 217, 253
Scipio Aemilianus: 124, 335
Scipio Africanus Maior: 135, 300
Scyths: 44
Sebastianus: 179, 224, 236, 242, 252, 262, 263, 274, 275
Seianus: 49
Sempronius, Ti. Gracchus: 124
Seneca: 87, 103
Seniauchus: 267, 322
Septimius Severus: 259, 260, 287
Sergius, M. – Silus: 83
Sicinius Dentatus: 82
Silvanus (usurpator): 65, 267, 296
Silvanus: 284, 289
Socrates: 86, 97, 103, 107
Solon: 100
Sophocles: 121
Spectatus: 14
Stilicho: 49
Strategius: 262, 309
Surena: 22
Taienes: 69

382 INDICES

Thalassius: 133, 150
Theoderic: 273
Theodora: 109
Theodosius: 20, 115, 125, 126, 198
Theodotus: 133
Theodulus: 150
Theolaifus: 101
Theophilus: 226
Thrasea Paetus: 87, 94, 103, 105
Thrasymachus: 95
Traianus: 259, 260, 274, 287
Trophonius and Agamedes: 90
Ursicinus: 212
Vadomarius: 6, 243
Valens: 96, 106, 115, 126, 130, 148, 172, 319
Valentinianus: 39, 46, 96, 111–113, 115, 120, 123, 126, 130, 132, 137, 148, 151, 154, 157, 172, 173, 176, 178, 185, 188, 267, 268, 319, 322, 325, 329
Valerianus: 298
Valerius Corvus: 134
Valerius, C.- Flaccus: 340
Varronianus puer: 331
Varronianus: 185–187, 192, 194, 341
Vetranio: 37, 296
Veturius, T. – Calvinus: 302
Victor: 171–173, 183, 230, 247, 248, 265
Vitalianus: 328
Vitellius: 126
Xenophanes: 51, 52
Zianni: 37

VI. *Military Matters*

acies: 188
agmen: 6
ala XVa Flavia Corduenorum: 236
ala: 10, 18
antesignanus: 62
aquila: 17
archers: 59, 63, 64, 79
armatura: 64
armorum magister: 268
auxilia palatina: 201
battle sounds: 80
candidati: 66
capita scholarum: 326
catafracti: 3, 23, 25, 60, 63, 201
clipeus: 73
cohors IX Maurorum Gordiana: 259
comitatenses: 186
comes domesticorum: 186
comes et magister equitum: 264
comes rei militaris: 186
comes: 42, 185, 328
contus: 25
cornu: 63, 84
crista: 79
cuneus: 32, 208

degradation: 18
discentes: 192
draco: 17
draconarius: 192
dux: 84, 171, 261, 268
elephants: 59, 63–65, 79, 222
equites tertii clibanarii Parthi: 16
equites tertii stablesiani: 16
equites tertio Dalmatae: 16
excursator: 5
exploratores: 221
gentilium rector: 267
globus: 63
gregarius miles: 44
hasta (pura): 17
Herculiani: 16, 200, 202
Heruli: 328
impedimentum: 18
inferior miles: 44
insignia: 17
Ioviani: 16, 192, 200, 202
Iovii: 16, 201
Lancearii: 16
legio comitatensis tertia Italica: 15
legio: 171, 200
legiones comitatenses: 16

INDICES 383

lorica: 3
magister armorum: 328
magister equitum: 264
magister equitum per Gallias: 265
magister equitum per Orientem: 265
magister equitum praesentalis: 265
magister peditum: 264
marching camps: 206
Mattiarii: 16
munifex miles: 44
munimenta praesidiaria: 303
numeri Gallicani: 201
numerus: 15, 19, 164, 248, 328
parma: 74
plebs: 202, 223
porta praetoria: 208
praesidium: 232
praetorium: 208
primates: 31
principalis: 192
procursator: 256
protecting the flanks: 60
protector: 195
punishment of military units: 17
rations, carried by the soldiers: 12

sacramenum: 18
sarcina: 18
Sasanian armour: 4
schola domesticorum: 327
schola Gentilium: 267
schola Scutariorum: 326
scholae: 326
scholae palatinae: 65, 66, 326
Scutarii: 85, 327
scutum: 73
Scythian or Parthian bow: 27
shield, sorts of -: 73
signifer: 192
signum: 17
size of Roman army: 223
soldiers' anger: 76
staple diet of soldiers: 43
Tertiaci(-ani): 15, 16, 18
tessera: 223
thorax: 3
tribunus: 18, 42, 202, 247, 248, 263, 274, 303
turma: 7, 18, 19, 210
vexillatio: 18
vexillum: 17
Victores: 16, 201
Zianni: 16

VII. *Various Topics*

acclamatio: 181
aer as the abode of the heroes: 53
agentes in rebus: 133
Ahura Mazda: 70
Alexander Mosaic: 281
Ammianus
  alleged participation in the election of Julian's successor: 177
  autopsy: 3, 80, 82, 209, 255, 309
  brevity in the description of Jovian's reign: 307
  carelessness in distinguishing army units: 201
  contempt for common soldiers: 42

criticism of Jovian: 233, 240, 244, 249
criticism of Julian's behaviour: 116
dislike of the palatina cohors: 173
ignores Julian's consecration: 115
impressionistic sketch of battle scenes: 33
influence of imperial biography on his work: 111
influence of panegyric on his work: 111
interest in naval matters: 254, 255
on the peace treaty of 363: 220

references to lost books: 259
use of exempla: 83
use of religious terms: 256
veracity: 180
views on divination: 46
apparitor: 85
Arianism: 308
aurum coronarium: 142, 289
battle sounds: 33
blood sacrifice: 155
boundary line between Roman and
    Persian territory: 213
bridges: 217, 225
burning of the ships: 10, 40
buying peace from barbarians: 211
Caesar: 230
camels: 261
Canicula: 213
cannibalism: 272
Caudine Forks: 301
celeritas: 167
censor: 130
censura morum: 130
chrysargyron: 143
civilitas: 94
    as an imperial virtue: 128
civitates foederatae liberae et
    immunes: 236
closure: 340
collatio lustralis: 143
comes: 185
comes domesticorum: 173, 186,
    264
comes rei militaris: 186
comets: 48, 49, 311
consiliarius: 85
consistorium: 85, 311
consolationes: 88
Constantine and Persia: 162, 164
cornucopia: 139
covering one's head in mourning:
    46
crossing rivers: 225, 255
Cunningham chalcedony: 70
curiositas: 153
deathbed scenes: 101
delaying tactics of the Persians: 212

demoralization Roman army: 213
designations of distance: 233
diadem: 188
dii caelestes: 90
discipline, lack of: 254
domestici: 185
dreams: 46, 341
dust in descriptions of battles: 78
dux Phoenices: 6
electio: 181, 184
election of Jovian: 180
elephants: 79, 199
embalming: 170
embedded focalisation: 207
emperor, his tasks: 316
epideictic oratory: 111, 295
eunuchs: 239
exchange of hostages: 247
exemplum: 127
expressions denoting a crisis: 180
felicitas: 138
fiscus: 145, 149
forma: 159
Fortuna: 139, 192, 294
furor
    of barbarians: 135
Genius (publicus): 39, 45, 46
gens: 236
gestures: 65
globe as a symbol of power: 311
Greek and Roman past: 81
greeting with a kiss: 275
haruspices: 54
haruspicina under Christian
    emperors: 198
heat: 36, 134
hierarchy of legions: 202
Homerica dispositio: 136
ideological debate between
    Christians and pagans: 69
imperator: 19
indicium: 127
indutiae: 39, 40
iudex: 340
Iustitia: 131
Jovian
    Christian convictions: 198, 338

INDICES

coinage: 269
ecclesiastical problems: 316
elogium: 336
personal qualities: 185
presentation of – in Christian
sources: 245
religious measures: 309
tolerance: 198, 339
Julian
activities at night: 126
admirer of Marcus Aurelius: 156
and Achilles: 115
as an avid reader: 129
as Caesar: 92
attitude towards the haruspices:
53
attitude towards the
philosophers: 55
beard: 160
birth date: 166
cautiousness: 136
compared to the Homeric
heroes: 114
compared to Epaminondas: 73
consecration: 114
courage: 134
death: 68, 87, 107
details of his wound: 71
direct knowledge of Plato: 117
disregard for omens: 54, 168
levitas: 152
location of his death: 75
loss of control: 66
military prudence: 94
necrology: 86
plan to march into the inner
parts of Persia: 138
posing as a philosopher: 124
presence on the battle field: 10
presentation as Caesar: 113
propensity to divination.: 54
purge of Constantius' court
clique: 172
rash behaviour: 66
recklessness: 134
resembles Hadrian: 43, 153
speeches in the Res Gestae: 87

tax measures: 141
temperantia: 42
ultima verba: 86
weapon that wounded –: 70, 99
wish to be buried in Tarsus: 319
year of birth: 108
Justice personified: 282
lamps: 126
legitimus princeps: 179
liberalitas: 140
magister officiorum: 66, 84
Mars: 39, 48, 49
medical experts: 72
medical terms: 106
Menander Rhetor: 111
Mesopotamia: 178
meteors: 49
Mithras: 70
modius: 273
munimenta: 241
musical instruments: 254
mutiny: 215
nobilissimus, title of: 109
notarius: 263
Numantia: 301
numen: 99, 227, 309
oath: 288
omina: 66
orbis Romanus: 294
oriens: 272
Paeanius' translation of Eutropius:
114
palatini: 172
Parthus: 244
Parthian campaign of Septimius
Severus: 259
Parthian campaigns of Traianus:
259
patricius, title of –: 109
peace of 363: 228, 246, 248
Persian archers: 26
Persian standards and banners:
280
Persian suits of armour: 23
Persian tactics: 212
Persians
cunning of –: 60

386 INDICES

physiognomy: 159, 336
Plato, Phaedo: 86, 87
PPO Italiae, Illyrici et Africae: 265
praefectus praetorio: 85
price of corn: 273
primicerius domesticorum: 185
primicerius notariorum: 172
principatus: 92
Procopius as a candidate for the
    throne: 179
provincials, plight of the –: 164
puer senilis: 129
puls: 43
pultes Iulianae: 43
rector: 102, 270
regiones Transtigritanae: 235
rex: 236, 280
rumours: 207, 270
Sapor-cameo in Paris: 249
Sapor
    despondency: 227
    mildness: 229
    rage: 229
satraps: 13, 80, 236, 248

scarcity of food: 41, 226, 231
scientific digressions: 312
sella curulis: 309
sexuality: 122
Sirius: 213
solidus: 273
sors: 76
sphragis: 341
stationes agrariae: 136
superstitio: 154
Surena: 227
Tacitus as Ammianus' model: 111
Taq-I Bustan, rock relief in –: 70
Tarquitiani libri: 54
temple lands: 148
topoi about death: 89
treaty of 298/9: 219, 233–236, 238
urbs aeterna: 320
vectigalia…cum fundis: 146
veritas: 162
virtues: 116, 119
vitaxa: 236
women in Amm.: 121
Xenophon's Cyropaedia: 107

VIII. *Passages referred to (Latin)*

Accius (Acc.)
    trag.   330: 7

Ambrosius (Ambr.)
    hex.   4.5.23: 7
    obit. Valent.
             21: 142

Anonymus (Anon.)
        de mach. bell. 2: 149

Anonymus Valesianus
    (Anon. Vales.)
             11.53: 273
             12.73: 273

Apicius (Apic.)
        5.186: 43

Apuleius (Apul.)
    Met.   2.2: 336, 337
             2.17: 21
             2.19: 313
             3.8.3: 108
             3.8: 293
             3.13: 176
             4.19: 126
             6.11: 286
             6.32: 273
             9.2: 35
             9.37: 6
             10.11: 342
    Soc.   122: 50

Arnobius (Arn.)
             2.15: 94

INDICES

Augustus (Aug.)
Anc. 21.3: 142

Augustinus (August.)
adult. coniug.
  1.26.33: 190
C.D. 1.15: 119
  5.21: 116
  7.6: 53
  21.5: 7
  21.8: 216
  22.8: 108
cat. rud. 22.40: 11
Conf. 2.5.11: 83
Ep. 143.10: 94

Ausonius (Aus.)
Caes. 80 Green: 195
Eph. 3.79: 195
Ludus sapientium
  61: 88
  204: 88

Bellum Africanum (B. Afr.)
  25.6: 77
  72.4: 28
  86.1: 28

Bibliotheca Hagiographica Latina
  (BHL)
  1427: 202

Caesar (Caes.)
Civ. 1.75.3: 217
  1.82.3: 223
  1.83.2: 10
  2.38.2: 35
Gal. 5.15.1: 199
  5.18.3: 205
  5.42.3: 217
  7.21.3: 223
  7.77.12: 272

Cato
fr 40.2: 286
orat. fr. 15–16 Iordan: 35
R.R. 85: 43

Carmina Epigraphica (CE)
  432.4: 103
  611.3–5: 104
  1109.15–6: 105
  1363.1: 104

Celsus (Cels.)
  5.26: 106
  7 pr: 247
  7.26: 106

Cicero (Cic.)
Amic. 32: 104
Att. 5.15.3: 199
  5.21.7: 322
  7.26.2: 342
Brutus 266: 166
Caec. 43: 34
Cael. 28: 153
Cat. 1.8: 162
  1.11: 257
  2. 7: 167
de Orat. 1.214: 128
  2.68: 136
  2.232: 51
  2.242: 206
  2.294: 286
  3.8: 178
  3.213: 202
Div. 1.47: 84
  2.117: 198
Fam. 2.65: 13
  3.11.4: 280
  7.10.2: 217
  15.1.6: 222
  15.16.2: 295
Fin. 2.26: 127
  3.18: 27
Font. 30: 288
  41: 133
Inv. 2.159: 117
  2.165: 154
Leg. 2.11: 55
Man. 28: 118
Mil. 16: 335
N.D. 2.114: 214
  3.80: 335

INDICES

Off. 1.20: 119
1.85: 95
1.93–8: 120
3.104: 288
Or. 53: 285
Parad. 42–52: 130
Phil. 10.16: 205
11.24: 139
Pis. 24: 160
44: 324
Quinct. 43: 329
Rep. 1.8: 98
1.11: 191
6.8: 26
Sen. 4: 127
9: 91
47: 121
78–9: 107
Sest. 2: 42
20: 191
Top. 63: 253
Tusc. 1.93: 89
2.11: 130
2.54: 91
3.16: 102
3.36–7: 119
3.69: 126
4.1: 298
4.26: 42
4.64: 152
5.32: 41
Ver. 2.4.45: 158
4.45: 41
5.118: 253

Pseudo-Cicero ([Cic.])
Sal. 2.7: 128

CIL 6.967: 145
6.1729: 335
6.32422: 335
9.1685: 338
13.7792: 139
13.12049: 139

Claudianus (Claud.)
Bell. Get. 2.333: 4

carm. min.
24.353: 28
28.571: 23
Cons. Stil.
1.45: 49
1.139: 269
in Eutr. 2.62–3: 121
2.487–8: 42
2.490–500: 50
In Ruf. 1.243: 342
1.283–4: 81
2.359–60: 25
IV Cons. Hon.
12–3: 332
569–70: 332
584: 332
Olyb. 197–8: 81

Claudius Quadrigarius
fr. 12: 336

Codex Iustinianus (Cod. Iust.)
1 40.5: 330
1.29.5: 235
8.11.4: 146, 147
11.70.1: 146, 147
11.70.1: 147
12.37.1: 43

Codex Theodosianus
(Cod. Theod.)
2.12.6: 289
5.13.1: 149
5.13.3: 147, 148
7.4.5: 12
7.4.6: 43
7.4.9: 308, 312, 316
8.5.1: 132
9.25.2: 339
10.1.8: 147, 148
10.1.8: 332, 339
10.3.1: 146, 147
10.19.2: 312, 316
11.12.2: 145
11.16.4: 326
11.16.10: 141, 144
11.20.1: 316, 318

INDICES

11.28.1: 142
11.28.1: 145
12.1.33: 149
12.1.50: 143
12.13.1: 144
12.13.4: 144
13.3.6: 332, 338
15.1.8: 146, 147
15.1.9: 146, 147
15.1.9: 147, 149
15.1.10: 147, 330

Curtius Rufus (Curt.)
3.3.16: 281
8.14.28: 65
9.2.19: 30
9.10.12: 273
9.10.13: 261

Dictys Cretensis (Dict.)
2.29: 212
2.32: 136

Digesta (Dig.)
33.7.12.23: 26
50.2.2 pr.: 329
50.16.197: 18

Ennius (Enn.)
Ann. 2 Sk.: 216
160 Sk: 80
266 Sk: 35
321 Sk: 334
584 Sk.: 34
scen. 172: 35

Epitome de Caesaribus (*epit.*)
12.12: 321
20.9: 334
42.12: 108
43.2: 59, 62
43.3: 64, 68
43.4: 71, 72, 100, 107
43.5: 129
43.7: 154, 156
43.8: 48
44.2: 341

44.3: 336, 340
44.4: 317, 335

Eutropius (Eutr.)
1.11.4: 342
4.17.1: 244
6.15.1: 83
7.22.2: 114
8.6.2: 299
8.14.2: 114
9.15.2: 114
10.1.2: 150
10.4.4: 319
10.8.1: 333
10.8.2: 114
10.9.4: 132
10.14.1–2: 167
10.14.1: 165
10.16.1: 184
10.16.2: 68, 114
10.16.3: 128, 129, 140, 141
10.17.1–2: 298
10.17.1: 181, 185, 186, 228, 231, 234, 244, 269
10.17.2–3: 245, 297
10.17.2: 301
10.17.3: 245, 296, 337
10.18.1: 335
10.18.2: 333, 335, 337

Exuperantius (Exup.)
7.42: 228

Festus (Fest.)
p. 27M: 18
p. 54M: 17
p. 101M: 17
p. 110M: 13

Firmicus Maternus (Firm. Mat.)
err. 24.7: 27

Florus (Flor.)
1.18.8: 200
1.34.7: 301

390   INDICES

2.8.16: 28
3.5.5: 257

Florentinus (Florent.)
  dig.   50.16.211: 147

Frontinus (Fron.)
  Str.   2.1.9: 32
          2.2.5: 32
          2.3.4: 32
          2.5.41: 134

Gaius
  Inst.   1.3: 114
          1.7: 157
          4.46: 54

Gellius (Gel.)
          1.3.1–3: 92
          1.5.1: 206
          1.12.17: 91
          2.11: 83
          2.24.1: 124
          4.6.1: 301
          4.8.4: 342
          4.9.12: 139
          4.10.8: 18
          7.13.2: 42
          9.2.4: 124
          9.4.8: 18
          9.11: 336
          10.27.3: 140
          12.4.1: 97
          17.9.3: 18
          19.14.1: 126

Historia Augusta (HA)
  A   39.7: 299
  AC   3.5: 83
  Ael.   3.9: 153
  AP   3.5: 341
          4.10: 143
  AS   24.3: 147
          26.3: 210
          32.5: 143
          47.1: 12
          61.3: 13

C   3.7: 127
Car   2.1: 298
DI   8.3: 176
Gall.   10.3: 287
          12.1: 287
          21.1: 152
          21.5: 126
Gd   10.6: 266
          26.6: 287
          27.6: 287
H   2.8: 153
          5.3: 299
          6.5: 143
          7.6: 145
          9.1: 299
          10.2: 43
          15.1: 150
          16.7: 153
MB   17.9: 268
P   15.7: 342
S   22.4: 228
T   15.3: 287
          30.3: 241
V   4.6: 127
Val.   5–6: 130

Hiëronymus (Hier.).
  Chron.   *a.* 363: 64, 185
          a. 364: 237, 245, 335
  ep.   66.3: 120
  Hom. Orig. in Ier.
          3.2: 97
  in Ephes. 1.2: 120
  Vit. Hil.   22: 66

Historia Acephala (Hist. Aceph.)
          3.1: 146
          4.4: 308

Horatius (Hor.)
  AP   198: 125
  Carm.   1.19.11: 35
          1.37.32: 104
          4.5.27–8: 178
          4.14.29–30: 23
  Ep.   1.10.16: 214
  S.   1.7.25: 214

INDICES

391

ILS   1254: 335
        4938: 335

Itinerarium Antonini Augustis
    (Itin. Anton. Aug.)
        142: 333
        142.4–143.1: 332
        143: 330
        144.1–145.2: 330

Itinerarium Burdigalense
    (Itin. Burdig.)
        574.5–575.1: 333
        575.5–12: 330
        575: 332

Iustinus (Iust.)
        6.8.11–2: 72

Jordanes (Jord.)
  Rom.   305: 185

Justiniani Novellae (Just. Nov.)
        1 pr.: 38
        28 pr.: 38

Juvenalis (Juv.)
        11.58: 43
        13.48: 20
        14.109: 195
        14.128: 286
        14.171: 43

Lactantius (Lact.)
  Inst.   6.23.4: 127
  mort. pers.
        33–4: 99

Livius (Liv.)
        1.4.6: 332
        1.16.6: 48
        1.29: 293
        2.48.8: 178
        3.13. 8: 230
        3.33.5: 157
        5.44.7: 216
        5.54.3: 293

6.36.7: 135
7.7.8: 220
7.26.10: 178
8.8.11: 212
8.30.12: 296
9.5.2: 302
10.30.10: 217
10.39.7: 135
22.29.5: 212
22.51.3: 180
22.51.5: 221
23.7.6: 6
24.16.13: 124
25.1.15: 201
25.13.12: 18
25.20.4: 78
25.36.15: 241
26.41.12: 223
27.8.6: 340
27.42.9: 309
27.49.1–2: 31
27.49.2: 201
28.2.6: 34
28.29.10: 77
28.31.5: 44
28.38.4: 300
28.41.6: 326
29.23.4: 66
29.25.5: 191
30.18.7: 29
30.18.12: 212
30.19.1: 321
31.20.4: 300
31.22.5: 228
34.57.6: 229
35.14.12: 229
35.29.3: 6
37.8.6: 317
37.13.5: 260
37.40.4: 79
37.42.1: 10
38.2.14: 246
39.17.1: 230
39.26.4: 191
39.48.5: 172
42.34.2: 293
44.31.13: 190

392 INDICES

44.34.3–4: 134
44.40.9: 7
per. 18: 84
19: 223
59: 335
98: 223
115: 222

Lucanus (Luc.)
1.529: 311
5.153–4: 50
5.562–3: 48
6.144: 202
6.272: 214
7.365–6: 63
7.599–600: 37
9.921: 260
9.951: 316

Lucretius (Lucr.)
1.29–30: 257
1.51: 316
2.836–7: 300
3.391 sqq: 89
3.410: 24
4.1161: 336
5.889: 160
6.428: 191

Macrobius (Macr.)
comm. 1.4.2: 26
1.6.41: 288
1.11.11: 103
1.21.35: 50
2.13.9: 312
2.14.22: 312
2.17.16: 45
Sat. 1.6.34: 152
3.7.2: 54
3.20.3: 54
5.17.7: 200
7.9.9: 285

Manilius (Man.)
1.847–51: 51
4.722: 313
5.146: 313

Martialis (Mart.)
3.9: 313
4.42: 313
5.78.9: 43
13.8: 43

Martianus Capella (Mart. Cap.)
8.815: 316
8.842: 52

Mauricius (Maur.)
1286: 205

Mela 1.102: 4

Notitia Dignitatum (Not. Dign.)
Occ. 5.88: 15
5.168: 201
5.184: 201
5.185: 201
5.186: 323
5.212: 201
5.237: 16
7. 42: 201
7. 154: 201
7.16: 201
7.17: 201
7.27: 201
7.48: 201
7.53: 16
7.72: 323
7.76: 201
7.126: 201
7.168: 323
Or. 5.40: 16
5.63: 201
6.40: 16
7.27: 16
7.30: 16
7.32: 16
8.17: 37
8.49: 38
36.34: 236
p. 101: 119

Orosius (Oros.)
hist. 4.18.12: 31

INDICES 393

7.31.2: 237
7.31: 244

Ovidius (Ov.)
am. 1.8.82: 271
Ars 1.6: 191
2.304: 313
2.615: 206
3.203: 320
Fast. 1.105–6: 52
2.741: 203
4.904: 214
Met. 2.321–2: 48
3.289: 8
4.399–401: 203
8.552: 24
8.784: 253
10.52: 2
11.682–3: 292
13.534: 292
13.765–6: 160
14.748–9: 293
15.845–9: 53
Pont. 2.2.28: 309
3.2.25: 2
3.6.60: 253
Rem. 465: 157
Tr. 5.10.52: 309

Pacuvius (Pac.)
trag. 158: 253

Palladius (Pallad.)
1.42.2: 29

Panegyrici Latini (Pan.)
2.4.5: 81
2.13.3: 125
2.17.1: 82
2.36.2: 253
3.3–4: 167
3.4.1: 165
3.6.4: 160, 161
3.9.1: 141
3.11.4: 124
3.11.13: 121
3.13.3: 126

3.13.3: 134
3.14.3: 123, 126, 127
3.21.4: 117
3.22.3: 140
3.28.1: 128
3.30.2: 332
4.8.2: 160
4.15.1: 82
10.3.4: 126

Paulinus Mediolanensis
(Paul. Med.)
vita Ambr.
46.1: 101

Petronius (Petr.)
59.3: 77
79.2: 101

Physiognomici Latini (Physiogn.)
37: 336

Plautus (Pl.)
As. 834–5: 120
Merc. 614: 228
Mil. 741: 309
802: 18
Truc. 885: 151
Most. 765: 59
Stich. 753: 91

Plinius Minor (Plin.).
Ep. 3.5.4: 341
6.8.1: 136
8.1.1: 7
8.24.6: 91
9.25.1: 135

Plinius Maior (Plin.)
Nat. 2.89: 313
6.176: 217
7.10: 317
7.92: 45
7.104: 83
8.5.12: 28
9.180: 309
13.126: 127

394 INDICES

18.83: 43
18.285: 214
21.160–2: 260
22.99: 261
24.142: 260
25.98: 317
27.23: 317
27.45–52: 260
28.11: 47
31.105: 152
37.80: 205

Polemo
Phgn.   p. 246: 336
p. 262: 336
p. 268: 160, 161

Priscianus (Prisc.)
gramm.   II 487.1: 142, 252

Propertius (Prop.)
2.1.71: 89

Prudentius (Prud.)
apoth.   449–52: 116
cath.   5.48: 23

Pseudo-Sergius (Ps. Serg.)
Gramm.   IV 559: 31, 163

Quintilianus (Quint.)
Inst.   3.7.1: 295
3.8.3: 301
5.11.41: 151
6.1.2: 152
6.2.13: 131
8.6.40: 42
8.6.44: 191
10.3.25: 126
11.1.63: 229

Pseudo-Quintilianus ([Quint.])
Decl.   3.13: 125
10.17: 44

Rhetorica ad Herennium
(Rhet. Her.)
1.2: 295
3.14.25: 285

Rufius (?) Festus (Ruf. Fest.)
14: 236
27: 29
28: 61, 64, 68, 70, 71,
78, 88
29.2: 245, 294, 296–298
29: 228, 229, 237

Rufinus (Rufin.)
hist.   10.9: 163
11.1: 227, 231, 248,
252, 309, 339

Rusticius
c. aceph.   p. 1233b: 268

Sallustius (Sal.)
Cat.   4.2: 152
5.3: 134
51.6: 246
Hist.   1.55.25: 244
1.67.7: 195
1.77.7: 324
2.44: 254
2.70.2: 297
2.87: 324
2.98.1: 226
3.21: 138
3.95: 180
Jug.   11.7: 290
85.4: 221
91.1: 217
108.1: 228

Seneca Maior (Sen.)
Contr.   1.17.10: 74
9.4.5: 272

Seneca Minor (Sen.)
Ben.   1.10: 168
3.27: 156

INDICES

Cons. Helv.
    6.8: 127
Cons. Marc.
    10.2: 89
    16.8: 172
Cons. Pol.
    6.2: 104
    11.3: 89
    11.4: 99
Ep.   14.16: 95
    18.10: 286
    47.2: 334
    89.3: 123
    93.1: 99
    95.21: 261
    120.14: 94
Her. O. 1005: 48
Nat.   1.1.3: 49
    1.1.9: 49
    2.32.2: 55
    2.55.3: 48
    7.8.1: 52
    7.11.3: 50
    7.12.1: 314
    7.17.1: 315
    7.17.2: 315
    7.20.2: 52
    7.21.1: 314
    7.21.2: 52
    7.22.1: 314
    7.25.3: 313
Tranq. 11.8: 295

Servius (Serv.)
A.   1.267: 298
    1.272: 298
    2.651: 190
    5.735: 105
    5.735: 108
    6.640: 105
    6.887: 105
    11.833: 285

Sidonius Apollinaris (Sidon.)
epist.   2.1.1: 83

Silius (Sil.)
    4.415–6: 135
    8.126: 203
    17.530: 203

Solinus (Sol.)
    1.73: 98
    1.102–7: 82
    1.102: 83
    1.105: 83
    1.107: 82
    27.39: 191

Pseudo-Solinus ([Sol].)
    53.12: 41

Statius (Stat.)
Silv.   2.1.4: 106
    2.2.60–2: 81
Th.   9.32–3: 270
    1.708: 311
    2.319: 77
    4.38–9: 316
    5.284–6: 53
    6. 766: 63
    6.274: 209
    12.548: 324

Suetonius (Suet.)
Aug.   24.2: 213
    91.1: 341
Cal.   15.6: 172
    54.2: 212
Cl.   33.1: 334
Jul.   44.4: 342
    56.5: 45
    58.1: 268
    61: 199
Nero   26.1: 127
    36.1: 311
    49.1: 170
    51.1: 336
Otho   9.3: 131
    10.1: 206
    11.2: 107
Tit.   10.1: 342
Vesp.   4.4: 212

396 INDICES

Vit.   17.2: 337

Symmachus (Symm.)
Ep.   2.18.2: 81
     4.29: 130
     4.45: 130
     5.9: 130
     7.58: 130
     9.112: 342
Or.   1.4: 264
     1.9: 82

Tabula Peutingeriana (Tab. Peut.)
     X 4: 274, 275
     X 4–5: 258, 273
     X 5: 262

Tacitus (Tac.)
Agr.   11.2: 313
     25.3: 259
Ann.   1.11.3: 190
     1.13.2: 101
     1.64.4: 260
     2.69.2: 189
     2.71.1: 88
     3.23.1: 190
     3.63.3: 158
     3.65.1: 91
     4.8.2: 190
     4.32.2: 139
     6.10.3: 342
     11.28.2: 135
     12.18.2: 305
     13.7.1: 257
     13.25.1: 127
     13.39.6: 35
     13.40.2: 63
     14.21.4: 202
     14.22.1: 311
     14.24.1: 7
     14.32.2: 48
     14.62.4: 342
     15.6.4: 195
     15.13.2: 301
     15.59.3: 326
     15.62: 103
     15.63–4: 87

     15.63.3: 105
     16.34–5: 87
     16.34.1: 105
     16.34: 103
Dial.   2.1: 317
     20.3: 160
Germ.   8.1: 135
Hist.   1.23.1: 244
     1.41.2: 71
     1.79.3: 25
     1.81.1: 24
     2.35.1: 215
     2.45.3: 190
     2.46–9: 87
     2.49.2: 107
     2.70.4: 2
     2.80.2: 66
     2.86.1: 77
     3.23.3: 47
     3.26.3: 224
     3.47.1: 323
     3.59.3: 176
     3.62.1: 254
     3.69.4: 2
     4.5.2: 130
     4.66.2: 215
     4.70.4: 202
     5.14.2: 215

Terentius (Ter.)
Eun.   1046: 139
Ph.   914: 191

Tertullianus (Tert.)
Pud.   16.23: 127

Valerius Maximus (V. Max.)
     1.8.1: 228
     2.5.5: 43
     2.8: 299
     2.8.4: 300
     2.8.4–5: 298, 300
     3.2 ext. 5: 73
     3.2.21: 15
     3.2.24: 82
     3.7 ext. 1: 128
     3.8 ext. 6: 320

INDICES   397

5.3.1a: 230   1.495: 47
5.3.2d: 335   1.641: 221
6.4. ext.1: 211   2.298: 292
7.6.2–3 ext: 272   2.489–90: 293
9.12.4: 333   2.697–8: 48
                                               3.351: 293
Valerius Flaccus (V.Fl.)   4.9: 44
        2.165: 77   4.379–80: 44
        5.324: 2   4.580: 25
                                               4.644: 7
Varro (Var.)   5.21–2: 50
  L.L.   5.105: 43   5.176–7: 191
                                               5.221: 4
Vegetius (Veg.)   5.844: 145
  mil.   1.20.7: 192   6.253: 24
                1.21.3: 205   6.268: 45
                1.22.2: 205   6.619: 126
                1.23.2: 208   6.873–4: 320
                1.24.2–4: 60, 205   7. 13: 126
                1.25.1: 60   7.106: 209
                2.1.2: 18   7.249–50: 47
                2.7.5: 192, 223   7.316: 135
                2.7.11: 66   7.687–8: 27
                2.7.12: 44   7.788: 285
                2.14.8: 3   8.64: 320
                2.19.1: 326   8.86–7: 214
                2.20.7: 192   8.709: 7
                2.25.6: 25   9.137: 135
                3.1.2: 223   9.422–45: 6
                3.5.9: 217   9.478: 292
                3.6.1: 12   10.18: 95
                3.6.14: 60   10.361: 35
                3.14.1: 78   11.253–4: 44
                3.19.3: 32   11.550–1: 255
                3.24.7–16: 65   11.833: 285
                3.24.7: 25   11.911: 80
                                               12.284: 35
Velleius (Vell.)   12.580–1: 126
        2.22.4: 333   12.670: 24
        2.48.3: 48   12.870: 292
        2.48.6: 342   *G.*   1.218: 214
        2.52.4: 35   1.477–8: 45
        2.104.3: 205   1.513–4: 25
                                               2.353: 214
Vergilius (Verg.)   3.31: 35
  A.   1.25: 77   3.111: 80
                1.87: 311

398 INDICES

Vitruvius (Vitr.)
9.5.2: 214
10.2.13: 26

IX. *Passages referred to (Greek, including Ephraem Syrus)*

Aelianus (Ael.)
NA   13.9: 29

Aëtius (Aet.)
Plac.   3.2.9: 50
3.2.10: 51
3.2.11: 51
p. 366.6–10: 315

Africanus (Afric.)
Cest.   1.18: 65

Agathias (Agath.).
4.25.7: 245

al-Tabari
Annales p. 843: 230
p. 843: 291

Alexander Aphrodisias
(Alex. Aphr.)
Fat.   16: 295

Anonymus Panegyricus Iuliani
Imperatoris (Anon. Paneg.
Iul. Imp.)
3.30: 123
10.10: 126
12.29–35: 134

Anthologia Graeca (Anth. Gr.)
7.747: 318
14.148: 108

Anthologia Palatina (AP)
7.64.4: 104

Appianus (App.)
BC   1.74: 333
Ib.   38: 300
Pun.   43: 28

Aristophanes (Ar.)
Ec.   1109–10: 26
Pax 832/3: 104

Aristoteles (Arist.)
EN   1160 b: 94
1160b2–3: 95
Mete. 342 a 10: 48
342b25–345 a 10: 313
342b28–9: 314
342b30–3: 315
344 a 10: 314

Arrianus (Arr.)
An.   2.4.7: 320

Artemii Passio (Art. pass.)
69: 71, 89
70: 240, 338

Athanasius (Athan.)
Hist. Ar. 5: 109

Seneca Maior (Sen.)
Contr. 1.17.10: 74
9.4.5: 272
V. Anton.
60.1–3: 108

Bacchylides (B.)
fr.   38 Maehler: 122

Basilius Seleucensis (Bas. Seleuc.)
PG   85: 37A, 310

Cedrenus
Chron. 1.516–7: 163

Chronicon Paschale (Chron. Pasch.)
a. 363: 76, 107, 170,
182, 185, 227, 228,

230, 231, 237, 241, 248, 280, 282–284, 290
a. 364: 333

Chronicle of Se'ert
p. 220–1 Scher: 11

Johannes Chrysostomus (Chrys.)
Laud. Paul.
4.6: 227
pan. Bab.
2.122.: 41
2.123: 287, 292

Consularia Constantinopolitana

(Cons. Const.)
a. 365: 306

Dio Chrysostomus (D. Chr.)
Or. 1.13: 126
3.136: 134

Dio Cassius (D.C.)
17.57.56: 300
36.6.1–8.1: 297
40.15.2: 25
40.22.2–3: 25
40.24.1: 25
51.21.4: 142
64.2.1: 127
67.18: 108
68.31: 259
69.8.1: 145
69.11.2: 153
73.1.4–5: 176
75.10.1: 259
76.11.1: 259
80.4.1–2: 165
80.13.2: 127

Diogenes Laertius (D.L.)
1.71: 92
7.95: 119
7.152: 314
10.118: 122

Diodorus Siculus (D.S.)
15.87.5–6: 72
15.87.6: 72
29.29: 151

Euripides (E.)
Andr. 266–7: 26
Med. 78–9: 156

Ephorus (Ephor.)
FrGrHist 70 F 149: 134

Ephraem Syrus (Ephr.)
Carm. Nis.
21: 281
HcJul. 2.18: 287
2.22–3: 290
2.26: 291
2.27: 290
3: 281
3.1: 248, 281
3.1–2.: 275
3.13–4: 69
Hist. S. Ephr.
10, col. 26: 290

Eunapius (Eun.)
fr. 14.2: 166, 167
16.2: 167
18: 167
19: 167
24: 143, 144
25.1: 130
27.8: 12, 23, 60, 63
28.1: 116, 169, 170, 171
28.2: 153
28.6: 98
29: 317, 335, 339, 340
29.1: 186, 237, 275, 287, 339
31: 290
VS 7.1.10: 106
7.1.11: 129
7.1.14: 106
7.2.12: 116
7.4.3–7: 106

7.4.4: 106
7.4.9: 106
7.4.11: 339
7.4.11–2: 106
8.1.11: 106
10.6.3: 174

Eusebius (Eus.)
VC   1.14: 151
     1.30: 342
     4.29: 126
     4.65: 169

Eustathius
ad D.P.
     766: 38

Excerpta Polyaeni
     3.8: 125

Galenus
De usu respirationis
     4.3: 334

Gregorius Nazianzenus
  (Greg. Naz.)
Carm.   1: 305
Or.   4.56: 160
        4.71: 123
        4.75: 142
        4.80–1: 159
        4.91: 174
        5.12: 41
        5.13: 68, 70
        5.14: 59, 61, 115
        5.15: 180, 228, 229,
          245, 252, 338
        5.18: 305, 319, 320
        5.23: 153, 160
        21.33: 305

Herodianus (Hdn.)
        2.3.3: 176
        3.1.3: 259
        3.6.10: 134
        3.9.1: 259
        3.9.3–8: 259

3.9.5: 30
Herodotus (Hdt.)
        1.32: 100
        1.136: 26
        2.104: 38
        3.25: 261, 272
        3.64.3–5: 76
        3.94: 38
        6.112: 32
        9.59: 280

Heraclides Ponticus (Heraclid. Pont.)
        fr. 116 Wehrli: 315

Heliodorus (Hld.)
        9.15.1: 3, 24, 25
        9.15.2–3: 3
        9.15.6: 25
        9.18.4: 29
        9.18.5: 29
        9.18.8: 28

Homerus (Hom.)
Il.   4.123: 27
        5.83: 319
Od.   12.342: 226

Iamblichus (Iamb.)
VP   31: 122
        82: 105

IG   1.2.945.6: 104
        2.2.1670.5: 26
        2.2.1672.176: 26
        7.3073.179: 26
        7.4255.15: 26
        9.1 271: 339

Josephus (J.)
BJ   1.42: 28
        3.79–84: 208
        3.95: 12

Johannes Antiochenus
  (Joh. Antioch.)
fr.   180: 156
        181: 186, 318

INDICES   401

Julianus (Jul. Caes.)
    313 a–b: 151
Caes. 332 d: 115
Ep. 4: 126
    13: 106
    14, 385 c: 19
    26: 415 c, 155
    26, 45 b–c: 133
    26, 415 b: 130
    28: 45, 126
    32, 381 b–c: 153
    59, 443 b: 89
    73, 428 c–d: 144
    80: 129
    89a, 452 c: 105
    96: 106
    98, 399 d: 156
    98, 401 b: 155
    98, 402 a: 132
    98, 402 b: 43
    111, 434 d: 108
    201, 412 c: 88
ad Ath. 270 c: 99
    271 a: 103
    277 d: 166
    278 a: 166
    278a–280d: 167
    281 a: 133
    281 b: 130
    281 d: 176
fr. 13: 159
Mis. 341 b–d: 334
    340 b: 123, 124
    347: 129
    352 b: 109
    363: 152
    365 b: 141, 145
    367 c–d: 145
    367 d: 143
Or. 1.10 c: 117
    1.11: 123
    1.11 a: 126
    1.27a–b: 291
    1.37 c–d: 23, 25
    1.38 a: 23
    3.57 c: 25
    3.86 b–92 d: 94

    3. 87 c: 126
    3.89 a: 97
    3. 101 d: 134
    4. 246 a: 97
    4. 252 a: 173
    7. 223 c: 90, 123
    7. 226 a: 123
    7. 226 c: 131
    7. 228 b: 149
    7. 234 b: 140
    8.166 d: 93
    8.180 a.: 90
    8. 180 c: 88
    9. 198 d: 123
    9. 199 d: 123
    11, 158 b: 88

Justinus (Just.)
apol. 43.2: 295

Libanius (Lib.)
Chria 1.5: 151
Ep. 369.8: 150
    724.2: 150
    757: 150
    760: 106
    763: 150
    803: 303
    819: 150
    828: 150
    947: 106
    1076: 106
    1119: 309
    1120.3: 132
    1180.1: 160
    1298: 176
    1364.7: 150
    1426: 106
    1428: 176
    1429: 176
    1436: 290, 309
    1439: 290
Or. 1.118: 124
    1.123: 106
    1.130: 126
    1.134: 192, 240, 242
    11.205–6: 310

402   INDICES

12.42–4: 166
12.43: 176
12.44–53: 167
12.55: 106
12.80: 155
12.85: 132
12.94: 126
12.95: 123
13.29: 125
13.44: 123
13.45: 146
14.32: 106
14.34: 106
15.8: 176
15.28: 129
15.36: 116
16.19: 132, 143
16.35: 116
16.56: 122
17.7: 150
17.23: 70
18.8–9: 109
18.10: 109
18.18: 150
18.21: 129
18.23: 150
18.31: 99
18.36: 166
18.37–81: 167
18.42: 166
18.58: 135
18.101: 132
18.126: 150
18.128: 155
18.157: 126
18.163: 145
18.171: 123
18.174–5: 123
18.175: 45, 126
18.178: 126
18.179: 121, 127
18.181: 127
18.182: 174
18.193: 143, 144
18.195: 131
18.198: 132
18.199–200: 132

18.201–2: 150
18.216: 125
18.242: 116
18.263: 37
18.264: 3–6, 12, 35
18.264: 7
18.265: 22
18.268: 61–63, 66, 70,
   71, 78
18.269: 71
18.270: 77
18.272: 86, 104, 105,
   107
18.273: 101
18.274–5: 69
18.277: 231
18.278: 234, 239, 240
18.279: 340
18.280: 273
18.281: 117, 118
18.282: 141
18.287: 339
18.297: 73
18.300: 139
18.304: 114
18.306: 321
18.308: 114
24.6: 69, 71
24.7: 71
24.9: 237
24.9: 242, 246
24.10: 319
24.13: 305
24.20: 230
30.6: 149
30.7: 339
30.38: 150
37.4: 116
59.69: 24
59.144: 126
62.8: 149

Anach.   24: 134

Lucianus
 Conscr. Hist.

      53–4: 341

 VH   1.29: 104

INDICES

403

Johannes Lydus (Lyd.)
Mag.   1.32: 332
     3.51.6–52.4: 236
     3.52.3: 227
Mens. 4.7: 138
     4.118: 70, 71, 88, 101,
      181

Malalas
Chron. 13.329: 5
     13.331: 75
     13.332: 61, 67, 68, 76,
      107
     13.333: 170, 185
     13.333–4: 107
     13.334: 188, 338
     13.335: 227, 228, 230,
      231
     13.336: 237, 241, 248,
      275, 280, 282–284,
      290
     13.337: 188

Menander Rhetor (Men. Rh.)
     331.15: 295
     373. 5–8: 117
     373.11: 128

Onasander
     33: 134

Oribasius (Orib.)
Coll. med.
     6.37.1: 122

Papyrus Fayum (P. Fay.)
     20: 142

Palladius (Pall.)
Dial. 13.169–70: 109
h. Laus. 4.4: 107

Peek GG 304.6: 104

Petrus Patricius (Petr. Patr.)
fr.   14: 235, 236, 238

     17: 14

Philostorgius (Philost.)
HE   7.15: 69, 88, 106
     8.1: 170, 237, 248, 304,
      319
     8.4–7: 308
     8.5: 338
     8.8: 331, 333, 335

Philostratus (Philostr.)
VA   1.13: 121, 122
     2.12: 29
     8.26: 108

Photius
Bibl. 96: 109
     484 b: 182

Plato (Pl.)
Ap.   42 a: 88
Cri.   50 c: 97
     51 a 7–9: 97
     51 b: 97
Euthphr. 2 c: 97
Grg. 471 c: 276
Phd. 70 b: 105
     117 d: 103
R.   329 c: 121
     342 e: 95
     427 e: 117
     488 b–489 a: 191
Tim. 41 d 8 – e 1: 104

Polybius (Plb.)
     2.56: 292
     10.3.7: 134
     10.13.1–2: 134
     10.24.2–3: 134
     10.32.9–11: 134
     10.33.4–5: 134
     11.33.7: 300

Plotinus (Plot.)
Enn. 1.7.3: 93
     2.1.5: 94
     6.4.14: 93

404 INDICES

Plutarchus (Plut.)
Alex. 77.6: 276
Caes. 17: 45
Cat. Min.
69–70: 87, 103
Cons.Apoll.
14: 90
Crass. 24.1: 3
24.3: 25, 26
24.5: 27
24.6: 35
25.7: 3, 25
25.8: 25
25.12: 25
27.1: 25
27.2: 25
fort. Rom.
317e–318a: 139
Luc. 32.3–4: 297
36.7: 297
Mar. 44.5: 333
Mor. 201 c: 125
525 a,: 121
788 e: 121
1094 e: 121
Otho 17.1: 107
Pomp. 14.1: 300

Polyaenus (Polyaen.)
8.16.2: 125
8.23.5: 28

Porphyrius (Porph.)
Abst. 1.47: 123
4.20: 123
4.20.3: 122

Procopius (Procop.)
Aed. 2.4.1: 238
Goth. 1.6.26: 249
2.25.21: 249
3.9.20: 249
Pers. 1.13.16: 22
1.15.21: 38
1.15.25: 38
1.19.29: 299
2.30.7: 22

Vand. 2.11.4: 249

**Pseudo Joshua the Stylite
(Ps. Josh. Styl.)**
Chron. 7: 248, 287

Pseudo P'awstos Buzand
4.21: 243

Pseudo Mauricius Tacticus
Str. 8.1.36: 284

Socrates (Socr.)
HE 1.19.3: 163
2.16.2: 174
3.1.8: 108
3.1.27: 166
3.1.27–8: 167
3.1.30: 166
3.21.12: 70
3.21.14: 69
3.21.17: 170
3.22: 338
3.22.1: 170, 179
3.22.1–2: 339
3.22.2: 185, 339
3.22.6: 231, 244
3.22.7: 237
3.23.23: 160
3.23.41–2: 115, 116
3.24–5: 309
3.24–6: 338
3.24.5: 338, 339
3.26.1: 333
3.26.1–2: 339
3.26.3: 331
3.26.4: 335
3.26.5: 333
4.2.4: 248

Soranus (Sor.)
Gynaec. 1.30.1: 122
1.32.1: 122

Sozomenus (Soz.)
HE 5.2.9: 108
5.2.21: 166

INDICES

5.2.21–2: 167
5.2.22: 166
5.4.5: 142
5.5.3–5: 149
5.5.5: 150
5.17.2–4: 159
6.2.1: 69
6.2.7: 107
6.3–5: 309, 338
6.3.1: 181, 339
6.3.2: 231, 234, 245
6.3.4: 338
6.6.1: 333, 335
6.7.10: 248

Stobaeus (Stob.)
1.49.61: 105
4.5.74: 96

Strabo (Str.)
15.1.52: 709C, 29

Suda   I 401: 317, 335

Stoicorum Veterum Fragmenta
(SVF)
3.264: 119
3.295: 119
3.299: 120

Synesius,
Or. de regno
3: 144

Tituli Asiae Minoris (TAM)
2.437: 26

Theodoretus (Thdt.)
h.rel.   1.11: 30
2.30: 30
2.30.14: 30
3.24.2: 107
3.25.3–4: 41
3.25.7: 70, 89
4.1.1: 171, 181
4.1–4: 338
4.1.2: 181, 182, 186,

337
4.1.4–6: 339
4.2–4: 309
4.2.2: 227, 231, 252
4.2.3: 248
4.4.1: 338
4.5.1: 333
4.24.3: 338
5.21.2: 338

Themistius (Them.)
Or.   5.3: 331, 343
5.6: 340
5.11: 331
5.63: 340
5.65 b: 186
5.65 c–d: 181
5.66 a: 196
5.66 b: 185
5.66 d: 276
5.69 b: 245
8.114 c: 245
13.12: 96
15.193 a: 126
15.195 b: 126

Theophylactus Simocatta
Hist.   3.14.5: 25

Xenophon (X.)
Ag.   7.1: 95
An.   1.10.12: 281
2.4.19: 177
4.8: 38
Cyr.   1.6.25: 134
4.5.27: 156
6.3.4: 280
7.1.4: 281
8.5.13: 280
8.7.4: 107

Zonaras (Zon.)
9.9: 31
13.13.12: 12, 13
13.13.14: 64
13.13.15: 63, 84
13.13.17: 62

INDICES

13.13.18: 70
13.13.20: 67, 68
13.13.21: 89
13.13.23: 304, 319
13.13.24: 318
13.13.25: 319
13.13.26: 153, 156
13.13.27: 123, 129
13.13.27–8: 117
13.13.29: 98
13.13.29–30: 75
13.14.1: 181, 185, 186
13.14.2–4: 339
13.14.4: 244
13.14.5: 237, 240
13.14.10: 318, 333
13.14.12: 333, 335
13.14.16: 174, 177
13.14.20: 340
13.14.23: 335
13.14.25: 336

Zosimus (Zos.)

1.39.1: 283, 287
2.40.2: 99
2.45.2: 264
3.1.1: 165
3.1.3: 166
3.2.2: 176
3.3.2–8.1: 167
3.3.4–5: 17
3.5.3: 166
3.8.2: 264
3.12.2: 143
3.22.4: 201
3.26.4: 4
3.26.5: 5, 6
3.27.1: 8, 9, 20, 21
3.27.2: 3, 10
3.27.2–3: 8
3.27.3: 12
3.27.4: 12, 13
3.28.1: 20, 21
3.28.2: 21, 37, 40

3.28.4: 60, 62–64
3.29.1: 64, 68, 70, 72
3.29.2: 80
3.29.2–3: 84
3.29.2–4: 84
3.29.3: 85
3.29.4: 85, 203, 204
3.30.1: 170, 171, 181, 186, 187
3.30.2: 61, 76, 188, 199, 200, 203
3.30.2–3: 200
3.30.3: 201
3.30.4: 84, 202, 203, 212
3.30.5: 215, 217, 231
3.31.1: 227, 230, 234, 236, 240, 241, 248
3.31.2: 242, 246, 256
3.32: 239, 245, 294
3.32.1: 299
3.32.2: 297, 299
3.32.2–3: 298
3.32.3: 299
3.32.5: 299
3.32.6: 299
3.33.1: 257, 262, 263
3.33.2: 275, 279, 282, 287
3.33.2–4: 288
3.33.3: 285, 286
3.33.4: 282–284
3.33.5: 283, 287
3.34.1: 280, 288, 290
3.34.2: 292
3.34.3: 308
3.34.3–4: 304
3.34.4: 318, 319
3.35.1: 264, 325
3.35.2: 263, 323, 325
3.35.3: 318, 333, 335
3.36.1: 174, 177
4.3.4: 140
4.34.1: 328

INDICES

407

X. *Passages referred to in Ammianus 14–24 and 26–31*

14.1.1: 189, 268, 294
14.1.3: 37
14.1.4: 142, 252
14.1.5: 315
14.1.7: 123
14.1.8: 156
14.1.10: 114
14.2.6: 180, 301
14.2.10: 35
14.2.14: 222
14.2.15: 79
14.2.17: 77
14.2.19: 59, 158
14.3.2: 126, 136, 210
14.4.2: 152
14.5.2: 281, 310
14.5.3: 277
14.5.6: 83
14.6.4: 187
14.6.5: 102
14.6.9: 315
14.6.10: 113
14.6.20: 2
14.6.24: 153
14.6.25: 44, 118
14.7.5: 137
14.7.6: 216, 226
14.7.9: 326
14.7.18: 305
14.7.20: 316
14.8.3: 51, 114, 318
14.8.4–5: 1
14.8.5: 216
14.8.12: 236
14.9.3: 46
14.10.7: 177
14.10.12: 96
14.10.13: 158
14.10.14: 284
14.11.1: 316
14.11.3: 128
14.11.4: 205
14.11.6: 272
14.11.8: 59
14.11.12: 202

14.11.14: 322
14.11.16: 224
14.11.19: 322
14.11.21: 264
14.11.22: 113
14.11.25: 139
14.11.32: 301
15.1.1: 162
15.1.3: 129
15.2.8: 114
15.2.9: 337
15.2.10: 83
15.3.8: 116
15.3.11: 212
15.4.10: 322, 328
15.4.12: 203
15.5.4: 208
15.5.6: 267
15.5.8: 283
15.5.10: 229
15.5.16: 17, 66
15.5.29: 203
15.5.33: 65
15.7.4: 208
15.7.6: 338
15.8.1: 195
15.8.2: 91
15.8.4: 17
15.8.13: 4, 54, 136
15.8.15: 77, 162
15.8.16: 14, 132, 160
15.9.8: 114
15.11.1: 153
15.11.3: 205
15.11.10: 323
15.12.4: 158
16.1.1: 294
16.1.2: 138
16.1.3: 113
16.1.4: 116, 118, 123, 127, 156
16.1.5: 166
16.2.6: 23
16.2.13: 32
16.3.1: 21, 305
16.4.5: 304

16.5.1–4: 123
16.5.1: 42, 120
16.5.3: 43, 44
16.5.4–8: 126
16.5.4: 44, 121
16.5.5: 47
16.5.6–8: 129
16.5.6: 45, 125, 129
16.5.8: 121
16.5.9: 128, 153
16.5.11: 159
16.5.12: 132
16.5.14: 141
16.5.15: 140, 144
16.7.4: 239
16.7.6: 152
16.10.3: 34
16.10.7: 28
16.10.8: 3, 23–25
16.10.10: 2
16.10.13: 189
16.10.21: 134, 159, 228
16.11.6: 304, 325
16.11.7: 161
16.11.8: 33
16.11.9: 5
16.11.13: 166, 208
16.12.3: 36, 271, 285
16.12.5: 214
16.12.7: 26, 200
16.12.11: 2
16.12.13: 77
16.12.15: 64, 137, 253
16.12.16: 145
16.12.21: 136
16.12.22: 210
16.12.24: 3
16.12.27: 268
16.12.31: 83
16.12.34: 202
16.12.36: 33, 287
16.12.37: 33, 34
16.12.39: 280
16.12.40–1: 135
16.12.43: 33
16.12.48: 36
16.12.49: 63

16.12.55: 214
16.12.56: 214
17.1.1: 166
17.1.2: 136
17.1.7: 303
17.1.8: 188
17.1.11: 204
17.1.13: 166, 316
17.1.14: 99
17.2.1: 60
17.2.2: 177, 320
17.3.1: 141
17.3.4: 12
17.3.5: 214
17.4.7: 252
17.4.10: 316
17.4.14: 165
17.5.2: 14, 327
17.5.6: 233
17.7.2: 253
17.7.3: 217
17.7.11: 244
17.8.3: 316
17.9.3: 261, 284
17.9.4: 226, 273
17.9.6: 137
17.10.1: 137
17.10.3: 200
17.10.8: 164
17.10.9: 271
17.11.1: 153, 206
17.11.3: 335
17.11.5: 76
17.12.4: 324
17.12.6: 325
17.12.11: 27
17.12.12: 132
17.12.15: 327
17.13.1: 213
17.13.6: 6
17.13.9: 50
17.13.12: 256
17.13.13: 132
17.13.15: 214
17.14.1: 233
17.14.2: 233
17.14.3: 303

INDICES

18.1.1: 141
18.1.2: 130, 131
18.1.3: 31
18.2.2: 252
18.2.4: 11
18.2.13: 6
18.2.14: 296
18.2.15: 333
18.2.16: 14
18.2.18–9: 166
18.3.1: 194
18.4.2: 208, 260
18.4.7: 123, 207, 330
18.5.1: 324
18.5.4: 173
18.5.6: 25
18.5.7: 37
18.6.2: 224
18.6.3: 198, 270
18.6.12: 10
18.6.13: 65, 216
18.6.20: 236
18.6.22: 295
18.7.7: 254
18.7.4: 280
18.7.5: 31
18.7.7: 228
18.7.9: 10
18.7.10: 303
18.8.4: 3
18.10.3: 120
18.10.4: 229
19.1.2: 23
19.2.5: 26
19.2.6: 16, 285
19.2.14: 7, 80
19.2.15: 41
19.3.1: 212
19.4.5: 51
19.5.2: 34
19.5.5: 28
19.5.8: 8
19.6.2: 65
19.6.7: 13
19.6.8: 80
19.6.9: 33, 79
19.7.1: 226

19.8.10: 59
19.9.2: 235, 305
19.9.3: 120
19.9.7: 12
19.9.8–9: 1
19.11.3: 19, 20, 285
19.11.4: 214, 297
19.11.11: 323
19.11.16: 37
19.11.17: 138
19.12.17: 127, 295
19.12.18: 96
19.13.2: 329
20.1.1: 297, 316
20.1.2: 211
20.1.3: 15, 124, 164, 325, 328
20.2.2: 84
20.2.3: 162
20.2.4: 254, 293, 325
20.2.5: 268, 282, 326, 327, 340
20.3.6: 315
20.3.10: 330
20.3.11: 50
20.3.12: 315
20.4.1: 62, 83, 135, 221
20.4.2: 133, 263
20.4.4: 162, 241, 277
20.4.5: 64, 244
20.4.6: 109, 172, 282, 296
20.4.8: 43, 92
20.4.9: 18, 275, 329
20.4.11: 172, 273, 322
20.4.12: 78
20.4.13: 158, 192, 277, 294
20.4.14: 77, 188
20.4.15: 98, 285
20.4.17: 188, 215, 224
20.4.18: 6, 42, 240, 289
20.4.18: 186
20.4.19: 125, 271, 337
20.4.22: 28, 35, 188, 195, 215,
    293, 311
20.5.1: 17, 31, 63, 260, 325
20.5.4: 96, 122, 166, 209, 306
20.5.7: 325, 340
20.5.8: 44, 77
20.5.9: 241

20.5.10: 39, 45, 46, 102, 343
20.6.1: 11, 41, 221, 229, 259
20.6.2: 308
20.6.3: 22, 36, 81, 303
20.6.4: 139
20.6.5: 13, 33, 214
20.6.6: 42, 202
20.6.7: 291, 292
20.6.9: 239, 271, 302
20.7.1: 88, 236
20.7.2: 3, 23, 63, 215
20.7.5: 41
20.7.6: 254
20.7.7: 256
20.7.11: 59
20.7.14: 23
20.8.1: 59
20.8.8: 315
20.8.9: 41, 98
20.8.10: 137
20.8.11: 109, 277
20.8.13: 51
20.8.15: 256
20.8.17: 94
20.8.19: 215
20.8.21: 257, 322
20.9.1: 119, 239, 305
20.9.4: 196
20.9.5: 232, 340
20.9.6: 14, 298
20.9.8: 84, 204, 329
20.9.9: 130
20.10.1: 32, 342
20.10.2: 222, 223
20.11.1: 14, 242
20.11.2: 91
20.11.5: 325
20.11.7: 33, 328
20.11.9: 41
20.11.11: 224
20.11.12: 14, 33, 64
20.11.16: 79
20.11.18: 210
20.11.19: 196
20.11.22: 216
20.11.24: 7, 80, 272
20.11.25: 34

20.11.26: 284, 314
20.11.29: 51, 52, 314, 315
20.11.31: 290
20.14.18: 328
20.15.2: 116
21.1.2: 285
21.1.4: 287
21.1.5: 121
21.1.6: 54
21.1.7: 129
21.1.8: 47, 95
21.1.10: 54
21.1.12: 341
21.1.14: 323
21.2.2: 107, 113
21.2.4: 54, 155
21.2.5: 309
21.3.2: 322
21.3.3: 4
21.3.4: 243
21.3.5: 6
21.4.4: 19
21.5.7: 188
21.5.9: 138
21.5.10: 301
21.5.13: 223
21.6.5: 85
21.6.6: 164, 326
21.6.7: 14, 235
21.6.8: 216, 234, 277
21.6.9: 327
21.7.1: 43, 51, 84
21.7.2: 27
21.7.4: 280
21.7.5: 304, 324
21.7.6: 199
21.8.1: 173, 259
21.8.3: 151, 325
21.9.1: 329
21.9.2: 42, 107, 123
21.9.3: 166
21.9.5–10.1: 133
21.9.5: 264, 265, 322
21.9.6: 167, 296
21.9.8: 44, 85
21.10.5: 203
21.10.7: 268

INDICES

411

21.10.8: 152, 158, 163, 173, 342
21.11.3: 137
21.12.3: 308
21.12.4: 198
21.12.5: 7
21.12.6: 33, 337
21.12.7: 98
21.12.9: 225
21.12.15: 34, 128
21.12.17: 20
21.12.22: 86
21.12.23: 129, 130, 158, 159, 317
21.12.24: 321
21.13.2: 215
21.13.3: 136, 266
21.13.4: 22, 81, 221
21.13.6: 31
21.13.9: 32, 63
21.13.10: 191
21.13.14: 194, 257, 309
21.14.1: 310
21.14.2: 39, 45, 46, 100
21.14.5: 93, 94
21.15.2: 318
21.15.4: 169, 324
21.15.5: 101
21.16.1: 118, 157, 337
21.16.2: 149, 261
21.16.3: 340
21.16.4: 157, 340
21.16.5–6: 340
21.16.5: 286
21.16 6: 96, 120, 123, 125
21.16.7: 128
21.16.8: 109, 151, 154, 172
21.16.9: 128, 161, 190
21.16.11: 156
21.16.12–3: 138
21.16.12: 124
21.16.13: 45
21.16.15: 285
21.16.17: 141, 164
21.16.18: 137, 154, 158
21.16.19: 13, 159
21.16.20: 170, 185
21.16.21: 195, 325
21.16: 111

22.1.1: 54, 284
22.1.2–3: 54
22.1.2: 310
22.2.1: 101
22.2.4: 128
22.2.5: 159, 166
22.3.1: 85
22.3.2: 171, 192, 274, 330
22.3.4: 151, 211, 301
22.4.3: 149
22.4.5: 206
22.4.8: 310
22.5.1: 158
22.5.2: 244
22.5.4: 108
22.6.1: 51, 292
22.6.2: 33
22.6.4: 340
22.7.1: 157, 331, 332
22.7.3: 116, 152, 157, 323
22.7.5: 217
22.7.7: 18
22.7.8: 131, 337
22.7.9: 118, 128
22.8.1: 316
22.8.2: 319, 333
22.8.3: 113
22.8.14: 59
22.8.26: 216
22.8.27: 322
22.8.30: 215
22.8.37: 322
22.8.42: 123, 330
22.8.46: 5
22.8.48: 316
22.9.1: 139, 167, 294
22.9.3: 31, 124, 322
22.9.4: 283
22.9.5: 329
22.9.7: 49
22.9.8: 62, 159, 330
22.9.9: 130, 145
22.9.10: 124, 292, 309, 337
22.9.12: 159
22.9.13: 275, 318
22.9.14: 309
22.10.1: 130

22.10.3: 19, 153
22.10.5: 132, 180
22.10.6: 100, 131, 155, 157
22.10.7: 158, 338
22.11.1: 133
22.11.2: 42, 262, 274
22.11.7: 2, 85, 99
22.11.8: 27
22.11.10: 303, 320
22.11.11: 153
22.12.: 153
22.12.1–2: 167
22.12.1: 163
22.12.2: 166, 167
22.12.3: 12, 161, 167
22.12.4: 115
22.12.5: 11
22.12.6–7: 154
22.12.6: 154, 155, 334
22.12.7–8: 153
22.12.7: 55, 125, 154, 155
22.12.8: 54
22.13.2: 335
22.13.3: 261
22.14.1: 157
22.14.2–3: 317
22.14.2: 131, 273
22.14.3: 31, 155, 159, 160, 189
22.14.4: 137
22.15.2: 9, 209, 305
22.15.3: 165
22.15.4: 174
22.15.5: 2, 138
22.15.6: 316
22.15.9: 282
22.15.20: 13
22.15.32: 114
22.16.6: 261
22.16.7: 47
22.16.14: 301
22.16.23: 292
23.1.1: 195, 342
23.1.6: 328
23.1.7: 54, 277
23.2.4: 189
23.2.5: 170, 304, 305, 318, 319
23.2.7: 138, 143, 178, 209, 261

23.2.8: 66, 207
23.3.2: 36, 63, 101, 164, 179, 239, 269, 274, 305
23.3.4: 7, 213, 256
23.3.5: 179, 223, 224, 274, 275
23.3.7: 89
23.3.8: 9, 69, 143, 209, 210
23.3.9: 18, 42, 262, 274
23.4.2: 52, 123
23.4.5: 123
23.4.14: 27
23.5.1–5: 5
23.5.1: 136
23.5.3–4: 1
23.5.3: 179
23.5.4: 47
23.5.5: 35, 168
23.5.6: 85
23.5.7: 99, 234
23.5.8–14: 53
23.5.8: 210
23.5.9: 98
23.5.10: 54, 198, 310
23.5.11: 55, 288, 310
23.5.14: 55, 116
23.5.16–23: 137, 167
23.5.16: 135, 161, 297
23.5.17: 259, 282
23.5.18: 41, 96, 164
23.5.19: 62, 94, 136, 139, 192, 294
23.5.20: 335
23.5.21: 257
23.6.14: 22
23.6.16: 4
23.6.19: 322
23.6.22: 64
23.6.33: 114, 316
23.6.35: 284, 301
23.6.42: 141
23.6.46: 124
23.6.61: 44
23.6.62: 200
23.6.65: 11
23.6.78: 254
23.6.79: 284
23.6.80: 24, 60
23.6.83: 59, 195

INDICES

413

23.6.84: 28
23.6.85: 163, 316
24.1.1: 16
24.1.2: 5, 9, 60, 171–173, 328
24.1.3: 188, 233
24.1.4: 18
24.1.5: 210
24.1.9: 18, 291
24.1.11: 209
24.1.12: 189
24.1.14: 282
24.1.15: 11
24.2.3: 20, 210
24.2.4: 52, 227
24.2.5: 3, 23, 32, 63, 66, 76
24.2.8: 255
24.2.9–22: 135
24.2.10: 23
24.2.12: 132
24.2.13: 27, 28
24.2.14: 35, 134
24.2.16: 335
24.2.18: 204
24.2.21: 248
24.3.1: 7, 17, 18, 262, 274
24.3.2: 17–20, 78, 132, 137
24.3.3: 14, 16
24.3.5: 130, 164
24.3.7: 79, 94, 137
24.3.8: 331
24.3.9: 98, 120, 167, 228
24.3.11: 217, 255
24.4.4: 14, 134
24.4.6–24: 135
24.4.6: 136
24.4.7: 8
24.4.9: 63
24.4.10: 200
24.4.11: 79, 93
24.4.13: 261
24.4.14: 254
24.4.15: 7, 23
24.4.17: 135
24.4.20: 33, 76, 77, 131
24.4.21–4: 276
24.4.21: 334
24.4.22: 80

24.4.23: 201, 276
24.4.24: 14, 317
24.4.27: 121, 151
24.4.30: 9
24.4.31: 22
24.5.2: 205
24.5.3: 11, 233
24.5.6: 19, 35
24.5.7: 4, 19
24.5.8: 2
24.5.9: 6, 254
24.5.10: 17, 18
24.5.11: 135
24.5.12: 205
24.6.1: 255
24.6.3: 108
24.6.5: 214
24.6.7: 214, 215
24.6.8: 23, 24, 32, 64, 79
24.6.9: 136, 188
24.6.10: 78
24.6.11: 32, 136
24.6.12: 14, 65
24.6.14: 115
24.6.15: 14
24.6.16: 39, 48
24.7.1: 31, 230
24.7.3: 138
24.7.4: 37, 40
24.7.5: 37, 40, 255
24.7.7: 4, 41
24.7.8: 3, 225, 242
24.8.2: 12, 101
24.8.3: 20, 36, 78
24.8.4: 4
24.8.5: 315
24.8.7: 5, 8, 136
26.1.3: 170, 171
26.1.5: 174, 329
26.1.11: 241
26.1.12: 299
26.2.3: 187, 289
26.2.7: 137
26.2.11: 132
26.3.1: 132
26.4.6: 243, 248
26.5.10: 137

26.6.1: 328
26.6.3: 101, 208, 268, 274, 276, 305
26.6.4: 305
26.6.15: 306
26.6.16: 33
26.7.1: 42, 187
26.7.4: 135
26.7.8: 244
26.7.13: 6, 201, 228
26.8.9: 52
26.9.5: 136
26.9.9: 294
26.10.5: 48
26.10.8: 114
26.10.9: 131
26.10.17: 8
27.1.5: 135
27.2.6: 65
27.2.10: 116
27.3.12: 217
27.3.15: 42
27.5.3: 36
27.5.10: 76
27.6.4: 189
27.6.9: 6
27.6.11: 289
27.7.5: 37
27.7.7: 178
27.8.7: 201
27.8.9: 36
27.9.7: 41
27.10.3: 162
27.10.13: 32
27.10.16: 83
27.11.1: 108
27.11.2: 139
27.11.4: 116
27.12.1: 243, 248, 284
27.12.5: 119
27.12.6: 158, 229
27.12.12: 317
27.12.17: 163
28.1.2: 152
28.1.13: 217
28.1.14: 37
28.1.18: 273

28.1.19: 216
28.1.35: 157
28.1.39: 250
28.1.44: 304
28.1.55: 28
28.2.5: 323
28.2.12: 216
28.2.13: 33
28.3.9: 189
28.4.14: 291
28.4.21: 7
28.4.24: 95
28.5.4–7: 284
28.5.4: 40
28.5.6: 33
29.1.4: 40
29.1.13: 59
29.1.20: 200
29.1.23: 129
29.1.34: 130
29.1.44: 212
29.2.2: 131
29.2.18: 96
29.2.21: 233
29.3.1: 96
29.3.2: 200
29.5.5: 136
29.5.15: 132
29.5.16: 275
29.5.17: 137
29.5.19: 208
29.5.20: 20
29.5.23: 20
29.5.24: 121
29.5.26: 137
29.5.34: 216
29.5.54: 256
29.5.56: 189
29.6.1: 233
29.6.7: 113
29.6.9: 41
29.6.17: 321
30.1.4: 272
30.1.5: 98
30.1.6: 233
30.1.16: 136
30.1.20: 42

INDICES

30.2.2: 228
30.2.8: 152
30.3.2: 230
30.3.5: 213
30.4.1: 323
30.4.20: 157
30.5.4: 116
30.5.16: 312, 313
30.5.18: 46
30.7–9: 111
30.7.4: 118, 185
30.7.5: 139
30.8.8: 151
30.8.13: 151
30.8.14: 96
30.9.1: 130
30.9.2: 120, 123
30.9.5: 206
30.10.1: 170
30.10.3: 253
30.10.5: 179
31.2.25: 134
31.3.8: 21
31.4.9: 202

31.5.10: 260
31.6.1: 212
31.6.2: 42
31.6.3: 98, 291
31.6.7: 293
31.7.6: 271
31.7.7: 36
31.7.8: 80
31.7.13: 214
31.8.8: 158, 192
31.10.5: 36
31.10.9: 3
31.10.12: 6, 224
31.10.21: 6
31.12.1: 177
31.13.4: 80
31.13.6: 213
31.13.7: 21, 35
31.13.18: 37
31.14.5: 130
31.15.8: 66
31.15.13: 199
31.16.6: 33
31.16.7: 200